Lecture Notes in Computer Science 11929

More information about this series at http://www.springer.com/series/7410

Martin Albrecht (Ed.)

Cryptography and Coding

17th IMA International Conference, IMACC 2019
Oxford, UK, December 16–18, 2019
Proceedings

Springer

Editor
Martin Albrecht
Royal Holloway, University of London
London, UK

ISSN 0302-9743 ISSN 1611-3349 (electronic)
Lecture Notes in Computer Science
ISBN 978-3-030-35198-4 ISBN 978-3-030-35199-1 (eBook)
https://doi.org/10.1007/978-3-030-35199-1

LNCS Sublibrary: SL4 – Security and Cryptology

This Springer imprint is published by the registered company Springer Nature Switzerland AG
The registered company address is: Gewerbestrasse 11, 6330 Cham, Switzerland

Preface

The International Conference on Cryptography and Coding is the biennial conference of the Institute of Mathematics and its Applications (IMA) on cryptography and coding theory. The conference series has been running for more than three decades and the 17th edition was held December 16–18, 2019, at St Anne's College, University of Oxford.

The Program Committee selected 17 submissions for presentation at the conference and inclusion in these proceedings. The review process was double-blind and rigorous. Each submission was reviewed independently by at least two reviewers in an individual review phase, and subsequently considered by the Program Committee in a discussion phase. Feedback from the reviews and discussions was given to the authors and their revised submissions are included in the proceedings.

In addition to the presentations of accepted papers, the conference also featured four keynote talks by internationally leading scientists on their research. I am grateful to Cas Cremers, Nadia Henninger, Clémentine Maurice, and Francesca Musiani for accepting our invitation and sharing the insights gathered from their exciting research. Finally, the conference featured several contributed presentations. However, these were not finalised by the time this preface went to print.

Running a conference like IMACC requires the effort of many people and many thanks are due. I would like to thank the Steering Committee for their trust and support. I thank the authors for their submissions and the Program Committee and the external reviewers for their effort in selecting the scientific program. Thanks also goes to the IACR for their cooperation. Finally, I am thankful to the conferences team – Maya Everson, Cerys Thompson, Pamela Bye, and colleagues – at the Institute of Mathematics and its Applications for handling all the practical matters of the conference.

September 2019 Martin Albrecht

Organization

Program Committee

Martin Albrecht	Royal Holloway, University of London, UK
Alex Davidson	Cloudflare Portugal, Portugal
Benjamin Dowling	ETH Zurich, Switzerland
Caroline Fontaine	CNRS (LSV), France
Julia Hesse	IBM Research Zurich, Switzerland
Christian Janson	TU Darmstadt, Germany
Cong Ling	Imperial College, UK
Emmanuela Orsini	Katholieke Universiteit Leuven, Belgium
Daniel Page	University of Bristol, UK
Christophe Petit	University of Oxford, UK
Rachel Player	Royal Holloway, University of London, UK
Elizabeth Quaglia	Royal Holloway, University of London, UK
Ciara Rafferty	Queen's University Belfast, UK
Christian Rechberger	TU Graz, Austria
Adeline Roux-Langlois	Univ Rennes, CNRS, IRISA, France
Christoph Striecks	AIT, Austria
Thyla van der Merwe	Mozilla, UK
Roope Vehkalahti	Aalto University, Finland
Carolyn Whitnall	University of Bristol, UK

Additional Reviewers

Bert, Pauline
Costache, Ana
Dalskov, Anders
Davies, Gareth
Dinur, Itai
Eaton, Edward
Fraser, Ashley
Garms, Lydia
Gryak, Jonathan
Howe, James
Kales, Daniel
Kutas, Peter
Kwiatkowski, Kris
Martindale, Chloe
Merz, Simon-Philipp
Persichetti, Edoardo
Qian, Chen
Ramacher, Sebastian
Renes, Joost
Slamanig, Daniel
van de Pol, Joop
Wen, Weiqiang
Yu, Yang

Contents

A Framework for UC-Secure Commitments from Publicly Computable Smooth Projective Hashing

Behzad Abdolmaleki[1(✉)], Hamidreza Khoshakhlagh[2], and Daniel Slamanig[3]

[1] University of Tartu, Tartu, Estonia
behzad.abdolmaleki@ut.ee
[2] Aarhus University, Aarhus, Denmark
hamidreza@cs.au.dk
[3] AIT Austrian Institute of Technology, Vienna, Austria
daniel.slamanig@ait.ac.at

Abstract. Hash proof systems or smooth projective hash functions (SPHFs) have been proposed by Cramer and Shoup (Eurocrypt'02) and can be seen as special type of zero-knowledge proof system for a language. While initially used to build efficient chosen-ciphertext secure public-key encryption, they found numerous applications in several other contexts. In this paper, we revisit the notion of SPHFs and introduce a new feature (a third mode of hashing) that allows to compute the hash value of an SPHF without having access to neither the witness nor the hashing key, but some additional auxiliary information. We call this new type publicly computable SPHFs (PC-SPHFs) and present a formal framework along with concrete instantiations from a large class of SPHFs.

We then show that this new tool generically leads to commitment schemes that are secure against adaptive adversaries, assuming erasures in the Universal Composability (UC) framework, yielding the first UC secure commitments build from a single SPHF instance. Instantiating our PC-SPHF with an SPHF for labeled Cramer-Shoup encryption gives the currently most efficient non-interactive UC-secure commitment. Finally, we also discuss additional applications to information retrieval based on anonymous credentials being UC secure against adaptive adversaries.

1 Introduction

Hash proof systems or smooth projective hash functions (SPHFs) were introduced by Cramer and Shoup [18] and can be considered as implicit designated-verifier proofs of membership [3,10]. Similarly to zero-knowledge proofs, SPHFs are defined for a NP language $\mathcal{L}$ and one considers membership of words $\mathsf{x} \in \mathcal{L}$. In SPHFs, a verifier can generate a secret hashing key hk and for any word x she can compute a hash value H by using the hashing key hk and x. In addition,

H. Khoshakhlagh—Majority of this work was done while working at the University of Tartu.

M. Albrecht (Ed.): IMACC 2019, LNCS 11929, pp. 1–21, 2019.
https://doi.org/10.1007/978-3-030-35199-1_1

the verifier can derive a projection key hp from the hashing key hk and send it to the prover. By knowing a witness $\mathtt{w}$ for membership of $\mathtt{x} \in \mathcal{L}$ and having the projection key hp, the prover is able to efficiently compute the projected hash pH for the word $\mathtt{x}$ such that it equals the hash H computed by the verifier. The smoothness property says that if $\mathtt{x} \notin \mathcal{L}$ one cannot guess the hash value H by knowing hp, or in other words, H looks completely random.

One of the very fundamental tools in cryptographic protocols are commitment schemes. They allow a committer C to pass an analogue of a sealed envelope of his message m to a receiver R. When the committer C then later reveals m with some additional opening information, R can verify whether the envelop contains m. It should be guaranteed that C cannot change the committed message m to some $m' \neq m$ later (binding property) and that R must not learn any information about the committed message m in the commit phase before the opening (hiding property). Some well known perfectly binding commitment are the Cramer-Shoup (CS) [18] and ElGamal [19] encryption schemes, or Pedersen commitments [28] for the case of perfectly hiding commitments.

To be suitable for the use within the universal composability (UC) framework [15], commitment schemes need to provide strong properties and in particular extractability and equivocability. The first one states that the simulator Sim can recover the committed value m by knowing a trapdoor and the latter means that Sim can open a commitment to any message $m' \neq m$ by means of a trapdoor. Satisfying both properties turns out to be a rather difficult task. In general, constructing efficient equivocable and extractable commitments falls into two categories: the one following the ideas of Canetti and Fischlin [15] including [2–4,6], and the ones using non-interactive zero-knowledge proofs as the opening information as the Fischlin-Libert-Manulis schemes [21] and improvements thereof [23]. In this paper, we go into latter direction, but instead of non-interactive zero-knowledge proofs, we use the PC-SPHF which allows us to improve the communication complexity.

Our Contribution. We first introduce an extension of classical SPHFs which we call publicly computable SPHFs (PC-SPHFs) in Sect. 3. Our focus is on SPHFs for languages of ciphertexts $\mathcal{L}_{\mathsf{aux}}$, parametrized by aux, instantiated in the source groups of a bilinear group, i.e., which are itself pairing-free. This covers many schemes such as (linear) ElGamal or (linear) CS. A PC-SPHF is such an SPHF with the following additional property: there is a third mode of hashing which allows to compute the hash value in the target group $\mathbb{G}_T$ of a bilinear group when neither having access to the hashing key hk nor the witness $\mathtt{w}$. This is achieved by adding some representations of the hashing key hk in the projection key hp such that by using aux, hp, and some public values ($\mathtt{crs}_{\mathcal{L}_{\mathsf{aux}}}$), one can compute the hash value in $\mathbb{G}_T$.

We then in Sect. 4 show how one can use PC-SPHFs built from any suitable SPHF for a labeled IND-CCA encryption scheme to construct a generic UC-secure commitment scheme. Following this approach, we construct the most efficient non-interactive UC-secure commitment by using the labeled CS encryption scheme ($\mathsf{PC\text{-}SPHF_{CS}}$). We compare the efficiency of $\mathsf{PC\text{-}SPHF_{CS}}$ with existing non-interactive UC-secure commitments in Table 1[1] and, as we discuss in Sect. 4.2, this gives us an improvement of around 30% over the UC-secure commitments in [2], which to the best of our knowledge represent the most efficient UC-secure commitments to date. Compared to the most efficient UC-secure commitments in bilinear groups, we obtain an improvement in the opening of a factor 4.

Table 1. Comparison with some existing non-interactive UC-secure commitments with a single global CRS when committing to a single message.

Scheme	|Commitment|	|Opening|	Assumption
[16]	$9 \times \mathbb{G}$	$2 \times \mathbb{Z}_p$	Plain DDH
[21], 1	$5 \times \mathbb{G}_1$	$16 \times \mathbb{G}_1$	DLIN
[21], 2	$37 \times \mathbb{G}_1$	$3 \times \mathbb{G}_1$	DLIN
[23]	$4 \times \mathbb{G}_1$	$3 \times \mathbb{G}_1 + 2 \times \mathbb{G}_2$	SXDH
[23]	$4 \times \mathbb{G}_1$	$4 \times \mathbb{G}_1$	DLIN
[1]	$8 \times \mathbb{G}_1 + \mathbb{G}_2$	$\mathbb{Z}_p$	SXDH
[2]	$7 \times \mathbb{G}$	$2 \times \mathbb{Z}_p$	Plain DDH
$\mathsf{PC\text{-}SPHF_{CS}}$	$4 \times \mathbb{G}_1$	$\mathbb{G}_1$	XDH

Finally, in Sect. 5 we show how PC-SPHFs help to improve the efficiency of information retrieval based on anonymous credentials (as proposed in [9]), which is UC secure against adaptive adversaries. In a nutshell, such protocols use anonymous credentials to securely retrieve a message without revealing the identity of the receiver to the sender.

2 Preliminaries

Let PPT denote probabilistic polynomial-time. Let $\lambda \in \mathbb{N}$ be the security parameter. All adversaries will be stateful. By $y \leftarrow \mathcal{A}(\mathtt{x}; r)$ we denote the fact that $\mathcal{A}$, given an input $\mathtt{x}$ and randomness r, outputs y. By $x \leftarrow\!\!\$\ \mathcal{D}$ we denote that x is sampled according to distribution $\mathcal{D}$ or uniformly random if $\mathcal{D}$ is a set. We denote by $\mathsf{negl}(\lambda)$ an arbitrary negligible function. A bilinear group generator $\mathsf{Pgen}(1^\lambda)$ returns $(p, \mathbb{G}_1, \mathbb{G}_2, \mathbb{G}_T, \bar{e})$, where $\mathbb{G}_1$, $\mathbb{G}_2$, and $\mathbb{G}_T$ are three cyclic groups of prime order p, and $\bar{e} : \mathbb{G}_1 \times \mathbb{G}_2 \rightarrow \mathbb{G}_T$ is a non-degenerate efficiently computable bilinear pairing. We use the implicit bracket notation of [20], that is, we write $[a]_\iota$ to denote ag_ι where g_ι is a fixed generator of $\mathbb{G}_\iota$. We denote $\bar{e}([a]_1, [b]_2)$ as $[a]_1 \bullet [b]_2$. Thus, $[a]_1 \bullet [b]_2 = [ab]_T$. We denote $s[a]_\iota = [sa]_\iota$ for $s \in \mathbb{Z}_p$ and $\iota \in \{1, 2, T\}$. We freely use the bracket notation together with matrix notation, for example, if $\boldsymbol{AB} = \boldsymbol{C}$ then $[\boldsymbol{A}]_1 \bullet [\boldsymbol{B}]_2 = [\boldsymbol{C}]_T$.

[1] We note that we follow existing literature and thus focus on the size of commitments and openings and exclude the message(s) in the opening information.

Labeled Public-Key Encryption. Labeled encryption is a variant of the public-key encryption notion where encryption and decryption take an additional label. Decryption should only work if the label used for decryption is identical to the one used when producing the ciphertext. More formally:

Definition 1. *A labeled (tagged) public-key encryption scheme* $\Pi = (\mathsf{KGen}, \mathsf{Enc}, \mathsf{Dec})$*, is defined by three algorithms:*

- $\mathsf{KGen}(1^\lambda)$ *given a security parameter* λ*, generates a public key* pk *and a secret key* sk.
- $\mathsf{Enc}^{\mathsf{t}}_{\mathsf{pk}}(M)$ *given the public key* pk*, a label* t *and a message* M*, outputs a ciphertext* $\mathbf{c}$.
- $\mathsf{Dec}^{\mathsf{t}}_{\mathsf{sk}}(\mathbf{c})$ *given a label* t*, the secret key* sk *and a ciphertext* $\mathbf{c}$*, with* $\mathbf{c} = \mathsf{Enc}^{\mathsf{t}}_{\mathsf{pk}}(M)$*, then outputs* M.

For correctness it is required that for all $(\mathsf{pk}, \mathsf{sk}) \in \mathsf{KGen}(1^\lambda)$, all labels t and all messages M, $\mathsf{Dec}^{\mathsf{t}}_{\mathsf{sk}}(\mathsf{Enc}^{\mathsf{t}}_{\mathsf{pk}}(M)) = M$. Henceforth, we use public-key encryption schemes that provide indistinguishability under chosen plaintext and adaptive chosen ciphertexts attacks, i.e., provide IND-CPA or IND-CCA security respectively.

Decisional Diffie-Hellman (DDH) Assumption. Let $\iota \in \{1, 2, T\}$. DDH holds relative to Pgen, for all λ, all PPT adversaries $\mathcal{A}$, $|\mathsf{Exp}^{\mathsf{DDH}}_{\mathcal{A}}(\mathsf{pars}) - 1/2| \approx_\lambda 0$, where $\mathsf{Exp}^{\mathsf{DDH}}_{\mathcal{A}}(\mathsf{pars}) :=$

$$\Pr\left[\begin{array}{l}\mathsf{pars} \leftarrow_{\$} \mathsf{Pgen}(1^\lambda); u, v, w \leftarrow_{\$} \mathbb{Z}_p; b \leftarrow_{\$} \{0,1\}; \\ b^* \leftarrow \mathcal{A}(\mathsf{pars}, [u]_\iota, [v]_\iota, [b \cdot uv + (1-b)w]_\iota)\end{array} : b = b^*\right].$$

Smooth Projective Hash Functions. Smooth projective hash functions (SPHFs) [18] are families of pairs of functions $(\mathsf{hash}, \mathsf{projhash})$ defined on a language $\mathcal{L}$. They are indexed by a pair of associated keys $(\mathsf{hk}, \mathsf{hp})$, where the hashing key hk may be viewed as the private key and the projection key hp as the public key. On a word $\mathtt{x} \in \mathcal{L}$, both functions need to yield the same result, that is, $\mathsf{hash}(\mathsf{hk}, \mathcal{L}, \mathtt{x}) = \mathsf{projhash}(\mathsf{hp}, \mathcal{L}, \mathtt{x}, \mathtt{w})$, where the latter evaluation additionally requires a witness $\mathtt{w}$ that $\mathtt{x} \in \mathcal{L}$. Thus, they can be seen as a tool for implicit designated-verifier proofs of membership [3]. Formally SPHFs are defined as follows (cf. [6]).

Definition 2. *A SPHF for a language* $\mathcal{L}$ *is a tuple of PPT algorithms* $(\mathsf{Pgen}, \mathsf{hashkg}, \mathsf{projkg}, \mathsf{hash}, \mathsf{projhash})$*, which are defined as follows:*

$\mathsf{Pgen}(1^\lambda)$: *Takes a security parameter* λ *and generates the global parameters* pars *(we assume that all algorithms have access to* pars*).*

$\mathsf{hashkg}(\mathcal{L})$: *Takes a language* $\mathcal{L}$ *and outputs a hashing key* hk *for* $\mathcal{L}$.

$\mathsf{projkg}(\mathsf{hk}, \mathcal{L}, \mathtt{x})$: *Takes a hashing key* hk*,* $\mathcal{L}$*, and a word* $\mathtt{x}$ *and outputs a projection key* hp*, possibly depending on* $\mathtt{x}$.

$\mathsf{hash}(\mathsf{hk}, \mathcal{L}, \mathtt{x})$: *Takes a hashing key* hk, $\mathcal{L}$, *and a word* $\mathtt{x}$ *and outputs a hash* H.
$\mathsf{projhash}(\mathsf{hp}, \mathcal{L}, \mathtt{x}, \mathtt{w})$: *Takes a projection key* hp, $\mathcal{L}$, *a word* $\mathtt{x}$, *and a witness* $\mathtt{w}$ *for* $\mathtt{x} \in \mathcal{L}$ *and outputs a hash* pH.

A SPHF needs to satisfy the following properties:

Correctness. It is required that $\mathsf{hash}(\mathsf{hk}, \mathcal{L}, \mathtt{x}) = \mathsf{projhash}(\mathsf{hp}, \mathcal{L}, \mathtt{x}, \mathtt{w})$ for all $\mathtt{x} \in \mathcal{L}$ and their corresponding witnesses $\mathtt{w}$.

Smoothness. It is required that for any pars and any word $\mathtt{x} \notin \mathcal{L}$, the following distributions are statistically indistinguishable:

$$\{(\mathsf{hp}, \mathsf{H}) : \mathsf{hk} \leftarrow \mathsf{hashkg}(\mathcal{L}), \mathsf{hp} \leftarrow \mathsf{projkg}(\mathsf{hk}, \mathcal{L}, \mathtt{x}), \mathsf{H} \leftarrow \mathsf{hash}(\mathsf{hk}, \mathcal{L}, \mathtt{x})\}$$
$$\{(\mathsf{hp}, \mathsf{H}) : \mathsf{hk} \leftarrow \mathsf{hashkg}(\mathcal{L}), \mathsf{hp} \leftarrow \mathsf{projkg}(\mathsf{hk}, \mathcal{L}, \mathtt{x}), \mathsf{H} \leftarrow_{\$} \Omega\}.$$

where Ω is the set of hash values.

Depending on the definition of smoothness, there are three types of SPHFs (cf. [6]):

GL-SPHF. The projection key hp can depend on word $\mathtt{x}$ and so the smoothness is correctly defined only if $\mathtt{x}$ is chosen before having seen hp.
KV-SPHF. hp does not depend on word $\mathtt{x}$ and the smoothness holds even if $\mathtt{x}$ is chosen after having seen hp.
CS-SPHF. hp does not depend on word $\mathtt{x}$ but the smoothness holds only if $\mathtt{x}$ is chosen before having seen hp.

Trapdoor Smooth Projective Hash Functions. Benhamouda et al. [6] proposed an extension of a classical SPHF, called TSPHF. Their construction has an additional algorithm tsetup, which takes as input the CRS $\mathtt{crs}$ (output by Pgen) and outputs an additional CRS $\mathtt{crs}_\tau$ with trapdoor τ, which can be used to compute the hash value of words $\mathtt{x}$ knowing hp and the trapdoor τ. We refer the reader to [6] for a rigorous formal definition of TSPHFs, and only briefly discuss their computational smoothness property.

Smoothness is the same as for SPHFs, except that after calling Pgen the trapdoor τ of the $\mathtt{crs}_\tau$ is dropped, but $\mathtt{crs}_\tau$ is forwarded to the adversary (together with $\mathtt{crs}_\mathcal{L}$ and even its trapdoor $\mathtt{tds}$). Notice that since hp now needs to contain enough information to compute the hash value of any word $\mathtt{x}$, the smoothness property of TSPHFs is no longer statistical but computational.

2.1 SPHFs on Languages of Ciphertexts

In this paper we mainly focus on SPHFs for languages of ciphertexts, whose corresponding plaintexts verify some relations. The language parameters parse in two parts $(\mathtt{crs}_\mathcal{L}, \mathsf{aux})$: the public part $\mathtt{crs}_\mathcal{L}$, known in advance, and the private part aux, possibly chosen later. More concretely, $\mathtt{crs}_\mathcal{L}$ represents the public values: it will define the (labeled) encryption scheme (and will thus contain the global parameters and the public key of the (labeled) encryption scheme) with the global format of both the tuple to be encrypted and the relations it should satisfy, and possibly additional public coefficients. While aux represents the private values: it will specify the relations, with more coefficients or constants that will remain private, i.e,. the message encrypted in the ciphertext in such languages. We will henceforth denote such languages by $\mathcal{L}_{\mathsf{aux}}$. Since in this paper we mostly focus on constructing a UC-secure commitment scheme where the $\mathtt{crs}$ is independent of the ciphertext (the word of the language), we focus on KV-SPHFs as used in [6,7,25].

Language Representation. Similar to [6], for a language $\mathcal{L}_{\mathsf{aux}}$, we assume there exist two positive integers k and n, a function $\Gamma : S \to \mathbb{G}^{k \times n}$, and a family of functions $\Theta_{\mathsf{aux}} : S \to \mathbb{G}^{1\times n}$, such that $\mathtt{x} \in S$ ($\mathtt{x} \in \mathcal{L}_{\mathsf{aux}}$) iff $\exists \boldsymbol{\lambda} \in \mathbb{Z}_p^{1\times k}$ such that $\Theta_{\mathsf{aux}}(\mathtt{x}) = \boldsymbol{\lambda}\Gamma(\mathtt{x})$. In other words, we assume that $\mathtt{x} \in \mathcal{L}_{\mathsf{aux}}$, if and only if, $\Theta_{\mathsf{aux}}(\mathtt{x})$ is a linear combination of (the exponents in) the rows of some matrix $\Gamma(\mathtt{x})$. For a KV-SPHF, $\boldsymbol{\Gamma}$ is supposed to be a constant function (independent of the word $\mathtt{x}$). Otherwise, one gets a GL-SPHF. We furthermore require that when knowing a witness $\mathtt{w}$ of the membership $\mathtt{x} \in \mathcal{L}_{\mathsf{aux}}$, one can efficiently compute the above linear combination $\boldsymbol{\lambda}$. This may seem a quite strong requirement, but this is actually satisfied by very expressive languages over ciphertexts such as ElGamal, CS and variants.

In the following, we briefly illustrate it on a KV-SPHF for the language of (labeled) CS ciphertexts encrypting a message $[m]_1 \in \mathbb{G}_1$ and $\mathsf{aux} := [m]_1$.

(Labeled) CS Ciphertext Language. The CS IND-CCA2 secure public-key encryption scheme in an abelian cyclic group $\mathbb{G}_1$ of order p is defined as follows: the secret key sk is $(x_1, x_2, y_1, y_2, z) \leftarrow_{\$} \mathbb{Z}_p^5$. Assume $[g_1]_1, [g_2]_1$ are two different independent generators of $\mathbb{G}_1$. Let H be a collision-resistant hash function. The public key is $\mathsf{pk} = ([g_1, g_2, h, c, d]_1, H)$, where $[c]_1 = x_1[g_1]_1 + x_2[g_2]_1$, $[d]_1 = y_1[g_1]_1 + y_2[g_2]_1$, $h = z[g_1]_1$. The encryption of $[m]_1$ with randomness $r \leftarrow_{\$} \mathbb{Z}_p$ is defined as $[\mathbf{c}]_1 = [u_1, u_2, e, v]_1$ where $[u_1]_1 = r[g_1]_1$, $[u_2]_1 = r[g_2]_1$, $[e]_1 = [m]_1 + r[h]_1$, $[v]_1 = r([c]_1 + \xi[d]_1)$, where $\xi = H([u_1]_1, [u_2]_1, [e]_1)$. In case of labeled CS with label t, the hash value is computed as $\xi = H(\mathsf{t}, [u_1]_1, [u_2]_1, [e]_1)$.

Smooth Projective Hash Function for (Labeled) CS Ciphertexts. With the notation introduced earlier, the hashing key is a vector $\mathsf{hk} = \boldsymbol{\alpha} \leftarrow_{\$} \mathbb{Z}_p^n$, while the projection key is, for a word $\mathtt{x}$, $\mathsf{hp} = [\Gamma(\mathtt{x})]_1\boldsymbol{\alpha} \in \mathbb{G}_1^k$ (if $\boldsymbol{\Gamma}$ depends on $\mathtt{x}$, this leads to a GL-SPHF, otherwise, one obtains a KV-SPHF). We have:

$$\mathsf{hash}(\mathsf{hk}, \mathcal{L}_{\mathsf{aux}}, \mathtt{x}) = \Theta_{\mathsf{aux}} \cdot \boldsymbol{\alpha} = \boldsymbol{\lambda} \cdot \mathsf{hp} = \mathsf{projhash}(\mathsf{hp}, \mathcal{L}_{\mathsf{aux}}, \mathtt{x}, \mathtt{w})$$

The parameters $\boldsymbol{\Gamma}$, $\boldsymbol{\lambda}$ and, $\Theta_{[m]_1}$ immediately lead to the KV-SPHF on (labeled) CS, introduced in [6]: with $\mathsf{hk} = (\eta_1, \eta_2, \theta, \mu, \iota) \leftarrow_{\$} \mathbb{Z}_p^5$, the product with Γ leads to, $\mathsf{hp} = (\mathsf{hp}_1 = \eta_1[g_1]_1 + \theta[g_2]_1 + \mu[h]_1 + \iota[\iota]_1, \mathsf{hp}_2 = \eta_2[g_1]_1 + \iota[d]_1)$ and,

$$\begin{aligned}\mathsf{H} &= \mathsf{hash}(\mathsf{hk}, (\mathsf{pk}, [m]_1), [\mathbf{c}]_1) = (\eta_1 + \xi\eta_2)[u_1]_1 + \theta[u_2]_1 + \mu([e]_1 - [m]_1) + \iota[v]_1 \\ &= r[\mathsf{hp}_1]_1 + r\xi[\mathsf{hp}_2]_1 = \mathsf{projhash}(\mathsf{hp}, (\mathsf{pk}, [m]_1), [\mathbf{c}]_1, r) = \mathsf{pH}.\end{aligned}$$

The analysis showing perfect smoothness can be found in [7].

3 Publicly Computable SPHFs

In this section we show how to construct Publicly Computable SPHFs (PC-SPHFs) in a bilinear group from SPHFs. Our PC-SPHF framework is similar to the generic framework for SPHFs in [6] with some slight modifications. Conceptually, the construction of PC-SPHF is inspired by TSPHFs [7], but with completely different motivations and algorithms. A PC-SPHF is an extension of a classical SPHF and in particular based upon an SPHF which can be constructed in the source groups of a bilinear group, i.e., the SPHF itself is pairing-free. The PC-SPHF builds upon the SPHF and is then instantiated in a bilinear group $(p, \mathbb{G}_1, \mathbb{G}_2, \mathbb{G}_T, \bar{e})$. The third mode of hashing provides a means to publicly compute a representation of the hash of the underlying SPHF in $\mathbb{G}_T$ without having access to secret information hk and $\mathtt{w}$. Also for PC-SPHFs, the algorithm projkg takes a hashing key hk, a language $\mathcal{L}_{\mathsf{aux}}$, and a word $\mathtt{x}$ and outputs a projection key $\mathsf{hp} = (\mathsf{hp}_1, \mathsf{hp}_2) \in \mathbb{G}_\iota^k \times \mathbb{G}_{3-\iota}^n$, where hp_1 is the projection key of the underlying SPHF and hp_2 is some representation of the hashing key hk. We note the the PC-SPHF is actually defined with respect to a family of languages $\{\mathcal{L}_{\mathsf{aux}}\}_{\mathsf{aux} \in \mathsf{AUX}}$ parametrized by aux, i.e., the message encrypted using the encryption scheme associated to the SPHF, but we will not make this explicit for the sake of readability and will always write $\mathcal{L}_{\mathsf{aux}}$ as well as aux.

Definition of PC-SPHFs. In the following we assume an SPHF on languages of ciphertexts (cf. Sect. 2.1 for the notation) instantiated in the source groups of a bilinear group $(p, \mathbb{G}_1, \mathbb{G}_2, \mathbb{G}_T, \bar{e})$ and let $\iota \in \{1, 2\}$ (depending on the concrete SPHF). We recall that the hashing key of the SPHF is a vector $\mathsf{hk} = \boldsymbol{\alpha} \leftarrow_\$ \mathbb{Z}_p^n$, while the projection key is, for a word $\mathtt{x}$, $\mathsf{hp} = [\Gamma(\mathtt{x})]_\iota \boldsymbol{\alpha} \in \mathbb{G}_\iota^k$.

Definition 3. *A PC-SPHF for language $\mathcal{L}_{\mathsf{aux}}$ based upon SPHF is defined by the following algorithms:*

$\mathsf{Pgen}(1^\lambda, \mathcal{L}_{\mathsf{aux}})$: *Takes a security parameter λ and language $\mathcal{L}_{\mathsf{aux}}$ and generates the global parameters* pars, *and the* $crs_{\mathcal{L}_{\mathsf{aux}}}$. *It outputs* $(\mathsf{pars}, \mathsf{aux}, crs_{\mathcal{L}_{\mathsf{aux}}})$.

$\mathsf{hashkg}(\mathcal{L}_{\mathsf{aux}})$: *Takes a language $\mathcal{L}_{\mathsf{aux}}$ and outputs a hashing key $\mathsf{hk} = \boldsymbol{\alpha} \leftarrow_\$ \mathbb{Z}_p^n$ for the language $\mathcal{L}_{\mathsf{aux}}$ of the underlying SPHF.*

$\mathsf{projkg}(\mathsf{hk}, crs_{\mathcal{L}_{\mathsf{aux}}}, \mathtt{x})$: *Takes a hashing key* hk, *a CRS* crs, *and possibly a word* $\mathtt{x}$ *and outputs a projection key $\mathsf{hp} = (\mathsf{hp}_1, \mathsf{hp}_2) \in \mathbb{G}_\iota^k \times \mathbb{G}_{3-\iota}^n$, possibly depending on* $\mathtt{x}$, *where* hp_1 *is the projection key of the underlying SPHF and* hp_2 *is some representation of* hk.

$\mathsf{hash}(\mathsf{hk}, crs_{\mathcal{L}_{\mathsf{aux}}}, \mathsf{aux}, \mathtt{x})$: *Takes a hashing key* hk, *a CRS* crs, aux, *and a word* x *and outputs a hash* $\mathsf{H} \in \mathbb{G}_\iota$, *being the hash of the underlying SPHF.*

$\mathsf{projhash}(\mathsf{hp}, crs_{\mathcal{L}_{\mathsf{aux}}}, \mathsf{aux}, \mathtt{x}, \mathtt{w})$: *Takes a projection key* hp, *a CRS* $crs_{\mathcal{L}_{\mathsf{aux}}}$, aux, *a word* x, *and a witness* w *for* $\mathtt{x} \in \mathcal{L}_{\mathsf{aux}}$ *and outputs a hash* $\mathsf{pH} \in \mathbb{G}_\iota$, *being the projective hash of the underlying SPHF.*

$\mathsf{pchash}(\mathsf{hp}, crs_{\mathcal{L}_{\mathsf{aux}}}, \mathsf{aux}, \mathtt{x})$: *Takes a projection key* hp, *a CRS* $crs_{\mathcal{L}_{\mathsf{aux}}}$, aux, *and a word* x, *and outputs a hash* $\mathsf{pcH} \in \mathbb{G}_T$.

A PC-SPHF must satisfy the following properties:

Perfect Correctness. For any $(\mathsf{pars}, \mathsf{aux}, \mathtt{crs}_{\mathcal{L}_{\mathsf{aux}}}) \leftarrow \mathsf{Pgen}(1^\lambda, \mathcal{L}_{\mathsf{aux}})$ and any word $\mathtt{x} \in \mathcal{L}_{\mathsf{aux}}$ with witness w, for any $\mathsf{hk} \leftarrow \mathsf{hashkg}(\mathcal{L}_{\mathsf{aux}})$ and for $\mathsf{hp} \leftarrow \mathsf{projkg}(\mathsf{hk}, \mathtt{crs}_{\mathcal{L}_{\mathsf{aux}}}, \mathtt{x})$:

$$\mathsf{pH} \bullet [1]_{3-\iota} = \mathsf{pcH}.$$

The (t, ϵ)-Soundness Property. For any $(\mathsf{pars}, \mathsf{aux}, \mathtt{crs}_{\mathcal{L}_{\mathsf{aux}}}) \leftarrow \mathsf{Pgen}(1^\lambda, \mathcal{L}_{\mathsf{aux}})$, given $\mathtt{crs}_{\mathcal{L}_{\mathsf{aux}}}$ and the projection key hp, no adversary running in time at most t can produce a value aux, a word x and valid witness w such that $\mathsf{projhash}(\mathsf{hp}, \mathtt{crs}_{\mathcal{L}_{\mathsf{aux}}}, \mathsf{aux}, \mathtt{x}, \mathtt{w}) \neq \mathsf{hash}(\mathsf{hk}, \mathtt{crs}_{\mathcal{L}_{\mathsf{aux}}}, \mathsf{aux}, \mathtt{x})$, with probability at least ϵ. Perfect soundness requires that this holds for any t and any $\epsilon > 0$.

Computational Smoothness. The computational smoothness experiment is provided in Fig. 1. For a language $\mathcal{L}_{\mathsf{aux}}$ and adversary $\mathcal{A}$, the advantage is defined as follows:

$$\mathsf{Adv}^{\text{csmooth}}_{\mathcal{L}_{\mathsf{aux}},\mathcal{A}}(\lambda) = |\Pr[\mathsf{Exp}^{csmooth-0}(\mathcal{A}, \lambda) = 1] - \Pr[\mathsf{Exp}^{csmooth-1}(\mathcal{A}, \lambda) = 1]|.$$

and we require that $\mathsf{Adv}^{\text{csmooth}}_{\mathcal{L}_{\mathsf{aux}},\mathcal{A}}(\lambda) \leq \mathsf{negl}(\lambda)$.

$\mathsf{Exp}^{csmooth\text{-}b}(\mathcal{A}, \lambda)$

- $(\mathsf{pars}, \mathsf{aux}, \mathtt{crs}_{\mathcal{L}_{\mathsf{aux}}}) \leftarrow \mathsf{Pgen}(1^\lambda, \mathcal{L}_{\mathsf{aux}})$, $\mathtt{x} \leftarrow_{\$} \mathcal{X}_{\mathsf{aux}} \setminus \mathcal{L}_{\mathsf{aux}}$, $\mathsf{hk} \leftarrow \mathsf{hashkg}(\mathcal{L}_{\mathsf{aux}})$, $\mathsf{hp} \leftarrow \mathsf{projkg}(\mathsf{hk}, \mathtt{crs}_{\mathcal{L}_{\mathsf{aux}}}, \mathtt{x})$;
- If $b = 0$, then $\mathsf{H} \leftarrow \mathsf{hash}(\mathsf{hk}, \mathtt{crs}_{\mathcal{L}_{\mathsf{aux}}}, \mathsf{aux}, \mathtt{x})$, else $\mathsf{H} \leftarrow_{\$} \Omega$;
- **return** $\mathcal{A}(\mathtt{crs}_{\mathcal{L}_{\mathsf{aux}}}, \mathtt{x}, \mathsf{hp}, \mathsf{H})$

Fig. 1. Experiments $\mathsf{Exp}^{csmooth\text{-}b}$ for computational smoothness.

Security Analysis. The correctness and the perfect soundness are easy to verify from the construction, and so the resulting PC-SPHF is correct and sound. Subsequently, we prove the computational smoothness of the PC-SPHF under the XDH assumption, i.e., the DDH assumption in $\mathbb{G}_\iota$. For the sake of exposition, we assume that the SPHF is instantiated in $\mathbb{G}_1$ below, i.e., $\iota = 1$.

$\mathsf{Exp}^{int}_{\mathcal{B}}(\mathsf{pars})$	$\mathsf{O}_0([\boldsymbol{\Gamma}]_1)$
$([\boldsymbol{\Gamma}]_1, \boldsymbol{\Gamma}) \leftarrow \mathsf{Pgen}^*(\mathsf{pars}, \mathcal{L}_{\mathsf{aux}})$; $b \leftarrow_\$ \{0,1\}$; $b' \leftarrow \mathcal{B}^{\mathsf{O}_b(\cdot,\cdot)}([\boldsymbol{\Gamma}]_1)$; **return** $b = b'$	$\boldsymbol{\alpha} \leftarrow_\$ \mathbb{Z}_p^n, [\boldsymbol{x}]_1 \leftarrow_\$ \mathcal{X}_{\mathsf{aux}} \setminus \mathcal{L}_{\mathsf{aux}}, [\boldsymbol{x}']_1 \leftarrow_\$ \mathbb{G}_1^n$; $R := \left(([\boldsymbol{\Gamma\alpha}]_1, [\boldsymbol{\alpha}]_1, [\boldsymbol{x}]_1, [x_i'\alpha_i]_1, [x_i'\alpha_i x_i]_1; [\boldsymbol{\alpha}]_2)\right)_{i\in[n]}$; **return** R
	$\mathsf{O}_1([\boldsymbol{\Gamma}]_1)$
	$\boldsymbol{\alpha} \leftarrow_\$ \mathbb{Z}_p^n; [\boldsymbol{x}]_1 \leftarrow_\$ \mathcal{X}_{\mathsf{aux}} \setminus \mathcal{L}_{\mathsf{aux}}, [\boldsymbol{x}']_1 \leftarrow_\$ \mathbb{G}_1^n, \boldsymbol{u} \leftarrow_\$ \mathbb{Z}_p^n$; $R := \left(([\boldsymbol{\Gamma\alpha}]_1, [\boldsymbol{\alpha}]_1, [\boldsymbol{x}]_1, [u_i]_1, [x_i'\alpha_i x_i]_1; [\boldsymbol{\alpha}]_2)\right)_{i\in[n]}$; **return** R

Fig. 2. Experiment $\mathsf{Exp}^{int}_{\mathcal{B}}(\mathsf{pars})$ for the proof of smoothness in Theorem 1.

Theorem 1. *Let* XDH *hold, then PC-SPHF is computationally smooth.*

Proof. We first reduce the smoothness to the following computational assumption: for all λ, $\mathsf{pars} \in \mathsf{Pgen}(1^\lambda)$, and PPT adversaries $\mathcal{B}$, $|\mathsf{Exp}^{int}_{\mathcal{B}}(\mathsf{pars}) - 1/2| \approx_\lambda 0$, where $\mathsf{Exp}^{int}_{\mathcal{B}}(\mathsf{pars})$ is depicted in Fig. 2. Let $\mathcal{B}$ be allowed to make only one query to the oracle O to obtain a tuple $(([\boldsymbol{\Gamma\alpha}]_1, [\boldsymbol{\alpha}]_1, [\boldsymbol{x}]_1, [x_i'\alpha_i]_1, [x_i'\alpha_i x_i]_1; [\boldsymbol{\alpha}]_2))_{i\in[n]}$.

Let $\mathcal{A}$ be the adversary against computational smoothness. We now construct the following adversary $\mathcal{B}$ against the *intermediate assumption*.

- $(([\boldsymbol{\Gamma\alpha}]_1, [\boldsymbol{\alpha}]_1, [\boldsymbol{x}]_1, [z_i]_1, [z_i x_i]_1; [\boldsymbol{\alpha}]_2))_{i\in[n]} \leftarrow \mathsf{O}_b([\boldsymbol{\Gamma}]_1)$; where if $b = 0$, $z_i = x_i'\alpha_i$ and $z_i \leftarrow_\$ \mathbb{Z}_p$ otherwise;
- $\mathsf{hp}_1 \leftarrow [\boldsymbol{\Gamma\alpha}]_1$; $\mathsf{hp}_2 \leftarrow [\boldsymbol{\alpha}]_2$;
- $\mathtt{crs}_{\mathcal{L}_{\mathsf{aux}}} = [\boldsymbol{\Gamma}]_1$;
- $H \leftarrow \sum_{i=1}^n [z_i]_1$; $\mathtt{x} \leftarrow [\boldsymbol{x}]_1$;
- $b_{\mathcal{A}} \leftarrow \mathcal{A}(\mathtt{crs}_{\mathcal{L}_{\mathsf{aux}}}, \mathsf{hp}, \mathtt{x}, H)$;
- **return**$b' \leftarrow b_{\mathcal{A}}$.

Thus, $\mathcal{A}$ is successful in breaking the soundness game iff $\mathcal{B}$ is successful in breaking the *intermediate assumption.*

We now show that the *intermediate assumption* can be reduced to the XDH problem, i.e., it is hard to distinguish the two distributions, $\{[1, a, b, ab]_1, [1]_2\}$ and $\{[1, a, u, ab]_1, [1]_2\}$ where $a, b, u \leftarrow_\$ \mathbb{Z}_p$. Let $\mathcal{D}$ be the adversary against this problem, such that given $T = \{[1, a, z, ab]_1, [1]_2\}$ it outputs 0 if $z = b$ and 1 otherwise. Given the tuple T, $\mathcal{D}$ uses $\mathcal{B}$ as a subroutine. In particular, $\mathcal{D}$ plays the role of the challenger for $\mathcal{B}$ in the experiment $\mathsf{Exp}^{int}_{\mathcal{B}}(\mathsf{pars})$ in Fig. 2 and on input $([\boldsymbol{\Gamma}]_1)$ works as follows:

1. By random self-reducibility of DDH, generate n DDH challenges $[u_i, v_i, w_i]_1$, for $i \in [1\,..\,n]$.
2. Let $[\boldsymbol{u}]_1 = ([u_1]_1, \ldots, [u_n]_1) \in \mathbb{G}^n$, $[\boldsymbol{v}]_1 = ([v_1]_1, \ldots, [v_n]_1) \in \mathbb{G}^n$, and $[\boldsymbol{w}]_1 = ([w_1]_1, \ldots, [w_n]_1) \in \mathbb{G}^n$.
3. Choose $\boldsymbol{\alpha} \leftarrow_\$ \mathbb{Z}_p^n$ and set $R \leftarrow (([\boldsymbol{\Gamma\alpha}]_1, [\boldsymbol{\alpha}]_1, [u_i]_1, [v_i\alpha_i]_1, [\alpha_i w_i]_1; [\boldsymbol{\alpha}]_2))_{i\in[n]}$.

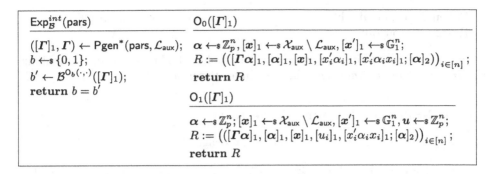

4. When $\mathcal{B}([\boldsymbol{\Gamma}]_1)$ calls the oracle O_b, the adversary $\mathcal{D}$ answers with R.
5. Return $\mathcal{B}$'s output.

Thus, $\mathcal{D}$ is successful in breaking the XDH problem iff $\mathcal{B}$ is successful in breaking the *intermediate assumption*. This concludes the proof. □

3.1 PC-SPHF on ElGamal Ciphertexts

We design a PC-SPHF for the ElGamal language,

$$\mathcal{L}_{[m]_1} = \left\{[\mathbf{c}]_1 = ([u]_1, [v]_1) \in \mathbb{G}_1^2 : \exists r \in \mathbb{Z}_p : ([u]_1 = r[g]_1, [v]_1 = [m]_1 + r[h]_1)\right\}.$$

The CRS $\mathtt{crs}_{\mathcal{L}_{\mathsf{aux}}}$ contains the ElGamal encryption public key $\mathsf{pk} = [g, h]_1 \in \mathbb{G}_1^2$. With the hashing key $\mathsf{hk} = (\eta, \theta) \leftarrow_{\$} \mathbb{Z}_p^2$ and the projection key $\mathsf{hp} = ([\mathsf{hp}_1]_1, [\mathsf{hp}_2]_2)$, where $[\mathsf{hp}_1]_1 = \eta[g]_1 + \theta[h]_1$, and $[\mathsf{hp}_2]_2 = [\eta, \theta]_2 \in \mathbb{G}_2^2$, and $\mathsf{aux} = [m]_1$, the hash values of the PC-SPHF are defined as follows:

$$\begin{aligned}
\mathsf{H} &= \mathsf{hash}(\mathsf{hk}, \mathtt{crs}_{\mathcal{L}_{\mathsf{aux}}}, [m]_1, [\mathbf{c}]_1) = \eta[u]_1 + \theta([v]_1 - [m]_1) \in \mathbb{G}_1 \\
\mathsf{pH} &= \mathsf{projhash}(\mathsf{hp}, \mathtt{crs}_{\mathcal{L}_{\mathsf{aux}}}, [m]_1, [\mathbf{c}]_1, r) = r[\mathsf{hp}_1]_1 \in \mathbb{G}_1 \\
\mathsf{pcH} &= \mathsf{pchash}(\mathsf{hp}, \mathtt{crs}_{\mathcal{L}_{\mathsf{aux}}}, [m]_1, [\mathbf{c}]_1) = [u]_1 \bullet [\mathsf{hp}_{21}]_2 + ([v]_1 - [m]_1) \bullet [\mathsf{hp}_{22}]_2 \in \mathbb{G}_T
\end{aligned}$$

where we observe that $\mathsf{H} \bullet [1]_2 = \mathsf{pH} \bullet [1]_2 = \mathsf{pcH}$.

3.2 PC-SPHF on (Labeled) Cramer-Shoup Ciphertexts

We show how to extend the SPHF on (labeled) CS ciphertexts into a PC-SPHF. The CRS $\mathtt{crs}_{\mathcal{L}_{\mathsf{aux}}}$ contains the encryption public key pk. With the hashing key $\mathsf{hk} = (\eta_1, \eta_2, \theta, \mu, \iota) \leftarrow_{\$} \mathbb{Z}_p^5$ and the projection key $\mathsf{hp} = ([\mathsf{hp}_1]_1, [\mathsf{hp}_2]_2)$, where $[\mathsf{hp}_{11}]_1 = \eta_1[g_1]_1 + \theta[g_2]_1 + \mu[h]_1 + \iota[c]_1$, and $[\mathsf{hp}_{12}]_1 = \eta_2[g_1]_1 + \iota[d]_1$, and $[\mathsf{hp}_2]_2 = [\eta_1, \eta_2, \theta, \mu, \iota]_2 \in \mathbb{G}_2^5$, and $\mathsf{aux} = [m]_1$, the hash values of the PC-SPHF are defined as follows:

$$\begin{aligned}
\mathsf{H} &= \mathsf{hash}(\mathsf{hk}, \mathtt{crs}_{\mathcal{L}_{\mathsf{aux}}}, [m]_1, [\mathbf{c}]_1) \\
&= (\eta_1 + \xi\eta_2)[u_1]_1 + \theta[u_2]_1 + \mu([e]_1 - [m]_1) + \iota[v]_1 \in \mathbb{G}_1 \\
\mathsf{pH} &= \mathsf{projhash}(\mathsf{hp}, \mathtt{crs}_{\mathcal{L}_{\mathsf{aux}}}, [m]_1, [\mathbf{c}]_1, r) = r[\mathsf{hp}_{11}]_1 + r\xi[\mathsf{hp}_{12}]_1 \in \mathbb{G}_1 \\
\mathsf{pcH} &= \mathsf{pchash}(\mathsf{hp}, \mathtt{crs}_{\mathcal{L}_{\mathsf{aux}}}, [m]_1, [\mathbf{c}]_1) \\
&= [u_1]_1 \bullet [\mathsf{hp}_{21}]_2 + [u_1]_1 \bullet \xi[\mathsf{hp}_{22}]_2 + [u_2]_1 \bullet [\mathsf{hp}_{23}]_2 + ([e]_1 - [m]_1) \bullet [\mathsf{hp}_{24}]_2 \\
&\quad + [v]_1 \bullet [\mathsf{hp}_{25}]_2 = [u_1]_1 \bullet [\eta_1]_2 + [u_1]_1 \bullet \xi[\eta_2]_2 + [u_2]_1 \bullet [\theta]_2 \\
&\quad + ([e]_1 - [m]_1) \bullet [\mu]_2 + [v]_1 \bullet [\iota]_2 \in \mathbb{G}_T
\end{aligned}$$

This PC-SPHF construction for labeled CS ciphertexts will be the core of constructing UC secure commitment scheme in the next section.

4 UC-Secure Commitment Scheme from PC-SPHFs

In this section, we introduce a direct application of the previous PC-SPHF on labeled CS ciphertexts to construct an efficient UC-secure commitment. Intuitively, the commit phase contains a labeled CS ciphertext. The projective hash pH will be revealed in the opening phase. The verification phase can be done by computing pcH. Finally, the simulator by having access to the trapdoor hk, computes the hash H as the simulated proof pH. Before presenting our concrete construction, we describe a generic UC-secure commitment scheme from any IND-CCA secure labeled encryption scheme with an associated PC-SPHF. Our efficient UC-secure commitment is an instantiation of this generic commitment.

4.1 Generic UC-Secure Commitment

The ideal functionality of a commitment scheme is depicted in Fig. 3. It has been proposed by Canetti and Fischlin [16]. Note that the functionality now takes another unique "commitment identifier" cid, which may be used if a sender commits to the same receiver multiple times within a session. We assume that the combination of sid and cid is globally unique. Our generic commitment, depicted in Fig. 4, is secure in the UC framework against adaptive corruptions (assuming reliable erasure), with a common reference string for any PC-SPHF on the language of a valid ciphertext on a message M under a labeled IND-CCA-secure encryption scheme. More formally, we show the following:

$\mathcal{F}_{\mathsf{mcom}}$, parameterized by a message space $\mathcal{M}$, interacts with adversary Sim and parties $P_1, \ldots, P_n$ as follows.

- Upon receiving $(\mathtt{commit}, \mathsf{sid}, \mathsf{cid}, P_i, P_j, M)$ from P_i, where $M \in \mathcal{M}$, proceed as follows: if a tuple $(\mathsf{sid}, \mathsf{cid}, \ldots)$ with the same $(\mathsf{sid}, \mathsf{cid})$ was previously recorded, do nothing. Otherwise, record $(\mathsf{sid}, \mathsf{cid}, P_i, P_j, M)$ and send $(\mathtt{receipt}, \mathsf{sid}, \mathsf{cid}, P_i, P_j)$ to P_j and Sim.
- Upon receiving $(\mathsf{open}, \mathsf{sid}, \mathsf{cid})$ from P_i, proceed as follows: if a tuple $(\mathsf{sid}, \mathsf{cid}, P_i, P_j, M)$ was previously recorded then send $(\mathsf{open}, \mathsf{sid}, \mathsf{cid}, P_i, P_j, M)$ to P_j and Sim. Otherwise do nothing.
- Upon receiving $(\mathtt{corrupt}, \mathsf{sid}, \mathsf{cid})$ from the adversary, send M to the adversary if there is already an entry $(\mathsf{sid}, \mathsf{cid}, P_i, P_j, M)$. Change the record to $(\mathsf{sid}, \mathsf{cid}, P_i, P_j, M^*)$, if the adversary provides some M^* and $(\mathtt{receipt}, \mathsf{sid}, \mathsf{cid}, P_i, P_j)$ has not yet been written on P_j's output tape.

Fig. 3. Functionality $\mathcal{F}_{\mathsf{mcom}}$ for committing multiple messages

Theorem 2. *The commitment scheme in Fig. 4 securely realizes $\mathcal{F}_{\mathsf{mcom}}$ in the CRS model against adaptive corruptions (assuming reliable erasure), provided that (i) $\Pi = (\mathsf{KGen}, \mathsf{Enc}, \mathsf{Dec})$, is an IND-CCA labeled PKE; (ii) the PC-SPHF is (t, ϵ)-sound and computationally smooth.*

$K_{crs}(1^\lambda)$: Generate a secret and public key $(\mathsf{sk}, \mathsf{pk})$ for a labeled IND-CCA encryption scheme, set $\mathtt{crs}_{\mathcal{L}_{\mathsf{aux}}} = \mathsf{pk}$. Compute $\mathsf{hk} \leftarrow \mathsf{hashkg}(\mathcal{L}_{\mathsf{aux}})$ and $\mathsf{hp} \leftarrow \mathsf{projkg}(\mathsf{hk}, \mathtt{crs}_{\mathcal{L}_{\mathsf{aux}}}, \cdot)$ and set $\mathtt{crs} := (\mathtt{crs}_{\mathcal{L}_{\mathsf{aux}}}, \mathsf{hp})$.
// Commit phase:
$\mathsf{Commit}(\mathtt{crs}, M, \mathsf{sid}, \mathsf{cid}, P_i, P_j)$: to commit to message $M \in \mathbb{G}_1$ for party P_j, upon receiving a command $(\mathtt{commit}, \mathsf{sid}, \mathsf{cid}, P_i, P_j, M)$, party P_i chooses randomness r and computes $\mathbf{c} = \mathsf{Enc}^{\mathsf{t}}_{\mathsf{pk}}(M; r)$ with $\mathsf{t} = (\mathsf{sid}, \mathsf{cid}, P_i)$ and $\mathsf{pH} \leftarrow \mathsf{projhash}(\mathsf{hp}, \mathtt{crs}_{\mathcal{L}_{\mathsf{aux}}}, M, \mathbf{c}, r)$. P_i erases r and sends $\mathbf{c}$ to P_j and stores pH. Upon receiving $(\mathtt{commit}, \mathsf{sid}, \mathsf{cid}, P_i, P_j, \mathbf{c})$ from P_i, party P_j verifies $\mathbf{c}$ is well-formed. If yes, P_j outputs $(\mathtt{receipt}, \mathsf{sid}, \mathsf{cid}, P_i, P_j)$. Otherwise, P_j ignores the message.
// Opening phase:
$\mathsf{Open}(M, \mathsf{pH}, \mathsf{sid}, \mathsf{cid}, P_i, P_j)$: when receiving a command $(\mathsf{open}, \mathsf{sid}, \mathsf{cid}, P_i, P_j, M)$, party P_i reveals M and his state information pH.
// Verification phase:
$\mathsf{Ver}(\mathtt{crs}, (\mathtt{commit}, \mathsf{sid}, \mathsf{cid}, \mathbf{c}), M, \mathsf{pH}, \mathsf{sid}, \mathsf{cid}, P_i, P_j)$: P_j computes $\mathsf{pcH} \leftarrow \mathsf{pchash}(\mathsf{hp}, \mathtt{crs}_{\mathcal{L}_{\mathsf{aux}}}, M, \mathbf{c})$ and verifies pH, i.e., whether $\mathsf{pH} \bullet [1]_2 = \mathsf{pcH}$, and ignores the opening if verification fails. If verification succeeds, P_j outputs $(\mathsf{open}, \mathsf{sid}, \mathsf{cid}, P_i, P_j, M)$ iff cid has not been used with this committer previously. Otherwise, P_j also ignores the message.

Fig. 4. Generic UC-Secure Commitment from PC-SPHFs.

For the proof we note that the simulator Sim first generates the CRS, with an encryption key pk, while knowing the decryption key sk for an IND-CCA-secure labeled encryption scheme, and the parameters for the PC-SPHF.

Proof. Intuitively, we construct an ideal-world adversary Sim that runs a black-box simulation of the real-world adversary $\mathcal{A}$ by simulating the protocol execution and relaying messages between $\mathcal{A}$ and the environment $\mathcal{Z}$. Sim proceeds as follows in experiment *IDEAL*:

- Upon the environment $\mathcal{Z}$ requires some uncorrupted party P_i to send $(\mathtt{commit}, \mathsf{sid}, \mathsf{cid}, P_i, P_j, M)$ to the functionality, Sim is informed that a commitment operation took place, without knowing the committed message M. Thus, Sim selects a fake random message $M' \leftarrow_{\$} \mathbb{G}_1$, and computes an encryption $\mathbf{c}$ of $M' \in \mathbb{G}_1$. Upon P_j' outputs $(\mathtt{receipt}, \mathsf{sid}, \mathsf{cid}, P_i, P_j)$, the adversary $\mathcal{A}$ is given $(\mathtt{commit}, \mathsf{sid}, \mathsf{cid}, \mathbf{c})$. Sim allows $\mathcal{F}_{\mathsf{mcom}}$ to proceed with the delivery of message $(\mathtt{commit}, \mathsf{sid}, \mathsf{cid}, P_i, P_j)$ to P_j.
- If $\mathcal{Z}$ requires some uncorrupted party P_i to open a previously generated commitment $\mathbf{c}$ to some message $M \in \mathbb{G}_1$, Sim learns M from $\mathcal{F}_{\mathsf{mcom}}$ and, using the trapdoor hk of the simulated PC-SPHF hp, generates a simulated proof H that satisfies the verification algorithm Ver for the message M obtained from $\mathcal{F}_{\mathsf{mcom}}$. The internal state of P_i' is modified to be H, which is also given to $\mathcal{A}$ as the real-world opening.
- When $\mathcal{A}$ delivers $(\mathtt{commit}, \mathsf{sid}', \mathsf{cid}', \mathbf{c}')$ for P_i' to P_j', (and P_j' still has not received a commitment with cid' from P_i'), Sim proceeds as follows:

(a) If P'_i is uncorrupted, Sim notifies $\mathcal{F}_{\mathsf{mcom}}$ that the commitment $(\mathsf{sid}', \mathsf{cid}')$ can be delivered. The `receipt` message from $\mathcal{F}_{\mathsf{mcom}}$ is delivered to the dummy P_j as soon as the simulated P'_j outputs his own `receipt` message.
(b) If P_i is a corrupted party, then $\mathbf{c}'$ has to be extracted. Indeed, Sim checks if $\mathbf{c}'$ is well-formed. It uses sk corresponding to pk to decrypt $\mathbf{c}'$.
(c) For an invalid $\mathbf{c}'$, the commitment is ignored. Otherwise, Sim receives M and sends $(\mathtt{commit}, \mathsf{sid}', \mathsf{cid}', P_i, P_j, M)$ to $\mathcal{F}_{\mathsf{mcom}}$, which causes $\mathcal{F}_{\mathsf{mcom}}$ to prepare a `receipt` message for P_j. The latter is delivered by Sim as soon as P'_j produces his own output.

- If $\mathcal{A}$ gets a simulated corrupted P'_i to correctly open a commitment $(\mathtt{commit}, \mathsf{sid}', \mathsf{cid}', \mathbf{c}')$ to M', Sim compares M' to M that was previously extracted from $\mathbf{c}'$ and aborts if $M \neq M'$. Otherwise, Sim sends $(\mathsf{open}, \mathsf{sid}, \mathsf{cid}, P_i, P_j, M)$ on behalf of P_i to $\mathcal{F}_{\mathsf{mcom}}$. If $\mathcal{A}$ provides an incorrect opening, Sim ignores this opening.
- If $\mathcal{A}$ decides to corrupt some party P'_i, Sim corrupts the corresponding party P_i in the ideal world and obtains all his internal information. In order to match the received opening information of P_i, Sim modifies all opening information about the unopened commitments generated by P'_i. This modified internal information is given to $\mathcal{A}$. For each commitment intended for P_j but for which P_j did not receive $(\mathtt{commit}, \mathsf{sid}, \mathsf{cid}, P_i, P_j)$, the newly corrupted P'_i is allowed to decide what the committed message will be. A new message M is thus provided by $\mathcal{A}$ and Sim informs $\mathcal{F}_{\mathsf{mcom}}$ that M supersedes the message chosen by P_i before his corruption.

We consider a sequence of *hybrid* games between the *real* and *ideal* worlds and show that the commitment scheme emulates the ideal functionality against adaptive corruptions with erasures. This is a general approach which one can follow to prove the security of a commitment scheme in the UC model. The games starts from the real game, adversary $\mathcal{A}$ interacts with real parties, and ends up with the ideal game. In the ideal game, we build Sim that interfaces between adversary $\mathcal{A}$ and ideal functionality $\mathcal{F}_{\mathsf{mcom}}$.

Game_0*:* This is called *real game* ($\text{HYBRID}^{\mathcal{F}_{\mathsf{mcom}}}$), which corresponds to the real world in the CRS model. In this game, the real protocol is executed between committer P_i and receiver P_j. Environment $\mathcal{Z}$ adaptively chooses the input for honest committer P_i and receives output of the honest parties. Naturally, there is an adversary $\mathcal{A}$ that attacks the real protocol in the real world, i.e., it can corrupt some parties and see all flows from parties. In the case of corruption, $\mathcal{A}$ can read the current inner state of the corrupted party and also can fully control it. In this game, environment $\mathcal{Z}$ can control adversary $\mathcal{A}$ and see exchanged messages among all honest parties, and all of $\mathcal{A}$'s interactions with other parties.

Game_1*:* In the setup phase of this game, simulator Sim chooses $\mathsf{hk} \hookleftarrow_{\$} \mathbb{Z}_p^n$, and generates $\mathsf{hp} \leftarrow \mathsf{projkg}(\mathsf{hk}, \mathtt{crs})$, $\mathtt{crs}_{\mathcal{L}_{\mathsf{aux}}}$ and sets $\mathtt{crs} = (\mathtt{crs}_{\mathcal{L}_{\mathsf{aux}}}, \mathsf{hp})$. In the commit phase, upon receiving a query $(\mathtt{commit}, \mathsf{sid}, \mathsf{cid}, P_i, P_j, M)$ from $\mathcal{Z}$, corrupted party P'_i computes $\mathbf{c}$ using the labeled IND-CCA encryption scheme and sends $(\mathtt{commit}, \mathsf{sid}, \mathsf{cid}, \mathbf{c})$ to receiver P_j. In the commit phase, after receiving $(\mathtt{commit}, \mathsf{sid}, \mathsf{cid}, P_i, P_j, \mathbf{c})$, Sim decrypts and stores $M' = \mathsf{Dec}^{\mathsf{t}}_{\mathsf{sk}}(\mathbf{c})$, where

$\mathsf{t} \leftarrow (\mathsf{sid}, \mathsf{cid}, P_i)$. In the opening phase, when P_i' successfully opens to message M, simulator Sim outputs $(\mathtt{reveal}, \mathsf{t}, M')$ to environment $\mathcal{Z}$.

Lemma 1. *If $\Pi = (\mathsf{KGen}, \mathsf{Enc}, \mathsf{Dec})$, the labeled PKE is IND-CCA secure, and PC-SPHF is computationally smooth, the output of $\mathcal{Z}$ in Game_0 and Game_1 is computationally indistinguishable.*

Proof. In Game_1, we observed that after P_i' opened commitment to message M, Sim reveals decrypted message M'. Suppose that bad defines the case that sender P_i' successfully opened message M but $M \neq M'$. Now, the claim states that if bad happens, that is the smoothness of PC-SPHF is broken; which it happens with a negligible probability. More precisely, let $M' \neq M$. Then, in the opening phase it uses $\pi = \mathsf{pH}$ and successfully opens the commitment to M'. The case impels party P_i' comes up with a valid proof for PC-SPHF where it turns that smoothness of PC-SPHF is broken.

Hence, the case bad happens only with a negligible probability and two games Game_0 and Game_1 are computationally indistinguishable in a view of $\mathcal{Z}$. □

Game_2*:* This game is the same with Game_1, the only difference is that simulator Sim modifies the simulation of an honest sender P_i. In the commit phase, after receiving a query $(\mathtt{commit}, \mathsf{sid}, \mathsf{cid}, P_i, P_j, M)$ from $\mathcal{Z}$, the simulator Sim computes $[\mathbf{c}]_1$ and sends $(\mathtt{commit}, \mathsf{sid}, \mathsf{cid}, \mathbf{c})$ to P_j (note that we assume that Sim knows M). In the opening phase, upon getting an Open query, Sim uses simulates a proof π by computing the hash value H. Finally, simulator Sim outputs $(\mathtt{reveal}, \pi, M)$ to the environment $\mathcal{Z}$.

Lemma 2. *The output of $\mathcal{Z}$ in Game_1 and Game_2 is computationally indistinguishable.*

Proof. The proof of this lemma is straightforward and lies in the soundness property of the PC-SPHF. Following the mentioned property, $\mathcal{Z}$'s views are statistically close in both games. □

Game_3*:* In this game, similar to last one, Sim again modifies the simulation of an honest sender P_i. But, in the commitment phase, Sim commits to message $M = [0]_1 = 1$. Accurately, upon receiving a query $(\mathtt{commit}, \mathsf{sid}, \mathsf{cid}, P_i, P_j, M)$ from $\mathcal{Z}$, the simulator Sim computes $\mathbf{c}$ with $M = 1$ and sends $(\mathtt{commit}, \mathsf{sid}, \mathsf{cid}, \mathbf{c})$ to P_j. In the opening phase, similar to Game_2, upon getting Open query, Sim simulates a π by computing the hash value H using the trapdoor keys (hk, τ). Finally, simulator Sim outputs $(\mathtt{reveal}, \pi, M)$ to the environment $\mathcal{Z}$.

Lemma 3. *Let $\Pi = (\mathsf{KGen}, \mathsf{Enc}, \mathsf{Dec})$, a labeled PKE, be IND-CCA. Then, the $\mathcal{Z}$'s view in Game_2 is computationally indistinguishable from Game_3.*

Proof. From the description of Game_3, we observe that the only difference with Game_2 is that, in this game the simulator Sim computes $\mathbf{c}$ with 1 instead of M. Actually, by having the trapdoor keys of the PC-SPHF, Sim can commit 1 in the commitment phase, and opens to M in the opening phase. Also by considering the IND-CCA property, we can say that Game_2 and Game_3 are statically close. As analyzed in Game_1, $\Pr[\mathsf{bad}_0] = \Pr[\mathsf{bad}_1] = \mathsf{negl}(\lambda)$. Similarly, in analysis of Game_2, we observed that Game_1 and Game_2 are statistically indistinguishable, so $\Pr[\mathsf{bad}_2] = \Pr[\mathsf{bad}_1] = \mathsf{negl}(\lambda)$. As already Game_2 and Game_3 are statically close, we conclude that the $\Pr[\mathsf{bad}_2] \approx \Pr[\mathsf{bad}_3] = \mathsf{negl}(\lambda)$. □

Game_4*:* This game corresponds to the *ideal world* in the CRS model. In the ideal world, there exists an ideal functionality $\mathcal{F}_{\mathsf{mcom}}$ and the task of the honest parties in the ideal world simply convey inputs from environment $\mathcal{Z}$ to the ideal functionalities and vice versa. In ideal word, the ideal honest parties interact only with the environment $\mathcal{Z}$ and the ideal functionalities. In this game, the ideal-world adversary Sim proceeds as follows:

- *Initialization step:* Sim chooses $\mathsf{hk} \leftarrow_{\$} \mathbb{Z}_p^n$, and generates $\mathsf{hp} \leftarrow \mathsf{projkg}(\mathsf{hk}, \mathtt{crs})$, $\mathtt{crs}_{\mathcal{L}_{\mathsf{aux}}}$ and sets $\mathtt{crs} = (\mathtt{crs}_{\mathcal{L}_{\mathsf{aux}}}, \mathsf{hp})$. In addition, it chooses a collision-resistant hash function H.
- *Simulating the communication with* $\mathcal{Z}$: Every input value that Sim receives from $\mathcal{Z}$ is written on $\mathcal{A}$'s input tape (as if coming from $\mathcal{Z}$) and vice versa.
- *Simulating the commit phase when committer P_i is honest:* Upon receiving the receipt message $(\mathtt{receipt}, \mathsf{sid}, \mathsf{cid}, P_i, P_j)$ from $\mathcal{F}_{\mathsf{mcom}}$, Sim computes $\mathbf{c}$ with $M = [0]_1$ and sends $(\mathtt{commit}, \mathsf{sid}, \mathsf{cid}, \mathbf{c})$ to P_j.
- *Simulating the opening phase when P_i is honest:* Upon receiving input $(\mathtt{open}, \mathsf{sid}, \mathsf{cid}, P_i, P_j, M)$ from $\mathcal{F}_{\mathsf{mcom}}$, simulator computes proof $\pi = \mathsf{pH}$, and sends $(\mathsf{sid}, \mathsf{cid}, P_i, M, \pi)$ to P_j.
- *Simulating adaptive corruption of P_i after the commit phase but before the opening phase:* When P_i is corrupted, Sim can immediately read ideal P_i's inner state and obtain M. Then, Sim produces $\mathbf{c}$ as in the case of the opening phase when P_i is honest and outputs $(\mathtt{reveal}, \mathsf{sid}, \mathsf{cid}, \mathbf{c}, \pi, M)$ to the P_j.
- *Simulating the commit phase when committer $\hat{P}_i$ is corrupted and the receiver P_j is honest:* After receiving $(\mathtt{commit}, \mathsf{sid}, \mathsf{cid}, \mathbf{c})$ from $\hat{P}_i$ controlled by $\mathcal{A}$ in the commit phase, Sim decrypts $M' = \mathsf{Dec}^{\mathsf{t}}_{\mathsf{sk}}(\mathbf{c})$, where $\mathsf{t} \leftarrow (\mathsf{sid}, \mathsf{cid}, P_i)$ and sends $(\mathtt{com}, \mathsf{t}, P_j, M')$ to $\mathcal{F}_{\mathsf{mcom}}$.
- *Simulating the opening phase when committer $\hat{P}_i$ is corrupted and receiver P_j is honest:* Upon receiving, $(\mathtt{open}, \mathsf{sid}, \mathsf{cid}, M, \pi)$ from corrupted committer $\hat{P}_i$ controlled by $\mathcal{A}$, as it expects to send to P_j, Sim sends $(\mathtt{open}, \mathsf{sid}, \mathsf{cid})$ to $\mathcal{F}_{\mathsf{mcom}}$. ($\mathcal{F}_{\mathsf{mcom}}$ follows its codes: If a tuple $(\mathsf{sid}, \mathsf{cid}, P_i', P_j, M')$ with the same $(\mathsf{sid}, \mathsf{cid})$ was previously stored by $\mathcal{F}_{\mathsf{mcom}}$, $\mathcal{F}_{\mathsf{mcom}}$ sends $(\mathtt{reveal}, \mathsf{sid}, \mathsf{cid}, P_i', M')$ to ideal receiver P_j and Sim. Then, ideal receiver P_j convey it to $\mathcal{Z}$).
- *Simulating adaptive corruption of P_j after the commit phase but before the opening phase:* When P_j is corrupted, Sim simply outputs $(\mathtt{reveal}, \mathsf{sid}, \mathsf{cid}, \mathbf{c})$.

By construction, Game_4 is identical to the Game_3. □

4.2 Efficient Instantiation

Let us now instantiate this generic commitment with the labeled CS encryption scheme and our PC-SPHF on labeled CS ciphertexts. The resulting scheme is depicted in Fig. 5. The commitment consists of 4 elements in $\mathbb{G}_1$ and the opening of one element in $\mathbb{G}_1$, which, to the best of our knowledge, makes it the most efficient non-interactive UC-secure commitment scheme.

For concrete figures, we compare our instantiation to the most efficient instantiation under the plain DDH assumption in [2]. For the comparison let us assume a type 3 bilinear group with a desired security level of 128 bit. A popular choice are Baretto-Naehrig (BN) or Barreto-Lynn-Scott (BLS) curves. A conservative estimate for this security level yields elements in $\mathbb{G}_1$, $\mathbb{G}_2$ and $\mathbb{G}_T$ of size $2 \cdot 384$, $4 \cdot 384$ and $12 \cdot 384$ bits for BN and BLS12 and $2 \cdot 320$, $4 \cdot 320$ and $24 \cdot 320$ for BLS24 (without point compression) respectively [26]. Assuming that we use elliptic curves over prime fields to instantiate the plain DDH setting, elements of $\mathbb{G}$ will have at least $2 \cdot 256$ bits (without point compression) when targeting 128 bit security. Consequently, assuming point compression is used in both schemes, the commitment and opening size of the UC-commitment in [2] is 1799 and 512 bits respectively. Our UC-secure commitment has a commitment and opening size of 1284 and 321 bit respectively, improving [2] by about 30%. Furthermore, compared to the most efficient construction in bilinear groups (i.e., [1]), we obtain an improvement in the opening size of a factor 4.

$K_{crs}(1^\lambda)$: Compute and return hp and the CRS $\mathtt{crs} = (\mathsf{pk}, \mathsf{hp})$. // similar to Fig 4

// Commit phase:

$\mathsf{Commit}(\mathtt{crs}, M, \mathsf{sid}, \mathsf{cid}, \mathsf{C}, \mathsf{R})$: to commit to message $M = [m]_1 \in \mathbb{G}_1$ for R, upon receiving a command $(\mathtt{commit}, \mathsf{sid}, \mathsf{cid}, \mathsf{C}, \mathsf{R}, M)$, C does the following,

(a) Choose $r \leftarrow_\$ \mathbb{Z}_p$ and compute $[\mathbf{c}]_1 = [u_1, u_2, e, v]_1 \in \mathbb{G}_1^4$ where $[u_1]_1 = r[g_1]_1$, $[u_2]_1 = r[g_2]_1$, $[e]_1 = [m]_1 + r[h]_1$, $[v]_1 = r([c]_1 + \xi[d]_1)$, where $\xi = H(\mathsf{t}, [u_1]_1, [u_2]_1, [e]_1)$ and $\mathsf{t} = (\mathsf{sid}, \mathsf{cid}, P_i)$.;

(b) Compute $\mathsf{pH} = r[\mathsf{hp}_{11}]_1 + r\xi[\mathsf{hp}_{12}]_1 \in \mathbb{G}_1$;

(c) Send $(\mathtt{commit}, \mathsf{sid}, \mathsf{cid}, \mathsf{C}, \mathsf{R}, [\mathbf{c}]_1)$ to R. Securely erase randomness r and store $\pi = \mathsf{pH}$.

(d) Upon receiving $(\mathtt{commit}, \mathsf{sid}, \mathsf{cid}, \mathsf{C}, \mathsf{R}, [\mathbf{c}]_1)$, R checks that $[\mathbf{c}]_1 \in \mathbb{G}_1^4$. If yes, outputs $(\mathtt{receipt}, \mathsf{sid}, \mathsf{cid}, \mathsf{C}, \mathsf{R})$ and stores $[\mathbf{c}]_1$. Otherwise, R ignores it.

// Opening phase:

$\mathsf{Open}([m]_1, \mathsf{pH}, \mathsf{sid}, \mathsf{cid}, \mathsf{C}, \mathsf{R})$: when receiving a command $(\mathsf{open}, \mathsf{sid}, \mathsf{cid}, \mathsf{C}, \mathsf{R}, [m]_1)$, party C reveals $[m]_1$ and his state information $\pi = \mathsf{pH}$.

// Verification phase:

$\mathsf{Ver}(\mathtt{crs}, (\mathtt{commit}, \mathsf{sid}, \mathsf{cid}, [\mathbf{c}]_1), [m]_1, \mathsf{pH}, \mathsf{sid}, \mathsf{cid}, \mathsf{C}, \mathsf{R})$: computes $\mathsf{pcH} = [u_1]_1 \bullet [\eta_1]_2 + [u_1]_1 \bullet \xi[\eta_2]_2 + [u_2]_1 \bullet [\theta]_2 + ([e]_1 - [m]_1) \bullet [\mu]_2 + [v]_1 \bullet [\iota]_2 \in \mathbb{G}_T$ and verifies $\pi \bullet [1]_2 = \mathsf{pcH}$. R ignores the opening if the verification fails. If verification succeeds, R outputs $(\mathsf{open}, \mathsf{sid}, \mathsf{cid}, \mathsf{C}, \mathsf{R}, [m]_1)$ iff cid has not been used with this committer previously. Otherwise, R also ignores the message.

Fig. 5. UC-Secure commitment from PC-SPHF for the labeled CS encryption scheme.

5 Anonymous Credential System-Based Message Transmission

Anonymous credentials (ACs) were introduced in the seminal work of Chaum [17], and allow users to anonymously authenticate to a variety of services. Typical use-cases of ACs involve three main parties, users, authorities (organizations), and verifiers (servers). Each user can receive credentials (which can be a set of attributes) from authorities, and register pseudonyms with authorities and verifiers. Then users can prove to verifiers that a subset of their attributes verifies some policy P. The pseudonyms associated to the identity of the user should be unlinkable to its exact identity, i.e., another entity should not be able to check whether two pseudonyms are associated with the same identity. Due to their wide range of real-world applications, anonymous credentials have received a lot of attention from the cryptographic community, e.g., [5,11–14,17,22].

CRS generation. Run $K_{crs}(1^\lambda)$ and generate hp and the CRS $\mathtt{crs}_{\mathcal{L}_{\mathsf{aux}}}$ and set $\mathtt{crs} = (\mathtt{crs}_{\mathcal{L}_{\mathsf{aux}}}, \mathsf{hp})$. // similar to Section 3.2

Pre-flow. The server generates a key pair $(\mathsf{pk}, \mathsf{sk})$ of a CPA secure encryption scheme. It stores sk and sends pk to user U.

Credential use by user U_i. The user U_i does the following:

(a) Choose a random value J. Compute $J_F \leftarrow F(J)$ and $c_J = \mathsf{Enc}^{cpa}_{\mathsf{pk}}(J)$, as an encryption of J under pk.

(b) Choose $r \leftarrow\!\!\$\, \mathbb{Z}_p$ and compute the CS ciphertext $[\mathbf{c}]_1 = [u_1, u_2, e, v]_1 \in \mathbb{G}_1^4$. Compute $\mathsf{pH} = (r[\mathsf{hp}_{11}]_1 + r\xi[\mathsf{hp}_{12}]_1) \in \mathbb{G}_1$ and $c_{\mathsf{Cred}} = \mathsf{Enc}^{cpa}_{\mathsf{pk}}([\mathsf{Cred}_i]_1)$.

(c) Send $(c_J, [\mathbf{c}]_1, c_m)$ to the server. Store pH (as the new witness) and J_F, and securely erase J and the randomnesses used in the encrypting processes.

Database input Doc with policy P. When receiving the messages $(c_J, [\mathbf{c}]_1, c_m)$ from U_i , the server S decrypts $J \leftarrow \mathsf{Dec}^{cpa}_{\mathsf{sk}}(c_J)$, $[m]_1 \leftarrow \mathsf{Dec}^{cpa}_{\mathsf{sk}}(c_m)$, and computes $F(J)$ and does the following:

(a) Compute $\mathsf{pcH} \in \mathbb{G}_T$. Choose $s \leftarrow\!\!\$\, \mathbb{Z}_p$ and compute $\mathsf{H}_S = s \cdot \mathsf{pcH} \in \mathbb{G}_T$ and $\mathsf{hp}_S = s[1]_2$. Compute $c_S = F(J) \oplus \mathsf{H}_S \oplus \mathsf{Doc}$.

(b) Erase everything except (c_S, hp_S) and send them over a secure channel.

Data recovery. When receiving the tuple (c_S, hp_S), the user U_i, first computes $\mathsf{pH}_D = \mathsf{pH} \bullet \mathsf{hp}_S \in \mathbb{G}_T$, and then retrieves $\mathsf{Doc} = c_S \oplus J_F \oplus \mathsf{pH}_D$.

Fig. 6. UC-Secure Anonymous Credential System-Based Message Transmission from an PC-SPHF.

In this section, we revisit the use of anonymous credentials for message recovery proposed in [9]. Similar to [9], we present a constant-size, round-optimal protocol that allows to use an anonymous credential to retrieve a message without revealing the identity of the receiver in a UC secure way, but more efficient than the one proposed in [9]. We follow the scenario of [9], and assume that different organization issue credentials to users. The full construction is shown in Fig. 6.

For the security analyzing, we first describe the ideal functionality $\mathcal{F}_{\mathsf{ac}}$ for Anonymous Credential-Based Message Transmission proposed by [9]. It is depicted in Fig. 7. The user U_i received Doc form the server S when her credentials Cred comply with the policy P.

$\mathcal{F}_{\mathsf{ac}}$, parameterized by a message space $\mathcal{D} \in \{0,1\}^\lambda$, interacts with adversary Sim and parties $P_1, \ldots, P_n$ as follows.

- **Upon receiving $(\mathtt{send}, \mathsf{sid}, \mathsf{cid}, P_i, P_j, \mathsf{Doc})$ from P_i, where $\mathsf{Doc} \in \mathcal{D}$, proceed as follows: if a tuple $(\mathsf{sid}, \mathsf{cid}, P_i, P_j, \mathsf{Doc})$ with the same $(\mathsf{sid}, \mathsf{cid})$ was previously recorded, do nothing. Otherwise, record $(\mathsf{sid}, \mathsf{cid}, P_i, P_j, M)$ and reveal $(\mathtt{send}, \mathsf{sid}, \mathsf{cid}, P_i, P_j)$ to Sim.**
- **Upon receiving $(\mathtt{receive}, \mathsf{sid}, \mathsf{cid}, \mathsf{Cred})$ from P_j, proceed as follows: if a tuple $(\mathsf{sid}, \mathsf{cid}, P_i, P_j, \mathsf{Doc})$ was previously recorded then send $(\mathtt{receive}, \mathsf{sid}, \mathsf{cid}, P_i, P_j)$ to Sim, and send $(\mathtt{receive}, \mathsf{sid}, \mathsf{cid}, P_i, P_j, \mathsf{Doc}')$ to P_J, where $\mathsf{Doc}' = \mathsf{Doc}$ if the credentials comply with the policy P, and $\mathsf{Doc}' = \perp$ otherwise. Ignore further receive messages with the same cid from P_j.**

Fig. 7. Functionality $\mathcal{F}_{\mathsf{ac}}$ for Ideal Functionality for Anonymous Credential-Based Message Transmission

Theorem 3. *The Anonymous Credential System-Based Message Transmission protocol described in Fig. 6 is UC secure in the presence of adaptive adversaries, assuming reliable erasures and authenticated channels.*

Proof. From a high level point of view, in the case of adaptive corruptions and for the simulating procedure we use an extractable and equivocable commitment, which allows the simulator Sim to simply open the commitment to any message (credential). Intuitively, the equivocability property of the commitment enables Sim to adapt the incorrect credential and the used randomness such that they seem to be in the language. By extractability property, when simulating the sever, Sim knows whether it has to send the correct message. Recall that by adaptive corruption we mean the adversary $\mathcal{A}$ is able to corrupt any player at any time during the execution of the protocol. Notice that the simulator Sim first generates the CRS $\mathtt{crs}$ and the PC-SPHF parameters. As usual, we can construct an ideal-world adversary Sim that runs a black-box simulation of the real-world adversary $\mathcal{A}$ by simulating the protocol execution and relaying messages between $\mathcal{A}$ and the environment $\mathcal{Z}$. Sim proceeds as follows in experiment *IDEAL*. The sketch of the proof is as follows,

- In pre-flow phase, upon receiving the $\mathtt{send}$ query from $\mathcal{F}_{\mathsf{ac}}$, Sim generates a key pair $(\mathsf{pk}, \mathsf{sk})$ (he knows it from an honest sender has sent a pre-flow).

- Upon receiving receivequery from $\mathcal{F}_{\mathsf{ac}}$, by using an equivocable commitment, Sim computes the tuple $(\mathsf{pH}, [\mathsf{c}]_1, \boldsymbol{c}_m)$ with label $(\mathsf{sid}, \mathsf{cid}, P_i, P_j)$ and a ciphertext $\boldsymbol{c}_J \leftarrow \mathsf{Enc}^{cpa}_{\mathsf{pk}}(J)$ where J_F is a random value. Note that Sim already has received a pre-flow pk from an honest or a corrupted sender.
- If $\mathcal{Z}$ requires uncorrupted server S who received the tuple $(\boldsymbol{c}_J, [\mathsf{c}]_1, \boldsymbol{c}_{\mathsf{Cred}})$ from a corrupted U_i, Sim decrypts the ciphertexts $\boldsymbol{c}_J$, and $\boldsymbol{c}_{\mathsf{Cred}}$, and obtains J and $[\mathsf{Cred_i}]_1$. Sim, and then computes $F(J)$. It extracts the committed values (Cred) and check if it is correct and sends receive to $\mathcal{F}_{\mathsf{ac}}$.
- When $\mathcal{Z}$ requires uncorrupted user U_i who received the tuple $(\boldsymbol{c}_S, \mathsf{hp}_S)$ from a corrupted S, Sim computes pH_D and obtains Doc and uses this value in a send query to $\mathcal{F}_{\mathsf{ac}}$.
- In the case of an honest server, when Sim receives a receive query and Doc from $\mathcal{F}_{\mathsf{ac}}$, it sends Doc to the corrupted user.
- When $\mathcal{Z}$ requires uncorrupted server S who is interacting with an uncorrupted user U_i, Sim sets Doc $= 0$ and choose J_F randomly instead of computing it correctly by $F(J)$. It computes the commitment $(\boldsymbol{c}_J, [\mathsf{c}]_1, \boldsymbol{c}_{\mathsf{Cred}})$. In case of corruption afterwards, due to equivocability property of the commitment the value J_F can be adapted during the simulation such that it gives the message Doc received by the user in case his credentials comply with the policy. □

6 Open Problem

In [24], Katz and Vaikuntanathan constructed the first (approximate) SPHF for a lattice-based language: the language of ciphertexts of some given plaintext for an LWE-based IND-CCA encryption scheme. Later, by using harmonic analysis, Benhamouda et al. [8] improved the Katz-Vaikuntanathan construction, where the construction is over a tag-based IND-CCA encryption scheme a la Micciancio-Peikert [27]. An interesting open question is the construction of PC-SPHFs for the class of lattice-based languages.

Acknowledgments. This work was supported by the EU's Horizon 2020 ECSEL Joint Undertaking project SECREDAS under grant agreement n°783119, the Austrian Science Fund (FWF) and netidee SCIENCE project PROFET (grant agreement P31621-N38) and the Estonian Research Council grant PRG49.

References

1. Abdalla, M., Benhamouda, F., Blazy, O., Chevalier, C., Pointcheval, D.: SPHF-friendly non-interactive commitments. In: Sako, K., Sarkar, P. (eds.) ASIACRYPT 2013, Part I. LNCS, vol. 8269, pp. 214–234. Springer, Heidelberg (2013). https://doi.org/10.1007/978-3-642-42033-7_12
2. Abdalla, M., Benhamouda, F., Pointcheval, D.: Removing erasures with explainable hash proof systems. In: Fehr, S. (ed.) PKC 2017, Part I. LNCS, vol. 10174, pp. 151–174. Springer, Heidelberg (2017). https://doi.org/10.1007/978-3-662-54365-8_7

3. Abdalla, M., Chevalier, C., Pointcheval, D.: Smooth projective hashing for conditionally extractable commitments. In: Halevi, S. (ed.) CRYPTO 2009. LNCS, vol. 5677, pp. 671–689. Springer, Heidelberg (2009). https://doi.org/10.1007/978-3-642-03356-8_39
4. Abdolmaleki, B., Baghery, K., Lipmaa, H., Siim, J., Zając, M.: DL-extractable UC-commitment schemes. In: Deng, R.H., Gauthier-Umaña, V., Ochoa, M., Yung, M. (eds.) ACNS 2019. LNCS, vol. 11464, pp. 385–405. Springer, Cham (2019). https://doi.org/10.1007/978-3-030-21568-2_19
5. Belenkiy, M., Camenisch, J., Chase, M., Kohlweiss, M., Lysyanskaya, A., Shacham, H.: Randomizable proofs and delegatable anonymous credentials. In: Halevi, S. (ed.) CRYPTO 2009. LNCS, vol. 5677, pp. 108–125. Springer, Heidelberg (2009). https://doi.org/10.1007/978-3-642-03356-8_7
6. Benhamouda, F., Blazy, O., Chevalier, C., Pointcheval, D., Vergnaud, D.: New techniques for SPHFs and efficient one-round PAKE protocols. In: Canetti, R., Garay, J.A. (eds.) CRYPTO 2013. LNCS, vol. 8042, pp. 449–475. Springer, Heidelberg (2013). https://doi.org/10.1007/978-3-642-40041-4_25
7. Benhamouda, F., Blazy, O., Chevalier, C., Pointcheval, D., Vergnaud, D.: New techniques for SPHFs and efficient one-round PAKE protocols. Cryptology ePrint Archive, Report 2015/188 (2015). http://eprint.iacr.org/2015/188
8. Benhamouda, F., Blazy, O., Ducas, L., Quach, W.: Hash proof systems over lattices revisited. In: Abdalla, M., Dahab, R. (eds.) PKC 2018, Part II. LNCS, vol. 10770, pp. 644–674. Springer, Cham (2018). https://doi.org/10.1007/978-3-319-76581-5_22
9. Blazy, O., Chevalier, C.: Structure-preserving smooth projective hashing. In: Cheon, J.H., Takagi, T. (eds.) ASIACRYPT 2016, Part II. LNCS, vol. 10032, pp. 339–369. Springer, Heidelberg (2016). https://doi.org/10.1007/978-3-662-53890-6_12
10. Blazy, O., Pointcheval, D., Vergnaud, D.: Round-optimal privacy-preserving protocols with smooth projective hash functions. In: Cramer, R. (ed.) TCC 2012. LNCS, vol. 7194, pp. 94–111. Springer, Heidelberg (2012). https://doi.org/10.1007/978-3-642-28914-9_6
11. Camenisch, J., Krenn, S., Lehmann, A., Mikkelsen, G.L., Neven, G., Pedersen, M.Ø.: Formal treatment of privacy-enhancing credential systems. In: Dunkelman, O., Keliher, L. (eds.) SAC 2015. LNCS, vol. 9566, pp. 3–24. Springer, Cham (2016). https://doi.org/10.1007/978-3-319-31301-6_1
12. Camenisch, J., Lysyanskaya, A.: An efficient system for non-transferable anonymous credentials with optional anonymity revocation. In: Pfitzmann, B. (ed.) EUROCRYPT 2001. LNCS, vol. 2045, pp. 93–118. Springer, Heidelberg (2001). https://doi.org/10.1007/3-540-44987-6_7
13. Camenisch, J., Lysyanskaya, A.: A signature scheme with efficient protocols. In: Cimato, S., Persiano, G., Galdi, C. (eds.) SCN 2002. LNCS, vol. 2576, pp. 268–289. Springer, Heidelberg (2003). https://doi.org/10.1007/3-540-36413-7_20
14. Camenisch, J., Lysyanskaya, A.: Signature schemes and anonymous credentials from bilinear maps. In: Franklin, M. (ed.) CRYPTO 2004. LNCS, vol. 3152, pp. 56–72. Springer, Heidelberg (2004). https://doi.org/10.1007/978-3-540-28628-8_4
15. Canetti, R.: Universally composable security: a new paradigm for cryptographic protocols. In: 42nd FOCS, pp. 136–145. IEEE Computer Society Press, October 2001
16. Canetti, R., Fischlin, M.: Universally composable commitments. In: Kilian, J. (ed.) CRYPTO 2001. LNCS, vol. 2139, pp. 19–40. Springer, Heidelberg (2001). https://doi.org/10.1007/3-540-44647-8_2

17. Chaum, D.: Showing credentials without identification. In: Pichler, F. (ed.) EUROCRYPT 1985. LNCS, vol. 219, pp. 241–244. Springer, Heidelberg (1986). https://doi.org/10.1007/3-540-39805-8_28
18. Cramer, R., Shoup, V.: Universal hash proofs and a paradigm for adaptive chosen ciphertext secure public-key encryption. In: Knudsen, L.R. (ed.) EUROCRYPT 2002. LNCS, vol. 2332, pp. 45–64. Springer, Heidelberg (2002). https://doi.org/10.1007/3-540-46035-7_4
19. ElGamal, T.: A public key cryptosystem and a signature scheme based on discrete logarithms. In: Blakley, G.R., Chaum, D. (eds.) CRYPTO 1984. LNCS, vol. 196, pp. 10–18. Springer, Heidelberg (1985). https://doi.org/10.1007/3-540-39568-7_2
20. Escala, A., Herold, G., Kiltz, E., Ràfols, C., Villar, J.: An algebraic framework for diffie-hellman assumptions. In: Canetti, R., Garay, J.A. (eds.) CRYPTO 2013, Part II. LNCS, vol. 8043, pp. 129–147. Springer, Heidelberg (2013). https://doi.org/10.1007/978-3-642-40084-1_8
21. Fischlin, M., Libert, B., Manulis, M.: Non-interactive and re-usable universally composable string commitments with adaptive security. In: Lee, D.H., Wang, X. (eds.) ASIACRYPT 2011. LNCS, vol. 7073, pp. 468–485. Springer, Heidelberg (2011). https://doi.org/10.1007/978-3-642-25385-0_25
22. Fuchsbauer, G., Hanser, C., Slamanig, D.: Structure-preserving signatures on equivalence classes and constant-size anonymous credentials. J. Cryptol. **32**(2), 498–546 (2019). https://doi.org/10.1007/s00145-018-9281-4
23. Jutla, C.S., Roy, A.: Shorter quasi-adaptive NIZK proofs for linear subspaces. In: Sako, K., Sarkar, P. (eds.) ASIACRYPT 2013, Part I. LNCS, vol. 8269, pp. 1–20. Springer, Heidelberg (2013). https://doi.org/10.1007/978-3-642-42033-7_1
24. Katz, J., Vaikuntanathan, V.: Smooth projective hashing and password-based authenticated key exchange from lattices. In: Matsui, M. (ed.) ASIACRYPT 2009. LNCS, vol. 5912, pp. 636–652. Springer, Heidelberg (2009). https://doi.org/10.1007/978-3-642-10366-7_37
25. Katz, J., Vaikuntanathan, V.: Round-optimal password-based authenticated key exchange. In: Ishai, Y. (ed.) TCC 2011. LNCS, vol. 6597, pp. 293–310. Springer, Heidelberg (2011). https://doi.org/10.1007/978-3-642-19571-6_18
26. Menezes, A., Sarkar, P., Singh, S.: Challenges with assessing the impact of NFS advances on the security of pairing-based cryptography. In: Phan, R.C.-W., Yung, M. (eds.) Mycrypt 2016. LNCS, vol. 10311, pp. 83–108. Springer, Cham (2017). https://doi.org/10.1007/978-3-319-61273-7_5
27. Micciancio, D., Peikert, C.: Trapdoors for lattices: simpler, tighter, faster, smaller. In: Pointcheval, D., Johansson, T. (eds.) EUROCRYPT 2012. LNCS, vol. 7237, pp. 700–718. Springer, Heidelberg (2012). https://doi.org/10.1007/978-3-642-29011-4_41
28. Pedersen, T.P.: Non-interactive and information-theoretic secure verifiable secret sharing. In: Feigenbaum, J. (ed.) CRYPTO 1991. LNCS, vol. 576, pp. 129–140. Springer, Heidelberg (1992). https://doi.org/10.1007/3-540-46766-1_9

Subverting Decryption in AEAD

Marcel Armour[1(✉)] and Bertram Poettering[2]

[1] Royal Holloway, University of London, Egham, UK
marcel.armour.2017@rhul.ac.uk
[2] IBM Research, Zurich, Switzerland
poe@zurich.ibm.com

Abstract. This work introduces a new class of Algorithm Substitution Attack (ASA) on Symmetric Encryption Schemes. ASAs were introduced by Bellare, Paterson and Rogaway in light of revelations concerning mass surveillance. An ASA replaces an encryption scheme with a subverted version that aims to reveal information to an adversary engaged in mass surveillance, while remaining undetected by users. Previous work posited that a particular class of AEAD scheme (satisfying certain correctness and uniqueness properties) is resilient against subversion. Many if not all real-world constructions – such as GCM, CCM and OCB – are members of this class. Our results stand in opposition to those prior results. We present a potent ASA that generically applies to *any* AEAD scheme, is undetectable in all previous frameworks and which achieves successful exfiltration of user keys. We give even more efficient *non-generic* attacks against a selection of AEAD implementations that are most used in practice. In contrast to prior work, our new class of attack targets the decryption algorithm rather than encryption. We argue that this attack represents an attractive opportunity for a mass surveillance adversary. Our work serves to refine the ASA model and contributes to a series of papers that raises awareness and understanding about what is possible with ASAs.

Keywords: Algorithm substitution attacks · Privacy · Symmetric encryption · Mass surveillance

1 Introduction

The Snowden revelations in 2013 exposed that mass surveillance is a reality. They also showed that even sophisticated adversaries with large resources have been unable to break well established cryptographic primitives and hardness assumptions, shifting their focus to circumventing cryptography. Together, these

The research of Armour was supported by the EPSRC and the UK government as part of the Centre for Doctoral Training in Cyber Security at Royal Holloway, University of London (EP/P009301/1). The research of Poettering was supported by the European Union's Horizon 2020 project FutureTPM (779391). The full version of this article is available at https://eprint.iacr.org/2019/987 [3].

M. Albrecht (Ed.): IMACC 2019, LNCS 11929, pp. 22–41, 2019.
https://doi.org/10.1007/978-3-030-35199-1_2

two facts suggest that the study of subverted implementations of cryptographic primitives and protocols is a fruitful area of research; Rogaway has gone so far as to call it a moral imperative [23]. The reader is referred to the survey by Schneier et al. [28], which provides a broad overview of subversion of cryptography, with some useful case studies. The idea that an adversary may embed a backdoor or otherwise tamper with the implementation or specification of a cryptographic scheme or primitive predates the Snowden revelations, and was initiated in a line of work by Young and Yung that they named *kleptography* [30,31]. This area of study can be traced back to Simmons' work on *subliminal channels*, e.g. [29], undertaken in the context of nuclear non-proliferation during the Cold War. In the original conception, kleptography considered a saboteur who designs a cryptographic algorithm whose outputs are computationally indistinguishable from the outputs of an unmodified trusted algorithm. The saboteur's algorithm should leak private key data through the output of the system, which was achieved using the same principles as Simmons' earlier subliminal channels.

PRECEDING WORK. Post-Snowden, work in this area was reignited by Bellare, Paterson and Rogaway (BPR) [8], who formalised study of so-called *algorithm substitution attacks* (ASAs) through the specific example of symmetric encryption schemes. In abstract terms, the adversary's goal in an ASA is to create a subverted implementation of a scheme that breaks some aspect of security (such as IND-CPA) while remaining undetected by the user. There is a tension for 'Big Brother' between mounting a successful attack and being detected; clearly an attack that simply replaces the encryption algorithm with one that outputs the messages in plaintext would be devastating yet trivially detectable. BPR stipulate that subverted schemes should at the very least decrypt correctly (according to the unmodified specification) in order to have some measure of resistance to detection, going on to define the success probability of a mass surveillance adversary in carrying out a successful attack, as well as the advantage of a user in detecting that an attack is taking place. BPR [8] demonstrate an attack against randomized schemes that relies on influencing the randomness generated in the course of encryption. Their attack applies to a sub-class of randomized schemes satisfying a property they call 'coin-injectivity'. Lastly, BPR also establish a positive result that shows that under certain assumptions, it is possible for authenticated encryption schemes to provide resistance against subversion attacks.

Degabriele, Farshim and Poettering (DFP) [12] critiqued the definitions and underlying assumptions of BPR. Their main insight is that perfect decryptability—as mandated by BPR—is a very strong requirement and artificially limits the adversary's set of available strategies. In practice, a subversion with negligible failure probability should be considered effectively correct.[1] As DFP note, decryption failures may happen for reasons other than subverted encryption, and if they occur sporadically may easily go unnoticed. DFP

[1] This is analogous to the fundamental notion in cryptography that a symmetric encryption scheme be considered secure even in the presence of adversaries with negligible advantage.

demonstrate how this can be achieved with an input-triggered subversion, where the trigger is some input (message, associated data, nonce, or a combination thereof) that is difficult to guess, making detection practically impossible.

Bellare, Jaeger and Kane (BJK) [6] improved on the attack of BPR, giving an attack which is effective against all randomized schemes. Whereas the attack of BPR is stateful and so vulnerable to detection through state reset, the BJK attack is stateless. BJK furthermore formalised that the desired outcome of an ASA from the point of view of a mass surveillance adversary is successful key recovery.

In concurrent work, we study the effects of subverting the receiver in the setting of message authentication codes [1,2]. Using similar techniques as in the current report, we provide ASAs that result in successful key exfiltration and thus universal forgeries.

CONTRIBUTIONS. Our work continues a line of investigation that serves to raise awareness of what is possible with ASAs, and highlights the importance of work countering subverted implementations. We consider ASAs from a new perspective that leads to results of practical importance. Recall that BPR established a covert channel through ciphertexts by manipulating the randomness generation; their model stipulated perfect decryptability, which resulted in their definitions being fragile. DFP identified this and proposed tolerating a (minimal) compromise of correctness, allowing trigger messages. We note that attacks employing trigger messages appear trivial to plant in formal security abstractions like IND-CPA where the adversary has full control over encrypted messages, associated data, and nonces. In practice, however, it is certainly questionable that adversaries have enough influence on any of the three to conduct DFP style attacks, as messages are chosen in special formats mandated by applications, nonces are implemented via counters, etc. We remove these dependencies, complementing the DFP approach, by attacking from a different angle: leaving perfect correctness intact, we (minimally) limit ciphertext integrity and establish a covert channel through decryption error events. Concretely, we manipulate the decryption algorithm to accept certain bogus ciphertexts. This requires the surveillance adversary to be able to observe whether a decryption implementation outputs a message or rejects the ciphertext. In many practical scenarios this is a mild assumption, for example if a decryption error results in a packet being dropped and automatically retransmitted. Furthermore, a subverted decryption algorithm could go beyond this by e.g. influencing timing information in future messages sent to the network. We conclude that this attack represents an attractive and easy to implement opportunity for a mass surveillance adversary.

Our results stand in opposition to previous work [6,8,12] which proposed subversion resilience of a large class of AEAD schemes to which many if not all real-world constructions such as GCM, CCM and OCB belong, as long as their nonces are generated deterministically via a shared state maintained by both encryptor and decryptor.[2] The key observation to resolve this apparent

[2] The members of this class of schemes are deterministic and satisfy certain technical correctness and uniqueness properties.

contradiction is that previous work has assumed, besides explicitly spelled out requirements like uniqueness of ciphertexts and perfect decryptability, implicit notions such as integrity of ciphertexts. In the ASA setting for AEAD where undermining the confidentiality of a scheme is the key goal of an adversary, it seems just as natural to assume that the adversary is also willing to compromise the integrity guarantees as well.

Related Work. We outlined the key publications on ASAs against symmetric encryption schemes above. Other works, briefly described here, consider subversion on different primitives and in different contexts. Berndt and Liskiewicz [9] reunite the fields of cryptography and steganography. Ateniese, Magri and Venturi [4] study ASAs on signature schemes. In a series of work, Russell, Tang, Yung and Zhou [24–27] consider ASAs on one-way functions, trapdoor one-way functions and key generation as well as defending randomized algorithms against ASAs. Goh, Boneh, Pinkas and Golle [18] show how to add key recovery to the SSL/TLS and SSH protocols. Dodis, Ganesh, Golovnev, Juels and Ristenpart [13] provide a formal treatment of backdooring PRGs, another form of subversion. Armour and Poettering [1,2] study subversion options for message authentication schemes (MAC). Cryptographic reverse firewalls [14,20,21] represent an architecture to counter ASAs via trusted code in network perimeter filters. Fischlin and Mazaheri show how to construct ASA-resistant encryption and signature algorithms given initial access to a trusted base scheme [17]. Fischlin, Janson and Mazaheri [16] show how to immunize (keyed and unkeyed) hash functions against subversion. Bellare, Kane and Rogaway [7] explore using large keys to prevent key exfiltration in the symmetric encryption setting. Bellare and Hoang [5] give public key encryption schemes that defend against the subversion of random number generators.

Camenisch, Drijvers and Lehmann [11] consider Direct Anonymous Attestation (DAA) in the presence of a subverted Trusted Platform Module (TPM). We note that subversion attacks on cryptographic primitives (on DAA, but just as well on message authentication as considered in the present article) manifest a major attack vector in particular against embedded cryptographic hardware modules like TPMs. This is because the main goal of such modules is to serve as a root of trust in exposed devices for which losing system integrity could be fatal. Subverting a TPM can thus have severe implications. As TPMs are widely available today, including for being embedded into virtually every modern PC, subverting them seems to be a promising option to conduct mass surveillance.

Structure. We first recall (Sect. 2) standard definitions for symmetric encryption schemes and their security. We next give definitions (Sect. 3) that provide a general framework in which to study ASAs. These have been refined and extended from prior work, crucially including the decryption oracle which had been ignored by previous work. Section 4 details our new type of attack, together with formal theorems quantifying the ability of an adversary to exfiltrate keys and the ability of the subversion to go undetected. We give two versions of our ASA: one for a passive adversary (the adversarial model considered by previous work), which we extend to a second ASA requiring an active trigger: a modified ciphertext provided to the decryption algorithm. We discuss the results of a proof-of-concept implementation in Sect. 5. Lastly, Sect. 6 explains how our attacks can be leveraged to compromise the security of popular practical schemes even more effectively, demonstrating how powerful ASAs become when conducted outside the clearly demarcated boundaries of a formal model. Concretely, we give evidence that ASAs against standardized AEAD constructions like GCM or OCB3 can be even more damaging than our attacks from Sect. 4.

2 Notation and Definitions

NOTATION. For a natural number $k \in \mathbb{N}$, we let $[k] = \{0, 1, \ldots, k-1\}$. We refer to an element $x \in \{0,1\}^*$ as a string, and denote its length by $|x|$. By ε we denote the empty string. The set of strings of length ℓ is denoted $\{0,1\}^\ell$. In addition we denote by $\bot \notin \{0,1\}^*$ a reserved special symbol. For $x \in \{0,1\}^*$, we let $x[i]$ denote the i-th bit of x, with the convention that we count from 0, i.e., we have $x = x[0] \ldots x[|x|-1]$. For two strings x, x' we denote by $x \parallel x'$ their concatenation. If S is a finite set, then $s \leftarrow_\$ S$ denotes choosing s uniformly at random from S. If $\mathcal{A}$ is a randomized algorithm, we write $y \leftarrow_\$ \mathcal{A}(x)$ to indicate that it is invoked on input x (and fresh random coins), and the result is assigned to variable y. In security games we write $\mathcal{A}^{\mathcal{O}_1,\ldots,\mathcal{O}_c} \Longrightarrow 1$ to denote the event that the adversary outputs 1 after being given access to the c oracles.

In Appendix A, we recall standard definitions for (length-preserving) pseudorandom functions and permutations.

2.1 Symmetric Encryption

We focus on the likely most widespread and practically useful encryption primitive: Authenticated Encryption with Associated Data (AEAD). We recall standard definitions of (deterministic) nonce-based AEAD, as per [22].

AEAD. A symmetric encryption scheme Π providing authenticated encryption with associated data is a triple of algorithms $(\Pi.\mathsf{Gen}, \Pi.\mathsf{Enc}, \Pi.\mathsf{Dec})$. Associated to Π are two parameters, $\Pi.\mathsf{kl}$ and $\Pi.\mathsf{nl}$, representing the key length and the nonce length. The key generation algorithm $\Pi.\mathsf{Gen}$ is a probabilistic algorithm that takes as input the key length $\Pi.\mathsf{kl}$ and returns a key $k \in \{0,1\}^{\Pi.\mathsf{kl}}$. Often $\Pi.\mathsf{Gen}$ is taken as the algorithm choosing k uniformly at random from $\{0,1\}^{\Pi.\mathsf{kl}}$. The encryption algorithm $\Pi.\mathsf{Enc}$ is deterministic and takes key k, message m, associated data d and nonce $n \in \{0,1\}^{\Pi.\mathsf{nl}}$ to deterministically obtain ciphertext $c \leftarrow \Pi.\mathsf{Enc}(k, m, d; n)$. Decryption algorithm $\Pi.\mathsf{Dec}$ is deterministic and $\Pi.\mathsf{Dec}(k, c, d; n)$ returns either a message m or the special symbol $\bot$. For simplicity, we assume that $|\Pi.\mathsf{Enc}(k, m, d; n)|$ is an affine function of the form $|m| + \tau$ where τ is some constant associated to the encryption scheme (all practical encryption schemes are of this type). We call τ the *stretch* of the encryption scheme. Lastly, where the context is clear, we drop the prefix Π.

Definition 1. *A symmetric encryption scheme* Π *is said to be* δ*-correct if for all tuples* $(m, d; n)$ *it holds that:*

$$\Pr\left[m \neq m' \mid k \leftarrow_{\$} \mathsf{Gen}(\mathsf{kl}), c \leftarrow \mathsf{Enc}(k, m, d; n), m' \leftarrow \mathsf{Dec}(k, c, d; n)\right] \leq \delta.$$

If $\delta = 0$ *the scheme is referred to as being perfectly correct.*

The classic privacy notion used for AEAD is indistinguishability from random bits under an adaptive chosen-plaintext-and-nonce attack, utilising standard game-based definitions. For the authenticity notion, we consider adversaries that aim to create (strong) forgeries. Security notions are as in [22]. Intuitively, the scheme provides confidentiality if the privacy advantage of any realistic adversary is negligible and authenticity if the forging advantage of any realistic adversary is negligible.

Definition 2. *The privacy advantage of an adversary* $\mathcal{A}$ *is given by*

$$\mathsf{Adv}_{\Pi}^{\mathrm{priv}}(\mathcal{A}) = \Pr\left[\mathcal{A}^{\mathsf{Enc}(k,\cdot,\cdot;\cdot)} \Longrightarrow 1 \mid k \leftarrow_{\$} \mathsf{Gen}(\mathsf{kl})\right] - \Pr\left[\mathcal{A}^{\$(\cdot,\cdot;\cdot)} \Longrightarrow 1\right],$$

where the $\$$ *oracle returns* $c \leftarrow_{\$} \{0,1\}^{|m|+\tau}$ *for any query* $\$(m, d; n)$*. We assume that* $\mathcal{A}$ *is nonce-respecting; that is,* $\mathcal{A}$ *does not make two queries with the same nonce.*

Definition 3. *The authenticity advantage of an adversary* $\mathcal{A}$ *is given by*

$$\mathsf{Adv}_{\Pi}^{\mathrm{auth}}(\mathcal{A}) = \Pr\left[\mathcal{A}^{\mathsf{Enc}(k,\cdot,\cdot;\cdot),\mathsf{Dec}(k,\cdot,\cdot;\cdot)} \textit{ forges} \mid k \leftarrow_{\$} \mathsf{Gen}(\mathsf{kl})\right],$$

where we say that $\mathcal{A}$ *forges if it receives any* $m' \neq \bot$ *from* Dec *where we require that* $(c, d; n)$ *is not the result of an encryption query* $(m, d; n)$*. We assume that* $\mathcal{A}$ *is nonce-respecting; that is,* $\mathcal{A}$ *does not make two encryption queries with the same nonce.*

3 ASAs on Symmetric Encryption Schemes

We now outline the framework which will allow us to describe our concrete ASAs in Sect. 4. The aim of an ASA is to replace a given (symmetric encryption) scheme with a compromised version; if the original scheme is denoted Π, we write $\widetilde{\Pi}$ for its subversion. The attacker may choose to replace one component of the scheme, or multiple. We model the subverted scheme as having an embedded attacker key which is shared with an external (mass surveillance) adversary. This approach was first used by BPR [8]. From the attacker's perspective, the ASA should be undetectable by the user and result in effective surveillance. We formalise these notions as detectability and key recovery. Our definitions are inherited from prior work [6,8,12]. Whereas previous work assumed that only the encryption algorithm might be subverted, we have generalised the definitions to reflect the possibility that any component (one or multiple) of the symmetric encryption

Game $\mathsf{Det}_{\Pi,\widetilde{\Pi}}(\mathcal{D})$	$\mathcal{O}_{\mathsf{Enc}}(k, m, d; n)$
$k_\mathsf{A} \leftarrow_\$ \mathsf{A.Gen}$	**if** $(b = 1)$ **then** $c \leftarrow \Pi.\mathsf{Enc}(k, m, d; n)$
$b \leftarrow_\$ \{0,1\}, b' \leftarrow_\$ \mathcal{D}^{\mathcal{O}_{\mathsf{Gen}}, \mathcal{O}_{\mathsf{Enc}}, \mathcal{O}_{\mathsf{Dec}}}$	**else** $c \leftarrow \widetilde{\Pi}.\mathsf{Enc}(k_\mathsf{A}, k, m, d; n)$
return $(b = b')$	return c
$\mathcal{O}_{\mathsf{Gen}}(\mathsf{kl})$	$\mathcal{O}_{\mathsf{Dec}}(k, c, d; n)$
if $(b = 1)$ **then** $k \leftarrow_\$ \Pi.\mathsf{Gen}(\mathsf{kl})$	**if** $(b = 1)$ **then** $m \leftarrow \Pi.\mathsf{Dec}(k, c, d; n)$
else $k \leftarrow_\$ \widetilde{\Pi}.\mathsf{Gen}(k_\mathsf{A}, \mathsf{kl})$	**else** $m \leftarrow \widetilde{\Pi}.\mathsf{Dec}(k_\mathsf{A}, k, c, d; n)$
return k	return m

Fig. 1. Game to define the detectability advantage of $\mathcal{D}$ with respect to $\widetilde{\Pi}, \Pi$.

scheme could be subverted, and adapted to explicitly consider AEAD schemes. We broadly follow the notational choices of BJK [6].

ASA SYNTAX. An algorithm substitution attack A on a scheme Π consists of a triple $(\mathsf{A.Gen}, \mathsf{A.Ext}, \widetilde{\Pi})$, where:

1. The attacker key generation algorithm $\mathsf{A.Gen}$ returns an attacker key $k_\mathsf{A} \in \{0,1\}^{\mathsf{A.kl}}$ for some constant $\mathsf{A.kl}$.
2. $\widetilde{\Pi} = (\widetilde{\Pi}.\mathsf{Gen}, \widetilde{\Pi}.\mathsf{Enc}, \widetilde{\Pi}.\mathsf{Dec})$ is a *subverted* symmetric encryption scheme.
   (a) The subverted key generation algorithm $\widetilde{\Pi}.\mathsf{Gen}$ is a probabilistic algorithm that takes as input the key length $\widetilde{\Pi}.\mathsf{kl}$ and the attacker key k_A, returning a key $k \in \{0,1\}^{\widetilde{\Pi}.\mathsf{kl}}$.
   (b) The subverted encryption algorithm $\widetilde{\Pi}.\mathsf{Enc}$ takes the attacker key k_A, user key k, message m, associated data d and nonce $n \in \{0,1\}^{\widetilde{\Pi}.\mathsf{nl}}$, outputting ciphertext $c \leftarrow \widetilde{\Pi}.\mathsf{Enc}(k_\mathsf{A}, k, m, d; n)$.
   (c) The subverted decryption algorithm $\widetilde{\Pi}.\mathsf{Dec}(k_\mathsf{A}, k, c, d; n)$ returns either a message m or the special symbol $\perp$.
3. The key extraction algorithm $\mathsf{A.Ext}$ takes as input k_A and has oracle access to both encryption and decryption oracles in the case of an active adversary, or to a transcript of ciphertexts in the case of a passive adversary. These notions are formalised in the key recovery game in Fig. 2. The output of this algorithm is a key $k \in \{0,1\}^{\widetilde{\Pi}.\mathsf{kl}}$.

We require that $\widetilde{\Pi}.\mathsf{kl} = \Pi.\mathsf{kl}$ and $\widetilde{\Pi}.\mathsf{nl} = \Pi.\mathsf{nl}$, as the subverted algorithm would otherwise be trivially detected. As in previous work, we assume throughout that the key generation is unsubverted, but we retain a syntax that allows for the more general case.

DETECTABILITY. In the formal notion of detectability, we allow a distinguisher $\mathcal{D}$ to interact with subverted encryption, subverted decryption and (for generality) subverted key generation. We assume that the distinguisher has access to its own reference copy of the unsubverted algorithms. It wins if it can distinguish between the base scheme and the subverted scheme in the game defined in Fig. 1. The detectability advantage of $\mathcal{D}$ with respect to Π, $\widetilde{\Pi}$ is given by

$$\mathsf{Adv}^{\mathrm{det}}_{\Pi,\widetilde{\Pi}}(\mathcal{D}) = 2 \cdot \Pr\left[\mathsf{Det}_{\Pi,\widetilde{\Pi}}(\mathcal{D})\right] - 1.$$

This definition is adapted from strong undetectability of [6]. Notice that (informally) a 'hard-to-detect' subversion of a perfectly correct base scheme necessarily satisfies some correctness condition. To see this, suppose that the subversion does not satisfy δ-correctness: it is detectable with probability at least δ.

KEY RECOVERY. Following [6], recovering the user's secret key is a strong property for an attacker. We give two flavours of the key recovery game, one for passive adversaries PassiveKR and one for active adversaries ActiveKR, as given in Fig. 2. In the passive case, we allow the adversary to observe ciphertexts and whether they are rejected. This is formalised through the transcript oracle $\mathcal{O}_{\mathsf{Trans}}$. For the active case, we allow the attacker to generate valid ciphertexts via $\mathcal{O}_{\mathsf{Enc}}$ and interact with a decryption oracle $\mathcal{O}_{\mathsf{Dec}}$ that reveals whether a submitted ciphertext is rejected. Both games are parametrised by a message sampler algorithm $\mathcal{M}$. Given its current state σ, $\mathcal{M}$ returns the next message with associated data (m, d) to be encrypted, together with a nonce $n \in \{0,1\}^{\Pi.\mathsf{nl}}$ and an updated state. It represents the choice of messages made by the sender. For simplicity, we model $\mathcal{M}$ as non-adaptive and nonce-respecting. It could be argued that a more realistic model might take into account that the adversary could influence the user's choice of messages to be encrypted. However, in constructing attacks we assume the weakest properties of the attacker.

Adversary A wins if A.Ext recovers the user's key k after interacting with the subverted encryption scheme. The key recovery advantage of A with respect to $\widetilde{\Pi}$ and $\mathcal{M}$ is given by

$$\mathsf{Adv}^{\mathrm{kr}}_{\widetilde{\Pi},\mathcal{M}}(\mathsf{A}) = \Pr\left[\mathsf{KR}_{\widetilde{\Pi},\mathcal{M}}(\mathsf{A})\right],$$

where $\mathsf{KR}_{\widetilde{\Pi},\mathcal{M}}(\mathsf{A})$ refers to the appropriate key recovery game according to whether the adversary is passive or active.

4 Mounting Attacks via Decryption Subversion

We now detail our ASAs, first for a passive surveillance adversary and then in the active case. It is easy to see that the attacks are undetectable according to the models in the literature [6,8,12], as the encryption algorithm is not subverted.

Imagine that Alice communicates with Bob. A passive adversary can observe ciphertexts from Alice to Bob. In addition, an active adversary can replace ciphertexts in transmission and submit its own (forged) ciphertexts to Bob. In the passive attack, the decryption algorithm is subverted so that it rejects a fraction of valid ciphertexts, bounded by an attacker controlled parameter. In the active attack, the decryption algorithm is subverted so that it accepts a (similarly bounded) fraction of invalid ciphertexts. The active attack requires the

Game $\mathsf{ActiveKR}_{\widetilde{\Pi},\mathcal{M}}$

$k_\mathsf{A} \leftarrow_\$ \mathsf{A.Gen}$
$k \leftarrow_\$ \widetilde{\Pi}.\mathsf{Gen}(\widetilde{\Pi}.\mathsf{kl}), \sigma \leftarrow \varepsilon$
$k' \leftarrow_\$ \mathsf{A.Ext}^{\mathcal{O}_{\mathsf{Enc}},\mathcal{O}_{\mathsf{Dec}}}(k_\mathsf{A})$
return $(k' = k)$

$\mathcal{O}_{\mathsf{Enc}}()$

$(m, d, n, \sigma) \leftarrow_\$ \mathcal{M}(\sigma)$
$c \leftarrow \widetilde{\Pi}.\mathsf{Enc}(k_\mathsf{A}, k, m, d; n)$
return (c, d, n)

$\mathcal{O}_{\mathsf{Dec}}(c, d; n)$

$m \leftarrow \widetilde{\Pi}.\mathsf{Dec}(k_\mathsf{A}, k, c, d; n)$
return $(m = \perp)$

Game $\mathsf{PassiveKR}_{\widetilde{\Pi},\mathcal{M}}$

$k_\mathsf{A} \leftarrow_\$ \mathsf{A.Gen}$
$k \leftarrow_\$ \widetilde{\Pi}.\mathsf{Gen}(\widetilde{\Pi}.\mathsf{kl}), \sigma \leftarrow \varepsilon$
$k' \leftarrow_\$ \mathsf{A.Ext}^{\mathcal{O}_{\mathsf{Trans}}}(k_\mathsf{A})$,
return $(k' = k)$

$\mathcal{O}_{\mathsf{Trans}}()$

$(m, d, n, \sigma) \leftarrow_\$ \mathcal{M}(\sigma)$
$c \leftarrow \widetilde{\Pi}.\mathsf{Enc}(k_\mathsf{A}, k, m, d; n)$
$m \leftarrow \widetilde{\Pi}.\mathsf{Dec}(k_\mathsf{A}, k, c, d; n)$
return $(c, d, n, (m = \perp))$

Fig. 2. Game to define the key recovery advantage of A with respect to $\widetilde{\Pi}$ and $\mathcal{M}$.

adversary to send Bob bogus ciphertexts (derived from genuine ciphertexts) that reveal Bob's secret key using decryption errors. Normally, these bogus ciphertexts are unlikely to decrypt correctly, i.e., they would be rejected. In both cases, if the decryptor is subverted then either real ciphertexts (in the passive case) or bogus ciphertexts (in the active case) can either be accepted or rejected, creating via the acceptance/rejection pattern a covert channel that will allow the key to be exfiltrated.

From the point of view of a mass surveillance adversary this is an attractive prospect: having passively collected all communications, triggered by some suspicion they can now target Alice and Bob's communication. By recovering Bob's key they may now decrypt all of the stored communication between Alice and Bob (and indeed from Bob to Alice as well).

We note that both of our attacks are stateless, which not only allows for much easier backdoor implementation from a technical perspective but also should decrease the likelihood that an implemented attack is detected through code review or observing memory usage.

4.1 Attack 1: Passive

Consider the following subversion of a given symmetric encryption scheme $(\Pi.\mathsf{Gen}, \Pi.\mathsf{Enc}, \Pi.\mathsf{Dec})$. Let $\widetilde{\Pi}.\mathsf{Gen} = \Pi.\mathsf{Gen}$ and $\widetilde{\Pi}.\mathsf{Enc} = \Pi.\mathsf{Enc}$. Let $\mathsf{A.Gen}$ choose a key k_A by $k_\mathsf{A} \leftarrow_\$ \{0,1\}^{\mathsf{A.kl}}$. Algorithms $\widetilde{\Pi}.\mathsf{Dec}$ and $\mathsf{A.Ext}$ are then specified in Fig. 3. The subverted decryptor $\widetilde{\Pi}.\mathsf{Dec}$ takes the same input as $\Pi.\mathsf{Dec}$ together with the attacker key, and utilises a pseudo-random function[3] F with $F\colon \{0,1\}^{\mathsf{A.kl}} \times \{0,1\}^* \to [\Pi.\mathsf{kl}] \times \{0,1\}$. In $\mathsf{A.Ext}$, we use the symbol $\star$ as a ternary

[3] See Appendix A for definitions of pseudo-random functions and length-preserving pseudo-random permutations.

Algorithm $\widetilde{\Pi}.\mathsf{Dec}(k_\mathsf{A}, k, c, d; n)$

1: parse $F(k_\mathsf{A}, c \parallel d)$ as $i \parallel b$
2: **if** $k[i] = b$ and $B(\delta)$ **then**
3:     return $\perp$
4: **else**
5:     return $\Pi.\mathsf{Dec}(k, c, d; n)$

Algorithm $\mathsf{A.Ext}^{\mathcal{O}_\mathsf{Trans}}(k_\mathsf{A})$

1: $\forall i \in [\Pi.\mathsf{kl}], \mathsf{key}[i] \leftarrow \star$
2: **while** $\exists j\colon \mathsf{key}[j] = \star$ **do**
3:     $(c, d, v) \leftarrow \mathcal{O}_\mathsf{Trans}$
4:     **if** $(v = 1)$ **then**
5:         parse $F(k_\mathsf{A}, c \parallel d)$ as $i \parallel b$
6:         **if** $(\mathsf{key}[i] = \star)$ **then**
7:             $\mathsf{key}[i] \leftarrow b$
8: return key

Fig. 3. Passive ASA against AEAD

symbol (neither 0 nor 1) to keep track of which key bits have been collected. In line 2 of the algorithm for $\widetilde{\Pi}.\mathsf{Dec}$, we write $B(\delta)$ to denote a Bernoulli trial which returns 1 with probability δ. Key extractor $\mathsf{A.Ext}$ takes as input the attacker key and the transcript, consisting of triples (c, d, n, v) where v is a bit representing whether or not the ciphertext decrypts to $\perp$.

Theorem 1. *Let* Π *be a perfectly-correct symmetric encryption scheme and let* $\ell = \Pi.\mathsf{kl}$. *Let* $\widetilde{\Pi}.\mathsf{Dec}$ *and* $\mathsf{A.Ext}$ *be defined as in Fig. 3. Let* $\mathcal{M}$ *be a message sampling algorithm, and* $F\colon \{0,1\}^{\mathsf{A.kl}} \times \{0,1\}^* \to [\ell] \times \{0,1\}$ *be a PRF with* $\mathsf{Adv}^{\mathrm{prf}}_F(\mathcal{F}) < \epsilon$ *for all efficient adversaries* $\mathcal{F}$. *Then*

(1) $\mathsf{Adv}^{\mathrm{kr}}_{\widetilde{\Pi},\mathcal{M}}(\mathsf{A}) \geq 1 - \ell e^{-\frac{q\delta}{2\ell}}$, *where* q *is the number of queries that* $\mathsf{A.Ext}$ *makes to the transcript oracle.*
(2) For all distinguishers $\mathcal{D}$, $\mathsf{Adv}^{\mathrm{det}}_{\Pi,\widetilde{\Pi}}(\mathcal{D}) \leq \frac{\delta q}{2}(1 + \epsilon)$ *where* $\mathcal{D}$ *makes* q *queries to its decryption oracle.*

Proof of (1). We use a combinatorial argument. Notice that this is essentially a coupon collection problem. We are looking for the probability that every key bit has been exfiltrated. If we fix i key bits that are not exfiltrated, there are $\binom{\ell}{i}$ ways to choose those fixed key bits. The probability that (at least) i of the key bits have not been exfiltrated is given by $\binom{\ell}{i}(1 - \frac{i\delta}{2\ell})^q$. Using the principle of inclusion exclusion, the probability that no key bit has not been exfiltrated is given by

$$\begin{aligned}
\mathsf{Adv}^{\mathrm{kr}}_{\widetilde{\Pi},\mathcal{M}}(\mathsf{A}) &= \sum_{i=0}^{\ell} (-1)^i \binom{\ell}{i} \left(1 - \frac{i\delta}{2\ell}\right)^q \\
&\geq 1 - \ell \left(1 - \frac{\delta}{2\ell}\right)^q \\
&\geq 1 - \ell e^{-\frac{q\delta}{2\ell}}.
\end{aligned}$$

□

Proof of (2). Clearly, the only way to distinguish between Π and $\widetilde{\Pi}$ is to observe $\widetilde{\Pi}.\mathsf{Dec}$ output $\perp$. Thus in order to distinguish, $\mathcal{D}$ must find $(m, d; n)$ such that $\perp = \mathcal{O}_{\mathsf{Dec}}(k, c, d; n)$ for $c \leftarrow \Pi.\mathsf{Enc}(k, m, d; n)$. This reduces to $\mathcal{D}$ finding some $c \parallel d$ such that $F(k_{\mathsf{A}}, c \parallel d) = i \parallel k[i]$ for some index i. Call this event W. Notice that for any F it holds that for all k_{A}, c, d we have $F(k_{\mathsf{A}}, c \parallel d) = i \parallel b$ for some index i and bit b.

We note that $\Pr[W] \leq \Pr[\mathsf{PRF}_F(\mathcal{F})]$ for all PRF adversaries $\mathcal{F}$. If not, it would be possible for $\mathcal{F}$ to act as a challenger to $\mathcal{D}$ and win its prf game whenever W occurs. Thus,

$$\begin{aligned}
\mathsf{Adv}^{\mathrm{det}}_{\Pi,\widetilde{\Pi}}(\mathcal{D}) &= \Pr\left[\mathsf{Det}_{\Pi,\widetilde{\Pi}}(\mathcal{D}) \mid b = 1\right] + \Pr\left[\mathsf{Det}_{\Pi,\widetilde{\Pi}}(\mathcal{D}) \mid b = 0\right] - 1 \\
&= 1 - (1 - \delta \cdot \Pr[W])^q \\
&\leq 1 - (1 - \delta \cdot \Pr[\mathsf{PRF}_F(\mathcal{D})])^q \\
&\leq 1 - \left(1 - \frac{\delta}{2}(1 + \mathsf{Adv}^{\mathrm{prf}}_F(\mathcal{D}))\right)^q \\
&\leq 1 - \left(1 - \frac{\delta}{2}(1 + \epsilon)\right)^q \\
&\leq \frac{\delta q}{2}(1 + \epsilon).
\end{aligned}$$

□

REMARK. Whereas (un)detectability does depend on the security of the PRF, the PRF can be quite weak without much impacting the adversary's key recovery advantage. If the base scheme Π's ciphertexts are indistinguishable from random (IND\$), then the PRF could simply choose the first $\lceil \log(\ell) \rceil + 1$ many bits of the ciphertext. This seems paradoxical, as strong privacy security is usually a desirable property but here it allows a simpler ASA to be successful.

We note that in practice, the subverted decryption algorithm $\widetilde{\Pi}.\mathsf{Dec}$ can be made more effective in a number of ways. Indeed, the model is very conservative and in practice it may be possible for $\mathsf{A.Ext}$ to observe a number of distinguishable error messages following [10].

4.2 Attack 2: Active

Consider algorithms $\widetilde{\Pi}.\mathsf{Dec}$ and $\mathsf{A.Ext}$ as specified in Fig. 4. The adversary $\mathsf{A.Ext}$ crafts special messages using a length-preserving pseudo-random permutation E under the attacker key[4]. We let $E : \{0,1\}^{\mathsf{A.kl}} \times \{0,1\}^* \to \{0,1\}^*$. The security of E will determine how easily the distinguisher $\mathcal{D}$ will be able to recreate a special message to trigger $\widetilde{\Pi}$. Furthermore, as in the passive attack, $\widetilde{\Pi}.\mathsf{Dec}$ makes use of a PRF F to determine whether or not to reject submitted ciphertexts. We let $F\colon \{0,1\}^{\mathsf{A.kl}} \times \{0,1\}^* \to [\Pi.\mathsf{kl}] \times \{0,1\}$. Although the notation implies keys are the

[4] See Appendix A for the definition of a length-preserving PRP.

Algorithm $\widetilde{\Pi}.\mathsf{Dec}(k_A, k, c, d; n)$	Algorithm $\mathsf{A}.\mathsf{Ext}^{\mathcal{O}_{\mathsf{Enc}}, \mathcal{O}_{\mathsf{Dec}}}(k_A)$
1: $m \leftarrow \Pi.\mathsf{Dec}(k, c, d; n)$	1: $\forall i \in [\Pi.\mathsf{kl}], \mathsf{key}[i] \leftarrow \star$
2: **if** $(m \neq \perp)$ **then**	2: **while** $\exists j: \mathsf{key}[j] = \star$ **do**
3: return m	3: $(c, d; n) \leftarrow \mathcal{O}_{\mathsf{Enc}}()$
4: $\widetilde{c} \leftarrow E^{-1}(k_A, c)$	4: parse $F(k_A, c \parallel d)$ as $i \parallel b$
5: $m \leftarrow \Pi.\mathsf{Dec}(k, \widetilde{c}, d; n)$	5: **if** $(\mathsf{key}[i] = \star)$ **then**
6: **if** $(m = \perp)$ **then**	6: $\widetilde{c} \leftarrow E(k_A, c)$
7: return $\perp$	7: $v \leftarrow \mathcal{O}_{\mathsf{Dec}}(\widetilde{c}, d; n)$
8: parse $F(k_A, \widetilde{c} \parallel d)$ as $i \parallel b$	8: $\mathsf{key}[i] \leftarrow b \oplus v$
9: **if** $(k[i] = b)$ **then**	9: return key
10: return m	
11: **else**	
12: return $\perp$	

Fig. 4. Active ASA against AEAD

same, we assume independent behaviour of F, E.[5] We analyse this construction in the formal model defined by game $\mathsf{ActiveKR}_{\widetilde{\Pi}, \mathcal{M}}$ in Fig. 2.

Theorem 2. *Let Π be a perfectly-correct symmetric encryption scheme and let $\ell = \Pi.\mathsf{kl}$. Let $\widetilde{\Pi}.\mathsf{Dec}$ and $\mathsf{A}.\mathsf{Ext}$ be defined as in Fig. 4. Let $\mathcal{M}$ be a message sampling algorithm. Let $\ell = \Pi.\mathsf{kl}$ and $\mathsf{Adv}_{\Pi}^{\mathrm{auth}} < \epsilon$. Let $F: \{0,1\}^{A.\mathsf{kl}} \times \{0,1\}^* \to [\ell] \times \{0,1\}$ be a PRF with $\mathsf{Adv}_F^{\mathrm{prf}}(\mathcal{F}) < 1$ for all efficient adversaries $\mathcal{F}$. Let E be a lp-PRP with $E: \{0,1\}^{A.\mathsf{kl}} \times \{0,1\}^* \to \{0,1\}^*$ and $\mathsf{Adv}_E^{\mathrm{prp}}(\mathcal{F}') < \epsilon'$ for all efficient PRP adversaries $\mathcal{F}'$. Then*

(1) $\mathsf{Adv}_{\widetilde{\Pi}, \mathcal{M}}^{\mathrm{kr}}(\mathsf{A}) \geq 1 - \ell e^{-\frac{q}{\ell}(1-\epsilon)}$, where $\mathsf{A}.\mathsf{Ext}$ makes exactly $\Pi.\mathsf{kl}$ calls to the decryption oracle and q calls to the encryption oracle.
(2) For every distinguisher $\mathcal{D}$, $\mathsf{Adv}_{\Pi, \widetilde{\Pi}}^{\mathrm{det}}(\mathcal{D}) \leq \frac{q}{2^\tau} + \epsilon'$, where $\mathcal{D}$ makes q queries to its decryption oracle.

Proof of (1). We use the same combinatorial argument as in Theorem 1. This time, the probability that (at least) i of the key bits have not been correctly exfiltrated is given by $\binom{\ell}{i} \left[(1 - \frac{i}{\ell}) + \frac{\alpha i}{2\ell}\right]^q$. Here α is the probability that $\Pi.\mathsf{Dec}(k, \widetilde{c}, d; n) \neq \perp$ given that $F^{-1}(k_A, \widetilde{c}) = j \parallel k[j]$ for j in the set of indices being counted. We note that $\mathsf{Adv}_{\Pi}^{\mathrm{auth}} \geq \alpha$.

$$\mathsf{Adv}_{\widetilde{\Pi}, \mathcal{M}}^{\mathrm{kr}}(\mathsf{A}) = \sum_{i=0}^{\ell} (-1)^i \binom{\ell}{i} \left[(1 - \frac{i}{\ell}) + \frac{\alpha i}{2\ell}\right]^q$$

$$\geq 1 - \ell \left(1 + \frac{1}{\ell}(\frac{\alpha}{2} - 1)\right)^q$$

$$\geq 1 - \ell e^{-\frac{q}{\ell}(1-\frac{\alpha}{2})}$$

$$\geq 1 - \ell e^{-\frac{q}{\ell}(1-\epsilon)}. \qquad \square$$

---

[5] Using only one key is just a trick to keep the notation compact.

Proof of (2). As in Theorem 1, the only way to distinguish between Π and $\widetilde{\Pi}$ is by observing $\widetilde{\Pi}.\mathsf{Dec}$ accepting a forged ciphertext. To do this, the distinguisher $\mathcal{D}$ must find some ciphertext c with associated data d such that $F(k_{\mathsf{A}}, \widetilde{c} \parallel d) = i \parallel k[i]$ for some $i \in [\ell]$ and where $\widetilde{c} = E^{-1}(k_{\mathsf{A}}, c)$. Noting that $\mathsf{Adv}_F^{\mathrm{prf}}(\mathcal{F}) < 1$, we thus obtain

$$\Pr\left[\mathsf{Det}_{\Pi,\widetilde{\Pi}}(\mathcal{D}) \mid b = 0\right] \leq \Pr\left[\begin{array}{c}\mathcal{D} \text{ finds } c \text{ with } E^{-1}(k_{\mathsf{A}}, c) = \widetilde{c} \text{ for some } \widetilde{c} \\ \text{with } \Pi.\mathsf{Dec}(k, \widetilde{c}, d; n) \neq \bot, \text{ for some } d, n\end{array}\right]$$

Consider the following game, which we will refer to as the pre-image game. For $b \in \{0,1\}$ we define experiment b as follows:

1. The challenger initially sets $C \leftarrow \emptyset$ and responds to query c_i in the following way:
   - if $(b = 0)$ then set $c_i' \leftarrow_{\$} \{0,1\}^{|c_i|} \setminus C$, update $C \xleftarrow{\cup} c_i'$ and return c_i'
   - if $(b = 1)$ then return $c_i' \leftarrow E^{-1}(k_{\mathsf{A}}, c_i)$.
2. The adversary $\mathcal{D}$ submits a sequence of queries $c_1, c_2, \ldots, c_q$ to the challenger and receives c_i' for $i \in [q]$.

For $b \in \{0,1\}$, let W_b be the event that $\mathcal{D}$ outputs 1 in experiment b; $\mathcal{D}$ outputs 1 if for some $d, n, \Pi.\mathsf{Dec}(k, c_i', d; n) \neq \bot$. The advantage of $\mathcal{D}$ in the pre-image game is clearly less than its advantage in distinguishing a lp-PRP from a random length preserving permutation. To see this, given $\mathcal{D}$ with some advantage playing the pre-image game we can construct an adversary $\mathcal{B}$ acting as a challenger to $\mathcal{D}$ such that $\mathcal{B}$ outputs 1 in the distinguishing game $\mathsf{PRP}_E(\mathcal{B})$ whenever $\mathcal{D}$ does in the pre-image game. Thus,

$$\Pr[W_0] - \Pr[W_1] \leq \mathsf{Adv}_E^{\mathrm{prp}}(\mathcal{B}).$$

Noting that $\Pr[W_1] = \frac{q}{2^\tau}$, where τ is the stretch of the encryption scheme, we conclude that

$$\mathsf{Adv}_{\Pi,\widetilde{\Pi}}^{\mathrm{det}}(\mathcal{D}) \leq \Pr[W_0] \leq \Pr[W_1] + \mathsf{Adv}_E^{\mathrm{prp}}(\mathcal{B}) \leq \frac{q}{2^\tau} + \epsilon'.$$

□

5 Implementation

We implemented our attacks in proof-of-concept Python code to verify their functionality and effectiveness.[6] The particular AEAD scheme we attack is AES-GCM [15], using black-box access to the implementation provided by [32]. We simulated both active and passive attacks 10,000 times, and recorded the number of queries for successful extraction of a 128-bit key (thus, $\ell = 128$). Messages, nonces and associated data were generated using the `random.getrandbits`

[6] We are happy to share our source code. Please contact the authors.

method from the `Crypto.Random` library. The plots below (Figs. 5 and 6) show the distribution (in blue) of the recorded number of queries q, and (in red) the cumulative success probability as a function of q. Our results confirm the theoretical estimates from Theorems 1 and 2; in particular, the exponential success rate. While the attacks have different application and success profiles, both reliably recover keys.

PASSIVE. The expected number of calls to the transcript oracle for successful exfiltration is given by $\frac{2\ell}{\delta}\sum_{i=1}^{\ell}\frac{1}{i}$ (see proof of Theorem 1). We set $\delta = 0.1$ for illustration. This gives us an expected value of $q = 13910$ compared to the recorded mean of 13920.59. Alternatively, the result from Theorem 1 gives a key recovery advantage of $\approx 1/2$ with $q = 14000$, compared to the recorded median of 13380. The discrepancy is due to the exponential approximation in the proof.

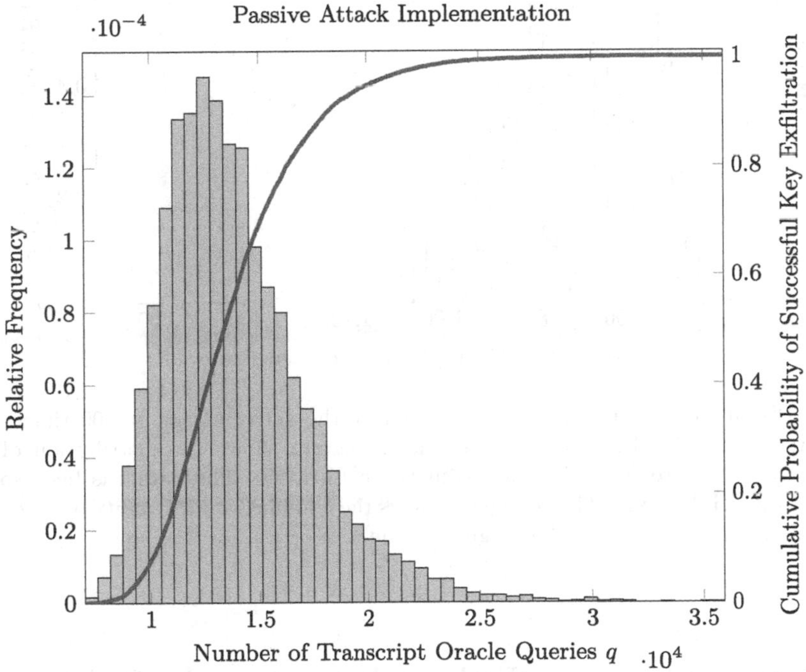

Fig. 5. Results of running an implementation of the passive attack 10,000 times. Key length $\ell = 128$, and parameter $\delta = 0.1$. **Left axis:** The blue histogram shows the distribution of the number of queries required for successful key exfiltration. The data has been sorted into 50 bins. **Right axis:** The red curve shows the cumulative probability of successful key exfiltration against q. (Colour figure online)

ACTIVE. We assume that for AES-GCM, $\mathsf{Adv}_{\Pi}^{\mathrm{auth}} \approx 0$ and set $\epsilon = 0$. The expected number of encryption calls for successful exfiltration is then $\ell\sum_{i=1}^{\ell}\frac{1}{i}$ (see proof of Theorem 2). This gives an expected value of $q = 696$ compared to the recorded mean of 695.05. Alternatively, the result from Theorem 2 gives a key recovery advantage of $\approx 1/2$ with $q = 710$ compared to the recorded median of 670. Again, the difference is due to exponential approximation.

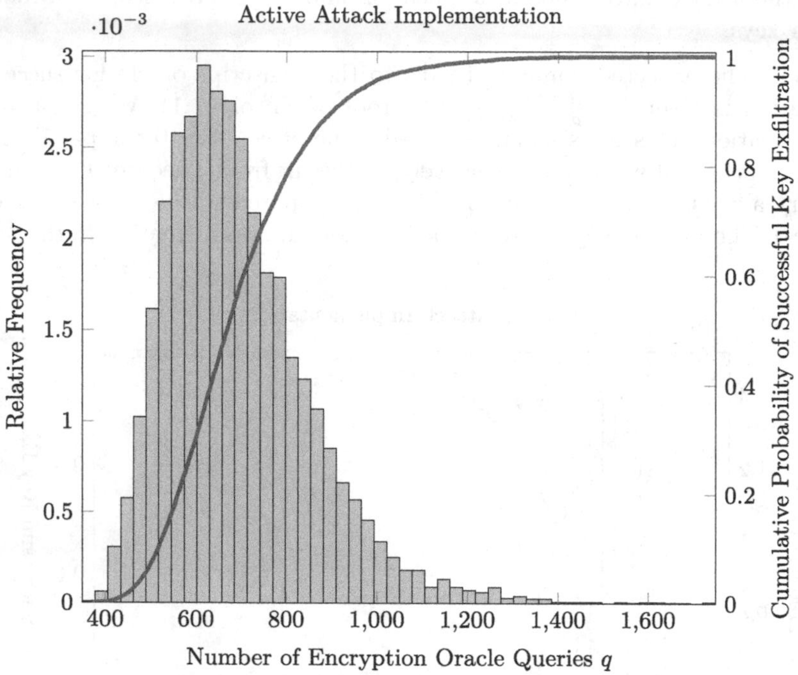

Fig. 6. Results of running an implementation of the active attack 10,000 times with key length $\ell = 128$. **Left axis:** The blue histogram shows the distribution of the number of queries required for successful key exfiltration. The data has been sorted into 50 bins. **Right axis:** The red curve shows the cumulative probability of successful key exfiltration against q. (Colour figure online)

6 Breaking Security Without Extracting the Full Key

The attacks presented in Sect. 4 are generic in that they are independent of the targeted AEAD scheme. Our approach, in common with previous work, was to extract the full key with which the AEAD instance is operated. Message recovery follows immediately by the definition of correctness. From this it is tempting to conclude that choosing longer keys, e.g. 256 bits instead of 128 in the case of AES-based encryption, gives better security against ASAs. (This approach is generally explored in big key cryptography [7].). In this section we show that this intuition is not necessarily correct. As we detail, many current AEAD schemes have inner building blocks that maintain their own secret values, and scaling up key sizes does not automatically also increase the sizes of these internal values. Note that ASAs in the style proposed in the previous section could easily be adapted to leak this internal information instead of the key. As the recovery of such values might not always directly lead to full message recovery, the assessment of whether the resulting overall attack is more or less effective than our generic attacks has to be made on a per scheme basis. We exemplify this on the basis of two of the currently best-performing AES-based AEAD schemes: GCM [15] and OCB3 [19]. In both cases, the size of the crucial internal value and the block size of the cipher have to coincide and the latter value is fixed to 128 bits for AES (independently of key size).

AES-GCM. We consider the following abstraction of GCM. The AEAD key k is used directly to create an instance E of the AES blockcipher. To encrypt a message m with respect to associated data d and nonce n, E is operated in counter mode, giving a pad $E(n+1) \parallel E(n+2) \parallel \ldots$, where a specific nonce encoding ensures there are no collisions between counter values of different encryption operations. The first part c_1 of the ciphertext $c = c_1c_2$ is obtained by XORing the pad into the message, and finally the authentication tag c_2 is derived by computing $c_2 \leftarrow E(n) + H_h(d, c_1)$. Here H_h is an instance of a universal hash function H indexed (that is, keyed) with the 128-bit value $h = E(0^{128})$. Concretely, $H_h(d, c_1) = \sum_{i=1}^{l} v_i h^{l-i+1}$, where coefficients $v_1, \ldots, v_l$ are such that a prefix $v_1 \ldots v_j$ is a length-padded copy of the associated data d, the middle part $v_{j+1} \cdots v_{l-1}$ is a length-padded copy of ciphertext component c_1, and the last item v_l is an encoding of the lengths of d and c_1. The addition and multiplication operations deployed in this computation are those of a specific representation of the Galois field $\mathrm{GF}(2^{128})$.

In executing a practical algorithm substitution attack against AES-GCM, it might suffice to leak the value h (which has length 128 independently of the AES key length, and furthermore stays invariant across encryption operations). The insight is that if the key of a universal hash function is known, then it becomes trivial to compute collisions. Concretely, assume the adversary is provided with the AES-GCM encryption $c = c_1c_2 = \mathsf{Enc}(k, m, d; n)$ for unknown k, m but chosen d, n. Then by the above we have $c_2 = R + \sum_{i=1}^{j} v_i h^{l-i+1}$ where the coefficients $v_1 \ldots v_j$ are an encoding of d and R is some residue. If, having been successfully leaked by the ASA, the internal value h is known, by solving a linear equation it is easy to find an associated data string $d' \neq d$, $|d'| = |d|$, such that for its encoding $v'_1 \ldots v'_j$ we have $\sum_{i=1}^{j} v'_i h^{l-i+1} = \sum_{i=1}^{j} v_i h^{l-i+1}$. Overall this means that we have found $d' \neq d$ such that $\mathsf{Enc}(k, m, d'; n) = c = \mathsf{Enc}(k, m, d; n)$. In a CCA attack the adversary can thus query for the decryption of c with associated data d' and nonce n, and thus fully recover the target message m. We finally note that this attack can be directly generalized to one where also the c_1 and c_2 components are modified, resulting in the decryption of a message $m' \neq m$ for which the XOR difference between $m = m'$ is controlled by the adversary.

OCB3. Multiple quite different versions of the OCB encryption scheme exist, but a common property is that the associated data input is incorporated via 'ciphertext translation' [22]. To encrypt a message m under key k with associated data d and nonce n, in a first step the message m is encrypted with a pure AE scheme (no AD!) to an intermediate ciphertext $c^* \leftarrow \mathsf{Enc}^*(k, m; n)$. Then to obtain the final ciphertext c, a pseudo-random function value $F_k(d)$ of the associated data string is XORed into the trailing bits of c^*. Concretely, in OCB3 we have $F_k(d) = \sum_{i=1}^{l} E(v_i + C_i)$ where all addition operations are XOR combinations of 128 bit values, $E(\cdot)$ stands for AES enciphering with key k, values $v_1, \ldots, v_l$ represent a length-padded copy of associated data d, and coefficients $C_1, \ldots, C_l$ are (secret) constants deterministically derived from the value $L = E(0^{128})$.

In the context of an ASA we argue that it is sufficient to leak the 128 bit value L. The attack procedure is, roughly, as in the AES-GCM case. Assume the adversary is provided with the OCB3 encryption $c = \mathsf{Enc}(k, m, d; n)$ for unknown k, m but chosen d, n, and assume the adversary knows L and thus $C_1, \ldots, C_l$. Now let $1 \leq s < t \leq l$ be any two indices, let $\Delta = C_s + C_t$ and let $d' \neq d$, $|d'| = |d|$, be the associated data string with encoding $v'_1, \ldots, v'_l$ such that we have $v'_s = v_t + \Delta$ and $v'_t = v_s + \Delta$ and $v'_i = v_i$ for all $i \neq s, t$. Then we have $E(v'_s + C_s) = E(v_t + \Delta + C_s) = E(v_t + C_t)$ and $E(v'_t + C_t) = E(v_s + \Delta + C_t) = E(v_s + C_s)$, which leads to $F_k(d) = F_k(d')$ and ultimately $\mathsf{Enc}(k, m, d'; n) = \mathsf{Enc}(k, m, d; n)$. In a CCA attack environment, this can immediately be leveraged to the full recovery of m. As in the AES-GCM case, we note that many variants of our attack exist (against all versions of OCB), including some that manipulate message bits in a controlled way.

7 Conclusion

This work examines subversion attacks against decryption only, providing two examples of a new class of Algorithm Substitution Attack that provides a mass surveillance adversary with a powerful and attractive strategy to compromise the confidentiality of mass communication. Previous models of ASA against symmetric encryption only considered subverting the encryption algorithm, and seemed to suggest that decryption could only be subverted together with encryption (and that analysing such "total subversion" is uninteresting, as this gives an adversary too much power).

Acknowledgements. Thanks to Jeroen Pijnenburg and Fabrizio De Santis for their early comments on this paper. Thanks also to the anonymous reviewers.

A Pseudo-Random Functions and Permutations

We recall standard notions of pseudo-random functions and permutations.

Definition 4. *A keyed pseudo-random function (PRF) for range R is an efficiently computable function $F\colon \{0,1\}^\ell \times \{0,1\}^* \to R$ taking a key $L \in \{0,1\}^\ell$*

and input $s \in \{0,1\}^*$ *to return an output* $F(L, s) \in R$. *Consider game* $\mathsf{PRF}_F(\mathcal{F})$ *in Fig. 7 associated to* F *and adversary* $\mathcal{F}$. *Let*

$$\mathsf{Adv}_F^{\mathrm{prf}}(\mathcal{F}) = 2 \cdot \Pr\left[\mathsf{PRF}_F(\mathcal{F})\right] - 1$$

be the prf advantage of adversary $\mathcal{F}$ *against function* F. *Intuitively, the function is pseudo-random if the prf advantage of any realistic adversary is negligible.*

Definition 5. *A keyed length-preserving pseudo-random permutation (lp-PRP) is an efficiently computable function* E *where* $E\colon \{0,1\}^\ell \times \{0,1\}^* \to \{0,1\}^*$ *takes a key* $L \in \{0,1\}^\ell$ *and input* $s \in \{0,1\}^*$ *to return an output* $E(L, s) \in \{0,1\}^{|s|}$. *We require that any keyed instance of* E *is a permutation on* $\{0,1\}^n$ *for all* $n \in \mathbb{N}$ *and also that its inverse* E^{-1} *is efficiently computable. Consider game* $\mathsf{PRP}_E(\mathcal{F})$ *in Fig. 7 associated to* E *and adversary* $\mathcal{F}$. *Let*

$$\mathsf{Adv}_E^{\mathrm{prp}}(\mathcal{F}) = 2 \cdot \Pr\left[\mathsf{PRP}_E(\mathcal{F})\right] - 1$$

be the prp advantage of adversary $\mathcal{F}$ *against function* E. *Intuitively, the permutation is pseudo-random if the prp advantage of any realistic adversary is negligible.*

Game $\mathsf{PRF}_F(\mathcal{F})$	Game $\mathsf{PRP}_E(\mathcal{F})$
$L \leftarrow_{\$} \{0,1\}^\ell, S \leftarrow \emptyset$	$L \leftarrow_{\$} \{0,1\}^\ell, S \leftarrow \emptyset$
$b \leftarrow_{\$} \{0,1\}, b' \leftarrow \mathcal{F}^{\mathcal{O}_{\mathsf{Fun}}}$	$b \leftarrow_{\$} \{0,1\}, b' \leftarrow \mathcal{F}^{\mathcal{O}_{\mathsf{Perm}}}$
return $(b = b')$	return $(b = b')$
$\mathcal{O}_{\mathsf{Fun}}(s)$	$\mathcal{O}_{\mathsf{Perm}}(s)$
if $(b = 1)$ **then** $y_s \leftarrow F(L, s)$	**if** $(b = 1)$ **then** $y_s \leftarrow E(L, s)$
else	**else**
if $s \notin S$ **then** $y_s \leftarrow_{\$} R$	**if** $s \notin S$ **then** $y_s \leftarrow_{\$} \{0,1\}^{|s|}$
$S \leftarrow S \cup \{s\}$	$S \leftarrow S \cup \{s\}$
return y_s	**return** y_s

Fig. 7. Game to define prf and prp advantage of $\mathcal{F}$ with respect to F, E.

References

1. Armour, M., Poettering, B.: Substitution attacks against message authentication. IACR Trans. Symmetric Cryptol. **2019**(3), 152–168 (2019). https://tosc.iacr.org/index.php/ToSC/article/view/8361
2. Armour, M., Poettering, B.: Substitution attacks against message authentication. Cryptology ePrint Archive, Report 2019/989 (2019). http://eprint.iacr.org/2019/989

3. Armour, M., Poettering, B.: Subverting decryption in AEAD. Cryptology ePrint Archive, Report 2019/987 (2019). http://eprint.iacr.org/2019/987
4. Ateniese, G., Magri, B., Venturi, D.: Subversion-resilient signature schemes. In: Ray, I., Li, N., Kruegel, C. (eds.) ACM CCS 2015: 22nd Conference on Computer and Communications Security, pp. 364–375. ACM Press, October 2015
5. Bellare, M., Hoang, V.T.: Resisting randomness subversion: fast deterministic and hedged public-key encryption in the standard model. In: Oswald, E., Fischlin, M. (eds.) EUROCRYPT 2015, Part II. LNCS, vol. 9057, pp. 627–656. Springer, Heidelberg (2015). https://doi.org/10.1007/978-3-662-46803-6_21
6. Bellare, M., Jaeger, J., Kane, D.: Mass-surveillance without the state: Strongly undetectable algorithm-substitution attacks. In: Ray, I., Li, N., Kruegel, C. (eds.) ACM CCS 2015: 22nd Conference on Computer and Communications Security, pp. 1431–1440. ACM Press, October 2015
7. Bellare, M., Kane, D., Rogaway, P.: Big-key symmetric encryption: resisting key exfiltration. In: Robshaw, M., Katz, J. (eds.) CRYPTO 2016, Part I. LNCS, vol. 9814, pp. 373–402. Springer, Heidelberg (2016). https://doi.org/10.1007/978-3-662-53018-4_14
8. Bellare, M., Paterson, K.G., Rogaway, P.: Security of symmetric encryption against mass surveillance. In: Garay, J.A., Gennaro, R. (eds.) CRYPTO 2014, Part I. LNCS, vol. 8616, pp. 1–19. Springer, Heidelberg (2014). https://doi.org/10.1007/978-3-662-44371-2_1
9. Berndt, S., Liskiewicz, M.: Algorithm substitution attacks from a steganographic perspective. In: Thuraisingham, B.M., Evans, D., Malkin, T., Xu, D. (eds.) ACM CCS 2017: 24th Conference on Computer and Communications Security, pp. 1649–1660. ACM Press (2017)
10. Boldyreva, A., Degabriele, J.P., Paterson, K.G., Stam, M.: On symmetric encryption with distinguishable decryption failures. In: Moriai, S. (ed.) FSE 2013. LNCS, vol. 8424, pp. 367–390. Springer, Heidelberg (2014). https://doi.org/10.1007/978-3-662-43933-3_19
11. Camenisch, J., Drijvers, M., Lehmann, A.: Anonymous attestation with subverted TPMs. In: Katz, J., Shacham, H. (eds.) CRYPTO 2017, Part III. LNCS, vol. 10403, pp. 427–461. Springer, Cham (2017). https://doi.org/10.1007/978-3-319-63697-9_15
12. Degabriele, J.P., Farshim, P., Poettering, B.: A more cautious approach to security against mass surveillance. In: Leander, G. (ed.) FSE 2015. LNCS, vol. 9054, pp. 579–598. Springer, Heidelberg (2015). https://doi.org/10.1007/978-3-662-48116-5_28
13. Dodis, Y., Ganesh, C., Golovnev, A., Juels, A., Ristenpart, T.: A formal treatment of backdoored pseudorandom generators. In: Oswald, E., Fischlin, M. (eds.) EUROCRYPT 2015, Part I. LNCS, vol. 9056, pp. 101–126. Springer, Heidelberg (2015). https://doi.org/10.1007/978-3-662-46800-5_5
14. Dodis, Y., Mironov, I., Stephens-Davidowitz, N.: Message transmission with reverse firewalls—secure communication on corrupted machines. In: Robshaw, M., Katz, J. (eds.) CRYPTO 2016, Part I. LNCS, vol. 9814, pp. 341–372. Springer, Heidelberg (2016). https://doi.org/10.1007/978-3-662-53018-4_13
15. Dworkin, M.J.: SP 800–38D: recommendation for block cipher modes of operation: Galois/Counter Mode (GCM) and GMAC. US National Institute of Standards and Technology (2007)
16. Fischlin, M., Janson, C., Mazaheri, S.: Backdoored hash functions: immunizing HMAC and HKDF. In: 2018 IEEE 31st Computer Security Foundations Symposium (CSF), pp. 105–118. IEEE (2018)

17. Fischlin, M., Mazaheri, S.: Self-guarding cryptographic protocols against algorithm substitution attacks. In: 2018 IEEE 31st Computer Security Foundations Symposium (CSF), pp. 76–90. IEEE (2018)
18. Goh, E.-J., Boneh, D., Pinkas, B., Golle, P.: The design and implementation of protocol-based hidden key recovery. In: Boyd, C., Mao, W. (eds.) ISC 2003. LNCS, vol. 2851, pp. 165–179. Springer, Heidelberg (2003). https://doi.org/10.1007/10958513_13
19. Krovetz, T., Rogaway, P.: The OCB authenticated-encryption algorithm (2014). https://tools.ietf.org/html/rfc7253
20. Ma, H., Zhang, R., Yang, G., Song, Z., Sun, S., Xiao, Y.: Concessive online/offline attribute based encryption with cryptographic reverse firewalls—secure and efficient fine-grained access control on corrupted machines. In: Lopez, J., Zhou, J., Soriano, M. (eds.) ESORICS 2018, Part II. LNCS, vol. 11099, pp. 507–526. Springer, Cham (2018). https://doi.org/10.1007/978-3-319-98989-1_25
21. Mironov, I., Stephens-Davidowitz, N.: Cryptographic reverse firewalls. In: Oswald, E., Fischlin, M. (eds.) EUROCRYPT 2015, Part II. LNCS, vol. 9057, pp. 657–686. Springer, Heidelberg (2015). https://doi.org/10.1007/978-3-662-46803-6_22
22. Rogaway, P.: Authenticated-encryption with associated-data. In: Atluri, V. (ed.) ACM CCS 2002: 9th Conference on Computer and Communications Security, pp. 98–107. ACM Press, November 2002
23. Rogaway, P.: The moral character of cryptographic work. Cryptology ePrint Archive, Report 2015/1162 (2015). http://eprint.iacr.org/2015/1162
24. Russell, A., Tang, Q., Yung, M., Zhou, H.-S.: Cliptography: clipping the power of kleptographic attacks. In: Cheon, J.H., Takagi, T. (eds.) ASIACRYPT 2016, Part II. LNCS, vol. 10032, pp. 34–64. Springer, Heidelberg (2016). https://doi.org/10.1007/978-3-662-53890-6_2
25. Russell, A., Tang, Q., Yung, M., Zhou, H.S.: Destroying steganography via amalgamation: kleptographically CPA secure public key encryption. Cryptology ePrint Archive, Report 2016/530 (2016). http://eprint.iacr.org/2016/530
26. Russell, A., Tang, Q., Yung, M., Zhou, H.S.: Generic semantic security against a kleptographic adversary. In: Thuraisingham, B.M., Evans, D., Malkin, T., Xu, D. (eds.) ACM CCS 2017: 24th Conference on Computer and Communications Security, pp. 907–922. ACM Press, October/November 2017
27. Russell, A., Tang, Q., Yung, M., Zhou, H.-S.: Correcting subverted random oracles. In: Shacham, H., Boldyreva, A. (eds.) CRYPTO 2018, Part II. LNCS, vol. 10992, pp. 241–271. Springer, Cham (2018). https://doi.org/10.1007/978-3-319-96881-0_9
28. Schneier, B., Fredrikson, M., Kohno, T., Ristenpart, T.: Surreptitiously weakening cryptographic systems. Cryptology ePrint Archive, Report 2015/097 (2015). http://eprint.iacr.org/2015/097
29. Simmons, G.J.: The prisoners' problem and the subliminal channel. In: Chaum, D. (ed.) Advances in Cryptology – CRYPTO'83, pp. 51–67. Plenum Press, New York (1983)
30. Young, A., Yung, M.: The dark side of "'black-box" cryptography or: should we trust capstone? In: Koblitz, N. (ed.) CRYPTO 1996. LNCS, vol. 1109, pp. 89–103. Springer, Heidelberg (1996). https://doi.org/10.1007/3-540-68697-5_8
31. Young, A., Yung, M.: Kleptography: using cryptography against cryptography. In: Fumy, W. (ed.) EUROCRYPT 1997. LNCS, vol. 1233, pp. 62–74. Springer, Heidelberg (1997). https://doi.org/10.1007/3-540-69053-0_6
32. Zhu, B.: AES-GCM-Python (2013). https://github.com/bozhu/AES-GCM-Python/blob/master/aes_gcm.py

Subversion-Resistant Simulation (Knowledge) Sound NIZKs

Karim Baghery(✉)

University of Tartu, Tartu, Estonia
karim.baghery@ut.ee

Abstract. In ASIACRYPT 2016, Bellare, Fuchsbauer and Scafuro studied security of non-interactive zero-knowledge (NIZK) arguments in the face of parameter subversion. They showed that achieving subversion soundness (soundness without trusting to the third party) and standard zero-knowledge is impossible at the same time. On the positive side, in the best case, they showed that one can achieve subversion zero-knowledge (zero-knowledge without trusting to the third party) and soundness at the same time. In this paper, we show that one can amplify their best positive result and construct NIZK arguments that can achieve subversion zero-knowledge and *simulation* (knowledge) soundness at the same time. Simulation (knowledge) soundness is a stronger notion in comparison with (knowledge) soundness, as it also guarantees non-malleability of proofs. Such stronger security guarantee is a must in practical systems. To prove the result, we show that given a NIZK argument that achieves Sub-ZK and (knowledge) soundness, one can use an OR-based construction to define a new language and build a NIZK argument that will guarantee Sub-ZK and *simulation* (knowledge) soundness at the same time. We instantiate the construction with the state-of-the-art zk-SNARK proposed by Groth [Eurocrypt 2016] and obtain an efficient SNARK that guarantees Sub-ZK and simulation knowledge soundness.

Keywords: NIZK · Subversion zero knowledge · zk-SNARK · Simulation extractability · CRS model

1 Introduction

Non-Interactive Zero-Knowledge (NIZK) proofs are one of the central design tools in cryptographically secure systems, allowing one to verify the veracity of statements without leaking extra information. Technically speaking, a NIZK allows a prover to prove that, for a public statement x she knows a witness w which hold in a relation $\mathbf{R}$, $(\mathsf{x}, \mathsf{w}) \in \mathbf{R}$, without leaking any information about her witness w. In the Common Reference String (CRS) model [BFM88], a NIZK requires a setup phase which is supposed to be done by a trusted third party. Under a trusted setup phase, usually a NIZK is required to guarantee

M. Albrecht (Ed.): IMACC 2019, LNCS 11929, pp. 42–63, 2019.
https://doi.org/10.1007/978-3-030-35199-1_3

three essential properties known as *completeness*, *zero-knowledge* and *soundness*. The property *completeness* guarantees that a honest prover always convinces a honest verifier. The *soundness* ensures that a malicious prover cannot convince the honest verifier except with negligible probability. Zero-knowledge property assures that the proof generated by prover does not leak any information about the witness w. Moreover, following some stronger requirements in practical systems, there have been various constructions for NIZKs that can achieve more stronger notions than bare soundness. The notions *knowledge soundness* and *simulation knowledge soundness* (a.k.a.simulation extractability) are two flavours of soundness that guarantee more security than what soundness achieves. Knowledge-soundness guarantees that if an adversarial prover manages to come out with an acceptable proof, there exists an efficient extractor which given some secret information can efficiently extract the witness from the proof. Zero-knowledge Succinct Non-interactive Arguments of Knowledge (zk-SNARKs) [Gro10,Lip12,PHGR13,BCTV13,Gro16,GM17,Lip19] are the most known and practically-interested NIZK arguments that guarantee knowledge soundness. By the date, the most efficient zk-SNARK is proposed by Groth [Gro16] in Eurocrypt 2016, which is constructed for Quadratic Arithmetic Programs (QAPs) and works in a biliner group. As an stronger notion, simulation knowledge soundness guarantees that knowledge-soundness is satisfied even if adversary already has seen arbitrary number of simulated proofs for any statements. Roughly speaking, simulation extractability guarantees that the proofs are also non-malleable and consequently secure against man-in-the-middle attacks. In Crypto 2017, Groth and Maller [GM17] proposed the first zk-SNARK in the CRS model for Square Arithmetic Programs (SAPs) that achieves (non-black-box) simulation extractability. Recently, Atapoor and Baghery [AB19] used a folklore OR technique [BG90] with a particular instantiation from CØCØ framework [KZM+15][1] and presented a variation of the state-of-the-art zk-SNARK proposed by Groth [Gro16] and showed that it can achieve (non-black-box) simulation extractability and outperforms Groth and Maller's zk-SNARK [GM17] considerably [AB19]. Concurrently, Lipmaa [Lip19] proposed several (non-black-box) simulation-extractable zk-SNARKs in the CRS model for different languages including QAPs, SAPs, Quadratic Span Programs (QSPs) and Square Span Programs (SSPs). By deploying zk-SNARKs in some bigger cryptographic systems that should guarantee universal composability (UC), some studies construct zk-SNARKs with black-box simulation extractability [KZM+15,Bag19a] which is a necessary requirement for using zk-SNARKs in the UC-secure protocols.

Importance of Setup Phase in the CRS Model. By deploying cryptographic primitives in various applications, recently there have been various attacks or flaw reports on the setup phase of cryptographic systems that rely on public parameters supposed to be generated honestly. In some cases, attacks are

[1] A framework with practically optimized primitives which given a sound NIZK lifts it to a universally composable or more precisely a black-box simulation extractable NIZK argument [KZM+15].

caused from maliciously (or incorrectly) generated public parameters or modifying cryptographic protocol specifications to embed backdoors, with intent to violate security of the main system [BBG+13, PLS13, Gre14, Gab19, LPT19, Hae19]. Specially, after the Snowden revelations, there have been various endeavours in constructing cryptographic primitives and protocols secure against active subversion. The primitives constructed in this setting, guarantee their pre-defined security with trusted parameters, even in the case that the public parameters are subverted. Initiated by Bellare et al. [BPR14] for symmetric encryption schemes, there have been various studies about subversion resistant of various cryptograph ic primitives, including signature schemes [AMV15], non-interactive zero-knowledge proofs [BFS16], public-key encryption schemes [ABK18] and commitment schemes [Bag19b].

Subversion Security in NIZK Arguments. In the context of NIZKs, in [BFS16], Bellare, Fuchsbauer and Scafuro tackled the discussed problem by studying how much security one can still achieve when the CRS generator cannot be trusted. They first defined three new notions called subversion witness indistinguishability (Sub-WI), subversion zero-knowledge (Sub-ZK) and subversion soundness (Sub-SND) as a variant of the standard notions witness indistinguishability (WI), zero-knowledge (ZK) and soundness (SND) in NIZK arguments. The main difference of proposed notions with the standard ones is that in the new ones the setup phase is compromised and the parameters can be generated maliciously. For instance, the notion Sub-ZK guarantees that even if an adversary generates the CRS elements, still the NIZK proof does not leak any information about the witness of the prover. Intuitively, Sub-ZK implies that the ZK is guaranteed even if an adversary generates the CRS. In the rest, Bellare et al. showed that the definitions of Sub-SND and ZK are not compatible; as the former requires that a prover should not be able to generate a fake proof even if he generates the CRS, but the later implies that there exists a simulation algorithm that given trapdoors of CRS can generate a (fake) simulated proof indistinguishable from the real ones. This resulted a negative result that we cannot construct a NIZK argument which will guarantee ZK and Sub-SND simultaneously.

The above negative result opened two possible directions for positive results on subversion-resistant proof systems. One direction was achieving Sub-ZK and a version of soundness (i.e. one of notions soundness, knowledge soundness or simulation knowledge soundness) and the second direction was achieving Sub-WI (the best notion weaker than ZK) and a notion of Sub-SND (one of notions subversion soundness, subversion knowledge soundness or subversion simulation knowledge soundness). Along the first direction, Bellare et al. showed that one can construct NIZK arguments which achieve Sub-ZK and SND at the same time [BFS16]. Their main idea to achieve Sub-ZK is to use a knowledge assumption in the proof of zero-knowledge to extract the trapdoors of CRS from untrusted CRS and then use them to simulate the argument. After this positive result, Abdolmaleki et al. [ABLZ17] showed that the state-of-the-art zk-SNARK [Gro16] can achieve Sub-ZK and *knowledge* soundness with minimal changes in the CRS and executing an efficient public algorithm to check the well-formedness of CRS elements. In a concurrent work, Fuchsbauer [Fuc18] showed that most of paring-based zk-SNARKs including Groth's scheme can achieve Sub-ZK and knowledge soundness simultaneously. In the same direction, Abdolmaleki et al. [ALSZ18] showed that one can achieve Sub-ZK and SND in the Quasi-Adaptive NIZK arguments which are a particular type of NIZK proof systems.

In the second direction of possible positive results, Bellare et al. [BFS16] showed that Zap schemes proposed by Groth, Ostrovsky and Sahai [GOS06] achieves Sub-WI and Sub-SND at the same time; as such proof systems do not require particular CRS (consequently they do not require a tru-sted setup phase) but provides weaker security guarantee than ZK. Recently, Fuchsbauer and Orru [FO18] showed that one can achieve even more in this direction, by presenting a Sub-WI and *knowledge* sound Zap scheme.

Problem Statement. By considering the summarized subversion-resistant constructions, one may ask if we can construct NIZK arguments with more stronger security guarantees in the face of subverted CRS. For instance, can we construct NIZK arguments that can guarantee Sub-ZK and *simulation* knowledge soundness at the same time, such that the prover will not trust a third party to achieve ZK and the verifier will obtain more security guarantee (more precisely non-malleable proofs) than knowledge soundness. In comparison with non-subversion-resistant simulation-extractable zk-SNARKs, our target constructions can eliminate the trust on CRS generators from prover side.

Our Contribution. We answer the question discussed above positively by constructing NIZK arguments that can achieve Sub-ZK and *simulation* knowledge soundness at the same time. Such construction guarantees that the prover does not need to trust a third party to achieve ZK, on the other side, extra from knowledge soundness verifier will get sure that the proofs are non-malleable. To construct such NIZK arguments, inspired by a folklore OR technique [BG90], we use a part of the C∅C∅ framework [BG90, DDO+01, KZM+15] that recently is also used by Atapoor and Baghery [AB19] to achieve simulation (knowledge) soundness in Gorth's zk-SNARK [Gro16]. We show that using such construction, given NIZK arguments that guarantees Sub-ZK and (knowledge) soundness, we can construct Sub-ZK and simulation (knowledge) sound NIZK arguments.

As an instantiation, we show that a recent variation of Groth's zk-SNARK proposed by Atapoor and Baghery [AB19] can achieve Sub-ZK with minimal extra computational cost. The cost is that similar to NIZK arguments that achieve Sub-ZK and (knowledge) soundness [ABLZ17, Fuc18], the prover only needs to execute an efficient algorithm (CRS verification) to check the well-formedness of CRS elements before using them. If CRS verification passed, the protocol ensures that the generated proof does not leak any information about the witnesses even if CRS generators collude with the verifier. This allows prover to achieve ZK without trusting to the CRS generators.

Table 1 summarizes current subversion-resistant constructions and compares with an instantiation of our result. First row shows the negative result that achieving Sub-SND and ZK at the same time is impossible as their definitions

Table 1. A comparison of our results with current subversion-resistant non-interactive proof systems and their security guarantees. WI: Witness Indistinguishable, ZK: Zero-Knowledge, SND: Soundness, KS: Knowledge Soundness, SS: Simulation Soundness, SKS: Simulation Knowledge Soundness, Sub-WI: Subversion Witness Indistinguishable, Sub-ZK: Subversion Zero-Knowledge, Sub-SND: Sub-Soundness, Sub-KS: Subversion Knowledge Soundness.

Achievable? ‖ Result in	Standard						Subversion resistant			
	WI	ZK	SND	KS	SS	SKS	Sub-WI	Sub-ZK	Sub-SND	Sub-KS
NO ‖ [BFS16]		✓							✓	
YES ‖ [BFS16]	✓		✓				✓		✓	
YES ‖ [FO18]	✓		✓	✓			✓		✓	✓
YES ‖ [BFS16]	✓	✓	✓				✓			
YES ‖ [BFS16]	✓	✓	✓				✓	✓		
YES ‖ [ALSZ18]	✓	✓	✓				✓	✓		
YES ‖ [ABLZ17,Fuc18]	✓	✓	✓	✓			✓	✓		
YES ‖ This work	✓	✓	✓	✓	✓	✓	✓	✓		

are incompatible [BFS16]. Next rows indicate the notions achieved in various presented non-interactive proof systems [ABLZ17,Fuc18,FO18,ALSZ18].

Our Technique. In the proposed construction, we use a part of the C∅C∅ framework and show that this part can be used to construct non-interactive arguments that will satisfies Sub-ZK and (non-black-box) simulation (knowledge) soundness. We define a new language $\mathbf{L}'$ based on an OR construction (that is added to achieve non-malleability) and the original language $\mathbf{L}$ in the input non-interactive argument that guarantees Sub-ZK. Then we use the basic property of an OR construction, i.e. that OR proofs can be simulated using the trapdoors of one branch. We show that if the input NIZK argument achieves Sub-ZK, then the lifted non-interactive argument also guarantees Sub-ZK. As in the notion of Sub-ZK the prover does not trust to the CRS generators and consequently the simulator does not trust to the simulation trapdoors, so in proof of Sub-ZK, different form C∅C∅ framework, we use a technique in subversion-resistant schemes and simulate the protocol. In this road, a key point is that the proofs for an OR-based language can be simulated by trapdoors of either first or second branch. Next, as an instantiation, we use the above result and show that since the state-of-the-art zk-SNARK proposed by Groth [Gro16] achieves Sub-ZK after some verifications on CRS elements [ABLZ17,Fuc18], its recent variation proposed in [AB19] (which uses the same OR construction) can achieve Sub-ZK after some efficient verifications on CRS elements.

Rest of the paper is organized as follows; Sect. 2 introduces notations and necessary preliminaries for the paper. The proposed transformation for constructing subversion-resistant simulation (knowledge) sound NIZK arguments is described in Sect. 3. In Sect. 4, we show that recent variation of Groth's zk-SNARK [Gro16] proposed by Atapoor and Baghery [AB19] can achieve Sub-ZK and simulation knowledge soundness with minimal extra computational cost. Finally, we conclude the paper in Sect. 5.

2 Preliminaries

Let PPT denote probabilistic polynomial-time. Let $\lambda \in \mathbb{N}$ be the information-theoretic security parameter, say $\lambda = 128$. All adversaries will be stateful. For an algorithm $\mathcal{A}$, let $\mathrm{im}(\mathcal{A})$ be the image of $\mathcal{A}$, i.e. the set of valid outputs of $\mathcal{A}$, let $\mathsf{RND}(\mathcal{A})$ denote the random tape of $\mathcal{A}$, and let $r \leftarrow_r \mathsf{RND}(\mathcal{A})$ denote sampling of a randomizer r of sufficient length for $\mathcal{A}$'s needs. By $y \leftarrow \mathcal{A}(x; r)$ we denote the fact that $\mathcal{A}$, given an input x and a randomizer r, outputs y. For algorithms $\mathcal{A}$ and $\mathsf{ext}_{\mathcal{A}}$, we write $(y \,\|\, y') \leftarrow (\mathcal{A} \,\|\, \mathsf{ext}_{\mathcal{A}})(x; r)$ as a shorthand for "$y \leftarrow \mathcal{A}(x; r)$, $y' \leftarrow \mathsf{ext}_{\mathcal{A}}(x; r)$". We denote by $\mathsf{negl}(\lambda)$ an arbitrary negligible function. For distributions A and B, $A \approx_c B$ means that they are computationally indistinguishable. In pairing-based groups, we use additive notation together with the bracket notation, i.e., in group $\mathbb{G}_\mu$, $[a]_\mu = a\,[1]_\mu$, where $[1]_\mu$ is a fixed generator of $\mathbb{G}_\mu$. A *bilinear group generator* $\mathsf{BGgen}(1^\lambda)$ returns $(p, \mathbb{G}_1, \mathbb{G}_2, \mathbb{G}_T, \hat{e}, [1]_1, [1]_2)$, where p (a large prime) is the order of cyclic abelian groups $\mathbb{G}_1$, $\mathbb{G}_2$, and $\mathbb{G}_T$. Finally, $\hat{e} : \mathbb{G}_1 \times \mathbb{G}_2 \rightarrow \mathbb{G}_T$ is an efficient non-degenerate bilinear pairing, s.t. $\hat{e}([a]_1, [b]_2) = [ab]_T$. Denote $[a]_1 \bullet [b]_2 = \hat{e}([a]_1, [b]_2)$.

Next we review QAPs that defines NP-complete language specified by a quadratic equation over polynomials and have reduction from the language Circuit-SAT [GGPR13, Gro16].

Quadratic Arithmetic Programs. QAP was introduced by Gennaro *et al.* [GGPR13] as a language where for an input x and witness w, $(\mathsf{x}, \mathsf{w}) \in \mathbf{R}$ can be verified by using a parallel quadratic check. Consequently, any efficient simulation-extractable zk-SNARK for QAP results in an efficient simulation-extractable zk-SNARK for Circuit-SAT.

An QAP instance $\mathcal{Q}_p$ is specified by the so defined $(\mathbb{Z}_p, m_0, \ell, \{u_j, v_j, w_j\}_{j=0}^{m})$, where m_0 is the length of the statement (e.g. public inputs and outputs in an arithmetic circuit), ℓ is a target polynomial (defined based on the number of constraints, e.g. number of multiplication gates in an arithmetic circuit), and u_j, v_j, w_j are three set of polynomials that encodes the wires in the target arithmetic circuit. More discussions about encoding an arithmetic circuit to an QAP instance can be found in [GGPR13]. A QAP instance $\mathcal{Q}_p$ defines the following relation, where we assume that $A_0 = 1$:

$$\mathbf{R} = \left\{ \begin{array}{l} (\mathsf{x}, \mathsf{w}) \colon \mathsf{x} = (A_1, \ldots, A_{m_0})^\top \wedge \mathsf{w} = (A_{m_0+1}, \ldots, A_m)^\top \wedge \\ \left(\sum_{j=0}^{m} A_j u_j(X)\right)\left(\sum_{j=0}^{m} A_j v_j(X)\right) \equiv \sum_{j=0}^{m} A_j w_j(X) \pmod{\ell(X)} \end{array} \right\}.$$

Alternatively, $(\mathsf{x}, \mathsf{w}) \in \mathbf{R}$ if there exists a (degree $\leq n-2$) polynomial $h(X)$, s.t.

$$\left(\sum_{j=0}^{m} A_j u_j(X)\right)\left(\sum_{j=0}^{m} A_j v_j(X)\right) - \sum_{j=0}^{m} A_j w_j(X) = h(X)\ell(X)$$

where $\ell(X) = \prod_{i=1}^{\mathsf{n}}(X - \omega^{i-1})$ is a polynomial related to Lagrange interpolation, and ω is an n-th primitive root of unity modulo p.

Roughly speaking, the goal of the prover of a zk-SNARK for QAP [GGPR13] is to prove that for public $(A_1, \ldots, A_{m_0})$ and $A_0 = 1$, she knows $(A_{m_0+1}, \ldots, A_m)$ and a degree $\leq n - 2$ polynomial $h(X)$, such that above equation holds.

2.1 Definitions

We use the definitions of subversion secure and standard NIZK arguments from [ABLZ17, Gro16, GM17]. Let $\mathcal{R}$ be a relation generator, such that $\mathcal{R}(1^\lambda)$ returns a polynomial-time decidable binary relation $\mathbf{R} = \{(\mathsf{x}, \mathsf{w})\}$. Here, x is the statement and w is the witness. Security parameter λ can be deduced from the description of $\mathbf{R}$. The relation generator also outputs auxiliary information ξ that will be given to the honest parties and the adversary. As in [Gro16, ABLZ17], ξ is the value returned by $\mathsf{BGgen}(1^\lambda)$, so ξ is given as an input to the honest parties; if needed, one can include an additional auxiliary input to the adversary. Let $\mathbf{L_R} = \{\mathsf{x} : \exists \mathsf{w}, (\mathsf{x}, \mathsf{w}) \in \mathbf{R}\}$ be an NP-language. A (subversion-resistant) *NIZK argument system* Ψ for $\mathcal{R}$ consists a tuple of PPT algorithms $(\mathsf{K}, \mathsf{CV}, \mathsf{P}, \mathsf{V}, \mathsf{Sim})$, such that:

CRS Generator: K is a PPT algorithm that, given $(\mathbf{R}, \xi)$ where $(\mathbf{R}, \xi) \in \mathrm{im}(\mathcal{R}(1^\lambda))$, outputs $\mathbf{crs} := (\mathbf{crs_P}, \mathbf{crs_V})$ and stores trapdoors of $\mathbf{crs}$ as $\mathbf{ts}$. We distinguish $\mathbf{crs_P}$ (needed by the prover) from $\mathbf{crs_V}$ (needed by the verifier).

CRS Verifier: CV is a PPT algorithm that, given $(\mathbf{R}, \xi, \mathbf{crs})$, returns either 0 (the CRS is incorrectly formed) or 1 (the CRS is correctly formed).

Prover: P is a PPT algorithm that, given $(\mathbf{R}, \xi, \mathbf{crs_P}, \mathsf{x}, \mathsf{w})$ for $\mathsf{CV}(\mathbf{R}, \xi, \mathbf{crs}) = 1$ and $(\mathsf{x}, \mathsf{w}) \in \mathbf{R}$, outputs an argument π. Otherwise, it outputs $\perp$.

Verifier: V is a PPT algorithm that, given $(\mathbf{R}, \xi, \mathbf{crs_V}, \mathsf{x}, \pi)$, returns either 0 (reject) or 1 (accept).

Simulator: Sim is a PPT algorithm that, given $(\mathbf{R}, \xi, \mathbf{crs}, \mathsf{x}, \mathbf{ts})$, outputs a simulated argument π.

Strictly speaking, a zk-SNARK system is required to be complete, (computationally) knowledge-sound, (statistically) ZK, and succinct as in the following definitions.

Definition 1 (Perfect Completeness). *A non-interactive argument Ψ is* perfectly complete for $\mathcal{R}$, *if for all λ, all $(\mathbf{R}, \xi) \in \mathrm{im}(\mathcal{R}(1^\lambda))$, and* $(\mathsf{x}, \mathsf{w}) \in \mathbf{R}$, $\Pr[\mathbf{crs} \leftarrow \mathsf{K}(\mathbf{R}, \xi),\ \pi \leftarrow \mathsf{P}(\mathbf{R}, \xi, \mathbf{crs_P}, \mathsf{x}, \mathsf{w}) : \mathsf{V}(\mathbf{R}, \xi, \mathbf{crs_V}, \mathsf{x}, \pi) = 1] = 1$.

Definition 2 (Computationally Knowledge-Soundness [Gro16]**).** *A non-interactive argument Ψ is computationally (adaptively)* knowledge-sound for $\mathcal{R}$, *if for every PPT $\mathcal{A}$, there exists a PPT extractor $\mathsf{ext}_\mathcal{A}$, s.t. for all λ,*

$$\Pr\left[\begin{array}{l}\mathbf{crs} \leftarrow \mathsf{K}(\mathbf{R}, \xi), r \leftarrow_r \mathsf{RND}(\mathcal{A}), ((\mathsf{x}, \pi) \parallel \mathsf{w}) \leftarrow (\mathcal{A} \parallel \mathsf{ext}_\mathcal{A})(\mathbf{R}, \xi, \mathbf{crs}; r) : \\ (\mathsf{x}, \mathsf{w}) \notin \mathbf{R} \wedge \mathsf{V}(\mathbf{R}, \xi, \mathbf{crs_V}, \mathsf{x}, \pi) = 1\end{array}\right] \approx_\lambda 0.$$

Here, ξ can be seen as a common auxiliary input to $\mathcal{A}$ and $\mathsf{ext}_\mathcal{A}$ that is generated by using a benign [BCPR14] relation generator.

Definition 3 (Statistically Zero-Knowledge (ZK) [Gro16]**).** *A non-interactive argument Ψ is* statistically ZK *for $\mathcal{R}$, if for all λ, all $(\mathbf{R}, \xi) \in \mathrm{im}(\mathcal{R}(1^\lambda))$, and for all PPT $\mathcal{A}$, $\varepsilon_0^{unb} \approx_\lambda \varepsilon_1^{unb}$, where*

$$\varepsilon_b = \Pr[(\mathbf{crs} \,\|\, \mathbf{ts}) \leftarrow \mathsf{K}(\mathbf{R}, \xi) : \mathcal{A}^{\mathsf{O}_b(\cdot,\cdot)}(\mathbf{R}, \xi, \mathbf{crs}) = 1].$$

Here, the oracle $\mathsf{O}_0(\mathsf{x}, \mathsf{w})$ returns $\perp$ (reject) if $(\mathsf{x}, \mathsf{w}) \notin \mathbf{R}$, and otherwise it returns $\mathsf{P}(\mathbf{R}, \xi, \mathbf{crs}_\mathsf{P}, \mathsf{x}, \mathsf{w})$. Similarly, $\mathsf{O}_1(\mathsf{x}, \mathsf{w})$ returns $\perp$ (reject) if $(\mathsf{x}, \mathsf{w}) \notin \mathbf{R}$, otherwise it returns $\mathsf{Sim}(\mathbf{R}, \xi, \mathbf{crs}, \mathbf{ts}, \mathsf{x})$. Ψ is perfect ZK *for $\mathcal{R}$ if one requires that $\varepsilon_0 = \varepsilon_1$.*

Definition 4 (Succinctness [GM17]**).** *A non-interactive argument Ψ is* succinct *if the proof size is polynominal in λ and the verifier's computation time is polynominal in security parameter λ and the size of instance x.*

In the rest, we recall the definition of (non-black-box) (or simulation knowledge soundness) and Sub-ZK [ABLZ17] that we aim to achieve in new constructions.

Definition 5 ((Non-Black-Box) Simulation Extractability [GM17]**).** *A non-interactive argument Ψ is* (non-black-box) simulation-extractable *for $\mathcal{R}$, if for any PPT $\mathcal{A}$, there exists a PPT extractor $\mathsf{ext}_\mathcal{A}$ s.t. for all λ,*

$$\Pr\left[\begin{array}{l}\mathbf{crs} \leftarrow \mathsf{K}(\mathbf{R}, \xi), r \leftarrow_r \mathsf{RND}(\mathcal{A}), ((\mathsf{x}, \pi) \,\|\, \mathsf{w}) \leftarrow (\mathcal{A}^{\mathsf{O}(.)} \,\|\, \mathsf{ext}_\mathcal{A})(\mathbf{R}, \xi, \mathbf{crs}; r) : \\ (\mathsf{x}, \pi) \notin Q \wedge (\mathsf{x}, \mathsf{w}) \notin \mathbf{R} \wedge \mathsf{V}(\mathbf{R}, \xi, \mathbf{crs}_\mathsf{V}, \mathsf{x}, \pi) = 1\end{array}\right] \approx_\lambda 0.$$

Here, Q is the set of (x, π)-pairs generated by the adversary's queries to $\mathsf{O}(.)$. Note that *(non-black-box) simulation extractability* implies *knowledge-soundness* (given in Definition 2), as the former additionally allows the adversary to send query to the proof simulation oracle.

Definition 6 (Statistically Subversion Zero-Knowledge [ABLZ17]**).** *A non-interactive argument Ψ is* statistically Sub-ZK *for $\mathcal{R}$, if for any PPT subverter X there exists a PPT extractor ext_X, such that for all λ, all $(\mathbf{R}, \xi) \in \mathrm{im}(\mathcal{R}(1^\lambda))$, and for all PPT $\mathcal{A}$, $\varepsilon_0 \approx_\lambda \varepsilon_1$, where*

$$\Pr\left[\begin{array}{l}r \leftarrow_r \mathsf{RND}(\mathsf{X}), (\mathbf{crs}, \xi_\mathsf{X} \,\|\, \mathbf{ts}) \leftarrow (\mathsf{X} \,\|\, \mathsf{ext}_\mathsf{X})(\mathbf{R}, \xi; r) : \\ \mathsf{CV}(\mathbf{R}, \xi, \mathbf{crs}) = 1 \wedge \mathcal{A}^{\mathsf{O}_b(\cdot,\cdot)}(\mathbf{R}, \xi, \mathbf{crs}, \mathbf{ts}, \xi_\mathsf{X}) = 1\end{array}\right].$$

Here, ξ_X is auxiliary information generated by subverter X, and the oracle $\mathsf{O}_0(\mathsf{x}, \mathsf{w})$ returns $\perp$ (reject) if $(\mathsf{x}, \mathsf{w}) \notin \mathbf{R}$, and otherwise it returns $\mathsf{P}(\mathbf{R}, \xi, \mathbf{crs}_\mathsf{P}, \mathsf{x}, \mathsf{w})$. Similarly, $\mathsf{O}_1(\mathsf{x}, \mathsf{w})$ returns $\perp$ (reject) if $(\mathsf{x}, \mathsf{w}) \notin \mathbf{R}$, and otherwise it returns $\mathsf{Sim}(\mathbf{R}, \xi, \mathbf{crs}, \mathbf{ts}, \mathsf{x})$. Ψ is perfectly Sub-ZK *for $\mathcal{R}$ if one requires that $\varepsilon_0 = \varepsilon_1$.*

3 Subversion-Resistant Simulation-Extractable NIZKs

As we discussed in the introduction, currently we have NIZK constructions that can achieve Sub-ZK (defined in Definition 6) and knowledge soundness (defined in Definition 2) at the same time [ABLZ17, Fuc18], which means prover achieves ZK *without trusting* to a third party and verifier achieves knowledge soundness but *with trusting* to the CRS generator. On the other hand, currently there are *simulation* knowledge sound (defined in Definition 5) NIZK arguments [GM17, Lip19, AB19] but none of them are known to achieve Sub-ZK, which means both prover and verifier needs to trust the CRS generators.

In this section, we aim to construct NIZK arguments that similar to NIZKs studied in [ABLZ17, Fuc18], the prover does not need to trust CRS generators to achieve ZK, but the protocol will guarantee *simulation* knowledge soundness, as in simulation-extractable zk-SNARKs [GM17, Lip19]. Recently, the scheme proposed in [Lip19] also was updated to achieve Sub-ZK. However, in the rest, we will observe that our proposed construction can be instantiated with any of current subversion-resistant NIZKs which basically allows to use it as a framework to achieve simulation (knowledge) soundness in all NIZKs that guarantee Sub-ZK and (knowledge) soundness. Subversion ZK in new constructions guarantees that even an adversary generates the CRS, still it cannot break the ZK of protocol. To mitigate the level of trust or to improve security in the setup phase even more, particularly for verifier, one can use Multi-Party Computation (MPC) protocols for CRS generation [BCG+15, ABL+19].

3.1 Construction

In this section, we presented the proposed construction which can act as a compiler that transforms Sub-ZK and (knowledge) sound NIZKs into ones that satisfy Sub-ZK and simulation (knowledge) soundness. We use a folklore OR technique with a particular instantiation proposed in [KZM+15, AB19]. Indeed, the proposed OR compiler can be viewed as using the Bellare-Goldwasser paradigm [BG90], which is proposed to construct signatures from NIZK arguments, in a non-black-box way.

Consider a subversion-resistant NIZK argument Ψ for $\mathcal{R}_\mathbf{L}$ which consists of PPT algorithms $(\mathsf{K}, \mathsf{CV}, \mathsf{P}, \mathsf{V}, \mathsf{Sim})$ and guarantees Sub-ZK and (knowledge) soundness. Let $(\mathsf{KGen}, \mathsf{Sign}, \mathsf{SigVerify})$ be a one-time secure signature scheme and $(\mathsf{Com}, \mathsf{ComVerify})$ be a perfectly binding commitment scheme. Using a variation of a construction proposed by Bellare-Goldwasser [BG90] (used in [KZM+15, AB19], given the language $\mathbf{L}$ with the corresponding NP relation $\mathbf{R_L}$, we define a new language $\mathbf{L}'$ such that $((\mathsf{x}, \mu, pk_{\mathsf{Sign}}, \rho), (\mathsf{w}, s, r)) \in \mathbf{R}_{\mathbf{L}'}$ iff:

$$((\mathsf{x}, \mathsf{w}) \in \mathbf{R_L} \vee (\mu = f_s(pk_{\mathsf{Sign}}) \wedge \rho = \mathsf{Com}(s, r))) \,,$$

where $\{f_s : \{0,1\}^* \rightarrow \{0,1\}^\lambda\}_{s \in \{0,1\}^\lambda}$ is a pseudo-random function family. Due to OR-based construction of new language $\mathbf{L}'$, a user to be able to generate an acceptable proof will require either the witness w or the trapdoors of CRS,

CRS Generator $\mathsf{K}'(\mathbf{R_L}, \xi)$: Call CRS generator of the subversion-resistant NIZK Ψ and sample $(\mathbf{crs} \parallel \mathbf{ts}) \leftarrow \mathsf{K}(\mathbf{R_{L'}}, \xi)$; $s, r \leftarrow_r \{0,1\}^\lambda$; $\rho := \mathsf{Com}(s, r)$; and output $\mathbf{crs}' := (\mathbf{crs}, \rho)$.

CRS Verifier $\mathsf{CV}'(\mathbf{R_L}, \xi, \mathbf{crs}')$: Parse $\mathbf{crs}' := (\mathbf{crs}, \rho)$; abort if $\rho = 0$; call CV algorithm of the subversion-resistant NIZK Ψ and return $b \leftarrow \mathsf{CV}(\mathbf{R_L}, \xi, \mathbf{crs})$.

Prover $\mathsf{P}'(\mathbf{R_L}, \xi, \mathbf{crs}', \mathsf{x}, \mathsf{w})$: Parse $\mathbf{crs}' := (\mathbf{crs}, \rho)$; abort if $\mathsf{CV}'(\mathbf{R_L}, \xi, \mathbf{crs}') \neq 1$ and $(\mathsf{x}, \mathsf{w}) \notin \mathbf{R_L}$; generate $(pk_{\mathsf{Sign}}, sk_{\mathsf{Sign}}) \leftarrow \mathsf{KGen}(1^\lambda)$; sample $z_0, z_1, z_2 \leftarrow_r \{0,1\}^\lambda$; generate $\pi \leftarrow \mathsf{P}(\mathbf{R_{L'}}, \xi, \mathbf{crs}, (\mathsf{x}, z_0, pk_{\mathsf{Sign}}, \rho), (\mathsf{w}, z_1, z_2))$ using the prover of subversion-resistant NIZK Ψ; sign $\sigma \leftarrow \mathsf{Sign}(sk_{\mathsf{Sign}}, (\mathsf{x}, z_0, \pi))$; and return $\pi' := (z_0, \pi, pk_{\mathsf{Sign}}, \sigma)$.

Verifier $\mathsf{V}'(\mathbf{R_L}, \xi, \mathbf{crs}', \mathsf{x}, \pi')$: Parse $\mathbf{crs}' := (\mathbf{crs}, \rho)$ and $\pi' := (z_0, \pi, pk_{\mathsf{Sign}}, \sigma)$; abort if $\mathsf{SigVerify}(pk_{\mathsf{Sign}}, (\mathsf{x}, z_0, \pi), \sigma) = 0$; call the verifier of input subversion-resistant NIZK argument $\mathsf{V}(\mathbf{R_{L'}}, \xi, \mathbf{crs}, (\mathsf{x}, z_0, pk_{\mathsf{Sign}}, \rho), \pi)$ and abort if it outputs 0.

Simulator $\mathsf{Sim}'(\mathbf{R_L}, \xi, \mathbf{crs}', \mathbf{ts}, \mathsf{x})$: Parse $\mathbf{crs}' := (\mathbf{crs}, \rho)$; call the extraction algorithm $\mathsf{ext_X}$ constructed in simulation of subversion-resistant NIZK Ψ and extract simulation trapdoors $\mathbf{ts}$ of Ψ from the CRS generator X; generate $(pk_{\mathsf{Sign}}, sk_{\mathsf{Sign}}) \leftarrow \mathsf{KGen}(1^\lambda)$; sample $z_0 \leftarrow_r \{0,1\}^\lambda$; generate $\pi \leftarrow \mathsf{Sim}(\mathbf{R_{L'}}, \xi, \mathbf{crs}, (\mathsf{x}, z_0, pk_{\mathsf{Sign}}, \rho), \mathbf{ts})$; sign $\sigma \leftarrow \mathsf{Sign}(sk_{\mathsf{Sign}}, (\mathsf{x}, z_0, \pi))$; and output $\pi' := (z_0, \pi, pk_{\mathsf{Sign}}, \sigma)$.

Fig. 1. An extension of the proposed construction in [AB19] that outputs a Sub-ZK and simulation (knowledge) sound NIZK argument Ψ'. Note that in our construction, we assumed that the input NIZK Ψ guarantees Sub-ZK and (knowledge) soundness. Due to this fact, we have a new algorithm CV' to verify the well-formedness of CRS elements, and a new simulation procedure by Sim' to simulate the proofs without trusting to the CRS generators.

and since it is assumed that the CRS trapdoors are kept secret, so soundness is guaranteed as long as CRS trapdoors are secret. We note that due to using the pseudo-random function f_s with a random secret trapdoor s, the output of f_s is indistinguishable from the outputs of a truly random function. By considering new language, the subversion-resistant NIZK argument Ψ for the relation $\mathbf{R_L}$ with PPT algorithms $(\mathsf{K}, \mathsf{CV}, \mathsf{P}, \mathsf{V}, \mathsf{Sim})$ that achieves Sub-ZK and (knowledge) soundness, can be lifted to a subversion-resistant NIZK Ψ' with PPT algorithms $(\mathsf{K}', \mathsf{CV}', \mathsf{P}', \mathsf{V}', \mathsf{Sim}')$ that guarantees Sub-ZK and *simulation* (knowledge) soundness. Based on the language $\mathbf{L}'$, the construction of NIZK Ψ' and the corresponding algorithms are described in Fig. 1.

Recently, Atapoor and Baghery [AB19] used the same construction to achieve *simulation knowledge soundness* in Groth's zk-SNARK [Gro16] which led to the most efficient zk-SNARK which also guarantees non-malleability of proofs. Here, we show that such OR-based language can be extended and used to build subversion-resistant NIZK arguments which will also guarantee simulation (knowledge) soundness.

Recall that one of two main differences between a Sub-ZK NIZK argument and a common NIZK argument is the existence of a public CRS verification algorithm CV in the former ones. Basically, given a CRS $\mathbf{crs}$ the algorithm CV verifies the well-formedness of its elements. Additionally, in simulation of a Sub-ZK NIZK argument there exists a (non-black-box) extractor $\mathsf{ext}_{\mathsf{X}}$ that can extract the simulation trapdoors from a (possibly malicious) CRS generator X. More detailed discussions can be found in [BFS16, ABLZ17, Fuc18, ALSZ18].

So similar to other subversion-resistant NIZK arguments, as we aim to achieve Sub-ZK (not standard ZK) and simulation (knowledge) soundness in our constructions, so there are two key differences between new proposed constructions and the one presented in [AB19] (that are shown in highlighted form in Fig. 1). The first key difference is that we have an extra algorithm CV' which will be used by prover to check the well-formedness of CRS elements before using them. This is actually the cost that prover needs to pay insted of trusting to the CRS generators. The second key difference is that in new constructions, the simulator Sim' does not get simulation trapdoors directly, as the prover does not trust to the CRS generators in this setting. Instead, the simulator Sim' calls the extraction algorithm $\mathsf{ext}_{\mathsf{X}}$ constructed for the input NIZK argument Ψ and extracts simulation trapdoors $\mathbf{ts}$ of it, and then uses them for the rest of simulation.

3.2 Efficiency

In the rest, by considering Fig. 1, we consider efficiency of new constructions for different important metrics in (subversion-resistant) NIZK arguments.

Setup Phase. The setup needs to be done for a new language $\mathbf{L}'$. Roughly speaking, it means the setup phase of original NIZK Ψ needs to be executed for a new arithmetic circuit that has slightly larger number of gates. Again with a particular instantiation [KMS+16, AB19], new changes will add around 52.000 multiplication gates to the QAP-based arithmetic circuits that encode $\mathbf{L}$. The number of gates comes from the case that both commitment scheme and pseduo-random function used in construction are instantiated with a SHA512 hash function [KMS+16, AB19]. Implementations show that this will add a constant amount (e.g. 10 megabyte) to the size of original CRS, that for arithmetic circuits with large number of gates (that usually is the case in practical application) the overhead is negligible [AB19].

CRS Verification. In new construction, in order to verify the well-formedness of CRS elements one needs to execute CV' algorithm which almost has the same efficiency as CV algorithm in original NIZK argument Ψ. In practice, it is shown that running time of CV can be less than running time of P [ABLZ17].

Prover. In new schemes, prover needs to give a proof for the new language $\mathbf{L}'$ and sign the proof with a one-time secure signature scheme. Empirical performances presented in [AB19] show that the overhead for a QAP-based zk-SNARK is very small in practical cases. For instance, in the fixed setting, for an arithmetic circuit that prover already needed 83 s to generate a proof, in new construction the proof generation took 90.1 s.

Proof Size. In new constructions the size of new proof $\pi' := (z_0, \pi, pk_{\mathsf{Sign}}, \sigma)$ will be equal to the size of original proof π plus the size of three elements (z_0, $pk_{\mathsf{Sign}}, \sigma$). Similarly, with a particular instantiation for 128-bit security (e.g. the one in [AB19]), these three elements totally can add less than 128 bytes to the size of original proof π.

Verifier. Extra from the verification of NIZK argument Ψ, the verifier of argument Ψ' will verify the validity of a one-time secure signature. Similarly, for a particular instantiation [AB19], verification of the signature scheme adds 1 equation to the verification of original scheme that needs two parings and one exponentiation. They show that a proper instantiation can even give a verification faster than the verification of current simulation knowledge sound NIZKs arguments in the CRS model [GM17,Lip19].

3.3 Security Proofs

In this section, we show that the given a subversion-resistant NIZK argument that guarantees completeness, Sub-ZK, and (knowledge) soundness, the described construction in Sect. 3.1 results a NIZK argument that achieves completeness, Sub-ZK and *simulation* (knowledge) soundness.

Theorem 1 (Completeness). *If the NIZK argument Ψ ensures completeness, Sub-ZK, and (knowledge) soundness, and the one-time signature scheme* $(\mathsf{KGen}, \mathsf{Sign}, \mathsf{SigVerify})$ *is secure, then the proposed construction in Fig. 1 guarantees completeness.*

Proof. By considering the completeness of NIZK argument Ψ and the fact that $\mathsf{SigVerify}(pk_{\mathsf{Sign}}, m, \mathsf{Sign}(m, sk_{\mathsf{Sign}})) = 1$, we conclude that the output NIZK argument Ψ' guarantees *completeness.* □

Theorem 2 (Subversion Zero-Knowledge). *If the NIZK argument Ψ guarantees completeness, Sub-ZK, and (knowledge) soundness, the pseudo-random function family is secure, and the one-time signature scheme is secure, then the proposed construction in Fig. 1 achieves Sub-ZK.*

Before going through the proof, it is worth to mention that proving Sub-ZK of a subversion-resistant NIZK argument is a bit tricky than proving standard notion of ZK. The reason is that in the proof of standard ZK, CRS generator is trusted and the CRS trapdoors (simulation trapdoors) are honestly provided to the simulator Sim. But in proving Sub-ZK, since the prover does not trust to the CRS generator any more, consequently the simulator Sim cannot trust to the provided trapdoors. To address this issue, the proposed solution [BFS16] is that the prover checks the well-formedness of CRS elements before using them and in simulating proofs, the simulator uses a non-black-box extraction procedure to extract the simulation trapdoors directly from the (possibly malicious) CRS generator and then uses them for the simulation [BFS16, ABLZ17, Fuc18, ALSZ18, Bag19b]. The non-black-box extraction usually is done using various knowledge assumptions [Dam92, BFS16]. For instance [ABLZ17] used Bilinear Diffie-Hellman Knowledge of Exponents (BDH-KE) assumption[2] to prove Sub-ZK of Groth's zk-SNARK [Gro16], while Fuchsbauer [Fuc18] did the same but with the Square Knowledge of Exponent (SKE) assumption[3] which led to prove Sub-ZK of Groth's zk-SNARK [Gro16] without modifying its CRS. But, intuitively in all cases one relies on the fact that if a (malicious) CRS generator manages to come out with some *well-formed* CRS elements, there exists a non-black-box extractor that given access to the source code and random coins of the (malicious) CRS generator, it can extract the simulation trapdoors. Once the simulation trapdoors are extracted, the simulator Sim can simulate the proofs. It is worth to mention that the well-formedness of CRS elements are checked by a public efficient CRS verification algorithm known as CV. Using different knowledge-assumptions in proving Sub-ZK of particular NIZK arguments might lead to different CV algorithms, as Abdolmaleki et al. [ABLZ17] and Fuchsbauer [Fuc18] proposed two different CV algorithms for Groth's zk-SNARK [Gro16].

Proof. Sub-ZK in the input NIZK implies that there exists a simulation algorithm Sim which first uses extraction algorithm $\mathsf{ext}_{\mathsf{X}}$ and extracts the simulation trapdoors from (malicious) CRS generator X and then uses the extracted trapdoors to simulate the argument. We note that due to OR-based construction of new language $\mathbf{L}'$, the proofs for new language can be simulated using either simulation trapdoors of NIZK argument Ψ (first branch) or simulation trapdoors (s, r) of that are hidden in the committed value $\rho := \mathsf{Com}(s, r)$ (second branch). Here for simulation we use simulation trapdoors of NIZK argument Ψ which can be extracted by $\mathsf{ext}_{\mathsf{X}}$. Now, consider the following experiences,

$\underline{\mathsf{EXP}_1^{zk}(\text{simulator})}$

- *Setup:* Sample $(\mathbf{crs} \| \mathbf{ts}) \leftarrow \mathsf{K}(\mathbf{R}_{\mathbf{L}'}, \xi)$; $s, r \leftarrow_r \{0,1\}^\lambda$; $\rho := Com(s, r)$; and output $\mathbf{crs}' := (\mathbf{crs}, \rho)$; where $\mathbf{ts}$ contains trapdoors of CRS $\mathbf{crs}$ and (s, r) are hidden trapdoors of the committed value ρ.
- *Define function* $\mathsf{O}(\mathsf{x}, \mathsf{w})$: Abort if $(\mathsf{x}, \mathsf{w}) \notin \mathbf{R}_{\mathbf{L}}$; call the extraction algorithm $\mathsf{ext}_{\mathsf{X}}$ constructed in simulation of subversion-resistant NIZK Ψ and extract simulation trapdoors $\mathbf{ts}$ of Ψ from CRS generator X; generate $(pk_{\mathsf{Sign}}, sk_{\mathsf{Sign}}) \leftarrow \mathsf{KGen}(1^\lambda)$; sample $z_0 \leftarrow_r \{0,1\}^\lambda$; generate $\pi \leftarrow \mathsf{Sim}(\mathbf{R}_{\mathbf{L}'}, \xi, \mathbf{crs}, (\mathsf{x}, z_0, pk_{\mathsf{Sign}}, \rho), \mathbf{ts})$; sign $\sigma \leftarrow \mathsf{Sign}(sk_{\mathsf{Sign}}, (\mathsf{x}, z_0, \pi))$; return $\pi' := (z_0, \pi, pk_{\mathsf{Sign}}, \sigma)$.
- $b \leftarrow \mathcal{A}^{\mathsf{O}(\mathsf{x},\mathsf{w})}(\mathbf{crs}')$

[2] It states that in an asymetric bilinear group, given $[1]_1$ and $[1]_1$, if an adversary manages to come out with $[a]_1$ and $[a]_2$, he must know a. Knowing a is formalized by showing that there exists an efficient non-black-box extractor that given access to source code and random coins of the adversary, it can extract a [Dam92].

[3] It states that in a symmetric bilinear group, given $[1]_1$, if an adversary manages to come out with $[a]_1$ and $[a^2]_1$, he must know a.

$\underline{\mathsf{EXP}_2^{zk}(\text{prover})}$

- *Setup:* Sample $(\mathbf{crs} \| \mathbf{ts}) \leftarrow \mathsf{K}(\mathbf{R_{L'}}, \xi)$; $s, r \leftarrow_r \{0,1\}^\lambda$; $\rho := Com(s, r)$; and output $\mathbf{crs}' := (\mathbf{crs}, \rho)$; where $\mathbf{ts}$ contains trapdoors of CRS $\mathbf{crs}$ and (s, r) are hidden trapdoors of the committed value ρ.
- *Define function* $\mathsf{O}(\mathsf{x}, \mathsf{w})$: Abort if $(\mathsf{x}, \mathsf{w}) \notin \mathbf{R_L}$; generate $(pk_{\mathsf{Sign}}, sk_{\mathsf{Sign}}) \leftarrow \mathsf{KGen}(1^\lambda)$; sample $z_0, z_1, z_2 \leftarrow_r \{0,1\}^\lambda$; generate $\pi \leftarrow \mathsf{P}(\mathbf{R_{L'}}, \xi, \mathbf{crs}, (\mathsf{x}, z_0, pk_{\mathsf{Sign}}, \rho), (\mathsf{w}, z_1, z_2))$; sign $\sigma \leftarrow \mathsf{Sign}(sk_{\mathsf{Sign}}, (\mathsf{x}, z_0, \pi))$; return $\pi' := (z_0, \pi, pk_{\mathsf{Sign}}, \sigma)$.
- $b \leftarrow \mathcal{A}^{\mathsf{O}(\mathsf{x},\mathsf{w})}(\mathbf{crs}')$

Lemma 1. *If the NIZK argument Ψ guarantees Sub-ZK, and the one-time signature scheme is secure, for two above experiments we have* $\Pr[\mathsf{EXP}_1^{zk}] \approx \Pr[\mathsf{EXP}_2^{zk}]$.

Proof. Two experiments EXP_2^{zk} and EXP_1^{zk} model the real prover and simulator of new construction described in Fig. 1. As the NIZK argument Ψ guarantees Sub-ZK it, consequently it guarantees ZK, so one can conclude that the proof generated by prover in experiment EXP_2^{zk} is indistinguishable from the proof generated by the simulator in EXP_1^{zk}. Intuitively, this is because of OR-based construction of new language $\mathbf{L}'$, and consequently the fact that all new elements added to the new construction are chosen randomly and independently. □

This results that the constructed NIZK arguments in Sect. 3.1 ensures Sub-ZK. □

Theorem 3 ((Non-black-Box) Simulation Knowledge Soundness). *If the NIZK argument Ψ is complete, Sub-ZK, and knowledge sound, then the proposed construction in Fig. 1 guarantees (non-black-box) simulation knowledge soundness.*

Before going through the proof of theorem, recall that simulation knowledge soundness states that given a honestly generated CRS $\mathbf{crs}$, an adversary cannot come out with a valid fresh proof, even if he access to an oracle which returns simulated proofs for an arbitrary statement, unless he knows the witness. The existing of an oracle which returns simulated proofs shows that the protocol is simulatable, so the proofs should be zero-knowledge. In the last theorem, we observed that the constructed NIZK argument in Sect. 3.1 guarantees Sub-ZK and consequently ZK. In proving this theorem, as verifier trusts to the CRS generator and as Sub-ZK implies ZK, so we use the simulator of standard ZK to prove this theorem.

Proof. The proof is simplified and generalized version of the proof of simulation knowledge soundness presented in [KZM+15] and in [AB19], respectively, but for all (Sub-)ZK and (knowledge) sound NIZK arguments. For the sake of completeness, we provide the proof in the rest. The proof is for the case that the input NIZK argument guarantees knowledge soundness. Similarly, we write consecutive hybrid experiments and at the end show that success probability of an adversary to break the simulation knowledge soundness of new constructions are negligible. Consider the following experiments,

$\underline{\mathsf{EXP}_1^{SimExt}(\text{main experiment})}$

- *Setup:* Sample $(\mathbf{crs} \,\|\, \mathsf{ts}) \leftarrow \mathsf{K}(\mathbf{R}_{\mathbf{L}'}, \xi)$; $s, r \leftarrow_r \{0,1\}^\lambda$; $\rho := \mathsf{Com}(s, r)$; and output $(\mathbf{crs}' \,\|\, \mathsf{ts}') := ((\mathbf{crs}, \rho) \,\|\, (\mathsf{ts}, (s, r)))$; where ts' is new CRS trapdoor.
- *Define function* $\mathsf{O}(\mathsf{x})$: $(pk_{\mathsf{Sign}}, sk_{\mathsf{Sign}}) \leftarrow \mathsf{KGen}(1^\lambda)$; set $\mu = f_s(pk_{\mathsf{Sign}})$; generate $\pi \leftarrow \mathsf{P}(\mathbf{R}_{\mathbf{L}'}, \xi, \mathbf{crs}, (\mathsf{x}, \mu, pk_{\mathsf{Sign}}, \rho), (s, r))$; sign $\sigma \leftarrow \mathsf{Sign}(sk_{\mathsf{Sign}}, (\mathsf{x}, \mu, \pi))$; return $\pi' := (\mu, \pi, pk_{\mathsf{Sign}}, \sigma)$.
- $(\mathsf{x}, \pi') \leftarrow \mathcal{A}^{\mathsf{O}(\mathsf{x})}(\mathbf{crs}')$.
- Parse $\pi' := (\mu, \pi, pk_{\mathsf{Sign}}, \sigma)$; $\mathsf{w} \leftarrow \mathsf{ext}_{\mathcal{A}}(\mathbf{crs}', \mathsf{x}, \pi, \xi)$.
- Return 1 iff $((\mathsf{x}, \pi') \notin Q) \wedge (\mathsf{V}'(\mathbf{R}_{\mathbf{L}}, \xi, \mathbf{crs}', \mathsf{x}, \pi') = 1) \wedge ((\mathsf{x}, \mathsf{w}) \notin \mathbf{R}_{\mathbf{L}})$; where Q shows the set of statment-proof pairs generated by $\mathsf{O}(\mathsf{x})$.

$\underline{\mathsf{EXP}_2^{SimExt}(\text{relaxing the return checking})}$

- *Setup:* Sample $(\mathbf{crs} \,\|\, \mathsf{ts}) \leftarrow \mathsf{K}(\mathbf{R}_{\mathbf{L}'}, \xi)$; $s, r \leftarrow_r \{0,1\}^\lambda$; $\rho := \mathsf{Com}(s, r)$; and output $(\mathbf{crs}' \,\|\, \mathsf{ts}') := ((\mathbf{crs}, \rho) \,\|\, (\mathsf{ts}, (s, r)))$; where ts' is new CRS trapdoor.
- *Define function* $\mathsf{O}(\mathsf{x})$: $(pk_{\mathsf{Sign}}, sk_{\mathsf{Sign}}) \leftarrow \mathsf{KGen}(1^\lambda)$; set $\mu = f_s(pk_{\mathsf{Sign}})$; generate $\pi \leftarrow \mathsf{P}(\mathbf{R}_{\mathbf{L}'}, \xi, \mathbf{crs}, (\mathsf{x}, \mu, pk_{\mathsf{Sign}}, \rho), (s, r))$; sign $\sigma \leftarrow \mathsf{Sign}(sk_{\mathsf{Sign}}, (\mathsf{x}, \mu, \pi))$; return $\pi' := (\mu, \pi, pk_{\mathsf{Sign}}, \sigma)$.
- $(\mathsf{x}, \pi') \leftarrow \mathcal{A}^{\mathsf{O}(\mathsf{x})}(\mathbf{crs}')$.
- Parse $\pi' := (\mu, \pi, pk_{\mathsf{Sign}}, \sigma)$; $\mathsf{w} \leftarrow \mathsf{ext}_{\mathcal{A}}(\mathbf{crs}', \mathsf{x}, \pi, \xi)$.
- Return 1 iff $((\mathsf{x}, \pi') \notin Q) \wedge (\mathsf{V}'(\mathbf{R}_{\mathbf{L}}, \xi, \mathbf{crs}', \mathsf{x}, \pi') = 1) \wedge (pk_{\mathsf{Sign}} \notin \mathcal{PK}) \wedge (\mu = f_s(pk_{\mathsf{Sign}}))$; where Q is the set of statment-proof pairs and $\mathcal{PK}$ is the set of signature verification keys, both generated by $\mathsf{O}(\mathsf{x})$.

Lemma 2. *If the underlying one-time signature scheme is strongly unforgeable, and the NIZK argument guarantees knowledge-soundness, then* $\Pr[\mathsf{EXP}_2^{SimExt}] \leq \Pr[\mathsf{EXP}_1^{SimExt}] + \mathsf{negl}(\lambda)$.

Proof. We note that if $(\mathsf{x}, \pi') \notin Q$ and "pk_{Sign} from (x, π'), has been generated by $\mathsf{O}(\cdot)$", then the (x, μ, π) is a valid message/signature pair. Therefore by security of the signature scheme, we know that $(\mathsf{x}, \pi) \notin Q$ and "pk_{Sign} has been generated by $\mathsf{O}(\cdot)$" happens with negligible probability, which allows us to focus on $pk_{\mathsf{Sign}} \notin \mathcal{PK}$.

Now, due to knowledge soundness of the original scheme (there is an extractor $\mathsf{ext}_{\mathcal{A}}$ where can extract witness from $\mathcal{A}$), if some witness is valid for $\mathbf{L}'$ and $(\mathsf{x}, \mathsf{w}) \notin \mathbf{R}_{\mathbf{L}}$, so we conclude it must be the case that there exists some s', such that ρ is valid commitment of s' and $\mu = f_{s'}(pk_{\mathsf{Sign}})$, which by perfectly binding property of the commitment scheme, it implies $\mu = f_s(pk_{\mathsf{Sign}})$. □

$\underline{\mathsf{EXP}_3^{SimExt}(\text{simulator})}$

- *Setup:* Sample $(\mathbf{crs} \,\|\, \mathsf{ts}) \leftarrow \mathsf{K}(\mathbf{R}_{\mathbf{L}'}, \xi)$; $s, r \leftarrow_r \{0,1\}^\lambda$; $\rho := Com(s, r)$; and output $(\mathbf{crs}' \,\|\, \mathsf{ts}') := ((\mathbf{crs}, \rho) \,\|\, (\mathsf{ts}, (s, r)))$; where ts' is new CRS trapdoor.

- *Define function* $\mathsf{O}(\mathsf{x})$: $(pk_{\mathsf{Sign}}, sk_{\mathsf{Sign}}) \leftarrow \mathsf{KGen}(1^\lambda)$; set $\mu = f_s(pk_{\mathsf{Sign}})$; generate $\pi \leftarrow \mathsf{Sim}(\mathbf{R}_{\mathbf{L}'}, \xi, \mathbf{crs}, (\mathsf{x}, \mu, pk_{\mathsf{Sign}}, \rho), (\mathsf{ts} \,\|\, (s, r)))$; sign $\sigma \leftarrow \mathsf{Sign}(sk_{\mathsf{Sign}}, (\mathsf{x}, \mu, \pi))$; return $\pi' := (\mu, \pi, pk_{\mathsf{Sign}}, \sigma)$.
- $(\mathsf{x}, \pi') \leftarrow \mathcal{A}^{\mathsf{O}(\mathsf{x})}(\mathbf{crs}')$.
- Parse $\pi' := (\mu, \pi, pk_{\mathsf{Sign}}, \sigma)$; $\mathsf{w} \leftarrow \mathsf{ext}_{\mathcal{A}}(\mathbf{crs}', \mathsf{x}, \pi, \xi)$.
- Return 1 iff $((\mathsf{x}, \pi') \notin Q) \wedge (\mathsf{V}'(\mathbf{R}_{\mathbf{L}}, \xi, \mathbf{crs}', \mathsf{x}, \pi') = 1) \wedge (pk_{\mathsf{Sign}} \notin \mathcal{PK}) \wedge (\mu = f_s(pk_{\mathsf{Sign}}))$; where Q is the set of statment-proof pairs and $\mathcal{PK}$ is the set of signature verification keys, both generated by $\mathsf{O}(\mathsf{x})$.

Lemma 3. *If the NIZK argument Ψ guarantees zero-knowledge, then for two experiments* EXP_3^{SimExt} *and* EXP_2^{SimExt}, *we have* $\Pr[\mathsf{EXP}_3^{SimExt}] \leq \Pr[\mathsf{EXP}_2^{SimExt}] + \mathsf{negl}(\lambda)$.

Proof. As the NIZK argument Ψ ensures Sub-ZK and consequently ZK, so it implies no polynomial time adversary can distinguish a proof generated by the simulator from a proof that is generated by the prover. So, as we are running in polynomial time, thus two experiments are indistinguishable. □

$\underline{\mathsf{EXP}_4^{SimExt}}$(separating secret key of pseudo random function)

- *Setup:* Sample $(\mathbf{crs} \,\|\, \mathsf{ts}) \leftarrow \mathsf{K}(\mathbf{R}_{\mathbf{L}'}, \xi)$; $s', s, r \leftarrow_r \{0,1\}^\lambda$; $\rho := \mathsf{com}(s', r)$; and output $(\mathbf{crs}' \,\|\, \mathsf{ts}') := ((\mathbf{crs}, \rho) \,\|\, (\mathsf{ts}, (s, s', r)))$; where ts' is new trapdoor.
- *Define function* $\mathsf{O}(\mathsf{x})$: $(pk_{\mathsf{Sign}}, sk_{\mathsf{Sign}}) \leftarrow \mathsf{KGen}(1^\lambda)$; set $\mu = f_s(pk_{\mathsf{Sign}})$; generate $\pi \leftarrow \mathsf{Sim}(\mathbf{R}_{\mathbf{L}'}, \xi, \mathbf{crs}, (\mathsf{x}, \mu, pk_{\mathsf{Sign}}, \rho), (\mathsf{ts} \,\|\, (s, r)))$; sign $\sigma \leftarrow \mathsf{Sign}(sk_{\mathsf{Sign}}, (\mathsf{x}, \mu, \pi))$; return $\pi' := (\mu, \pi, pk_{\mathsf{Sign}}, \sigma)$.
- $(\mathsf{x}, \pi') \leftarrow \mathcal{A}^{\mathsf{O}(\mathsf{x})}(\mathbf{crs}')$.
- Parse $\pi' := (\mu, \pi, pk_{\mathsf{Sign}}, \sigma)$; $\mathsf{w} \leftarrow \mathsf{ext}_{\mathcal{A}}(\mathbf{crs}', \mathsf{x}, \pi, \xi)$.
- Return 1 iff $((\mathsf{x}, \pi') \notin Q) \wedge (\mathsf{V}'(\mathbf{R}_{\mathbf{L}}, \xi, \mathbf{crs}', \mathsf{x}, \pi') = 1) \wedge (pk_{\mathsf{Sign}} \notin \mathcal{PK}) \wedge (\mu = f_s(pk_{\mathsf{Sign}}))$; where Q is the set of statment-proof pairs and $\mathcal{PK}$ is the set of signature verification keys, both generated by $\mathsf{O}(\mathsf{x})$.

Lemma 4. *If the commitment scheme used in the CRS generation is computationally hiding, then* $\Pr[\mathsf{EXP}_4^{SimExt}] \leq \Pr[\mathsf{EXP}_3^{SimExt}] + \mathsf{negl}(\lambda)$.

Proof. Computationally hiding of a commitment scheme implies that $Com(m_1, r)$ and $Com(m_2, r)$ are computationally indistinguishable, as in this lemma. □

$\underline{\mathsf{EXP}_5^{SimExt}}$(replace pseudo random function $f_s(\cdot)$ with true random function $F(\cdot)$):

- *Setup:* Sample $(\mathbf{crs}||\mathsf{ts}) \leftarrow \mathsf{K}(\mathbf{R}_{\mathbf{L}'}, \xi)$; s', $\not{s}$, $r \leftarrow_r \{0,1\}^\lambda$; $\rho := \mathsf{Com}(s', r)$; and output $(\mathbf{crs}'||\mathsf{ts}') := ((\mathbf{crs}, \rho)||(\mathsf{ts}, (\not{s}, s', r)))$; where ts' is new CRS trapdoor.
- *Define function* $\mathsf{O}(\mathsf{x})$: $(pk_{\mathsf{Sign}}, sk_{\mathsf{Sign}}) \leftarrow \mathsf{KGen}(1^\lambda)$; set $\mu = F(pk_{\mathsf{Sign}})$; generate $\pi \leftarrow \mathsf{Sim}(\mathbf{R}_{\mathbf{L}'}, \xi, \mathbf{crs}, (\mathsf{x}, \mu, pk_{\mathsf{Sign}}, \rho), (\mathsf{ts}||(s, r)))$; sign $\sigma \leftarrow \mathsf{Sign}(sk_{\mathsf{Sign}}, (\mathsf{x}, \mu, \pi))$; return $\pi' := (\mu, \pi, pk_{\mathsf{Sign}}, \sigma)$.

- $(\mathsf{x}, \pi') \leftarrow \mathcal{A}^{\mathsf{O}(\mathsf{x})}(\mathbf{crs}')$.
- Parse $\pi' := (\mu, \pi, pk_{\mathsf{Sign}}, \sigma)$; $\mathsf{w} \leftarrow \mathsf{ext}_{\mathcal{A}}(\mathbf{crs}', \mathsf{x}, \pi, \xi)$.
- Return 1 iff $((\mathsf{x}, \pi') \notin Q) \wedge (\mathsf{V}'(\mathbf{R_L}, \xi, \mathbf{crs}', \mathsf{x}, \pi') = 1) \wedge (pk_{\mathsf{Sign}} \notin \mathcal{PK}) \wedge (\mu = F(pk_{\mathsf{Sign}}))$; where Q is the set of statment-proof pairs and $\mathcal{PK}$ is the set of signature verification keys, both generated by $\mathsf{O}(\mathsf{x})$.

Lemma 5. *If the underlying truly random function $F(\cdot)$ is secure, then* $\Pr[\mathsf{EXP}_4^{SimExt}] \leq \Pr[\mathsf{EXP}_5^{SimExt}]$.

Proof. By assuming function $F(\cdot)$ is secure, we can conclude no polynomial time adversary can distinguish an output of the true random function $F(\cdot)$ from an output of the pseudo random function $f_s(\cdot)$. Indeed, experiment EXP_5^{SimExt} can be converted to an adversary for the game of a *true random function.* □

Claim. For experiment EXP_5^{SimExt}, we have $\Pr[\mathsf{EXP}_5^{SimExt}] \leq 2^{-\lambda}$.

Proof. From verification we know $pk_{\mathsf{Sign}} \notin \mathcal{PK}$, therefore $F(pk_{\mathsf{Sign}})$ has not been queried already. Thus, we will see $F(pk_{\mathsf{Sign}})$ as a newly generated random string independent from μ, which implies adversary only can guess. □

This completes proof of the main theorem. □

4 A Sub-ZK Simulation-Extractable SNARK

In this section, we aim to instantiate the construction proposed in Sect. 3.1, and achieve a NIZK argument that can guarantee Sub-ZK and simulation knowledge soundness. In such a scheme, the prover will get sure that the proof is ZK without trusting to the CRS generators but to achieve simulation knowledge soundness they will trust the CRS generators. Based on discussions in Sect. 3.1 and Fig. 1, we need to instantiate some primitives including the pseudo-random function, the commitment scheme, and the one-time secure signature scheme and also use a subversion-resistant NIZK argument as a subroutine.

A Subversion-Resistant NIZK. Currently Groth's zk-SNARK is the most efficient subversion-resistant NIZK argument that is proven to achieve Sub-ZK [ABLZ17,Fuc18] and knowledge soundness [Gro16] in the generic group model. While proving Sub-ZK, Abdolmaleki et al. [ABLZ17] and Fuchsbauer [Fuc18] have proposed two different CRS verification CV algorithms for Groth's zk-SNARK, which the later works for original version but the first one requires some changes in the CRS of Groth's zk-SNARK.

Instantiation of Primitives. As mentioned before, recently Atapoor and Baghery [AB19] used a similar construction to achieve simulation knowledge soundness in Groth's zk-SNARK [Gro16]. Their main goal was to construct an efficient version of Groth's zk-SNARK that can also guarantee non-malleability of proofs and outperforms Groth and Maller's zk-SNARK [GM17]. They instantiate pseudo-random function and commitment scheme with SHA512 hash

CRS of Groth's zk-SNARK [Gro16]:

$$(\mathsf{crs_P}, \mathsf{crs_V}) := \mathsf{crs} \leftarrow \begin{pmatrix} [\alpha, \beta, \delta, (\chi^i)_{i=0}^{n-1}, (\frac{u_j(\chi)\beta + v_j(\chi)\alpha + w_j(\chi)}{\gamma})_{j=0}^{m_0}, \\ (\frac{u_j(\chi)\beta + v_j(\chi)\alpha + w_j(\chi)}{\delta})_{j=m_0+1}^{m}, (\chi^i \ell(\chi)/\delta)_{i=0}^{n-2}]_1, \\ [\beta, \gamma, \delta, (\chi^i)_{i=0}^{n-1}]_2, \ [\alpha\beta]_T \end{pmatrix}.$$

CRS of the variation of Groth's zk-SNARK in [AB19]: $\mathsf{crs}' := (\mathsf{crs}, \rho)$.

$\mathsf{CV}'(\mathbf{R_L}, \xi, \mathsf{crs}' := (\mathsf{crs}, \rho))$:

1. For $\iota \in \{1, \alpha, \beta, \delta, \ell(\chi)/\delta\}$ and $\iota' \in \{1, \gamma\}$: check that $[\iota]_1 \neq [0]_1$ and $[\iota']_2 \neq [0]_1$
2. For $i = 1$ to $n-1$: check that $[\chi^i]_1 \bullet [1]_2 = [1]_1 \bullet [\chi^i]_2$, and $[\chi^i]_1 \bullet [1]_2 = [\chi^{i-1}]_1 \bullet [\chi]_2$,
3. For $\iota \in \{\alpha, \beta, \delta\}$: check that $[\iota]_1 \bullet [1]_2 = [1]_1 \bullet [\iota]_2$,
4. For $j = m_0 + 1$ to m: check that $[(u_j(\chi)\beta + v_j(\chi)\alpha + w_j(\chi))/\delta]_1 \bullet [\delta]_2 = [u_j(\chi)]_1 \bullet [\beta]_2 + [\alpha]_1 \bullet [v_j(\chi)]_2 + [w_j(\chi)]_1 \bullet [1]_2$,
5. For $i = 0$ to $n-2$: check that $[\chi^i \ell(\chi)/\delta]_1 \bullet [\delta]_2 = \sum_{j=0}^{n-1} L_j [\chi^j]_1 \bullet [\chi^i]_2$,
6. For $j = 0$ to m_0: check that $[(u_j(\chi)\beta + v_j(\chi)\alpha + w_j(\chi))/\gamma]_1 \bullet [\gamma]_2 = [u_j(\chi)]_1 \bullet [\beta]_2 + [\alpha]_1 \bullet [v_j(\chi)]_2 + [w_j(\chi)]_1 \bullet [1]_2$,
7. Check that $[\alpha]_1 \bullet [\beta]_2 = [\alpha\beta]_T$, and $[\delta]_2$ in $\mathsf{crs_P}$ and $\mathsf{crs_V}$ are the same,
8. Check that $\rho \neq 0$.

If all above checks succeeded then return 1 (the CRS is correctly formed) and otherwise 0 (the CRS is incorrectly formed).

Fig. 2. A CRS verification algorithm for the variation of Groth's zk-SNARK [Gro16] proposed by Atapoor and Baghery [AB19]. Note that $\mathsf{crs}' := (\mathsf{crs}, \rho)$, where $\rho := Com(s, r)$ and crs is the CRS of Groth's zk-SNARK that is shown above the figure.

function which requires an arithmetic circuit with ≈26.000 multiplication gates [KMS+16]. They used Boneh and Boyen's signature scheme [BB08] to instantiate the one-time secure signature scheme which is a paring-based signature scheme and works as follows:

Key Generation, $(\mathsf{pk_{Sign}}, \mathsf{sk_{Sign}}) \leftarrow \mathsf{KGen}(1^\lambda)$: Given a bilinear group description $(p, \mathbb{G}_1, \mathbb{G}_2, \mathbb{G}_T, \hat{e}, [1]_1, [1]_2)$, selects $\mathsf{sk} \leftarrow_r \mathbb{Z}_p^*$, and returns $(\mathsf{pk_{Sign}}, \mathsf{sk_{Sign}}) := ([\mathsf{sk}]_1, \mathsf{sk})$.

Signing, $[\sigma]_2 \leftarrow \mathsf{Sign}(\mathsf{sk_{Sign}}, m)$: Given the group description, $\mathsf{sk_{Sign}}$, and a message m, returns $[\sigma]_2 = [1/(m + \mathsf{sk})]_2$.

Verification, $\{1, 0\} \leftarrow \mathsf{SigVerify}(\mathsf{pk_{Sign}}, [\sigma]_2)$: Given $\mathsf{pk_{Sign}}$, m, and $[\sigma]_2$, checks whether $[m + \mathsf{sk}]_1 \bullet [1/(m + \mathsf{sk})]_2 = [1]_T$ and returns either 1 or 0.

Subversion-Resistant Simulatioo-Extractable SNARK. In the rest, we use the instantiations used in [AB19] and the CV algorithm proposed by Fuchsbauer [Fuc18] to construct a variation of Groth's zk-SNARK that will guarantee

Sub-ZK and simulation knowledge soundness. In Fig. 2 we presented a CRS verification algorithm CV' which basically is a minimally changed version of the CV algorithm proposed by Fuchsbauer [Fuc18]. In CV' we also check whether $\rho \neq 0$, and basically this is the only difference between CV' and CV algorithms.

Finally, as we used the same instantiations used in [AB19], so the other three algorithms $(\mathsf{K}', \mathsf{P}', \mathsf{V}')$ will be the same as in the variation of Groth's zk-SNARK proposed in [AB19]. Basically, we propose to add the new algorithm CV' to their variation and with minimal computational cost, achieve Sub-ZK as well. To this end, the prover first needs to check the well-formedness of CRS elements with executing the algorithm CV' (shown in Fig. 2) and if it returned 1 (the CRS is well-formed) it continues and generates the proof as described in Fig. 1. Abodlmaleki et al. [ABLZ17] showed that using batching techniques a similar CV' algorithm can be executed very efficiently; specially faster than running time of prover.

5 Conclusion

Recently, Atapoor and Baghery [AB19] used a folklore OR technique [BG90] with a particular instantiation [KZM+15, AB19] to construct a variation of Groth's zk-SNARK [Gro16] that achieves simulation knowledge soundness; consequently it guarantees non-malleability of proofs.

In this paper, we showed that the same technique can be used to amplify the best result in constructing subversion-resistant NIZK arguments [BFS16, ABLZ17, Fuc18, FO18, ALSZ18]. Technically speaking, we proved that if the input NIZK argument already achieves Sub-ZK (ZK without trusting to a third party) and (knowledge) soundness, by applying the mentioned technique, the lifted NIZK argument will *also* guarantee Sub-ZK and *simulation* (knowledge) soundness. Simulation knowledge soundness (a.k.a. simulation-extractability) ensures non-malleability of proofs which is a necessary requirement in practical applications.

We emphasize that, the used compiler can be applied on any subversion-resistant NIZK argument, e.g. the ones studied in [Fuc18], but we focused on the state-of-the-art zk-SNARK which is proposed by Groth in [Gro16]. From a different perspective, basically we showed that the recent construction proposed by Atapoor and Baghery [AB19] can also achieve Sub-ZK with minimal efficiency loss. The cost is that prover will check the well-formedness of CRS elements by an efficient CRS verification algorithm before using them.

To sum up, we note that as currently Atapoor and Baghery's variation [AB19] of Groth's zk-SNARK is the most efficient simulation-extractable zk-SNARK in the CRS model, so adding Sub-ZK to their scheme will result the most efficient SNARK that can guarantee Sub-ZK and simulation-extractability.

Acknowledgement. This work was supported in part by the Estonian Research Council grant PRG49.

References

[AB19] Atapoor, S., Baghery, K.: Simulation extractability in groth's zk-SNARK. In: Pérez-Solá, C., Navarro-Arribas, G., Biryukov, A., Garcia-Alfaro, J. (eds.) DPM/CBT-2019. LNCS, vol. 11737, pp. 336–354. Springer, Cham (2019). https://doi.org/10.1007/978-3-030-31500-9_22

[ABK18] Auerbach, B., Bellare, M., Kiltz, E.: Public-key encryption resistant to parameter subversion and its realization from efficiently-embeddable groups. In: Abdalla, M., Dahab, R. (eds.) PKC 2018, Part I. LNCS, vol. 10769, pp. 348–377. Springer, Cham (2018). https://doi.org/10.1007/978-3-319-76578-5_12

[ABL+19] Abdolmaleki, B., Baghery, K., Lipmaa, H., Siim, J., Zając, M.: UC-secure CRS generation for SNARKs. In: Buchmann, J., Nitaj, A., Rachidi, T. (eds.) AFRICACRYPT 2019. LNCS, vol. 11627, pp. 99–117. Springer, Cham (2019). https://doi.org/10.1007/978-3-030-23696-0_6

[ABLZ17] Abdolmaleki, B., Baghery, K., Lipmaa, H., Zając, M.: A subversion-resistant SNARK. In: Takagi, T., Peyrin, T. (eds.) ASIACRYPT 2017, Part III. LNCS, vol. 10626, pp. 3–33. Springer, Cham (2017). https://doi.org/10.1007/978-3-319-70700-6_1

[ALSZ18] Abdolmaleki, B., Lipmaa, H., Siim, J. and Zajac, M.: On QA-NIZK in the BPK model. IACR Cryptology ePrint Archive, 2018:877 (2018). http://eprint.iacr.org/2018/877

[AMV15] Ateniese, G., Magri, B., Venturi, D.: Subversion-resilient signatures: definitions, constructions and applications. Cryptology ePrint Archive, Report 2015/517 (2015). http://eprint.iacr.org/2015/517

[Bag19a] Baghery, K.: On the efficiency of privacy-preserving smart contract systems. In: Buchmann, J., Nitaj, A., Rachidi, T. (eds.) AFRICACRYPT 2019. LNCS, vol. 11627, pp. 118–136. Springer, Cham (2019). https://doi.org/10.1007/978-3-030-23696-0_7

[Bag19b] Baghery, K.: Subversion-resistant commitment schemes: definitions and constructions. Cryptology ePrint Archive, Report 2019/1065 (2019). http://eprint.iacr.org/2019/1065

[BB08] Boneh, D., Boyen, X.: Short signatures without random oracles and the SDH assumption in bilinear groups. J. Cryptol. **21**(2), 149–177 (2008)

[BBG+13] Ball, J., Borger, J., Greenwald, G., et al.: Revealed: how us and uk spy agencies defeat internet privacy and security. The Guardian **6**, 2–8 (2013)

[BCG+15] Ben-Sasson, E., Chiesa, A., Green, M., Tromer, E., Virza, M.: Secure sampling of public parameters for succinct zero knowledge proofs. In: 2015 IEEE Symposium on Security and Privacy, pp. 287–304. IEEE Computer Society Press (2015)

[BCPR14] Bitansky, N., Canetti, R., Paneth, O., Rosen, A.: On the existence of extractable one-way functions. In: Shmoys, D.B. (ed.) 46th ACM STOC, pp. 505–514. ACM Press, May/June 2014

[BCTV13] Ben-Sasson, E., Chiesa, A., Tromer, E., Virza, M.: Succinct non-interactive arguments for a von neumann architecture. Cryptology ePrint Archive, Report 2013/879 (2013). http://eprint.iacr.org/2013/879

[BFM88] Blum, M., Feldman, P., Micali, S.: Non-interactive zero-knowledge and its applications (extended abstract). In: 20th ACM STOC, pp. 103–112. ACM Press, May 1988

[BFS16] Bellare, M., Fuchsbauer, G., Scafuro, A.: NIZKs with an untrusted CRS: security in the face of parameter subversion. In: Cheon, J.H., Takagi, T. (eds.) ASIACRYPT 2016, Part II. LNCS, vol. 10032, pp. 777–804. Springer, Heidelberg (2016). https://doi.org/10.1007/978-3-662-53890-6_26

[BG90] Bellare, M., Goldwasser, S.: New paradigms for digital signatures and message authentication based on non-interactive zero knowledge proofs. In: Brassard, G. (ed.) CRYPTO 1989. LNCS, vol. 435, pp. 194–211. Springer, New York (1990). https://doi.org/10.1007/0-387-34805-0_19

[BPR14] Bellare, M., Paterson, K.G., Rogaway, P.: Security of symmetric encryption against mass surveillance. In: Garay, J.A., Gennaro, R. (eds.) CRYPTO 2014, Part I. LNCS, vol. 8616, pp. 1–19. Springer, Heidelberg (2014). https://doi.org/10.1007/978-3-662-44371-2_1

[Dam92] Damgård, I.: Towards practical public key systems secure against chosen ciphertext attacks. In: Feigenbaum, J. (ed.) CRYPTO 1991. LNCS, vol. 576, pp. 445–456. Springer, Heidelberg (1992). https://doi.org/10.1007/3-540-46766-1_36

[DDO+01] De Santis, A., Di Crescenzo, G., Ostrovsky, R., Persiano, G., Sahai, A.: Robust non-interactive zero knowledge. In: Kilian, J. (ed.) CRYPTO 2001. LNCS, vol. 2139, pp. 566–598. Springer, Heidelberg (2001). https://doi.org/10.1007/3-540-44647-8_33

[FO18] Fuchsbauer, G., Orrù, M.: Non-interactive zaps of knowledge. In: Preneel, B., Vercauteren, F. (eds.) ACNS 2018. LNCS, vol. 10892, pp. 44–62. Springer, Cham (2018). https://doi.org/10.1007/978-3-319-93387-0_3

[Fuc18] Fuchsbauer, G.: Subversion-zero-knowledge SNARKs. In: Abdalla, M., Dahab, R. (eds.) PKC 2018, Part I. LNCS, vol. 10769, pp. 315–347. Springer, Cham (2018). https://doi.org/10.1007/978-3-319-76578-5_11

[Gab19] Gabizon, A.: On the security of the BCTV pinocchio zk-SNARK variant. IACR Cryptology ePrint Archive, 2019:119 (2019)

[GGPR13] Gennaro, R., Gentry, C., Parno, B., Raykova, M.: Quadratic span programs and succinct NIZKs without PCPs. In: Johansson, T., Nguyen, P.Q. (eds.) EUROCRYPT 2013. LNCS, vol. 7881, pp. 626–645. Springer, Heidelberg (2013). https://doi.org/10.1007/978-3-642-38348-9_37

[GM17] Groth, J., Maller, M.: Snarky Signatures: minimal signatures of knowledge from simulation-extractable SNARKs. In: Katz, J., Shacham, H. (eds.) CRYPTO 2017, Part II. LNCS, vol. 10402, pp. 581–612. Springer, Cham (2017). https://doi.org/10.1007/978-3-319-63715-0_20

[GOS06] Groth, J., Ostrovsky, R., Sahai, A.: Non-interactive zaps and new techniques for NIZK. In: Dwork, C. (ed.) CRYPTO 2006. LNCS, vol. 4117, pp. 97–111. Springer, Heidelberg (2006). https://doi.org/10.1007/11818175_6

[Gre14] Greenwald, G.: No Place to Hide: Edward Snowden, the NSA, and the US Surveillance State. Macmillan, London (2014)

[Gro10] Groth, J.: Short pairing-based non-interactive zero-knowledge arguments. In: Abe, M. (ed.) ASIACRYPT 2010. LNCS, vol. 6477, pp. 321–340. Springer, Heidelberg (2010). https://doi.org/10.1007/978-3-642-17373-8_19

[Gro16] Groth, J.: On the size of pairing-based non-interactive arguments. In: Fischlin, M., Coron, J.-S. (eds.) EUROCRYPT 2016, Part II. LNCS, vol. 9666, pp. 305–326. Springer, Heidelberg (2016). https://doi.org/10.1007/978-3-662-49896-5_11

[Hae19] Haenni, R.: Swiss post public intrusion test: undetectable attack against vote integrity and secrecy (2019). https://e-voting.bfh.ch/app/download/7833162361/PIT2.pdf?t=1552395691

[KMS+16] Kosba, A., Miller, A.: The blockchain model of cryptography and privacy-preserving smart contracts. In: 2016 IEEE Symposium on Security and Privacy, pp. 839–858. IEEE Computer Society Press, May 2016

[KZM+15] Kosba, A.E., et al.: A framework for building composable zero-knowledge proofs. Technical report 2015/1093, 10 November 2015. http://eprint.iacr.org/2015/1093. Accessed 9 Apr 2017

[Lip12] Lipmaa, H.: Progression-free sets and sublinear pairing-based non-interactive zero-knowledge arguments. In: Cramer, R. (ed.) TCC 2012. LNCS, vol. 7194, pp. 169–189. Springer, Heidelberg (2012). https://doi.org/10.1007/978-3-642-28914-9_10

[Lip19] Lipmaa, H.: Simulation-extractable SNARKs revisited. Cryptology ePrint Archive, Report 2019/612 (2019). http://eprint.iacr.org/2019/612

[LPT19] Lewis, S.J., Pereira, O., Teague, V.: Trapdoor commitments in the swisspost e-voting shuffle proof (2019). https://people.eng.unimelb.edu.au/vjteague/SwissVote

[PHGR13] Parno, B., Howell, J., Gentry, C., Raykova, M.: Pinocchio: nearly practical verifiable computation. In: 2013 IEEE Symposium on Security and Privacy, pp. 238–252. IEEE Computer Society Press, May 2013

[PLS13] Perlroth, N., Larson, J., Shane, S.: NSA able to foil basic safeguards of privacy on web. The New York Times, 5 (2013)

Classification of Self-dual Codes of Length 20 over $\mathbb{Z}_4$ and Length at Most 18 over $\mathbb{F}_2 + u\mathbb{F}_2$

Rowena Alma L. Betty[1(✉)] and Akihiro Munemasa[2]

[1] Institute of Mathematics, University of the Philippines-Diliman, Quezon City 1101, Philippines
rabetty@math.upd.edu.ph

[2] Graduate School of Information Sciences, Tohoku University, Sendai 980–8579, Japan
munemasa@math.is.tohoku.ac.jp

Abstract. In this paper, we give a precise description of Rains' algorithm for classifying self-dual $\mathbb{Z}_4$-codes with a given residue code. We will use this to classify self-dual $\mathbb{Z}_4$-codes of length 20. A similar method is used to classify self-dual codes over $\mathbb{F}_2 + u\mathbb{F}_2$. We will update the table given by Han, Lee and Lee, of the data regarding the classification of self-dual codes over $\mathbb{F}_2 + u\mathbb{F}_2$.

Keywords: Self-dual code · Self-orthogonal code · Automorphism group

1 Introduction

In recent years, the study of self-dual codes over rings had been of great interest to many researchers. This was ignited by the work of Hammons, Kumar, Calderbank, Sloane and Solé [7], who showed that some famous classes of binary nonlinear codes can be obtained as the image under the Gray map from linear codes over $\mathbb{Z}_4$. As in the case for codes over finite fields, it is a fundamental problem to classify self-dual codes of a given length. In [13], Rains studied self-dual codes over $\mathbb{Z}_4$, via their residue codes, that is, their reduction modulo 2. We will give a precise description of Rains' algorithm (see [13, Theorem 3]) for classifying self-dual codes with a given binary doubly-even residue code, and use this to classify self-dual $\mathbb{Z}_4$-codes of length 20. Classification of self-dual $\mathbb{Z}_4$-codes of lengths up to 9 were given in [3], and [5] gave a classification for lengths 10 up to 15. Type II codes over $\mathbb{Z}_4$ of length 16 were classified in [12], while classification for Type I codes of length 16, as well as self-dual codes over $\mathbb{Z}_4$ of lengths 17 up to 19 have been established in [9].

We can use a similar method to classify self-dual codes over $\mathbb{F}_2 + u\mathbb{F}_2$ up to lengths 17 and 18, with binary self-orthogonal residue code. Self-dual codes over

R. A. L. Betty—Partially supported by Philippine National Oil Company.

M. Albrecht (Ed.): IMACC 2019, LNCS 11929, pp. 64–77, 2019.
https://doi.org/10.1007/978-3-030-35199-1_4

$\mathbb{F}_2 + u\mathbb{F}_2$ were classified for lengths up to 8 in [4]. Classification of Type II codes of lengths 12 and 16 are given in [1].

The organization of the paper is as follows. In Sect. 2, we recall basic results. In Sect. 3, we investigate how the automorphism group of the residue codes acts on the set of self-dual $\mathbb{Z}_4$-codes having the same residue. In Sect. 4, we will describe Rains' algorithm for self-dual $\mathbb{Z}_4$-codes as our main theorem, and give a classification of self-dual $\mathbb{Z}_4$-codes of length 20. In Sect. 5, we give a classification of self-dual codes over $\mathbb{F}_2 + u\mathbb{F}_2$.

2 Preliminaries

Let R denote the ring $\mathbb{Z}_m$ of integers modulo m or the commutative ring $\mathbb{F}_2 + u\mathbb{F}_2 = \{0, 1, u, 1+u\}$, with $u^2 = 0$. A (linear) R-code of length n is an R-submodule of R^n. Two codes $\mathcal{C}$ and $\mathcal{C}'$ over $\mathbb{Z}_m$ (respectively, over $\mathbb{F}_2 + u\mathbb{F}_2$) are equivalent if there exists a monomial $(\pm 1, 0)$-matrix (respectively, monomial $(1, 1+u, 0)$-matrix) P such that $\mathcal{C}' = \mathcal{C} \cdot P = \{c \cdot P \mid c \in \mathcal{C}\}$. An automorphism of $\mathcal{C}$ is a monomial matrix P with $\mathcal{C} = \mathcal{C} \cdot P$, and the automorphism group $\mathrm{Aut}(\mathcal{C})$ of $\mathcal{C}$ is the group of all automorphisms. A matrix $G \in M_{k \times n}(R)$ whose rows generate the code $\mathcal{C}$ is called a generator matrix of $\mathcal{C}$. We denote by $R^k G$ the R-code with generator matrix G.

The Hamming weight of $x \in R^n$ denoted by $\mathrm{wt}(x)$ is the number of its nonzero components. The Lee weight $\mathrm{wt}_L(x)$ of an element $x \in \mathbb{Z}_4$ is defined by $\mathrm{wt}_L(0) = 0$, $\mathrm{wt}_L(1) = \mathrm{wt}_L(3) = 1$ and $\mathrm{wt}_L(2) = 2$. The Lee weight $\mathrm{wt}_L(x)$ of an element $x \in \mathbb{F}_2 + u\mathbb{F}_2$ is defined by $\mathrm{wt}_L(0) = 0$, $\mathrm{wt}_L(1) = \mathrm{wt}_L(1+u) = 1$ and $\mathrm{wt}_L(u) = 2$. The Lee weight of a vector in R^n is the integral sum of the Lee weights of its components. The minimum Hamming and Lee weight of a code $\mathcal{C}$ are the smallest Hamming and Lee weights among all nonzero codewords of $\mathcal{C}$, respectively. The symmetrized weight enumerator for Lee weights of a code $\mathcal{C}$ of length n over $\mathbb{F}_2 + u\mathbb{F}_2$ is defined as

$$\mathrm{swe}(a, b, c) = \sum_{x \in \mathcal{C}} a^{n_0(x)} b^{n_1(x)} c^{n_2(x)},$$

where $n_0(x)$ is the number of $x_i = 0$, $n_2(x)$ is the number of $x_i = u$, and $n_1(x) = n - n_0(x) - n_2(x)$, for $x = (x_1, \dots, x_n) \in \mathcal{C}$.

We equip R^n with the standard inner product $x \cdot y = \sum_{i=1}^n x_i y_i$, for $x = (x_1, \dots, x_n)$, $y = (y_1, \dots, y_n) \in R^n$. The dual of an R-code $\mathcal{C}$ is defined as $\mathcal{C}^\perp = \{v \in R^n \mid u \cdot v = 0 \text{ for all } u \in \mathcal{C}\}$. We say that a code $\mathcal{C}$ is self-orthogonal if $\mathcal{C} \subseteq \mathcal{C}^\perp$, and self-dual if $\mathcal{C} = \mathcal{C}^\perp$. We say that a self-dual code is Hamming-optimal if it has the largest possible minimum Hamming weight among self-dual codes of the same length, and Lee-optimal self-dual codes are defined in a similar manner.

3 The Automorphism Group of the Residue Code of a Self-dual $\mathbb{Z}_4$-code

There are two binary codes $\mathrm{res}(\mathcal{C})$ and $\mathrm{tor}(\mathcal{C})$ associated with every $\mathbb{Z}_4$-code $\mathcal{C}$:

$$\mathrm{res}(\mathcal{C}) = \{c \bmod 2 \mid c \in \mathcal{C}\} \text{ and } \mathrm{tor}(\mathcal{C}) = \{c \bmod 2 \mid c \in \mathbb{Z}_4^n,\ 2c \in \mathcal{C}\}.$$

The codes $\mathrm{res}(\mathcal{C})$ and $\mathrm{tor}(\mathcal{C})$ are called the residue and torsion codes of $\mathcal{C}$, respectively. A $\mathbb{Z}_4$-code $\mathcal{C}$ is said to be free if $\mathrm{res}(\mathcal{C}) = \mathrm{tor}(\mathcal{C})$. If $\mathcal{C}$ is self-dual, then $\mathrm{res}(\mathcal{C})$ is a binary doubly-even code with $\mathrm{tor}(\mathcal{C}) = \mathrm{res}(\mathcal{C})^{\perp}$ [3]. In this section, we investigate how the automorphism group of $\mathrm{res}(\mathcal{C})$ acts on the set of all self-dual $\mathbb{Z}_4$-codes having the residue code $\mathrm{res}(\mathcal{C})$.

Let k and n be positive integers with $2k \le n$, and set $\mathcal{M} = M_{k\times n}(\mathbb{Z}_2)$. Let C be a doubly-even binary $[n, k]$ code with generator matrix $A \in \mathcal{M}$ and

$$\begin{bmatrix} A \\ B \end{bmatrix}$$

be a generator matrix of $C^{\perp}$, where $B \in M_{(n-2k)\times n}(\mathbb{Z}_2)$. Therefore, we have

$$AA^{\top} = 0, \tag{1}$$
$$BA^{\top} = 0. \tag{2}$$

We denote by $\iota : \mathbb{Z}_2 \to \mathbb{Z}_4$ the section defined by $\iota(0) = 0$ and $\iota(1) = 1$. Note that for $x, y \in \mathbb{Z}_2$, $2\iota(xy) = 2\iota(x)\iota(y)$ and $2\iota(x + y) = 2\iota(x) + 2\iota(y)$. Therefore, for matrices X, Y over $\mathbb{Z}_2$, we have

$$2\iota(X + Y) = 2\iota(X) + 2\iota(Y),$$
$$2\iota(XY) = 2\iota(X)\iota(Y) = \iota(X) \cdot 2\iota(Y).$$

We shall use these properties of ι freely.

Let $\tilde{A}$ be a $k \times n$ matrix over $\mathbb{Z}_4$ such that the code generated by $\tilde{A}$ is self-orthogonal and $\tilde{A} \bmod 2 = A$. Then

$$\tilde{A}\tilde{A}^{\top} = 0, \tag{3}$$
$$2\tilde{A} = 2\iota(A). \tag{4}$$

In particular, the $\mathbb{Z}_4$-code generated by

$$\begin{bmatrix} \tilde{A} \\ 2\iota(B) \end{bmatrix}$$

is self-dual.

Let

$$V_0 = \{M \in \mathcal{M} \mid MA^{\top} + AM^{\top} = 0\}, \tag{5}$$
$$W_0 = \langle \{M \in \mathcal{M} \mid MA^{\top} = 0\}, \{AE_{ii} \mid 1 \le i \le n\} \rangle, \tag{6}$$
$$V = V_0 \oplus \mathbb{Z}_2, \tag{7}$$
$$W = W_0 \oplus \{0\}, \tag{8}$$

where matrix E_{ij} has 1 in the (i,j)-entry and zeros in all other entries. Observe that $W_0 \subset V_0$, and hence $W \subset V$.

Suppose $P \in \mathrm{Aut}(C)$. Recall that $\mathrm{GL}(k, \mathbb{Z}_2)$ denote the group of invertible $k \times k$ matrices over $\mathbb{Z}_2$. Since A has full row rank, there exists a unique matrix $E_1(P) \in \mathrm{GL}(k, \mathbb{Z}_2)$ such that

$$AP = E_1(P)A. \tag{9}$$

Clearly,

$$E_1(PQ) = E_1(P)E_1(Q) \quad (P, Q \in \mathrm{Aut}(C)). \tag{10}$$

Since $\mathrm{Aut}(C)$ consists of permutation matrices, we have

$$\iota(PQ) = \iota(P)\iota(Q) \quad (P, Q \in \mathrm{Aut}(C)). \tag{11}$$

Also, there exists a unique matrix $E_2(P) \in \mathcal{M}$ such that

$$2\iota(E_2(P)) = \iota(E_1(P)^{-1})\tilde{A}\iota(P) - \tilde{A}. \tag{12}$$

Note that

$$E_1(I) = I \text{ and } E_2(I) = 0. \tag{13}$$

Lemma 1. *Let $P \in \mathrm{Aut}(C)$ and $M \in V_0$. Then*

$$E_1(P)^{-1}MP \in V_0, \tag{14}$$
$$E_2(P) \in V_0. \tag{15}$$

Proof. Set $N = E_1(P)^{-1}MP + E_2(P)$. Then

$$\begin{aligned} \tilde{A} + 2\iota(N) &= \tilde{A} + 2\iota(E_2(P)) + 2\iota(E_1(P)^{-1}MP) \\ &= \iota(E_1(P)^{-1})\tilde{A}\iota(P) + 2\iota(E_1(P)^{-1}MP) \quad \text{(by (12))}. \end{aligned} \tag{16}$$

From (11), we have

$$\iota(P)\iota(P)^\top = I. \tag{17}$$

Since

$$\begin{aligned}
&2\iota(NA^\top + AN^\top) \\
&= 2\iota(N)\tilde{A}^\top + \tilde{A} \cdot 2\iota(N)^\top && \text{(by (4))} \\
&= (\tilde{A} + 2\iota(N))(\tilde{A} + 2\iota(N))^\top && \text{(by (3))} \\
&= (\iota(E_1(P)^{-1})\tilde{A}\iota(P) + 2\iota(E_1(P)^{-1}MP)) \\
&\quad \cdot (\iota(E_1(P)^{-1})\tilde{A}\iota(P) + 2\iota(E_1(P)^{-1}MP))^\top && \text{(by (16))} \\
&= \iota(E_1(P)^{-1})\tilde{A}\iota(P)(2\iota(E_1(P)^{-1}MP))^\top \\
&\quad + 2\iota(E_1(P)^{-1}MP)(\iota(E_1(P)^{-1})\tilde{A}\iota(P))^\top && \text{(by (3), (17))} \\
&= 2\iota(E_1(P)^{-1}AM^\top(E_1(P)^{-1})^\top) \\
&\quad + 2\iota(E_1(P)^{-1}MA^\top(E_1(P)^{-1})^\top) && \text{(by (4))} \\
&= 2\iota(E_1(P)^{-1}(AM^\top + MA^\top)(E_1(P)^{-1})^\top) = 0,
\end{aligned}$$

we have $NA^\top + AN^\top = 0$. This implies $N \in V_0$. Setting $M = 0$, we obtain (15). Since $N \in V_0$, we also obtain (14). □

Lemma 2. *Let $P \in \mathrm{Aut}(C)$. If $M \in W_0$, then $E_1(P)^{-1}MP \in W_0$.*

Proof. Suppose first $MA^\top = 0$. Since $AP^{-1} = E_1(P^{-1})A$ by (9), we have $PA^\top = A^\top E_1(P^{-1})^\top$. Thus

$$E_1(P)^{-1}MPA^\top = E_1(P)^{-1}MA^\top E_1(P^{-1})^\top = 0.$$

This implies $E_1(P)^{-1}MP \in W_0$.

Next, suppose $M = AE_{ii}$, where $i \in \{1, \ldots, n\}$. Then there exists a unique $j \in \{1, \ldots, n\}$ such that $P_{ij} = 1$. Now, by (9), we have

$$E_1(P)^{-1}MP = E_1(P)^{-1}APE_{jj} = AE_{jj} \in W_0.$$

□

Lemma 3. *Let $P, Q \in \mathrm{Aut}(C)$. Then $E_1(Q)^{-1}E_2(P)Q + E_2(Q) + E_2(PQ) \in W_0$.*

Proof. From (10), we have $2\iota(E_1(PQ)^{-1}) = 2\iota(E_1(Q)^{-1})\iota(E_1(P)^{-1})$. This implies that there exists $X \in M_k(\mathbb{Z}_2)$ such that

$$\iota(E_1(PQ)^{-1}) = \iota(E_1(Q)^{-1})\iota(E_1(P)^{-1}) + 2\iota(X). \tag{18}$$

Then

$$\begin{aligned}
&2\iota(E_2(PQ)) \\
&= \iota(E_1(PQ)^{-1})\tilde{A}\iota(PQ) - \tilde{A} && \text{(by (12))} \\
&= (\iota(E_1(Q)^{-1})\iota(E_1(P)^{-1}) + 2\iota(X))\tilde{A}\iota(PQ) - \tilde{A} && \text{(by (18))} \\
&= \iota(E_1(Q)^{-1})\iota(E_1(P)^{-1})\tilde{A}\iota(P)\iota(Q) \\
&\quad + \iota(X) \cdot 2\tilde{A}\iota(PQ) - \tilde{A} && \text{(by (11))} \\
&= \iota(E_1(Q)^{-1})(\tilde{A} + 2\iota(E_2(P)))\iota(Q) + 2\iota(XAPQ) - \tilde{A} && \text{(by (4), (12))} \\
&= \iota(E_1(Q)^{-1})\tilde{A}\iota(Q) + 2\iota(E_1(Q)^{-1}E_2(P)Q) + 2\iota(XAPQ) - \tilde{A} \\
&= 2\iota(E_2(Q) + E_1(Q)^{-1}E_2(P)Q + XAPQ) && \text{(by (12))}.
\end{aligned}$$

Hence

$$E_2(PQ) = E_1(Q)^{-1}E_2(P)Q + E_2(Q) + XAPQ.$$

Since $APQA^\top = E_1(PQ)AA^\top = 0$ by (1), we have $XAPQ \in \{M \in \mathcal{M} \mid MA^\top = 0\} \subset W_0$. The result then follows. □

Lemma 4. *Let $M, M' \in \mathcal{M}$. Then*

$$\mathbb{Z}_4^{n-k} \begin{bmatrix} \tilde{A} + 2\iota(M) \\ 2\iota(B) \end{bmatrix} = \mathbb{Z}_4^{n-k} \begin{bmatrix} \tilde{A} + 2\iota(M') \\ 2\iota(B) \end{bmatrix} \tag{19}$$

if and only if

$$(M + M')A^\top = 0. \tag{20}$$

Proof. If (19) holds, then there exist matrices P, Q, R, S over $\mathbb{Z}_4$ such that

$$\begin{bmatrix} \tilde{A} + 2\iota(M) \\ 2\iota(B) \end{bmatrix} = \begin{bmatrix} P & Q \\ R & S \end{bmatrix} \begin{bmatrix} \tilde{A} + 2\iota(M') \\ 2\iota(B) \end{bmatrix}.$$

Thus

$$2\iota(M) = (P - I)\tilde{A} + 2P\iota(M') + 2Q\iota(B). \tag{21}$$

Moreover, this implies $\tilde{A} \equiv P\tilde{A} \pmod 2$, hence $A = (P \bmod 2)A$. Since $A \in M_{k\times n}(\mathbb{Z}_2)$ has rank k, this implies

$$P \equiv I \pmod 2. \tag{22}$$

Thus we have

$$\begin{aligned}
&2\iota((M + M')A^\top) \\
&= \iota(M + M') \cdot 2\iota(A^\top) \\
&= \iota(M + M') \cdot 2\tilde{A}^\top && \text{(by (4))} \\
&= (2\iota(M) + 2\iota(M'))\tilde{A}^\top \\
&= ((P - I)\tilde{A} + 2P\iota(M') + 2Q\iota(B) + 2\iota(M'))\tilde{A}^\top && \text{(by (21))} \\
&= 2(P + I)\iota(M')\tilde{A}^\top + 2Q\iota(B)\tilde{A}^\top && \text{(by (3))} \\
&= Q\iota(B) \cdot 2\tilde{A}^\top && \text{(by (22))} \\
&= Q\iota(B) \cdot 2\iota(A^\top) && \text{(by (4))} \\
&= Q \cdot 2\iota(BA^\top) \\
&= 0 && \text{(by (2))}.
\end{aligned}$$

Therefore, (20) holds.

Conversely, suppose (20) holds. Then

$$\mathbb{Z}_2^k(M + M') \subset C^\perp = \mathbb{Z}_2^{n-k} \begin{bmatrix} A \\ B \end{bmatrix}.$$

This implies

$$2\mathbb{Z}_4^k\iota(M + M') \subset 2\mathbb{Z}_4^{n-k} \begin{bmatrix} \iota(A) \\ \iota(B) \end{bmatrix} = \mathbb{Z}_4^{n-k} \begin{bmatrix} 2(\tilde{A} + 2\iota(M')) \\ 2\iota(B) \end{bmatrix},$$

and hence

$$\begin{aligned}
\mathbb{Z}_4^{n-k} \begin{bmatrix} \tilde{A} + 2\iota(M) \\ 2\iota(B) \end{bmatrix} &\subset \mathbb{Z}_4^{n-k} \begin{bmatrix} \tilde{A} + 2\iota(M') \\ 2\iota(B) \end{bmatrix} + 2\mathbb{Z}_4^{n-2k}\iota(M + M') \\
&= \mathbb{Z}_4^{n-k} \begin{bmatrix} \tilde{A} + 2\iota(M') \\ 2\iota(B) \end{bmatrix}.
\end{aligned}$$

Switching the roles of M and M', we obtain the reverse containment. Therefore, (19) holds. □

Lemma 5. *Let $M \in \mathcal{M}$ and $P \in \mathrm{Aut}(C)$. Then*

$$\mathbb{Z}_4^{n-k}\begin{bmatrix}\tilde{A}+2\iota(M)\\ 2\iota(BP)\end{bmatrix} = \mathbb{Z}_4^{n-k}\begin{bmatrix}\tilde{A}+2\iota(M)\\ 2\iota(B)\end{bmatrix}.$$

Proof. Since $P \in \mathrm{Aut}(C) = \mathrm{Aut}(C^\perp)$, there exists $F \in \mathrm{GL}(n-k, \mathbb{Z}_2)$ such that

$$\begin{bmatrix}AP\\ BP\end{bmatrix} = F\begin{bmatrix}A\\ B\end{bmatrix}.$$

Since A has full row rank, (9) implies that

$$F = \begin{bmatrix}E_1(P) & 0\\ E_3 & E_4\end{bmatrix}$$

for some matrix E_3 and some nonsingular matrix E_4. Then $BP = E_3A + E_4B$, so

$$\begin{aligned}\mathbb{Z}_4^{n-k}\begin{bmatrix}\tilde{A}+2\iota(M)\\ 2\iota(BP)\end{bmatrix} &= \mathbb{Z}_4^{n-k}\begin{bmatrix}\tilde{A}+2\iota(M)\\ 2\iota(E_3A+E_4B)\end{bmatrix}\\ &= \mathbb{Z}_4^{n-k}\begin{bmatrix}I & 0\\ 2\iota(E_3) & \iota(E_4)\end{bmatrix}\begin{bmatrix}\tilde{A}+2\iota(M)\\ 2\iota(B)\end{bmatrix}\\ &= \mathbb{Z}_4^{n-k}\begin{bmatrix}\tilde{A}+2\iota(M)\\ 2\iota(B)\end{bmatrix}.\end{aligned}$$

□

We define matrices F_{ij} over $\mathbb{Z}_4$ by $F_{ij} = I + 2E_{ij}$. Note that the matrices F_{ij} are pairwise commutative, that is,

$$F_{ij}F_{kl} = F_{kl}F_{ij} = I + 2(E_{ij} + E_{kl}). \tag{23}$$

Note also that the matrix F_{ii} is the diagonal matrix whose diagonal entries are all 1 except its (i,i)-entry which is -1. For a subset Λ of $\{1, 2, \ldots, n\}$ and a permutation matrix P, we denote by Λ^P the subset satisfying

$$P^{-1}\sum_{i\in\Lambda} E_{ii}P = \sum_{i\in\Lambda^P} E_{ii}.$$

Lemma 6. *For $M \in \mathcal{M}$, $P \in \mathrm{Aut}(C)$ and $\Lambda \subset \{1, 2, \ldots, n\}$, we have*

$$\begin{aligned}&\mathbb{Z}_4^{n-k}\begin{bmatrix}\tilde{A}+2\iota(M)\\ 2\iota(B)\end{bmatrix}\left(\prod_{i\in\Lambda} F_{ii}\right)\iota(P)\\ &= \mathbb{Z}_4^{n-k}\begin{bmatrix}\tilde{A}+2\iota(E_1(P)^{-1}MP + E_2(P) + A\sum_{i\in\Lambda^P} E_{ii})\\ 2\iota(B)\end{bmatrix}.\end{aligned}$$

Proof. Since

$$\begin{aligned}(\tilde{A}+2\iota(M))\prod_{i\in\Lambda}F_{ii}\iota(P) &= \tilde{A}\prod_{i\in\Lambda}F_{ii}\iota(P)+2\iota(MP)\\ &= (\tilde{A}+2\tilde{A}\sum_{i\in\Lambda}E_{ii})\iota(P)+2\iota(MP)\\ &= \tilde{A}\iota(P)+2\iota(A\sum_{i\in\Lambda}E_{ii}P+MP)\\ &= \tilde{A}\iota(P)+2\iota(AP\sum_{i\in\Lambda^P}E_{ii}+MP),\end{aligned}$$

we have

$$\begin{aligned}&\iota(E_1(P)^{-1})(\tilde{A}+2\iota(M))\prod_{i\in\Lambda}F_{ii}\iota(P)\\ &= \iota(E_1(P)^{-1})(\tilde{A}\iota(P)+2\iota(AP\sum_{i\in\Lambda^P}E_{ii}+MP))\\ &= \tilde{A}+2\iota(E_2(P)+E_1(P)^{-1}AP\sum_{i\in\Lambda^P}E_{ii}+E_1(P)^{-1}MP) \qquad \text{(by (12))}\\ &= \tilde{A}+2\iota(E_1(P)^{-1}MP+E_2(P)+A\sum_{i\in\Lambda^P}E_{ii}) \qquad \text{(by (9))}.\end{aligned}$$

Thus

$$\begin{aligned}&\mathbb{Z}_4^{n-k}\begin{bmatrix}\tilde{A}+2\iota(M)\\ 2\iota(B)\end{bmatrix}\left(\prod_{i\in\Lambda}F_{ii}\right)\iota(P)\\ &= \mathbb{Z}_4^{n-k}\begin{bmatrix}\iota(E_1(P)^{-1})(\tilde{A}+2\iota(M))\prod_{i\in\Lambda}F_{ii}\iota(P)\\ 2\iota(BP)\end{bmatrix}\\ &= \mathbb{Z}_4^{n-k}\begin{bmatrix}\tilde{A}+2\iota(E_1(P)^{-1}MP+E_2(P)+A\sum_{i\in\Lambda^P}E_{ii})\\ 2\iota(B)\end{bmatrix}\end{aligned}$$

by Lemma 5. □

Lemma 7. *For $M, M' \in \mathcal{M}$ and $P \in \mathrm{Aut}(C)$, there exists a subset Λ of $\{1, 2, \ldots, n\}$ such that*

$$\mathbb{Z}_4^{n-k}\begin{bmatrix}\tilde{A}+2\iota(M)\\ 2\iota(B)\end{bmatrix}\left(\prod_{i\in\Lambda}F_{ii}\right)\iota(P) = \mathbb{Z}_4^{n-k}\begin{bmatrix}\tilde{A}+2\iota(M')\\ 2\iota(B)\end{bmatrix} \qquad (24)$$

if and only if

$$M'+E_1(P)^{-1}MP+E_2(P)\in W_0. \qquad (25)$$

Proof. By Lemmas 4 and 6, (24) is equivalent to

$$(M'+E_1(P)^{-1}MP+E_2(P)+A\sum_{i\in\Lambda_0}E_{ii})A^{\top}=0, \qquad (26)$$

where $\Lambda_0 = \Lambda^P$. Assuming (26), we obtain (25) using (6).

Conversely, if (25) holds, then there exists a subset Λ_0 of $\{1, 2, \dots, n\}$ such that (26) holds. Setting $\Lambda = \Lambda_0^{P^{-1}}$, we recover (24) by Lemmas 4 and 6. □

4 Classification of Self-dual $\mathbb{Z}_4$-codes with Given Residue

In this section, we state and prove our main theorems about classification of self-dual $\mathbb{Z}_4$-codes with given residue, in terms of the action of the automorphism group of the residue code.

Theorem 1. *Let C be a binary doubly-even $[n, k]$ code with generator matrix A. Define V_0, W_0, V, W by (5)–(8). Then the group* $\mathrm{Aut}(C)$ *acts on V/W linearly by*

$$((M, a) + W)^P = (E_1(P)^{-1}MP + aE_2(P), a) + W, \tag{27}$$

for $P \in \mathrm{Aut}(C)$. Moreover, $\mathrm{Aut}(C)$ *leaves the subset*

$$\Omega = \{(M, 1) + W \mid M \in V_0\}$$

invariant, and the orbits of $\mathrm{Aut}(C)$ *on Ω are in one-to-one correspondence with the equivalence classes of self-dual codes over $\mathbb{Z}_4$ with residue code C.*

Proof. Suppose $(M_1, a_1), (M_2, a_2) \in V$ and $(M_1, a_1) + W = (M_2, a_2) + W$. Then $M_1 - M_2 \in W_0$ and $a_1 - a_2 = 0$. We have

$$\begin{aligned}
&(E_1(P)^{-1}M_1P + a_1E_2(P), a_1) - (E_1(P)^{-1}M_2P + a_2E_2(P), a_2) \\
&= (E_1(P)^{-1}(M_1 - M_2)P, 0) \in W,
\end{aligned}$$

by Lemma 2.

Observe that for $P, Q \in \mathrm{Aut}(C)$,

$$\begin{aligned}
&(((M, a) + W)^P)^Q \\
&= \left((E_1(P)^{-1}MP + aE_2(P), a) + W\right)^Q \\
&= (E_1(Q)^{-1}(E_1(P)^{-1}MP + aE_2(P))Q + aE_2(Q), a) + W \\
&= (E_1(Q)^{-1}E_1(P)^{-1}MPQ + a(E_1(Q)^{-1}E_2(P)Q + E_2(Q)), a) + W \\
&= (E_1(Q)^{-1}E_1(P)^{-1}MPQ + aE_2(PQ), a) + W
\end{aligned}$$

by Lemma 3, while

$$\begin{aligned}
((M, a) + W)^{PQ} &= (E_1(PQ)^{-1}MPQ + aE_2(PQ), a) + W \\
&= (E_1(Q)^{-1}E_1(P)^{-1}MPQ + aE_2(PQ), a) + W
\end{aligned}$$

by (10). Thus, $((M, a) + W)^{PQ} = (((M, a) + W)^P)^Q$.

Also, (13) implies $((M, a) + W)^I = (M, a) + W$. Therefore, (27) defines an action of $\mathrm{Aut}(C)$ on V/W. Moreover, it is easy to see that this action is linear.

Next, we show that Aut(C) leaves Ω invariant. By Lemma 1, for $P \in \mathrm{Aut}(C)$ and $M \in V_0$, $E_1(P)^{-1}MP + E_2(P) \in V_0$. Therefore, if $(M,1) + W \in \Omega$, then

$$((M,1)+W)^P = (E_1(P)^{-1}MP + E_2(P), 1) + W \in \Omega.$$

Let $(M,1)+W, (M',1)+W \in \Omega$. Note that two codes

$$\mathbb{Z}_4^{n-k}\begin{bmatrix}\tilde{A}+2\iota(M)\\ 2\iota(B)\end{bmatrix} \text{ and } \mathbb{Z}_4^{n-k}\begin{bmatrix}\tilde{A}+2\iota(M')\\ 2\iota(B)\end{bmatrix}$$

are equivalent if and only if (24) holds for some subset Λ of $\{1,2,\dots,n\}$ and a permutation matrix P. Reducing modulo 2, we see that $P \in \mathrm{Aut}(C)$. Then by Lemma 7, this is equivalent to (25), or $(M',1)+W = ((M,1)+W)^P$. Therefore, the orbits of Aut(C) on Ω are in one-to-one correspondence with the equivalence classes of self-dual codes over $\mathbb{Z}_4$ with residue code C. □

By modifying the proof of Theorem 1, we can determine the order of the automorphism group of a $\mathbb{Z}_4$-code. For $x, y \in \mathbb{Z}_2^n$, we denote by $x*y$ the entrywise product of x and y. The linear span of all $x*y$, for $x,y \in C$, is denoted by $C*C$. Note that by Theorem 1, we have an action of Aut(C) on Ω, so we can speak of the stabilizer in Aut(C) of an element $(M,1)+W \in \Omega$. This is the subgroup of Aut(C) consisting of elements fixing $(M,1)+W \in \Omega$, and is denoted by $\mathrm{Stab}_{\mathrm{Aut}(C)}((M,1)+W)$.

Theorem 2. *For $M \in V_0$, let*

$$\mathcal{C} = \mathbb{Z}_4^{n-k}\begin{bmatrix}\tilde{A}+2\iota(M)\\ 2\iota(B)\end{bmatrix}.$$

Then

$$|\mathrm{Aut}(\mathcal{C})| = |\mathrm{Stab}_{\mathrm{Aut}(C)}((M,1)+W)||(C*C)^{\perp}|, \tag{28}$$

where $C = \mathrm{res}(\mathcal{C})$.

Proof. We consider the homomorphism

$$\begin{aligned}\pi : \mathrm{Aut}(\mathcal{C}) &\to \mathrm{Aut}(C)\\ \tilde{P} &\mapsto \tilde{P} \bmod 2,\end{aligned}$$

so that $|\mathrm{Aut}(\mathcal{C})| = |\mathrm{Im}\,\pi||\mathrm{Ker}\,\pi|$. Note that $\mathrm{Im}\,\pi = \mathrm{Stab}_{\mathrm{Aut}(C)}((M,1)+W)$ by Lemma 7.

Observe that, by Lemma 6,

$$\mathbb{Z}_4^{n-k}\begin{bmatrix}\tilde{A}+2\iota(M)\\ 2\iota(B)\end{bmatrix}\left(\prod_{i\in\Lambda} F_{ii}\right) = \mathbb{Z}_4^{n-k}\begin{bmatrix}\tilde{A}+2\iota(M+A\sum_{i\in\Lambda}E_{ii})\\ 2\iota(B)\end{bmatrix}.$$

Then, by Lemma 4, $\prod_{i\in\Lambda} F_{ii} \in \mathrm{Aut}(\mathcal{C})$ is equivalent to $A\sum_{i\in\Lambda}E_{ii}A^{\top} = 0$. The latter is equivalent to $\lambda \in (C*C)^{\perp}$, where $\lambda = \sum_{i\in\Lambda} e_i$. Hence $|\mathrm{Ker}\,\pi| = |(C*C)^{\perp}|$, and (28) holds. □

By Theorem 1, we can classify self-dual $\mathbb{Z}_4$-codes with given residue code C. Letting C run through all doubly-even binary codes of length 20, a complete classification of self-dual $\mathbb{Z}_4$-codes of length 20 can be obtained. To this end, we use a database of doubly-even binary codes found in [10]. Let C be a doubly-even code of length 20 and dimension k with generator matrix A. Let $\tilde{A}$, B be as in Sect. 3. Define V_0, W_0, V, W by (5)–(8). Let

$$\{(M_i, 1) + W \mid 1 \le i \le M_r\}$$

be a set of representatives for the action of $\mathrm{Aut}(C)$ on Ω. The proof of Theorem 1 shows that the codes

$$\mathbb{Z}_4^{n-k} \begin{bmatrix} \tilde{A} + 2\iota(M_i) \\ 2\iota(B) \end{bmatrix} \quad (1 \le i \le r)$$

form a complete set of representatives for equivalence classes of self-dual $\mathbb{Z}_4$-codes with residue code C.

We also obtain inequivalent self-dual Hamming-optimal codes and inequivalent self-dual Lee-optimal codes over $\mathbb{Z}_4$ of length 20 from three inequivalent doubly-even binary residue codes with highest possible dual distance 4 (see [13, Theorem 2]). All computer calculations in this paper were done with the help of MAGMA [2].

Theorem 3. *There are 183,948 inequivalent self-dual $\mathbb{Z}_4$-codes of length 20, where 596 of these codes are Hamming-optimal and 237 of these codes are Lee-optimal.*

It is well known that every self-dual code gives rise to a unimodular lattice [9]. More precisely, given a self-dual $\mathbb{Z}_4$-code of length 20,

$$A_4(\mathcal{C}) = \frac{1}{2}\{(x_1, \ldots, x_{20}) \in \mathbb{Z}^{20} \mid (x_1 \bmod 4, \ldots, x_{20} \bmod 4) \in \mathcal{C}\}$$

is a unimodular lattice of rank 20. This construction of lattices from codes is called Construction A. The number of isomorphism classes of unimodular lattices of rank 20 is significantly smaller than the number 183,948 of self-dual $\mathbb{Z}_4$-codes of length 20. This means that the set of these codes are partitioned into equivalence classes according to the associated lattice. In Table 1, we give the number of inequivalent self-dual $\mathbb{Z}_4$-codes $\mathcal{C}$, with $A_4(\mathcal{C}) \simeq L$ for each unimodular lattice L of rank 20, having a given dimension k of the binary doubly-even residue codes $\mathrm{res}(\mathcal{C})$.

5 Classification of Self-dual $\mathbb{F}_2 + u\mathbb{F}_2$-codes with Given Residue

In the previous sections, we considered self-dual codes over the ring $\mathbb{Z}_4$. The ring $\mathbb{F}_2 + u\mathbb{F}_2$ is very similar to $\mathbb{Z}_4$, where u in $\mathbb{F}_2 + u\mathbb{F}_2$ plays almost the same role

Table 1. Number of inequivalent self-dual $\mathbb{Z}_4$-codes of length 20

$L\backslash k$	0	1	2	3	4	5	6	7	8	9	Total
D_{20}	0	1	1	2	5	9	13	20	19	12	82
$D_{12}E_8$	0	0	1	4	13	38	86	143	160	86	531
$D_{12}D_8$	0	0	2	8	30	97	259	516	649	378	1939
$E_7^2D_6$	0	0	0	2	15	81	308	794	1191	780	3171
$A_{15}D_5$	0	0	0	0	2	13	61	195	352	263	886
$D_8^2D_4$	0	0	1	9	57	284	1085	2913	4732	3306	12387
$A_{11}E_6A_3$	0	0	0	0	2	26	190	804	1770	1475	4267
$D_6^3A_1^2$	0	0	0	3	33	274	1583	5874	11964	9780	29511
$A_9^2A_1^2$	0	0	0	0	1	14	129	688	1844	1831	4507
$A_7^2D_5O_1$	0	0	0	0	5	74	671	3591	9772	9600	23713
D_4^5	0	0	0	2	20	152	930	3762	8486	7362	20714
A_5^4	0	0	0	0	2	31	340	2172	6931	7374	16850
$E_6^3O_1 \oplus \mathbb{Z}$	0	0	0	1	8	49	216	610	955	590	2429
$A_{11}D_7O_1 \oplus \mathbb{Z}$	0	0	0	1	9	66	332	1044	1762	1114	4328
$A_7^2D_5 \oplus \mathbb{Z}$	0	0	0	1	14	130	828	3239	6288	4158	14658
$A_{17}A_1 \oplus \mathbb{Z}^2$	0	0	0	0	1	6	27	71	101	53	259
$D_{10}E_7A_1 \oplus \mathbb{Z}^2$	0	0	1	9	53	229	733	1609	2074	1123	5831
$D_6^3 \oplus \mathbb{Z}^2$	0	0	1	7	56	348	1576	4487	7023	4234	17732
$A_9^2 \oplus \mathbb{Z}^2$	0	0	0	0	2	22	170	674	1272	750	2890
$A_{11}E_6 \oplus \mathbb{Z}^3$	0	0	0	1	10	75	351	950	1238	527	3152
$E_8^2 \oplus \mathbb{Z}^4$	0	0	1	4	16	46	98	154	155	70	544
$D_{16} \oplus \mathbb{Z}^4$	0	1	3	9	24	54	106	157	153	66	573
$D_8^2 \oplus \mathbb{Z}^4$	0	0	2	14	80	347	1097	2321	2808	1375	8044
$\mathbb{Z}^{20}$	1	1	2	4	7	10	15	16	12	3	71
$E_8 \oplus \mathbb{Z}^{12}$	0	1	3	9	25	54	95	122	94	27	430
$D_{12} \oplus \mathbb{Z}^8$	0	1	4	16	52	140	291	436	382	131	1453
$E_7^2 \oplus \mathbb{Z}^6$	0	0	1	7	37	140	395	713	728	283	2304
$A_{15} \oplus \mathbb{Z}^5$	0	0	0	1	7	32	107	225	239	81	692

as 2 in $\mathbb{Z}_4$. Therefore, the method we used in $\mathbb{Z}_4$ can also be used for $\mathbb{F}_2 + u\mathbb{F}_2$. For a code $\mathcal{C}$ over $\mathbb{F}_2 + u\mathbb{F}_2$, we define its residue code and torsion code as

$$\begin{aligned}\mathrm{res}(\mathcal{C}) &= \{x \in \mathbb{F}_2^n \mid \exists y \in \mathbb{F}_2^n,\ x + uy \in \mathcal{C}\},\\ \mathrm{tor}(\mathcal{C}) &= \{x \in \mathbb{F}_2^n \mid ux \in \mathcal{C}\}.\end{aligned}$$

If $\mathcal{C}$ is self-dual, then $\mathrm{res}(\mathcal{C})$ is a binary self-orthogonal code with $\mathrm{tor}(\mathcal{C}) = \mathrm{res}(\mathcal{C})^{\perp}$ (see [6]). Thus, instead of specifying a doubly-even binary codes as a residue code of a $\mathbb{Z}_4$-code, we fix a binary self-orthogonal code C and classify self-dual codes $\mathcal{C}$

over $\mathbb{F}_2 + u\mathbb{F}_2$ with $\mathrm{res}(\mathcal{C}) = C$. Classification of binary maximal self-orthogonal codes of length up to 18 were given in [11], from which all binary self-orthogonal codes of length up to 18 can be enumerated.

A self-dual code over $\mathbb{F}_2 + u\mathbb{F}_2$ is Type II if the Lee weight of every codeword is divisible by 4, and Type I otherwise. Type II self-dual codes over $\mathbb{F}_2 + u\mathbb{F}_2$ exist only for lengths a multiple of 4 (see [4]).

Table I of [4] shows 10 inequivalent Type II codes of length 8, but the code whose automorphism group of order equal to $2^9 \cdot 3$ has symmetrized weight enumerator given by

$$12a^4b^4 + 12a^5b^2c + 4a^6c^2 + 16b^8 + 64ab^6c + 72a^2b^4c^2 + 40a^3b^2c^3 + 6a^4c^4 \\ + 12b^4c^4 + 12ab^2c^5 + c^8 + 4a^2c^6 + a^8.$$

Table IV of [4] gives 20 inequivalent Type I codes of length 8 which contain no code with generator matrix (u) as a subcode of length 1, but there are in fact only 19 such codes. Table 2 lists the order of their automorphism groups and symmetrized weight enumerators.

Table 2. Type I codes of length 8 without trivial component

Group Order	Symmetrized Weight Enumerators								
	b^2	c	b^4	b^2c	c^2	b^6	b^4c	b^2c^2	c^3
$2^{11} \cdot 3^2 \cdot 5$	2	0	0	0	16	32	0	30	0
$2^{13} \cdot 3^2$	0	0	0	0	12	0	64	0	0
$2^{11} \cdot 3$	0	0	4	0	8	32	16	0	16
$2^{11} \cdot 3$	4	0	12	0	8	32	0	28	0
$2^{10} \cdot 3$	2	0	0	8	8	16	32	14	0
$2^{11} \cdot 3$	0	0	4	0	8	32	0	32	0
$2^{10} \cdot 3$	0	0	0	4	8	16	32	16	0
$2^9 \cdot 3$	2	0	12	0	4	24	24	6	8
2^9	0	0	4	4	4	24	24	8	8
2^{11}	0	0	8	0	4	0	64	0	0
$2^{11} \cdot 3$	8	0	24	0	4	32	0	24	0
2^{10}	4	0	8	8	4	16	32	12	0
2^9	2	0	4	8	4	16	32	14	0
$2^9 \cdot 3$	2	0	12	0	4	32	0	30	0
2^{10}	0	0	8	0	4	16	32	16	0
2^9	0	0	0	8	4	16	32	16	0
2^9	0	0	4	4	4	16	32	16	0
2^{11}	0	0	8	0	4	32	0	32	0
$2^7 \cdot 3$	0	0	12	0	0	0	64	0	0

Table 3 shows the current status of the classification of self-dual codes over $\mathbb{F}_2 + u\mathbb{F}_2$, including our results, for length n, $8 \leq n \leq 18$. The data is an update of [8, Table 1], where they gave a lower bound for the number of inequivalent self-dual codes for lengths 9 and 10. Note that an incorrect number for the number of Type I codes of length 8 was given in [4].

Table 3. Number of inequivalent self-dual codes over $\mathbb{F}_2 + u\mathbb{F}_2$ of length n, $8 \leq n \leq 18$

n	Type I	Type II	n	Type I	Type II
8	33	10	14	5,768	
9	46 (≥46 in [8])		15	7,611	
10	158 (≥157 in [8])		16	68,649	1,894
11	179		17	107,479	
12	725	82	18	1,680,292	
13	960				

References

1. Bannai, E., Harada, M., Munemasa, A., Ibukiyama, T., Oura, M.: Type II codes over $\mathbb{F}_2 + u\mathbb{F}_2$ and applications to Hermitian modular forms. Abh. Math. Semin. Univ. Hambg. **73**, 13–42 (2003)
2. Bosma, W., Cannon, J., Playoust, C.: The Magma algebra system I: the user language. J. Symb. Comput. **24**, 235–265 (1997)
3. Conway, J.H., Sloane, N.J.A.: Self-dual codes over the integers modulo 4. J. Comb. Theory Ser. A **62**, 30–45 (1993)
4. Dougherty, S.T., Gaborit, P., Harada, M., Solé, P.: Type II codes over $\mathbb{F}_2 + u\mathbb{F}_2$. IEEE Trans. Inf. Theory **45**, 32–45 (1999)
5. Fields, J., Gaborit, P., Leon, J.S., Pless, V.: All self-dual $\mathbb{Z}_4$ codes of length 15 or less are known. IEEE Trans. Inf. Theory **44**, 311–322 (1998)
6. Gaborit, P.: Mass formulas for self-dual codes over $\mathbb{Z}_4$ and $\mathbb{F}_q + u\mathbb{F}_q$. IEEE Trans. Inf. Theory **42**, 1222–1228 (1996)
7. Hammons, A.R., Kumar, P.V., Calderbank, A.R., Sloane, N.J.A., Solé, P.: The $\mathbb{Z}_4$-linearity of Kerdock, Preparata, Goethals, and related codes. IEEE Trans. Inf. Theory **40**, 301–319 (1994)
8. Han, S., Lee, H., Lee, Y.: Construction of self-dual codes over $\mathbb{F}_2 + u\mathbb{F}_2$. Bull. Korean Math. Soc. **49**, 135–143 (2012)
9. Harada, M., Munemasa, A.: On the classification of self-dual $\mathbb{Z}_k$-codes. In: Parker, M.G. (ed.) IMACC 2009. LNCS, vol. 5921, pp. 78–90. Springer, Heidelberg (2009)
10. Miller, R.L.: Doubly-Even Codes. https://rlmill.github.io/de_codes/
11. Pless, V.: A classification of self-orthogonal codes over $GF(2)$. Discrete Math. **3**, 209–246 (1972)
12. Pless, V., Leon, J.S., Fields, J.: All $\mathbb{Z}_4$ codes of Type II and length 16 are known. J. Comb. Theory, Ser. A. **78**, 32–50 (1997)
13. Rains, E.M.: Optimal self-dual codes over $\mathbb{Z}_4$. Discrete Math. **203**, 215–228 (1999)

A Framework for Universally Composable Oblivious Transfer from One-Round Key-Exchange

Pedro Branco[1,2(✉)], Jintai Ding[3], Manuel Goulão[1,2], and Paulo Mateus[1,2]

[1] SQIG-Instituto de Telecomunicações, Lisbon, Portugal
pmbranco@math.tecnico.ulisboa.pt
[2] Department of Mathematics, IST-University of Lisbon, Lisbon, Portugal
[3] University of Cincinnati, Cincinnati, USA

Abstract. Oblivious transfer is one of the main pillars of modern cryptography and plays a major role as a building block for other more complex cryptographic primitives. In this work, we present an efficient and versatile framework for oblivious transfer (OT) using one-round key-exchange (ORKE), a special class of key exchange (KE) where only one message is sent from each party to the other. Our contributions can be summarized as follows:

- We analyze carefully ORKE schemes and introduce new security definitions. Namely, we introduce a new class of ORKE schemes, called Alice-Bob one-round key-exchange (A-B ORKE), and the definitions of message and key indistinguishability.
- We show that OT can be obtained from A-B ORKE schemes fulfilling message and key indistinguishability. We accomplish this by designing a new efficient, versatile and universally composable framework for OT in the Random Oracle Model (ROM). The efficiency of the framework presented depends almost exclusively on the efficiency of the A-B ORKE scheme used since all other operations are linear in the security parameter. Universally composable OT schemes in the ROM based on new hardness assumptions can be obtained from instantiating our framework.

Examples are presented using the classical Diffie-Hellman KE, RLWE-based KE and Supersingular Isogeny Diffie-Hellman KE.

Keywords: Oblivious transfer · Universal Composability · Key exchange

1 Introduction

Oblivious transfer (OT), introduced in the 80s by Rabin [33], is one of the main pillars of modern cryptography. It involves two parties: the sender, which receives as input two messages M_0 and M_1, and the receiver, which receives as input a bit $b \in \{0, 1\}$. Security for the receiver is guaranteed if the sender

M. Albrecht (Ed.): IMACC 2019, LNCS 11929, pp. 78–101, 2019.
https://doi.org/10.1007/978-3-030-35199-1_5

gets no information on b whereas security for the sender is guaranteed if the receiver gets M_b but no information on M_{1-b}. Despite its simplicity, OT can be employed as a building block to construct other more complex cryptographic primitives [26], such as secure multiparty computation (MPC) [35], privacy-preserving keyword search [22], or private information retrieval [27]. However, for practical purposes, the efficiency and number of OT executions needed to perform these tasks, specially MPC protocols, is a clear bottleneck, even using optimizations, such as OT extensions [3]. Hence, the development of efficient OT protocols is crucial to make MPC protocols ubiquitous, which is the motivation of this work.

Recall that key-exchange (KE) allows two parties, usually called Alice and Bob, to share a key while preventing an eavesdropper to get any information about the key. It is probably the oldest public-key cryptographic primitive and its study goes back to the seminal paper of Diffie and Hellman [19]. In this work, we consider a special type of KE, called one-round key-exchange (ORKE), where only one message is sent from each party to the other (see, for example, [7,25]). That is, to share a key using an ORKE scheme, Alice sends one message to Bob and Bob sends one message back.

Our main result is the construction of a new efficient and Universally Composable [12] framework for OT from ORKE, with very low overhead. Since, it is impossible to achieve universally composable OT in the plain model [13], our framework is proven secure in the random oracle model (ROM). In order to design the framework, we carefully analyze ORKE schemes to understand which are the additional conditions required to construct OT.

1.1 Related Work

Although it is quite difficult to come up with UC-secure OT protocols, several proposals have been made in recent years. We highlight the ones which use public-key encryption (PKE) schemes as a building block [5,11,17,18,32] (an idea firstly presented in [6]). However, the use of PKE schemes to perform OT is, in most cases, too inefficient, especially in a scenario where one has to create a new pair of public and secret keys for each execution of the OT. This also affects the communication complexity since, for example, post-quantum PKE schemes have very large public keys, and all the above mentioned OT protocols require a public key to be sent from one party to the other. Our approach is to use a special type of key exchange and symmetric-key primitives to implement an OT protocol. To this end, we adapt some techniques of [5] to the symmetric setting, as it is discussed in the next section.

In real life applications, key exchange (KE) schemes are often used to exchange keys in order to securely communicate using a symmetric-key encryption (SKE) scheme. Hence, the idea of using KE and SKE schemes to design OT protocols seems to follow naturally. This idea was introduced in [16,30] and applied in [8,21,23], using the Diffie-Hellman protocol and, later, post-quantum versions were presented using the Supersingular Isogeny Diffie-Hellman (SIDH) protocol [4] and using RLWE-based KE [9]. The main advantage of using KE over PKE schemes to construct OT is that exchanging keys and communicating via SKE is usually much more efficient than communicating using PKE schemes (many times, the decryption algorithm of PKE schemes is much more inefficient than the encryption algorithm. By using KE and SKE over PKE, we avoid the use of the decryption algorithm of PKE). We remark that both the schemes [4,16] do not provide UC-security.

1.2 Our Contribution

A-B ORKE. Our first contribution is the definition of a new class of key-exchange protocols, called *Alice-Bob one-round key-exchange* (A-B ORKE). An A-B ORKE is an ORKE where the message sent by one party (say Bob) might depend on the message previously sent by the other party (Alice). The specific case when Bob's message does not depend on Alice's is the standard ORKE (as in [7]). Thus, it is obvious that ORKE is a particular case of A-B ORKE. More precisely, it is the non-interactive case of A-B ORKE. To encompass more instances of our OT framework, we work with A-B ORKE schemes. However, we remark that any vanilla ORKE scheme with the same security properties can also be used in our construction.[1]

We introduce new security definitions for A-B ORKE: (i) key indistinguishable, meaning that, if Alice sends a uniformly random message (instead of message computed using her secret key), then the shared key computed by Bob is indistinguishable from a uniformly chosen value to her; and (ii) message indistinguishable, which means that Alice's message should be indistinguishable from a uniformly random value from Bob's point-of-view. These concepts cannot be trivially defined in a formal way since Alice's message may be composed by several smaller messages, some of them indistinguishable from uniformly random values, but others not.

Hence, consider the set of messages $\mathcal{M}$ that can be computed by Alice. Suppose that there is a group $\mathbb{M}$ and a set $\overline{\mathcal{M}}$ such that $\mathcal{M} \subseteq \overline{\mathcal{M}}$ and consider a group action $\psi : \overline{\mathcal{M}} \times \mathbb{M} \to \overline{\mathcal{M}}$. We define message indistinguishability to be the incapability of an adversary in distinguishing $m \in \mathcal{M}$ from $m' = \psi(m, h)$ where h was sampled uniformly from $\mathbb{M}$. Key indistinguishability is defined similarly as the infeasibility of a adversary to distinguish a key computed by Bob using m' sent by Alice (instead of m) from a uniformly chosen value.

A New Framework for OT. As our main result, we present a new framework for building an OT from any A-B ORKE scheme. Our construction shows that it is possible to construct OT from an A-B ORKE that is message and key indistinguishable. The framework is proven to be universally composable in the Random Oracle Model (ROM), and can be seen as a generalization of the protocol in [9].

The framework has four rounds and it is extremely efficient, as the overhead is very low. It only requires: (i) three messages of the A-B ORKE scheme to

[1] Remark that a Key Encapsulation Mechanism (KEM) is an A-B ORKE, however the opposite is not known to be true. Note that Key Exchanges (KE) and KEM are not comparable primitives and that some KE are A-B ORKE.

be created, and exchanged; (ii) a challenge that takes linear-time to create in the security parameter; and (iii) two ciphertexts of SKE to be exchanged. Thus, the efficiency of the framework depends almost exclusively on the A-B ORKE scheme used.

Comparing with other recently proposed frameworks [5,32], we conclude our construction is more efficient, since we rely on ORKE and SKE, while they rely on PKE schemes. Moreover, our framework can be used to create OT protocols based on hard problems which cannot be achieved when using the frameworks of [5,32] (such as Supersingular Isogeny-based OT), making our proposal extremely versatile.

Concretely, in our OT framework, the sender and the receiver use, in an ingenious way, the A-B ORKE such that the sender is able to compute two keys k_0 and k_1, one of them (k_b) shared with the receiver. The messages are encrypted by the sender with these keys using a SKE scheme and the receiver can only decrypt one of them.

More precisely, the receiver computes m_{R}^b, where b is its input, and chooses a random seed t. It computes m_{R}^{1-b} such that $m_{\mathsf{R}}^1 = \psi(m_{\mathsf{R}}^0, \mathsf{H}_1(t))$, where H_1 is a random oracle with range $\mathbb{M}$, and sends t and m_{R}^0 to the sender. The sender recovers m_{R}^1 from both t and m_{R}^0 and computes two shared keys. The messages M_0 and M_1 are encrypted using these keys. A challenge has to be sent from the sender to the receiver in order to guarantee security in the UC-framework (we give a detailed explanation for this in the next paragraph). As mentioned before, this paradigm was firstly used to design the simplest OT protocol [16]. However, unlike [4,16], in our protocol the interaction starts with the receiver which allows to save one round. We remark that this strategy was already used in [9].

By now, it is well-known that the protocol of [16] does not guarantee security in the UC-framework due to subtle timing attacks [5,11,21] (in particular, it does not guarantee security against a corrupted receiver). Here, to achieve UC-security, we have to extract the inputs when only the sender and when only the receiver are corrupted. The extraction of the inputs of the sender is done by programming the random oracle in such a way that the simulator will be able to compute both keys. The extraction of the input of the receiver is a more subtle problem. We solve it using a similar strategy as the one used in [5], where a challenge is made to the receiver in such a way that it needs to ask the random oracle for information that reveals the input bit to the simulator. However, in [5], PKE schemes are used to make this challenge. In our protocol we use SKE schemes, so we adapt the technique of [5] using symmetric primitives. To this end, we add two more rounds where a challenge is sent from the sender to the receiver, which can only answer correctly if it queries the random oracle. These queries will be fundamental to design the simulator and avoid attacks from a corrupted receiver. These two extra rounds do not reveal any information about the bit b to the sender since the receiver is able to answer correctly to the challenge no matter its input. On the other hand, the receiver only gets information on the outputs of the secret keys by a random oracle. Observe that the output of the secret key k_{1-b} by the random oracle is not correlated at all with the key. Thus, the receiver does not get any information on the key it does not have.

2 Preliminaries

If $\mathcal{A}$ is an algorithm, we denote by $y \leftarrow \mathcal{A}(x)$ the output of the experiment of running $\mathcal{A}$ on input x. If S is a set and χ is a probabilistic distribution over S, we denote by $x \leftarrow\!\!\$\, S$ the experiment of choosing uniformly at random an element x from S and by $x \leftarrow\!\!\$\, \chi$ the experiment of choosing x from S according to χ. If x and y are two binary strings, we denote by $x|y$ their concatenation and by $x \oplus y$ their bit-wise XOR. If X and Y are two probability distributions, $X \approx Y$ means that they are computationally indistinguishable. A negligible function $\mathsf{negl}(n)$ is a function such that $\mathsf{negl}(n) < 1/\mathsf{poly}(n)$ for every polynomial $\mathsf{poly}(n)$ and sufficiently large n. By a PPT algorithm we mean a probabilistic polynomial-time algorithm. By $\mathsf{Pr}[A : B_1, \ldots, B_n]$ we mean the probability of event A given that events $B_1, \ldots, B_n$ happened sequentially. Throughout this work, the security parameter will be denoted by κ.

In this work, we use symmetric-key encryption schemes. Below, we present the definition of a symmetric-key encryption scheme.

Definition 1. A *symmetric-key encryption* (SKE) scheme $\Delta = (\mathsf{Enc}_\Delta, \mathsf{Dec}_\Delta)$ is a pair of algorithms such that:

- $c \leftarrow \mathsf{Enc}_\Delta(k, M; r)$ is a PPT algorithm that takes as input a shared key k, a message to encrypt M and randomness r and outputs a ciphertext c. Whenever r is omitted, it means that it was chosen uniformly at random;
- $M/ \perp \leftarrow \mathsf{Dec}_\Delta(k, c)$ is a PPT algorithm that takes as input a key k and a ciphertext c and outputs a message M, if c was encrypted using k, or an error message $\perp$, otherwise.

A SKE scheme must be sound, that is, $M \leftarrow \mathsf{Dec}_\Delta\left(k, \mathsf{Enc}_\Delta\left(k, M; r\right)\right)$ for any message M and any r. Also, it should be secure, that is, it should be infeasible for an adversary, without knowledge of the secret key, to recover a message from its ciphertext. The security notion that we consider in this work is the one of IND-CPA secure.

Let Δ be a SKE and consider the following game between a challenger $\mathcal{C}$ and an adversary $\mathcal{A}$: (i) $\mathcal{C}$ creates a key k. (ii) $\mathcal{A}$ has access to an encryption oracle that it can query a polynomial number of times. (iii) At some point, $\mathcal{A}$ outputs two messages M_0 and M_1. (iv) A bit b is chosen uniformly by $\mathcal{C}$ and it encrypts M_b and returns the corresponding ciphertext to $\mathcal{A}$. (v) Again, $\mathcal{A}$ has access to an encryption oracle that it can query a polynomial number of times. (vi) The game ends with $\mathcal{A}$ outputting a bit b'.

We say that Δ is IND-CPA secure if the advantage of $\mathcal{A}$ in the game above, defined as $\left|\Pr\left[b = b'\right] - \frac{1}{2}\right|$, is negligible in the security parameter.

2.1 One-Round Key-Exchange

One-round key-exchange (ORKE) is a cryptographic primitive that allows two parties to agree on a shared key while an eavesdropper gets no information on that key, by sending only one message from each party to the other. We present the definition of ORKE as a variant of the one presented in [7].

Definition 2. A *one-round key-exchange* (ORKE) scheme Π is defined by a tuple of algorithms $(\mathsf{Gen}_\Pi, \mathsf{Msg}_\Pi, \mathsf{Key}_\Pi)$ where:

- $\mathsf{sk} \leftarrow \mathsf{Gen}_\Pi(1^\kappa, r)$ is an algorithm that takes as input a security parameter κ and a random value r and outputs a secret keys sk. Whenever r is omitted, it means that it is chosen uniformly at random.
- $m_i \leftarrow \mathsf{Msg}_\Pi(r_i, \mathsf{sk}_i)$ is an algorithm that takes as input a random value r_i and secret key sk_i, and outputs a message m_i.
- $k \leftarrow \mathsf{Key}_\Pi(r_i, \mathsf{sk}_i, m_j)$ is an algorithm that takes as input a secret key sk_i, a random r_i and a message m_j and outputs a key k.

A ORKE scheme Π should be *sound*. That is, if for all $\mathsf{sk}_i \leftarrow \mathsf{Gen}_\Pi(1^\kappa)$ and $\mathsf{sk}_j \leftarrow \mathsf{Gen}_\Pi(1^\kappa)$ and for all $r_i, r_j \leftarrow \{0,1\}^\kappa$, it holds that

$$\mathsf{Key}_\Pi(r_i, \mathsf{sk}_i, m_j) = \mathsf{Key}_\Pi(r_j, \mathsf{sk}_j, m_i)$$

where $m_i \leftarrow \mathsf{Msg}_\Pi(r_i, \mathsf{sk}_i)$ and $m_j \leftarrow \mathsf{Msg}_\Pi(r_j, \mathsf{sk}_j)$.

ORKE structure

Alice		**Bob**
$r_\mathsf{A} \leftarrow_\$ \{0,1\}^\kappa$		$r_\mathsf{B} \leftarrow_\$ \{0,1\}^\kappa$
$\mathsf{sk}_\mathsf{A} \leftarrow \mathsf{Gen}_\Pi(1^\kappa)$		$\mathsf{sk}_\mathsf{B} \leftarrow \mathsf{Gen}_\Pi(1^\kappa)$
$m_\mathsf{A} \leftarrow \mathsf{Msg}_\Pi(r_\mathsf{A}, \mathsf{sk}_\mathsf{A})$	$\xrightarrow{m_\mathsf{A}}$	$m_\mathsf{B} \leftarrow \mathsf{Msg}_\Pi(r_\mathsf{B}, \mathsf{sk}_\mathsf{B})$
	$\xleftarrow{m_\mathsf{B}}$	
$k_\mathsf{A} \leftarrow \mathsf{Key}_\Pi(r_\mathsf{A}, \mathsf{sk}_\mathsf{A}, m_\mathsf{B})$		$k_\mathsf{B} \leftarrow \mathsf{Key}_\Pi(r_\mathsf{B}, \mathsf{sk}_\mathsf{B}, m_\mathsf{A})$

We want our framework to be as general as possible, so we define a new type of ORKE scheme which we call Alice-Bob one-round key-exchange (A-B ORKE). An A-B ORKE scheme is an ORKE scheme where Alice sends her message m_A first. So, Bob's message m_B can depend on m_A. An A-B ORKE can be seen as a generalization of the concept of ORKE. It is obvious that every ORKE scheme is an A-B ORKE scheme. However, the converse is not true in general: in Ding's KE [20] or in New Hope KE [1], Bob's message depends on Alice's, and thus, they are A-B ORKE schemes but not ORKE schemes.

Definition 3. An *Alice-Bob one-round key-exchange* (A-B ORKE) scheme Π is defined by three algorithms $(\mathsf{Gen}_\Pi, \mathsf{Msg}_\Pi, \mathsf{Key}_\Pi)$, where $\mathsf{Msg}_\Pi = (\mathsf{Msg}_\Pi^\mathsf{A}, \mathsf{Msg}_\Pi^\mathsf{B})$, such that

- $\mathsf{sk} \leftarrow \mathsf{Gen}_\Pi(1^\kappa, r)$ is an algorithm that takes as input a security parameter κ and a random value r and outputs a secret key sk.
- $m_i \leftarrow \mathsf{Msg}_\Pi^\mathsf{A}(r_i, \mathsf{sk}_i)$ is an algorithm that takes as input a random value r_i and secret key sk_i, and outputs a message m_i.
- $m_j \leftarrow \mathsf{Msg}_\Pi^\mathsf{B}(r_j, \mathsf{sk}_j, m_i)$ is an algorithm that takes as input a random value r_i, and secret key sk_i and a message m_i previously sent by the other party and outputs a message m_j.
- $k \leftarrow \mathsf{Key}_\Pi(r_i, \mathsf{sk}_i, m_j)$ is an algorithm that takes as input a secret key sk_i, a random r_i and a message m_j and outputs a key k.

A-B ORKE structure

Alice		**Bob**
$r_\mathsf{A} \leftarrow_\$ \{0,1\}^\kappa$		$r_\mathsf{B} \leftarrow_\$ \{0,1\}^\kappa$
$\mathsf{sk}_\mathsf{A} \leftarrow \mathsf{Gen}_\Pi(1^\kappa, r_\mathsf{A})$		$\mathsf{sk}_\mathsf{B} \leftarrow \mathsf{Gen}_\Pi(1^\kappa, r_\mathsf{B})$
$m_\mathsf{A} \leftarrow \mathsf{Msg}_\Pi^\mathsf{A}(r_\mathsf{A}, \mathsf{sk}_\mathsf{A})$	$\xrightarrow{m_\mathsf{A}}$	
	$\xleftarrow{m_\mathsf{B}}$	$m_\mathsf{B} \leftarrow \mathsf{Msg}_\Pi^\mathsf{B}(r_\mathsf{B}, \mathsf{sk}_\mathsf{B}, m_\mathsf{A})$
$k_\mathsf{A} \leftarrow \mathsf{Key}_\Pi(r_\mathsf{A}, \mathsf{sk}_\mathsf{A}, m_\mathsf{B})$		$k_\mathsf{B} \leftarrow \mathsf{Key}_\Pi(r_\mathsf{B}, \mathsf{sk}_\mathsf{B}, m_\mathsf{A})$

To design our framework for OT, we need that the A-B ORKE scheme used fulfills certain properties which we have called *message indistinguishability* and *key indistinguishability*.

First, we need to introduce the notion of *non-redundant message for key generation*. Intuitively, a non-redundant message output by the algorithm Msg_Π is a message such that every part of it is used to construct the shared key. We define such property for messages sent by Alice:

Definition 4. Let κ be the security parameter, $\Pi = (\mathsf{Gen}_\Pi, \mathsf{Msg}_\Pi, \mathsf{Key}_\Pi)$ be an A-B ORKE scheme and $a \in \mathbb{N}$. Let $m = (m_1, \dots, m_a) \leftarrow \mathsf{Msg}_\Pi^\mathsf{A}(r_\mathsf{A}, \mathsf{sk}_\mathsf{A})$, and $m_\mathsf{B} \leftarrow \mathsf{Msg}_\Pi^\mathsf{B}(r_\mathsf{B}, \mathsf{sk}_\mathsf{B}, m)$. Let $m' = (m_{i_1}, \dots, m_{i_b})$ for any proper subset $\{i_1, \dots, i_b\} = S \subset \{1, \dots, a\}$. We say that $m = (m_1, \dots, m_a)$ is *non-redundant for key generation* (NRKG) if

$$\begin{aligned}\mathsf{Pr}\,[k_\mathsf{B} \neq k'_\mathsf{B} \wedge k_\mathsf{B} = k_\mathsf{A} : k_\mathsf{B} \leftarrow \mathsf{Key}_\Pi(r_\mathsf{B}, \mathsf{sk}_\mathsf{B}, m),\\ k'_\mathsf{B} \leftarrow \mathsf{Key}_\Pi(r_\mathsf{B}, \mathsf{sk}_\mathsf{B}, m'), k_\mathsf{A} \leftarrow \mathsf{Key}_\Pi(r_\mathsf{A}, \mathsf{sk}_\mathsf{A}, m_\mathsf{B})] \geq 1 - \mathsf{negl}(\kappa)\end{aligned}$$

for $\mathsf{sk}_\mathsf{A} \leftarrow \mathsf{Gen}_\Pi(1^\kappa)$, $\mathsf{sk}_\mathsf{B} \leftarrow \mathsf{Gen}_\Pi(1^\kappa)$, $r_\mathsf{A}, r_\mathsf{B} \leftarrow_\$ \{0,1\}^\kappa$.

We introduce the concept of *message indistinguishable* for an A-B ORKE scheme. Again, we define this property for messages sent by Alice.

Recall that, if $(\mathbb{G}, *)$ is a group with operation $*$ and X is a set, then a right group action $\psi : X \times \mathbb{G} \to X$ is a function that satisfies: (i) $\psi(x, e) = x$ for every $x \in X$ and the identity element e of $\mathbb{G}$; and (ii) $\psi(\psi(x, g), h) = \psi(x, g * h)$ for every $x \in X$ and $g, h \in \mathbb{G}$.

In the following, let $(\mathbb{M}, *)$ be a group and $\mathcal{M}$ be the space of non-redundant messages for key generation outputted by the algorithm $\mathsf{Msg}_{\Pi}^{\mathsf{A}}$. Let $\psi : \overline{\mathcal{M}} \times (\mathbb{M}, *) \rightarrow \overline{\mathcal{M}}$ be a right group action of $(\mathbb{M}, *)$ on $\overline{\mathcal{M}}$, where $\overline{\mathcal{M}}$ is a set such that $\mathcal{M} \subseteq \overline{\mathcal{M}}$.

Definition 5. Let κ be the security parameter, $\Pi = (\mathsf{Gen}_{\Pi}, \mathsf{Msg}_{\Pi}, \mathsf{Key}_{\Pi})$ be an A-B ORKE scheme that is NRKG and ψ, $\mathbb{M}$ and $\mathcal{M}$ be as described above. We say that an A-B ORKE protocol is *ψ-message indistinguishable* (or fulfills the *ψ-message indistinguishability* property) if, for any PPT adversary $\mathcal{A}$, we have that

$$\Pr\left[1 \leftarrow \mathcal{A}(x, \mathsf{sk}_{\mathsf{B}}, h) : x \leftarrow \mathsf{Msg}_{\Pi}^{\mathsf{A}}(r_{\mathsf{A}}, \mathsf{sk}_{\mathsf{A}}), h \leftarrow_{\$} \mathbb{M}\right]$$
$$-\Pr\left[1 \leftarrow \mathcal{A}(x, \mathsf{sk}_{\mathsf{B}}, h) : y \leftarrow \mathsf{Msg}_{\Pi}^{\mathsf{A}}(r_{\mathsf{A}}, \mathsf{sk}_{\mathsf{A}}), h \leftarrow_{\$} \mathbb{M}, x \leftarrow \psi(y, h)\right] \leq \mathsf{negl}(\kappa)$$

where $\mathsf{sk}_{\mathsf{A}} \leftarrow \mathsf{Gen}_{\Pi}(1^{\kappa})$, $\mathsf{sk}_{\mathsf{B}} \leftarrow \mathsf{Gen}_{\Pi}(1^{\kappa})$, $r_{\mathsf{A}} \leftarrow_{\$} \{0,1\}^{\kappa}$.

The intuition behind this definition is that we need $x = \psi(y, h)$ to be indistinguishable from uniformly chosen elements from some set, where $y \in \mathcal{M}$ and h is an element in a set $\mathbb{M}$. We also need h to have inverse in $\mathbb{M}$, to be able to recover y. One possible solution is to consider A-B ORKE schemes for which the set $\mathcal{M}$ (the set of outputs of $\mathsf{Msg}_{\Pi}^{\mathsf{A}}$) forms a group, and consider $\mathcal{M}$ to be $\mathbb{M}$. This happens when we consider the Diffie-Hellman KE, for example. However, there are cases where the set $\mathcal{M}$ may not have inverses or, even worse, it may not be closed under any operation (e.g., consider $\mathcal{M}$ to be the set of LWE samples [34], as in the A-B ORKE schemes of [1,20,31]). But observe that cases like these LWE-based schemes also have some type of indistinguishability (see Example 6). From this example, we conclude that we only need the elements in $\mathcal{M}$ to be indistinguishable from elements in $\overline{\mathcal{M}}$, where $\overline{\mathcal{M}}$ is a set such that $\mathcal{M} \subseteq \overline{\mathcal{M}}$. Again, for the framework to be as general as possible, we define message indistinguishability as the incapability to distinguish elements of $\mathcal{M}$ from elements of $\overline{\mathcal{M}}$. This definition also includes the cases where $m = (m_1, \ldots, m_a) \in \mathcal{M}$ is composed by several smaller messages m_i and where only part of these coordinates are affected by the action of the group $(\mathbb{M}, *)$ (while the other coordinates remain the same).

Example 6. *Consider $\mathcal{M}$ to be the the set of* LWE *samples in $\mathbb{Z}_q^n = (\mathbb{Z}/q\mathbb{Z})^n$ for some $n \in \mathbb{N}$ and some $q \in \mathbb{N}$, as in several lattice-based A-B ORKE schemes [1, 20, 31]. Now consider $\overline{\mathcal{M}}$ and $\mathbb{M}$ to be $\mathbb{Z}_q^n$ and the operation $*$ to be the sum $+$ in $\mathbb{Z}_q^n$. Observe that, when the action $\psi : \overline{\mathcal{M}} \times (\mathbb{Z}_q^n, +) \rightarrow \overline{\mathcal{M}}$ is defined as $\psi(x, h) = x + h$, then $\psi(x, h)$ is uniformly chosen at random in $\mathbb{Z}_q^n$ when $h \leftarrow_{\$} \mathbb{M}$. From the* LWE *assumption [34], which states that* LWE *samples are indistinguishable from uniformly chosen values from $\mathbb{Z}_p^n$, we conclude that the schemes [1, 20, 31] are ψ-message indistinguishable. The definition above generalizes this notion of indistinguishability of messages.*

Finally, we also need that the key obtained by Bob is indistinguishable from a uniformly chosen value, when it is given a uniformly chosen value instead of the message obtained by Alice when running $\mathsf{Msg}_{\Pi}^{\mathsf{A}}$.

Definition 7. Let κ be the security parameter, $\Pi = (\mathsf{Gen}_\Pi, \mathsf{Msg}_\Pi, \mathsf{Key}_\Pi)$ be an A-B ORKE scheme that is NRKG, ψ, $\mathbb{M}$ and $\mathcal{M}$ be as above and $\mathcal{K} = \{0,1\}^\beta$, where β is the length of the key output by the Key_Π algorithm. We say that an A-B ORKE protocol is *ψ-key indistinguishable* (or fulfills the *ψ-key indistinguishability* property) if, for any PPT adversary $\mathcal{A}$, we have that

$$\Pr\left[1 \leftarrow \mathcal{A}(k, \mathsf{sk}_\mathsf{A}, m, m', h) : k \leftarrow \mathsf{Key}_\Pi(r_\mathsf{B}, \mathsf{sk}_\mathsf{B}, m')\right] \\ - \Pr[1 \leftarrow \mathcal{A}(k, \mathsf{sk}_\mathsf{A}, m, m', h) : k \leftarrow_\$ \mathcal{K}] \leq \mathsf{negl}(\kappa)$$

where $\mathsf{sk}_\mathsf{A} \leftarrow \mathsf{Gen}_\Pi(1^\kappa)$, $\mathsf{sk}_\mathsf{B} \leftarrow \mathsf{Gen}_\Pi(1^\kappa)$, $m' \leftarrow \psi(m, h)$ with $m \leftarrow \mathsf{Msg}^\mathsf{A}_\Pi(r_\mathsf{A}, \mathsf{sk}_\mathsf{A})$ and $h \leftarrow_\$ \mathbb{M}$.

As an example, KE protocols fulfilling AM security, as in [14], also fulfill key indistinguishability. However, we remark that AM security is stronger than key indistinguishability.

Examples of A-B ORKE schemes that fulfill both of these conditions are Diffie-Hellman [19], the lattice-based protocols of [1,20], and the Supersingular Isogeny Diffie-Hellman [24] (we discuss these cases in Sect. B).

3 A Framework for OT Using ORKE

In this section, we present the framework for OT. Let κ be the security parameter. Let $\overline{\mathcal{M}}$ and $\psi : \overline{\mathcal{M}} \times (\mathbb{M}, *) \to \overline{\mathcal{M}}$ be the right group action as defined in Sect. 2.1, where $\mathcal{M}$ is the set of outputs of algorithm $\mathsf{Msg}^\mathsf{A}_\Pi$ and let $(\mathbb{M}, *)$ be a group. We assume that, given $x, y \in \overline{\mathcal{M}}$, it is computationally easy to find $h \in \mathbb{M}$ such that $x \leftarrow \psi(y, h)$. Let $\Pi = (\mathsf{Gen}_\Pi, \mathsf{Msg}_\Pi, \mathsf{Key}_\Pi)$ be an A-B ORKE protocol that is ψ-message indistinguishable and ψ-key indistinguishable, and $\Delta = (\mathsf{Enc}_\Delta, \mathsf{Dec}_\Delta)$ be an IND-CPA secure symmetric-key encryption protocol. Suppose that the sender S wants to obliviously send M_0 and M_1, and that the receiver R wants to receive the message M_b, where $b \in \{0,1\}$ is its input. Both S and R start by generating a secret key, $\mathsf{sk}_\mathsf{S} \leftarrow \mathsf{Gen}_\Pi(1^\kappa)$ and $\mathsf{sk}_\mathsf{R} \leftarrow \mathsf{Gen}_\Pi(1^\kappa)$, respectively.

Let H_i, for $i = 1, \ldots, 4$ be four different instances of the random oracle functionality $\mathcal{F}_\mathsf{RO}$. More precisely, $\mathsf{H}_1 : \{0,1\}^* \to \mathbb{M}$ is used to create a random message from a honestly created message (for the receiver), $\mathsf{H}_2 : \{0,1\}^* \to \mathcal{K} = \{0,1\}^\beta$ where β is the size of the keys outputted by the Key_Π algorithm, and $\mathsf{H}_3 : \{0,1\}^* \to \{0,1\}^{2\kappa+\beta}$ and $\mathsf{H}_4 : \{0,1\}^* \to \{0,1\}^\kappa$ for a challenge-response interaction.

The Framework. The scheme has four communication rounds and the receiver R sends the first message.

1. When activated with its input, the receiver R:
   - Chooses at random $t, r_\mathsf{R} \leftarrow_\$ \{0,1\}^\kappa$;
   - Queries H_1 on (sid, t) and sets the output to $h \in \mathbb{M}$;
   - Computes $m_\mathsf{R}^b \leftarrow \mathsf{Msg}_\Pi^\mathsf{A}(r_\mathsf{R}, \mathsf{sk}_\mathsf{R})$;
   - If $b = 1$, it computes $m_\mathsf{R}^0 \leftarrow \psi(m_\mathsf{R}^1, h^{-1})$. Else, it continues;
   - Sends $(\mathsf{sid}, t, m_\mathsf{R}^0)$ to S.
2. Upon receiving $(\mathsf{sid}, t, m_\mathsf{R}^0)$ from R, the sender S:
   - Chooses $r_\mathsf{S} \leftarrow \{0,1\}^\kappa$;
   - Queries H_1 on (sid, t) and sets the output to $h' \in \mathbb{M}$;
   - Computes $m_\mathsf{R}^1 \leftarrow \psi(m_\mathsf{R}^0, h')$;
   - Computes $m_\mathsf{S}^0 \leftarrow \mathsf{Msg}_\Pi^\mathsf{B}(r_\mathsf{S}, \mathsf{sk}_\mathsf{S}, m_\mathsf{R}^0)$ and $m_\mathsf{S}^1 \leftarrow \mathsf{Msg}_\Pi^\mathsf{B}(r_\mathsf{S}, \mathsf{sk}_\mathsf{S}, m_\mathsf{R}^1)$;
   - Computes the keys $k_\mathsf{S}^0 \leftarrow \mathsf{Key}_\Pi(r_\mathsf{S}, \mathsf{sk}_\mathsf{S}, m_\mathsf{R}^0)$ and $k_\mathsf{S}^1 \leftarrow \mathsf{Key}_\Pi(r_\mathsf{S}, \mathsf{sk}_\mathsf{S}, m_\mathsf{R}^1)$;
   - Chooses $w_0, z_0, w_1, z_1 \leftarrow \{0,1\}^\kappa$;
   - Queries H_2 on $(\mathsf{sid}, k_\mathsf{S}^0)$ setting the output to $\bar{k}_\mathsf{S}^0$, and on $(\mathsf{sid}, k_\mathsf{S}^1)$ setting the output to $\bar{k}_\mathsf{S}^1$;
   - Queries H_3 on (sid, w_0) setting the output to $\bar{w}_0$, and on (sid, w_1) setting the output to $\bar{w}_1$;
   - Computes $a_0 \leftarrow \mathsf{Enc}_\Delta(\bar{k}_\mathsf{S}^0, w_0; z_0)$ and $a_1 \leftarrow \mathsf{Enc}_\Delta(\bar{k}_\mathsf{S}^1, w_1; z_1)$;
   - Sets $u_0 \leftarrow \bar{w}_0 \oplus (w_1 | \bar{k}_\mathsf{S}^1 | z_1)$ and $u_1 \leftarrow \bar{w}_1 \oplus (w_0 | \bar{k}_\mathsf{S}^0 | z_0)$;
   - Queries H_4 on $(\mathsf{sid}, w_0, w_1, z_0, z_1)$ setting the output to ch;
   - Sends $(\mathsf{sid}, m_\mathsf{S}^0, m_\mathsf{S}^1, a_0, a_1, u_0, u_1)$ to R.
3. Upon receiving $(\mathsf{sid}, m_\mathsf{S}^0, m_\mathsf{S}^1, a_0, a_1, u_0, u_1)$ from S, the receiver R:
   - Computes $k_\mathsf{R} \leftarrow \mathsf{Key}_\Pi(r_\mathsf{R}, \mathsf{sk}_\mathsf{R}, m_\mathsf{S}^b)$;
   - Queries H_2 on $(\mathsf{sid}, k_\mathsf{R})$ setting the output to $\bar{k}_\mathsf{R}$;
   - Decrypts $x_b \leftarrow \mathsf{Dec}_\Delta(\bar{k}_\mathsf{R}, a_b)$;
   - Queries H_3 on (sid, x_b) setting the output to $\bar{x}_b$;
   - Computes $(x_{1-b} | \bar{k}_\mathsf{R}^{1-b} | y_{1-b}) = u_b \oplus \bar{x}_b$;
   - Queries H_3 on (sid, x_{1-b}) setting the output to $\bar{x}_{1-b}$;
   - Recovers $(x_b' | \bar{k}_\mathsf{R}^b | y_b) = u_{1-b} \oplus \bar{x}_{1-b}$;
   - Checks if $a_0 = \mathsf{Enc}_\Delta(\bar{k}_\mathsf{R}^0, x_0; y_0)$, if $a_1 = \mathsf{Enc}_\Delta(\bar{k}_\mathsf{R}^1, x_1; y_1)$, if $\bar{k}_\mathsf{R}^b = \bar{k}_\mathsf{R}$ and if $x_b' = x_b$. It aborts if any of these conditions fail;
   - Queries H_4 on $(\mathsf{sid}, x_0, x_1, y_0, y_1)$ and sets the output to ch';
   - Sends (sid, ch') to S.
4. Upon receiving (sid, ch') from R, the sender S:
   - Checks if $ch = ch'$. It aborts, if the test fails;
   - Encrypts $c_0 \leftarrow \mathsf{Enc}_\Delta(k_\mathsf{S}^0, M_0)$ and $c_1 \leftarrow \mathsf{Enc}_\Delta(k_\mathsf{S}^1, M_1)$;
   - Sends (sid, c_0, c_1) to R and halts.
5. Upon receiving (sid, c_0, c_1) from S, the receiver R:
   - Decrypts $M_b \leftarrow \mathsf{Dec}_\Delta(k_\mathsf{R}, c_b)$;
   - Outputs M_b and halts.

We call this framework π_{OT}. In the first two rounds, a key exchange is used in a ingenious way that allows the sender and the receiver to share a common key such that: (i) the sender does not know which of the two keys it has computed is shared with the receiver; and (ii) the receiver has no information about the other key.

In the proof of security in the UC-framework, the extraction of the inputs of the sender (the messages M_0 and M_1) is done by programming the random oracle H_1 in such a way that the simulator has both keys and is able to decrypt both ciphertexts c_0 and c_1.

The challenge that the sender sends to the receiver is necessary to extract the input bit b of the receiver. The extraction is possible when the receiver asks k_{R} to the random oracle. Here, the simulator is able to know the bit b by comparing this value with the keys the dummy sender has computed. Note that this challenge does not carry any information about the key k_{S}^{1-b}: the only values that the receiver gets from this challenge are random values x_0, x_1, y_0, y_1 and the output of the secret keys by the random oracle, which, by definition, are completely uncorrelated with the keys.

Extension to $\binom{N}{1}$*-OT.* It is straightforward to extend the framework above to an $\binom{N}{1}$-OT, where S's input is composed by N messages $M_0, \dots M_{N-1}$ and R's input is $b \in \{0, \dots, N-1\}$ such that R receives M_b.

In the first message, the receiver R, instead of just sending t, sends $t_1, \dots, t_{N-2}$ along with m_{R}^0. S computes $h_i' \leftarrow \mathsf{H}_1(t_i)$ and the messages $m_{\mathsf{R}}^i \leftarrow \psi(m_{\mathsf{R}}^0, h_i')$ for $i = 1, \dots, N-1$. From these messages, S computes N keys such that one of them is shared with R.

Also, S chooses $w_0, \dots, w_{N-1}, z_0, \dots, z_{N-1} \leftarrow_{\$} \{0,1\}^{\kappa}$ and sets the challenge to be

$$ch \leftarrow \mathsf{H}_4(\mathsf{sid}, w_0, \dots, w_{N-1}, z_0, \dots, z_{N-1}),$$

instead of just $(\mathsf{sid}, w_0, w_1, z_0, z_1)$. Furthermore, S needs to compute

$$a_i \leftarrow \mathsf{SEnc}_{\Delta}(\bar{\mathsf{sk}}_{\mathsf{S}}^i, w_i; z_i)$$

and

$$u_i \leftarrow \bar{w}_i \oplus (w_{i+1 \mod N} | \bar{\mathsf{sk}}_{\mathsf{S}}^{i+1 \mod N} | z_{i+1 \mod N})$$

for $i = 0, \dots, N-1$. Finally, it sends $(a_0, \cdots, a_{N-1}, u_0, \cdots, u_{N-1})$ to R. The remaining steps can be easily adapted from the version presented above.

Security for the Receiver. Security for R is guaranteed by the ψ-message indistinguishability of the A-B ORKE scheme used. Note that S receives two messages from R. In the first one, it receives m_{R}^0 (from which it can recover m_{R}^1) but, by the ψ-message indistinguishability property, S has no information on which message was the one computed using the $\mathsf{Msg}_{\Pi}^{\mathsf{A}}$ algorithm and which one is a random value. Thus, it does not know which message R uses to compute its key.

The second message sent by R to S is ch', but note that R can compute ch' regardless of its input, given that S has behaved honestly. Observe that when S does not behave honestly, then R aborts the execution. We conclude that it is infeasible for S to know the input of the receiver.

Security for the Sender. The first message that S sends to R is $(m_{\mathsf{S}}^0, m_{\mathsf{S}}^1, a_0, a_1, u_0, u_1)$. By the ψ-key indistinguishability of the A-B ORKE scheme used, R is not able to derive a key from m_{S}^{1-b}, since this key looks uniform to R. Otherwise, it could break the ψ-key indistinguishability property of the underlying A-B ORKE. To see this, consider the following hybrid game where S replaces k_{S}^{1-b} by a uniformly random value $a \leftarrow_{\$} \mathcal{K}$. It is easy to see that if R can distinguish these two games with non-negligible probability ε, then we can break the ψ-key indistinguishability of the underlying A-B ORKE with the same probability.

Moreover, the only information R gets from a_0, a_1, u_0, u_1 about k_{S}^{1-b} is its output by H_2, that is $\bar{k}_{\mathsf{S}}^{1-b}$. Since H_2 is modeled as a random oracle, the values k_{S}^{1-b} and $\bar{k}_{\mathsf{S}}^{1-b}$ are not correlated.

The second message sent from S to R is composed by the ciphertexts c_0, c_1. Given that the SKE scheme Δ is secure, it is infeasible for R to get information about M_{1-b} if it does not have the corresponding secret key. We conclude that it is infeasible for the receiver to get both messages.

UC-Security. We prove the main result of this paper which guarantees the UC-security of the proposed OT protocol π_{OT}.[2]

Theorem 8. *The protocol π_{OT} UC-realizes $\mathcal{F}_{OT}$ in the $\mathcal{F}_{RO}$-hybrid model against static malicious adversaries, given that Δ is* IND-CPA *secure and the A-B ORKE scheme used is ψ-message indistinguishable and ψ-key indistinguishable.*

We begin with the trivial case: When the adversary is corrupting both the sender and the receiver then the simulator just runs internally the adversary which generates the messages for both the sender and the receiver.

When the adversary is not corrupting any party, then the simulator just follows the protocol with the random inputs, forwarding every message to $\mathcal{A}$. Observe that the obtained transcript is indistinguishable from any other transcript (with other inputs) from the point-of-view of $\mathcal{A}$ and thus, $\mathcal{E}$.

Lemma 9. *Given any PPT adversary $\mathcal{A}(\mathsf{R})$ corrupting the receiver R, there is a PPT simulator Sim such that for every PPT environment $\mathcal{E}$ we have*

$$\mathsf{IDEAL}_{\mathcal{F}_{OT},\mathsf{Sim},\mathcal{E}} \approx \mathsf{EXEC}^{\mathcal{F}_{RO}}_{\pi_{OT},\mathcal{A}(\mathsf{R}),\mathcal{E}},$$

given that Δ is IND-CPA *secure and the A-B ORKE scheme used is ψ-message indistinguishable and ψ-key indistinguishable.*

Proof. To prove security against a corrupted receiver, we have to construct a simulator that is able to extract the input of a corrupted receiver, given any adversary $\mathcal{A}(\mathsf{R})$ corrupting the receiver.

[2] The full proof of the theorem is thoroughly described in the full version [10].

1. Upon activating the adversary, the simulator Sim simulates the random oracles H_1, H_2, H_3 and H_4 in the following way: Sim keeps a list L_i for each H_i, for $i = 1, \ldots, 4$, which is initially empty. Whenever $\mathcal{A}(\mathsf{R})$ queries H_i on (sid, q), Sim checks if there is $(q, h) \in L_i$. If so, it returns h. Else, it chooses h uniformly at random, records the pair (q, h) in L_i and returns h.
2. Upon receiving $(\mathsf{sid}, t, m_\mathsf{R}^0)$ from the adversary $\mathcal{A}(\mathsf{R})$, the simulator Sim:
   - Follows the protocol and sends $(\mathsf{sid}, m_\mathsf{S}^0, m_\mathsf{S}^1, a_0, a_1, u_0, u_1)$ to $\mathcal{A}$;
   - Sets $b \leftarrow \perp$. When $k_\mathsf{S}^{\bar{b}}$ is asked to the random oracle H_2, it sets $b \leftarrow \bar{b}$;
   - Aborts, if w_{1-b} is asked to the random oracle H_3 before w_b or if k_S^{1-b} is asked to H_2.
3. Upon receiving (sid, ch') from the adversary $\mathcal{A}(\mathsf{R})$, the simulator Sim:
   - Aborts, if $ch \neq ch'$;
   - If $b = \perp$, sets $b \leftarrow_\$ \{0, 1\}$;
   - Sends (sid, b) to the ideal functionality $\mathcal{F}_{\mathrm{OT}}$.
4. Upon receiving (sid, M_b) from $\mathcal{F}_{\mathrm{OT}}$, the simulator Sim:
   - Encrypts $c_b \leftarrow \mathsf{Enc}_\Delta(k_\mathsf{S}^b, M_b)$ and $c_{1-b} \leftarrow \mathsf{Enc}_\Delta(k_\mathsf{S}^{1-b}, 0^\lambda)$;
   - Sends (sid, c_0, c_1) to $\mathcal{A}(\mathsf{R})$;
   - Halts whenever $\mathcal{A}(\mathsf{R})$ halts.

The executions differ when Sim aborts if $\mathcal{A}$ asks the key k_S^{1-b} to H_2, or if it asks w_{1-b} to H_3 before w_b, or even if none of the keys k_S^0 and k_S^1 are queried. The first two cases happen with a negligible probability. The last case also has negligible probability of happening since, without asking any of the keys, the adversary has negligible probability of guessing ch. □

Lemma 10. *Given any adversary $\mathcal{A}(\mathsf{S})$ corrupting the sender S, there is a simulator Sim such that for every environment $\mathcal{E}$ we have*

$$\mathsf{IDEAL}_{\mathcal{F}_{OT}, \mathsf{Sim}, \mathcal{E}} \approx \mathsf{EXEC}^{\mathcal{F}_{RO}}_{\pi_{OT}, \mathcal{A}(\mathsf{S}), \mathcal{E}},$$

given that Δ is IND-CPA *secure and the A-B ORKE scheme used is ψ-message indistinguishable and ψ-key indistinguishable.*

Proof. The goal of the simulator is, given any adversary $\mathcal{A}(\mathsf{S})$ corrupting the sender, to extract the messages M_0 and M_1. Recall that, by assumption, given $x, y \in \overline{\mathcal{M}}$, it is computationally easy to find $h \in \mathbb{M}$ such that $x \leftarrow \psi(y, h)$.

1. Before activating the adversary, the simulator Sim:
   - Chooses $r_\mathsf{R}^0 \leftarrow_\$ \{0, 1\}^\kappa$ and $r_\mathsf{R}^1 \leftarrow_\$ \{0, 1\}^\kappa$;
   - Computes $m_\mathsf{R}^0 \leftarrow \mathsf{Msg}_\Pi(r_\mathsf{R}^0, \mathsf{sk}_\mathsf{R})$ and $m_\mathsf{R}^1 \leftarrow \mathsf{Msg}_\Pi(r_\mathsf{R}^1, \mathsf{sk}_\mathsf{R})$.

2. Upon activating the adversary, the simulator Sim sends $(\mathsf{sid}, t, m_{\mathsf{R}}^0)$:
   - Simulates H_2, H_3 and H_4 in the following way: Sim keeps a list L_i for each H_i, for $i = 2, 3, 4$, which is initially empty. Whenever $\mathcal{A}(\mathsf{S})$ queries H_i on (sid, q), Sim checks if there is $(q, h) \in L_i$. If so, it returns h. Else, it chooses h uniformly at random, records the pair (q, h) in L_i and returns h.
   - Simulates H_1 in the following way: when the adversary queries H_1 with (sid, t), the simulator answers h such that $m_{\mathsf{R}}^1 = \psi(m_{\mathsf{R}}^0, h)$. For all other queries to H_1, it answers as the ideal functionality would.
3. Upon receiving $(\mathsf{sid}, m_{\mathsf{S}}^0, m_{\mathsf{S}}^1, a_0, a_1, u_0, u_1)$ from $\mathcal{A}$, the simulator Sim:
   - Computes the keys $k_{\mathsf{R}}^0 \leftarrow \mathsf{Key}_{\Pi}(r_{\mathsf{R}}^0, \mathsf{sk}_{\mathsf{R}}, m_{\mathsf{S}}^0)$ and $k_{\mathsf{R}}^1 \leftarrow \mathsf{Key}_{\Pi}(r_{\mathsf{R}}^1, \mathsf{sk}_{\mathsf{R}}, m_{\mathsf{S}}^1)$;
   - Proceeds as the honest receiver would do and computes ch';
   - Sends (sid, ch') to $\mathcal{A}$.
4. Upon receiving (sid, c_0, c_1) from $\mathcal{A}$, the simulator Sim:
   - Computes $M_0 \leftarrow \mathsf{Dec}_{\Delta}(k_{\mathsf{R}}^0, c_0)$ and $M_1 \leftarrow \mathsf{Dec}_{\Delta}(k_{\mathsf{R}}^1, c_1)$;
   - Sends (sid, M_0, M_1) to the ideal functionality $\mathcal{F}_{\mathrm{OT}}$.
5. Upon receiving $(\mathsf{sid}, \mathit{receipt})$ from $\mathcal{F}_{\mathrm{OT}}$, the simulator Sim halts whenever the adversary halts.

Note that the executions differ in the outputs given by the random oracle H_1. But the value h, returned by the simulator to the adversary, is computationally indistinguishable from uniformly chosen values since the A-B ORKE scheme used is message indistinguishable. □

4 Efficiency and Comparison

Efficiency of the Framework. Let κ be the security parameter. To ease the presentation, we assume the SKE protocol Δ has keys of size κ and ciphertexts are of the same size as plaintexts. Suppose the messages being sent by the sender are of size λ. Let α be the size of the binary representation of elements of $\mathcal{M}$.

Although our scheme has four rounds, it has a low communication complexity since it only requires the exchange of $2\alpha + 2\lambda + 10\kappa$ bits of information, per iteration of the protocol. The first message by the sender carries $\alpha + \kappa$ bits of information, the second $2\alpha + 2\kappa + 6\kappa$ bits of information, the third message is just the answer to the challenge which is of size κ and, finally, the fourth message carries 2λ bits of information.

Our protocol is also very efficient in terms of computational complexity since it only requires to run twice the Gen_{Π} algorithm and the Msg_{Π} algorithm and three times the Key_{Π} algorithm. It requires 11 calls to the random oracle. All other operations (sum modulo 2 and concatenation of strings) are linear in the security parameter and should be quite fast to perform (Table 1).

Table 1. Comparison between different composable OT frameworks.

	Rounds	Building block	Assumption
[32]	2	Dual-Mode PKE	CRS
[5]	3	PKE	ROM
Ours	4	ORKE + SKE	ROM

Comparison with Other Frameworks. The framework of [32] requires the use of a dual-mode public-key encryption (PKE) scheme. However, very few dual-mode PKE are known. For example, finding a dual-mode RLWE PKE scheme is stated as an open problem in [28]. Their framework has just two rounds. However, since it relies on PKE schemes, a public key needs to be sent from the receiver to the sender. For post-quantum PKE schemes, this key can be too large, which makes the communication and the computational complexity rather cumbersome and the scheme impractical for real-life uses. Another bottleneck regarding the framework of [32] is that it relies its security in the Common Reference String (CRS) model. In practice, the common reference string needs to be generated using a third party (which always raises security issues) or by some multiparty computation protocol, which is too inefficient.

The work of Barreto *et al.* [5] presents a framework for OT in the ROM, which can be instantiated using a PKE scheme with certain properties. One of these properties is that the space of public keys of the PKE scheme used must have a group structure for a certain operation. This property is too exclusive and immediately discards some of the most important post-quantum PKE schemes such as LWE [34] or RLWE [29] PKE schemes. Note that both the public keys of these schemes do not have a group structure for any operation (e.g., this set is not closed under addition). However, we think that this condition is too strong and, perhaps, it could be weaken to accept LWE and RLWE-based instances. The framework of [5] has three rounds. But again, a public key needs to be sent from the receiver to the sender which will be reflected in a high communication complexity. Besides that, the framework requires six encryptions and two decryptions, which is usually more expensive than exchanging a symmetric key.

Since it is difficult to compare frameworks generically as the building blocks are different, we compare these frameworks when instantiated from the Decisional Diffie-Hellman assumption. The framework of [32] needs 7 exponentiations to be carried in a execution of the protocol, and the framework of [5] needs 14. On the other hand, our framework needs only 3 exponentiations.

Acknowledgment. The first author thanks the support from DP-PMI and FCT (Portugal) through the grant PD/BD/ 135181/2017. This work was done while visiting the University of Cincinnati. The third author thanks the support from DP-PMI and FCT (Portugal) through the grand PD/BD/135182/2017. This work was funded by the project UID/EEA/50008/2019.

Appendix

A UC-Security and Ideal Functionalities

The Universal Composability (UC) framework, firstly introduced by Canetti [12], allows us to analyze the security of protocols, not just *per se*, but also when composed with other protocols. Due to the lack of space, only a brief introduction on the UC-framework is presented. For more details on this subject we refer the reader to [12].

In a nutshell, to prove UC security of a protocol π (usually called the real-world execution) one compares it to an ideal version of the primitive, defined *a priori* (usually called the ideal-world execution). The entities involved in the ideal-world execution are dummy parties which interact via an ideal functionality $\mathcal{F}$. These dummy parties may or may not be corrupted by an ideal adversary Sim, usually called the simulator. The functionality works as a trusted party: it receives inputs from all the entities involved and returns to each one something, depending on the primitive being implemented. In this way, each of the parties learns nothing but its own input and output. In the real-world execution, several parties interact between them via some protocol π, which implements the desired primitive. These parties may or may not be corrupted by some adversary $\mathcal{A}$. An entity $\mathcal{E}$, often called the environment, oversees the executions in both the ideal and the real worlds. At the end of the executions, the environment is asked to distinguish them. The intuition of the UC-framework is that a protocol π is secure if the environment $\mathcal{E}$ is not able to distinguish the real-world execution of π from the ideal-world execution of $\mathcal{F}$. If this happens, we can conclude that a real-world adversary $\mathcal{A}$ does not have more power than an ideal-world adversary Sim. Hence, whatever strategy a real-world adversary $\mathcal{A}$ uses to cheat in the execution of π, it can also be used by an ideal-world adversary Sim. Since we define the ideal functionality in order to avoid attacks from any adversary, we can conclude that there is no strategy for the real-world adversary $\mathcal{A}$ that allows it to know more than its own input and output.

Formally, let π be a protocol where n parties and an adversary $\mathcal{A}$ are involved. We denote the output of the environment $\mathcal{E}$ in the end of the real-world execution of π with adversary $\mathcal{A}$ by $\mathsf{EXEC}_{\pi,\mathcal{A},\mathcal{E}}$. The output of $\mathcal{E}$ at the end of the ideal-world execution of a functionality $\mathcal{F}$ with adversary Sim is denoted by $\mathsf{IDEAL}_{\mathcal{F},\mathsf{Sim},\mathcal{E}}$. The following definition introduces the notion of a protocol emulating (in a secure way) some ideal functionality.

Definition 11. We say that a protocol π *UC-realizes* $\mathcal{F}$ if for every PPT adversary $\mathcal{A}$ there is a PPT simulator Sim such that for all PPT environments $\mathcal{E}$,

$$\mathsf{IDEAL}_{\mathcal{F},\mathsf{Sim},\mathcal{E}} \approx \mathsf{EXEC}_{\pi,\mathcal{A},\mathcal{E}}$$

where $\mathcal{F}$ is an ideal functionality.

Oblivious transfer (OT), firstly introduced by Rabin [33], is a crucial primitive in cryptography. We describe the $\binom{2}{1}$-OT ideal functionality $\mathcal{F}_{\mathrm{OT}}$, as presented in [15]. Let $\lambda \in \mathbb{N}$ be a fixed value known to both parties, $M_0, M_1 \in \{0,1\}^\lambda$

and $b \in \{0,1\}$. The value sid represents the session ID and the ID of the parties involved in the protocol.

$\mathcal{F}_{OT}$ functionality

Parameters: $\mathsf{sid}, \lambda \in \mathbb{N}$ known to both parties.

- Upon receiving (sid, M_0, M_1) from S, $\mathcal{F}_{OT}$ stores M_0, M_1 and ignores future messages from S with the same sid;
- Upon receiving (sid, b) from R, $\mathcal{F}_{OT}$ checks if it has recorded (sid, M_0, M_1). If so, returns (sid, M_b) to R and $(\mathsf{sid}, \mathit{receipt})$ to S and halts. Else, it sends nothing but continues running.

Unfortunately, it is impossible to design universally composable OT protocols in the plain model, that is, without any setup assumption [13]. Hence, we use the random oracle model (ROM) to construct our UC-secure OT protocol. To this end, we work on the $\mathcal{F}_{\mathrm{RO}}$-hybrid model in order to model random oracles in the UC framework. The random oracle ideal functionality $\mathcal{F}_{\mathrm{RO}}$ is presented below.

$\mathcal{F}_{\mathrm{RO}}$ functionality

Parameters: Let $\mathcal{D}$ be the range of $\mathcal{F}_{\mathrm{RO}}$ and L be a list initially empty.

- Upon receiving a query (sid, q) from a party $\mathcal{P}$ or from an adversary $\mathcal{A}$, $\mathcal{F}_{\mathrm{RO}}$ proceeds as follows:
  - If there is a pair $(q, h) \in L$, it returns (sid, h);
  - Else, it chooses $h \leftarrow_{\$} \mathcal{D}$, stores the pair $(q, h) \in L$ and returns (sid, h).

The idea behind the $\mathcal{F}_{\mathrm{RO}}$-hybrid model is that every party involved in both the ideal-world execution of $\mathcal{F}$ and the real-world execution of the protocol π (including the adversary) have access to an ideal functionality $\mathcal{F}_{\mathrm{RO}}$, which behaves as a random oracle. The environment can access this ideal functionality through the adversary. We denote by $\mathsf{EXEC}^{\mathcal{F}_{\mathrm{RO}}}_{\pi,\mathcal{A},\mathcal{E}}$ the output of the environment after the real-world execution of the protocol π with an adversary $\mathcal{A}$ in the real-world, with the ideal functionality $\mathcal{F}_{\mathrm{RO}}$. The notion of a protocol securely emulating an ideal functionality can be adapted to this model.

Definition 12. We say that a protocol π *UC-realizes* $\mathcal{F}$ *in the* $\mathcal{F}_{\mathrm{RO}}$*-hybrid model* if for every PPT adversary $\mathcal{A}$ there is a PPT simulator Sim such that for all PPT environments $\mathcal{E}$,

$$\mathsf{IDEAL}_{\mathcal{F},\mathsf{Sim},\mathcal{E}} \approx \mathsf{EXEC}^{\mathcal{F}_{\mathrm{RO}}}_{\pi,\mathcal{A},\mathcal{E}}.$$

In this work, we consider static malicious adversaries. That is, an adversary corrupting any of the parties can deviate arbitrarily as it wishes from the protocol. However the parties are corrupted by the adversary before the beginning of the protocol and they remain so until the end of the protocol.

B Framework Instantiations

In the following section we provide relevant cases of ORKE schemes that can be used to instantiate our framework. More concretely, we show that our framework can be used with Diffie-Hellman, Ding's KE and Supersingular Isogeny Diffie-Hellman.

B.1 DH-Based OT

Consider the Diffie-Hellman (DH) KE protocol [19]. Let p be a prime and consider the group $\mathbb{Z}_p = \mathbb{Z}/p\mathbb{Z}$. Let $g \in \mathbb{Z}_p$ be a generator of the multiplicative group $\mathbb{Z}_p^*$. We assume g to be a public parameter of the system (e.g. a standard one), known by all parties. The DH KE is defined by three algorithms:

- $\mathsf{Gen}_{\mathrm{DH}}(1^\kappa)$ outputs a secret key $\mathsf{sk} = x \in \mathbb{Z}_p^*$ and a public key $\mathsf{pk} \leftarrow g$.
- $\mathsf{Msg}_{\mathrm{DH}}(r_i, \mathsf{sk}_i)[= \mathsf{Msg}_{\mathrm{DH}}^{\mathsf{A}}(r_i, \mathsf{sk}_i) = \mathsf{Msg}_{\mathrm{DH}}^{\mathsf{B}}(r_j, \mathsf{sk}_j, \cdot)]$ which takes as input the secret $\mathsf{sk}_i = x_i$ and generator g and outputs g^{x_i}.
- $\mathsf{Key}_{\mathrm{DH}}(r_i, \mathsf{sk}_i, m_j)$ which takes as input a message $m_j \leftarrow g^{x_j}$ and a secret key $\mathsf{sk}_i = x_i$ and outputs $m_j^{x_i}$.

Note that DH KE is an ORKE scheme, which means that $\mathsf{Msg}_{\mathrm{DH}}$ is the same for both parties.

Recall that the Decisional Diffie-Hellman (DDH) assumption assumes that (g, g^x, g^y, g^{xy}) is computationally indistinguishable from (g, g^x, g^y, z) when $z \leftarrow_\$ \mathbb{Z}_p^*$.

Using the notation of Sect. 2.1, consider $\mathcal{M} = \overline{\mathcal{M}} = \mathbb{M} = \mathbb{Z}_p^*$, the operation $*$ to be the product modulo p and $\psi : \mathbb{Z}_p^* \times (\mathbb{Z}_p^*, *) \to \mathbb{Z}_p^*$ to be the action group defined as $\psi(y, h) = y * h \mod p$.

The properties of ψ-message indistinguishability and ψ-key indistinguishability follow directly from the hardness of DDH of base g in the group $\mathbb{Z}_p^*$. Consider the notation of Definition 5.

Lemma 13. *The DH KE protocol is ψ-message indistinguishable.*

Proof. Since g is a generator of $\mathbb{Z}_p^*$, the message sent by Alice to Bob is a random element from $\mathbb{Z}_p^*$ when it is computed using Msg_Π or using ψ. □

Lemma 14. *The DH KE protocol is ψ-key indistinguishable, given that the DDH assumption holds.*

Proof. Any key obtained using the $\mathsf{Key}_{\mathrm{DH}}$ algorithm should be of the form g^{xy}, where g^x is the output of the other party's $\mathsf{Msg}_{\mathrm{DH}}$, and y is the secret key of the party running this algorithm. As before, g^{xy} is a random element in $\mathbb{Z}_p^*$, and so indistinguishable from a uniform chosen values from $\mathbb{Z}_p^*$, given that the hardness of the DDH assumption holds. □

Therefore, we conclude that the DH KE can be used to instantiate the framework presented in this paper.

B.2 RLWE-Based OT

The instantiation of this framework using Ding's KE was presented previously in [9] and this framework can be viewed as a generalization of their work. Here, we present a more generic instantiation using any RLWE-based KE scheme, such as [1,20,31].

Let $q > 2$ be a prime such that $q \equiv 1 \mod 2n$, $n \in N$ be a power of 2 and $R_q = \mathbb{Z}_q[x]/\langle(x^n + 1)\rangle$. Let χ_α be a discrete Gaussian distribution with parameter α.

Let $s \leftarrow_\$ R_q$. The RLWE assumption asks to distinguish $(a, as + e)$ where $e \leftarrow_\$ \chi_\alpha$ from (a, u) where $u \leftarrow_\$ R_q$ [29]. The HNF-RLWE assumption is similar to the RLWE assumption, but $s \leftarrow_\$ \chi_\alpha$ [2].

Consider an RLWE-based KE scheme, which is secure given that the HNF-RLWE problem is hard. Let $(\mathsf{recMsg}, \mathsf{recKey})$ be any reconciliation mechanism, as the ones presented in [20,31], where recMsg receives as input a value $x_1 \in R_q$ and outputs the signal w of x_1 and a key K, and recKey receives as input a value $x_2 \in R_q$ and a signal w and it outputs a key K. Recall that a reconciliation mechanism is parameterized by a bound ξ_{rec} such that if x_1 and x_2 are close (meaning that $|x_1 - x_2| \leq \xi_{\mathsf{rec}}$), then

$$\Pr\left[K_1 = K_2 : (w, K_1) \leftarrow \mathsf{recMsg}(x_1), K_2 \leftarrow \mathsf{recKey}(x_2, w)\right] \geq 1 - \mathsf{negl}(\kappa).$$

It is also required that, if x_1 is uniform, then K_1 is indistinguishable from a uniform value, even when given w, where $(w, K_1) \leftarrow \mathsf{recMsg}(x_1)$.

Let $a \leftarrow_\$ R_q$ be a public polynomial. The four algorithms that define any RLWE-based KE based are the following:

- $\mathsf{Gen}_{RLWE}(1^\kappa)$ chooses $s \leftarrow_\$ \chi_\alpha$ and outputs a secret key $\mathsf{sk} \leftarrow_\$ s$ and a public key $\mathsf{pk} \leftarrow as + 2e \mod q$ where $e \leftarrow_\$ \chi_\alpha$.
- $\mathsf{Msg}^{\mathsf{A}}_{RLWE}(r_{\mathsf{A}}, \mathsf{sk}_{\mathsf{A}})$ outputs the message $m_{\mathsf{A}} = \mathsf{pk}_{\mathsf{A}}$.
- $\mathsf{Msg}^{\mathsf{B}}_{RLWE}(r_{\mathsf{B}}, \mathsf{sk}_{\mathsf{B}}, m_{\mathsf{A}})$ computes $(w, K) \leftarrow \mathsf{recMsg}(m_A \mathsf{sk}_B + 2e')$, where $e' \leftarrow_\$ \chi_\alpha$, and outputs $m_{\mathsf{B}} = (\mathsf{pk}_{\mathsf{B}}, w)$.
- $\mathsf{Key}_{RLWE}(r_i, \mathsf{sk}_i, m_j)$ computes $k_i \leftarrow s_i \mathsf{pk}_j + 2e'_i$, where $e' \leftarrow_\$ \chi_\alpha$, and outputs the shared key $K \leftarrow \mathsf{recKey}(k_i, w)$.

RLWE-based KE schemes [1,20,31] are A-B ORKE scheme since Bob's message depends on Alice message.

Using the notation of Sect. 2.1, consider $\mathcal{M}$ to be the set of RLWE samples, that is, $\mathcal{M} = \{x : x = as + e \wedge s, e \leftarrow_\$ \chi_\alpha\}$, and $\overline{\mathcal{M}} = \mathbb{M} = R_q$, the operation $*$ to be the sum in R_q and $\psi : R_q \times (R_q, +) \to R_q$ to be the action group defined as $\psi(y, h) = y + h$.

Lemma 15. *RLWE-based KE is ψ-message indistinguishable given that the HNF-RLWE assumption holds.*

Proof. The message algorithm of Alice ($\mathsf{Msg}^{\mathsf{A}}_{RLWE}$) in this key exchange protocol outputs messages which are HNF-RLWE samples, thus, it is trivial to reduce the problem of breaking ψ-message indistinguishability of an RLWE-based KE to the problem of deciding the HNF-RLWE problem. □

For the ψ-key indistinguishability property, let K_A and K_B be the output of the algorithm Key_{DingKE} when run by party A and B respectively.

Lemma 16. *RLWE-based KE protocol is ψ-key indistinguishable, given that the HNF-RLWE assumption holds.*

Proof. This follows directly from the security of the KE protocol. As proved in [20, Theorem 3], to computationally distinguish K_A or K_B from uniformly random in R_q reduces to the HNF-RLWE assumption. Thus, if the HNF-RLWE assumption holds, the protocol is ψ-key indistinguishable. □

We conclude that RLWE-based KE schemes [1,20,31] can be used to instantiate the framework of this article.

B.3 SIDH-Based OT

Following the work of [4], where it is presented an OT protocol based on the Supersingular Isogeny Diffie-Hellman (SIDH) of [24], we adapt the same techniques to achieve the first UC OT based on Supersingular Isogeny cryptography. Although we use the same techniques to instantiate our framework using this key exchange, we work in the ROM instead of using the secure coin flip they use.

As defined in [24], let $p = \ell_A^{e_A} \ell_B^{e_B} \cdot f \pm 1$ where ℓ_A, ℓ_B are small primes and f is a cofactor such that p is prime. Let E_0 be a supersingular curve defined over $\mathbb{F}_{p^2}$, and let P_A, Q_A be a basis generating $E_0[\ell_A^{e_A}]$ and P_B, Q_B a basis generating $E_0[\ell_B^{e_B}]$, where $E[\ell]$ is the ℓ-torsion group of E, i.e. the set of all points $P \in E(\overline{\mathbb{F}}_q)$ such that ℓP is the identity. As in [4], we consider $(P_A, Q_A), (P_B, Q_B)$ as public parameters of the cryptosystem.

Like the DH scheme, this is a vanilla ORKE scheme, since Msg_{SIDH} is the same for both parties, and does not depend on the message previously exchanged by the other party. The three algorithms that define the KE are:

- $\mathsf{Gen}_{SIDH}(1^\kappa, r)$ pick $m_i, n_i \in \mathbb{Z}/\ell_i^{e_i}\mathbb{Z}$, where at most one of them is divisible by ℓ_i, and compute an isogeny $\phi_i : E_0 \to E_i$ with kernel $K_i = \langle [m_i]P_i + [n_i]Q_i \rangle$. Set $\mathsf{sk} \leftarrow (m_i, n_i, \phi_i)$.
- $\mathsf{Msg}_{SIDH}(r_i, \mathsf{sk}_i)[= \mathsf{Msg}^{\mathsf{A}}_{SIDH}(r_A, \mathsf{sk}_A) = \mathsf{Msg}^{\mathsf{B}}_{SIDH}(r_B, \mathsf{sk}_B, \cdot)]$ compute images
$$\{\phi_i(P_j), \phi_i(Q_j)\} \subset E_i$$
and outputs the message $m = (E_i, \phi_i(P_j), \phi_i(Q_j))$.
- $\mathsf{Key}_{SIDH}(r_i, \mathsf{sk}_i, m_j)$ since $m_j \leftarrow (E_j, \phi_j(P_i), \phi_j(Q_i))$, compute an isogeny $\phi'_i : E_j \to E_{ij}$ considering its kernel $\langle [m_i]\phi_j(P_i) + [n_i]\phi_j(Q_i) \rangle$. Return the *j-invariant* of
$$\begin{aligned} E_{AB} &= \phi'_A(\phi_B(E_0)) = \phi'_B(\phi_A(E_0)) \\ &= {E_0}/{\langle [m_A]P_A + [n_A]Q_A, [m_B]P_A + [n_B]Q_B \rangle}. \end{aligned}$$

Now, we prove that there exists the group action ψ as stated in Definition 5. Again, we base our group action on the assumptions of [4] and follow their notation. Consider $\mathcal{M} = \overline{\mathcal{M}}$ to be the set of elements of the form (E, G, H), where G and H are elements of the ℓ-torsion group of E. In [4], it is assumed that (E, G, H) is computationally indistinguishable from $(E, G+U, H+V)$ when U, V are randomly chosen among $E[\ell]$ such that the Weil paring of (G, H) and $(G+U, H+V)$ coincides. Moreover, they also show that such U, V can be sampled in polynomial time among the elements of $E[\ell]$, namely $U \leftarrow \alpha G_B + \beta H_B$, $V \leftarrow -(\alpha/\beta)U$, where $G_B \leftarrow \phi_B(P_A)$, $H_B \leftarrow \phi_B(Q_A)$, and $\alpha, \beta \in \mathbb{Z}/\ell\mathbb{Z}$.

We are now able to propose the required group action ψ. Let $\mathbb{M}$ be the group of elements of the form $(U, V) \in E[\ell]$ with group law $*$ being the coordinate-wise usual sum of the ellipic curve points. This group acts on $\overline{\mathcal{M}}$, $\psi : \overline{\mathcal{M}} \times (\mathbb{M}, *) \to \overline{\mathcal{M}}$, by modifying G and H, as $\psi(y, h) = (E, G + U, H + V)$, where y is of the form of (E, G, H) and h of the form (U, V), and G, H, U, V are all elements in $E[\ell]$, such that U, V are sampled accordingly with [4].

Lemma 17. *The SIDH KE protocol is ψ-message indistinguishable given the security assumptions in [24, Section 5] and the parameters are chosen as to prevent any distinguisher based attack [4].*

Proof. In order to achieve the property of ψ-message indistinguishability, we must prevent any distinguisher from figuring out if the first message from the receiver is (E, G, H) or $(E, G+U, H+V)$. As in [4], we can choose the parameters to avoid the paring-based distinguisher using the Weil pairing, and so prevent the sender from finding out the secret bit of the receiver. If their conjecture that there is no other polynomial-time distinguisher for schemes of this form holds, then our OT protocol is ψ-message indistinguishable. □

Note that, differently from [4], in our proposal the receiver sends either (E, G, H) or $(E, G + U, H + V)$, together with the nounce t such that $(U, V) \leftarrow \mathsf{H}(t)$. In fact, [4] uses a secure coin flip procedure to generate U, V, while in this work we obtain U, V from the random oracle. This means that the receiver has the ability to try a polynomial number of queries to the RO in order to choose U, V, in contrast to the single possibility of [4]. Notwithstanding, if it would be possible for the receiver to obtain a *good* U, V in polynomial many tries, then the probability of the secure coin flip would be non-negligible. Therefore, the two approaches are equivalent with regard to the security of this procedure.

Lemma 18. *The SIDH KE is ψ-key indistinguishable given the assumptions in [24, Section 5].*

Proof. This follows from the proof of security of the key exchange in [24]. The shared key must be a *j-invariant* uniformly random in the set *j-invariants*, i.e. a random curve in the isogeny graph, which according to the assumptions in [24, Section 5] is difficult to compute without knowledge of the private isogenies. □

Therefore, we conclude that SIDH KE protocol of [24] can be used to instantiate the framework in this article.

References

1. Alkim, E., Ducas, L., Pöppelmann, T., Schwabe, P.: Post-quantum key exchange—a new hope. In: 25th USENIX Security Symposium (USENIX Security 16), pp. 327–343. USENIX Association, Austin, TX (2016). https://www.usenix.org/conference/usenixsecurity16/technical-sessions/presentation/alkim
2. Applebaum, B., Cash, D., Peikert, C., Sahai, A.: Fast cryptographic primitives and circular-secure encryption based on hard learning problems. In: Halevi, S. (ed.) CRYPTO 2009. LNCS, vol. 5677, pp. 595–618. Springer, Heidelberg (2009). https://doi.org/10.1007/978-3-642-03356-8_35
3. Asharov, G., Lindell, Y., Schneider, T., Zohner, M.: More efficient oblivious transfer extensions. J. Cryptol. **30**(3), 805–858 (2017)
4. Barreto, P., Oliveira, G., Benits, W.: Supersingular isogeny oblivious transfer. Cryptology ePrint Archive, Report 2018/459 (2018). https://eprint.iacr.org/2018/459
5. Barreto, P.S.L.M., David, B., Dowsley, R., Morozov, K., Nascimento, A.C.A.: A framework for efficient adaptively secure composable oblivious transfer in the ROM. Cryptology ePrint Archive, Report 2017/993 (2017). https://eprint.iacr.org/2017/993
6. Bellare, M., Micali, S.: Non-interactive oblivious transfer and applications. In: Brassard, G. (ed.) CRYPTO 1989. LNCS, vol. 435, pp. 547–557. Springer, New York (1990). https://doi.org/10.1007/0-387-34805-0_48
7. Bergsma, F., Jager, T., Schwenk, J.: One-round key exchange with strong security: an efficient and generic construction in the standard model. In: Katz, J. (ed.) PKC 2015. LNCS, vol. 9020, pp. 477–494. Springer, Heidelberg (2015). https://doi.org/10.1007/978-3-662-46447-2_21
8. Blazy, O., Chevalier, C., Germouty, P.: Almost optimal oblivious transfer from QA-NIZK. In: Gollmann, D., Miyaji, A., Kikuchi, H. (eds.) ACNS 2017. LNCS, vol. 10355, pp. 579–598. Springer, Cham (2017). https://doi.org/10.1007/978-3-319-61204-1_29
9. Branco, P., Ding, J., Goulão, M., Mateus, P.: Universally composable oblivious transfer protocol based on the RLWE assumption. Cryptology ePrint Archive, Report 2018/1155 (2018). https://eprint.iacr.org/2018/1155
10. Branco, P., Ding, J., Goulão, M., Mateus, P.: A framework for universally composable oblivious transfer from one-round key-exchange. Cryptology ePrint Archive, Report 2019/726 (2019). https://eprint.iacr.org/2019/726
11. Byali, M., Patra, A., Ravi, D., Sarkar, P.: Fast and universally-composable oblivious transfer and commitment scheme with adaptive security. Cryptology ePrint Archive, Report 2017/1165 (2017). https://eprint.iacr.org/2017/1165
12. Canetti, R.: Universally composable security: a new paradigm for cryptographic protocols. In: Proceedings of the 42nd IEEE Symposium on Foundations of Computer Science, FOCS 2001, p. 136. IEEE Computer Society, Washington, DC, USA (2001). http://dl.acm.org/citation.cfm?id=874063.875553
13. Canetti, R., Fischlin, M.: Universally composable commitments. In: Kilian, J. (ed.) CRYPTO 2001. LNCS, vol. 2139, pp. 19–40. Springer, Heidelberg (2001). https://doi.org/10.1007/3-540-44647-8_2
14. Canetti, R., Krawczyk, H.: Analysis of key-exchange protocols and their use for building secure channels. In: Pfitzmann, B. (ed.) EUROCRYPT 2001. LNCS, vol. 2045, pp. 453–474. Springer, Heidelberg (2001). https://doi.org/10.1007/3-540-44987-6_28

15. Canetti, R., Lindell, Y., Ostrovsky, R., Sahai, A.: Universally composable two-party and multi-party secure computation. In: Proceedings of the Thiry-fourth Annual ACM Symposium on Theory of Computing, STOC 2002, pp. 494–503. ACM, New York, NY, USA (2002). http://doi.acm.org/10.1145/509907.509980
16. Chou, T., Orlandi, C.: The simplest protocol for oblivious transfer. In: Lauter, K., Rodríguez-Henríquez, F. (eds.) LATINCRYPT 2015. LNCS, vol. 9230, pp. 40–58. Springer, Cham (2015). https://doi.org/10.1007/978-3-319-22174-8_3
17. David, B., Dowsley, R., Nascimento, A.C.A.: Universally composable oblivious transfer based on a variant of LPN. In: Gritzalis, D., Kiayias, A., Askoxylakis, I. (eds.) CANS 2014. LNCS, vol. 8813, pp. 143–158. Springer, Cham (2014). https://doi.org/10.1007/978-3-319-12280-9_10
18. David, B.M., Nascimento, A.C.A., Müller-Quade, J.: Universally composable oblivious transfer from lossy encryption and the McEliece assumptions. In: Smith, A. (ed.) ICITS 2012. LNCS, vol. 7412, pp. 80–99. Springer, Heidelberg (2012). https://doi.org/10.1007/978-3-642-32284-6_5
19. Diffie, W., Hellman, M.: New directions in cryptography. IEEE Trans. Inf. Theory **22**(6), 644–654 (1976)
20. Ding, J., Xie, X., Lin, X.: A simple provably secure key exchange scheme based on the learning with errors problem. Cryptology ePrint Archive, Report 2012/688 (2012). https://eprint.iacr.org/2012/688
21. Doerner, J., Kondi, Y., Lee, E., Shelat, A.: Secure two-party threshold ECDSA from ECDSA assumptions. In: 2018 IEEE Symposium on Security and Privacy (SP), vol. 00, pp. 595–612 (2018). doi.ieeecomputersociety.org/10.1109/SP.2018.00036
22. Freedman, M.J., Ishai, Y., Pinkas, B., Reingold, O.: Keyword search and oblivious pseudorandom functions. In: Kilian, J. (ed.) TCC 2005. LNCS, vol. 3378, pp. 303–324. Springer, Heidelberg (2005). https://doi.org/10.1007/978-3-540-30576-7_17
23. Hauck, E., Loss, J.: Efficient and universally composable protocols for oblivious transfer from the CDH assumption. Cryptology ePrint Archive, Report 2017/1011 (2017). https://eprint.iacr.org/2017/1011
24. Jao, D., De Feo, L.: Towards quantum-resistant cryptosystems from supersingular elliptic curve isogenies. In: Yang, B.-Y. (ed.) PQCrypto 2011. LNCS, vol. 7071, pp. 19–34. Springer, Heidelberg (2011). https://doi.org/10.1007/978-3-642-25405-5_2
25. Jeong, I.R., Katz, J., Lee, D.H.: One-round protocols for two-party authenticated key exchange. In: Jakobsson, M., Yung, M., Zhou, J. (eds.) ACNS 2004. LNCS, vol. 3089, pp. 220–232. Springer, Heidelberg (2004). https://doi.org/10.1007/978-3-540-24852-1_16
26. Kilian, J.: Founding cryptography on oblivious transfer. In: Proceedings of the Twentieth Annual ACM Symposium on Theory of Computing, STOC 2088, pp. 20–31. ACM, New York, NY, USA (1988). http://doi.acm.org/10.1145/62212.62215
27. Kushilevitz, E., Ostrovsky, R.: Replication is not needed: single database, computationally-private information retrieval. In: Proceedings 38th Annual Symposium on Foundations of Computer Science, pp. 364–373, October 1997
28. Liu, M.m., Krämer, J., Hu, Y.p., Buchmann, J.: Quantum security analysis of a lattice-based oblivious transfer protocol. Front. Inf. Technol. Electron. Eng. **18**(9), 1348–1369 (2017). https://doi.org/10.1631/FITEE.1700039
29. Lyubashevsky, V., Peikert, C., Regev, O.: On ideal lattices and learning with errors over rings. In: Gilbert, H. (ed.) EUROCRYPT 2010. LNCS, vol. 6110, pp. 1–23. Springer, Heidelberg (2010). https://doi.org/10.1007/978-3-642-13190-5_1
30. Parakh, A.: Oblivious transfer based on key exchange. Cryptologia **32**(1), 37–44 (2008). https://doi.org/10.1080/01611190701593228

31. Peikert, C.: Lattice cryptography for the internet. In: Mosca, M. (ed.) PQCrypto 2014. LNCS, vol. 8772, pp. 197–219. Springer, Cham (2014). https://doi.org/10.1007/978-3-319-11659-4_12
32. Peikert, C., Vaikuntanathan, V., Waters, B.: A framework for efficient and composable oblivious transfer. In: Wagner, D. (ed.) CRYPTO 2008. LNCS, vol. 5157, pp. 554–571. Springer, Heidelberg (2008). https://doi.org/10.1007/978-3-540-85174-5_31
33. Rabin, M.O.: How to exchange secrets with oblivious transfer (1981)
34. Regev, O.: On lattices, learning with errors, random linear codes, and cryptography. In: Proceedings of the Thirty-seventh Annual ACM Symposium on Theory of Computing, STOC 2005, pp. 84–93. ACM, New York, NY, USA (2005). http://doi.acm.org/10.1145/1060590.1060603
35. Yao, A.C.C.: How to generate and exchange secrets. In: Proceedings of the 27th Annual Symposium on Foundations of Computer Science, SFCS 1986, pp. 162–167. IEEE Computer Society, Washington, DC, USA (1986). https://doi.org/10.1109/SFCS.1986.25

Efficient Fully Secure Leakage-Deterring Encryption

Jan Camenisch[1], Maria Dubovitskaya[1], and Patrick Towa[2,3](✉)

[1] DFINITY, Zurich, Switzerland
{jan,maria}@dfinity.org
[2] IBM Research – Zurich, Rüschlikon, Switzerland
tow@zurich.ibm.com
[3] ENS and PSL Research University, Paris, France

Abstract. Encryption is an indispensable tool for securing digital infrastructures as it reduces the problem of protecting the data to just protecting decryption keys. Unfortunately, this also makes it easier for users to share protected data by simply sharing decryption keys.

Kiayias and Tang (ACM CCS 2013) were the first to address this important issue pre-emptively rather than a posteriori like traitor tracing schemes do. They proposed *leakage-deterring* encryption schemes that work as follows. For each user, a piece of secret information valuable to her is embedded into her public key. As long as she does not share her ability to decrypt with someone else, her secret is safe. As soon as she does, her secret is revealed to her beneficiaries. However, their solution suffers from serious drawbacks: (1) their model requires a fully-trusted registration authority that is privy to user secrets; (2) it only captures a CPA-type of privacy for user secrets, which is a very weak guarantee; (3) in their construction which turns any public-key encryption scheme into a leakage-deterring one, the new public keys consist of linearly (in the bit-size of the secrets) many public keys of the original scheme, and the ciphertexts are large.

In this paper, we redefine leakage-deterring schemes. We remove the trust in the authority and guarantee full protection of user secrets under CCA attacks. Furthermore, in our construction, all keys and ciphertexts are short and constant in the size of the secrets. We achieve this by taking a different approach: we require users to periodically refresh their secret keys by running a protocol with a third party. Users do so anonymously, which ensures that they cannot be linked, and that the third party cannot perform selective failure attacks. We then leverage this refresh protocol to allow for the retrieval of user secrets in case they share their decryption capabilities. This refresh protocol also allows for the revocation of user keys and for the protection of user secrets in case of loss or theft of a decryption device. We provide security definitions for our new model as well as efficient instantiations that we prove secure.

M. Albrecht (Ed.): IMACC 2019, LNCS 11929, pp. 102–127, 2019.
https://doi.org/10.1007/978-3-030-35199-1_6

1 Introduction

Encryption is a powerful instrument to ensure data confidentiality and to ease data protection: only decryption keys need to be protected. However, it makes sharing protected data much easier as well, just by sharing secret keys only. Users might share decryption keys for different reasons: out of convenience or malice, or accidentally due to poor key management. For example, malicious users might share access to paid services or sell access to company confidential information. Therefore, preventing users from sharing their secret keys, either in the clear or by providing a possibly obfuscated decryption algorithm, is an important problem in deploying cryptographic systems, in particular in corporate environments.

To address this issue, one could use pieces of tamper-proof hardware. However, these are expensive and strenuous to build, deploy and manage. A better approach is a software only solution as proposed by Kiayias and Tang: Leakage-Deterring Encryption (LDE) schemes [17]. The main idea behind LDE schemes is to have an authority embed into each user's public key some valuable secret information that she would rather keep private, and which is revealed as soon as she shares her decryption capabilities. Such secret information could for instance be bitcoin-account secret key [18]. In addition to the secrecy of messages against chosen-ciphertext attacks, an LDE scheme should at least satisfy the following properties:

Privacy of user secrets: provided that a user does not share her decryption capabilities, her secret must not be recoverable from her public key, even if all other parties (including the registration authority which embeds the secrets) are malicious. Ideally, privacy should hold even under CCA attacks.

Recoverability: anyone with a device capable of decrypting, with non-negligible probability, a non-negligible amount of ciphertexts of a user should be able to retrieve her secret.

There precisely lies the complexity of designing LDE schemes: two seemingly antagonistic properties must be bridged, in a context in which users are adversarial and have knowledge of secret information. In cryptography, to overcome apparent paradoxes, one usually assumes the adversary not to be privy to crucial secret information. In the present case, an adversarial user does not only know her secret information but also the device meant to be used against her. She could implement a decryption device that rejects any decryption query that results in the secret, and this rejection would not contradict the fact that her device decrypts a non-negligible amount of ciphertext computed with her public key. Given this observation, to hope to recover user secrets, recovery queries made to decryption devices must be indistinguishable from decryption queries accepted by rogue devices; hence the difficulty to design LDE schemes.

Kiayias and Tang provide schemes [17,18] that partially satisfy those requirements. Namely, they provide two constructions of LDE schemes which turn any public-key encryption scheme into an LDE scheme. The first construction requires the original encryption scheme to be additively homomorphic and is efficient, and the second one applies to any encryption scheme (i.e., is generic) but is prohibitively inefficient. Indeed, the public keys of their generic construction of LDE schemes grow linearly (even with the use of error-correcting codes) in the bit-size of the secrets, and the ciphertexts grow with a factor (log of the inverse) that depends on the assumed minimal correctness rate of pirate decryption devices. It already means that if a user designs a pirate decryption device with a decryption success probability that is non-negligibly smaller than the assumed minimal correctness rate though non-negligible, recoverability is not assured. In addition to that, for secrets of sensible length (e.g., 128 bits) and a decryption device with a conceivable correctness rate (e.g., 50%), the scheme is impractical. Moreover, their model only captures a CPA-type of privacy of user secrets: an attacker that can launch a chosen-ciphertext attacks on a user can also recover her secret. Lastly, in their model of LDE schemes, the registration authority is privy to user secrets, which weakens even further user privacy.

1.1 Contributions

We redefine LDE schemes and design a new model that encompasses all the security properties that an LDE scheme should satisfy. The new model captures a CCA-type of privacy of user secrets (even with respect to the registration authority), recoverability and secrecy of messages under CCA attacks:

- We first show that a CCA-type of privacy of user secrets and recoverability can simultaneously be achieved. As noted by Kiayias and Tang, the fact that recovery queries made must be indistinguishable from standard decryption queries implies that a CCA-type of privacy of user secrets and recoverability cannot a priori coexist: any decryption oracle in a privacy security game could be used to perform recovery queries and surely win the game. It comes as a disappointment as it means that an honest user would put her secret at risk under CCA attacks for the sake of protecting the data of a company or of a service provider; data which would withstand those same attacks. A sensible user would clearly not want to use such a system as it does not guarantee the same protection for user secrets as for the encrypted data. Except that this observation is not entirely true: we point out that *a CCA-type of privacy and recoverability can coexist if recovery queries involve a step that cannot be performed with a definition oracle.* We point that since adversaries do not control the randomness of oracles in security definitions, CCA privacy and recoverability[1] can actually be bridged: if recovery queries require to control the randomness of rogue decryption devices, the previous impossibility result does not apply.

  In our construction, the idea is to leverage rewinding to extract secrets from decryption devices. Note that rewinding an algorithm, which solely consists

[1] Of course, if adversaries were to know the randomness used by security-game oracles, the outputs of those would be deterministic in the view of the adversaries, and even simple properties like IND-CPA would not be satisfiable.

in controlling randomness and not reverse-engineering it, is a black-box technique [2,4]. Rewinding is used in the context of zero-knowledge proofs to extract witnesses, hence our idea of introducing a third party (which may as well be the embedding authority) that assists users with decryption. To decrypt ciphertexts, users are required to perform a zero-knowledge proof involving their secrets. We prove that any partially functional decryption device needs to do so as well with non-negligible probability, and can therefore be employed to extract secrets.

To reduce communication, we introduce leakage-deterring systems that operate in time periods. We call them time-based leakage-deterring encryption (TB-LDE) schemes. The first time (and only the first time) a user wishes to decrypt a ciphertext in a given time period, she needs to request from the third party a key for the time period by executing a key-derivation protocol. The frequency at which the key-derivation protocol is to be executed (i.e., the length of a time period, e.g., a week) can be adjusted by the system manager. A rogue decryption device that can decrypt ciphertexts in a time period must then also hold the key for it.

Note that a *minimal requirement* to ensure recoverability via interaction while guaranteeing CCA privacy is that the device must be able to decrypt a ciphertext for a future time period, i.e., for which the user does not have the key yet[2]. Indeed, if a user already has the key for a time period, she can hard-code it in the device and avoid any interaction for this period; making the recovery of her secret with ciphertexts encrypted for the period impossible. To ensure recoverability via interaction, users must not always possess all the information required to decrypt. It is an aspect *inherent* to any LDE scheme that leverages interaction to bridge CCA privacy and recoverability. In Sect. 4, we construct a TB-LDE scheme that satisfies both properties under this minimal requirement.

Despite the introduction of a third party that assists users with decryption, in our model, users remain anonymous and untraceable when they request keys to the third party. The presence of a third party also allows for the revocation of user keys in case of misconduct, or loss or theft of a decryption device. These untraceability and revocation properties are also properly modelled and formally defined in Sects. 3 and 8 respectively.

- Secondly, in comparison to Kiayias and Tang's model [17], we do not assume the authority to be privy to the secrets (it only receive commitments), and thus guarantee more privacy. The authority is only used to ensure that the secrets are correctly integrated into the public keys and to vouch for the latter. One may however think that only seeing a commitment prevents the authority from making sure that the secret is indeed valuable to the user and not just garbage. In fact, the same issue already arises when the authority sees the secrets in the clear. If the secret is a bitcoin-account secret key, the authority can check that it is the valid secret key for a given account, but cannot know whether the money is later moved from the account without

[2] If time periods are short, then any useful device should be able to do so.

resorting to a form of tracing scheme (e.g., by regularly checking a public ledger). However, deterring schemes exactly aim to avoid tracing. Moreover, even if the authority were to see secrets in clear, value lies in the eyes of the beholder: the authority cannot tell if the user is concerned about the money in that account, if she has for instance other sources of income. We therefore assume that there is higher-level mechanism that ascertains the value of the secret. In the case of a bitcoin account, it could for example be a mechanism that verifies that the commitment the authority receives is indeed a commitment to the secret key of an account on which the user will receive her *future* salary, assuming that the user cares about it. (Using future salary frees the authority from the need to regularly check a public ledger since the money is yet to come.)

- Lastly, we provide efficient constructions that fulfill all these security requirements. The first time-based construction (in Sect. 4) is proved secure in the plain model, and the second one (in Sect. 6), which is even more efficient, is proved secure in the Random Oracle Model (ROM). In Sect. 7, we give a definition of LDE schemes which satisfy CCA privacy of user secrets and recoverability thanks to interaction, but which require users to interact every time a ciphertext is to be decrypted. Such schemes are relevant when only few ciphertexts are to be decrypted compared to the provided bandwidth, as the burden of interaction would not be prohibitive.

  Furthermore, we show in Sect. 9 how, in combination with revocation, interaction with the key-derivation party in the recovery process can be enforced and leveraged to protect a user's secret and prevent misuse of her legitimate decryption device in case she was simply lost it or was stolen. Those are critical functionalities for deploying such a system.

1.2 Related Work

Kiayias and Tang were the first to consider typical public-key-infrastructure functionalities such as encryption, signatures and identification [17] in the context of leakage-deterrence. Nevertheless, deterring users from sharing their keys has been prominently considered in the context of broadcast encryption, in which malicious accredited users might implement pirate decoders. In such a scenario, traitor-tracing schemes [13] were introduced. They aim at identifying at least one of possibly many users that colluded to produce a pirate decryption device. Several efficiency improvements have been proposed thereupon [7–9,19,20], and variants such as public traitor tracing or anonymous traitor tracing [23] have also been considered. Contrary to traitor-tracing schemes, leakage-deterring schemes follow a proactive approach rather than rely on the identification of malicious users to enforce penalties.

A concept closer to the leakage-deterrence paradigm is that of *self enforcement* [15], which also involves private user pieces of information. In a multi-user encryption system, the adversary controls a set of malicious-user keys, and wishes to redistribute a plaintext. A self-enforcing schemes ensures that the adversary has to either send a message as long as the plaintext or leak some information about the private information of the traitors. However, recovery in those systems assumes direct access to user keys, i.e., white-box access, and the proposed construction relies on an unfalsifiable assumption.

2 Preliminaries

This section introduces the notations and the building blocks used in the paper. See Appendix A for hardness assumptions and instantiations.

2.1 Notations

Unless stated otherwise, p is a prime number, and $\mathbb{Z}_p$ denotes the p-order field. For an integer $n \geq 1$, $\mathrm{GL}_n(\mathbb{Z}_p)$ denotes the set of invertible $n \times n$ $\mathbb{Z}_p$-matrices, and $\mathbf{I}_n$ its neutral element. Given an n-dimensional $\mathbb{Z}_p$ vector space $\mathbb{V} \cong \mathbb{Z}_p^n$, $(\mathbf{e}_i)_i$ denotes its canonical basis. For a family $\mathbb{V}_k$ of N_k-dimensional vector spaces, the canonical basis of $\mathbb{V}_k$ is denoted by $(\mathbf{e}_{k,i})_i$. For $g \in \mathbb{G}$, $\mathrm{diag}(g)$ represents the matrix with g on the diagonal and $1_{\mathbb{G}}$ elsewhere. Besides, for $x \in \mathbb{Z}_p$ and $\mathbf{g} \in \mathbb{G}^n$, define $x\mathbf{g} := \mathbf{g}^x$. For an integer $k \geq 1$, a matrix $\mathbf{A} \in \mathbb{G}^{n \times k}$ and a vector $\mathbf{x} \in \mathbb{Z}_p^k$, $(\mathbf{A}\mathbf{x})_i = \left(\prod_j \mathbf{x}_j \mathbf{A}_{ij}\right)_i = \left(\prod_j \mathbf{A}_{ij}^{\mathbf{x}_j}\right)_i$. Likewise, for $\mathbf{y} \in \mathbb{Z}_p^n$, $(\mathbf{y}\mathbf{A})_j = \left(\prod_i \mathbf{y}_i \mathbf{A}_{ij}\right)_j = \left(\prod_i \mathbf{A}_{ij}^{\mathbf{y}_i}\right)_j$. To indicate that a random variable X has a distribution $\mathcal{D}$, the notation $X \leftarrow_{\$} \mathcal{D}$ is used. When $\mathcal{D}$ is the uniform distribution over a finite set $\mathcal{X}$, the notation $X \in_R \mathcal{X}$ is used instead. The predictive probability $p(\mathcal{D})$ of a distribution $\mathcal{D}$ is defined as $\max_{x \in \mathcal{X}} p_x$, with p_x being the probability that a $\mathcal{D}$-distributed random variable takes value $x \in \mathcal{X}$. Given a relation $\mathcal{R}$, the notation $\mathsf{PoK}\{w\colon (x, w) \in \mathcal{R}\}$ is used for a Proof of Knowledge (PoK) for the corresponding language; and its extractor is denoted $\mathcal{K}$.

2.2 Ciphertext-Policy Attribute-Based Encryption Schemes

Formally, a CP-ABE scheme is a tuple of algorithms (Setup, KeyDer, Enc, Dec) such that

$\mathsf{Setup}(1^\lambda, aux) \to (\mathcal{PP}, pk, msk)$: takes as an input a security parameter 1^λ and an auxiliary input aux (used to define attribute sets), and outputs public parameters, a public key and a master secret key;

$\mathsf{KeyDer}(msk, \mathcal{A}) \to sk_{\mathcal{A}}$: takes as an input a master secret key and a set of attributes, and outputs a corresponding secret key;

$\mathsf{Enc}(pk, m, \mathbb{S}) \to ct$: takes as an input a public key pk, a plaintext m and an access structure $\mathbb{S}$, and outputs a ciphertext ct; and

$\mathsf{Dec}(sk_{\mathcal{A}}, ct) \to m$: takes as an input a secret key corresponding to a set of a attributes $\mathcal{A}$ and a ciphertext, and outputs a plaintext m or $\perp$.

The CP-ABE schemes considered herein are required to be correct and adaptively Payload Hiding against Chosen-Plaintext Attacks [25, Definition 9] (or adaptively PH-CPA secure).

3 Definitions and Security Model

Leakage-deterring encryption (LDE) schemes are encryption schemes that deter users from sharing their decryption capabilities. To do so, user secrets are embedded into their public keys by an authority. As long as a user is honest, her secret remains private, but as soon as she produces a decryption device, anyone with access to it can recover her secret.

More precisely, we introduce Time-Based Leakage-Deterring Encryption (TB-LDE) schemes in which a third party $\mathcal{T}$ (which may as well be the embedding authority) assists users with decryption. The first time a user $\mathcal{U}$ wishes to decrypt a ciphertext in a given time period, she needs to request from $\mathcal{T}$ a key for the time period by executing a key-derivation protocol KeyDer. From then on until the end of the time period, *the decryption process is non-interactive.* The frequency at which the key-derivation protocol KeyDer is to be executed (i.e., the length of a time period, e.g., a week) can be adjusted at will by the system manager.

Yet, this does not affect in any way the ability to recover $\mathcal{U}$'s secret from a rogue decryption device B *at any time*: recovering a secret from an algorithm B will only be considered if it can decrypt ciphertexts for at least one time period subsequent to the current one, i.e., one for which $\mathcal{U}$ does not yet have a key. To recover a secret from a rogue algorithm B, one need not wait until that future time period, it suffices to locally submit (i.e., without involving $\mathcal{T}$) to B ciphertexts encrypted for that future time period. This will prompt B to interact, and perform, with non-negligible probability, a valid zero-knowledge proof on secret of the user who owns B, allowing for the extraction of her secret.

3.1 Time-Based Leakage-Deterring Encryption Schemes

We now formally define TB-LDE schemes. Let $\mathcal{T} \subseteq \mathbb{N}$ denote a non-empty time-period set. Assume that all parties are roughly synchronized, i.e., that there is always a consensus among them on the current time period $t_c \in \mathcal{T}$ (to make sure that users cannot obtain keys for future time periods from the third-party). A TB-LDE scheme $\mathcal{E}$ consists of the following algorithms:

$\mathsf{Setup}(1^\lambda, aux) \to (\mathcal{PP}, ck)$: an algorithm that generates public parameters and a commitment key on the input of a security parameter 1^λ and of an auxiliary input aux (used to define a time-period set $\mathcal{T}$ and other parameters)

$\mathsf{KeyGen.U}(\mathcal{PP}) \to (pk_{\mathcal{U}}, sk_{\mathcal{U}})$: a user key-generation algorithm

$\mathsf{KeyGen.T}(\mathcal{PP}) \to (pk_{\mathcal{T}}, sk_{\mathcal{T}})$: a user third-party key-generation algorithm

$\mathsf{KeyEn} = (\mathsf{KeyEn.U}(ck, c, s, o, pk_{\mathcal{U}}, sk_{\mathcal{U}}), \mathsf{KeyEn.A}(ck, c, pk_{\mathcal{U}})) \to ((epk, esk), epk)$: a key-enhancement protocol between a user key-enhancement algorithm $\mathsf{KeyEn.U}$ and an authority key-enhancement algorithm $\mathsf{KeyEn.A}$. In addition to cryptographic keys, these algorithms take as an input a commitment c to a secret s, the secret s itself and an opening o. At the end of the protocol, $\mathsf{KeyEn.U}$ outputs a pair of "enhanced" keys (epk, esk), and $\mathsf{KeyEn.A}$ outputs epk

$\mathsf{Enc}(epk, pk_{\mathcal{T}}, m \in \mathcal{M}, t \in \mathcal{T}) \rightarrow ct$: a probabilistic encryption algorithm

$\mathsf{KeyDer} = (\mathsf{KeyDer.U}(esk, t), \mathsf{KeyDer.T}(sk_{\mathcal{T}}, ck, t_c)) \rightarrow (sk_{\mathcal{T}}^{t,u}, \bot)$: an interactive protocol between a user key-derivation algorithm KeyDer.U and a third-party key-derivation algorithm KeyDer.T. *For every current time period* t_c, *if* $t > t_c$, *then* $sk_{\mathcal{T}}^{t,u} \leftarrow \bot$ (i.e., users cannot obtain keys for future time periods). Otherwise, at the end of the protocol, KeyDer.U outputs a third-party decryption key $sk_{\mathcal{T}}^{t,u}$

$\mathsf{Dec}(esk, sk_{\mathcal{T}}^{t,u}, ct) \rightarrow m$: a deterministic decryption algorithm

$\mathsf{Rec}(\mathsf{B}, epk, pk_{\mathcal{T}}, \mathcal{D}, t) \rightarrow s$: a recovery algorithm that takes as input an algorithm B (a "decryption box"), two keys epk and $pk_{\mathcal{T}}$, the description of a distribution $\mathcal{D}$ and a time period t, and outputs a secret s or $\bot$.

Commitment c may at first seem superfluous to the syntax, but the authority needs to receive some information bound to s (so that it can later be recovered given a decryption device) and that hides it (to ensure the privacy of s). Such information is nothing but a commitment.

3.2 Security Definitions

In this section, we define the security properties that an LDE scheme should satisfy. The security definitions are first given in a single-user case for simplicity, and are straightforwardly extended to the multi-user case in the full version. In every security experiment, the adversary is assumed to be stateful.

Correctness. Correctness states that the decryption of a plaintext encrypted for a certain time period, on the input of secret key for that time period, results in the plaintext with probability one.

To model algorithms which can decrypt only certain ciphertexts, a "partial"-correctness definition must be given. In the following, for any two functions f and g of λ, the notation $f \gtrsim g$ means that there exists a negligible function negl such that $f \geq g - \text{negl}$.

Definition 1 (δ-Correctness). *For* $\delta \in [0, 1]$, *given public keys* epk *and* $pk_{\mathcal{T}}$, *an algorithm* B *is said to be* δ*-correct in time period* t *with respect to a distribution* $\mathcal{D}$ *if for* $m \leftarrow_{\$} \mathcal{D}$,

$$\Pr\left[\mathsf{B}^{\mathsf{KeyDer.T}(sk_{\mathcal{T}}, ck, t)}(\mathsf{Enc}(epk, pk_{\mathcal{T}}, m, t)) = m\right] \gtrsim \delta.$$

Note that the clock of algorithm KeyDer.T *is here set to time period* t *(so that it does not systematically reject every key request for future time periods).*

To define privacy and untraceability, consider the experiments in Fig. 1.

Privacy. Privacy guarantees that not even the authority that the user interacts with in the key-enhancement protocol can infer any information about her secret.

$\mathbf{Exp}^{\text{priv}-\beta}_{\mathcal{E},\lambda}(\mathcal{A})$:	$\mathbf{Exp}^{\text{trace}-\beta}_{\mathcal{E},\lambda}(\mathcal{A})$:
1. $(\mathcal{PP}, ck) \leftarrow \mathsf{Setup}(1^\lambda)$ $(pk_{\mathcal{U}}, sk_{\mathcal{U}}) \leftarrow \mathsf{KeyGen.U}(\mathcal{PP})$	1. $(\mathcal{PP}, ck) \leftarrow \mathsf{Setup}(1^\lambda)$
2. $(s_0, s_1) \leftarrow \mathcal{A}(ck, pk_{\mathcal{U}})$	2. $(esk_0, esk_1, t) \leftarrow \mathcal{A}(\mathcal{PP}, ck)$
3. $(c, o) \leftarrow \mathsf{Com}(ck, s_\beta)$	3. $b \leftarrow \mathcal{A}^{\mathcal{O}_{\mathcal{U}}(esk_\beta, t)}$
4. $(\cdot, (epk, esk)) \leftarrow (\mathcal{A}(c), \mathsf{KeyEn.U}(ck, c, s_\beta, o, pk_{\mathcal{U}}, sk_{\mathcal{U}}))$	
5. $b \leftarrow \mathcal{A}^{\mathcal{O}_{\mathcal{U}}(esk)}$	

Fig. 1. Privacy and traceability experiments for a TB-LDE scheme $\mathcal{E}$. In the privacy experiment, oracle $\mathcal{O}_{\mathcal{U}}(esk)$ can be requested to execute either $\mathsf{KeyDer.U}(esk, \cdot)$ on arbitrary time periods or $\mathsf{Dec}(esk, \cdot, \cdot)$ on arbitrary third-party derived keys and ciphertexts, and return the outputs to $\mathcal{A}$. In the traceability experiment, oracle $\mathcal{O}_{\mathcal{U}}(esk_\beta, t)$ runs $\mathsf{KeyDer.U}(esk_\beta, t)$.

Definition 2 (Privacy (of the User Secret)). *$\mathcal{E}$ satisfies privacy of user secrets if for every efficient adversary $\mathcal{A}(1^\lambda)$, there exists a negligible function* negl *such that*

$$\mathbf{Adv}^{\text{priv}}_{\mathcal{E},\lambda}(\mathcal{A}) = \left|\Pr\left[\mathbf{Exp}^{\text{priv}-0}_{\mathcal{E},\lambda}(\mathcal{A}) = 1\right] - \Pr\left[\mathbf{Exp}^{\text{priv}-1}_{\mathcal{E},\lambda}(\mathcal{A}) = 1\right]\right| \leq \text{negl}(\lambda).$$

LD-IND-CCA Security. As for classical cryptosystems, the secrecy of the user's messages should be retained even when the key-enhancement protocol is taken into account. This requirement is captured by the LD-IND-CCA property.

Definition 3 (LD-IND-CCA Security). *$\mathcal{E}$ satisfies Leakage-Deterring Indistinguishability under Chosen-Ciphertext Attacks (LD-IND-CCA) if for every efficient adversary $\mathcal{A}(1^\lambda)$, there exists a negligible function* negl *such that*

$$\mathbf{Adv}^{\text{ld-cca}}_{\mathcal{E},\lambda}(\mathcal{A}) = \left|\Pr\left[b' = b\colon \begin{array}{r} (\mathcal{PP}, ck) \leftarrow \mathsf{Setup}(1^\lambda),\ (pk_{\mathcal{U}}, sk_{\mathcal{U}}) \leftarrow \mathsf{KeyGen.U}(\mathcal{PP}), \\ (c, s, o) \leftarrow \mathcal{A}(ck, pk_{\mathcal{U}}), \\ (\cdot, (epk, esk)) \leftarrow (\mathcal{A}(c),\ \mathsf{KeyEn.U}(ck, c, s, o, pk_{\mathcal{U}}, sk_{\mathcal{U}})), \\ (m_0, m_1, t, pk_{\mathcal{T}}) \leftarrow \mathcal{A}^{\mathcal{O}_{\mathcal{U}_1}(esk)}(epk),\ b \in_R \{0,1\}, \\ ct^* \leftarrow \mathsf{Enc}(epk, pk_{\mathcal{T}}, m_b, t),\ b' \leftarrow \mathcal{A}^{\mathcal{O}_{\mathcal{U}_2}(esk, ct^*)}(ct^*) \end{array}\right] - \frac{1}{2}\right| \leq \text{negl}(\lambda),$$

with $\mathcal{O}_{\mathcal{U}_1}(esk)$ an oracle that can be requested by $\mathcal{A}$ to execute either $\mathsf{KeyDer.U}(esk, \cdot)$ *or* $\mathsf{Dec}(esk, \cdot, \cdot)$ *and return the outputs to $\mathcal{A}$, and $\mathcal{O}_{\mathcal{U}_2}(esk, ct^*)$ an oracle that can be requested by $\mathcal{A}$ to execute either* $\mathsf{KeyDer.U}(esk, \cdot)$ *or* $\mathsf{Dec}(esk, \cdot, \cdot)$ *on arbitrary ciphertexts ct such that $ct_0 \neq ct_0^*$ (only the first part of the ciphertext, the one that the user can decrypt on her own, must be different) and return the outputs.*

Untraceability. Untraceability ensures that the protocol in which the third party helps the user decrypt ciphertexts should preserve her anonymity.

Definition 4 (Untraceability). *$\mathcal{E}$ satisfies untraceability if for every efficient adversary $\mathcal{A}(1^\lambda)$, there exists a negligible function* negl *such that*

$$\mathbf{Adv}_{\mathcal{E},\lambda}^{\mathrm{trace}}(\mathcal{A}) = \left|\Pr\left[\mathbf{Exp}_{\mathcal{E},\lambda}^{\mathrm{trace}-0}(\mathcal{A}) = 1\right] - \Pr\left[\mathbf{Exp}_{\mathcal{E},\lambda}^{\mathrm{trace}-1}(\mathcal{A}) = 1\right]\right| \leq \mathrm{negl}(\lambda).$$

Recoverability. Given that the authority correctly executes its key-enhancement algorithm and that the third party keys are correctly generated, a TB-LDE scheme should ensure that the secret output by the recovery algorithm is the one the user committed to during the key-enhancement protocol. Note that the truthful generation of third party keys is necessary to enforce that the user, to decrypt ciphertexts, must to interact at least once per time period.

Definition 5 (Recoverability (of the User Secret)). *$\mathcal{E}$ satisfies (rewinding black-box) recoverability of the user secret (with respect to a distribution class $\mathscr{D}$) if for every efficient adversary $\mathcal{A}(1^\lambda)$, for every current time period t_c, there exists a negligible function* negl *such that*

$$\Pr\left[s \neq s', \mathcal{D} \in \mathscr{D}, t > t_c, \mathsf{B} \text{ is } \delta\text{-correct in time period } t \text{ w.r.t. } \mathcal{D}: \begin{array}{c} (\mathcal{PP}, ck) \leftarrow \mathsf{Setup}(1^\lambda), (pk_{\mathcal{T}}, sk_{\mathcal{T}}) \leftarrow \mathsf{KeyGen.T}(\mathcal{PP}), \\ (s, pk_{\mathcal{U}}) \leftarrow \mathcal{A}(\mathcal{PP}, ck, pk_{\mathcal{T}}), (c, o) \leftarrow \mathsf{Com}(ck, s), \\ (\cdot, epk) \leftarrow (\mathcal{A}(c, o), \mathsf{KeyEn.A}(ck, c, pk_{\mathcal{U}})), \\ (\mathsf{B}, \mathcal{D}, t) \leftarrow \mathcal{A}^{\mathsf{KeyDer.T}(sk_{\mathcal{T}}, ck, t_c)}, s' \leftarrow \mathsf{Rec}(\mathsf{B}, epk, pk_{\mathcal{T}}, \mathcal{D}, t) \end{array}\right] \leq \mathrm{negl}(\lambda).$$

Remark 1. The maximal class $\mathscr{D}$ for which it is possible to successfully deter users from delegating their decryption capabilities is the class of distributions $\mathcal{D}$ such that $\delta > p(\mathcal{D})$ and $\delta - p(\mathcal{D})$ is non-negligible. Indeed, for a distribution $\mathcal{D}$ such that $p(\mathcal{D}) > \delta$ or $\delta - p(\mathcal{D})$ is negligible, any decryption algorithm B can merely output a message with probability mass $p(\mathcal{D})$, and readily satisfy δ-correctness as pointed out by Kiayias and Tang [17]; in which case recoverability cannot be achieved since the user secret is not involved in the decryption process.

Remark 2. The restriction $t > t_c$ is crucial. Would it not be the case, an adversary could request a decryption key for a time period $t \leq t_c$ from third-party $\mathcal{T}$, hard-code it in B, and thereby achieve 1-correctness for time period t without ever having to interact.

4 Generic Construction of a TB-LDE Scheme

In this section, we give a generic construction which turns any PKE scheme into a TB-LDE scheme. The main ideas are as follows. We use the original PKE scheme to encrypt a one-time-pad encryption of the plaintext, and encrypt the one-time-pad key with a CP-ABE scheme for which third party $\mathcal{T}$ holds the master secret key. The CP-ABE allows to specify a recipient user and a time-period in which the whole ciphertext can be decrypted. Users are thereby compelled to interact with the third party at least once per time-period to obtain the secret key corresponding to the time period indicated by the ciphertext policy. This interaction requires users to perform a proof on the secrets to which they committed during the key-enhancement protocol, and it allows, via rewinding, for the recoverability of those secrets by anyone with a decryption device.

In more detail, during the key-enhancement protocol, a user $\mathcal{U}$ commits to a secret, sends a commitment to the authority, and after proving knowledge of the secret to the latter, she receives a random identity and a signature on it and the commitment. Ciphertexts consist of two parts: a first that $\mathcal{U}$ can decrypt on her own and another (the CP-ABE part) that she can only decrypt with a key derived from $\mathcal{T}$'s master secret key. To obtain such a key, $\mathcal{U}$ encrypts her identity and must prove, to $\mathcal{T}$, knowledge of a signature on the encrypted identity and on a commitment to which she knows an opening. As the signature scheme is assumed unforgeable, $\mathcal{U}$ has to use the commitment that she sent to the authority during the key-enhancement protocol. Any pirate decryption algorithm B that can decrypt a non-negligible amount of ciphertexts generated with $\mathcal{U}$'s key must perform the same proof with non-negligible probability. The extractor of the proof system can then recover $\mathcal{U}$'s secret.

Formal Description. Let $\mathcal{T}$ be a set of natural integers, the time-period set, and $\mathcal{ID}$ a non-empty identity set. Our construction uses as building blocks

- $\mathcal{C}$ a commitment scheme with which users commit to their secrets,
- $\mathcal{S}$ a signature scheme used to sign user commitments and identities
- $\mathcal{E}_0$ a public-key encryption scheme to compute ciphertext parts that the user can decrypt on her own,
- $\mathcal{E}_1$ a CP-ABE scheme with attribute space $\mathcal{T} \times \mathcal{ID}$ and equality as access policy used to compute the ciphertext parts for which $\mathcal{U}$ needs assistance from $\mathcal{T}$,
- $\mathcal{E}_2$ a PKE scheme with message space $\mathcal{ID}$ is used to encrypt $\mathcal{U}$'s identity when she interacts with $\mathcal{T}$.

Suppose that $\mathcal{E}_0$ and $\mathcal{E}_1$ share the same message space $\mathcal{M}$, on which there exists an internal composition law $\oplus$ such that for all $m \in \mathcal{M}$, the map $\cdot \oplus m$ is a permutation of $\mathcal{M}$. Let $\cdot \ominus m$ stand for its inverse. To turn the key-derivation algorithm of CP-ABE $\mathcal{E}_1$ into an interactive protocol between $\mathcal{U}$ and $\mathcal{T}$, assume that there exists probabilistic algorithms Der_0 and Der_2 (Der_2 will be used for simulation in the proof of recoverability – see Theorem 5), and a deterministic algorithm Der_1 such that

1. for all $sk_{\mathcal{T}}$, t, $(ek, dk) \leftarrow \mathcal{E}_2.\mathsf{KeyGen}(\mathcal{PP})$, id, $ct^{id} \leftarrow \mathcal{E}_2.\mathsf{Enc}(ek, id; r_{\mathcal{U}})$, variables $(ek, dk, r_{\mathcal{U}}, \mathsf{Der}_0(sk_{\mathcal{T}}, t, ek, ct^{id}))$ and $(ek, dk, r_{\mathcal{U}}, \mathsf{Der}_2(sk_{\mathcal{T}}^{t,id}, ek))$ have the same distribution; and
2. for all $sk_{\mathcal{T}}$, t, $(ek, dk) \leftarrow \mathcal{E}_2.\mathsf{KeyGen}(\mathcal{PP})$, id, $ct^{id} \leftarrow \mathcal{E}_2.\mathsf{Enc}(ek, id)$, $sk_{\mathcal{T}}'^{t,id} \leftarrow \mathsf{Der}_0(sk_{\mathcal{T}}, t, ek, ct^{id})$, $\mathsf{Der}_1(dk, sk_{\mathcal{T}}'^{t,id}) = \mathcal{E}_1.\mathsf{KeyDer}(sk_{\mathcal{T}}, \{t, id\})$.

We then construct a TB-LDE scheme $\mathcal{E}$, parametrized by the time-period set $\mathcal{T}$ and the identity set $\mathcal{ID}$, such that

$\mathsf{Setup}(1^\lambda, (\mathcal{T}, \mathcal{ID})) \rightarrow (\mathcal{PP}, ck)$: generates public parameters, by running algorithms $\mathcal{E}_0.\mathsf{Setup}(1^\lambda)$, $\mathcal{E}_1.\mathsf{Setup}(1^\lambda, (\mathcal{T}, \mathcal{ID}))$, $\mathcal{C}.\mathsf{Setup}(1^\lambda)$, $\mathcal{S}.\mathsf{Setup}(1^\lambda)$, and computes a commitment key $ck \leftarrow \mathsf{ComKeyGen}(\mathcal{PP})$

$\mathsf{KeyGen.U}(\mathcal{PP}) \rightarrow (pk_{\mathcal{U}}, sk_{\mathcal{U}})$: runs $\mathcal{E}_0.\mathsf{KeyGen}(\mathcal{PP})$

$\mathsf{KeyGen.T}(\mathcal{PP}) \rightarrow (pk_{\mathcal{T}}, sk_{\mathcal{T}})$: runs $(pk_{\mathcal{T}}, sk_{\mathcal{T}}) \leftarrow (pk, msk) \leftarrow \mathcal{E}_1.\mathsf{KeyGen}(\mathcal{PP})$

$\mathsf{KeyEn} = (\mathsf{KeyEn.U}(ck, c, s, o, pk_{\mathcal{U}}, sk_{\mathcal{U}}), \mathsf{KeyEn.A}(ck, c, pk_{\mathcal{U}})) \rightarrow ((epk, esk), epk)$: is the following protocol between KeyEn.U and KeyEn.A:

1. KeyEn.U and KeyEn.A run protocol $\mathsf{PoK}\{(s, o) \colon \mathsf{Open}(ck, c, s, o) = 1\}$ as prover and verifier respectively. If it fails, the overall key-enhancement protocol is aborted, i.e., $epk \leftarrow esk \leftarrow \perp$, otherwise
2. KeyEn.A generates $(sk, vk) \leftarrow \mathcal{S}.\mathsf{KeyGen}(\mathcal{PP})$, $id \in_R \mathcal{ID}$, computes $\sigma = \mathsf{Sign}(sk, (c, id))$, sets $epk \leftarrow (pk_{\mathcal{U}}, c, id, \sigma)$, and sends id and σ to KeyEn.U
3. KeyEn.U sets epk as KeyEn.A, and sets $esk \leftarrow (sk_{\mathcal{U}}, c, s, o, id, \sigma)$.

$\mathsf{Enc}(epk, pk_{\mathcal{T}}, m \in \mathcal{M}, t \in \mathcal{T}) \rightarrow ct$: generates $m_1 \in_R \mathcal{M}$, sets $m_0 \leftarrow m \oplus m_1$, and outputs $ct \leftarrow (\mathcal{E}_0.\mathsf{Enc}(pk_{\mathcal{U}}, m_0), \mathcal{E}_1.\mathsf{Enc}(pk_{\mathcal{T}}, m_1, \mathbb{S} = \{t, id\}))$

$\mathsf{KeyDer} = (\mathsf{KeyDer.U}(esk, t), \mathsf{KeyDer.T}(sk_{\mathcal{T}}, ck, vk, t_c)) \rightarrow (sk_{\mathcal{T}}^{t,id}, \perp)$: is a two-party interactive equivalent of algorithm $\mathcal{E}_1.\mathsf{KeyDer}(sk_{\mathcal{T}}, \{t, id\})$. More precisely, it is a protocol in which KeyDer.U and KeyDer.T proceed as follows.

1. KeyDer.U generates and stores a pair of keys $(ek, dk) \leftarrow \mathcal{E}_2.\mathsf{KeyGen}(\mathcal{PP})$ if none was priorly stored (otherwise reuses such a pair), computes $ct^{id} \leftarrow \mathcal{E}_2.\mathsf{Enc}(ck, id; r_{\mathcal{U}})$, and sends (ek, t, ct^{id}) to KeyDer.T
2. if $t > t_c$, then KeyDer.T returns $\perp$, and KeyDer.U outputs $\perp$; otherwise algorithms KeyDer.U and KeyDer.T run protocol

$$\mathsf{PoK}\{(c, s, o, id, \sigma, r_{\mathcal{U}}) \colon \mathsf{Open}(ck, c, s, o) = 1, \mathsf{Verify}(vk, (c, id), \sigma) = 1, ct^{id} = \mathcal{E}_2.\mathsf{Enc}(ek, id; r_{\mathcal{U}})\} \quad (1)$$

   as prover and verifier respectively. If protocol PoK fails, the overall protocol is aborted, i.e., $sk_{\mathcal{T}}^{t,id} \leftarrow \perp$; otherwise
3. KeyDer.T computes $sk_{\mathcal{T}}^{\prime t,id} \leftarrow \mathsf{Der}_0(sk_{\mathcal{T}}, t, ek, ct^{id})$ and sends it to KeyDer.U
4. KeyDer.U outputs $sk_{\mathcal{T}}^{t,id} = \mathsf{Der}_1(dk, sk_{\mathcal{T}}^{\prime t,id})$.

$\mathsf{Dec}(esk, sk_{\mathcal{T}}^{t,id}, ct) \rightarrow m$: returns $m = \mathcal{E}_0.\mathsf{Dec}(sk, ct_0) \ominus \mathcal{E}_1.\mathsf{Dec}(sk_{\mathcal{T}}^{t,id}, ct_1)$ (outputs $\perp$ instead if either $\mathcal{E}_0.\mathsf{Dec}(sk, ct_0) = \perp$ or $\mathcal{E}_1.\mathsf{Dec}(sk_{\mathcal{T}}^{t,id}, ct_1) = \perp$)

$\mathsf{Rec}(\mathsf{B}, epk, pk_{\mathcal{T}}, \mathcal{D}, t) \rightarrow s$: generates messages $m \leftarrow_{\$} \mathcal{D}$, computes $\mathsf{Enc}(epk, pk_{\mathcal{T}}, m, t)$ and runs B on it until the latter engages in protocol PoK as prover, and succeeds in it. Once this event occurs (it is yet to be proved that it does indeed occur), algorithm Rec runs extractor $\mathcal{K}$, which can rewind B, to extract a witness that contains a secret s to which c is a commitment. Note that algorithm Rec runs B *locally*, i.e., B does not interact with KeyDer.T, but rather Rec which plays the role of the verifier. *Importantly,* Rec *does not reject the key-request from* B *if it is for a time period* $t > t_c$. This allows for recoverability without having to wait until a future time period in which B is claimed to be δ-correct.

Correctness & Security. We now state the security properties achieved by our construction.

Theorem 1 (Correctness). *$\mathcal{E}$ is correct if $\mathcal{E}_0$ and $\mathcal{E}_1$ are correct and if* PoK *is complete.*

Proof. If PoK is complete, then, for any ciphertext, KeyDer.U successfully obtains a secret key corresponding to the time period indicated in the access structure of the ciphertext. The correctness of $\mathcal{E}_0$ and $\mathcal{E}_1$ then implies that of $\mathcal{E}$. □

Complete proofs for Theorems 2, 3 and 4 are given in the full version.

Theorem 2 (Privacy). *$\mathcal{E}$ satisfies privacy if $\mathcal{C}$ is hiding, protocol* PoK *is zero knowledge, and $\mathcal{E}_2$ is IND-CPA secure.*

Proof (Sketch). If the commitment scheme is hiding, the authority cannot infer any information about user secrets. If PoK is zero-knowledge and $\mathcal{E}_2$ is IND-CPA, the third-party cannot infer any information about the user identities related which are related to commitments to user secrets. □

Theorem 3 (LD-IND-CCA Security). *$\mathcal{E}$ is LD-IND-CCA secure if $\mathcal{E}_0$ is IND-CCA secure.*

Proof (Sketch). Reducing the LD-IND-CCA security of $\mathcal{E}$ to the IND-CCA security of $\mathcal{E}_0$ is straightforward since without the user public key, even the third party can tell apart an encryption of $m \oplus m_0$ from an encryption of $m \oplus m_1$, where m is a uniformly random bit-string, only with non-negligible probability.

Theorem 4 (Untraceability). *$\mathcal{E}$ satisfies untraceability if proof system* PoK *is zero knowledge and $\mathcal{E}_2$ is IND-CPA secure.*

Proof (Sketch). As users encrypt their identities to request keys, if $\mathcal{E}_2$ is IND-CPA secure and PoK is ZK, then the third-party cannot infer any information about the user identities during protocol KeyDer. □

Theorem 5 (Recoverability). *$\mathcal{E}$ satisfies recoverability with respect to the class of distributions $\mathcal{D}$ such that $\delta > p(\mathcal{D})$ and $\delta - p(\mathcal{D})$ is non-negligible assuming $\mathcal{C}$ to be binding, $\mathcal{S}$ to be existentially unforgeable and $\mathcal{E}_1$ to be adaptively PH-CPA secure.*

Proof (Sketch). It suffices to prove that with a probability close to δ, when given ciphertexts generated for the time period and the identity for which Rec is δ-correct, and encrypting messages with distribution $\mathcal{D}$, algorithm B requests the third-party secret key corresponding to the time period and the identity. This is the crucial part of the proof.

As soon as this event occurs, algorithm Rec runs extractor $\mathcal{K}$ to extract a secret. Since the commitment and the identity used in the witness for the proof are signed by the key-enhancement authority, algorithm Rec must send, with overwhelming probability, the commitment and an encryption of the identity that are in the user enhanced public key. As the commitment scheme is binding, the extracted secret is the one that was used in the key-enhancement protocol. □

5 Instantiation

We now instantiate each of the building blocks of the construction in Sect. 4.

Let $(p, \mathbb{G}_1 = \langle P_1 \rangle, \mathbb{G}_2 = \langle P_2 \rangle, \mathbb{G}_T, e)$ be a pairing group such that the DLOG assumption holds in $\mathbb{G}_1$, the Decisional Diffie–Hellman (DDH) assumption holds in $\mathbb{G}_2$ and $\mathbb{G}_T$, the DLIN assumption holds in $\mathbb{G}_1$ and $\mathbb{G}_2$, and the qSDH problem in intractable in $(\mathbb{G}_1, \mathbb{G}_2)$ (see Appendix A.1). Set

- $\mathcal{C}$ as the standard Pedersen commitment scheme over $\mathbb{G}_1$
- $\mathcal{E}_0$ as the Cramer–Shoup encryption scheme [14] with message space $\mathbb{G}_T$
- $\mathcal{E}_1$ as the Okamoto–Takashima CP-ABE scheme (Appendix A.4)
- $\mathcal{E}_2$ as the Elgamal encryption scheme with message space $\mathbb{Z}_p$ and $\mathcal{S}$ as the BBS+ signature scheme (Appendix A.2) in the case $n = 3$ (to sign a secret s, an opening o and an identity id).

Note that the Okamoto–Takashima scheme remains PH-CPA secure under the same assumptions if generator $\mathcal{G}_{\mathrm{ob}}$ outputs matrices $\mathbf{V}_k$ instead of matrices $\mathbf{B}_k^*$, and its setup algorithm includes matrices $\hat{\mathbf{V}}_k$ (defined similarly to $\hat{\mathbf{B}}_k^*$) instead of matrices $\hat{\mathbf{B}}_k^*$ in the master secret key. In this section, the Okamato–Takashima scheme is considered with this modification.

It remains to provide algorithms Der_0, Der_1, Der_2 for protocol KeyDer and a proof system (P, V) for the language of Eq. 1. Consider then the following algorithms:

$\mathsf{Der}_0(sk_{\mathcal{T}}, t, ek = (P_2, Q_2), ct^{id} = (C_0^{id}, C_1^{id})) \rightarrow sk_{\mathcal{T}}^{\prime t, id}$: generate $\lambda_1, \ldots, \lambda_7$, α, $y_0 \in \mathbb{Z}_p$, $\mathbf{y}_1, \mathbf{y}_2 \in_R \mathbb{Z}_p^2$, compute $\mathbf{k}_0^* = [\alpha\ 1\ y_0]\, \hat{\mathbf{B}}_0^*$, $\mathbf{k}_1^* = [\alpha \mathbf{x}_1\ \mathbf{y}_1]\, \hat{\mathbf{B}}_1^*$,

$$\mathbf{k}_2^{\prime *} = \left[\left(P_2^{\lambda_j} \left(C_0^{id}\right)^{\alpha \hat{\mathbf{V}}_{2,2,j}}, Q_2^{\lambda_j} P_2^{\alpha \hat{\mathbf{V}}_{2,1,j}} \left(C_1^{id}\right)^{\alpha \hat{\mathbf{V}}_{2,2,j}} P_2^{\mathbf{y}_{2,1} \hat{\mathbf{V}}_{2,3,j}} P_2^{\mathbf{y}_{2,2} \hat{\mathbf{V}}_{2,4,j}}\right)\right]_j,$$

and return $sk_{\mathcal{T}}^{\prime t, id} = (\mathbf{k}_0^*, \mathbf{k}_1^*, \mathbf{k}_2^{\prime *})$

$\mathsf{Der}_1(dk = q = \mathrm{dlog}_{P_2}(Q_2), sk_{\mathcal{T}}^{\prime t, id}) \rightarrow sk_{\mathcal{T}}^{t, id}$: parse $\mathbf{k}_2^{\prime *}$ as $\left[\left(\mathbf{k}_{2,j,0}^{\prime *}, \mathbf{k}_{2,j,1}^{\prime *}\right)\right]_j$, compute $\mathbf{k}_2^* = \left[\mathbf{k}_{2,j,1}^{\prime *} / \left(\mathbf{k}_{2,j,0}^{\prime *}\right)^q\right]_j$, and return $sk_{\mathcal{T}}^{t, id} = (\mathbf{k}_0^*, \mathbf{k}_1^*, \mathbf{k}_2^*)$

$\mathsf{Der}_2(sk_{\mathcal{T}}^{t, id}, ek) \rightarrow sk_{\mathcal{T}}^{\prime t, id}$: generate $\lambda_1, \ldots, \lambda_7 \in_R \mathbb{Z}_p$, compute a vector $\mathbf{k}_2^{\prime *} = \left[\left(P_2^{\lambda_j}, Q_2^{\lambda_j} \mathbf{k}_{2,j}^*\right)\right]_j$, and return $sk_{\mathcal{T}}^{\prime t, id} = (\mathbf{k}_0^*, \mathbf{k}_1^*, \mathbf{k}_2^{\prime *})$.

Notice that requirements in Sect. 4 for Der_0, Der_1 and Der_2 are met.

Moreover, in the key-derivation protocol KeyDer, protocol PoK should be a ZKPoK protocol for the language

$$(s, o, \overbrace{\mathbf{x}_{2,2}}^{id}, \overbrace{W, y, z}^{\sigma}, \overbrace{\gamma}^{r_u}) \colon e(W, U P_2^y) = e(P_1 H_0^z H_1^r H_2^s H_3^{\mathbf{x}_{2,2}}, P_2),$$
$$C_0^{id} = P_2^{\gamma},\ C_1^{id} = Q_2^{\gamma} P_2^{\mathbf{x}_{2,2}}.$$

A standard ZK protocol for proving knowledge of a preimage of a group homomorphism is then a suitable ZKPoK protocol.

Theorems 1, 2, 3, 4, 5 imply that this instantiation satisfies correctness, privacy, LD-IND-CCA security, untraceability and recoverability (Fig. 2).

	$\mathbb{Z}$	$\mathbb{Z}_p$	$\mathbb{G}_1$	$\mathbb{G}_2$	$\mathbb{G}_T$
Keys and Ciphertexts					
$pk_{\mathcal{U}}$	1	8	2	0	5
$sk_{\mathcal{U}}$	1	10	1	0	0
$pk_{\mathcal{T}}$	3	0	57	0	1
$sk_{\mathcal{T}}$	3	71	0	0	0
$sk_{\mathcal{T}}^{t,id}$	0	0	0	19	0
ct	0	2	19	0	5
Protocols					
KeyEn	0	6	1	0	0
KeyDer	0	12	2	32	0

	(Multi-)Exp.	Pairing
Der_0	26 in $\mathbb{G}_2$	0
Der_1	7 in $\mathbb{G}_2$	0
Enc	27 (26 in $\mathbb{G}_1$, 1 in $\mathbb{G}_T$)	0
Dec	1 (in $\mathbb{G}_T$)	19

Fig. 2. Efficiency of our instantiation. On the left, for keys and ciphertexts, the figures represent the number of elements they comprise. As for the protocols, it is their bandwidth that is represented, i.e., the number of elements exchanged between the parties. The table on the right indicates the number of operations (multi-exponentiation and pairing) performed by each of the algorithms.

Comparison with Kiayias and Tang's Generic Construction. The only existing leakage-deterring scheme in the literature is Kiayias and Tang's. They did not provide an instantiation of their generic construction of an LD-IND-CPA scheme [17, Section 4]. Yet, it can naturally be instantiated with the Elgamal encryption scheme. In that case, for secrets of 128 bits, a partial correctness $\delta = 4/2^3 = 50\%$ and the error correcting code that they propose [16, Figure 1, No 1], their enhanced public keys consist of $162 = 2*81$ Elgamal public keys and ciphertexts consist of $30 = 2*15$ Elgamal ciphertexts (i.e., 60 group elements). To make their scheme LD-IND-CCA secure, they compose it with a standard CCA-secure scheme which must then encrypt a vector of group elements, and the keys of which must be accounted for in the overall enhanced public key.

Section 6 gives construction a more efficient construction of our scheme in the ROM. The message space of $\mathcal{E}_0$ is $\mathbb{G}_1$ and the ciphertexts consist of 2 $\mathbb{Z}_p$ elements, 23 $\mathbb{G}_1$ and 1 $\mathbb{G}_T$ elements. Our enhanced public keys and ciphertexts in the ROM are therefore much shorter than those of Kiayias and Tang. However, computing our ciphertexts is more expensive because of the pairings of the Okamoto–Takashima CP-ABE scheme.

6 Construction in the Random Oracle Model

The main drawback, in terms of computation time and ciphertext size, of the Sect. 4 construction is that the message spaces of $\mathcal{E}_0$ and $\mathcal{E}_1$ must match. As a result, the Sect. 5 instantiation requires the Cramer–Shoup encryption scheme (with ciphertexts consisting of 4 plaintext-group elements) to have $\mathbb{G}_T$ as message space since the message space of the Okamoto–Takashima CP-ABE is $\mathbb{G}_T$. However, target group elements are typically large (around 10 times larger than $\mathbb{G}_1$ elements) and operations in $\mathbb{G}_T$ are much slower than in $\mathbb{G}_1$. It would thus be preferable to have $\mathbb{G}_1$ as a message space for $\mathcal{E}_0$. Consider then the following construction which is proved secure in the ROM. The RO is further denoted by Hash). It is identical to that of Sect. 4 except for its message space that is now $\{0,1\}^{n(\lambda)}$, the message space $\mathcal{M}_0$ of $\mathcal{E}_0$, the message space $\mathcal{M}_1$ of $\mathcal{E}_1$, and for algorithms Enc and Dec. Those latter algorithms are now[3]

$\mathsf{Enc}(epk, pk_{\mathcal{T}}, m \in \{0,1\}^n, t \in \mathcal{T}) \to ct$: that generates $K_{\mathcal{U}} \in_R \mathcal{M}_0$, $K_{\mathcal{T}} \in_R \mathcal{M}_1$, and outputs a ciphertext $ct = (\mathcal{E}_0.\mathsf{Enc}(pk_{\mathcal{U}}, K_{\mathcal{U}}), \mathcal{E}_1.\mathsf{Enc}(pk_{\mathcal{T}}, K_{\mathcal{T}}, \{t, id\}), m \oplus \mathsf{Hash}(K_{\mathcal{U}}, K_{\mathcal{T}}))$;

$\mathsf{Dec}(esk, ct) \to m$: an algorithm that parses ct as (ct_0, ct_1, ct_2), and computes and outputs $ct_2 \oplus \mathsf{Hash}(\mathcal{E}_0.\mathsf{Dec}(sk_{\mathcal{U}}, ct_0), \mathcal{E}_1.\mathsf{Dec}(sk_{\mathcal{T}}^{t,id}, ct_1))$.

With this alteration, the proofs of correctness, privacy and untraceability are straightforwardly adapted from those of the scheme in Sect. 4. As for LD-IND-CCA security and recoverability, their proofs require a more elaborate (although simple) argumentation, and are given in the full version. Note that still no proof of knowledge on the ciphertexts is required (only on an encrypted identity at the beginning of each time period). Therefore, no proof of circuit satisfiability for the RO must be computed.

7 Non–Time-Based LDE Schemes

In case only few ciphertexts are expected to be decrypted, communication during decryption might not be a major hindrance. LDE schemes in which users need to interact whenever they wish to decrypt a ciphertext are conceivable, and could spare the need for a CP-ABE scheme which incurs larger keys and ciphertexts than regular encryption schemes. Time periods and synchronization would then be unnecessary. In such a system, compared to the Sect. 3 definition of a TB-LDE scheme, $\mathcal{T}$ does not send a key to $\mathcal{U}$ (i.e., protocol KeyDer is obsolete), and $\mathsf{Dec} = (\mathsf{Dec.U}(esk, ct), \mathsf{Dec.T}(sk_{\mathcal{T}}, ck))$ is an interactive protocol between a user decryption algorithm Dec.U and a third-party decryption algorithm Dec.T, at the end of which Dec.U outputs a plaintext m or $\perp$, and Dec.T outputs $\perp$.

7.1 Security Definitions

The privacy definition remains the same, the traceability experiments and the LD-IND-CCA security game are only modified not to incorporate a time period t in the challenge tuples, and the oracles are redefined to execute Dec.U.

In the traceability experiment, the adversary now outputs a tuple $((epk_0, esk_0), (epk_1, esk_0), m)$, the challenger computes $\mathsf{Enc}(epk_\beta, pk_{\mathcal{T}}, m)$, and the adversary can request the challenger to run Dec.U.

δ-correctness is not defined with respect to a time period anymore, and concerning recoverability, $\mathcal{A}$ need then not specify a time period $t > t_c$ in which B is δ-correct (equivalently, $\mathcal{A}$ could specify any dummy time period so long as t_c is set to $-\infty$), and algorithm B does not receive a time period t as an input.

The multi-user-case definitions are derived accordingly.

[3] $\oplus$ here denotes the traditional XOR operation.

7.2 Generic Construction

Let Rand be a commitment re-randomization algorithm. Following the notation of Sect. 4, except that $\mathcal{E}_1$ is now an encryption scheme supporting labels (from every ciphertext of which the corresponding label can be efficiently computed), let $\mathcal{E}$ be an LDE scheme such that

$\mathsf{KeyEn} = (\mathsf{KeyEn.U}(ck, c, s, o, pk_{\mathcal{U}}, sk_{\mathcal{U}}), \mathsf{KeyEn.A}(ck, c, pk_{\mathcal{U}})) \to ((epk, esk), epk)$: is a protocol between $\mathsf{KeyEn.U}$ and $\mathsf{KeyEn.A}$, which proceed as follows.

1. $\mathsf{KeyEn.U}(ck, c, s, o, pk_{\mathcal{U}}, sk_{\mathcal{U}})$ and $\mathsf{KeyEn.A}(ck, c, pk_{\mathcal{U}})$ run the interactive protocol $\mathsf{PoK}\{(s, o) \colon \mathsf{Open}(ck, c, s, o) = 1\}$ as prover and verifier respectively. If the protocol fails, the overall protocol is aborted, i.e., $epk = esk \leftarrow \perp$; otherwise
2. both algorithms set $epk = (pk_{\mathcal{U}}, c)$, and $\mathsf{KeyEn.U}$ sets $esk = (sk_{\mathcal{U}}, c, o)$

$\mathsf{Enc}(epk, pk_{\mathcal{T}}, m \in \mathcal{M}) \to ct$: generates $m_1 \in_R \mathcal{M}$, sets $m_0 = m \oplus m_1$, and outputs $ct = (\mathcal{E}_0.\mathsf{Enc}(pk_{\mathcal{U}}, m_0), \mathcal{E}_1.\mathsf{Enc}(pk_{\mathcal{T}}, m_1, l = \mathsf{Rand}(ck, c; r)), r)$

$\mathsf{Dec} = (\mathsf{Dec.U}(esk, ct), \mathsf{Dec.T}(sk_{\mathcal{T}}, ck))$: is an interactive protocol between $\mathsf{Dec.U}$ and $\mathsf{Dec.T}$ which proceed as follows.

1. Algorithm $\mathsf{Dec.U}$ sends (ct_1, l) to $\mathsf{Dec.T}$
2. algorithms $\mathsf{Dec.U}$ and $\mathsf{Dec.T}$ run protocol

$$\mathsf{PoK}\{(c, s, o, r) \colon \mathsf{Open}(ck, c, s, o) = 1,\, l = \mathsf{Rand}(ck, c; r)\}$$

   as prover and verifier respectively. If the protocol fails, $\mathsf{Dec.U}$ outputs $\perp$; otherwise
3. $\mathsf{Dec.T}$ sends $m_1 = \mathcal{E}_1.\mathsf{Dec}(sk_{\mathcal{T}}, ct_1, l)$ to $\mathsf{Dec.U}$; and
4. $\mathsf{Dec.U}$ outputs $\mathcal{E}_0.\mathsf{Enc}(sk, ct_0) \ominus m_1$ if $m_1 \neq \perp$ (outputs $\perp$ otherwise).

The other algorithms remain the same up to the omission of time periods. Observe that $\mathcal{E}_2$ and $\mathcal{S}$ are not used since the user need not encrypt her identity and prove that she knows a signature on it.

Similar proofs to those of Sect. 4 entail that $\mathcal{E}$ is correct if $\mathcal{E}_0$ and $\mathcal{E}_1$ are correct and if PoK is complete; that it satisfies privacy if $\mathcal{C}$ is hiding, and protocol PoK is ZK; that $\mathcal{E}$ is LD-IND-CCA secure if $\mathcal{E}_0$ is IND-CCA secure; and that untraceability is also satisfied if PoK is ZK. Scheme $\mathcal{E}$ also satisfies recoverability with respect to the class of distributions $\mathcal{D}$ such that $\delta > p(\mathcal{D})$ and $\delta - p(\mathcal{D})$ is non-negligible assuming $\mathcal{C}$ to be binding and $\mathcal{E}_1$ to be secure against chosen-ciphertext attacks [12, Section 2.4]. To prove it, it suffices to prove, as in Theorem 5 that with non-negligible probability, a δ-correct algorithm B sends the (third-party part of the) ciphertext and the label that it was given, and succeeds in the subsequent proof of knowledge. The knowledge extractor can then be used to retrieve the user secret.

7.3 Instantiation

Set $\mathcal{C}$ as the standard Pedersen commitment scheme and Rand as the algorithm that generates $r \in_r \mathbb{Z}_p$, and maps $c = g_1^s g_2^o$ to $c g_3^r$ for pairwise distinct g_1, g_2

and g_3. Let $\mathcal{E}_0$ be the Cramer–Shoup encryption scheme, and $\mathcal{E}_1$ be the Cramer–Shoup encryption scheme supporting labels [14]. Both schemes may have any group (in which the DDH assumption holds) with short representation as a common message space. The resulting ciphertexts are then composed of 9 group elements (one of which is a re-randomized commitment as a label), and decryption only requires exponentiations and two hash computations.

8 Revocation

Besides the scenario in which a decryption box was intentionally distributed by a user, the scenario in which a decryption device was stolen from an honest user or in which a user simply lost it is also relevant. In this case, the user should be able to prevent misuse of her device, i.e., unauthorized decryption. This can be achieve by adding a revocation functionality to LDE schemes. The interaction with the third party allows to easily add such a functionality: the third party need only also verify that the user's public key was not revoked without putting her anonymity at risk. Camenisch et al. [11] proposed a generic key-revocation component, which can be added to any system to enable a privacy-preserving revocation functionality. It is referred to as an Anonymous Revocation Component (ARC).

An ARC requires an entity called Revocation Authority (RA). In the present case, the RA can be the key-enhancement authority itself, the decryption third party or any other party in the system. The RA partakes in the key-enhancement protocol, maintains some revocation information, and changes the revocation status of the enhanced public keys.

Camenisch et al. [11, Section 4.4] provided definitions and a description of interfaces of an ARC, and instantiated it with the revocation scheme of Nakanishi et al. [22]. Baldimtsi et al. [3] gave an instance with accumulators. Both those instances are suitable for LDE schemes.

We first recall the definition of an ARC as proposed by Camenisch et al. [11], then we show how to add an ARC to our constructions without compromising the privacy of users' secrets or their anonymity.

8.1 Anonymous Revocation Components

In an ARC, revocation is achieved via a *revocation handle* $rh \in \mathcal{RH}$ that is embedded into the key to be revoked. An ARC $\mathcal{ARC}$ is a tuple of algorithms $(\mathsf{SPGen}, \mathsf{RKGen}, \mathsf{Revoke}, \mathsf{RevTokenGen}, \mathsf{RevTokenVer})$ such that

$\mathsf{SPGen}(1^\lambda) \rightarrow \mathcal{PP}_r$: is an algorithm that generates revocation parameters $\mathcal{PP}_r$

$\mathsf{RKGen}(\mathcal{PP}_r) \rightarrow (rpk, rsk, RI)$: is an algorithm that generates the RA's secret and public keys, and an initial revocation information RI

$\mathsf{Revoke}(rsk, RI, rh) \rightarrow RI'$: is an algorithm that revokes rh, and outputs an update RI' of the revocation information RI

$\mathsf{RevTokenGen}(rpk, RI, c, rh, o) \rightarrow rt$: is an algorithm which generates a publicly-verifiable revocation token proving that handle rh has not been revoked and that c is a commitment to rh

$\mathsf{RevTokenVer}(rpk, RI, c, rt) \rightarrow \{0,1\}$: is a revocation token verification algorithm.

The security requirements of an ARC can be informally stated as follows. *Correctness* states that any revocation token rt generated with a non-revoked handle rh and an honestly computed information RI is accepted by RevTokenVer. *Soundness* ensures that RevTokenVer accepts rt and c on input RI and rpk only if rt was computed with rh and a valid opening o to c. Moreover, no party other than the RA can publish a valid revocation information RI, i.e., it is always authentic. *Revocation privacy* guarantees that given a revocation token rt, no information about the underlying revocation handle rh can be inferred.

8.2 Revocable (TB-)LDE Schemes

To add an ARC to the generic constructions of Sects. 4, 6 and 7, it suffices to have the RA – recall that it partakes in the key-enhancement protocol – assign to each user, in addition to her secret, a revocation handle. In the case of TB-LDE schemes, this handle is signed by the key-enhancement authority together with the user's identity and commitment to her secret. To revoke a key, the corresponding handle is added to the publicly available revocation information. In (non–time-based) LDE schemes, the handle is also included in the computation of the label. During the key-derivation protocol for TB-LDE schemes or the decryption protocol for LDE schemes, the user computes a fresh (to be untraceable) commitment to the handle of her enhanced public key, and a revocation token, both sent to the third party. In addition to the proofs of those constructions, the user also proves that the handle of which she just sent a fresh commitment is not revoked, and that it was signed with the encrypted identity (for TB-LDE schemes) or used for the computation of the label (for LDE schemes).

Generic Construction of a Revocable TB-LDE Scheme. Let $\mathcal{E}$ be either of the Sect. 4 or the Sect. 6 TB-LDE scheme. Consider $\mathcal{E}_R$, a revocable TB-LDE scheme that has the same algorithms as $\mathcal{E}$, except for $\mathcal{E}_R.\mathsf{Setup}(1^\lambda)$ which also runs $\mathcal{ARC}.\mathsf{SPGen}(1^\lambda)$, for an additional algorithm $\mathcal{E}_R.\mathsf{Revoke} = \mathcal{ARC}.\mathsf{Revoke}$, and for its KeyEn and KeyDer protocols. Assuming, without loss of generality, the key-enhancement authority to also be the RA, those protocols are now

$\mathsf{KeyEn} = (\mathsf{KeyEn.U}(ck, c, s, o, pk_{\mathcal{U}}, sk_{\mathcal{U}}), \mathsf{KeyEn.A}(ck, c, pk_{\mathcal{U}})) \rightarrow ((epk, esk), epk)$: a protocol between KeyEn.U and KeyEn.T, which proceed as follows.

1. KeyEn.U and KeyEn.T run protocol $\mathsf{PoK}\{(s, o)\colon \mathsf{Open}(ck, c, s, o) = 1\}$ as prover and verifier respectively. If it fails, the overall key-enhancement protocol is aborted, i.e., $epk = esk \leftarrow \perp$; otherwise

2. KeyEn.A generates $(sk, vk) \leftarrow \mathcal{S}.\mathsf{KeyGen}(\mathcal{PP})$, $id \in_R \mathcal{ID}$, $rh \in_R \mathcal{RH}$, computes $\sigma = \mathsf{Sign}(sk, (c, id, rh))$, sets $epk = (pk_{\mathcal{U}}, c, id, rh, \sigma)$, and sends id and σ to KeyEn.U, which sets epk as KeyEn.A and $esk = (sk_{\mathcal{U}}, c, s, o, id, rh, \sigma)$

$\mathsf{KeyDer} = (\mathsf{KeyDer.U}(esk, t), \mathsf{KeyDer.T}(sk_{\mathcal{T}}, ck, vk, rpk, RI)) \rightarrow (sk_{\mathcal{T}}^{t,id}, \perp)$: a protocol between KeyDer.U and KeyDer.T, which proceed as follows.

1. Algorithm KeyDer.U generates and stores a pair of encryption keys $(ek, dk) \leftarrow \mathcal{E}_2.\mathsf{KeyGen}(\mathcal{PP})$ if none was priorly stored, and otherwise reuses such a pair, computes a ciphertext $ct^{id} = \mathcal{E}_2.\mathsf{Enc}(ek, id; r_{\mathcal{U}})$, a commitment and an opening $(c_{rh}, o_{rh}) = \mathsf{Com}(ck, rh)$, and a revocation token $rt = \mathcal{ARC}.\mathsf{RevTokenGen}(rpk, RI, c_{rh}, rt)$, and sends $(ek, t, ct^{id}, c_{rh}, rt)$ to algorithm KeyDer.T
2. if $t > t_c$, then KeyDer.T returns $\perp$, and KeyDer.U outputs $\perp$; otherwise, algorithms KeyDer.U and KeyDer.T run protocol

$$\begin{aligned}\mathsf{PoK}\{(c,s,o,id,rh,o_{rh},\sigma,r_{\mathcal{U}})\colon\ & \mathsf{Open}(ck,c,s,o)=1,\\ & \mathsf{Open}(ck,c_{rh},rh,o_{rh})=1,\ \mathsf{Verify}(vk,(c,id,rh),\sigma)=1,\\ & ct^{id}=\mathcal{E}_2.\mathsf{Enc}(ek,id;r_{\mathcal{U}}),\ \mathsf{RevTokenGen}(rpk,RI,c_{rh},rh,o_{rh})=1\}\end{aligned}$$

   as prover and verifier respectively. If protocol PoK fails, the overall protocol is aborted, i.e., $sk_{\mathcal{T}}^{t,id} \leftarrow \perp$; otherwise
3. KeyDer.T computes $sk_{\mathcal{T}}^{\prime t,id} \leftarrow \mathsf{Der}_0(sk_{\mathcal{T}}, t, ek, ct^{id})$, and sends it to KeyDer.U.
   Finally, KeyDer.U outputs $sk_{\mathcal{T}}^{t,id} = \mathsf{Der}_1(dk, sk_{\mathcal{T}}^{\prime t,id})$.

In the full version, we show how to add recovaction to the construction of Sect. 7.

9 Interactive Recoverability

A key-revocation component only allows a user to prevent further use of her device in case of loss or theft.[7] Nevertheless, as the Sect. 4 Rec algorithm is not interactive, a user's secret can still be recovered by anyone in possession of her device even if she has requested to have her public key revoked. To also protect user secrets in case she lost her device, local recoverability must be prevented, i.e., recoverability without interaction with the decryption third party $\mathcal{T}$ which checks that user public keys are not revoked.

To add interaction soundness to Sects. 7 and 4 (TB-)LDE scheme, it suffices to make the Dec.T (KeyDer.T) algorithm sign the first messages sent by Dec.U (KeyDer.U) and its challenges with an existentially unforgeable scheme $\mathcal{S}'$. Before answering the challenge, algorithm Dec.U (KeyDer.U) verifies the signature with the public verification key. It follows that unless an adversary, which does not possess the third-party signing key, can forge a signature, protocol PoK will never terminate, and algorithm Rec will never produce any output, and the user secret cannot be recovered. The existential unforgeability of $\mathcal{S}'$ then implies the interaction soundness of the (TB-)LDE scheme.

10 Conclusion

We first argued that in leakage-deterring schemes, a CCA type of privacy of user secrets is compatible with their recoverability. We therefore redefined leakage-deterring schemes with security guarantees stronger than existing ones. We then gave a construction that turns any CCA-secure encryption scheme into a leakage deterring one that achieves those stronger guarantees and has constant-size ciphertexts in the size of user secrets.

The main drawback of our construction is the need to interaction once per epoch (e.g., a week) with a party that helps users decrypt. However, this very same interaction is needed to guarantee a CCA type of privacy of user secrets together with their recoverability, and can even be leveraged to revoke user keys and protect their secrets in case or loss or theft.

Acknowledgements. This work supported by the ERC Grant PERCY #321310, and was done while the first two authors were at IBM Research – Zurich.

A Preliminaries

We here give the hardness assumptions and instantiations of the building blocks on which our constructions rely.

A.1 Pairing Groups and Hardness Assumptions

This section introduces pairing groups and classical hardness assumptions underlying our constructions.

Asymmetric Bilinear Pairing Groups. An asymmetric bilinear pairing group (or simply pairing group) consists of a tuple $(p, \mathbb{G}_1 = \langle P_1 \rangle, \mathbb{G}_2 = \langle P_2 \rangle, \mathbb{G}_T, e)$ such that p is a prime number, $\mathbb{G}_1, \mathbb{G}_2$ and $\mathbb{G}_T$ are (cyclic) p-order groups, and $e\colon \mathbb{G}_1 \times \mathbb{G}_2 \to \mathbb{G}_T$ is an efficiently-computable non-degenerate bilinear map (also called pairing), i.e., $e(P_1, P_2) \neq 1_{\mathbb{G}_T}$, and $\forall a, b \in \mathbb{Z}_p, e(P_1^a, P_2^b) = e(P_1, P_2)^{ab}$. Let $\mathcal{G}_{\text{bpg}}(1^\lambda)$ denote an algorithm that takes as an input a security parameter 1^λ, and outputs the description $\mathcal{PP}_{\mathbb{G}}$ of a pairing group.

q-Strong Diffie–Hellman Assumption. Let $\mathbb{G}_1 = \langle P_1 \rangle$ and $\mathbb{G}_2 = \langle P_2 \rangle$ be two p-order groups. The q-Strong Diffie–Hellman (qSDH) problem [5] in $(\mathbb{G}_1, \mathbb{G}_2)$ consists in computing a pair $\left(y, P_1^{1/(u+y)}\right) \in \mathbb{Z}_p \backslash \{-u\} \times \mathbb{G}_1$ given a $(p+3)$-tuple $(P_1, P_1^u, P_1^{u^2}, \ldots, P_1^{u^q}, P_2, P_2^u) \in \mathbb{G}_1^{p+1} \times \mathbb{G}_2^2$. The qSDH assumption over $(\mathbb{G}_1, \mathbb{G}_2)$ is that no efficient algorithm has a non-negligible probability to solve the qSDH problem in $(\mathbb{G}_1, \mathbb{G}_2)$.

Decisional Linear Assumption. The (2-)Decisional Linear (DLIN) assumption [6] over a p-order group $\mathbb{G} = \langle P \rangle$ is that, for $a, b, x, y, z \in_R \mathbb{Z}_p$, the distributions of $(P, P^a, P^b, P^{ax}, P^{by}, P^{x+y})$ and $(P, P^a, P^b, P^{ax}, P^{by}, P^z)$ are computationally indistinguishable.

A.2 BBS+ Signature Scheme

The BBS+ signature scheme (as described by Au et al. [1] and inspired by a group signature [6] introduced by Boneh et al.) is a tuple of algorithms (SignSetup, SignKeyGen, Sign, Verify) with

SignSetup$(1^\lambda) \to \mathcal{PP}$: output $\mathcal{PP} = \mathcal{PP}_\mathbb{G}$ the description of a pairing group $(p, \mathbb{G}_1 = \langle P_1 \rangle, \mathbb{G}_2 = \langle P_2 \rangle, \mathbb{G}_T, e)$ calling on $\mathcal{G}_{\text{bpg}}(1^\lambda)$

SignKeyGen$(\mathcal{PP}, n) \to (sk, vk)$: generate $H_0, \ldots, H_n \in_R \mathbb{G}_1, u \in_R \mathbb{Z}_p$, computes $U = P_2^u$, and output $sk = u, vk = (U, H_0, \ldots, H_n)$

Sign$(sk, \mathbf{m} \in \mathbb{Z}_p^n) \to \sigma$: generate $y, z \in_R \mathbb{Z}_p$, compute $V = P_1 H_0^z \prod_{i \geq 1} H_i^{m_i}$ and $W = V^{1/(u+y)}$, and outputs $\sigma = (W, y, z)$

Verify$(vk, \mathbf{m}, \sigma) \to b \in \{0, 1\}$: output 1 if $\mathbf{m} \in \mathbb{Z}_p^n$, σ can be parsed as (W, y, z) and $e(W, UP_2^y) = e\left(P_1 H_0^z \prod_{i \geq 1} H_i^{m_i}, P_2\right)$, and otherwise 0.

Camenisch et al. [10, Lemma 1] proved that the BBS+ signature scheme is existentially unforgeable against chosen-message attacks under the qSDH assumption over $(\mathbb{G}_1, \mathbb{G}_2)$. They showed [10, Section 4.5] how to prove knowledge of a BBS+ signature. We recall it in the full version.

A.3 Dual Pairing Vector Spaces

Dual Pairing Vector Spaces (DPVSs) were introduced by Okamoto and Takashima [24]. They provide a mechanism for parameter hiding [21] in prime-order pairing groups. The latter feature allows to proves the full security of functional encryption schemes in prime-order settings.

Definition 6 (Dual Pairing Vector Space). *Let $N \geq 1$ be an integer. A dual pairing vector space by direct product of a pairing group $(p, \mathbb{G}_1 = \langle P_1 \rangle, \mathbb{G}_2 = \langle P_2 \rangle, \mathbb{G}_T, e)$ is a tuple $(p, \mathbb{V}, \mathbb{V}^*, \mathbb{G}_T, \mathbb{A}, \mathbb{A}^*, e)$ such that $\mathbb{V} = \mathbb{G}_1^N$ and $\mathbb{V}^* = \mathbb{G}_2^N$ are two N-dimensional $\mathbb{Z}_p$ vector spaces, $\mathbb{A} = (\mathbf{a}_1, \ldots, \mathbf{a}_N)$ is the canonical basis of $\mathbb{V}$ (i.e., $\mathbf{a}_i = (\mathbf{1}_{\mathbb{G}_1^{i-1}}, P_1, \mathbf{1}_{\mathbb{G}_1^{N-i}})$), $\mathbb{A}^* = (\mathbf{a}_1^*, \ldots, \mathbf{a}_N^*)$ is the canonical basis of $\mathbb{V}^*$ (i.e., $\mathbf{a}_i^* = (\mathbf{1}_{\mathbb{G}_2^{i-1}}, P_2, \mathbf{1}_{\mathbb{G}_2^{N-i}})$) and*

$$e \colon \mathbb{V} \times \mathbb{V}^* \to \mathbb{G}_T$$
$$(\mathbf{x} = (X_1, \ldots, X_N), \mathbf{y} = (Y_1, \ldots, Y_N)) \mapsto \prod_i e(X_i, Y_i)$$

(note the abuse of notation) is a pairing, i.e., $\mathbf{x} = \mathbf{1}_{\mathbb{G}_1^N}$ if $e(\mathbf{x}, \cdot)$ is the $1_{\mathbb{G}_T}$ map, and $\forall a, b \in \mathbb{Z}_p, \mathbf{x} \in \mathbb{V}, \mathbf{y} \in \mathbb{V}^*, e(\mathbf{x}^a, \mathbf{y}^b) = e(\mathbf{x}, \mathbf{y})^{ab}$.

Note that for all $1 \leq i, j \leq N, e(\mathbf{a}_i, \mathbf{a}_j^*) = e(P_1, P_2)^{\delta_{ij}}$, with δ_{ij} being the Kronecker delta, i.e., $\delta_{ij} = 1$ if $i = j$, and otherwise 0.

Let $\mathcal{G}_{\text{dpvs}}(1^\lambda, \mathcal{PP}_\mathbb{G}, N)$ denote an algorithm that takes as an input a security parameter 1^λ, the description $\mathcal{PP}_\mathbb{G}$ of a pairing group $(p, \mathbb{G}_1 = \langle P_1 \rangle, \mathbb{G}_2 = \langle P_2 \rangle, \mathbb{G}_T, e)$ and an integer N, and outputs the description $\mathcal{PP}_\mathbb{V}$ of a DPVS $(p, \mathbb{V}, \mathbb{V}^*, \mathbb{G}_T, \mathbb{A}, \mathbb{A}^*, e)$.

A.4 Okamoto–Takashima Adaptively-Secure CP-ABE Scheme

Let $\mathcal{G}_{\mathrm{ob}}(1^\lambda, \mathbf{n} = (d; n_1, \ldots, n_d))$ be a dual-orthonormal-basis generator which proceeds as follows:

1. it generates a pairing group $\mathcal{PP}_{\mathbb{G}} = (p, \mathbb{G}_1 = \langle P_1 \rangle, \mathbb{G}_2 = \langle P_2 \rangle, \mathbb{G}_T, e) \leftarrow \mathcal{G}_{\mathrm{bpg}}(1^\lambda)$, a value $\psi \in_R \mathbb{Z}_p^*$, and sets $N_0 = 5$ and $N_k = 3n_k + 1$ for $1 \leq k \leq d$
2. for $0 \leq k \leq d$, it generates a Dual Pairing Vector Space (DPVS) (see Appendix A.3) $\mathcal{PP}_{\mathbb{V}_k} = (p, \mathbb{V}_k, \mathbb{V}_k^*, \mathbb{G}_T, \mathbb{A}_k, \mathbb{A}_k^*, e) \leftarrow \mathcal{G}_{\mathrm{dpvs}}(1^\lambda, \mathcal{PP}_{\mathbb{G}}, N_k)$, generates a matrix $\mathbf{X}_k \in_R \mathrm{GL}_{N_k}(\mathbb{Z}_p)$, and computes $\mathbf{V}_k = \psi \left(\mathbf{X}_k^{\mathrm{T}}\right)^{-1}$. Let $\mathbf{M}_{\mathbb{A}_k}$ and $\mathbf{M}_{\mathbb{A}_k^*}$ respectively denote the diagonal matrices $\mathrm{diag}(P_1) \in \mathbb{G}_1^{N_k \times N_k}$ and $\mathrm{diag}(P_2) \in \mathbb{G}_2^{N_k \times N_k}$. Generator $\mathcal{G}_{\mathrm{ob}}$ computes $\mathbf{B}_k = \begin{bmatrix} \mathbf{b}_{k,1} \\ \vdots \\ \mathbf{b}_{k,n} \end{bmatrix} = \mathbf{X}_k \mathbf{M}_{\mathbb{A}_k} \in \mathbb{G}_1^{N_k \times N_k}$ and $\mathbf{B}_k^* = \begin{bmatrix} \mathbf{b}_{k,1}^* \\ \vdots \\ \mathbf{b}_{k,n}^* \end{bmatrix} = \mathbf{V}_k \mathbf{M}_{\mathbb{A}_k^*} \in \mathbb{G}_2^{N_k \times N_k}$ with $\mathbf{b}_{k,i} = (\mathbf{e}_i \cdot \mathbf{X}_k) \mathbf{M}_{\mathbb{A}_k} = \begin{bmatrix} P_1^{\mathbf{X}_{k,i,1}} \ldots P_1^{\mathbf{X}_{k,i,N_k}} \end{bmatrix}$ and $\mathbf{b}_{k,i}^* = (\mathbf{e}_i \cdot \mathbf{V}_k) \mathbf{M}_{\mathbb{A}_k^*} = \begin{bmatrix} P_2^{\mathbf{V}_{k,i,1}} \cdots P_2^{\mathbf{V}_{k,i,N_k}} \end{bmatrix}$
3. it computes $G_T = e(P_1, P_2)^\psi$, sets $\mathcal{PP}_{\mathbf{n}} = \{\mathcal{PP}_{\mathbb{V}_k}\}_{0 \leq k \leq d}$, and eventually outputs $(G_T, \mathcal{PP}_{\mathbf{n}}, \{\mathbf{B}_k, \mathbf{B}_k^*\}_{0 \leq k \leq d})$.

Notice that for all $i, k, G_T = e(\mathbf{b}_{k,i}, \mathbf{b}_{k,i}^*)$. Indeed,

$$e(\mathbf{b}_{k,i}, \mathbf{b}_{k,i}^*) = e\left(\prod_j \mathbf{a}_j^{\mathbf{X}_{ij}}, \prod_l \mathbf{a}_l^{*\mathbf{V}_{il}}\right) = \prod_{j,l} e(\mathbf{a}_j, \mathbf{a}_l^*)^{\mathbf{X}_{ij}\mathbf{V}_{il}}$$
$$= \prod_{j,l} e(P_1, P_2)^{\delta_{jl}\mathbf{X}_{ij}\mathbf{V}_{il}} = e(P_1, P_2)^\psi = G_T.$$

Consider now the (monotone-span-program) Okamato–Takashima CP-ABE scheme [25, Section 7.1] in the case $d = 2$. The access structure associated to a ciphertext is determined by two 2-dimensional vectors $\mathbf{v}_1$ and $\mathbf{v}_2$. A pair of attributes (a pair of $\mathbb{Z}_p$-lines) represented by a pair of vectors $(\mathbf{x}_1, \mathbf{x}_2)$ is "accepted" by the structure if and only if $\mathbf{x}_k \cdot \mathbf{v}_k^{\mathrm{T}} = 0$: that is, the structure specifies two accepted $\mathbb{Z}_p$-lines. Their CP-ABE scheme is defined as follows:

$\mathsf{Setup}(1^\lambda, \mathbf{n} = (2; n_1 = 2, n_2 = 2)) \rightarrow (pk, msk)$: generate an orthonormal basis $(G_T, \mathcal{PP}_{\mathbf{n}}, \{\mathbf{B}_k, \mathbf{B}_k^*\}_{0 \leq k \leq 2}) \leftarrow \mathcal{G}_{\mathrm{ob}}(1^\lambda, \mathbf{n})$, set $\hat{\mathbf{B}}_0 = \begin{bmatrix} \mathbf{b}_{0,1} \\ \mathbf{b}_{0,3} \\ \mathbf{b}_{0,5} \end{bmatrix}, \hat{\mathbf{B}}_0^* = \begin{bmatrix} \mathbf{b}_{0,1}^* \\ \mathbf{b}_{0,3}^* \\ \mathbf{b}_{0,4}^* \end{bmatrix}$, $\hat{\mathbf{B}}_k = \begin{bmatrix} \mathbf{b}_{k,1} \\ \mathbf{b}_{k,2} \\ \mathbf{b}_{k,7} \end{bmatrix}, \hat{\mathbf{B}}_k^* = \begin{bmatrix} \mathbf{b}_{k,1}^* \\ \mathbf{b}_{k,2}^* \\ \mathbf{b}_{k,5}^* \\ \mathbf{b}_{k,6}^* \end{bmatrix}$ for $k = 1, 2$, and then output $pk = (G_T, \mathcal{PP}_{\mathbf{n}}, \{\hat{\mathbf{B}}_k\}_{k=0,\ldots,2})$, $msk = (pk, \{\hat{\mathbf{B}}_k^*\}_{k=0,\ldots,2})$

KeyDer($msk, \mathcal{A} = \{\mathbf{x}_{k=1,2} \in \mathbb{Z}_p^2 \colon \mathbf{x}_{k,1} = 1\}) \to sk_{\mathcal{A}}$: generate $\alpha, y_0 \in_R \mathbb{Z}_p$, $\mathbf{y}_k \in_R \mathbb{Z}_p^2$ for $k = 1, 2$, compute vectors $\mathbf{k}_0^* = \left[\alpha\ 0\ 1\ y_0\ 0\right] \mathbf{B}_0^* = \left[\alpha\ 1\ y_0\right] \hat{\mathbf{B}}_0^*$, $\mathbf{k}_k^* = \left[\alpha \mathbf{x}_k\ \mathbf{0}_{\mathbb{Z}_p^2}\ \mathbf{y}_k\ 0\right] \mathbf{B}_k^* = \left[\alpha \mathbf{x}_k\ \mathbf{y}_k\right] \hat{\mathbf{B}}_k^*$, and output secret key $sk_{\mathcal{A}} = (pk, \mathcal{A}, \{\mathbf{k}_k^*\}_{k=0,\ldots,2})$

Enc($pk, M \in \mathbb{G}_T, \mathbb{S} = (\mathbf{v}_1, \mathbf{v}_2)) \to ct$: generate uniformly random values a_1, a_2, ζ, η_0, η_k, θ_k for $k = 1, 2$ from $\mathbb{Z}_p$, computes $a = a_1 + a_2$,

$$\mathbf{c}_0 = \left[-a\ 0\ \zeta\ 0\ \eta_0\right] \mathbf{B}_0 = \left[-a\ \zeta\ \eta_0\right] \hat{\mathbf{B}}_0,$$
$$\mathbf{c}_k = \left[a_k \mathbf{e}_{k,1} + \theta_k \mathbf{v}_k\ \mathbf{0}_{\mathbb{Z}_p^4}\ \eta_1\right] \mathbf{B}_k = \left[a_k \mathbf{e}_{k,1} + \theta_k \mathbf{v}_k\ \eta_1\right] \hat{\mathbf{B}}_k \quad \text{for } k = 1, 2,$$
$$c_3 = G_T^{\zeta} M,$$

and output $ct = (\mathbb{S}, \mathbf{c}_0, \mathbf{c}_1, \mathbf{c}_2, c_3) \in \mathbb{Z}_p^4 \times \mathbb{G}_1^{19} \times \mathbb{G}_T$ and

Dec($sk_{\mathcal{A}}, ct) \to M$: output $M = c_3 / e(\mathbf{c}_0, \mathbf{k}_0^*) e(\mathbf{c}_1, \mathbf{k}_1^*) e(\mathbf{c}_2, \mathbf{k}_2^*)$ if the key and the ciphertext can be properly parsed and $\mathbf{x}_k \cdot \mathbf{v}_k^{\mathrm{T}} = 0 \mod p$ for $k = 1, 2$, and otherwise output $\perp$.

Since attribute vectors have their first coordinates set to 1, (the second coordinates specify the slopes of the $\mathbb{Z}_p$-lines accepted by the access structure), the attribute set may be identified with $\mathbb{Z}_p^2$. Okamoto and Takashima proved that this CP-ABE scheme is correct and adaptively payload-hiding against chosen-message attacks under the DLIN assumption over $\mathbb{G}_1$ and $\mathbb{G}_2$ [25, Theorem 2].

References

1. Au, M.H., Susilo, W., Mu, Y.: Constant-size dynamic k-TAA. Cryptology ePrint Archive, Report 2008/136 (2008). http://eprint.iacr.org/2008/136
2. Backes, M., Müller-Quade, J., Unruh, D.: On the necessity of rewinding in secure multiparty computation. In: Vadhan, S.P. (ed.) TCC 2007. LNCS, vol. 4392, pp. 157–173. Springer, Heidelberg (2007). https://doi.org/10.1007/978-3-540-70936-7_9
3. Baldimtsi, F., et al.: Accumulators with applications to anonymity-preserving revocation. In: EuroS&P (2017)
4. Barak, B.: How to go beyond the black-box simulation barrier. In: 42nd FOCS, pp. 106–115. IEEE Computer Society Press, October 2001
5. Boneh, D., Boyen, X.: Short signatures without random oracles and the SDH assumption in bilinear groups. J. Cryptol. **21**(2), 149–177 (2008)
6. Boneh, D., Boyen, X., Shacham, H.: Short group signatures. In: Franklin, M. (ed.) CRYPTO 2004. LNCS, vol. 3152, pp. 41–55. Springer, Heidelberg (2004). https://doi.org/10.1007/978-3-540-28628-8_3
7. Boneh, D., Franklin, M.: An efficient public key traitor tracing scheme. In: Wiener, M. (ed.) CRYPTO 1999. LNCS, vol. 1666, pp. 338–353. Springer, Heidelberg (1999). https://doi.org/10.1007/3-540-48405-1_22
8. Boneh, D., Sahai, A., Waters, B.: Fully collusion resistant traitor tracing with short ciphertexts and private keys. In: Vaudenay, S. (ed.) EUROCRYPT 2006. LNCS, vol. 4004, pp. 573–592. Springer, Heidelberg (2006). https://doi.org/10.1007/11761679_34

9. Boneh, D., Zhandry, M.: Multiparty key exchange, efficient traitor tracing, and more from indistinguishability obfuscation. In: Garay, J.A., Gennaro, R. (eds.) CRYPTO 2014, Part I. LNCS, vol. 8616, pp. 480–499. Springer, Heidelberg (2014). https://doi.org/10.1007/978-3-662-44371-2_27
10. Camenisch, J., Drijvers, M., Lehmann, A.: Anonymous attestation using the strong Diffie Hellman assumption revisited. Cryptology ePrint Archive, Report 2016/663 (2016). http://eprint.iacr.org/2016/663
11. Camenisch, J., Krenn, S., Lehmann, A., Mikkelsen, G.L., Neven, G., Pedersen, M.Ø.: Formal treatment of privacy-enhancing credential systems. In: Dunkelman, O., Keliher, L. (eds.) SAC 2015. LNCS, vol. 9566, pp. 3–24. Springer, Cham (2016). https://doi.org/10.1007/978-3-319-31301-6_1
12. Camenisch, J., Shoup, V.: Practical verifiable encryption and decryption of discrete logarithms. In: Boneh, D. (ed.) CRYPTO 2003. LNCS, vol. 2729, pp. 126–144. Springer, Heidelberg (2003). https://doi.org/10.1007/978-3-540-45146-4_8
13. Chor, B., Fiat, A., Naor, M.: Tracing traitors. In: Desmedt, Y.G. (ed.) CRYPTO 1994. LNCS, vol. 839, pp. 257–270. Springer, Heidelberg (1994). https://doi.org/10.1007/3-540-48658-5_25
14. Cramer, R., Shoup, V.: A practical public key cryptosystem provably secure against adaptive chosen ciphertext attack. In: Krawczyk, H. (ed.) CRYPTO 1998. LNCS, vol. 1462, pp. 13–25. Springer, Heidelberg (1998). https://doi.org/10.1007/BFb0055717
15. Dwork, C., Lotspiech, J.B., Naor, M.: Digital signets: self-enforcing protection of digital information (preliminary version). In: 28th ACM STOC, pp. 489–498. ACM Press, May 1996
16. Guruswami, V., Indyk, P.: Expander-based constructions of efficiently decodable codes. In: 42nd FOCS, pp. 658–667. IEEE Computer Society Press, October 2001
17. Kiayias, A., Tang, Q.: How to keep a secret: leakage deterring public-key cryptosystems. In: Sadeghi, A.-R., Gligor, V.D., Yung, M. (eds.) ACM CCS 2013, pp. 943–954. ACM Press, New York (2013)
18. Kiayias, A., Tang, Q.: Traitor deterring schemes: using bitcoin as collateral for digital content. In: Ray, I., Li, N., Kruegel, C. (eds.) ACM CCS 2015, pp. 231–242. ACM Press, New York (2015)
19. Kiayias, A., Yung, M.: Traitor tracing with constant transmission rate. In: Knudsen, L.R. (ed.) EUROCRYPT 2002. LNCS, vol. 2332, pp. 450–465. Springer, Heidelberg (2002). https://doi.org/10.1007/3-540-46035-7_30
20. Kurosawa, K., Desmedt, Y.: Optimum traitor tracing and asymmetric schemes. In: Nyberg, K. (ed.) EUROCRYPT 1998. LNCS, vol. 1403, pp. 145–157. Springer, Heidelberg (1998). https://doi.org/10.1007/BFb0054123
21. Lewko, A.: Tools for simulating features of composite order bilinear groups in the prime order setting. Cryptology ePrint Archive, Report 2011/490 (2011). http://eprint.iacr.org/2011/490
22. Nakanishi, T., Fujii, H., Hira, Y., Funabiki, N.: Revocable group signature schemes with constant costs for signing and verifying. In: Jarecki, S., Tsudik, G. (eds.) PKC 2009. LNCS, vol. 5443, pp. 463–480. Springer, Heidelberg (2009). https://doi.org/10.1007/978-3-642-00468-1_26
23. Nishimaki, R., Wichs, D., Zhandry, M.: Anonymous traitor tracing: how to embed arbitrary information in a key. In: Fischlin, M., Coron, J.-S. (eds.) EUROCRYPT 2016, Part II. LNCS, vol. 9666, pp. 388–419. Springer, Heidelberg (2016). https://doi.org/10.1007/978-3-662-49896-5_14

24. Okamoto, T., Takashima, K.: Homomorphic encryption and signatures from vector decomposition. In: Galbraith, S.D., Paterson, K.G. (eds.) Pairing 2008. LNCS, vol. 5209, pp. 57–74. Springer, Heidelberg (2008). https://doi.org/10.1007/978-3-540-85538-5_4
25. Okamoto, T., Takashima, K.: Fully secure functional encryption with general relations from the decisional linear assumption. In: Rabin, T. (ed.) CRYPTO 2010. LNCS, vol. 6223, pp. 191–208. Springer, Heidelberg (2010). https://doi.org/10.1007/978-3-642-14623-7_11

Sharing the LUOV: Threshold Post-quantum Signatures

Daniele Cozzo[1] and Nigel P. Smart[1,2(✉)]

[1] imec-COSIC, KU Leuven, Leuven, Belgium
{daniele.cozzo,nigel.smart}@kuleuven.be
[2] University of Bristol, Bristol, UK

Abstract. We examine all of the signature submissions to Round-2 of the NIST PQC "competition" in the context of whether one can transform them into threshold signature schemes in a relatively straight forward manner. We conclude that all schemes, except the ones in the MQ family, have significant issues when one wishes to convert them using relatively generic MPC techniques. The lattice based schemes are hampered by requiring a mix of operations which are suited to both linear secret shared schemes (LSSS)-based and garbled circuits (GC)-based MPC techniques (thus requiring costly transfers between the two paradigms). The Picnic and SPHINCS+ algorithms are hampered by the need to compute a large number of hash function queries on secret data. Of the nine submissions the two which would appear to be most suitable for using in a threshold like manner are Rainbow and LUOV, with LUOV requiring less rounds and less data storage.

1 Introduction

Ever since the late 1980s there has been interest in threshold cryptography [13]. Constructions for threshold signatures have received particular interest; these allow the distribution of signing power to several authorities using different access structures. For example, the 1990s and early 2000s saw work on threshold RSA signatures [11,48] and DSA/EC-DSA signatures [19,38].

The case of distributed EC-DSA signature gathered renewed interest [8,16–18,33–35], due to applications in blockchain. Furthermore, general distributed solutions for decryption and signature operations are attracting more attention, such as the recent NIST workshop in this space[1].

However, solutions for distributed RSA and EC-DSA signatures do not provide resistance against quantum computers. Thus if one is to provide threshold signatures in a post-quantum world, then one needs to examine how to "thresholdize" post-quantum signatures. The techniques to create threshold versions of RSA and EC-DSA signatures make strong use of the number-theoretic structure

[1] https://www.nist.gov/news-events/events/2019/03/nist-threshold-cryptography-workshop-2019.

M. Albrecht (Ed.): IMACC 2019, LNCS 11929, pp. 128–153, 2019.
https://doi.org/10.1007/978-3-030-35199-1_7

of such schemes; however this structure is not available for many of the proposed post-quantum signature algorithms.

The NIST post-quantum cryptography "competition" aims to find replacement public key encryption and signature algorithms for the current number-theoretic solutions based on integer factoring and discrete logarithms. There are nine solutions which have been selected for the second round of this process, and these can be divided into four classes, according to the underlying hard problem on which they are based:

- Lattice-based: there are three submissions in this category; Dilithium [37], qTesla [4], and Falconal [44]
- Hash-based: there is one submission in this category, SPHINCS+ [27].
- MPC-in-the-Head (MPC-in-H)-based: here there is also one submission Picnic [51].
- Multivariate Quadratic-based: here we have four submissions GeMSS [5], LUOV [3], MQDSS [47] and Rainbow [14].

Generic MPC techniques are now developed enough that one could simply apply them here in a black-box manner, but not all proposed post-quantum schemes would be equally suited to this approach. In this work we therefore examine the proposed post-quantum signature schemes submitted to Round 2 of the NIST project in the context of this problem.

Our Contribution: Looking only at the underlying assumptions one would suspect Picnic would be the algorithm which best lends itself to being converted into an MPC threshold version; after all it is based on MPC-in-the-Head. However, closer examination reveals that this is not the case. Indeed we examine all the post-quantum signature submissions from the point of view of whether one can easily turn them into threshold versions. It turns out that the ones which are most amenable to "thresholdizing" are those based on the MQ family of problems, in particular Rainbow and LUOV, see Table 1 for a summary.

In this version we discuss in detail Crystal-Dilithium, Picnic, SPHINCS+, Rainbow and LUOV. In the full version we cover the other Round-2 submissions.

The main issues with lattice-based techniques are the need to perform rejection sampling, which means intermediate values need to be kept secret until after the rejection sampling has been accomplished, and they need to be compared to given constants. This results in a number of operations suitable for garbled circuit operation to be performed. However, the rest of the algorithms require operations which are linear. Thus one has both a large number of garbled circuits (GC)-based operations to perform, as well as conversions to-and-from linear secret sharing scheme (LSSS) based representations to help mitigate the number of GC operations needed. This conversion turns out to be a major bottleneck.

Picnic on the other hand requires the signer to privately evaluate a set of PRFs and then reveal the associated keys for a given subset of the PRFs when obtaining the challenge value. This means that the PRFs need to be securely

Table 1. Summary of NIST Round 2 post-quantum signature schemes

Name	Underlying assumption	Issues in obtaining a threshold variant
Dilithium	Lattice	A mix of linear operations (suitable for LSSS-based MPC) and non-linear operations (suitable for GC-based MPC) requires costly transferring between the two representations. We expect this to take around 12 s to execute
qTesla	Lattice	A mix of linear operations (suitable for LSSS-based MPC) and non-linear operations (suitable for GC-based MPC) requires costly transferring between the two representations. We expect to take at least 16 s to execute
Falcon	Lattice	A mix of linear operations (suitable for LSSS-based MPC) and non-linear operations (suitable for GC-based MPC) requires costly transferring between the two representations. We expect to take at least 6 s to execute
Picnic	MPC-in-H	Applying SHA-3 to obtain the necessary randomness in the views of the MPC parties
SPHINCS+	Hash	Applying SHA-3 to obtain the data structures needed
MQDSS	MQ	Applying SHA-3 to obtain the commitments
GeMSS	MQ	Potential for threshold implementation, implementation is tricky due to need to extract polynomial roots via Berlekamp algorithm
Rainbow	MQ	Simple LSSS based MPC solution which requires 12 rounds of communication. We expect a signature can be generated in around three seconds
LUOV	MQ	Simple LSSS based MPC solution which requires 6 rounds of communication. We expect a signature can be generated in just over a second

evaluated in a threshold manner. Since the PRFs used in Picnic are not specifically designed to be evaluated in this way one is left applying generic MPC techniques. These become very expensive due to the gate counts of the underlying PRFs specified by the proposal.

The hash-based signature scheme SPHINCS+ has a similar issue in that one needs to securely evaluate the underlying hash functions in a threshold manner; this again leads to huge gate counts.

One of the MQ schemes (MQDSS) also requires to evaluate hash functions on secret data, and so suffers from the same problems as the previous schemes. One MQ scheme (GeMSS) is a plausible candidate to be implemented via MPC, but any implementation would be highly non-trivial due to the need to evaluate Berlekamps' algorithm to extract roots of a univariate polynomial.

This leaves us with the two remaining MQ schemes (LUOV and Rainbow). These are based on the FDH signature construction and hence the main issue is implementing generic MPC for arithmetic circuits over the given finite fields. This would lead to threshold variants relatively easily. In this case Rainbow requires more rounds of interaction than LUOV, on the other hand Rainbow requires less secure multiplications. In addition, LUOV requires less data to store the shared secret key state.

In all of our analyses we try to give a best estimate as to the *minimum* amount of time a threshold implementation would take for each of the candidates. This is assuming the current best run-times for evaluating the SHA-3 internal function in an MPC system. These estimates are given for the schemes at the security level denoted Level 3 by NIST; when a scheme does not have parameters at Level 3 we pick the set at Level 4. Level 3 corresponds to the difficulty of breaking AES-192 on a quantum computer. This provides less than 192-bits of quantum security (due to Grover's algorithm), and hence seems a reasonable compromise since current (classical) security levels are usually picked to be equivalent to AES-128.

2 Preliminaries

In this section we define various notations and notions which will be needed in future sections. In particular we describe the underlying MPC systems which we will assume 'as given'. In particular our focus will be on MPC solutions which are actively secure (with abort) against static corruptions.

We assume that all involved parties are probabilistic polynomial time Turing machines. Given a positive integer n, we denote by $[n]$ the set $\{1, \ldots, n\}$. We let $x \leftarrow X$ denote the uniformly random assignment to the variable x from the set X, assuming a uniform distribution over X. We also write $x \leftarrow y$ as shorthand for $x \leftarrow \{y\}$. If $\mathcal{D}$ is a probability distribution over a set X, then we let $x \leftarrow \mathcal{D}$ denote sampling from X with respect to the distribution $\mathcal{D}$. If A is a (probabilistic) algorithm then we denote by $a \leftarrow A$ the assignment of the output of A where the probability distribution is over the random tape of A.

Signature Schemes: Digital signature schemes which are defined by

Definition 2.1. *A* digital signature scheme *is given by a tuple of probabilistic algorithms* $(\mathsf{KeyGen}, \mathsf{Sign}, \mathsf{Verify})$*:*

- $\mathsf{KeyGen}\left(1^{\lambda}\right)$ *is a randomized algorithm that takes as input the security parameter and returns the public key* pk *and the private key* sk.
- $\mathsf{Sign}\left(\mathsf{sk}, \mu\right)$ *is a randomized signing algorithm that takes as inputs the private key and a message and returns a signature on the message.*
- $\mathsf{Verify}\left(\mathsf{pk}, (\sigma, \mu)\right)$ *is a deterministic verification algorithm that takes as inputs the public key and a signature* σ *on a message* μ *and outputs a bit which is equal to one if and only if the signature on* μ *is valid.*

Correctness and security (EU-CMA) are defined in the usual manner, and all signature scheme submitted to NIST in Round-2 meet this security definition.

A threshold signature scheme with respect to some access structure Γ is defined by the following definition

Definition 2.2. *A* threshold digital signature scheme *is given by a tuple of probabilistic algorithms* (KeyGen, Sign, Verify)*:*

- $\mathsf{KeyGen}\left(1^\lambda\right)$ *is a randomized algorithm that takes as input the security parameter and returns the public key* pk *and a set of secret keys* sk_i*, one secret key for every party in the access structure.*
- $\mathsf{Sign}(\mathsf{sk}, \mu)$ *is a randomized signing algorithm that takes as inputs a* qualified set *of private keys and a message and returns a signature on the message.*
- $\mathsf{Verify}(\mathsf{pk}, (\sigma, \mu))$ *is a deterministic verification algorithm that takes as inputs the public key and a signature* σ *on a message* μ *and outputs a bit which is equal to one if and only if the signature on* μ *is valid.*

Informally security for a threshold signature scheme is that an unqualified set of parties cannot produce a signature. An additional requirement is often that a valid output signature should be indistinguishable from the signature produced by the signing algorithm of equivalent the non-thresholdized scheme with the same public key.

Multi-party Computation: As mentioned above we consider actively secure (with abort) MPC for static adversaries in this work. We assume a generic black

---

The ideal functionality $\mathcal{F}_{\mathsf{MPC}}$ for MPC over $\mathbb{F}_q$

Initialize: On input $(init, \mathbb{K})$ from all parties, the functionality stores $(domain, \mathbb{K})$.

Input: On input $(input, P_i, varid, x)$ from P_i and $(input, P_i, varid, ?)$ from all other parties, with $varid$ a fresh identifier, the functionality stores $(varid, x)$.

Random: On input of $(random, varid)$, if $varid$ is not present in memory then the functionality picks a random value in $\mathbb{K}$ and stores it in $varid$.

Add: On command $(add, varid_1, varid_2, varid_3)$ from all parties, if $varid_1$ and $varid_2$ are present in memory and $varid_3$ is not then the functionality retrieves $(varid_1, x)$ and $(varid_2, y)$ and stores $(varid_3, x + y)$. Otherwise does nothing.

Multiply: On input $(multiply, varid_1, varid_2, varid_3)$ from all parties, if $varid_1$ and $varid_2$ are present in memory and $varid_3$ is not then retrieve $(varid_1, x)$ and $(varid_2, y)$ and store $(varid_3, x \cdot y)$. Otherwise do nothing.

Output: On input $(output, varid, i)$ from all honest parties, if $varid$ is present in memory then retrieve $(varid, y)$ and output it to the environment. It then waits for an input from the environment. If this input is Deliver then y is output to all players if $i = 0$, or y is output to party i if $i \neq 0$. If the input is not equal to Deliver then $\perp$ is output to all parties.

Fig. 1. The ideal functionality $\mathcal{F}_{\mathsf{MPC}}$ for MPC over $\mathbb{F}_q$

box for MPC, abstracted in the functionality $\mathcal{F}_{\mathsf{MPC}}$ of Fig. 1, which defines MPC over a given finite field $\mathbb{K}$ (or indeed sometimes a finite ring). When instantiating this abstract MPC functionality with state-of-the-art protocols one needs to consider aspects such as the access structure, the field used $\mathbb{K}$, and the computational/communication model. We summarize many of the state-of-the-art of MPC protocols in Table 2.

Table 2. Summary of main practical MPC protocols

Protocol name	Field $\mathbb{K}$	Access structure	Pre-Proc model	Rounds	Example reference
SPDZ family	Large $\mathbb{K}$	Full threshold	✓	$\approx \mathsf{depth}(C)$	[12]
Tiny-OT family	$\mathbb{F}_2$	Full threshold	✓	$\approx \mathsf{depth}(C)$	[32,42]
SPDZ-2k	$(\mathbb{Z}/2^k\mathbb{Z})$	Full threshold	✓	$\approx \mathsf{depth}(C)$	[9]
n-party GC family	$\mathbb{F}_2$	Full threshold	✓	constant	[25,50]
General Q2	Any	Q2	✓	$\approx \mathsf{depth}(C)$	[49]
General Q2	Any	Q2	–	$\approx \mathsf{depth}(C)$	[7]
Special GC	$\mathbb{F}_2$	$(t, n) = (1, 3)$	–	constant	[41]

In terms of access structures the main ones in use are full threshold (for example in the SPDZ protocol family [12]) and Q2-access structures (which includes standard threshold protocols for which $t < n/2$). A Q2-access structure is one in which the union of no two unqualified sets cover the entire set of players. In terms of the field $\mathbb{K}$ for evaluating binary circuits one usually utilizes MPC over $\mathbb{K} = \mathbb{F}_2$. However, for some applications (in particular the MQ signature schemes considered later) it is better to take $\mathbb{K}$ to be a specific finite field taylored to the application. Some protocols are tailored to very specific access structures (for example using threshold $(t, n) = (1, 3)$).

The functionality has a command to produce random values in $\mathbb{K}$. This can always be achieved using interaction (via the input command), however, for LSSS based protocols in the Q2 setting (with small numbers of parties) such a command can be executed for free using a PRSS.

To make it simpler to describe MPC protocols, in what follows we use the notation $\langle x \rangle$ for $x \in \mathbb{K}$ to denote a value x stored in the MPC engine (the reader can think of this as $\langle x \rangle$ being the secret sharing of x). The MPC functionality Fig. 1 enables one to compute $\langle x \rangle + \langle y \rangle$, $\lambda \cdot \langle x \rangle$ and $\langle x \rangle \cdot \langle y \rangle$. We extend this notation to vectors and matrices of elements in $\mathbb{K}$ in the obvious manner.

In terms of computational model we find the set of practical MPC protocols divided into distinct classes. In some protocols there is a function-independent offline phase, and then a fast offline phase. Other protocols have no offline phase but then pay a small cost in the online phase. In some instances one can choose which class one wants to be in. For example, for Q2 access structures over a general finite field one can use the protocol of [49] if one wishes to utilize an offline phase, but the protocol in [7] if ones wants to avoid the offline phase (but have a slightly slower "online" phase). Although the performance of [7] degrades considerably for small finite fields, whereas that of [49] does not degrade at all (however [49]'s offline phase performance degrades if the finite field is small). Note [7] is expressed in terms of $t < n/2$ threshold adversaries but it can be trivially extended to any Q2 access structure.

The communication model also plays a part with protocols based on Garbled Circuits using a constant number of rounds, whereas protocols based on linear-secret sharing (LSSS) requiring rounds (roughly) proportional to the circuit depth. In all cases the total amount of communication, and computation, is roughly proportional to the number of multiplication gates with the arithmetic circuit over $\mathbb{K}$ which represents the function to be computed[2]. The LSSS based protocols cost (essentially) one round of communication per each multiplicative depth, and communication cost linear in the number of multiplication gates.

It is possible to mix GC and LSSS based MPC in one application, and pass between the two representations. For special access structures one can define special protocols for this purpose, see [30] for example. For general access structures one can apply the technique of doubly-authenticated bits (so called daBits) introduced in [46]. This latter method however comes with a cost. Assuming we are converting ℓ bit numbers, then not only does one need to generate (at least) ℓ daBits, but when transforming from the LSSS to the GC world one requires to evaluate a garbled circuit with roughly $3 \cdot \ell$ AND gates. The more expensive part is actually computing the daBits themselves. The paper [30] claims a cost of 0.163 ms per daBit, for fields of size 2^{128}. Whilst the fields used in the lattice based post-quantum signature algorithms are much smaller (of the order of 2^{20}) we use the same estimate[3].

Of course one could execute bitwise operations in an LSSS-based MPC for an odd modulus q using the methods described in [6,10]. But these are generally slower than performing the conversion to a garbled circuit representation and then performing the garbled circuit based operation. Especially when different operations are needed to be performed on the same bit of data.

MPC of Standard Functionalities: A number of the signature schemes submitted to NIST make use of keyed (and unkeyed) symmetric functions which need to be applied in any threshold implementation to secret data. Thus any threshold implementation will need to also enable a threshold variant of these symmetric primitives. Here we recap, from the literature, the best timings and costs one can achieve for such primitives. We will use these estimates to examine potential performance in our discussions which follow.

In [30] the authors give details, also within the context of thresholdizing a NIST PQC submission (this time an encryption algorithm), of an MPC

[2] This is not strictly true as one often does not represent the function as a pure arithmetic circuit. But as a first order approximation this holds.

[3] Arithmetic modulo a prime of size 2^{20} is faster, but on the other hand one then has to perform more work to obtain the same level of active security.

implementation of the SHA-3 round function (within the context of executing the KMAC algorithm). The round function f for SHA-3 requires a total of 38,400 AND gates, and using a variant of the three party honest majority method from [41], the authors were able to achieve a latency of 16 ms per execution of f, for a LAN style setting. This equates to around 0.4 µs per AND gate. Any actual application of SHA-3 requires multiple executions of the round function f; depending on how much data is being absorbed and how much is being squeezed.

In [50] give timings for a full-threshold garbled circuit based evaluation of various functions. Concentrating on the case of AES and SHA-256, and three party protocols, the authors obtain a latency of 95 ms (13 ms online) for the 6800 AND gate AES circuit, and 618 ms (111 ms online) for the 90825 AND gate SHA-256 circuit, again for a LAN setting. These times correspond to between 1 µ and 2 µs per AND gate, thus the three party full threshold setting is slightly slower than the honest majority setting (as is to be expected).

For general arithmetic circuits the estimates in [7] in the honest majority three party setting for a 61-bit prime field give a time of 826 ms to evaluate a depth 20 circuit with one million multiplication gates, in a LAN setting. Thus we see that when using arithmetic circuits over such a finite field one can deal we obtain a similar throughput, in terms of multiplications per second, as one has when looking at binary circuits using garbled circuit techniques. However, the fields are of course much larger and we are performing more "bit operations" per second in some sense.

However, the protocol in [7] for 61-bit prime fields assumes a statistical security of 61-bits, i.e. the adversary can pass one of the checks on secure multiplications probability $1/2^{61} = 1/\#\mathbb{K}$. For smaller finite fields the performance degrades as one needs to perform more checks. A back-of-the-envelope calculation reveals one would expect a throughput of roughly 250,000 multiplications per second in the case of $\mathbb{F}_{2^8}$.

Whilst these times are comparing apples and oranges, they do give an order of magnitude estimate of the time needed to compute these functions. Generally speaking, one is looking for operations which involve a few number of multiplications. Almost all NIST signature submissions make use of SHAKE-256, as a randomness expander, or hash-function. The SHAKE-256 algorithm is based on SHA-3. Recall that an application of SHA-3/SHAKE-256 on an input of ℓ_i bits, to produce an output of ℓ_o bits, will require (ignoring issues when extra padding results in more blocks being processed) a total of

$$\mathsf{rounds}(\ell_i, \ell_o) := \left\lceil \frac{\ell_i}{1088} \right\rceil + \left\lceil \frac{\ell_o}{1088} \right\rceil - 1$$

iterations of the main Keccak round function, since the rate of SHA3-256 is $r = 1088$ bits. In what follows we use the current best MPC evaluation time for this function (of 16 ms from [30]) to obtain an estimate of how a specific application of SHAKE-256/SHA-3 will take.

3 Lattice Based Schemes

Lattice based signature schemes have a long history, going back to the early days of lattice based cryptography. Early examples such as NTRUSign [26] were quickly shown to be insecure due to each signature leaking information about the private key [21]. In recent years following the work of Lyubashevsky [36] the standard defence against such problems has been to adopt a methodology of Fiat–Shamir-with-aborts. All of the three lattice based submissions to NIST Round-2 follow this paradigm. However, we shall see that this means that they are all not particularly tuned to turning into threshold variants; for roughly the same reasons; although Falcon is slightly better in this regard. In all our lattice descriptions we will make use of a ring R_q, which one can take to be the cyclotomic ring $\mathbb{Z}[X]/(X^N+1)$ reduced modulo q.

3.1 Crystals-Dilithium

The Dilithium [37] signature scheme is based on the Module-LWE problem. The secret key is two "short" vectors (s_1, s_2) with $s_1 \in R_q^l$ and $s_2 \in R_q^k$, and the public key is a matrix $A \in R_q^{k \times l}$ and a vector $t \in R_q^k$ such that $t = A \cdot s_1 + s_2$. The high-level view of the signature algorithm for signing a message μ is given in Fig. 2, for precise details see the main Dilithium specification. We do not discuss the optimization in the Dilithium specification of the MakeHint function, to incorporate this will involve a few more AND gates in our discussion below. To aid exposition we concentrate on the basic signature scheme above. At the Level-3 security level the main parameters are set to be $N = \deg R_q = 256$, $q = 2^{23} - 2^{13} + 1$ and $(k, l) = (5, 4)$. There are a number of other parameters which are derived from these, in particular $\gamma_1 = (q-1)/16$ and $\gamma_2 = (q-1)/32$.

The Dilithium Signature Algorithm

1. $z \leftarrow \perp$
2. While $(z = \perp)$ do
   - (a) Sample a "short" $y \in R_q^l$ with $\|y\|_\infty \leq \gamma_1$.
   - (b) $v \leftarrow A \cdot y$.
   - (c) Let w be the topbits of v.
   - (d) $c \leftarrow H(\mu \| w) \in R_q$.
   - (e) $z \leftarrow y + c \cdot s_1$.
   - (f) If z or the lower bits of $v - c \cdot s_2$ are too big then set $z \leftarrow \perp$.
3. Return $\sigma \leftarrow (z, c)$.

Fig. 2. The Dilithium signature algorithm

From our point of view we see that Dilithium is a signature scheme in the Fiat-Shamir-with-aborts family. If we did not have the while-loop in the signature algorithm, then the values of z and $v - c \cdot s_2$ would leak information to the adversary. Thus it is clear that *any* distributed version of Dilithium signatures should maintain the secrecy of these intermediate values. Only values which pass the size check and are output as a valid signature, can be revealed.

The parameters of the algorithm are selected so that the probability of needing two iterations of the while loop is less than one percent. Thus we can concentrate on the case of only executing one iteration of the loop. We assume that the secret key has been shared in an LSSS scheme over $\mathbb{F}_q$ which supports one of the MPC algorithms for LSSS schemes discussed in the introduction. The main issue with Dilithium, and indeed all the other lattice based schemes, is that some operations are best suited to linear secret sharing based MPC over the underlying finite field $\mathbb{F}_q$ (e.g. lines 2b and 2e), whereas some are more suited to evaluation using a binary circuit (e.g. lines 2c and 2d). The main cost therefore comes in switching between the two types of MPC systems. For full details see the full version.

3.2 qTesla

qTesla is a signature scheme based on the ring-LWE problem, and like the previous one it too uses rejection sampling to avoid information leakage from signatures. The secret key is a pair $s, e \in R_q$, where e is small and R_q has degree N. The public key is a value $a \in R_q$ in R_q along with the value $t = a \cdot s + e$. The high level view of the signature algorithm is given in Fig. 3. For the Level-3 security level we have the parameters $N = \deg R_q = 1024$, $B = 2^{21} - 1$, $q = 8404993$, and $d = 22$.

The qTesla Signature Algorithm

1. $z \leftarrow \perp$.
2. While $(z = \perp)$ do
   (a) Sample a "short" $y \in R_q$ with $\|y\|_\infty \leq B$.
   (b) $b \leftarrow [a \cdot y]_M \in R_q$.
   (c) $c \leftarrow H(b \| G(\mu)) \in R_q$.
   (d) $z \leftarrow y + s \cdot c$.
   (e) If z is not short or $a \cdot y - e \cdot c$ is not "well-rounded" then set $z \leftarrow \perp$.
3. Return $\sigma \leftarrow (z, c)$.

Fig. 3. The qTesla signature algorithm

The operation $[x]_M$ applied to $x \in R_q$ provides a rounding operation akin to taking the top $(\log_2 q - d)$ bits of x in each coefficient. We define $[x]_M = (x \pmod q) - x \pmod{2^d})/2^d$ where the two modular operations perform a centered reduction (i.e. in the range $(-q/2, \ldots, q/2]$. The values of $[x]_M$ are stored in one byte per coefficient.

The function G is a hash function which maps messages to 512 bit values, and H is a hash function which maps elements in $R_q \times \{0,1\}^{512}$ to a 512-bit string c, which is then treated as a trinary polynomial. The functions H and G being variants of SHAKE-256 (or SHAKE-128 for the low security variants). Again much like the Dilithium, due to the rejection sampling the computation of y and the evaluation of H must be done in shared format.

The analysis of the cost of qTesla in a threshold system follows much the same as the analysis done above for Crystals-Dilithium, thus we leave the full discussion to the full version.

3.3 Falcon

Falcon [44] is another lattice based scheme, and the only one to have NTRU-like public keys. It is based on the GPV framework [20]. The private key is a set of four "short" polynomials $f, g, F, G \in R_q$ such that $f \cdot G = g \cdot F$ in the ring R_q. The public key is the polynomial $h \leftarrow g/f$, which will have "large" coefficients in general. Associated to the private key is the private lattice basis in the FFT domain

$$\overline{B} = \begin{pmatrix} \mathsf{FFT}(g) & -\mathsf{FFT}(f) \\ \mathsf{FFT}(G) & -\mathsf{FFT}(F) \end{pmatrix}.$$

There is also a data structure T, called the *Falcon Tree* associated to the private key, which can be thought of as a set of elements in the ring R_q. At the Level-3 security level one has $N = \deg R_q = 768$ and $q = 18435$. A high level view of the signature algorithm is given in Fig. 4.

The Falcon Signature Algorithm

1. $r \leftarrow \{0,1\}^{320}$.
2. $c \leftarrow H(r\|\mu)$.
3. $t \leftarrow (\mathsf{FFT}(c), \mathsf{FFT}(0)) \cdot \overline{B}^{-1}$.
4. $z \leftarrow \perp$.
5. While $(z = \perp)$ do
   (a) $z \leftarrow \mathsf{ffSampling}_n(t, T)$.
   (b) $s \leftarrow (t - z) \cdot \overline{B}$.
   (c) If s is not short then set $z = \perp$.
6. $(s_1, s_2) \leftarrow \mathsf{FFT}^{-1}(s)$.
7. $s \leftarrow \mathsf{Compress}(s_2)$.
8. Return $\sigma = (r, s)$.

Fig. 4. The Falcon signature algorithm

Again, we assume that the secret key has been shared in an LSSS scheme over $\mathbb{F}_q$, and we go through each line in turn. The specification document says that how the discrete Gaussian is evaluated is "arbitrary" and "outside the scope of this specification" [44], bar needing to be close in terms of the Rényi divergence. However, a Gaussian sampler is defined within the specification, [44, Section 4.4], for use in the reference implementation. It turns out that this sampler is the main impediment to producing an efficient threshold version of Falcon. We leave the details to the full version.

4 MPC-in-the-Head Based Scheme

The MPC-in-the-Head paradigm for producing zero-knowledge proofs was developed in [28]. The prover, to prove knowledge of a preimage x of some function $\Phi(x) = y$ (where Φ and y are public), simulates an MPC protocol to compute the functionality Φ, with the input x shared among the simulated parties. The prover executes the protocol (in it's head), then commits to the state and the transcripts of all players. Then it sends the verifier these commitments and randomly opens a (non-qualified) subset of them (the precise subset is chosen by the verifier). The verifier checks that the simulated protocol was correctly executed using the opened values. If everything is consistent, it then accepts the statement that the prover knows x, otherwise it rejects. Typically, the proof has to repeated several times in order to achieve high security. Clearly to obtain a signature scheme we apply the Fiat–Shamir transform so that the verifier's choices are obtained by hashing the commitments with the message.

4.1 Picnic

Picnic is a digital signature scheme whose security entirely relies on the security only of symmetric key primitives, in particular the security of SHA-3 and a low-complexity block cipher called Low-MC [1]. The core construction is a zero-knowledge proof of knowledge of a preimage for a one-way function $y = f_k(x)$, where f is the Low-MC block cipher, the values x and y are public and the key k is the value being proved. Using the Fiat–Shamir and MPC-in-the-Head paradigms we obtain a signature scheme with public key (x, y) and private key k.

The Picnic Signature Algorithm (High Level)

1. Generate $3 \cdot T$ secret seeds $\mathsf{seed}_{i,j}$ for $i = 0, \ldots, T-1$ and $j = 0, 1, 2$.
2. Using a KDF expand the $\mathsf{seed}_{i,j}$ values to a sequence of random tapes $\mathsf{rand}_{i,j}$.
3. For each i use the three random tapes $\mathsf{rand}_{i,j}$ as the random input to a player P_j for an MPC protocol to evaluate the function $f_k(x)$.
4. Commit to the resulting views, and hash them with a message to obtain a set of challenges $e_0, \ldots, e_t \in \{0, 1, 2\}$.
5. Reveal all seeds $\mathsf{seed}_{i,j}$ bar seed_{i,e_i}.

Fig. 5. The Picnic signature algorithm (high level)

In this paper we concentrate on Picnic-1, but a similar discussion also applies to the Picnic-2 construction. The specific proof system that implements the MPC-in-the-Head for Picnic-1 is ZKBoo++ [1], which is itself an extension of the original ZKBoo framework from [22]. The simulated MPC protocol is between three parties, and is executed at a high level as in Fig. 5.

In our analysis we will ignore any hashing needed to produce commitments and the challenge, and we will simply examine the operation of the key derivation in step 2 of Fig. 5. It is clear that in the MPC-in-the-Head paradigm the seeds need to be kept secret until the final reveal phase, thus the derivation of the random tape from the seed needs to be done in a secure manner in a any threshold implementation.

In Picnic the precise method used to derive the random tape is to use

$$\mathsf{rand}_{i,j} = \mathsf{KDF}\left(H_2\left(\mathsf{seed}_{i,j}\right) \|\mathsf{salt}\|i\|j\|\mathsf{length}\right)$$

where

- The seeds are S bits long.
- The salt is 256 bits long.
- The integers i, j and length are encoded as 16-bit values.
- The output length (length), of the KDF, is $n+3\cdot r\cdot s$ when $j=0,1$ and $3\cdot r\cdot s$ when $j=2$.

We again concentrate on the NIST security Level-3, which is instantiated with the parameters $S=n=192$, $T=329$, $s=10$ and $r=30$. The hash function H_2 is SHAKE-256 based with an output length of 384 bits. Thus the execution of H_2 requires only two executions of the SHA-3 round function. Each KDF operation is also cheap, requiring either two or three rounds. The problem is we need to execute these operations so many times. The total number of executions of the round function of SHA-3 is given by

$$\begin{aligned} T\cdot\Big(2 + 2\cdot \mathsf{rounds}(384+256+32+32, n+3\cdot r\cdot s) \\ + \mathsf{rounds}(384+256+32+32, 3\cdot r\cdot s)\Big) \\ = 329\cdot\Big(2+2\cdot\mathsf{rounds}(704,1092)+\mathsf{rounds}(704,900)\Big) \\ = 329\cdot(2+2\cdot(3-1)+(2-1)) = 2303. \end{aligned}$$

Thus given our estimate of a minimum of 16 ms for a SHA-3 round execution in MPC we see that even this part of the Picnic algorithm is expected to take $16\cdot 3290$ ms, i.e. 37 s!

5 Hash Based Scheme

Hash based signatures have a long history going back to the initial one-time signature scheme of Lamport [31]. A more efficient variant of the one-time signature attributed to Winternitz is given in [40], where a method is also given to turn the one-time signatures into many-time signatures via so-called Merkle-trees. The problem with these purely Merkle tree based constructions is that they are strictly a stateful signature scheme. The signer needs to maintain a changing state between each signature issued, and the number of signatures able to be issued is bounded as a function of the height of the Merkle tree.

To overcome these issues with state the SPHINCS signature scheme was introduced in 2015 [2], which itself builds upon ideas of Goldreich elaborated in [24], and going back to [23]. In the SPHINCS construction messages are still signed by Winternitz one-time signatures, but the public keys of such signatures are then authenticated via another (similar) structure called a Forest of Random Subsets (which is itself based on earlier work in [45]).

5.1 SPHINCS+

The only hash based signature scheme to make it into the second round of the NIST competition is SPHINCS+ [27]. We refer the reader to the design document [27] for a full description. For our purposes we recall that messages are signed using Winternitz one-time signatures which are then authenticated using a FORS tree. The parameters which are of interest to us are: n the security parameter in bytes, w a parameter related to the underlying Winternitz signature, h the height of the hypertree, d the number of layers in the hypertree, k the number of trees in a FORS, t the number of leaves in a FORS tree. From these two length functions are defined[4]

$$\mathsf{len}_1 = \left\lceil \frac{8 \cdot n}{\log_2 w} \right\rceil, \qquad \mathsf{len}_2 = \left\lfloor \frac{\log(\mathsf{len}_1 \cdot (w-1))}{\log w} \right\rfloor + 1, \qquad \text{and} \qquad \mathsf{len} = \mathsf{len}_1 + \mathsf{len}_2.$$

The scheme uses (essentially) four hash functions labelled **F**, **H**, **PRF** and T_{len}. The function **F** is used as the main function in the Winternitz signature scheme, as well as the FORs signature. The underlying expansion the secret key into secret keys of the trees is done via the function **PRF**. The function **H** is used to construct a root of the associated binary trees, where as T_{len} is used to compress the len Winternitz public key values into a single n-bit value for use as a leaf in the Merkle tree. The evaluation of the **F** and **PRF** calls within a single signature needs to be performed on secret data, even though eventually some of the input/outputs become part of the public signature. The calls to **H** and T_{len} appear to be able to be performed on public data, and will not concern us here.

In what follows we concentrate on the SHAKE-256 based instantiation of SPHINCS+ (to be comparable with other signature schemes in this paper). In the SHAKE instantiation the execution of the function **F** requires two calls to the underlying SHA-3 permutation, where as **H** requires three calls to the underlying SHA-3 permutation, and **PRF** requires one call to the SHA-3 permutation.

[4] Note the definition of len_1 in the specification is wrong and need correcting which we do below.

To sign a message requires $k \cdot t + d \cdot w \cdot \mathsf{len} \cdot 2^{h/d}$ calls to $\mathbf{F}$ and $k \cdot t + d \cdot \mathsf{len} \cdot 2^{h/d} + 1$ calls to **PRF**. When instantiated with the parameters at the NIST Level-3 security level (for fast signing) we have $(n, w, h, d, k, t) = (24, 16, 66, 22, 33, 256)$. Leading to $\mathsf{len}_1 = 48$, $\mathsf{len}_2 = 3$ and $\mathsf{len} = 51$. This leads to a grand total of 152064 calls to **F** and 17425 calls to **PRF**. This leads to a total of 321553 calls to the SHA-3 internal permutation which need to be performed securely. With current best garbled circuit implementations this on its own would require 85 min to execute. Of course a complete threshold implementation would take longer as we have not looked at other aspects of the signature algorithm.

6 MQ Based Schemes

The history of MQ cryptography, is almost as old as that of hash-based signatures. The first MQ based scheme was presented in 1988 [39]. In terms of signature schemes based on the MQ problem, the original works were due to Patarin and were given the name "Oil and Vinegar" [29,43]. The basic idea is to define a set of multivariate quadratic equations (hence the name MQ) $P : \mathbb{F}_q^m \longrightarrow \mathbb{F}_q^n$ and the hard problem is to invert this map, where q is a power of two[5]. The intuition being that inverting this map is (for a general quadratic map P) is an instance of the circuit satisfiability problem, which is known to be NP-Complete.

In three of the NIST candidate signature schemes the function P is generated so that there is an efficient trapdoor algorithm which allows the key holder to invert the map P using the secret key. In such situations the secret key is usually chosen to be two affine transforms $S : \mathbb{F}_q^n \longrightarrow \mathbb{F}_q^n$ and $T : \mathbb{F}_q^m \longrightarrow \mathbb{F}_q^m$, plus an easy to invert map $P' : \mathbb{F}_q^m \longrightarrow \mathbb{F}_q^n$ consisting of quadratic functions (note any function can be expressed in terms of quadratic functions by simple term rewriting). Then the public map is defined by $P = S \circ P' \circ T$. Of course the precise definition of this construction implies that one is not using a generic circuit satisfiability problem. However, for specific choices of P', q, n and m the construction is believed to provide a trapdoor one-way function.

Given we have a trapdoor one way function the standard Full Domain Hash construction gives us a signature scheme. Namely to sign a message μ, the signer hashes μ to an element $y \in \mathbb{F}_q^m$ and then exhibits a preimage of y under P as the signature s. To verify the signature the verifier simply checks that $P(s) = y$. Note, that many preimages can exist for y under P, thus every message could have multiple valid signatures. From this basic outline one can define a number of signature scheme depending on the definition of the "central map" P'. All of the Round-2 MQ based signature schemes, with the exception of MQDSS, follow this general construction method. In this version we discuss Rainbow and LUOV, leaving MQDSS and GeMSS to the full version.

[5] To enable comparison with the NIST submissions we use the same notation in the sections which follow as used in the submissions. We hope this does not confuse the reader.

Method for solving $\langle A\rangle \cdot \langle \mathbf{x}\rangle = \langle \mathbf{b}\rangle$

Input: $\langle A\rangle, \langle \mathbf{b}\rangle$ with $A \in F_q^{n\times n}$ and $\mathbf{b} \in \mathbb{F}_q^n$.
Output: $\perp$ or $\langle \mathbf{x}\rangle$ such that $A \cdot \mathbf{x} = \mathbf{b}$.

1. Generate a random $n \times n$ shared matrix $\langle R\rangle$. Generation of random elements in LSSS based MPC systems can *usually* be done for free in the online phase with no communication costs.
2. Compute $\langle T\rangle \leftarrow \langle A\rangle \cdot \langle R\rangle$. This requires one round of communication and the secure multiplication of n^3 elements.
3. Open the matrix $\langle T\rangle$. This requires one round of communication.
4. In the clear, compute T^{-1}. If $\det(T) = 0$ then we return $\perp$.
5. Compute $\langle \mathbf{t}\rangle \leftarrow T^{-1} \cdot \langle \mathbf{b}\rangle$, which is a linear operation and hence free.
6. Finally compute $\langle \mathbf{x}\rangle \leftarrow \langle R\rangle \cdot \langle \mathbf{t}\rangle = \langle R \cdot T^{-1} \cdot \mathbf{b}\rangle = \langle R \cdot R^{-1} \cdot A^{-1} \cdot \mathbf{b}\rangle = \langle A^{-1} \cdot \mathbf{b}\rangle$. This step requires one round of communication, and n^2 secure multiplications.

Fig. 6. Method for solving $\langle A\rangle \cdot \langle \mathbf{x}\rangle = \langle \mathbf{b}\rangle$

Inverting Linear Systems in MPC. Before proceeding we present a trick which enables us to efficiently solve linear systems in an LSSS based MPC system. We will use this in our analysis of two of the submissions, so we present it here first. Suppose we have a shared $n \times n$ matrix $\langle A\rangle$ over $\mathbb{F}_q$ and an n-dimensional shared vector $\langle \mathbf{b}\rangle$. We would like to determine $\langle \mathbf{x}\rangle$ such that $A \cdot \mathbf{x} = \mathbf{b}$. We do this using the algorithm in Fig. 6. This algorithm either returns the secret shared solution or the $\perp$ symbol. This latter either happens because the input matrix has determinant zero, or the random matrix used in the algorithm has determinant zero (which occurs with probability $1/q$). The algorithm requires a total of three rounds of communication and $n^3 + n^2$ secure multiplications.

6.1 Rainbow

The Rainbow signature scheme can be seen as a multilayer version of the original UOV. In its original version, the number of layers is determined by a parameter u. For $u = 1$ this is just the basic UOV scheme, whereas the candidate submission chooses $u = 2$. As described earlier we pick for the secret key two affine transforms $\mathcal{S} : \mathbb{F}_q^m \to \mathbb{F}_q^m$ and $\mathcal{T} : \mathbb{F}_q^n \to \mathbb{F}_q^n$. Along with a function $\mathcal{F}$, called the central map, which can be defined by quadratic functions. The public key is then the map $\mathcal{P} = \mathcal{S} \circ \mathcal{F} \circ \mathcal{T} : \mathbb{F}_q^n \to \mathbb{F}_q^m$.

In the Rainbow specification the affine maps $\mathcal{S}$ and $\mathcal{T}$ are chosen to be given by matrix multiplication by upper triangular matrices S and T. This means that the inverse matrices S^{-1} and T^{-1} are also upper triangular. In particular the inverses are selected to have the following block form

$$S^{-1} = \begin{pmatrix} \mathbf{1}_{o_1} & S_{o_1\times o_2} \\ \mathbf{0}_{o_2\times o_1} & \mathbf{1}_{o_2} \end{pmatrix} \quad \text{and} \quad T^{-1} = \begin{pmatrix} \mathbf{1}_{v_1} & T_{v_1\times o_1} & T'_{v_1\times o_2} \\ \mathbf{0}_{o_2\times v_1} & \mathbf{1}_{o_1} & T''_{o_1\times o_2} \\ \mathbf{0}_{o_2\times v_1} & \mathbf{0}_{o_2\times o_1} & \mathbf{1}_{o_2} \end{pmatrix}$$

where $S_{a\times b}$ etc. denotes a matrix of dimension $a \times b$, $\mathbf{0}_{a\times b}$ denotes the zero matrix of dimension $a \times b$ and $\mathbf{1}_a$ denotes the identity matrix of dimension a.

To define the central map we define three constants (v_1, o_1, o_2), which at the Level-3 security level are chosen to be $(68, 36, 36)$. From these we define further parameters given by $v_2 = v_1 + o_1, n = v_3 = v_2 + o_2$ and $m = o_1 + o_2$. Note this means that $n = v_1 + m$. We then define the sets $V_i = \{1, \ldots, v_i\}$ and $O_i = \{v_i + 1, \ldots, v_{i+1}\}$, for $i = 1, 2$, which will be referred to as the vinegar (resp. oil) variables of the ith layer.

The Rainbow central map $\mathcal{F} : \mathbb{F}_q^n \to \mathbb{F}_q^m$ can then be defined by the set of m quadratic polynomials $f^{(v_1+1)}, \ldots, f^{(n)}$ having the form

$$f^{(k)} = \begin{cases} \sum_{i,j\in V_1, i\leq j} \alpha_{ij}^{(k)} x_i \cdot x_j + \sum_{i\in V_1} \sum_{j\in O_1} \beta_{ij}^{(k)} x_i \cdot x_j & k = v_1 + 1, \ldots, v_2, \\ \sum_{i,j\in V_2, i\leq j} \alpha_{ij}^{(k)} x_i \cdot x_j + \sum_{i\in V_2} \sum_{j\in O_2} \beta_{ij}^{(k)} x_i \cdot x_j & k = v_2 + 1, \ldots, n, \end{cases}$$

where the coefficients $\alpha_{i,j}^{(k)}, \beta_{i,j}^{(k)}$ are randomly chosen from $\mathbb{F}_q$.

Inversion of the Rainbow central map

Input: The central map $\mathcal{F} = \left(f^{(v_1+1)}, \ldots, f^{(n)}\right)$, a vector $\mathbf{x} \in \mathbb{F}_q^m$
Output: A vector $\mathbf{y} \in \mathbb{F}_q^n$ satisfying $\mathcal{F}(\mathbf{y}) = \mathbf{x}$.

1. Choose random values for the variables $\hat{y}_1, \ldots, \hat{y}_{v_1}$ and substitute these values into the polynomials $f^{(v_1+1)}, \ldots, f^{(v_2)}$.
2. Perform Gaussian elimination on the system
$$f^{(v_1+1)}(\hat{y}_1, \ldots, \hat{y}_{v_1}, y_{v_1+1}, \ldots, y_n) = x_{v_1+1}$$
$$\vdots$$
$$f^{(v_2)}(\hat{y}_1, \ldots, \hat{y}_{v_1}, y_{v_1+1}, \ldots, y_n) = x_{v_2}$$
to obtain the values of the variables $y_{v_1+1}, \ldots, y_{v_2}$, say $\hat{y}_{v_1+1}, \ldots, \hat{y}_{v_2}$.
3. Substitute the values $\hat{y}_{v_1}, \ldots, \hat{y}_{v_2}$ into the polynomials $f^{(v_2+1)}, \ldots, f^{(n)}$.
4. Perform Gaussian elimination on the system
$$f^{(v_2)}(\hat{y}_1, \ldots, \hat{y}_{v_2}, y_{v_2+1}, \ldots, y_n) = x_{v_2+1}$$
$$\vdots$$
$$f^{(n)}(\hat{y}_1, \ldots, \hat{y}_{v_2}, y_{v_2+1}, \ldots, y_n) = x_n$$
to obtain the values of the variables $y_{v_2+1}, \ldots, y_n$, say $\hat{y}_{v_2+1}, \ldots, \hat{y}_n$.
5. Return $\mathbf{y} = (\hat{y}_1, \ldots, \hat{y}_n)$.

Fig. 7. Inversion of the Rainbow central map

Signature generation (for the EUF-CMA scheme) is done by the steps

1. Compute the hash value $\mathbf{h} \leftarrow H\left(H\left(\mu\right) \| \mathsf{salt}\right) \in \mathbb{F}_q^m$, where μ is the message, salt is a random l-bit string and $H : \{0, 1\} \to \mathbb{F}_q^m$ is an hash function.

2. Compute $\mathbf{x} \leftarrow S^{-1} \cdot \mathbf{h} \in \mathbb{F}_q^m$,
3. Compute a preimage $\mathbf{y} \in \mathbb{F}_q^n$ of $\mathbf{x}$ under the central map $\mathcal{F}$.
4. Compute $\mathbf{z} \leftarrow T^{-1} \cdot \mathbf{y} \in \mathbb{F}_q^n$.
5. Output $(\mathbf{z}, \mathsf{salt})$.

The main work of the signing algorithm occurs in step 3 which is done using the method described in Fig. 7. As all the components $f^{(k)}$ of the central map are homogeneous polynomials of degree two, we can represent them using matrices. Specifically, substituting the first layer of the vinegar variables $\hat{y}_1, \ldots, \hat{y}_{v_1}$ into the first o_1 components of $\mathcal{F}$ is equivalent to computing

$$(\hat{y}_1, \ldots, \hat{y}_{v_1}) \cdot \begin{pmatrix} \alpha_{11}^{(k)} & \cdots & \alpha_{1v_1}^{(k)} \\ & \ddots & \vdots \\ & & \alpha_{v_1v_1}^{(k)} \end{pmatrix} \cdot \begin{pmatrix} \hat{y}_1 \\ \vdots \\ \hat{y}_{v_1} \end{pmatrix}$$

$$+ (\hat{y}_1, \ldots, \hat{y}_{v_1}) \cdot \begin{pmatrix} \beta_{1v_1+1}^{(k)} & \cdots & \beta_{1v_2}^{(k)} \\ \vdots & & \vdots \\ \beta_{v_1v_1+1}^{(k)} & \cdots & \beta_{v_1v_2}^{(k)} \end{pmatrix} \cdot \begin{pmatrix} y_{v_1+1} \\ \vdots \\ y_{v_2} \end{pmatrix},$$

for $k = v_1 + 1, \ldots, v_2$. With a similar equation occurring for the second layer, namely,

$$(\hat{y}_1, \ldots, \hat{y}_{v_2}) \cdot \begin{pmatrix} \alpha_{11}^{(k)} & \cdots & \alpha_{1v_2}^{(k)} \\ & \ddots & \vdots \\ & & \alpha_{v_1v_2}^{(k)} \end{pmatrix} \cdot \begin{pmatrix} \hat{y}_1 \\ \vdots \\ \hat{y}_{v_2} \end{pmatrix}$$

$$+ (\hat{y}_1, \ldots, \hat{y}_{v_2}) \cdot \begin{pmatrix} \beta_{1v_2+1}^{(k)} & \cdots & \beta_{1n}^{(k)} \\ \vdots & & \vdots \\ \beta_{v_2v_2+1}^{(k)} & \cdots & \beta_{v_2n}^{(k)} \end{pmatrix} \cdot \begin{pmatrix} y_{v_2+1} \\ \vdots \\ y_n \end{pmatrix}$$

for $k = v_2+1, \ldots, n$. We call the $2 \cdot (n - v_1)$ matrices in these equations $A^{(k)}, B^{(k)}$. So (abusing notation a bit) we write the equations as $f_k = \hat{\mathbf{y}} \cdot A^{(k)} \cdot \hat{\mathbf{y}}^\mathsf{T} + \hat{\mathbf{y}} \cdot A^{(k)} \cdot \mathbf{y}^\mathsf{T}$. Recall at any stage we know $\hat{\mathbf{y}}$ and we want to solve the equations for $\mathbf{y}$.

It is clear that signing, given $\mathbf{h} \in \mathbb{F}_q^m$, is a purely algebraic operation over $\mathbb{F}_q$. Thus it can be accomplished in a threshold manner via any LSSS based MPC protocol which evaluates arithmetic circuits over $\mathbb{F}_q$, such as those mentioned earlier. We assume that the private key already exists in secret shared form, i.e. we have sharings $\langle S^{-1} \rangle$, $\langle T^{-1} \rangle$, $\langle \alpha_{i,j}^{(k)} \rangle$ and $\langle \beta_{i,j}^{(k)} \rangle$.

We now look at the signing algorithm's complexity from the point of view of MPC evaluation. We count both the multiplicative depth, as well the number of secure $\mathbb{F}_q$ multiplications needed.

- The first two operations of the signing algorithm come for free, as they are a public hash calculation, followed by the linear operation $\langle \mathbf{x} \rangle \leftarrow \langle S^{-1} \rangle \cdot \mathbf{h}$.
- We then need to evaluate the map $\mathcal{F}$. This executes in a number of phases.
  - We generate shared values $\langle y_1 \rangle, \ldots, \langle y_{v_1} \rangle$ at random.
  - We then translate the first level of o_2 equations $f_k = \mathbf{x}^{(k)}$ for $k = v_1 + 1, \ldots, v_2$ into a linear system to solve for $\mathbf{y}_1 = (y_{v_1+1}, \ldots, y_{v_2})$. Thus we find an $o_1 \times o_1$ shared matrix $\langle C \rangle$ and a vector $\langle \mathbf{b} \rangle$ such that $C \cdot \mathbf{y}_1 = \mathbf{b}$. To *determine* this system requires two rounds of communication and

$$\begin{aligned} M_1 &= o_1 \cdot \left(\sum_{i=1}^{v_1} i + v_1 + (v_2 - v_1) \cdot v_1 \right) \\ &= o_1 \cdot (v_1 \cdot (v_1 + 1)/2 + v_1 + o_1 \cdot v_1) \\ &= o_1 \cdot (o_1 \cdot v_1 + v_1 \cdot (v_1 + 3)/2) = 175032 \end{aligned}$$

    secure multiplications.
  - Solving our linear system to obtain $\langle \mathbf{y}_1 \rangle$ using our method from Fig. 6, which requires three rounds of communication and $M_2 = o_1^3 + o_1^2 = 47952$ secure multiplications.
  - We then repeat with the second layer of the central map, which requires

$$\begin{aligned} M_3 &= o_2 \cdot \left(\sum_{i=1}^{v_2} i + v_2 + (n - v_2) \cdot v_2 \right) \\ &= o_2 \cdot (v_2 \cdot (v_2 + 1)/2 + v_2 + o_2 \cdot v_2) \\ &= o_2 \cdot (o_2 \cdot v_2 + v_2 \cdot (v_2 + 3)/2) = 335088. \end{aligned}$$

    secure multiplications, and another two rounds of communication.
  - We now solve this new linear system to obtain $\langle \mathbf{y}_2 \rangle$ using Fig. 6. Again this requires three rounds of communication and $M_4 = M_2$ secure multiplications.
- We then compute $\langle \mathbf{z} \rangle \leftarrow \langle T^{-1} \rangle \cdot \langle \mathbf{y} \rangle$. This requires one round of communication, and due to the special form of T^{-1} it requires $M_5 = v_1 \cdot (o_1 + o_2) + o_1 \cdot o_2 = 6192$ secure multiplications.
- Finally we need to open $\langle \mathbf{z} \rangle$ to obtain the signature in the clear which takes one round of communication.

In summary we require $2 + 3 + 2 + 3 + 1 + 1 = 12$ rounds of communication and $M_1 + M_2 + M_3 + M_4 + M_5 = 612216$ secure multiplications. Note the last two steps could be computed by opening the last o_2 variables (one round), and then computing $v_1 \cdot o_1 = 2448$ secure multiplications (one round), with another round of communication to open the first $v_1 + o_1$ variables. In practice we expect the extra round to be more costly than the extra multiplications.

If the above algorithm aborts, which can happen if the linear systems have zero determinant, or the random matrices in the trick to solve the linear systems also have zero determinant, then we simply repeat the signing algorithm again. The probability of an abort is bounded by $4/q$. The Rainbow specification uses

$q = 2^8$, thus we expect to need to repeat the signing process with probability about 1.5%. As mentioned in the introduction a LSSS based MPC protocol can process at least a 250,000 secure multiplications per second over the field $\mathbb{F}_{2^8}$ in the honest majority setting. Thus we expect an implementation of a threshold version of Rainbow to take around three seconds. A *major* disadvantage of this threshold variant of Rainbow is the need to store so much data in secret shared form, namely $\langle S^{-1}\rangle$, $\langle T^{-1}\rangle$, $\langle \alpha_{i,j}^{(k)}\rangle$ and $\langle \beta_{i,j}^{(k)}\rangle$.

6.2 LUOV

Here we present the LUOV signature scheme [3]. As we shall see this is almost entirely made up of low depth algebraic operations, making this scheme a prefect candidate for a threshold variant. The main non-linear component is a map $\mathcal{F} : \mathbb{F}_{2^r}^n \rightarrow \mathbb{F}_{2^r}^m$ with components $(f_1, \ldots, f_m)$ where

$$f_k(\mathbf{x}) = \sum_{i=1}^{v} \sum_{j=1}^{n} \alpha_{i,j,k} x_i x_j + \sum_{i=1}^{n} \beta_{i,k} x_i + \gamma_k,$$

with the coefficients $\alpha_{i,j,k}$, $\beta_{i,k}$ and γ_k being chosen from the field $\mathbb{F}_{2^r}$ by expanding a seed which forms part of the secret key. The integers n, m and v are related by the $v = n - m$. The elements in $\{x_1, \ldots, x_v\}$ are called the *vinegar* variables and that the ones in $\{x_{v+1}, \ldots, x_n\}$ are the *oil* variables. Note that the polynomials $f_1, \ldots, f_m$ contain no quadratic terms $x_i \cdot x_j$ with both x_i and x_j oil variables.

The central map $\mathcal{F}$ has to be secret and in order to hide the structure of $\mathcal{F}$ in the public key, one composes $\mathcal{F}$ with an affine map $\mathcal{T} : \mathbb{F}_{2^r}^n \rightarrow \mathbb{F}_{2^r}^m$. The public key consisting of composition $\mathcal{P} = \mathcal{F} \circ \mathcal{T} : \mathbb{F}_{2^r}^n \rightarrow \mathbb{F}_{2^r}^m$, and the private key being $\mathcal{P}$. At the Level-4 security level (Level-3 is not provided for LUOV) there are two sets of parameters $(r, m, v) = (8, 82, 323)$ and $(64, 61, 302)$.

The LUOV signature generation

Input: The message to be signed μ, and the data $\mathbf{C}, \mathbf{L}, \mathbf{Q}_1$ and $\mathbf{T}$.
Output: A signature $(\mathbf{s}, \mathsf{salt})$ on the message μ.

1. $\mathsf{salt} \leftarrow \{0,1\}^{16 \cdot 8}$.
2. $\mathbf{h} \leftarrow H(\mu \| \mathsf{0x00} \| \mathsf{salt})$
3. While no solution $\mathbf{s}'$ for the system $\mathcal{F}(\mathbf{s}) = \mathbf{h}$ is found
   (a) $\mathbf{v} \leftarrow \mathbb{F}_{2^r}^v$.
   (b) $\mathbf{RHS} \| \mathbf{LHS} \leftarrow \mathrm{BuildAugmentedMatrix}(\mathbf{C}, \mathbf{L}, \mathbf{Q}_1, \mathbf{T}, \mathbf{h}, \mathbf{v})$
   (c) If $\det(\mathbf{LHS}) \neq 0$ set $\mathbf{o} \leftarrow \mathbf{LHS}^{-1} \cdot \mathbf{RHS}$.
4. $\mathbf{s} \leftarrow \begin{pmatrix} \mathbf{1}_v & -\mathbf{T} \\ \mathbf{0} & \mathbf{1}_m \end{pmatrix} \cdot \begin{pmatrix} \mathbf{v} \\ \mathbf{o} \end{pmatrix}$
5. Return $(\mathbf{s}, \mathsf{salt})$.

Fig. 8. The LUOV signature generation

The LUOV public and private keys are in practice expanded from a random seed to define the actual data defining the various maps. However, for our threshold variant we assume this expansion has already happened and we have the following data values $\mathbf{C} \in \mathbb{F}_{2^r}^m$, $\mathbf{L} \in \mathbb{F}_{2^r}^{m \times n}$, $\mathbf{Q}_1 \in \mathbb{F}_{2^r}^{m \times (\frac{v(v+1)}{2} + v \cdot m)}$, and $\mathbf{T} \in \mathbb{F}_{2^r}^{v \times m}$, where $\mathbf{C}$, $\mathbf{L}$, and $\mathbf{Q}_1$ are public values and the matrix $\mathbf{T}$ is a secret parameter. In our threshold variant the parameter $\mathbf{T}$ will be held in secret shared form $\langle \mathbf{T} \rangle$. There is another matrix $\mathbf{Q}_2$, but that will not concern us as it is only related to verification. The signing algorithm is given in Fig. 8, and makes use of an auxilary algorithm given in Fig. 9 and a hash function $H : \{0,1\}^* \longrightarrow \mathbb{F}_{2^r}^m$. The auxiliary algorithm builds a linear system $\mathbf{LHS} \cdot \mathbf{o} = \mathbf{RHS}$ which we solve to obtain the oil variables.

BuildAugmentedMatrix

Input: The data $\mathbf{C}, \mathbf{L}, \mathbf{Q}_1$ and $\mathbf{T}$, the hashed message $\mathbf{h} \in \mathbb{F}_{2^r}^m$, and an assignment to the vinegar variables $\mathbf{v} \in \mathbb{F}_{2^r}^v$.
Output: $\mathbf{LHS} \| \mathbf{RHS} \in \mathbb{F}_{2^r}^{m \times m+1}$, the augmented matrix for $\mathcal{F}(\mathbf{v} \| \mathbf{o}) = \mathbf{h}$.

1. $\mathbf{RHS} \leftarrow \mathbf{h} - \mathbf{C} - \mathbf{L} \cdot \begin{pmatrix} \mathbf{v} \\ \mathbf{0} \end{pmatrix}$
2. $\mathbf{LHS} \leftarrow \mathbf{L} \cdot \begin{pmatrix} -\mathbf{T} \\ \mathbf{1}_m \end{pmatrix}$
3. For k from 1 to m
   (a) From $\mathbf{Q}_1$ build a public matrix $\mathbf{P}_{k,1} \in \mathbb{F}_2^{v \times v}$ (for details see the LUOV specification).
   (b) From $\mathbf{Q}_1$ build $\mathbf{P}_{k,2} \in \mathbb{F}_2^{v \times m}$ (again see the specification).
   (c) $\mathbf{RHS}[k] \leftarrow \mathbf{RHS}[k] - \mathbf{v}^\mathsf{T} \cdot \mathbf{P}_{k,1} \cdot \mathbf{v}$.
   (d) $\mathbf{F}_{k,2} \leftarrow -\left(\mathbf{P}_{k,1} + \mathbf{P}_{k,1}^\mathsf{T}\right) \cdot \mathbf{T} + \mathbf{P}_{k,2}$.
   (e) $\mathbf{LHS}[k] \leftarrow \mathbf{LHS}[k] + \mathbf{v} \cdot \mathbf{F}_{k,2}$.
4. Return $\mathbf{LHS} \| \mathbf{RHS}$

Fig. 9. BuildAugmentedMatrix

We now examine the above algorithm from the point of view of how one could implement it in a threshold manner given a generic MPC functionality for arithmetic circuits over $\mathbb{F}_{2^r}$. We assume that the secret matrix $\mathbf{T}$ is presented in secret shared form $\langle \mathbf{T} \rangle$. First note that the hash function is only called to compute the hash digest, which does not involve any shared input.

In the main while loop we assume the vinegar variables are generated in a shared manner in secret shared form $\langle \mathbf{v} \rangle$. Thus the main call to the BuiltAugmentedMatrix routine has two secret shared input $\langle \mathbf{T} \rangle$ and $\langle \mathbf{v} \rangle$, with the other values being public. The key lines in this algorithm then requiring secure multiplications are lines 3c and 3e to compute $\langle \mathbf{v} \rangle^\mathsf{T} \cdot \mathbf{P}_{k,1} \cdot \langle \mathbf{v} \rangle$ and $\langle \mathbf{v} \rangle \cdot \mathbf{F}_{k,2}$ respectively. The first of these takes v secure multiplications, whereas the latter requires $v \cdot m$

secure multiplications. Giving a total of $v \cdot m \cdot (m + 1)$ secure multiplications in total, which can be performed in parallel in one round of communication.

Solving the nonlinear system in line 3c is done using the method in Fig. 6, which requires three rounds of interaction and $m^3 + m^2$ secure multiplications. Note the probability that this procedure fails is roughly 2^{-r+1}, which can be essentially ignored for the parameter set with $r = 64$ and is under one percent for the parameter set with $r = 8$. But if it does fail, then we simply repeat the signing algorithm with new shared vinegar variables.

We then need to compute the matrix multiplication $\langle \mathbf{T} \rangle \cdot \langle \mathbf{o} \rangle$. However, note that we can save some secure multiplications by opening the oil variables $\mathbf{o}$ after the matrix inversion (since they are going to be released in any case in the clear). This will require anyway a round of interaction, but we are then able to save the $v \cdot m$ secure multiplications required to multiply $\mathbf{T}$ by $\mathbf{o}$, since that operation then becomes a linear operation. Finally, we open the resulting shared signature in order to transmit it in the clear. This requires one round of interaction.

Thus the overall cost of LUOV signature algorithm is $1+3+1+1 = 6$ rounds of interaction and $(m^3+m^2)+v \cdot m \cdot (m+1)$ secure multiplications. Choosing the Level-4 parameter set with $(r, m, v) = (8, 82, 323)$ this gives a total of 2756430 secure multiplications. Whereas for the parameter set $(r, m, v) = (64, 61, 302)$ this gives us 1372866 secure multiplications. In the former case, where arithmetic is over $\mathbb{F}_{2^8}$ and we expect to perform 250,000 secure multiplications per second, signing will take about 10 s. In the latter case, where arithmetic is over $\mathbb{F}_{2^{64}}$ and we expect to perform 1,000,000 secure multiplications per second, signing will take about 1.3 s. Another advantage of LUOV is that our threshold variant requires less storage of secret key material. We only need to store $\langle \mathbf{T} \rangle$ in secret shared form.

It is worth mentioning that at the NIST second PQC Standardization Conference a new attack has been presented [15] against LUOV. This attack crucially exploits the existence intermediate subfields in $\mathbb{F}_{2^r}$. Consequently, the authors proposed new sets of parameters to ensure the extension degree r is prime. Our expected run times above are likely to be similar for the new prime power finite fields. However, the other parameters are now a little smaller, resulting in the need for fewer secure multiplications. Thus we expect the new version of LUOV will be more efficient as a threshold variant.

Acknowledgments. This work has been supported in part by ERC Advanced Grant ERC-2015-AdG-IMPaCT, by the Defense Advanced Research Projects Agency (DARPA) and Space and Naval Warfare Systems Center, Pacific (SSC Pacific) under contracts No. N66001-15-C-4070 and FA8750-19-C-0502, and by the FWO under an Odysseus project GOH9718N. Any opinions, findings and conclusions or recommendations expressed in this material are those of the author(s) and do not necessarily reflect the views of the ERC, United States Air Force, DARPA or FWO. The authors would like to thank Cyprien Delpech de Saint Guilhem and Dragos Rotaru for helpful discussions whilst this work was carried out.

References

1. Albrecht, M.R., Rechberger, C., Schneider, T., Tiessen, T., Zohner, M.: Ciphers for MPC and FHE. In: Oswald, E., Fischlin, M. (eds.) EUROCRYPT 2015, Part I. LNCS, vol. 9056, pp. 430–454. Springer, Heidelberg (2015). https://doi.org/10.1007/978-3-662-46800-5_17
2. Bernstein, D.J., et al.: SPHINCS: practical stateless hash-based signatures. In: Oswald, E., Fischlin, M. (eds.) EUROCRYPT 2015, Part I. LNCS, vol. 9056, pp. 368–397. Springer, Heidelberg (2015). https://doi.org/10.1007/978-3-662-46800-5_15
3. Beullens, W., Preneel, B., Szepieniec, A., Vercauteren, F.: LUOV (2019). Submission to NIST PQC "competition" Round-2
4. Bindel, N., et al.: Lattice-based digital signature scheme qTESLA (2019). Submission to NIST PQC "competition" Round-2
5. Casanova, A., Faugère, J.C., Patarin, G.M.R.J., Perret, L., Ryckeghem, J.: GeMSS: a great multivariate short signature (2019). Submission to NIST PQC "competition" Round-2
6. Catrina, O., de Hoogh, S.: Improved primitives for secure multiparty integer computation. In: Garay, J.A., De Prisco, R. (eds.) SCN 2010. LNCS, vol. 6280, pp. 182–199. Springer, Heidelberg (2010). https://doi.org/10.1007/978-3-642-15317-4_13
7. Chida, K., et al.: Fast large-scale honest-majority MPC for malicious adversaries. In: Shacham, H., Boldyreva, A. (eds.) CRYPTO 2018, Part III. LNCS, vol. 10993, pp. 34–64. Springer, Cham (2018). https://doi.org/10.1007/978-3-319-96878-0_2
8. Cogliati, B., et al.: Provable security of (tweakable) block ciphers based on substitution-permutation networks. In: Shacham, H., Boldyreva, A. (eds.) CRYPTO 2018, Part I. LNCS, vol. 10991, pp. 722–753. Springer, Cham (2018). https://doi.org/10.1007/978-3-319-96884-1_24
9. Cramer, R., Damgård, I., Escudero, D., Scholl, P., Xing, C.: SPD $\mathbb{Z}_{2^k}$: efficient MPC mod 2^k for dishonest majority. In: Shacham, H., Boldyreva, A. (eds.) CRYPTO 2018, Part II. LNCS, vol. 10992, pp. 769–798. Springer, Cham (2018). https://doi.org/10.1007/978-3-319-96881-0_26
10. Damgård, I., Fitzi, M., Kiltz, E., Nielsen, J.B., Toft, T.: Unconditionally secure constant-rounds multi-party computation for equality, comparison, bits and exponentiation. In: Halevi, S., Rabin, T. (eds.) TCC 2006. LNCS, vol. 3876, pp. 285–304. Springer, Heidelberg (2006). https://doi.org/10.1007/11681878_15
11. Damgård, I., Koprowski, M.: Practical threshold RSA signatures without a trusted dealer. In: Pfitzmann, B. (ed.) EUROCRYPT 2001. LNCS, vol. 2045, pp. 152–165. Springer, Heidelberg (2001). https://doi.org/10.1007/3-540-44987-6_10
12. Damgård, I., Pastro, V., Smart, N., Zakarias, S.: Multiparty computation from somewhat homomorphic encryption. In: Safavi-Naini, R., Canetti, R. (eds.) CRYPTO 2012. LNCS, vol. 7417, pp. 643–662. Springer, Heidelberg (2012). https://doi.org/10.1007/978-3-642-32009-5_38
13. Desmedt, Y., Frankel, Y.: Threshold cryptosystems. In: Brassard, G. (ed.) CRYPTO 1989. LNCS, vol. 435, pp. 307–315. Springer, New York (1990). https://doi.org/10.1007/0-387-34805-0_28
14. Ding, J., Chen, M.S., Petzoldt, A., Schmidt, D., Yang, B.Y.: Rainbow (2019). Submission to NIST PQC "competition" Round-2
15. Ding, J., Zhang, Z., Deaton, J., Schmidt, K., Vishakha, F.: New attacks on lifted unbalanced oil vinegar. In: The 2nd NIST PQC Standardization Conference (2019)

16. Doerner, J., Kondi, Y., Lee, E., Shelat, A.: Secure two-party threshold ECDSA from ECDSA assumptions. In: 2018 IEEE Symposium on Security and Privacy, pp. 980–997. IEEE Computer Society Press, May 2018
17. Gennaro, R., Goldfeder, S.: Fast multiparty threshold ECDSA with fast trustless setup. In: Lie, D., Mannan, M., Backes, M., Wang, X. (eds.) ACM CCS 2018, pp. 1179–1194. ACM Press, New York (2018)
18. Gennaro, R., Goldfeder, S., Narayanan, A.: Threshold-optimal DSA/ECDSA signatures and an application to bitcoin wallet security. In: Manulis, M., Sadeghi, A.-R., Schneider, S. (eds.) ACNS 2016. LNCS, vol. 9696, pp. 156–174. Springer, Cham (2016). https://doi.org/10.1007/978-3-319-39555-5_9
19. Gennaro, R., Jarecki, S., Krawczyk, H., Rabin, T.: Robust threshold DSS signatures. In: Maurer, U. (ed.) EUROCRYPT 1996. LNCS, vol. 1070, pp. 354–371. Springer, Heidelberg (1996). https://doi.org/10.1007/3-540-68339-9_31
20. Gentry, C., Peikert, C., Vaikuntanathan, V.: Trapdoors for hard lattices and new cryptographic constructions. In: Ladner, R.E., Dwork, C. (eds.) 40th ACM STOC, pp. 197–206. ACM Press, New York (2008)
21. Gentry, C., Szydlo, M.: Cryptanalysis of the revised NTRU signature scheme. In: Knudsen, L.R. (ed.) EUROCRYPT 2002. LNCS, vol. 2332, pp. 299–320. Springer, Heidelberg (2002). https://doi.org/10.1007/3-540-46035-7_20
22. Giacomelli, I., Madsen, J., Orlandi, C.: ZKBoo: faster zero-knowledge for boolean circuits. In: Holz, T., Savage, S. (eds.) USENIX Security 2016, pp. 1069–1083. USENIX Association, Berkeley (2016)
23. Goldreich, O.: Two remarks concerning the Goldwasser-Micali-Rivest signature scheme. In: Odlyzko, A.M. (ed.) CRYPTO 1986. LNCS, vol. 263, pp. 104–110. Springer, Heidelberg (1987). https://doi.org/10.1007/3-540-47721-7_8
24. Goldreich, O.: Foundations of Cryptography: Basic Applications, vol. 2. Cambridge University Press, Cambridge (2004)
25. Hazay, C., Scholl, P., Soria-Vazquez, E.: Low cost constant round MPC combining BMR and oblivious transfer. In: Takagi, T., Peyrin, T. (eds.) ASIACRYPT 2017, Part I. LNCS, vol. 10624, pp. 598–628. Springer, Cham (2017). https://doi.org/10.1007/978-3-319-70694-8_21
26. Hoffstein, J., Howgrave-Graham, N., Pipher, J., Silverman, J.H., Whyte, W.: NTRUSign: digital signatures using the NTRU lattice. In: Joye, M. (ed.) CT-RSA 2003. LNCS, vol. 2612, pp. 122–140. Springer, Heidelberg (2003). https://doi.org/10.1007/3-540-36563-X_9
27. Hulsing, A., et al.: SPHINCS+ (2019). Submission to NIST PQC "competition" Round-2
28. Ishai, Y., Kushilevitz, E., Ostrovsky, R., Sahai, A.: Zero-knowledge from secure multiparty computation. In: Johnson, D.S., Feige, U. (eds.) 39th ACM STOC, pp. 21–30. ACM Press, New York (2007)
29. Kipnis, A., Patarin, J., Goubin, L.: Unbalanced oil and vinegar signature schemes. In: Stern, J. (ed.) EUROCRYPT 1999. LNCS, vol. 1592, pp. 206–222. Springer, Heidelberg (1999). https://doi.org/10.1007/3-540-48910-X_15
30. Kraitsberg, M., Lindell, Y., Osheter, V., Smart, N.P., Talibi Alaoui, Y.: Adding Distributed Decryption and Key Generation to a Ring-LWE Based CCA Encryption Scheme. In: Jang-Jaccard, J., Guo, F. (eds.) ACISP 2019. LNCS, vol. 11547, pp. 192–210. Springer, Cham (2019). https://doi.org/10.1007/978-3-030-21548-4_11
31. Lamport, L.: Constructing digital signatures from a one-way function. Technical report SRI-CSL-98, SRI International Computer Science Laboratory, October 1979

32. Larraia, E., Orsini, E., Smart, N.P.: Dishonest majority multi-party computation for binary circuits. In: Garay, J.A., Gennaro, R. (eds.) CRYPTO 2014, Part II. LNCS, vol. 8617, pp. 495–512. Springer, Heidelberg (2014). https://doi.org/10.1007/978-3-662-44381-1_28
33. Lindell, Y.: Fast secure two-party ECDSA signing. In: Katz, J., Shacham, H. (eds.) CRYPTO 2017, Part II. LNCS, vol. 10402, pp. 613–644. Springer, Cham (2017). https://doi.org/10.1007/978-3-319-63715-0_21
34. Lindell, Y., Nof, A.: Fast secure multiparty ECDSA with practical distributed key generation and applications to cryptocurrency custody. In: Lie, D., Mannan, M., Backes, M., Wang, X. (eds.) ACM CCS 2018, pp. 1837–1854. ACM Press, New York (2018)
35. Lindell, Y., Nof, A., Ranellucci, S.: Fast secure multiparty ECDSA with practical distributed key generation and applications to cryptocurrency custody. IACR Cryptology ePrint Archive 2018, 987 (2018). https://eprint.iacr.org/2018/987
36. Lyubashevsky, V.: Fiat-Shamir with aborts: applications to lattice and factoring-based signatures. In: Matsui, M. (ed.) ASIACRYPT 2009. LNCS, vol. 5912, pp. 598–616. Springer, Heidelberg (2009). https://doi.org/10.1007/978-3-642-10366-7_35
37. Lyubashevsky, V., et al.: Crystals-dilithium (2019). Submission to NIST PQC "competition" Round-2
38. MacKenzie, P., Reiter, M.K.: Two-party generation of DSA signatures. In: Kilian, J. (ed.) CRYPTO 2001. LNCS, vol. 2139, pp. 137–154. Springer, Heidelberg (2001). https://doi.org/10.1007/3-540-44647-8_8
39. Matsumoto, T., Imai, H.: Public quadratic polynomial-tuples for efficient signature-verification and message-encryption. In: Barstow, D., et al. (eds.) EUROCRYPT 1988. LNCS, vol. 330, pp. 419–453. Springer, Heidelberg (1988). https://doi.org/10.1007/3-540-45961-8_39
40. Merkle, R.C.: A certified digital signature. In: Brassard, G. (ed.) CRYPTO 1989. LNCS, vol. 435, pp. 218–238. Springer, New York (1990). https://doi.org/10.1007/0-387-34805-0_21
41. Mohassel, P., Rosulek, M., Zhang, Y.: Fast and secure three-party computation: the garbled circuit approach. In: Ray, I., Li, N., Kruegel, C. (eds.) ACM CCS 2015, pp. 591–602. ACM Press, New York (2015)
42. Nielsen, J.B., Nordholt, P.S., Orlandi, C., Burra, S.S.: A new approach to practical active-secure two-party computation. In: Safavi-Naini, R., Canetti, R. (eds.) CRYPTO 2012. LNCS, vol. 7417, pp. 681–700. Springer, Heidelberg (2012). https://doi.org/10.1007/978-3-642-32009-5_40
43. Patarin, J.: The oil and vinegar signature scheme. In: Presentation at the Dagstuhl Workshop on Cryptography (1997)
44. Prest, T., et al.: Falcon: fast-Fourier lattice-based compact signatures over NTRU (2019). Submission to NIST PQC "competition" Round-2
45. Reyzin, L., Reyzin, N.: Better than BiBa: short one-time signatures with fast signing and verifying. In: Batten, L., Seberry, J. (eds.) ACISP 2002. LNCS, vol. 2384, pp. 144–153. Springer, Heidelberg (2002). https://doi.org/10.1007/3-540-45450-0_11
46. Rotaru, D., Wood, T.: Marbled circuits: mixing arithmetic and boolean circuits with active security. IACR Cryptology ePrint Archive 2019, 207 (2019). https://eprint.iacr.org/2019/207
47. Samardjiska, S., Chen, M.S., Hulsing, A., Rijneveld, J., Schwabe, P.: MQDSS (2019). Submission to NIST PQC "competition" Round-2

48. Shoup, V.: Practical threshold signatures. In: Preneel, B. (ed.) EUROCRYPT 2000. LNCS, vol. 1807, pp. 207–220. Springer, Heidelberg (2000). https://doi.org/10.1007/3-540-45539-6_15
49. Smart, N.P., Wood, T.: Error detection in monotone span programs with application to communication-efficient multi-party computation. In: Matsui, M. (ed.) CT-RSA 2019. LNCS, vol. 11405, pp. 210–229. Springer, Cham (2019). https://doi.org/10.1007/978-3-030-12612-4_11
50. Wang, X., Ranellucci, S., Katz, J.: Global-scale secure multiparty computation. In: Thuraisingham, B.M., Evans, D., Malkin, T., Xu, D. (eds.) ACM CCS 2017, pp. 39–56. ACM Press, New York (2017)
51. Zaverucha, G., et al.: The picnic signature scheme (2019). Submission to NIST PQC "competition" Round-2

Commodity-Based 2PC for Arithmetic Circuits

Ivan Damgård, Helene Haagh, Michael Nielsen, and Claudio Orlandi(✉)

Department of Computer Science, DIGIT, Aarhus University, Aarhus, Denmark
{ivan,orlandi}@cs.au.dk

Abstract. We revisit the framework of Commodity-based Cryptography presented by Beaver (STOC'97) with a focus on updating the framework to fit with modern multiparty computation (MPC) protocols. We study the possibility of replacing the well-known preprocessing model with a commodity-based setting, where a set of *independent* servers (some of which may be corrupt) provide clients with correlated randomness. From this, the clients then distill correct and secure correlated randomness that they can use during the online phase of the MPC protocol. Beaver showed how to do OT with semi-honest security in the commodity setting. We improve on Beaver's result as follows: In a model where one of two clients and a constant fraction of the servers may be maliciously corrupted, we obtain unconditionally secure multiplication triples and oblivious linear evaluations (OLEs) such that the amortized communication cost of one triple/OLE is a constant number of field elements (when the field is sufficiently large). We also report on results from an implementation of the OLE protocol. Finally, we suggest an approach to practical realization of a commodity based system where servers need no memory and can be accessed asynchronously by clients, but still a maliciously corrupt client cannot get data he should not have access to.

Keywords: Secure two-party computation · Information theoretic security · Oblivious linear evaluation · Commodity-based cryptography

1 Introduction

In commodity-based cryptography as defined in [Bea97], we have a set of clients (typically 2) and a set of servers. The clients want to use the servers to help them implement some cryptographic primitive in a way that is faster or more secure

Research funded by: the Concordium Blockhain Research Center, Aarhus University, Denmark; the Carlsberg Foundation under the Semper Ardens Research Project CF18-112 (BCM); the European Research Council (ERC) under the European Unions's Horizon 2020 research and innovation programme under grant agreement No. 669255 (MPPRO), No. 803096 (SPEC) and No. 731583 (SODA); the Danish Independent Research Council under Grant-ID DFF-6108-00169 (FoCC).

M. Albrecht (Ed.): IMACC 2019, LNCS 11929, pp. 154–177, 2019.
https://doi.org/10.1007/978-3-030-35199-1_8

than if the clients were on their own – even if some of the servers and clients are corrupted. The primitive we focus on here is secure function evaluation, or primitives that are complete for this purpose, such as creation of random Beaver triples or oblivious linear evaluations (OLEs) (see more details on these below).

While the client-server model has been used multiple times to improve performances of MPC protocols (e.g. [BLW08,BCD+09,JNO14]), the commodity-based model is significantly different. In particular, what sets the commodity-based model apart from other client-server models are the requirements made on the communication between servers and clients (we recall the formal definition in Appendix B.2):

- Each server should be oblivious to the existence, identities and number of other servers, so no communication takes place between servers.
- The interaction between client i and server j should take the form of a 2-message protocol where the client sends a request $q_{i,j}$ and the server returns a response $r_{i,j}$.
- $q_{i,j}$ should be independent of the client's input (apart from its length) and of any previous communications with the servers.

The idea behind the commodity-based model is that it should be easy for a server to set up a business where it provides resources to anyone who is willing to pay, and on the other hand clients can decide to access as many servers as they see fit in order to gain confidence that at least some fraction of the material received is securely and correctly generated.

In [Bea97] it was shown how to do 2-party OT and hence 2-party secure computation in the commodity model, assuming *only passive corruption* of one client and a minority of the servers.[1] Note that in [Bea97] it is also claimed that the protocol can be modified to tolerate active corruptions, but no full protocol description nor security proof is provided.

In this paper, we revisit the commodity-based model and improve on Beaver's original result in several ways.[2] We present two protocols: one that produces batches of OLEs for two clients over any field. The protocol has statistical security against a bounded number of *maliciously* corrupted servers and 1 *maliciously* corrupted client. This improves on Beaver's result since: we can deal with arbitrary fields, the mechanism for dealing with active security is more efficient and (crucially) proven secure and, we modify the protocol so that it allows to produce *batches* of OLEs at the price of tolerating fewer corruptions, thus allowing for meaningful security-efficiency tradeoff. Our second protocol produces multiplication triples over any field for two clients with statistical security against a bounded number of *maliciously* corrupted servers *or* 1 *maliciously* corrupted client. While the security guarantees of this protocol are weaker than the first

[1] This corruption bound is clearly optimal for information theoretic security: if one of the two clients and half the servers could be corrupt, then we would immediately get a 2-party information theoretically secure OT which is well known to be impossible.

[2] In 2015, Tonicelli et al. [TND+15] proposed a protocol which they claim to be in the commodity-based model. However, their construction assumes that the servers are trusted, as oppose to our constructions and the original paper by Beaver.

one, the protocol is more efficient and therefore it could provide an interesting security-efficiency tradeoffs in some application. In Appendix A we illustrate how our constructions fit in the bigger picture of performing secure 2-party computation. Furthermore, we suggest an approach to practical realization of a commodity-based system where servers can be fully stateless and can be accessed asynchronously by clients.

Constructing Commodity-Based OLEs. Our first contribution (in Sect. 2) is a novel protocol that produces batches of m OLEs[3] over any field for two clients with statistical security against t *maliciously* corrupted servers and one client assuming that there are $n = 2t + 2m + 1$ servers. This protocol works in the commitment hybrid model. We also show how to do without commitments if we assume $n = 2t + 2m + 3$ servers. Thus, we can achieve essentially the optimal corruption threshold by setting the batch size to be $m = 1$, while if one is willing to assume a larger number of honest players it is possible to achieve higher amortized efficiency. When the underlying field is large (of size exponential in the security parameter), our protocol requires each server to supply just one OLE to the clients, and sending a constant number of field elements between the clients. This means that we can set both t and m to be $\Theta(n)$ and obtain an amortized communication cost per OLE corresponding to a constant number of field elements while still tolerating a constant fraction of corrupted servers. The computational work is dominated by polynomial interpolation, so by standard FFT techniques the computational complexity for $m \in \Theta(n)$ OLEs is $n \cdot \text{polylog}(n)$ elementary field operations.

We emphasize that the protocol between the clients and each individual server is independent of n, t and m. Thus the clients can collect data from any number of servers and later decide on the fly how many OLE's they think it will be secure to extract. Concretely, the clients may agree on number of servers n and corruption threshold t which determine the maximum m by our main theorem. Now, to obtain a total of M OLEs, the clients run $l = M/m$ parallel instances of the whole protocol, which is secure by parallel UC composition.

Although the goal of our protocol is OLE, we construct an equivalent but randomized version, called ROLE. This randomized primitive outputs to the clients random a, b as well as c_A and c_B where $ab = c_A + c_B$ (see Appendix B.4). This is sufficient for 2-party computation with good concrete efficiency: ROLE trivially implies passively secure multiplication. But we can also use the ROLEs to produce authenticated multiplication triples allowing us to achieve malicious (and information theoretic) security.

In [DGN+17], it was shown that actively secure 2-party computation can be built from actively secure OLE at an amortized price of 22 OLEs per multiplication. It was recently announced that this has been now improved to 14[4]. Using

[3] The OLE (Oblivious Linear Evaluation) primitive is defined as follows: Alice inputs values a and b in some field $\mathbb{F}$ and Bob inputs $x \in \mathbb{F}$. Alice learns nothing and Bob learns $y = ax + b$.

[4] Personal communication.

our protocol, this translates to asking for 14 ROLEs from each server per secure multiplication (Given our ROLE protocol, it is also possible to implement secure computation for more than two parties, by having each pair of parties constructing the necessary number of ROLEs with the help of the commodity servers). The construction from [DGN+17] works by building authenticated multiplication triples from OLE. Such a triple consists of random values x, y, z with $xy = z$ as well as additive sharings among Alice and Bob of the three values. Moreover, the shares are authenticated using an unconditionally secure MAC scheme to prevent cheating.

In more details, our protocol for ROLE works as follows: the clients ask each server for a ROLE $(a_i, b_i, c_{A,i}, c_{B,i})$, where Alice holds $(a_i, c_{A,i})$ and Bob holds $(b_i, c_{B,i})$. Alice and Bob then create two polynomials $A(X)$ and $B(X)$ of degree d by using some of the a_i's and b_i's. Then they jointly create two polynomials $C_A(X)$ and $C_B(X)$ of degree $2d$ by using some of the $c_{A,i}$'s and $c_{B,i}$'s, and to get the rest of the points they use the remaining unused ROLEs from the servers to multiply $A(X)$ and $B(X)$. If every party behaved honestly, then Alice and Bob will now hold four polynomials that satisfy the following equation:

$$A(x) \cdot B(x) = C_A(x) + C_B(x) \quad \text{for all } x \in \mathbb{F}.$$

However, if one of the servers provided a bad ROLE or one of the clients behaved inconsistently during the protocol, then some of the polynomials might not be well defined, and hence the input/output is not be well defined either. To be able to detect cheating, we introduce a check phase, where each client chooses a random challenge (a random field element), where the other client must prove that the equation holds when evaluating the polynomials on the challenge value. The non-trivial part of our proof is to show that just one such check in each direction is sufficient to ensure that well-defined polynomials exist for a corrupt client (whenever the protocol does not abort). If the protocol does not abort, then the clients can output a valid ROLE by computing $A(\sigma) \cdot B(\sigma) = C_A(\sigma) + C_B(\sigma)$ where σ is a predefined and unused field element. The check for dealing with active adversaries, as well as its analysis, are the main changes we introduce to the original protocol by Beaver, which was only proved to be passive secure.

Implementation of Commodity-Based OLEs. We experimentally validate our OLE protocol in Sect. 3, by implementing it and testing it on Amazon Cloud. The servers were spread over different locations (5 different continents). We give detailed timings for different settings of parameters. As an example, when we want to tolerate 5 corrupt servers and hence involve 13 servers in total, the latency for generating an OLE is about 1 ms. The amortized time for one OLE ranges from 0.02 ms to 0.5 ms when the field size in bits ranges from 32 to 2048. Note that a growth in wall clock time when the field size grows is to be expected: although the number of field elements to send is constant in the field size, we need to send and process more bits when the field size is larger. These timings are for the case where each instance of the protocol runs with $m = 1$, so we can increase m and decrease t and get better amortized times. For instance, if we are willing to assume at most 1 corrupted server out of 13, one instance of the same protocol can produce batches of 5 OLEs at the time and the amortized times instead vary between 0.004 and 0.1 ms.

With the known reductions from multiplication triples to OLE, our performance numbers show that we can preprocess a secure multiplication triple in amortized time between 0.08 and 0.4 ms for a field size of 128 bits, depending on the assumed corruption threshold. For a very rough comparison, the recent "Overdrive" protocol [KPR18], which does the same task using only communication between the two clients, takes roughly 0.03 ms per multiplication in a LAN setting. We emphasize that it does not make sense to compare the timings directly because the hardware set-ups are different and the achieved types of security are different: computational security in the "Overdrive" protocol versus unconditional security assuming an honest server majority in our protocol. Nevertheless, we believe the numbers show that our protocol is indeed applicable in a practical setting.

Constructing Commodity-Based Multiplication Triples. As an additional contribution (in the full version [DHNO19]) we present a novel protocol for constructing multiplication triples directly (instead of producing OLE first and then using known reductions). For malicious (and information theoretic) security the standard goal is to produce authenticated multiplication triples. So it may seem natural to ask the servers for such triples and try to extract a secure triple from what we get. However, this does not work: the authentication in a triple involves unconditionally secure MACs and a server will of course know the MAC keys involved in its own triples. If this server as well as, say, Alice is corrupt, then Alice can cheat with those MACs. This problem can be solved in a weaker corruption model where *either* some servers *or* a client can be corrupt (but not both).

The high-level idea of the triple protocol closely follows the structure of the OLE protocol with some variation. The clients obtain random triples authenticated under different global keys from the servers, which means that the triples cannot be combined. To solve this, we observe that the MACs are key-homomorphic, which allows the clients to adjust the global MAC key with one round of interaction. Once the MACs are adjusted to use the same key, the clients can combine the triples in a similar manner as the OLE protocol.

Allowing Servers to Be Memoryless. As a final contribution, we suggest an approach for the practical realization of a commodity based system. For the sake of presentation, we assume in most of the paper that there are secure channels between each pair of client and server. Also, we allow servers to remember which clients they talked to and what was sent (so that output to different clients can be properly correlated). Those assumptions are inconvenient in practice and therefore, in Appendix D, we show how to get rid of both requirements. It will clearly be an advantage if the servers do not need memory in the sense that they do not have to remember who they talked to or what was sent. This would mean that a server will not have to administrate identities and log-in credentials, and could simply generate the required data on the fly, say, against payment in some cryptocurrency.

An obvious problem with this goal is that the data sent to two clients Alice and Bob must be correlated and a memoryless server cannot make this happen on its own. We solve this by letting Alice and Bob interact before talking to the severs, in order to choose a common nonce n_{AB}. Then Alice can send ("Alice", n_{AB}) to the server who will use this and a private PRF key to generate Alice's data. We can do something similar for Bob. However, this is not secure: if Alice is corrupt, she can send both ("Alice", n_{AB}) and ("Bob", n_{AB}) to each honest server, get Bob's data and break the protocol. We show how this can be solved by generating the nonce such that Alice and Bob each know different secrets relating to the nonce and hence cannot impersonate the other party towards the server.

Alternatives to the Commodity Model. The commodity model has not received much attention since its introduction, but a very large amount of work has been done on secure computation in general. So we should of course ask ourselves, if some of this work has made the model redundant. Now, if two clients want to do secure computation, two obvious alternatives are well known that allow the clients to do it themselves: first, one could use garbled circuits. This will be constant round, but introduces an overhead on communication that depends on security parameter and also grows with the size of the underlying field (if the goal is arithmetic computation). A second alternative is to do GMW style arithmetic computation using authenticated multiplication triples that the clients generate themselves. If the underlying field is not too large, the triples can be built very efficiently using OT extension [KOS16], but we get an overhead that grows linearly with the bit-size of a field element. Another recent approach generates OLEs from noisy encoding-style assumptions with constant overhead [ADI+17], but only with passive security. For specific applications that use scalar-vector multiplication with long vectors, one may consider the generation of vector-OLE[5] as in [ADI+17] obtaining rate 1/3. This primitive was recently improved to rate 1/2 using compression [BCGI18], that utilize function secret-sharing to enable a small "sparse" vector-OLE to be locally expanded to larger width.

Since it is clear that any solution involving only the two clients must be based on some intractability assumption, such solutions are incomparable to the commodity model with respect to security: we are replacing trust in a computational assumption by trust in some fraction of the servers. But even if we ignore this issue, what we can do in the commodity model seems to be competitive because our protocol has active security and the overhead of doing a secure multiplication is constant as the field size grows. We do not know any solution with these properties that the clients could execute themselves.

---

[5] In the width-w vector-OLE primitive, Alice inputs $\boldsymbol{a}, \boldsymbol{b} \in \mathbb{F}^w$ and Bob $x \in \mathbb{F}$. Alice learns nothing and Bob learns $\boldsymbol{y} = \boldsymbol{a}x + \boldsymbol{b}$.

The commodity model is somewhat related to the idea of *combiners*: for instance, an Oblivious Transfer (OT) combiner [HIKN08,HKN+05] is a protocol that gets (black-box) access to a number of OT implementations, some of which may be faulty, and the goal is now is to build a secure OT. One may think of the given OT implementations as corresponding to the servers in the commodity model. However, the models are incomparable: on one hand, the combiner model is more restrictive since its "servers" are assumed to only implement a certain primitive. On the other hand, a combiner may make many correlated calls to the "servers".

2 Commodity-Based Oblivious Linear Evaluation

In this section, we present a commodity-based protocol for ROLE, which will combine commodities in the form of ROLE's from n servers into a secure ROLE (see Appendix B.4 for the formal definition). We consider the setting where one client and up to t of the servers are maliciously corrupt. The protocol is presented in the commitment-hybrid model. In Appendix C, we show as a corollary a protocol that does not use commitments, at the expense of slightly worse parameters. In the appendix, we furthermore discuss the concrete efficiency of the protocol and how to deal with smaller fields.

The high-level idea of the protocol is to first obtain the ROLE commodities from each server. The clients will use $d+1$ of these to fully define two degree d polynomials $A(X)$ and $B(X)$ held by each party respectively and define points on two degree $2d$ polynomials $C_1(X)$ and $C_2(X)$, which shall form a secret sharing of $A(X) \cdot B(X)$. The clients will use the remaining ROLEs to securely compute $A(X) \cdot B(X)$ on agreed upon points until we have obtained enough points to fully define $C_1(X)$ and $C_2(X)$. After constructing these polynomials, the clients perform a check that with high probability reveals whether the polynomials are valid, that is the equation $A(\gamma) \cdot B(\gamma) = C_1(\gamma) + C_2(\gamma)$ holds for all $\gamma \in \mathbb{F}$. The resulting ROLEs of the protocol will be defined by a fixed set of points $\sigma_1, ..., \sigma_m \in \mathbb{F}$ on these polynomials:

$$\boldsymbol{u} = (A(\sigma_1), ..., A(\sigma_m)) \qquad \boldsymbol{v} = (B(\sigma_1), ..., B(\sigma_m))$$
$$\boldsymbol{w}_1 = (C_1(\sigma_1), ..., C_1(\sigma_m)) \quad \boldsymbol{w}_2 = (C_2(\sigma_1), ..., C_2(\sigma_m))$$

Here, one client will output $\boldsymbol{u}, \boldsymbol{w}_1 \in \mathbb{F}^m$ and the other $\boldsymbol{v}, \boldsymbol{w}_2 \in \mathbb{F}^m$ such that $\boldsymbol{u} * \boldsymbol{v} = \boldsymbol{w}_1 + \boldsymbol{w}_2$. The complete protocol π_{ROLE} is presented in Protocol 1.

Theorem 1. *Assume that $n = 2t + 2m + 1$ and that $|\mathbb{F}|$ is exponential in the security parameter. Then protocol π^m_{ROLE} is an implementation of $\mathcal{F}^m_{\text{ROLE}}$ in the $\mathcal{F}_{\text{COMMIT}}$-hybrid model with statistical UC-security. The protocol tolerates a static adversary corrupting one client and at most $t \leq \frac{n-2m-1}{2}$ servers. The simulation is perfect unless an error event occurs, which has probability at most $\frac{n}{|\mathbb{F}|-(n+m)}$.*

Protocol π^m_{ROLE}

Public: Let $d = t + m$ and $n = 2d + 1$ and let $\mathcal{U} = \{\gamma_1, \ldots, \gamma_n\}$, $\mathcal{V} = \{\sigma_1, ..., \sigma_m\}$ be sets of publicly known distinct points in $\mathbb{F}$. Let $\{\mathtt{S}_1, \ldots, \mathtt{S}_n\}$ be the servers and {Alice, Bob} the clients.
Output: Alice gets $\boldsymbol{u}, \boldsymbol{w}_1 \in \mathbb{F}^m$ and Bob get $\boldsymbol{v}, \boldsymbol{w}_2 \in \mathbb{F}^m$ such that $\boldsymbol{u} * \boldsymbol{v} = \boldsymbol{w}_1 + \boldsymbol{w}_2$.
Protocol:
Stateless oblivious RPC:

1. Alice and Bob: send a request to each server $\mathtt{S}_i$ for $i \in [n]$;
2. Server $\mathtt{S}_i$ for $i \in [n]$:
   - creates a ROLE $(a_i, b_i, c_{1,i}, c_{2,i}) \xleftarrow{\$} \mathbb{F}^4$ such that $a_i \cdot b_i = c_{1,i} + c_{2,i}$;
   - sends $(a_i, c_{1,i})$ to Alice and sends $(b_i, c_{2,i})$ to Bob;

Computation phase:

3. Alice:
   - interpolates polynomial A of degree d by setting $A(\gamma_i) = a_i$ for $i \in [d+1]$;
   - prepares polynomial C_1 of degree $2d$ by setting $C_1(\gamma_i) = c_{1,i}$ for $i \in [d+1]$;
4. Bob:
   - interpolates polynomial B of degree d by setting $B(\gamma_i) = b_i$ for $i \in [d+1]$;
   - prepares polynomial C_2 of degree $2d$ by setting $C_2(\gamma_i) = c_{2,i}$ for $i \in [d+1]$;
5. For $i = d + 2, \ldots, n$
   a. Alice: sends $k_i = A(\gamma_i) - a_i$ to Bob;
   b. Bob:
      - sends $\ell_i = B(\gamma_i) - b_i$ to Alice;
      - sets $C_2(\gamma_i) = c_{2,i} + B(\gamma_i) \cdot k_i$;
   c. Alice: sets $C_1(\gamma_i) = c_{1,i} + A(\gamma_i) \cdot \ell_i - k_i \cdot \ell_i$;
6. Alice: interpolates polynomial C_1 by the $2d + 1$ defined points;
7. Bob: interpolates polynomial C_2 by the $2d + 1$ defined points;

Check phase:

8. Alice: draw $t_A \xleftarrow{\$} \mathbb{F} \backslash (\mathcal{U} \cup \mathcal{V})$ uniformly at random and send t_A to Bob;
9. Bob:
   - draw $t_B \xleftarrow{\$} \mathbb{F} \backslash (\mathcal{U} \cup \mathcal{V})$ uniformly at random;
   - Execute COMMIT$(B(t_A), C_2(t_A))$ and send t_B to Alice;
10. Alice: once commitment has been done, send $(A(t_B), C_1(t_B))$ to Bob;
11. Bob:
    - check if $A(t_B) \cdot B(t_B) = C_1(t_B) + C_2(t_B)$ and abort if not;
    - execute OPEN$(B(t_A), C_2(t_A))$;
12. Alice:
    - receive $(B(t_A), C_2(t_A))$ from the opening of the commitment, abort if nothing is received;
    - check if $A(t_A) \cdot B(t_A) = C_1(t_A) + C_2(t_A)$ and abort if not;

Output phase:

13. Alice: output $\boldsymbol{u} = (A(\sigma_1), ..., A(\sigma_m))$ and $\boldsymbol{w}_1 = (C_1(\sigma_1), ..., C_1(\sigma_m))$;
14. Bob: output $\boldsymbol{v} = (B(\sigma_1), ..., B(\sigma_m))$ and $\boldsymbol{w}_2 = (C_2(\sigma_1), ..., C_2(\sigma_m))$.

Protocol 1: Protocol for commodity-based ROLE

Proof. The environment corrupts one client and a subset of the servers $\mathcal{C} \subset [n]$ with $|\mathcal{C}| \leq t$. Thus, the environment learns at most t points on all polynomials, and one extra from the check phase. After seeing these points, the environment still cannot distinguish whether it is interacting with the ideal world or the real world – that is, the output of the computation (which is m extra points on the polynomial) is compatible with the points that it already received from the simulator (which does not learn the output of the honest party). In other words, a necessary condition for being able to prove unconditional security is to set the degree to $d = t + m$ (since a random such polynomial has $t + m + 1$ random coefficients). The protocol uses $2d + 1$ ROLEs in total and thus we need the number of servers to be at least $n \geq 2d + 1 = 2t + 2m + 1$. In other words, we have that $t \leq \frac{n-2m-1}{2}$.

The protocol is essentially symmetric, i.e. the only difference is that in the proof for corrupt Bob we need to exploit that Bob has to commit to his answer to Alice's challenge before he sees $A(t_B)$, and hence a corrupt Bob also knows only t points of Alice's polynomial. Thus, in the following we prove security against corrupt Alice.

Let $\mathcal{C} \subset [n]$ denote the set of corrupt servers and $\mathcal{H} \subseteq [n]$ the set of honest servers. For these sets it hold that $|\mathcal{C}| \leq t$, $\mathcal{C} \cup \mathcal{H} = [n]$, and $\mathcal{C} \cap \mathcal{H} = 0$. Note that the servers play two different roles in the protocol: the first $d + 1$ servers are used to define the polynomials $A(x)$ and $B(x)$, and the last $n - d - 1$ servers are used to compute the remaining points on $C_1(x)$ and $C_2(x)$.

We start by presenting some facts about the protocol.

Definition 1. *For an honest server $i \in \mathcal{H}$, Alice gets a_i from the server and (if $i \geq d + 2$) sends a value k_i to Bob. Note that if Alice follows the protocol, then the values $\{a_i\}_{i \in \mathcal{H}, i \leq d+1}$ and $\{k_i + a_i\}_{i \in \mathcal{H}, i \geq d+2}$ are all consistent with a polynomial of degree at most d (namely $A(x)$ if Alice was honest). We say that Alice* behaves consistently *if such a polynomial $A^*(x)$ of degree at most d exists.*

Lemma 1. *If Alice is corrupt, but behaves consistently, then from her interaction with honest servers and Bob, one can compute a uniquely defined view for Alice and all corrupt servers that is consistent with them having followed the protocol up to (but not including) the check phase. This includes polynomials $A^*(x), C_1^*(x)$ of degree at most d and $2d$ respectively, where if Alice is honest we have $A^*(x) = A(x)$ and $C_1^*(x) = C_1(x)$.*

Proof. Since Alice behaves consistently this uniquely defines a polynomial $A^*(x)$ of degree at most d, by the above definition. Now we define a view $(a_i, b_i, c_{1,i}, c_{2,i})$ for each corrupt server $i \in \mathcal{C}$: The server sent $b_i, c_{2,i}$ to honest Bob, so these are fixed. Then if $1 \leq i \leq d + 1$, there is no interaction between Alice and Bob so we set $a_i = A^*(\gamma_i)$ and $c_{1,i} = a_i b_i - c_{2-i}$. If $d + 2 \leq i \leq n$, Alice sent k_i and received ℓ_i from Bob. So we set $a_i = A^*(\gamma_i) - k_i$, and $c_{1,i} = a_i b_i - c_{2-i}$. This gives a view for each corrupt server which is consistent with $A^*(x)$ and honest behaviour. Each honest server i, has sent $a_i, c_{1,i}$ to Alice and (if $i \geq d + 2$) she has received a value ℓ_i from Bob and has sent k_i to Bob.

In particular, $c_{1,i}$ is now defined for all i and k_i, ℓ_i are defined for $i \geq d+2$. Therefore we can define the polynomial $C_1^*(x)$ by simply following the specification of the protocol, namely we set $C_1^*(\gamma_i) = c_{1,i}$ for $1 \leq i \leq d+1$ and otherwise $C_1^*(\gamma_i) = c_{1,i} + A^*(\gamma_i)\ell_i - k_i\ell_i$, and finally we interpolate $C_1^*(x)$ from these values. □

Lemma 2. *If Alice is corrupt and does not behave consistently, then the protocol aborts in the check phase except with probability at most* $\frac{n}{|\mathbb{F}|-(m+n)}$.

Proof. Consider the values $Q = \{a_i\}_{i\in\mathcal{H},i\leq d+1} \cup \{k_i + a_i\}_{i\in\mathcal{H},i\geq d+2}$ (see Definition 1). Since Alice does not behave consistently these values are not all consistent with a polynomial of degree at most d. We nevertheless define a polynomial $A'(x)$ by interpolating from the first $d+1$ values in Q.[6] For all the remaining values in Q, we define δ_i by

$$k_i + a_i = A'(\gamma_i) + \delta_i.$$

Note that, by assumption, there exists an index $j \in \mathcal{H}$ and $j > d+2$ such that $\delta_j \neq 0$. To simplify the notation, let $\mathcal{H}_1$ be the first $d+1$ indexes of the honest servers, i.e. those used for defining polynomial $A'(x)$, and let $\mathcal{H}_2$ be the remaining honest servers.

On the other hand, for the corrupt servers, one can always fix a view that is consistent with $A'(x)$ and with the interaction with (honest) Bob, exactly as in the proof of the previous lemma. Thus we assume (for notational convenience) that a_i for $i \in \mathcal{C}$ is defined this way such that $A'(\gamma_i) = a_i$.

Now, from the communication in the computation phase, for each index i the outcome for Alice and Bob consists of two field elements $C_1(\gamma_i)$ and $C_2(\gamma_i)$ (of course, corrupt Alice does not necessarily store the $C_1(\gamma_i)$'s, all we mean to say is that they can be computed from the adversary's view). Now, from our definition of $A'(x)$ and δ_i and the protocol specification, it is easy to see that $C_1(\gamma_i) + C_2(\gamma_i) = A'(\gamma_i)B(\gamma_i)$ if $i \in \mathcal{C} \cup \mathcal{H}_1$, and otherwise $C_1(\gamma_i) + C_2(\gamma_i) = (A'(\gamma_i)+\delta_i)B(\gamma_i) = A'(\gamma_i)B(\gamma_i)+\delta_i B(\gamma_i)$ if $i \in \mathcal{H}_2$. For notational convenience, we will define $\delta_i = 0$ for $i \in \mathcal{C} \cup \mathcal{H}_1$, so we have

$$C_1(\gamma_i) + C_2(\gamma_i) = A'(\gamma_i)B(\gamma_i) + \delta_i B(\gamma_i) \text{ for } i \in [n]$$

We can now interpolate polynomials of degree at most $2d$ from the $C_1(\gamma_i)$'s, the $C_2(\gamma_i)$'s and the $C_1(\gamma_i) + C_2(\gamma_i) = A'(\gamma_i)B(\gamma_i) + \delta_i B(\gamma_i)$-values. Because interpolation is linear, this results in polynomials $C_1(x)$, $C_2(x)$ such that

$$C_1(x) + C_2(x) = A'(x)B(x) + \Delta(x), \text{ where } \Delta(\gamma_i) = B(\gamma_i)\delta_i \text{ for } i \in [n].$$

[6] The choice to interpolate from the first $d+1$ values is completely arbitrary, the following argument will work no matter the choice of subset.

In the test phase, Bob sends a point t_B and Alice returns two field elements, that are "supposed to be" $A'(t_B)$ and $C_1(t_B)$. We can always write what she actually sends as $\alpha + A'(t_B)$ and $\beta + C_1(t_B)$, for some α, β that the adversary can compute. Bob will check the equation

$$(\beta + C_1(t_B)) + C_2(t_B) = (\alpha + A'(t_B))B(t_B)$$

which easily simplifies to $\beta + \Delta(t_B) = \alpha B(t_B)$.

So what we need to argue is that the adversary can guess α, β satisfying this equation with only negligible probability. This will turn out to be because he does not have sufficient information about the polynomial $B(x)$. Note that the adversary has seen t values of $B(x)$ from Bob's interaction with the corrupt servers ($B(t_A)$ has been committed to but is not revealed yet). Since the degree is $d = t + m$ and $m \geq 1$, the adversary is at least 2 points short of being able to determine $B(x)$. We can therefore assume that the values $B(t_B)$ and $B(\gamma_j)$ are independent and uniform in the view of the adversary, namely γ_j is the index of an honest server and t_B is chosen such that it is never the index of a corrupt server. To emphasize that the values are unknown, we will write $X = B(t_B)$ and $Y = B(\gamma_j)$.

We can imagine giving the adversary extra points so he knows exactly $d - 1$ points on $B(x)$, this can only help him. Therefore, using the formulas of interpolation, the adversary can write any value of $B(x)$ as an affine linear combination of X and Y with known coefficients. In particular, this means there exist field elements $\omega_i, \eta_i, \sigma_i$ such that $\Delta(\gamma_i) = B(\gamma_i)\delta_i = \omega_i X + \eta_i Y + \sigma_i$. From the values $\omega_1, ..., \omega_n$ we can interpolate exactly one polynomial of degree at most $2d$, which we call $F(x)$. Likewise we interpolate $G(x)$ from the η_i's and $H(x)$ from the σ_i's. This immediately implies that

$$\Delta(x) = F(x)X + G(x)Y + H(x)$$

The meaning of this equation is that the polynomials $F(x), G(x)$ and $H(x)$ are fixed in the sense that they do not depend on the choice of $B(x)$ (and hence of X, Y). So in the adversary's view, the polynomial $\Delta(x)$ depends linearly on the two (random) values X, Y as described by the equation.

Note that for $i = j$, we have $\delta_j B(\gamma_j) = \delta_j Y = \omega_j X + \eta_j Y + \sigma_j$ which can only be true for random X and Y if $\omega_j = \sigma_j = 0$ and $\eta_j = \delta_j \neq 0$. So this implies that $G(x)$ is not the 0-polynomial. Hence the above equation that the adversary must try to satisfy becomes:

$$\beta + F(t_B)X + G(t_B)Y + H(t_B) = \alpha X$$

Which can be rewritten as $(F(t_B) - \alpha)X + G(t_B)Y + \beta + H(t_B) = 0$.

Note that we can think of the experiment done as follows: first we choose t_B at random from a set of size $|\mathbb{F}| - (m + n)$, then the adversary chooses α, β and then we choose X, Y independently and uniformly at random in $\mathbb{F}$. It is then clear that if $(F(t_B) - \alpha) \neq 0$ then the left-hand side is uniformly random and so is 0 with probability $1/|\mathbb{F}|$. On the other hand, if $(F(t_B) - \alpha) = 0$, we can use the fact that $G(x)$ is non-zero and has degree at most $2d$ to conclude that $G(t_B) = 0$ with probability at most $2d/(|\mathbb{F}| - (m+n))$. But if $G(t_B) \neq 0$, then again the left-hand side is uniformly random and is 0 with probability $1/|\mathbb{F}|$. We conclude that the equation is satisfied with probability at most

$$\frac{2d}{|\mathbb{F}| - (m+n)} + \frac{1}{|\mathbb{F}|} \leq \frac{n}{|\mathbb{F}| - (m+n)}$$

□

Having proved the lemmas, we present a simulator $\mathcal{S}_A$ (see Simulator 1) which provides statistically indistinguishable simulation of the protocol π_{ROLE} against a malicious adversary that corrupts Alice and t servers. The simulator basically runs its own instance of the protocol with corrupt Alice and servers, playing honestly for Bob and the honest servers. There is, however, an important difference: During the check phase, the simulator aborts under a different condition than in the real protocol: While an honest Bob in the real protocol aborts only if the values sent by Alice do not satisfy the right relation with the polynomials held by Bob, the simulator will also abort if Alice does not behave consistently. Now, there two cases to consider:

1. Alice behaves consistently: in this case, the simulator follows the protocol until the end, so it is clear that simulation of the adversary's view of the protocol is perfect. Furthermore, it follows by Lemma 1 that the simulator extracts the only possible candidate for Alice's output shares, given the interaction with honest players, so what it sends to the functionality is correct. Hence the only difference between the real and the ideal process is that in the real process, Bob's output is extracted from his view of the protocol, whereas in the ideal process it is chosen by the functionality (but consistently with Alice's shares). This makes no difference: Alice has seen $t+1$ points on the polynomial $B(x)$ and since the degree is $d = t + m$ this leaves m degrees of freedom which means that the values $B(\sigma_1), ..., B(\sigma_m)$ are random and independent of the adversary/environment's view of the protocol. So in this case, the real and ideal process are perfectly indistinguishable.
2. Alice does not behave consistently: in this case the ideal process always aborts, but by Lemma 2 the real process does the same, except with negligible probability. Thus in this case, the processes are statistically indistinguishable. □

Simulator 1: Simulator $\mathcal{S}_A$ against corrupt Alice

The simulator starts by initializing copies of the code for the honest servers, for honest Bob, and for $\mathcal{F}_{\text{COMMIT}}$. Then the simulation proceeds as follows:

Stateless oblivious RPC and Computation phase:

1. Let the simulator's copies of the honest servers and Bob interact with corrupt Alice and the corrupt servers (which are controlled by the environment).
2. When the computation phase is done, check whether Alice has acted consistently (see Definition 1).
3. If Alice has not acted consistently, set a flag `will-abort` = `true`. Else (Alice has acted consistently), do as follows:
   (a) Compute polynomials $A^*(x), C_1^*(x)$ as guaranteed by Lemma 1.
   (b) Compute $\hat{\boldsymbol{u}} = (A^*(\sigma_1), ..., A^*(\sigma_m))$. $\hat{\boldsymbol{w}}_1 = (C_1^*(\sigma_1), ..., C_1^*(\sigma_m))$. Send $(\texttt{corrupt}, \texttt{A}, (\hat{\boldsymbol{u}}, \hat{\boldsymbol{w}}_1))$ to the ideal functionality $\mathcal{F}^m_{\text{ROLE}}$;

Check phase:

1. Let the simulator's copies of Bob and $\mathcal{F}_{\text{COMMIT}}$ do the check phase with corrupt Alice. If the test done by Bob fails, set the flag `will-abort` = `true`.

Output phase:

1. If `will-abort` = `true`, abort the protocol.
   Else, send $(\texttt{deliver}, \texttt{A})$ and $(\texttt{deliver}, \texttt{B})$ to the ideal functionality $\mathcal{F}^m_{\text{ROLE}}$.

3 Implementation

We implement and measure timings for the commodity-based OLE protocol.[7] The two clients Alice and Bob are set up on a basic LAN and will connect to some number of servers around the world. Since the experiments are identical up to the output for different tradeoff choices of t and m, we implement the setting of generating one OLE $m = 1$ with maximum adversarial threshold $t \leq \frac{n-3}{2}$.

Instantiations. We use a basic OpenSSL (version 1.1.0) setup to implement a public key infrastructure for the clients to authenticate servers. Our setting consists of a single root certificate authority, trusted by each client, and who have signed certificates to each server. This setup is easily used in the real world, as two clients can simply agree on some domain name and rely on root certificates already included in the system to do hostname validation.

All finite fields are implemented using GNU Multiple Precision Arithmetic Library and when testing a b-bit prime field, we refer to $\mathbb{Z}_p$ for the largest $p < 2^b$. We instantiate the hash function $\mathcal{H}$ as SHA256. For sampling random numbers, we construct a PRG by using the AES instruction set in counter mode. This PRG takes a seed s of arbitrary length and set the AES key to be the 128 first bits of $\mathcal{H}(s)$. To generate a random field element from $\mathbb{Z}_p$, we sample $b = \lceil \log_2 p \rceil$ random bits from the PRG repeatedly until it represents a valid element.

[7] The sources used for the benchmark implementation are available at `[source hidden for anonymity]`.

We fix the polynomial evaluation points $\gamma_1, \ldots, \gamma_n$ to be $1, \ldots, n$, and set the extraction point $\sigma_1 = 0$. We use the following preprocessed variant of Lagrange interpolation to fast[8] evaluate $f(x)$ where f is a degree d polynomial represented by $d+1$ points $y_1, \ldots, y_n$ and $y_i = f(i)$. First preprocess $\delta_{ij} = (i-j)^{-1}$ and $\lambda_{ij} = j \cdot \delta_{ij}$ for $i, j \in [d+1]$, and then compute the point $f(x)$ as:

$$f(x) = \sum_{i=1}^{d+1} y_i \prod_{\substack{j=1 \\ j \neq i}}^{d+1} x\delta_{ij} - \lambda_{ij}$$

Set-Up and Results. The two clients are tested on a basic LAN setup consisting of two identical machines each with a i7-3770K CPU running at 3.5 GHz, 32 GB of RAM and connected via 1 GbE with a 0.15 ms delay. The servers are set up on Amazon Cloud using M4.LARGE instances with 2 vCPUs and are spread across five continents namely North America (N. Virginia), South America (São Paulo), Europe (Ireland), Asia (Mumbai) and Australia (Sydney). The Internet connection for all servers and clients was measured to vary between 200–500 Mbps up and down at the time of testing.

We test the protocol with different field sizes ranging from 32 to 2048 bit and tolerating up to 1, 5 or 10 malicious servers colluding with one malicious client. This implies the number of servers used in each setting being 5, 13 and 23 respectively. Both clients run a producer-consumer program where the producer is connected to all servers and produce batches of shares from each server to be used for the protocol. The consumer is connected to the other client and consumes a batch by running the protocol in parallel for each OLE to be corrected. All measurements are done as an average over 30 s.

First we measure sequential timings for protocol, namely how long time a single consumer (thread) takes to compute a corrected ROLE given the raw material. We test this in two versions, one where the clients are only interested in a single ROLE and another where they want a batch of 1000. The first version (Table 1) may be interesting in a real-world application where clients wants a single OLE, and serves well as a baseline for OLE protocol comparison. The second version (Table 2) on the contrary shows what to expect, if our protocol is to be used in a subsequent protocol requiring 1000 OLEs. Here, one would expect a batch of 1000 to take 1000 times as long – however the numbers show that this vary between roughly 200 to 900 depending on the field size and number of servers, which is partly due to less network delay. Finally, amortized timings for the protocol are measured (Table 3). These timings show how many ROLEs we can generate per second. We simply let the machines generate as many ROLEs as possible by turning up the number of consumers. Note that our tests was done on a university network and on shared cloud nodes, which meant inconsistency in available resources. This, together with different parameter choices to maximize parallelization (number of threads and batch size), means that we can expect to

[8] Fast in practice for low-degree polynomials, but theoretically inferior to the Fast Fourier Transform.

see jumps in the amortized table, for example for 23 servers and $b = 256$ and $b = 512$.

Table 1. Sequential timings for one OLE

	$n = 5$ $t = 1$	$n = 13$ $t = 5$	$n = 23$ $t = 10$
$b = 32$	0.301 ms	0.460 ms	0.930 ms
$b = 64$	0.317 ms	0.465 ms	1.162 ms
$b = 128$	0.333 ms	0.803 ms	1.294 ms
$b = 256$	0.980 ms	1.388 ms	2.311 ms
$b = 512$	1.372 ms	1.891 ms	3.301 ms
$b = 1024$	1.491 ms	2.625 ms	5.228 ms
$b = 2048$	1.856 ms	4.252 ms	9.311 ms

Table 2. Sequential timings for batch of 1000 OLEs

	$n = 5$ $t = 1$	$n = 13$ $t = 5$	$n = 23$ $t = 10$
$b = 32$	13.450 ms	86.103 ms	370.984 ms
$b = 64$	13.356 ms	136.978 ms	405.691 ms
$b = 128$	15.334 ms	171.623 ms	468.540 ms
$b = 256$	24.716 ms	317.403 ms	829.741 ms
$b = 512$	51.997 ms	410.123 ms	1792.491 ms
$b = 1024$	151.008 ms	858.411 ms	2820.248 ms
$b = 2048$	371.269 ms	2188.804 ms	7970.499 ms

Using the tradeoff, one can increase m and decrease t to get a protocol with same sequential running time, but with higher throughput i.e. lower amortized timings. For example, the second column for the amortized timings represent $n = 13, t = 5$ and $m = 1$ – but we can get a five time increase in throughput by running the protocol with $n = 13, t = 1$ and $m = 5$. Likewise, for the case of $m = 2$, one can decrease t by one to obtain a column with half the amortized timings.

Table 3. Amortized timing for generating one OLE

	$n = 5$ $t = 1$	$n = 13$ $t = 5$	$n = 23$ $t = 10$
$b = 32$	3.570 µs	23.657 µs	89.055 µs
$b = 64$	5.801 µs	23.362 µs	105.628 µs
$b = 128$	16.867 µs	28.201 µs	106.868 µs
$b = 256$	33.101 µs	56.197 µs	191.985 µs
$b = 512$	69.297 µs	115.180 µs	2160.664 µs
$b = 1024$	118.353 µs	230.487 µs	4938.348 µs
$b = 2048$	249.018 µs	516.934 µs	7709.943 µs

In the case of 128-bit fields, existing protocols providing computational security like the "Overdrive" LowGear protocol [KPR18] achieve a secure 128-bit multiplication in roughly 0.03 ms. To compare our protocol roughly, one can set

$n = 13$ and assume a 14 times overhead by using the optimized[9] TinyOLE variant, we can compute roughly a secure multiplication between 0.4 and 0.08 ms with a choice of $(t = 5, m = 1)$ and $(t = 1, m = 5)$ respectively. We stress the difference between the models used by us and "Overdrive": ours provide unconditional security (assuming $\leq t$ malicious servers colluding) rather than computational security - and we believe these numbers show that our protocol is indeed applicable in a practical setting.

A Our Constructions in the Big Picture

In this section we present a graphical overview of how our constructions fits in the bigger picture of performing secure 2-party computation (Fig. 1).

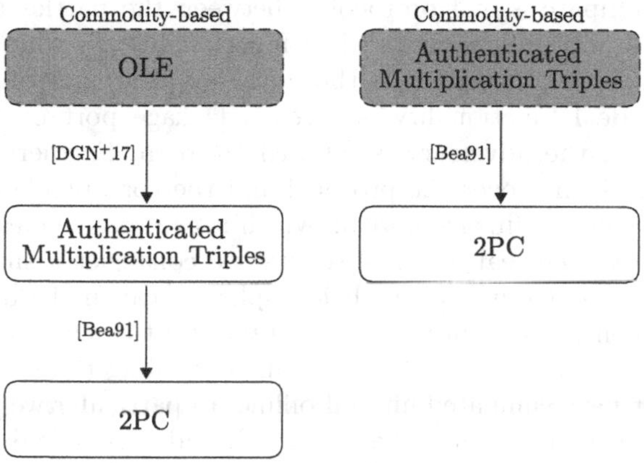

Fig. 1. An overview of how our constructions (the blue boxes with dashed lines) fits in the bigger picture of performing secure 2-party computation. (Color figure online)

Construction 1: Commodity-Based OLEs. We construct commodity-based OLEs in the commitment-hybrid model with active, statistical security and in the standard model with active, information theoretic security (with slightly worse parameter). In this construction we allow a corrupt client to collude with a minority of the servers. Using the result from [DGN+17], we can use the commodity-based OLEs to construct authenticated multiplication triples, which are complete for multiparty computation.

Construction 2: Commodity-Based Multiplication Triples. We construct commodity-based authenticated multiplication triples in the standard model with active, information theoretic security. This construction has a slightly weaker corruption model: we do not allow collusion between clients and servers. Thus, the adversary can corrupt either one client or a minority of the servers.

[9] Which requires 14 OLEs to produce a secure multiplication, by personal communication.

B Preliminaries

Let $[n]$ be the set of integers $\{1, \ldots, n\}$. Denote a field of size q as $\mathbb{F}_q$ and the set of all polynomials over such field as $\mathbb{F}_q[X]$. All variables and operations are over $\mathbb{F}_q$ unless stated otherwise. $\boldsymbol{v}$ denotes a vector with entries in $\mathbb{F}_q$, the entries are usually denoted $v_1, v_2...$ If $\boldsymbol{u}, \boldsymbol{v}$ are vectors of the same length, say m, then $\boldsymbol{v} * \boldsymbol{u}$ denotes the vector containing the coordinate-wise products, $\boldsymbol{v} * \boldsymbol{u} = (v_1u_1, v_2u_2, ..., v_mu_m)$. As a shorthand, we denote $\mathbb{F}$ to be a field of arbitrary size.

B.1 Security Model

We will use the UC framework of Canetti [Can01] to prove our protocols secure. Informally, we compare a real protocol π between the parties to a setting in which the parties only talk with an ideal functionality $\mathcal{F}$, which by definition is secure. To model the information the adversary learns during the protocol execution, each ideal functionality is given a leakage port on which it leaks all the information the adversary is allowed to learn. Furthermore, to model the adversary's influence over the protocol and the corrupt players, each ideal functionality is given a influence port on which it can receive messages from the adversary. To prove the real protocol secure, we construct a simulator $\mathcal{S}$ such that no adversary controlling all malicious players can make an environment distinguish between the real protocol execution and the simulator's transcript. Intuitively, the adversary gains nothing from controlling the malicious players, that he could not have simulated himself offline. In particular we use the variant in which the environment plays the role of the adversary and will prove our protocols secure under static corruption for malicious adversaries.

B.2 Commodity Model

Commodity-based cryptography works in a client-server model, where a group of clients obtain some information (called commodities) from a set of servers. In the basic setting, the clients will send a request to a server, who will reply with a single response computed from the request, whereas other settings may extend this to multiple rounds.

Following the work of Beaver, we define a two-tiered (c, n)-protocol $\pi = (\mathcal{C}, \mathcal{S})$ as a collection of $c + n$ probabilistic interactive Turing machines (PTM), which are divided into two groups: the clients $\mathcal{C}$ and the servers $\mathcal{S}$. The clients must be polynomial time PTM's and are assigned a unique id $i \in [c]$, and the servers are likewise assigned a unique id $j \in [n]$. We consider the basic form of two clients $c = 2$ and a variable number of servers n, with the servers being polynomial time PTM's. Other settings, which we shall not consider, may include a variable number of clients, computationally unbounded servers, multiple rounds between clients and servers or even allowing communication between servers.

Definition 2 (Stateless Oblivious RPC, [Bea97]**).** *Given a two-pass protocol between client $C_i \in \mathcal{C}$ and server $S_j \in \mathcal{S}$, where the C_i sends a request $q_{i,j}$ to the S_j, who send back the response $r_{i,j}$. This protocol is called a* stateless oblivious remote procedure call (RPC) *if $q_{i,j}$ is independent of C_i's input x_i (apart from the length) and of any previous communications with S_j or any other servers (apart from including tags for identifying and authenticating C_i and S_j).*

Definition 3 (Commodity-based Protocol, [Bea97]**).** *A two-tiered protocol π is* commodity-based *if*

1. *No communication between servers is necessary.*
2. *Servers do not need to know the identities, numbers of, or existence of other servers.*
3. *For each client $C_i \in \mathcal{C}$ and server $S_j \in \mathcal{S}$, C_i interacts with S_j only through stateless oblivious RPC's.*

B.3 Commitments

Some of our protocol make use of a UC-secure commitment scheme, which is modelled by an ideal functionality $\mathcal{F}_{\text{COMMIT}}$. Committing to a value x is denoted $\text{COMMIT}(x)$ and means that the committer sends x to the commit functionality which notifies the other party that the commitment has been made. Opening is denoted $\text{OPEN}(x)$ and means the committer sends an open command to the functionality which then sends x to the other party. In a practical implementation, $\mathcal{F}_{\text{COMMIT}}$ can be implemented using a random oracle (it is well known, and trivial to prove, that applying a random oracle to the string to commit to, concatenated by random coins, gives a UC-secure commitment scheme).

B.4 Oblivious Linear Evaluation

An oblivious linear evaluation (OLE) over the finite field $\mathbb{F}$ is a primitive in which Alice inputs $a, b \in \mathbb{F}$ and Bob inputs $x \in \mathbb{F}$. Alice learns nothing and Bob learns $y = ax + b$. This primitive can be seen as a natural generalization of Oblivious Transfer (OT) [Rab05] for the case $\mathbb{F} = \mathbb{F}_2$ or as a special case of Oblivious Polynomial Evaluation (OPE) [NP99] for the case of degree 1 polynomials. The ideal UC-functionality $\mathcal{F}^m_{\text{OLE}}$ is defined in Fig. 2. It implements m OLEs in parallel.

A variant called random oblivious linear evaluation (ROLE) is a similar primitive, but where Alice receives random values $u, w_1 \xleftarrow{\$} \mathbb{F}$ and Bob $v, w_2 \xleftarrow{\$} \mathbb{F}$ such that $uv = w_1 + w_2$. The ideal UC-functionality $\mathcal{F}^m_{\text{ROLE}}$ is defined in Fig. 3. We show that a random oblivious linear evaluation (ROLE) is equivalent to an oblivious linear evaluation (OLE) in the same way oblivious transfer is shown to be equal to a random oblivious transfer. We define a protocol π^m_{OLE} that realizes $\mathcal{F}^m_{\text{OLE}}$ with access to $\mathcal{F}^m_{\text{ROLE}}$. This protocol (which is folklore) is formally given in Fig. 4 and can be proven secure as stated in the following:

Lemma 3. *The protocol π^m_{OLE} UC-realizes $\mathcal{F}^m_{\text{OLE}}$ in the $\mathcal{F}^m_{\text{ROLE}}$-hybrid model.*

Correctness of the protocol can be trivially checked. Security can be proven similarly to other protocols in the correlated randomness model [IKM+13]: if Bob is corrupted, the simulator emulates the ROLE by picking random $\boldsymbol{v}, \boldsymbol{w}_2$, extracts $\boldsymbol{x}$ from $\boldsymbol{e}$ and $\boldsymbol{v}$ and feeds it to the ideal functionality to receive $\boldsymbol{y}$. Finally the simulator chooses a random $\boldsymbol{s}$ and computes $\boldsymbol{d} = \boldsymbol{v}^{-1} * (\boldsymbol{y} - \boldsymbol{w}_2 - \boldsymbol{s})$, thus producing a view which is distributed identically as in the real world. Here, $\boldsymbol{v}^{-1}$ means the vector with entries $v_1^{-1}, v_2^{-1}, \ldots$ In the case where Alice is corrupted, the simulator emulates the ROLE by picking random $\boldsymbol{u}, \boldsymbol{w}_1$ and sends

Functionality $\mathcal{F}_{\text{OLE}}^m$

1. Upon receiving message $(\texttt{inputA}, a, b)$ from Alice with $\boldsymbol{a}, \boldsymbol{b} \in \mathbb{F}^m$: if there already is a stored tuple from Alice, then ignore the message. Otherwise, store $\boldsymbol{a}$ and $\boldsymbol{b}$ and send message $(\texttt{inputA})$ on leakage port.
2. Upon receiving message $(\texttt{inputB}, \boldsymbol{x})$ from Bob with $\boldsymbol{x} \in \mathbb{F}^m$: if there already is a stored tuple from Bob, then ignore the message. Otherwise, store $\boldsymbol{x}$ and send message $(\texttt{inputB})$ on leakage port.
3. Upon receiving message $(\texttt{deliver}, \texttt{A})$ on influence port: if $\boldsymbol{a}, \boldsymbol{b}$ and $\boldsymbol{x}$ have been stored, then send $(\texttt{delivered})$ to Alice. Otherwise, ignore the message.
4. Upon receiving message $(\texttt{deliver}, \texttt{B})$ on influence port: if $\boldsymbol{a}, \boldsymbol{b}$ and $\boldsymbol{x}$ have been stored, then set $\boldsymbol{y} = \boldsymbol{a} * \boldsymbol{x} + \boldsymbol{b}$ and send $(\texttt{output}, \boldsymbol{y})$ to Bob. Otherwise, ignore the message.

Fig. 2. Ideal functionality $\mathcal{F}_{\text{OLE}}^m$ for Oblivious Linear Evaluation (OLE).

Functionality $\mathcal{F}_{\text{ROLE}}^m$

1. Upon receiving message $(\texttt{init})$ from both Alice and Bob, store $\texttt{init} = \textit{true}$ and send message $(\texttt{init})$ on leakage port.
2. Upon receiving message $(\texttt{corrupt}, \texttt{A}, (\boldsymbol{u}, \boldsymbol{w}_1))$ on influence port with $\boldsymbol{u}, \boldsymbol{w}_1 \in \mathbb{F}^m$: if no values for $\boldsymbol{u}, \boldsymbol{w}_1$ have been stored, draw and store uniformly random $\boldsymbol{v} \in \mathbb{F}^m$ and compute and store $\boldsymbol{w}_2 := \boldsymbol{u} * \boldsymbol{v} - \boldsymbol{w}_1$.
3. Upon receiving message $(\texttt{corrupt}, \texttt{B}, (\boldsymbol{v}, \boldsymbol{w}_2))$ on influence port with $\boldsymbol{v}, \boldsymbol{w}_2 \in \mathbb{F}^m$: if no values for $\boldsymbol{v}, \boldsymbol{w}_2$ have been stored, draw and store uniformly random $\boldsymbol{u} \in \mathbb{F}^m$ and compute and store $\boldsymbol{w}_1 := \boldsymbol{u} * \boldsymbol{v} - \boldsymbol{w}_2$.
4. Upon receiving message $(\texttt{deliver}, \texttt{A})$ on influence port, if $\texttt{init} = \textit{true}$: if no values for $\boldsymbol{u}, \boldsymbol{v}, \boldsymbol{w}_1$ and $\boldsymbol{w}_2$ have been stored, draw and store uniformly random $\boldsymbol{u}, \boldsymbol{v}, \boldsymbol{w}_1 \in \mathbb{F}^m$ and compute and store $\boldsymbol{w}_2 := \boldsymbol{u} * \boldsymbol{v} - \boldsymbol{w}_1$. Send $(\texttt{output}, (\boldsymbol{u}, \boldsymbol{w}_1))$ to Alice.
5. Upon receiving message $(\texttt{deliver}, \texttt{B})$ on influence port, if $\texttt{init} = \textit{true}$: if no values for $\boldsymbol{u}, \boldsymbol{v}, \boldsymbol{w}_1$ and $\boldsymbol{w}_2$ have been stored, draw and store uniformly random $\boldsymbol{u}, \boldsymbol{v}, \boldsymbol{w}_1 \in \mathbb{F}^m$ and compute and store $\boldsymbol{w}_2 := \boldsymbol{u} * \boldsymbol{v} - \boldsymbol{w}_1$. Send $(\texttt{output}, (\boldsymbol{v}, \boldsymbol{w}_2))$ to Bob.

Fig. 3. Ideal functionality $\mathcal{F}_{\text{ROLE}}^m$ for Random Oblivious Linear Evaluation (ROLE). It chooses random outputs for the parties, but lets a corrupt party choose his own outputs.

a random $\boldsymbol{e}$. Then, upon receiving $\boldsymbol{d}$ and $\boldsymbol{s}$ the simulator extracts $\boldsymbol{a} = \boldsymbol{d} + \boldsymbol{u}$ and $\boldsymbol{b} = \boldsymbol{s} - \boldsymbol{w}_1 - \boldsymbol{a} * \boldsymbol{e}$ and feeds them to the ideal functionality.

Protocol π^m_{OLE}

Input: Alice inputs $\boldsymbol{a}, \boldsymbol{b} \in \mathbb{F}^m$ and Bob inputs $\boldsymbol{x} \in \mathbb{F}^m$
Output: Bob outputs $\boldsymbol{y}$ such that $\boldsymbol{y} = \boldsymbol{a} * \boldsymbol{x} + \boldsymbol{b}$

Protocol:
1. Both run $\mathcal{F}^m_{\mathrm{ROLE}}$ such that Alice gets $\boldsymbol{u}, \boldsymbol{w}_1$ and Bob $\boldsymbol{v}, \boldsymbol{w}_2$
2. Bob computes and sends $\boldsymbol{e} = \boldsymbol{x} - \boldsymbol{v}$;
3. Alice computes and sends $\boldsymbol{d} = \boldsymbol{a} - \boldsymbol{u}$ and $\boldsymbol{s} = \boldsymbol{w}_1 + \boldsymbol{a} * \boldsymbol{e} + \boldsymbol{b}$;
4. Bob returns $\boldsymbol{y} = \boldsymbol{w}_2 + \boldsymbol{x} * \boldsymbol{d} - \boldsymbol{d} * \boldsymbol{e} + \boldsymbol{s}$.

Fig. 4. Protocol for OLE in the $\mathcal{F}^m_{\mathrm{ROLE}}$-hybrid model.

C More Details on Commodity-Based OLE

Concrete Efficiency. We remark on the overall communication of the OLE protocol: For a single OLE instance, the *oblivious RPC's* consist of one tuple $\mathbb{F}^2$ sent from each server to each client totaling $4n \log_2 |\mathbb{F}|$ bits. In the *computation phase*, both parties send to each other one field element for each evaluation point from $d + 2, \ldots, n$, which totals $2(n - (t + m + 2) + 1)$ field elements as $d = t + m$. In the *check phase*, each party sends 3 field elements to the other, and in addition we send a commitment (and its decommitting information). Let κ be the security parameter (e.g., if SHA256 is used for the commitment $\kappa = 256$). Then, the overall communication complexity (including the communication from the servers to the clients, and the communication between the two clients) for generating m OLEs using n servers tolerating up to t corruptions boils down to

$$2(3n - t - m + 2) \log_2 |\mathbb{F}| + 2\kappa.$$

Doing Without Commitments. The only reason we use a commitment is that if Bob would immediately send $B(t_A)$ to Alice, the proof of Lemma 2 would break down because Alice would now know $t+1$ and not t points on $B(x)$, at the time where she has to answer Bob's challenge. Therefore, in the view of Alice, there is only 1 degree of freedom for $B(x)$ instead of 2, as we need in the proof. We can even show that there is an attack on the protocol in this case.

However, this is easy to fix, we just set the degree of polynomials $A(x), B(x)$ to be $d = t + m + 1$ instead of $t + m$, and change the protocol such that in the Check Phase, Bob sends $B(t_A), C_2(t_A)$ in the clear along with t_B. Alice can now do her check immediately and return her answer $A(t_B), C_1(t_B)$ to Bob. We can prove the equivalent of Lemma 2 for the modified protocol using the same proof: even if Alice now learns $B(t_A)$ before she has to answer she is still at least 2 points short of being able to determine $B(x)$, and this is the crucial property that makes the proof go through. The simulation for the modified protocol and the proof that it works is the same as before. The price we pay for this is that we need $n = 2d + 1 = 2t + 2m + 3$, so we need 2 servers more than before. In summary, we have

Corollary 1. *Assume that* $n = 2t + 2m + 3$ *and that* $|\mathbb{F}|$ *is exponential in the security parameter. Then protocol* π^m_{ROLE} *is an implementation of* $\mathcal{F}^m_{\text{ROLE}}$ *with statistical UC-security. The protocol tolerates a static adversary corrupting one client and at most* $t \leq \frac{n-2m-3}{2}$ *servers. The simulation is perfect unless an error event occurs, which has probability at most* $\frac{n}{|\mathbb{F}|-(n+m)}$.

Smaller Fields. The protocol can be modified to work even with small fields where $|\mathbb{F}|$ is not exponentially large in the security parameter: the argument that the check phase makes a mistake with probability a most $n/(|\mathbb{F}| - (m+n))$ holds for any field. In particular, we will get at most constant error probability p as long as $|\mathbb{F}| > n/p + m + n$. Then we can get negligible error probability if we repeat the check phase κ times where κ is the security parameter. This will give error probability at most p^κ.

D Allowing Servers to Be Memoryless

We now look at practical aspect of the commodity model. As mentioned in the introduction, it will clearly be an advantage if the servers in our model do not need memory in the sense that they do not have to remember who they talked to or what was sent. This would mean that a server will not have to administrate identities and log-in credentials, and could simply generate the required data on the fly, say, against payment in some cryptocurrency. An obvious problem with this goal is that the data sent to two clients Alice and Bob must be correlated and a memoryless server cannot make this happen on its own. We now informally sketch a solution to this: We will assume that clients can communicate with servers such that clients can authenticate the identity of servers, but not necessarily the other way around (in practice, one may think of 1-way TLS here).

We also assume that Alice and Bob interact before talking to the servers – indeed this is necessary to create any correlation if the servers have no memory. We assume a 2-way authenticated channel for this, indeed this seems necessary if there are several clients, otherwise an honest Alice could not know with whom she is doing secure computation. Alice and Bob would then agree on a common nonce n_{AB}, as well as a parameter *par* specifying what they will request from the server, as well as the identity *id* of the server. For the case of our protocol, we would have $par = (\mathbb{F}, s, id)$ where $\mathbb{F}$ is the field to use for the OLEs, s is the number of OLEs to request and *id* is the server identifier.

In a naive solution, Alice would send (“A”, par, n_{AB}) to the server who will use this and a private PRF key K to generate Alice's data, and something similar is done for Bob. However, this is clearly not secure: if Alice is corrupt, she can send both (“A”, par, n_{AB}) and (“B”, par, n_{AB}) to each honest server, get Bob's data and break the protocol.

We solve this by generating the nonce such that Alice and Bob each know different secrets relating to the nonce and hence cannot impersonate the other party towards the server. In the simplest case where a nonce is used for only one server, a straightforward way to do this is to make use of a one-way function $f : \{0,1\}^k \mapsto \{0,1\}^k$ where k is a security parameter. Then Alice chooses $x_A \in \{0,1\}^k$ at random, similarly Bob chooses x_B and we let $n_{A,B} = f(x_A)||f(x_B)$ where $||$ denotes concatenation.

Now, party $P \in \{A, B\}$ would send (“P”, par, x_P, n_{AB}). The server checks that x_P is correct with respect to n_{AB} and only then will it send data to P. In this case we can instantiate f efficiently using a hash function, for instance.

For the security of this solution, note that we just need to make sure that the data sent from an honest server to an honest client is secure, since all other data is known and can be modified by the adversary anyway. So assume Alice is honest and agrees on nonce n_{AB} and *par* with corrupt Bob, and let d_A be the data that honest server S will returns to Alice. Now, if Bob sends any request to S that contains something different from par, n_{AB} then S will return something that is (pseudo)uncorrelated to d_A. If the request does contain par, n_{AB}, then S may return either nothing or the data Bob is allowed to get, which is fine. It will only return d_A if the request contains x_A, and this happens only with negligible probability since f is one-way.

It is also possible to use one nonce for all servers. In that case we cannot let Alice simply reveal a preimage to the server. If the server is corrupt it can send x_A to Bob who can then do the same attack as before on honest servers. Instead we can let Alice generate a public key vk_A for a secure signature scheme, while Bob generates vk_B. Now, the request sent by Alice will be of form (“A”, par, σ_A, n_{AB}), where σ_A is a signature on n_{AB} and *par*, and where $par = (\mathbb{F}, s, id, vk_A, vk_B)$. The server only sends back data if the signature verifies under the public key found in *par*, and if its own name occurs in *par*. Note that this last checks prevents a corrupt server from replaying a request to an honest server, and hence security can be argued in a similar way as before.

We remark that a practical implementation of any information theoretically secure MPC needs to implement the secure channels using encryption and (usually) a PKI, which is only computationally secure. We are in a similar situation, only we consider also the authentication aspect: if we assumed ideal authentic channels, the servers could generate data based on the ID's of the parties they know they are talking to. If we do not assume this, we have to use computational assumptions.

References

[ADI+17] Applebaum, B., Damgård, I., Ishai, Y., Nielsen, M., Zichron, L.: Secure arithmetic computation with constant computational overhead. In: Katz, J., Shacham, H. (eds.) CRYPTO 2017. LNCS, vol. 10401, pp. 223–254. Springer, Cham (2017). https://doi.org/10.1007/978-3-319-63688-7_8

[BCD+09] Bogetoft, P., et al.: Secure multiparty computation goes live. In: Dingledine, R., Golle, P. (eds.) FC 2009. LNCS, vol. 5628, pp. 325–343. Springer, Heidelberg (2009). https://doi.org/10.1007/978-3-642-03549-4_20

[BCGI18] Boyle, E., Couteau, G., Gilboa, N., Ishai, Y.: Compressing vector OLE. In: Proceedings of the 2018 ACM SIGSAC Conference on Computer and Communications Security, CCS 2018, Toronto, ON, Canada, 15–19 October 2018, pp. 896–912 (2018)

[Bea97] Beaver, D.: Commodity-based cryptography (extended abstract). In: Proceedings of the Twenty-Ninth Annual ACM Symposium on the Theory of Computing, El Paso, Texas, USA, 4–6 May 1997, pp. 446–455 (1997)

[BLW08] Bogdanov, D., Laur, S., Willemson, J.: Sharemind: a framework for fast privacy-preserving computations. In: Jajodia, S., Lopez, J. (eds.) ESORICS 2008. LNCS, vol. 5283, pp. 192–206. Springer, Heidelberg (2008). https://doi.org/10.1007/978-3-540-88313-5_13

[Can01] Canetti, R.: Universally composable security: a new paradigm for cryptographic protocols. In: FOCS, pp. 136–145 (2001)

[DGN+17] Döttling, N., Ghosh, S., Nielsen, J.B., Nilges, T., Trifiletti, R.: Tinyole: efficient actively secure two-party computation from oblivious linear function evaluation. In: CCS, pp. 2263–2276. ACM (2017)

[DHNO19] Damgård, I., Haagh, H., Nielsen, M., Orlandi, C.: Commodity-based 2PC for arithmetic circuits. Cryptology ePrint Archive, Report 2019/705 (2019). https://eprint.iacr.org/2019/705

[HIKN08] Harnik, D., Ishai, Y., Kushilevitz, E., Nielsen, J.B.: OT-combiners via secure computation. In: Canetti, R. (ed.) TCC 2008. LNCS, vol. 4948, pp. 393–411. Springer, Heidelberg (2008). https://doi.org/10.1007/978-3-540-78524-8_22

[HKN+05] Harnik, D., Kilian, J., Naor, M., Reingold, O., Rosen, A.: On robust combiners for oblivious transfer and other primitives. In: Cramer, R. (ed.) EUROCRYPT 2005. LNCS, vol. 3494, pp. 96–113. Springer, Heidelberg (2005). https://doi.org/10.1007/11426639_6

[IKM+13] Ishai, Y., Kushilevitz, E., Meldgaard, S., Orlandi, C., Paskin-Cherniavsky, A.: On the power of correlated randomness in secure computation. In: Sahai, A. (ed.) TCC 2013. LNCS, vol. 7785, pp. 600–620. Springer, Heidelberg (2013). https://doi.org/10.1007/978-3-642-36594-2_34

[JNO14] Jakobsen, T.P., Nielsen, J.B., Orlandi, C.: A framework for outsourcing of secure computation. In: Proceedings of the 6th Edition of the ACM Workshop on Cloud Computing Security, CCSW 2014, Scottsdale, Arizona, USA, 7 November 2014, pp. 81–92 (2014)

[KOS16] Keller, M., Orsini, E., Scholl, P.: MASCOT: faster malicious arithmetic secure computation with oblivious transfer. In: ACM Conference on Computer and Communications Security, pp. 830–842. ACM (2016)

[KPR18] Keller, M., Pastro, V., Rotaru, D.: Overdrive: making SPDZ great again. In: Nielsen, J.B., Rijmen, V. (eds.) EUROCRYPT 2018. LNCS, vol. 10822, pp. 158–189. Springer, Cham (2018). https://doi.org/10.1007/978-3-319-78372-7_6

[NP99] Naor, M., Pinkas, B.: Oblivious transfer and polynomial evaluation. In: Proceedings of the Thirty-First Annual ACM Symposium on Theory of Computing, Atlanta, Georgia, USA, 1–4 May 1999, pp. 245–254 (1999)

[Rab05] Rabin, M.O.: How to exchange secrets with oblivious transfer. IACR Cryptology ePrint Archive 2005:187 (2005)

[TND+15] Rafael, T., et al.: Information-theoretically secure oblivious polynomial evaluation in the commodity-based model. Int. J. Inf. Secur. **14**(1), 73–84 (2015)

Improved Low-Memory Subset Sum and LPN Algorithms via Multiple Collisions

Claire Delaplace, Andre Esser(✉), and Alexander May

Ruhr University Bochum, Bochum, Germany
{claire.delaplace,andre.esser,alex.may}@rub.de

Abstract. For enabling post-quantum cryptanalytic experiments on a meaningful scale, there is a strong need for low-memory algorithms. We show that the combination of techniques from representations, multiple collision finding, and the Schroeppel-Shamir algorithm leads to improved low-memory algorithms.

For random subset sum instances $(a_1, \ldots, a_n, t)$ defined modulo 2^n, our algorithms improve over the Dissection technique for small memory $M < 2^{0.02n}$ and in the mid-memory regime $2^{0.13n} < M < 2^{0.2n}$.

An application of our technique to LPN of dimension k and constant error p yields significant time complexity improvements over the Dissection-BKW algorithm from Crypto 2018 for all memory parameters $M < 2^{0.35 \frac{k}{\log k}}$.

Keywords: Time-memory trade-off · Representations · Parallel Collision Search

1 Introduction

We are now in a transition phase to post-quantum cryptography, where we have to determine reliably strong parameters for prospective schemes (e.g. for the 2nd round candidates of NIST's post-quantum standardization process [1]). This requires mid-scaled cryptanalytic experiments from which we can safely extrapolate to the desired security levels. However, a major drawback for cryptanalytic analysis of most post-quantum systems, for example in comparison to their number-theoretic counterparts, is the large memory consumption of today's best attack algorithms.

For instance, the famous BKW algorithm [10] for attacking coding/lattice-based schemes [3,16,18,23] as well as lattice sieving [2,8] require huge memory, which prevents their application even for medium-sized parameters. Thus, there is a strong need for developing general techniques that sacrifices a bit of run time at the sake of having a manageable memory consumption. These time-memory trade-offs are well-studied for the subset sum problem [4,6,7,13], which usually serves as a meta-problem to sharpen our tools and techniques. Then,

M. Albrecht (Ed.): IMACC 2019, LNCS 11929, pp. 178–199, 2019.
https://doi.org/10.1007/978-3-030-35199-1_9

these techniques are often transferred to the coding and lattice world [5,8,9,25], where we solve similar vectorial versions of the subset sum problem.

In the subset sum context, the best memory-saving techniques are Schroeppel-Shamir [28] and the elegant Dissection technique from Dinur, Dunkelman, Keller, Shamir [13]. The Schroeppel-Shamir algorithm is a remarkable technique that allows to save memory without sacrificing time at all. Namely, solving subset sum via the usual Meet-in-the-Middle technique using the Horowitz-Sahni algorithm [20] requires time and space $\tilde{\mathcal{O}}(2^{n/2})$, whereas the Schroeppel-Shamir algorithm needs the same time but only $\tilde{\mathcal{O}}(2^{n/4})$ memory. The Dissection technique can be seen as a natural generalization of Schroeppel-Shamir, where Schroeppel-Shamir is the special case of a 4-Dissection. Indeed, one of the original applications of Dissection in [13] is the today's best time-memory trade-off for subset sum. More recently, Esser et al. [15] used Dissection for also designing time-memory trade-offs for the LPN (and LWE) problem.

Without memory restrictions, the currently best algorithm for solving random subset sum instances $\mathbf{a} = (a_1, \ldots, a_n) \in \mathbb{Z}_{2^n}^n, t \in \mathbb{Z}_{2^n}$—with some weight-$\frac{n}{2}$ solution $\mathbf{e} \in \{0,1\}^n$ satisfying $\langle \mathbf{a}, \mathbf{e} \rangle = t \bmod 2^n$—is the Becker-Coron-Joux algorithm [7] with time and space complexity $2^{0.291n}$. The core idea of this algorithm is the so-called representation technique, where the search space for $\mathbf{e}$ is enhanced by R redundant representations of $\mathbf{e}$. Then one enumerates a $\frac{1}{R}$-fraction of the search space such that on expectation one representation survives.

Moreover, Becker, Coron and Joux also provide a polynomial memory algorithm that solves random subset sum instances in time $2^{0.72n}$. This low-memory algorithm represents $\mathbf{e} = \mathbf{e}_1 + \mathbf{e}_2$ with weight-$\frac{n}{4}$ vectors and samples (via a random walk) weight-$\frac{n}{4}$ vectors $\mathbf{e}_1', \mathbf{e}_2'$ until one finds a collision $\langle \mathbf{a}, \mathbf{e}_1' \rangle = t - \langle \mathbf{a}, \mathbf{e}_2' \rangle$. Thus, the low-memory algorithm uses collision finding to recover a 2-sum representation $\mathbf{e}_1' + \mathbf{e}_2' = \mathbf{e}$ of the solution.

Our Contribution. First, we show that multiple collision finding easily provides a time-memory trade-off for the low-memory 2-sum Becker-Coron-Joux algorithm. We benefit basically from the well-known fact that multiple collision finding algorithms like Parallel Collision Search (PCS) [30] provide 2^m collisions for an r-bit function $f : \mathbb{F}_2^r \to \mathbb{F}_2^r$ in time only $2^{\frac{r+m}{2}}$ instead of the trivial $2^m \cdot 2^{\frac{r}{2}}$ for 2^m applications of simple collision finding.

Second, we develop a more involved 4-sum subset sum algorithm that represents $\mathbf{e} = \mathbf{e}_1 + \ldots + \mathbf{e}_4$ with weight-$\frac{n}{8}$ vectors $\mathbf{e}_i$, thereby profiting from the increased amount of representations. We sample all candidates $\mathbf{e}_i'$ for $\mathbf{e}_i$ via PCS as the sum of two weight-$\frac{n}{16}$ vectors, again exploiting the benefits of representations. When having sampled sufficiently many candidate tuple $(\mathbf{e}_1', \ldots, \mathbf{e}_4')$, one of them is a representation of $\mathbf{e}$ with high probability. We then efficiently construct this solution $\mathbf{e}$ using the Schroeppel-Shamir algorithm.

Our improved algorithms' time-memory behaviours are depicted in Fig. 1. Our 2-sum subset sum algorithm provides some improvement in the small memory regime $M < 2^{0.02n}$, whereas our 4-sum algorithm improves on the Dissection technique in the mid-size memory regime $2^{0.13n} < M < 2^{0.2n}$.

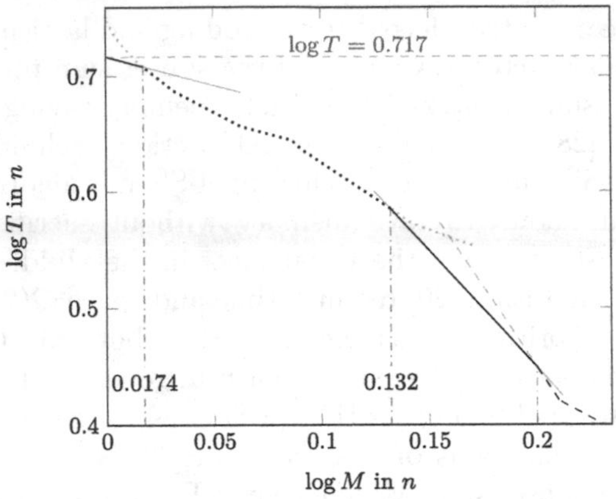

Fig. 1. Comparison of our trade-offs and the previous best trade-offs. The dotted line represent the trade-off obtained via Dissection [13], while the dashed one was obtained in [21] using representations. Our new trade-offs are depicted as solid lines.

Third, for the LPN problem with dimension k and constant error probability p, we build on the Dissection-BKW algorithm proposed by Esser et al. [15]. The authors of [15] show that any algorithm for a certain c-sum problem can be turned into an LPN algorithm. The c-sum problem is solved in [15] via the Dissection framework to obtain efficient time-memory trade-offs.

In this work, we express the c-sum problem from [15] as a multiple collision problem of two $\frac{c}{2}$-sums, which again is solved via sampling collisions with PCS. This results in quite significant time improvements for the whole memory region $M < 2^{0.35\frac{k}{\log k}}$ when compared to the Dissection technique (see Fig. 2). For small memory regimes, the time complexity of our new `PCS-BKW` algorithm even comes close to the best quantum algorithm `Quantum-BKW`, which makes use of a highly memory-efficient Grover search.

In the commonly used time-memory notion, we achieve the results from Table 1. Notice that our `PCS-BKW` algorithm has the same linear dependency on c as `Quantum-BKW`.

Table 1. Our LPN-trade-off `PCS-BKW` in comparison to [15].

Tradeoff	$2^{\log c \cdot \frac{k}{\log k}}$
`PCS-BKW`	$T \cdot M^{\frac{c-2}{4}}$
`Dissection-BKW` [15]	$T \cdot M^{\sqrt{c}}$
`Quantum-BKW` [15]	$T \cdot M^{\frac{c-2}{2}}$

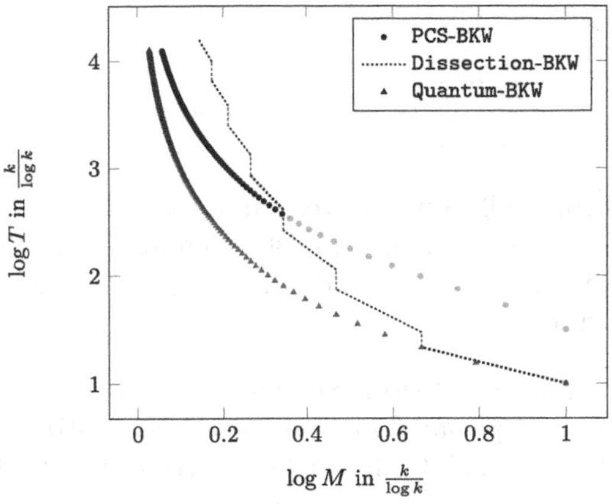

Fig. 2. The dotted marks depict our trade-off PCS-BKW, which improves for memory $M < 2^{0.35\frac{k}{\log k}}$ on the so far best classical algorithm Dissection-BKW from [15]. The triangle marks depict the best known quantum trade-off [15].

Related Work. Parallel Collision Search (PCS), introduced by van Oorschot and Wiener [30], is a widely applied tool in cryptanalysis for achieving good time-memory trade-offs [12,17,22,26,27]. It has been thoroughly analyzed in the context of finding multiple collisions [17,24,29].

Nikolić and Sasaki [26] applied PCS sampling in a similar scenario to ours, namely for constructing improved time-memory trade-offs for the Generalized Birthday Problem based on Wagners k-tree algorithm [31]. Dinur [12] later generalized the Nikolić-Sasaki approach using the Dissection technique.

2 Preliminaries

Let us denote by $\mathbb{Z}_q$ the ring of integers modulo q. $\mathcal{U}_S$ is the uniform distribution over a finite set S. Ber_p is the Bernoulli distribution with parameter p, i.e. for $X \sim \mathrm{Ber}_p$ we have $\Pr[X = 1] = p$ and $\Pr[X = 0] = 1 - p$. We denote by Geo_p the geometric distribution with parameter p, which is the amount of independent Bernoulli trials needed for the first success.

We define lists $L = \{\ell_1, \ell_2, \ldots, \ell_n\}$ as multisets over some universe S. For $\mathbf{x} \in \{0,1\}^n$ we refer to the i-th coordinate of $\mathbf{x}$ by x_i. By $\mathrm{wt}(\mathbf{x})$ we refer to the Hamming weight of $\mathbf{x}$.

For complexity statements we use soft-Oh notation, where $\tilde{\mathcal{O}}(f(k))$ is a shorthand for $\mathcal{O}(\log(f(k))^i \cdot f(k))$ for some constant i. An algorithm succeeds with high probability $p(n)$ if $p(n) \geq 1 - \frac{1}{\mathrm{poly}(n)}$.

We refer to the binary entropy function by $H(\alpha)$, $\alpha \in [0, 1]$. We also make use of the approximation of binomial coefficients derived from Stirlings formula, which is $\binom{n}{m} \simeq 2^{n \cdot H(\frac{m}{n})}$, where $\simeq$ is used to suppress polynomial factors in n.

More precisely we have

$$\frac{2^{n \cdot H(\frac{m}{n})}}{n+1} \leq \binom{n}{m} \leq 2^{n \cdot H(\frac{m}{n})}.$$

For finding multiple collisions between functions $f, g : \mathbb{F}_2^r \to \mathbb{F}_2^r$ we apply the Parallel Collision Search algorithm [30], denoted PCS. We call procedure $\texttt{PCS}(f, g, \alpha r)$ for finding $2^{\alpha r}, 0 \leq \alpha \leq 1$ distinct collisions. The following theorem states PCS's complexities.

Theorem 2.1 (Parallel Collision Search). *Let $r \in \mathbb{N}$, $0 \leq \alpha \leq 1$, and $m := \alpha r$. Given two independent random functions $f\colon \{0,1\}^r \to \{0,1\}^r$ and $g\colon \{0,1\}^r \to \{0,1\}^r$,* Parallel Collision Search *returns 2^m distinct collisions between f and g using expected time $T = \tilde{\mathcal{O}}\left(2^{\frac{r+m}{2}}\right)$ and memory $M = \tilde{\mathcal{O}}\left(2^m\right)$.*

For more details on PCS the reader is referred to [29,30]. A complexity analysis for multiple collisions is given in [17,24,29]. As we apply PCS several times to the same functions, we technically get some dependency problems between the returned collisions of multiple executions. To mitigate this issue, we introduce the notion of flavours, similar to [7,14].

Definition 2.1 (Flavour of a function). *Let f be a function with $f\colon \mathcal{T} \to \mathcal{T}$, where $\mathcal{T} \subseteq \{0,1\}^n$. Let $P_k : \mathcal{T} \to \mathcal{T}$ be a family of bijective functions addressed by k. Then the kth flavour of f is defined as*

$$f^{[k]}(\mathbf{x}) := P_k(f(\mathbf{x})).$$

Note that any collision (x, y) in $f^{[k]}$ is also a collision in f. However, flavoured versions $f^{[k]}$ invoke different function graphs. Therefore we heuristically treat different flavours $f^{[k]}$ of f as independent functions, which yields the independence of output collisions of multiple executions of PCS on different flavours of the same function.

We apply PCS on random subset sum, defined as follows.

Definition 2.2 (Random Subset Sum). *Let $\mathbf{a} \in (\mathbb{Z}_{2^n})^n$ be chosen uniformly at random. For a random $\mathbf{e} \in \mathbb{F}_2^n$ with $\mathrm{wt}(\mathbf{e}) = \frac{n}{2}$ compute $t = \langle \mathbf{a}, \mathbf{e} \rangle \bmod 2^n$. Then $(\mathbf{a}, t) \in (\mathbb{Z}_{2^n})^{n+1}$ is called a random subset sum instance, while each $\mathbf{e}' \in \mathbb{F}_2^n$ with $\langle \mathbf{a}, \mathbf{e}' \rangle = t$ is called a solution.*

Following Howgrave-Graham and Joux [21], we represent a subset sum solution in a redundant manner as sums of vectors, called *representations*.

Definition 2.3 (Representation). *Let $\mathbf{e} \in \{0,1\}^n$ with $\mathrm{wt}(\mathbf{e}) = \beta n$. Any tuple $(\mathbf{e}_1, \mathbf{e}_2, \ldots, \mathbf{e}_k) \in \left(\{0,1\}^n\right)^k$ with $\mathrm{wt}(\mathbf{e}_i) = \frac{\beta n}{k}$ for all $i = 1, \ldots, k$ is called a* representation *of $\mathbf{e}$ if $\mathbf{e} = \mathbf{e}_1 + \mathbf{e}_2 + \ldots + \mathbf{e}_k$.*

The Schroeppel-Shamir Algorithm [28]. We use the algorithm by Schroeppel and Shamir to solve the following problem: Given four lists $L_1, \ldots, L_4$ of equal size 2^m containing uniformly at random drawn elements from $\mathbb{Z}_{2^n}$ together with a target $t \in \mathbb{Z}_{2^n}$, compute the solution set

$$\mathcal{C} = \{(x_{i_1}, \ldots, x_{i_4}) \in L_1 \times \ldots \times L_4 \mid x_{i_1} + \ldots + x_{i_4} = t \mod 2^n\}.$$

While the original algorithm uses involved data structures to guarantee worst case complexities, we use a heuristic simplification by Howgrave-Graham and Joux [21] at the cost of obtaining only expected complexities. However, we still refer to the algorithm as `Schroeppel-Shamir`.

`Schroeppel-Shamir` merges two lists at a time. The lists L_1 and L_2 are merged into a new list

$$L_{12} = \{x + y \mid x \in L_1, y \in L_2, x + y = R \mod 2^m\} \text{ for some } R \in \mathbb{Z}_{2^m}.$$

The constraint R enforces expected size $|L_{12}| = 2^m$. Similarly, we merge L_3, L_4 into L_{34} with the constraint $t - R \bmod 2^m$. Eventually, we merge L_{12}, L_{34} such that their elements sum up to $t \bmod 2^n$. To compute the complete solution set $\mathcal{C}$ the algorithm iterates over all $R \in \mathbb{Z}_{2^m}$.

Since the elements in $L_1, \ldots, L_4$ are uniformly distributed, we have $\mathbb{E}[|C|] = 2^{4m-n}$. Thus $\mathbb{E}[|C|] \leq 2^m$ if $n \geq 3m$. Since each merge can be performed in expected time and memory $\tilde{\mathcal{O}}(2^m)$ the total expected time complexity by iterating over all constraints is $\tilde{\mathcal{O}}(2^{2m})$, while the expected memory complexity is $\tilde{\mathcal{O}}(2^m)$.

Lemma 2.1 (Schroeppel-Shamir). *Let $m, n \in \mathbb{N}$ with $n \geq 3m$. Given four lists $L_1, \ldots, L_4$ of equal size 2^m containing uniformly at random drawn elements from $\mathbb{Z}_{2^n}$ together with a target $t \in \mathbb{Z}_{2^n}$,* `Schroeppel-Shamir` *returns the solution set C in expected time $\tilde{\mathcal{O}}\left(2^{2m}\right)$ and memory $\tilde{\mathcal{O}}\left(2^m\right)$.*

We also apply multiple collision search to the LPN problem, which is defined as follows.

Definition 2.4 (Search LPN Problem). *Let $k \in \mathbb{N}$, $\mathbf{s} \in \mathbb{F}_2^k$ and $p \in [0, \frac{1}{2})$ be a constant. Let* `Sample` *denote an oracle that, when queried, samples $\mathbf{a} \sim \mathcal{U}_{\mathbb{F}_2^k}$, $e \sim Ber_p$ and outputs a* sample *of the form $(\mathbf{a}, b) := (\mathbf{a}, \langle \mathbf{a}, \mathbf{s} \rangle + e)$. The* $\mathtt{LPN}_k$ problem *consists of recovering* $\mathbf{s}$ *given access to* `Sample`.

3 New Subset-Sum Trade-Offs Using PCS

We introduce two new trade-offs for the random subset sum problem from Definition 2.2. The first one, SS-PCS, uses the representation technique together with the PCS algorithm and provides time improvements in the sparse memory area with memory $M < 2^{0.02n}$. The second one, SS-PCS_4, combines representations with Schroeppel-Shamir and PCS to achieve time improvements in the (quite large) memory regime $2^{0.13n} < M < 2^{0.2n}$. Notice that a memory $M = 2^{0.291n}$ is sufficient to run the best algorithm by Becker-Coron-Joux [7] with time $T = M$. All in all, we achieve improvements in a large parameter range of M (for roughly a third of the meaningful exponents).

3.1 Algorithm SS-PCS

Our algorithm SS-PCS builds on the memoryless BCJ-algorithm [7] for which we replace its simple collision search procedure by PCS.

The idea of the BCJ-algorithm is to split the solution vector $\mathbf{e}$ with $\mathrm{wt}(\mathbf{e}) = \frac{n}{2}$ in two vectors $\mathbf{e}_1, \mathbf{e}_2 \in \mathbb{F}_2^n$ each of weight $\frac{n}{4}$. Let $(\mathbf{a}, t)$ be a random subset sum instance and $\mathcal{T} := \{\mathbf{x} \in \mathbb{F}_2^n \mid \mathrm{wt}(\mathbf{x}) = \frac{n}{4}\}$, where $|\mathcal{T}| \simeq 2^{H(\frac{1}{4})n}$ and define the two functions.

$$g, g_t \colon \mathcal{T} \to \mathbb{Z}_{2^{H(1/4)n}}, \text{where}$$

$$g(\mathbf{x}) = \sum_{i=1}^{n} x_i a_i \mod 2^{H(\frac{1}{4})n} \text{ and } g_t(\mathbf{x}) = t - \sum_{i=1}^{n} x_i a_i \mod 2^{H(\frac{1}{4})n}.$$

Note that any representation $(\mathbf{e}_1, \mathbf{e}_2)$ of our solution $\mathbf{e}$ satisfies $g(\mathbf{e}_1) = g_t(\mathbf{e}_2)$. The algorithm now simply searches for collisions $(\mathbf{e}_1', \mathbf{e}_2')$ between g and g_t until $\mathbf{e}_1' + \mathbf{e}_2'$ yields a solution to the subset sum instance.

We expect to have $2^{H(1/4)n}$ collisions between g and g_t, whereas the number of representations $(\mathbf{e}_1, \mathbf{e}_2)$ is $\binom{n/2}{n/4} \simeq 2^{\frac{n}{2}}$. Thus, a random collision solves the subset sum instance with probability $p = 2^{(1/2-H(1/4))n}$. Equivalently, we need to compute on expectation $2^{(H(1/4)-1/2)n} = 2^{0.31n}$ collisions before we find the solution. The BCJ-algorithm uses standard cycle-finding for computing a collision in $2^{H(1/4)\frac{n}{2}}$, resulting in total run time $2^{\frac{3H(1/4)-1}{2}n} = 2^{0.717n}$.

Since we have to compute an exponential amount of collisions, obviously PCS can be utilized to improve on run time if we are willing to spend some memory. In the following, we show that (under some mild heuristic assumption) algorithm SS-PCS (Algorithm 1) solves random subset sum instances in time $2^{(0.717-\frac{\gamma}{2})n}$ using memory $\tilde{\mathcal{O}}(2^{\gamma n})$.

Algorithm 1. SS-PCS$((\mathbf{a}, t), \gamma)$

Input: subset sum instance $(\mathbf{a}, t)$, memory parameter γ
Output: solution $\mathbf{e} \in \mathbb{F}_2^n$ to instance $(\mathbf{a}, t)$ or $\perp$

```
for i = 1 to n^3 · 2^{(H(1/4) - 1/2 - γ)n} do
    choose random flavour k
    L ← PCS(g^[k], g_t^[k], γn)
    if ∃(e_1, e_2) ∈ L, such that e = e_1 + e_2 ∈ {0,1}^n and ⟨a, e⟩ = t then
        return e
return ⊥
```

Notice that for rigorously analyzing the time complexity of SS-PCS, we have to lower bound the probability p for success in each iteration. This in turn requires an upper bound on the number of collisions between g and g_t, which is shown in the following lemma.

Lemma 3.1 (Number of collisions between g and g_t). *Let $n \in \mathbb{N}$ and $(\mathbf{a}, t)$ be a random subset sum instance. Then with high probability the number of collisions between g and g_t is at most $n \cdot 2^{H(1/4)n}$.*

Proof. By definition a collision between g and g_t is a tuple $(\mathbf{x}_1, \mathbf{x}_2) \in \mathcal{T}^2$ with $g(\mathbf{x}_1) + g(\mathbf{x}_2) = t \bmod 2^{H(1/4)n}$. Let us define indicator variables $X_{i,j}$ with $X_{i,j} = 1$ iff $g(\mathbf{x}_i) + g(\mathbf{x}_j) = t \bmod 2^{H(1/4)n}$ and let $X = \sum_{1 \le i,j \le |\mathcal{T}|} X_{i,j}$.

Let $i \neq j$ and $\mathbf{c} = \mathbf{x}_i + \mathbf{x}_j \in \{0, 1, 2\}^n$. Then $\mathbf{c}$ contains at least one 1-coefficient, wlog $c_1 = 1$. By the randomness of $\mathbf{a}$ in our subset sum instance we have.

$$\begin{aligned}\Pr\left[X_{i,j} = 1 \mid i \neq j\right] &= \Pr\left[\langle \mathbf{a}, \mathbf{c}\rangle = t \bmod 2^{H(1/4)n}\right] \\ &= \Pr\left[a_1 = t - \sum_{i=2}^{n} c_i a_i \bmod 2^{H(1/4)n}\right] = \frac{1}{2^{H(1/4)n}}.\end{aligned}$$

Thus, $X_{i,j} \sim \mathrm{Ber}_{2^{-\mathrm{H}(1/4)n}}$ for $i \neq j$. Using $|\mathcal{T}| = \binom{n}{n/4} \le 2^{H(1/4)n}$, we obtain

$$\mathbb{E}[X] \le (|\mathcal{T}|^2 - |\mathcal{T}|) \cdot 2^{-\mathrm{H}(1/4)n} + |\mathcal{T}| \le 2^{H(1/4)n+1}.$$

An application of Markov's inequality yields

$$\Pr\left[X > n2^{H(1/4)n}\right] \le \frac{\mathbb{E}[X]}{n2^{H(1/4)n}} \le \frac{2}{n}.$$

□

Assumptions of the Analysis. For the proof of the complexity of SS-PCS we rely on commonly used heuristics in the context of PCS [13,30] and collision search [7].

Heuristic 1.

(1) PCS returns uniformly random collisions.
(2) PCS behaves on input functions g and g_t as on independent random functions.

We validate Heuristic 1 experimentally in Sect. 5.

Theorem 3.1 (Complexity of SS-PCS). *Let $(\mathbf{a}, t)$ be a random subset sum instance and let $0 \le \gamma \le 0.31$. Then under Heuristic 1 with high probability SS-PCS finds a solution to $(\mathbf{a}, t)$ in expected time $2^{(0.717 - \frac{\gamma}{2})n}$ and memory $\tilde{\mathcal{O}}(2^{\gamma n})$.*

Proof. The time complexity of one iteration of the loop is dominated by the execution of PCS. By Theorem 2.1 PCS finds $2^{\gamma n}$ collisions between g and g_t in expected time $\tilde{\mathcal{O}}\left(2^{\frac{H(1/4)+\gamma}{2}n}\right)$. Therefore the overall expected time complexity is

$$
\begin{aligned}
T &= n^3 \cdot 2^{\frac{2H(1/4)-1-2\gamma}{2}n} \cdot \tilde{\mathcal{O}}\left(2^{\frac{H(1/4)+\gamma}{2}n}\right) \\
&= \tilde{\mathcal{O}}\left(2^{\frac{3H\left(\frac{1}{4}\right)-1-\gamma}{2}n}\right) = 2^{(0.717-\frac{\gamma}{2})n}.
\end{aligned}
$$

Here, the restriction $\gamma \leq 0.31$ ensures that the exponent $H(\frac{1}{4}) - \frac{1}{2} - \gamma$ of the number of iterations of the **for**-loop is positive. Regarding memory, we need to store $|L| = 2^{\gamma n}$ elements.

It remains to show that SS-PCS succeeds with high probability. An iteration is successful whenever list L contains a representation $(\mathbf{e}_1, \mathbf{e}_2)$ of the desired solution $\mathbf{e}$. Let us denote by $\mathcal{R}_{\frac{n}{2},2}$ the number of representations of $\mathbf{e}$ with weight $\frac{n}{2}$ as a decomposition in two vectors $(\mathbf{e}_1, \mathbf{e}_2)$. Via Definition 2.3 and Stirling's formula we obtain

$$
\mathcal{R}_{\frac{n}{2},2} = \binom{n/2}{n/4} \geq \frac{2^{\frac{n}{2}}}{n}.
$$

By construction, each representation $(\mathbf{e}_1, \mathbf{e}_2)$ forms a collision between g and g_t. Thus, a collision sampled uniformly at random from the whole set of collisions C_{g,g_t} is a solution with probability

$$
q := \frac{\mathcal{R}_{\frac{n}{2},2}}{|C_{g,g_t}|}.
$$

Since by Lemma 3.1 with high probability the total amount of collisions is $|C_{g,g_t}| \leq n \cdot 2^{H(\frac{1}{4})n}$, we obtain

$$
q \geq \frac{1}{n^2} \cdot 2^{-(H(\frac{1}{4})-\frac{1}{2})n}.
$$

Let Y denote the amount of sampled collisions until we hit a solution, where $Y \sim \mathrm{Geo}_q$. Then

$$
\mathbb{E}[Y] = \frac{1}{q} \leq n^2 \cdot 2^{(H(\frac{1}{4})-\frac{1}{2})n}.
$$

In total, SS-PCS samples $2^{\gamma n} \cdot n^3 \cdot 2^{(H(\frac{1}{4})-\frac{1}{2}-\gamma)n} = n^3 \cdot 2^{(H(\frac{1}{4})-\frac{1}{2})n}$ collisions. Under Heuristic 1 these are independently and uniformly at random drawn from the whole set of collisions.

Thus, by Markov's inequality SS-PCS does not recover the solution with probability at most

$$
\Pr\left[Y > n^3 \cdot 2^{(H(\frac{1}{4})-\frac{1}{2})n}\right] \leq \frac{\mathbb{E}[Y]}{n^3 \cdot 2^{(H(\frac{1}{4})-\frac{1}{2})n}} \leq \frac{1}{n}.
$$

□

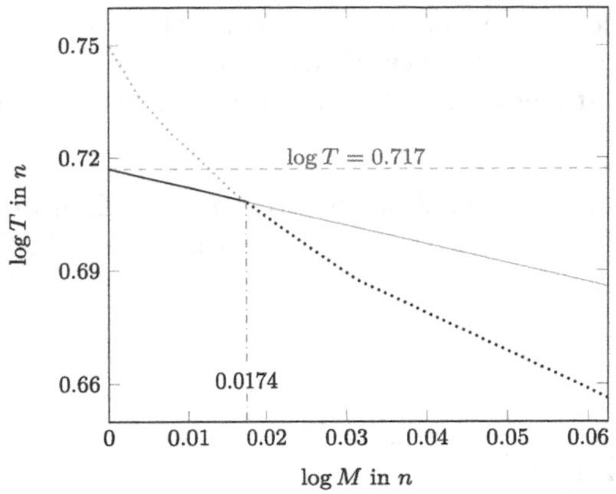

Fig. 3. Comparison of our trade-off and the previous best trade-off for small available memory. The dotted line represents the trade-off obtained in [13], while the solid line is our trade-off achieved by using PCS.

The achieved trade-off is illustrated in Fig. 3. As discussed before, it contains as special case the memoryless algorithm by Becker et al. [7] and is superior to the previously best trade-off based on a combination of PCS and the Dissection framework [13] for any memory $M \leq 2^{0.0174n}$.

3.2 Algorithm SS-PCS$_4$

In this section we introduce a more involved trade-off based on a combination of PCS, the representation technique and the Schroeppel-Shamir algorithm that achieves time improvements for an available memory of $2^{0.13n} < M < 2^{0.2n}$.

Idea of SS-PCS$_4$. We represent our solution $\mathbf{e}$ as a sum of four vectors $\mathbf{e} = \mathbf{e}_1 + \cdots + \mathbf{e}_4$, such that $\mathrm{wt}(\mathbf{e}_j) = \frac{n}{8}$ for all j. We choose random restrictions $R_1, R_2, R_3 \in \mathbb{Z}_{2^{\lambda n}}$ and $R_4 = t - (R_1 + R_2 + R_3) \mod 2^{\lambda n}$, for some $0 < \lambda < 1$.

Using PCS, we compute four lists $L_i \subseteq Z_i$, $i = 1, \ldots, 4$, where

$$Z_i = \left\{ u_i = \langle \mathbf{a}, \mathbf{e}_i' \rangle \mid \mathrm{wt}(\mathbf{e}_i') = \frac{n}{8},\ u_i = R_i \bmod 2^{\lambda n} \right\}.$$

Note that by construction every $(u_1, u_2, u_3, u_4) \in L_1 \times L_2 \times L_3 \times L_4$ satisfies $u_1 + u_2 + u_3 + u_4 = t \bmod 2^{\lambda n}$. We now use the Schroeppel-Shamir algorithm to search for $(u_1, u_2, u_3, u_4) \in L_1 \times L_2 \times L_3 \times L_4$, such that also $u_1 + u_2 + u_3 + u_4 = t \bmod 2^n$, which yields

$$\langle \mathbf{a}, \mathbf{e}_1' \rangle + \langle \mathbf{a}, \mathbf{e}_2' \rangle + \langle \mathbf{a}, \mathbf{e}_3' \rangle + \langle \mathbf{a}, \mathbf{e}_4' \rangle = \langle \mathbf{a}, \mathbf{e}_1' + \mathbf{e}_2' + \mathbf{e}_3' + \mathbf{e}_4' \rangle = t \bmod 2^n.$$

This implies that $\mathbf{e}_1' + \mathbf{e}_2' + \mathbf{e}_3' + \mathbf{e}_4' \in \{0,1,2,3,4\}^n$ solves our subset sum instance iff it defines a vector in $\{0,1\}^n$. We iterate our process until we find a solution.

Remark 3.1. In order to be able to reconstruct the solution, the Schroeppel-Shamir algorithm has to keep track of the vectors $\mathbf{e}'_i$ that were used to produce the corresponding list elements $u_i \in L_i$. For ease of notation, we ignore this in the following.

Let us elaborate a bit on how we construct $L_1, \ldots, L_4$ using PCS. We denote by $\mathcal{S}$ the set $\mathcal{S} := \{\mathbf{x} \in \mathbb{F}_2^n \mid \mathrm{wt}(\mathbf{x}) = n/16\}$ with $|\mathcal{S}| = \binom{n}{n/16} \simeq 2^{H(1/16)n}$ and define the function f as

$$\begin{aligned} f\colon \mathcal{S} &\rightarrow \mathbb{Z}_{2^{H(1/16)n}} \\ \mathbf{x} &\mapsto \sum_{i=1}^{n} x_i a_i \mod 2^{H(1/16)n} = \langle \mathbf{a}, \mathbf{x} \rangle \mod 2^{H(1/16)n}. \end{aligned}$$

Analogously, given an arbitrary value $R \in \mathbb{Z}_{2^{H(1/16)n}}$ we define

$$\begin{aligned} f_R\colon \mathcal{S} &\rightarrow \mathbb{Z}_{2^{H(1/16)n}} \\ \mathbf{x} &\mapsto R - \sum_{i=1}^{n} x_i a_i \mod 2^{H(1/16)n} = R - \langle \mathbf{a}, \mathbf{x} \rangle \mod 2^{H(1/16)n}. \end{aligned}$$

Thus, any collision $(\mathbf{x}, \mathbf{y}) \in \mathcal{S}^2$ between f and f_R satisfies.

$$\begin{aligned} f(\mathbf{x}) = f_R(\mathbf{y}) \Leftrightarrow \sum_{i=1}^{n} x_i a_i &= R - \sum_{i=1}^{n} y_i a_i \mod 2^{H(1/16)n} \\ \Leftrightarrow \sum_{i=1}^{n} (x_i + y_i) a_i &= R \mod 2^{H(1/16)n}. \end{aligned}$$

Since eventually we look for a solution $\mathbf{e} \in \{0,1\}^n$, we filter out non-binary vectors $\mathbf{x} + \mathbf{y}$ in every iteration of our algorithm.

Definition 3.1. *Let* $\mathbf{x}, \mathbf{y} \in \{0,1\}^n$. *We call* $(\mathbf{x}, \mathbf{y})$ consistent *if* $\mathbf{x} + \mathbf{y} \in \{0,1\}^n$, *otherwise we call* $(\mathbf{x}, \mathbf{y})$ inconsistent.

Notice that for consistent $(\mathbf{x}, \mathbf{y})$ we have $\mathrm{wt}(\mathbf{x} + \mathbf{y}) = \mathrm{wt}(\mathbf{x}) + \mathrm{wt}(\mathbf{y})$.

Now, our algorithm proceeds as follows (see also Fig. 4). We fill all lists L_i with collisions provided by PCS, where we filter out inconsistent collisions immediately. Notice that this filter does not discard any representation of the desired solution, since representations are consistent by definition. The whole algorithm is summarized in Algorithm 2.

For the analysis, we use a heuristic similar to Heuristic 1, where we additionally assume that representations of a solution are sufficiently uniform, as commonly done in the context of the representation technique [7,19,21].

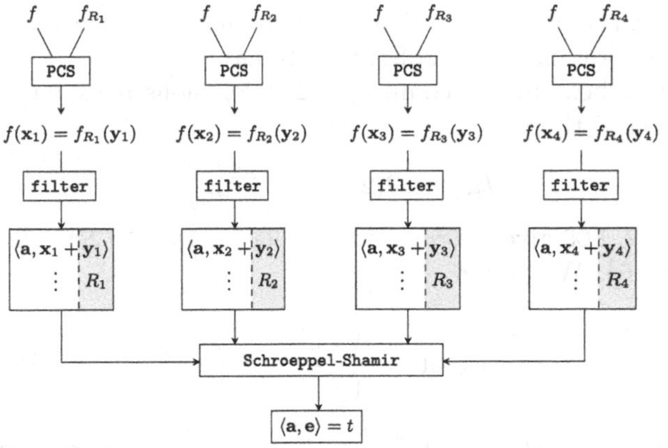

Fig. 4. One iteration of the SS-PCS$_4$ Algorithm.

Algorithm 2. SS-PCS$_4((\mathbf{a}, t), \gamma)$

Input: subset sum instance $(\mathbf{a}, t)$, memory parameter γ
Output: solution $\mathbf{e} \in \mathbb{F}_2^n$ to instance $(\mathbf{a}, t)$ or $\perp$

1: **for** $i = 1$ to $n^4 \cdot 2^{(3 \cdot H(1/16)-1)n}$ **do**
2: choose $R_1, R_2, R_3 \in \mathbb{Z}_{2^{H(1/16)n}}$ uniformly at random
3: $R_4 \leftarrow t - R_1 - R_2 - R_3 \mod 2^{H(1/16)n}$
4: **for** $i = 1$ to $n^9 \cdot 2^{(4H(1/16)-\frac{1}{2}-4\gamma)n}$ **do**
5: choose random flavour k
6: $L_i \leftarrow \texttt{PCS}(f^{[k]}, f_{R_i}^{[k]}, \gamma n)$ for $i = 1, 2, 3, 4$
7: $\texttt{Filter}(L_i)$ for $i = 1, 2, 3, 4$ ▷ Filter out inconsistent vectors.
8: $L \leftarrow \texttt{Schroeppel-Shamir}(L_1, L_2, L_3, L_4, t)$
9: **if** $\exists(u_1, u_2, u_3, u_4) \in L$, such that $\mathbf{e} = \mathbf{e}_1' + \mathbf{e}_2' + \mathbf{e}_3' + \mathbf{e}_4'$ is in $\{0,1\}^n$ **then**
10: **return e**
11: **return** $\perp$

Heuristic 2.

(1) PCS returns uniformly random collisions.
(2) PCS behaves on input functions f and f_R as on independent random functions.
(3) Let $(\mathbf{e}_1, \ldots, \mathbf{e}_4)$ be a representation of the solution $\mathbf{e}$ of a random subset sum instance $(\mathbf{a}, t)$. Then the values of $\langle \mathbf{a}, \mathbf{e}_i \rangle \mod 2^{H(1/16)n}$, $i = 1, 2, 3$, are independently and uniformly distributed.

Theorem 3.2 (Complexity of SS-PCS$_4$**).** *Let* $(\mathbf{a}, t)$ *be a random subset sum instance and let* $\frac{1}{8} \leq \gamma \leq 0.21$. *Then under Heuristic 2 with high probability* SS-PCS$_4$ *finds a solution to* $(\mathbf{a}, t)$ *in expected time* $2^{(0.849-2\gamma)n}$ *and memory* $\tilde{\mathcal{O}}(2^{\gamma n})$.

Proof. We start by analyzing the time complexity of the algorithm. The running time $T_{\mathtt{it}}$ of each iteration of the second **for**-loop of Algorithm 2 (steps 6–10) is dominated by creating $L_1, \ldots, L_4$ via PCS and checking for a solution with

Schroeppel-Shamir. In the following we show that by our choice of γ the run time $T_{\mathtt{it}}$ is solely dominated by Schroeppel-Shamir.

According to Theorem 2.1, computing $2^{\gamma n}$ collisions between f and f_{R_i} can be done in expected time

$$T_{\mathsf{PCS}} = \tilde{\mathcal{O}}(2^{\frac{(H(1/16)+\gamma)n}{2}}).$$

By Heuristic 2, PCS gives us random collisions $(\mathbf{x}, \mathbf{y}) \in_R \mathcal{S}^2$, where $\mathcal{S} := \{\mathbf{x} \in \mathbb{F}_2^n \mid \text{wt}(\mathbf{x}) = n/16\}$. We obtain

$$\Pr\left[(\mathbf{x}, \mathbf{y}) \in_R \mathcal{S}^2 \text{ is consistent}\right] = \frac{\binom{\frac{15}{16}n}{\frac{1}{16}n}}{\binom{n}{\frac{1}{16}n}} = \tilde{\Theta}\left(2^{(\frac{15}{16}H(1/15)-H(1/16))n}\right).$$

Let $\delta = (H(1/16) - \frac{15}{16}H(1/15))n$. Thus, the input lists for Schroeppel-Shamir have expected size $\tilde{\mathcal{O}}(2^{(\gamma-\delta)n})$. An easy calculation shows that the prerequisite of Lemma 2.1 is met. Therefore, an application of Lemma 2.1 yields that Schroeppel-Shamir takes expected time $T_{\mathsf{SS}} = \tilde{\mathcal{O}}(2^{2(\gamma-\delta)n})$. One also easily verifies that our restriction $\gamma \geq \frac{1}{8}$ from Theorem 3.2 implies $T_{\mathsf{SS}} \geq T_{\mathsf{PCS}}$, which entails that T_{SS} dominates $T_{\mathtt{it}}$. Moreover, the prerequisite $\gamma \leq 0.21$ guarantees that the exponent $4H(1/16) - \frac{1}{2} - 4\gamma$ of the number of iterations of the second **for**-loop is positive.

Therefore, the total expected time complexity is

$$T = \tilde{\mathcal{O}}(2^{(7\cdot H(1/16)-3/2-4\gamma)n} \cdot T_{\mathtt{it}}) = \tilde{\mathcal{O}}(2^{(7\cdot H(1/16)-3/2-2\gamma-2\delta)n}) = 2^{(0.849-2\gamma)n}.$$

Concerning memory, we require to store $|L_i| = 2^{\gamma n}$ elements.

It remains to show that Algorithm 2 succeeds with high probability. Let us define the event E_1 that we find within the first **for**-loop a choice of $R_1, \ldots, R_3$ for which a representation $(\mathbf{e}_1, \ldots, \mathbf{e}_4)$ of our solution $\mathbf{e}$ exists. Further, let E_2 be the event that $(\mathbf{e}_1, \ldots, \mathbf{e}_4)$ is found within the second **for**-loop. We show that $E_1 \cap E_2$ happens with high probability in at least one of the iterations of the algorithm.

Let us start with event E_1. Let $\mathcal{R}_{\frac{n}{2},4}$ denote the number of representations of a vector with weight $\frac{n}{2}$ into four vectors, i.e.

$$\mathcal{R}_{\frac{n}{2},4} = \binom{n/2}{n/8, n/8, n/8, n/8} \geq \frac{2^n}{n^3}.$$

By Heuristic 2 for a representation $(\mathbf{e}_1, \mathbf{e}_2, \mathbf{e}_3, \mathbf{e}_4)$ the values $\langle \mathbf{a}, \mathbf{e}_i \rangle \bmod 2^{H(1/16)n}$, for $i = 1, 2, 3$ are independently and uniformly distributed over $\mathbb{Z}_{2^{H(1/16)n}}$. Thus, a fixed choice of $R_1, R_2, R_3 \in \mathbb{Z}_{2^{H(1/16)n}}$ does not yield a representation with probability.

$$\Pr\left[R_1, R_2, R_3 \text{ bad}\right] = (1 - 2^{-3H(1/16)n})^{\mathcal{R}_{\frac{n}{2},4}} \leq (1 - 2^{-3H(1/16)n})^{\frac{2^n}{n^3}}.$$

Using $1 - x \leq e^{-x}$, in all $n^4 \cdot 2^{(3\cdot H(1/16)-1)n}$ iterations of the first **for**-loop we find no representation with probability.

$$\Pr\left[\bar{E_1}\right] \leq (1 - 2^{-3H(1/16)n})^{n\cdot 2^{3H(1/16)n}} \leq e^{-n}.$$

It remains to show that $E_2|E_1$ happens with high probability. As we condition on E_1, we already fixed R_1, R_2, R_3 for which there exist a representation $(\mathbf{e}_1, \ldots, \mathbf{e}_4)$ with $\langle \mathbf{a}, \mathbf{e}_i \rangle = R_i \mod 2^{H(1/16)n}$ for $i = 1, 2, 3$. We now have to lower bound the probability that $(\mathbf{e}_1, \ldots, \mathbf{e}_4) \in L_1 \times \ldots \times L_4$.

Each element from L_i is constructed via PCS, where by Heuristic 2 PCS returns independently and uniformly at random drawn collisions. Let us represent $\mathbf{e}_i$ as $(\mathbf{e}_i^{(1)}, \mathbf{e}_i^{(2)})$, which can be done in $R_{\frac{n}{8},2} = \binom{n/8}{n/16} \geq \frac{1}{n} \cdot 2^{\frac{n}{8}}$ many ways.

Moreover, similar to the proof of Lemma 3.1 we know that with high probability the number of collisions between f and f_{R_i} is upper-bounded by $n \cdot 2^{\mathrm{H}(1/16)n}$. Hence, a random collision from PCS yields $\mathbf{e}_i$ with probability.

$$q \geq \frac{\mathcal{R}_{\frac{n}{8},2}}{n \cdot 2^{\mathrm{H}(1/16)n}} \geq \frac{1}{n^2} \cdot 2^{(-\mathrm{H}(1/16)+1/8)n}.$$

As an execution of PCS provides us $2^{\gamma n}$ collisions we obtain

$$p := \Pr\left[L_i \text{ contains } \mathbf{e}_i\right] = 1 - (1-q)^{2^{\gamma n}}.$$

It follows that

$$\Pr\left[(\mathbf{e}_1, \ldots, \mathbf{e}_4) \in L_1 \times \ldots \times L_4\right] = p^4 = \left(1 - (1-q)^{2^{\gamma n}}\right)^4.$$

Let $Y \sim \mathrm{Geo}_{p^4}$ be a random variable for the number of iterations until $(\mathbf{e}_1, \ldots, \mathbf{e}_4) \in L_1 \times \ldots \times L_4$. Using Bernoulli's inequality $(1-x)^n \geq 1 - xn$ we obtain

$$\mathbb{E}[Y] = \frac{1}{((1-q)^{2^{\gamma n}} - 1)^4} \leq \frac{1}{(1 - q \cdot 2^{\gamma n} - 1)^4} \leq n^8 \cdot 2^{(4H(1/16) - \frac{1}{2} - 4\gamma)n}.$$

Using Markov's inequality, SS-PCS$_4$ does not succeed to find a solution to the random subset sum instance $(\mathbf{a}, t)$ in its $n^9 \cdot 2^{(4H(1/16) - \frac{1}{2} - 4\gamma)n}$ iterations of the second **for**-loop with

$$\Pr\left[\bar{E}_2 \mid E_1\right] = \Pr\left[Y > n^9 \cdot 2^{(4H(1/16) - \frac{1}{2} - 4\gamma)n}\right] \leq \frac{\mathbb{E}[Y]}{n^9 \cdot 2^{(4H(1/16) - \frac{1}{2} - 4\gamma)n}} \leq \frac{1}{n}.$$

□

Our new trade-offs are illustrated in Fig. 5. By Theorem 3.2, SS-PCS$_4$ gives us for memory $2^{\gamma n}$ within the interval $\frac{1}{8} \leq \gamma \leq 0.21$ a line with slope -2 (solid line in Fig. 5). For $\gamma \geq 0.132$ our algorithm improves on the trade-off based on the Dissection framework obtained in Dinur et al. [13] (dotted lines in Fig. 5). Moreover, for $\gamma \leq 0.2$, our algorithm improves on a trade-off by Howgrave-Graham and Joux [21] (dashed line in Fig. 5).

Remark 3.2. We also generalized our 4-sum algorithm SS-PCS$_4$ to a 7- and 11-sum algorithm in a natural way, thereby replacing `Schroeppel-Shamir` with a 7- respectively 11-Dissection. While our 7-sum algorithm gave us an additional (tiny) improvement, the 11-sum algorithm could no longer provide any improvements.

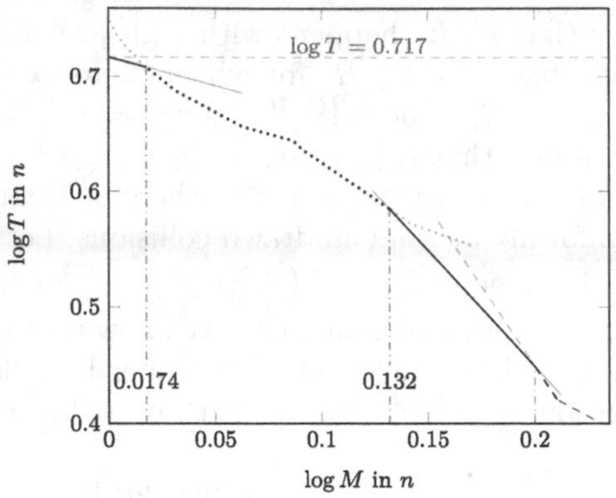

Fig. 5. Comparison of our trade-offs and the previous best trade-offs. The dotted line represent the trade-off obtained in [13], while the dashed one was obtained in [21]. Our new trade-offs are depicted as solid lines.

4 Application to LPN

The results from Sect. 3 show that the subset sum problem formulated as a 4-sum problem in combination with PCS leads to improved time-memory trade-offs. This technique is even superior to the quite involved time-memory Dissection framework for many parameter sets.

Since c-sum applications appear quite often in cryptanalysis, it is natural to ask whether other problems enjoy similar advantages. At Crypto'18, Esser et al. [15] proposed time-memory trade-offs for the LPN problem of dimension k using c-sums in combination with Dissection. In the following, we show that the combination of c-sums with PCS also for LPN provides significant improvements for the whole memory region $M < 2^{0.35\frac{k}{\log k}}$.

The BKW algorithm [10] achieves for $\mathtt{LPN}_k$ time and memory complexity of $2^{\frac{k}{\log k}(1+o(1))}$ using 2-sums. Esser et al. [15] achieved time-memory trade-offs for $\mathtt{LPN}_k$ by using BKW in combination with c-sums for $c > 2$ and the Dissection technique. The resulting algorithm is called Dissection-BKW in [15]. Let us define the c-sum problem underlying $\mathtt{LPN}_k$ more formally.

Definition 4.1 (The c-Sum-Problem ($\mathtt{c\text{-}SP}$)). *Let $b, c, N \in \mathbb{N}$ with $c \geq 2$. Let $L := \{\boldsymbol{\ell}_1, \ldots, \boldsymbol{\ell}_N\}$, where each list element $\boldsymbol{\ell}_i \sim \mathcal{U}_{\mathbb{F}_2^b}$. A* single-solution *of the $\mathtt{c\text{-}SP}_b$ is a size-c set $\mathcal{L} \subset \{1, \ldots, N\}$ such that*

$$\sum_{j \in \mathcal{L}} \boldsymbol{\ell}_j = 0^b.$$

A solution *is a set of at least N distinct single-solutions. The* c-sum-problem *$\mathtt{c\text{-}SP}_b$ consists in finding a solution when given L.*

Hence, we have to find N different combinations of c out of all N b-bit vectors in L such that each of them sums up to the all-zero vector. In the BKW algorithm applied to $\mathtt{LPN}_k$, the block-size b is chosen as $b := \log c \cdot \frac{k}{\log k}$. Esser et al. [15] showed that the running time of their Dissection-BKW on $\mathtt{LPN}_k$ is dominated by the time to solve the $\mathtt{c\text{-}SP}_b$, as formulated in the next theorem.

Here, we use the following heuristic from Esser et al. [15] for analyzing c-sum algorithms. This heuristic is backed up theoretically for $c = 2$ by results in [11] and experimentally for $c > 2$ in [15].

Independence Heuristic [15]. We treat c-sums as independent in the run time analysis.

Algorithm 3. $\mathtt{c\text{-}sum\text{-}PCS}(L)$

Input: list $L = \{\boldsymbol{\ell}_1, \ldots \boldsymbol{\ell}_N\}$ with $\boldsymbol{\ell}_i \in \mathbb{F}_2^b$, where $N = c \cdot 2^{\frac{2b}{c}}$
Output: solution S to the $\mathtt{c\text{-}SP}_b$ instance L
1: split L in c lists L_i of equal size $2^{\frac{2b}{c}}$
2: $S \leftarrow \mathtt{PCS}(f_0, f_1, \log N)$
3: **return** S

Theorem 4.1 [15, Theorem 3.2]. *Let $k, c \in \mathbb{N}$ and $0 < \varepsilon < 1$. Let us define $b := \frac{\log c}{1-\varepsilon} \cdot \frac{k}{\log k}$. Under the Independence Heuristic the following holds: If there is an algorithm solving the $\mathtt{c\text{-}SP}_b$ for an input list of size N in expected time T and memory M, then it is possible to solve the $\mathtt{LPN}_k$ problem with high probability in time $T^{1+o(1)}$ and memory $M^{1+o(1)}$ using $N^{1+o(1)}$ samples, as long as $\log(N) \geq \frac{b + c\log c + 1}{c}$.*

Theorem 4.1 states that N (roughly) denotes the number of samples from our $\mathtt{LPN}_k$ oracle. By Definition 2.4, N can be freely chosen, since we are given full access to `Sample`. However, Lemma 4.1 provides a lower bound on N, which basically guarantees the existence of a solution to the $\mathtt{c\text{-}SP}_b$ as specified in Definition 4.1.

4.1 Computing c-sums with PCS

We choose list size $N = |L| = c \cdot 2^{\frac{2b}{c}}$, which satisfies the constraint from Lemma 4.1. For simplicity of notation, we assume in the following that $c \in \mathbb{N}$ is even. We first split L in c lists of equal size $|L_i| = 2^{\frac{2b}{c}}$, $i = 1, \ldots, c$. Let us denote by $L_i[k]$ the kth element in list L_i. For $j = 0, 1$ we define the functions

$$\begin{aligned} f_j \colon \left(\mathbb{F}_2^{\frac{2b}{c}}\right)^{\frac{c}{2}} &\to \mathbb{F}_2^b, \\ (x_1, \ldots, x_{\frac{c}{2}}) &\mapsto L_{1+j\frac{c}{2}}[x_1] + L_{2+j\frac{c}{2}}[x_2] \ldots + L_{(1+j)\frac{c}{2}}[x_{\frac{c}{2}}]. \end{aligned}$$

Hence, f_0 maps $\frac{c}{2}$ indices to a $\frac{c}{2}$-sum over the first half of all lists, where f_1 computes a $\frac{c}{2}$-sum over the second half. Therefore a collision $f_0(x_1, \ldots, x_{\frac{c}{2}}) = f_1(x_{\frac{c}{2}+1}, \ldots, x_c)$ yields a c-sum satisfying.

$$L_1[x_1] + \ldots + L_c[x_c] = 0^b,$$

as desired for a single-solution in Definition 4.1. A solution to the c-SP$_b$ requires according to Definition 4.1 N distinct single-solutions. Thus, we apply PCS to find $N = c \cdot 2^{\frac{2b}{c}}$ different collisions between f_0 and f_1. The resulting procedure is given in Algorithm 3.

Lemma 4.1 (Complexity of c-sum-PCS). *Let c be even, and let L be a c-SP$_b$-instance with $|L| = N := c \cdot 2^{\frac{2b}{c}}$. Under the Independence Heuristic* c-sum-PCS *solves the* c-SP$_b$ *in expected time $T = \tilde{\mathcal{O}}\left(2^{(\frac{1}{2}+\frac{1}{c})b}\right)$ and memory $M = \tilde{\mathcal{O}}(2^{\frac{2b}{c}})$.*

Proof. The time complexity of c-sum-PCS is dominated by the application of PCS. Since list elements from L are from $\mathcal{U}_{\mathbb{F}_2^b}$, under the Independence Heuristic the functions f_0 and f_1 behave like independent random functions. By Theorem 2.1 the PCS algorithm finds $N = c \cdot 2^{\frac{2b}{c}}$ collisions between f_0 and f_1 with range $\mathbb{F}_2^b$ using memory $M = \tilde{\mathcal{O}}(N) = \tilde{\mathcal{O}}(2^{\frac{2b}{c}})$ and expected time.

$$T = \tilde{\mathcal{O}}(N^{\frac{1}{2}} \cdot 2^{\frac{b}{2}}) = \tilde{\mathcal{O}}(2^{\frac{b}{c}} \cdot 2^{\frac{b}{2}}) = \tilde{\mathcal{O}}(2^{(\frac{1}{2}+\frac{1}{c})b}).$$

Since PCS by definition returns N distinct collisions, this solves the c-SP$_b$. □

Putting Theorem 4.1 with its choice $b := \frac{\log c}{1-\varepsilon} \cdot \frac{k}{\log k}$ and Lemma 4.1 together, we immediately obtain the following LPN trade-off.

Theorem 4.2 (PCS-BKW). *Let $\varepsilon > 0$, $c \in \mathbb{N}$ be even and $k \in \mathbb{N}$ be sufficiently large. Under the Independence Heuristic* LPN$_k$ *can be solved with high probability in time*

$$T = 2^{\left(\frac{1}{2}+\frac{1}{c}\right)\cdot \log c \cdot \frac{k}{\log k}(1+\varepsilon)} \text{ using } M = 2^{\frac{2}{c}\cdot \log c \cdot \frac{k}{\log k}(1+\varepsilon)}$$

memory and samples.

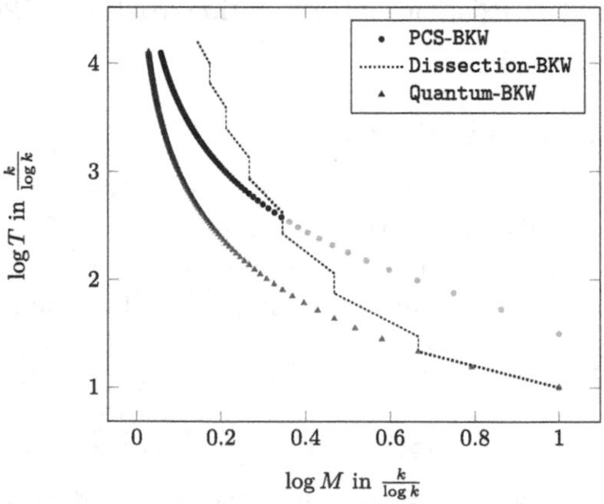

Fig. 6. The dotted marks depict our trade-off PCS-BKW, which improves for memory $M < 2^{0.35\frac{k}{\log k}}$ on the so far best classical algorithm Dissection-BKW from [15]. The triangle marks depict the best known quantum trade-off [15].

Table 2. Our LPN-trade-off PCS-BKW in comparison to [15].

Tradeoff	$2^{\log c \cdot \frac{k}{\log k}} =$
`PCS-BKW`	$T \cdot M^{\frac{c-2}{4}}$
`Dissection-BKW` [15]	$T \cdot M^{\sqrt{c}}$
`Quantum-BKW` [15]	$T \cdot M^{\frac{c-2}{2}}$

In Fig. 6, we compare our new trade-off, called `PCS-BKW`, to `Dissection-BKW` and `Quantum-BKW` from Esser et al. [15]. In comparison to the so far best classical trade-off `Dissection-BKW`, based on the Dissection technique, our `PCS-BKW` improves on the run-time for any memory less than $2^{0.35\frac{k}{\log k}}$, or in other words it improves over any Dissection larger than an 11-Dissection. For very small memory we even come close to the time requirement of the quantum version `Quantum-BKW` with its highly memory-efficient Grover search.

In the commonly used time-memory trade-off notation, we obtain Table 2. We see that `PCS-BKW` shares with `Quantum-BKW` the linear dependency on c, whereas the previously best classical trade-off `Dissection-BKW` had only a square root dependency on c. In comparison with `Quantum-BKW`, for fixed T our algorithm needs only a square of the space requirement.

5 Experimental Verification of Heuristic 1

In this section we present experimental results that verify the used heuristic assumptions.

Distribution of Collisions. Our analyses assume that collision sampling via PCS yields independently and uniformly distributed collisions. Let C be the set of all collisions of some function g and let $S \subseteq C$ be a distinguished subset. By our assumption we hit S with probability $p = \frac{|S|}{|C|}$.

We tested this heuristic for functions with domain size 2^n, where $n \in \{14, 18, 22\}$ by measuring the amount of collisions until we hit S for the first time, which exactly determines the running time of our algorithms in Sect. 3 and should be geometrically distributed with parameter p. To this end we generated a random subset sum instance $(\mathbf{a}, t)$ and constructed a function g mapping $\mathbf{x} \in \mathbb{F}_2^n$ to $\langle \mathbf{a}, \mathbf{x} \rangle \bmod 2^n$. We then enumerated all collisions C of g and randomly chose $S \subseteq C$.

We experimentally observed that the distribution of required collisions until we first hit S is indeed geometric. Moreover, for various different functions g_i we compared the experimentally observed geometric parameters p_i to the expected p. Let $\ell_i = \frac{p}{p_i}$ denote their quotient, so ℓ_i should be close to 1. In Fig. 7 we show the distribution of the ℓ_i in our experiments, where the dots represent the relative frequencies of the ℓ_i. The ℓ_i closely follow a logarithmic-normal distribution – depicted as a solid line – centered around the desired value of one. Moreover,

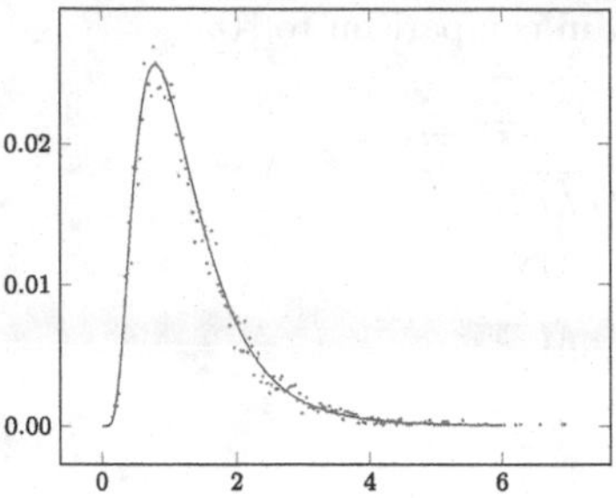

(a) $n = 14$, $|S| = 16$, $\mathbb{E}[\ell_i] = 1.312$, $\mathrm{Var}[\ell_i] = 0.598$. Parameters of log-normal distribution $\mu = 0.118, \sigma^2 = 0.311$. Sample size 10,000

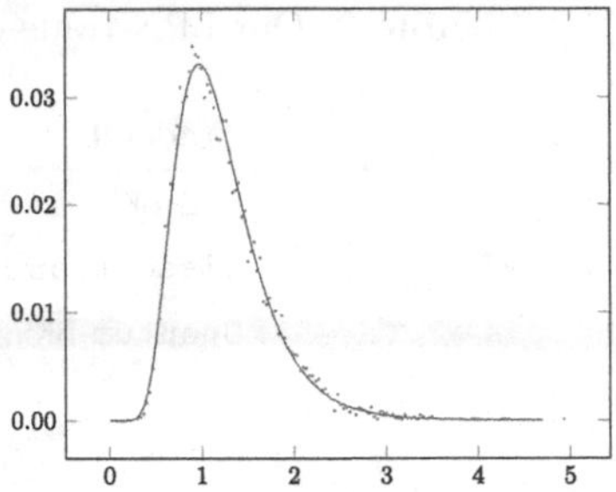

(b) $n = 18$, $|S| = 32$, $\mathbb{E}[\ell_i] = 1.214$, $\mathrm{Var}[\ell_i] = 0.236$. Parameters of log-normal distribution $\mu = 0.120, \sigma^2 = 0.147$. Sample size 10,000

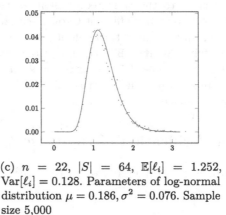

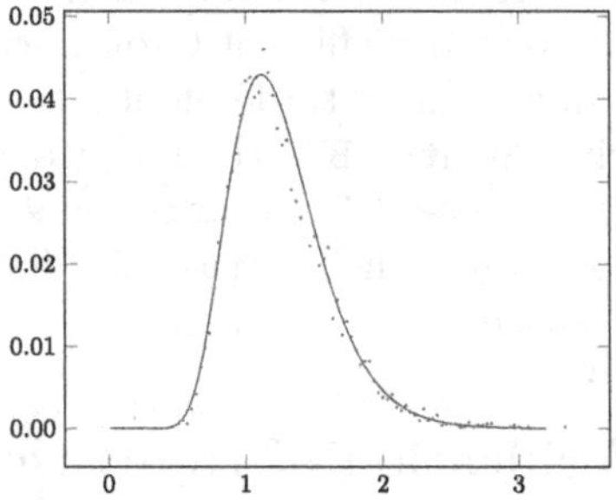

(c) $n = 22$, $|S| = 64$, $\mathbb{E}[\ell_i] = 1.252$, $\mathrm{Var}[\ell_i] = 0.128$. Parameters of log-normal distribution $\mu = 0.186, \sigma^2 = 0.076$. Sample size 5,000

Fig. 7. Distribution of the ℓ_i for $(n, \log|S|) \in \{(14, 4), (18, 5), (22, 6)\}$.

we see that for increasing n the variance of the distribution decreases. Thus, ℓ_i becomes sharply centred around one.

Complexity of PCS Algorithm Applied to Subset Sum Functions. According to Theorem 2.1, the PCS algorithm performs on independent random functions (roughly) $2^{\frac{r+m}{2}}$ evaluations for finding 2^m collisions. This implies on average $2^{\frac{r-m}{2}}$ evaluations per collision.

We verify this asymptotic behaviour experimentally for our subset sum functions g and g_t from Sect. 3.1. We implemented g, g_t for $n \in \{28, 40\}$ and measured the average amount of function evaluations to obtain a specific number of collisions via PCS. Figure 8 shows the results in logarithmic scale, where the dots represent the experimental data averaged over multiple executions. The solid line represents the asymptotic prediction of $\frac{r-m}{2}$ (shifted by a small additive

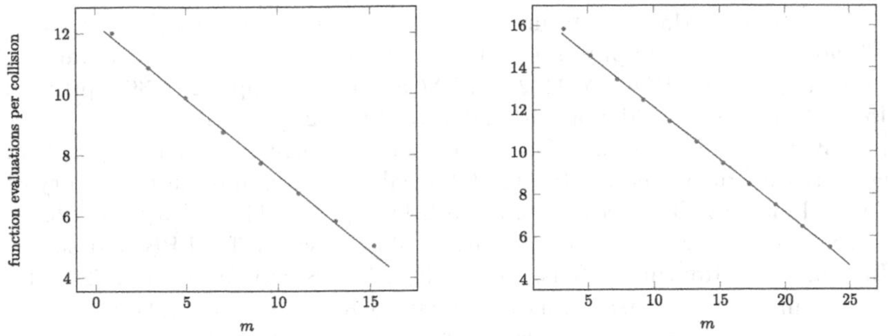

(a) $n = 28$, $r = \log\binom{28}{7} \approx 20$. Each data point is averaged over 30 executions

(b) $n = 40$, $r = \log\binom{40}{10} \approx 30$. Each data point is averaged over 15 executions

Fig. 8. Average number of function evaluations per collision (in logarithmic scale, y-axis) for generating 2^m collisions (x-axis) for $n \in \{28, 40\}$.

constant that stems from the $\tilde{\mathcal{O}}$-notion). We see that the average cost of multiple collision finding in g and g_t closely matches the prediction from Theorem 2.1, and thus g, g_t behave with respect to multiple collision finding like independent random functions.

References

1. http://csrc.nist.gov/groups/ST/post-quantum-crypto/
2. Aggarwal, D., Dadush, D., Regev, O., Stephens-Davidowitz, N.: Solving the shortest vector problem in 2^n time using discrete Gaussian sampling: extended abstract. In: Servedio, R.A., Rubinfeld, R. (eds.) 47th Annual ACM Symposium on Theory of Computing, Portland, OR, USA, 14–17 June 2015, pp. 733–742. ACM Press (2015)
3. Albrecht, M.R., Cid, C., Faugere, J.C., Fitzpatrick, R., Perret, L.: On the complexity of the BKW algorithm on LWE. Des. Codes Crypt. **74**(2), 325–354 (2015)
4. Austrin, P., Kaski, P., Koivisto, M., Määttä, J.: Space-time tradeoffs for subset sum: an improved worst case algorithm. In: Fomin, F.V., Freivalds, R., Kwiatkowska, M.Z., Peleg, D. (eds.) ICALP 2013. LNCS, vol. 7965, pp. 45–56. Springer, Heidelberg (2013). https://doi.org/10.1007/978-3-642-39206-1_5
5. Bai, S., Laarhoven, T., Stehlé, D.: Tuple lattice sieving. LMS J. Comput. Math. **19**(A), 146–162 (2016)
6. Bansal, N., Garg, S., Nederlof, J., Vyas, N.: Faster space-efficient algorithms for subset sum and k-sum. In: Hatami, H., McKenzie, P., King, V. (eds.) 49th Annual ACM Symposium on Theory of Computing, Montreal, QC, Canada, 19–23 June 2017, pp. 198–209. ACM Press (2017)
7. Becker, A., Coron, J.S., Joux, A.: Improved generic algorithms for hard knapsacks. In: Paterson, K.G. (ed.) EUROCRYPT 2011. LNCS, vol. 6632, pp. 364–385. Springer, Heidelberg (2011). https://doi.org/10.1007/978-3-642-20465-4_21
8. Becker, A., Ducas, L., Gama, N., Laarhoven, T.: New directions in nearest neighbor searching with applications to lattice sieving. In: Krauthgamer, R. (ed.) 27th Annual ACM-SIAM Symposium on Discrete Algorithms, Arlington, VA, USA, 10–12 January 2016, pp. 10–24. ACM-SIAM (2016)

9. Becker, A., Joux, A., May, A., Meurer, A.: Decoding random binary linear codes in $2^{n/20}$: how $1 + 1 = 0$ improves information set decoding. In: Pointcheval, D., Johansson, T. (eds.) EUROCRYPT 2012. LNCS, vol. 7237, pp. 520–536. Springer, Heidelberg (2012). https://doi.org/10.1007/978-3-642-29011-4_31
10. Blum, A., Kalai, A., Wasserman, H.: Noise-tolerant learning, the parity problem, and the statistical query model. In: 32nd Annual ACM Symposium on Theory of Computing, Portland, OR, USA, 21–23 May 2000, pp. 435–440. ACM Press (2000)
11. Devadas, S., Ren, L., Xiao, H.: On iterative collision search for LPN and subset sum. In: Kalai, Y., Reyzin, L. (eds.) TCC 2017. LNCS, vol. 10678, pp. 729–746. Springer, Cham (2017). https://doi.org/10.1007/978-3-319-70503-3_24
12. Dinur, I.: An algorithmic framework for the generalized birthday problem. Des. Codes Crypt. **27**(8), 1–30 (2018)
13. Dinur, I., Dunkelman, O., Keller, N., Shamir, A.: Efficient dissection of composite problems, with applications to cryptanalysis, knapsacks, and combinatorial search problems. In: Safavi-Naini, R., Canetti, R. (eds.) CRYPTO 2012. LNCS, vol. 7417, pp. 719–740. Springer, Heidelberg (2012). https://doi.org/10.1007/978-3-642-32009-5_42
14. Dinur, I., Dunkelman, O., Keller, N., Shamir, A.: Memory-efficient algorithms for finding needles in haystacks. In: Robshaw, M., Katz, J. (eds.) CRYPTO 2016. LNCS, vol. 9815, pp. 185–206. Springer, Heidelberg (2016). https://doi.org/10.1007/978-3-662-53008-5_7
15. Esser, A., Heuer, F., Kübler, R., May, A., Sohler, C.: Dissection-BKW. In: Shacham, H., Boldyreva, A. (eds.) CRYPTO 2018. LNCS, vol. 10992, pp. 638–666. Springer, Cham (2018). https://doi.org/10.1007/978-3-319-96881-0_22
16. Esser, A., Kübler, R., May, A.: LPN decoded. In: Katz, J., Shacham, H. (eds.) CRYPTO 2017. LNCS, vol. 10402, pp. 486–514. Springer, Cham (2017). https://doi.org/10.1007/978-3-319-63715-0_17
17. Fouque, P.A., Joux, A., Mavromati, C.: Multi-user collisions: applications to discrete logarithm, Even-Mansour and PRINCE. In: Sarkar, P., Iwata, T. (eds.) ASIACRYPT 2014. LNCS, vol. 8873, pp. 420–438. Springer, Heidelberg (2014). https://doi.org/10.1007/978-3-662-45611-8_22
18. Guo, Q., Johansson, T., Stankovski, P.: Coded-BKW: solving LWE using lattice codes. In: Gennaro, R., Robshaw, M.J.B. (eds.) CRYPTO 2015. LNCS, vol. 9215, pp. 23–42. Springer, Heidelberg (2015). https://doi.org/10.1007/978-3-662-47989-6_2
19. Helm, A., May, A.: Subset sum quantumly in 1.17^n. In: 13th Conference on the Theory of Quantum Computation, Communication and Cryptography (TQC 2018). Schloss Dagstuhl-Leibniz-Zentrum fuer Informatik (2018)
20. Horowitz, E., Sahni, S.: Computing partitions with applications to the knapsack problem. J. ACM (JACM) **21**(2), 277–292 (1974)
21. Howgrave-Graham, N., Joux, A.: New generic algorithms for hard knapsacks. In: Gilbert, H. (ed.) EUROCRYPT 2010. LNCS, vol. 6110, pp. 235–256. Springer, Heidelberg (2010). https://doi.org/10.1007/978-3-642-13190-5_12
22. Joux, A., Lucks, S.: Improved generic algorithms for 3-collisions. In: Matsui, M. (ed.) ASIACRYPT 2009. LNCS, vol. 5912, pp. 347–363. Springer, Heidelberg (2009). https://doi.org/10.1007/978-3-642-10366-7_21
23. Kirchner, P., Fouque, P.A.: An improved BKW algorithm for LWE with applications to cryptography and lattices. In: Gennaro, R., Robshaw, M. (eds.) CRYPTO 2015. LNCS, vol. 9215, pp. 43–62. Springer, Heidelberg (2015). https://doi.org/10.1007/978-3-662-47989-6_3

24. Kuhn, F., Struik, R.: Random walks revisited: extensions of Pollard's rho algorithm for computing multiple discrete logarithms. In: Vaudenay, S., Youssef, A.M. (eds.) SAC 2001. LNCS, vol. 2259, pp. 212–229. Springer, Heidelberg (2001). https://doi.org/10.1007/3-540-45537-X_17
25. May, A., Meurer, A., Thomae, E.: Decoding random linear codes in $\tilde{\mathcal{O}}(2^{0.054n})$. In: Lee, D.H., Wang, X. (eds.) ASIACRYPT 2011. LNCS, vol. 7073, pp. 107–124. Springer, Heidelberg (2011). https://doi.org/10.1007/978-3-642-25385-0_6
26. Nikolić, I., Sasaki, Y.: Refinements of the k-tree algorithm for the generalized birthday problem. In: Iwata, T., Cheon, J.H. (eds.) ASIACRYPT 2015. LNCS, vol. 9453, pp. 683–703. Springer, Heidelberg (2015). https://doi.org/10.1007/978-3-662-48800-3_28
27. Nikolić, I., Sasaki, Y.: A new algorithm for the unbalanced meet-in-the-middle problem. In: Cheon, J.H., Takagi, T. (eds.) ASIACRYPT 2016. LNCS, vol. 10031, pp. 627–647. Springer, Heidelberg (2016). https://doi.org/10.1007/978-3-662-53887-6_23
28. Schroeppel, R., Shamir, A.: A $\mathrm{t} = \mathrm{o}(2^{\mathrm{n}/2})$, $\mathrm{s} = \mathrm{o}(2^{\mathrm{n}/4})$ algorithm for certain NP-complete problems. SIAM J. Comput. **10**(3), 456–464 (1981). https://doi.org/10.1137/0210033
29. Trimoska, M., Ionica, S., Dequen, G.: Time-memory trade-offs for parallel collision search algorithms. Cryptology ePrint Archive, Report 2017/581 (2017). https://eprint.iacr.org/2017/581
30. van Oorschot, P.C., Wiener, M.J.: Parallel collision search with cryptanalytic applications. J. Cryptol. **12**(1), 1–28 (1999)
31. Wagner, D.: A generalized birthday problem. In: Yung, M. (ed.) CRYPTO 2002. LNCS, vol. 2442, pp. 288–304. Springer, Heidelberg (2002). https://doi.org/10.1007/3-540-45708-9_19

Forgery Attacks on FlexAE and FlexAEAD

Maria Eichlseder, Daniel Kales(✉), and Markus Schofnegger

Graz University of Technology, Graz, Austria
{maria.eichlseder,daniel.kales,markus.schofnegger}@iaik.tugraz.at

Abstract. FlexAEAD is one of the round-1 candidates in the ongoing NIST Lightweight Cryptography standardization project and an evolution of the previously published FlexAE scheme. For each data block, the mode performs multiple calls to a permutation in an Even-Mansour construction. The designers argue that the mode permits using a permutation with slightly suboptimal properties in order to increase performance, such as allowing differential distinguishers which cannot be extended to attacks on the full construction.

We first show that this claim is incorrect since differences can not only be introduced via the processed data, but also via the mode's control flow. Second, by exploiting a strong differential clustering effect in the permutation, we propose several forgery attacks on FlexAEAD with complexity less than the security bound given by the designers, such as a block reordering attack on full FlexAEAD-128 with estimated success probability about 2^{-54}. Additionally, we discuss some trivial forgeries and point out domain separation issues.

Keywords: Authenticated encryption · NIST LWC · Forgery · Differential

1 Introduction

FlexAEAD [13] is one of the round-1 candidate algorithms of the ongoing NIST Lightweight Cryptography (LWC) standardization project [15]. The FlexAEAD family of authenticated encryption (AEAD) algorithms is based on the previously published authenticated encryption design FlexAE [10–12]. Compared to FlexAE, FlexAEAD was modified to also handle associated data blocks, and the generation of the ciphertext blocks was amended by an additional call to their internal keyed permutation to better resist reordering attacks.

One noteworthy property of the FlexAEAD design is its use of a primitive with certain non-ideal properties, in particular the possibility to find differential distinguishers. This primitive, the Even-Mansour-keyed permutation PF_K, is essentially used in a triple-encryption construction with different keys K_0, K_1, K_2 to encrypt plaintext blocks into ciphertext blocks, while the intermediate encryption results are accumulated to later derive the tag. For this reason, the designers argue that it is sufficient to ensure that no differential distinguishers can be found for the combined number of rounds. They derive corresponding bounds

M. Albrecht (Ed.): IMACC 2019, LNCS 11929, pp. 200–214, 2019.
https://doi.org/10.1007/978-3-030-35199-1_10

on the maximum expected differential probability of differential characteristics based on the excellent properties of the underlying AES S-box and the (weaker) diffusion properties of the (more lightweight) linear layer.

This approach deviates from the classical separation of mode and primitive, where the security proof of the first relies on well-defined security assumptions regarding the latter. However, related ideas have for example enjoyed considerable popularity in the CAESAR competition for authenticated encryption schemes, since they allow secure designs with a very lightweight footprint (e.g., [1]) or very high performance (e.g., [18]), and can also be found in several other NIST LWC submissions. In these examples, unlike FlexAEAD, the reduced primitives typically serve as state update functions where the state size is considerably larger than the absorbed data block size.

Contributions. We show that all proposed variants of FlexAEAD are vulnerable to different forgery attacks with complexity below the claimed security level. We propose forgeries which reorder the associated data blocks, truncate the ciphertext, or reorder the ciphertext blocks. These attacks work despite several countermeasures included by the designers against such reordering attacks when developing FlexAEAD based on FlexAE.

Our two main observations are (1) that the designers' rationale to combine the mode with a non-ideal primitive and to rely on multiple encryption to hide distinguishing properties is not sound, and (2) that the attacks can be made significantly more efficient by taking advantage of the strong clustering effect of the sparse differential characteristics permitted by the non-ideal primitive. We also discuss applicability to the original FlexAE design, as well as several domain separation problems in FlexAEAD.

Related Work. This note was originally posted on NIST's LWC mailing list [4]. Independent observations on this list include an iterated truncated differential attack and Yoyo distinguisher on the underlying block cipher by Rahman et al. [16,17] and a trivial padding domain separation attack for associated data by Mège [8] that we also mention in Sect. 4.1. The designers of FlexAEAD have responded to these observations with a series of suggested tweaks intended to mitigate all attacks. We briefly discuss these new tweaks in Sect. 4.5.

Outline. We first recall the FlexAEAD and FlexAE designs in Sect. 2. In Sect. 3, we first propose a differential characteristic for the keyed permutation. Then, we show how to apply the resulting counter differential to obtain several forgery attacks on FlexAEAD-64, FlexAEAD-128, and FlexAEAD-256. In Sect. 4, we discuss some additional issues with the FlexAEAD mode of operation that are independent of the underlying primitive PF, as well as the applicability of our results to FlexAE, their practical verification, and the designers' proposed tweaks. Finally, we conclude in Sect. 5.

2 Description of FlexAE and FlexAEAD

In this section, we summarize the construction of FlexAEAD [13].

The main building block of FlexAE and FlexAEAD is a keyed permutation PF_K. PF_K is an Even-Mansour construction with whitening keys K_A, K_B, where the master key is $K = K_A \,||\, K_B$. The inner permutation is built using a nibble shuffling layer reminiscent of Tree-Structured SPNs [7] and several parallel applications of the 8-bit AES S-Box [2]. The full construction of PF_K is given in Fig. 1. For a more detailed description of the building blocks, we refer to the NIST submission document [13].

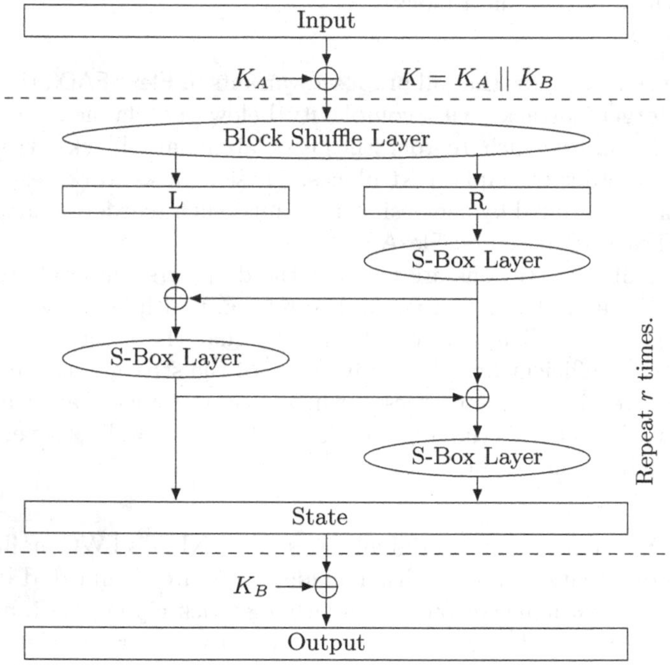

Fig. 1. Keyed permutation PF_K [13] with $r \in \{5, 6, 7\}$ for FlexAEAD-$\{64, 128, 256\}$.

PF_K is used with four different keys in the FlexAEAD construction. These four keys are derived from a master key K^* by applying PF_{K^*} three times to an initial state of 0^n, iterating this process to generate enough bits for the four subkeys K_0, K_1, K_2, K_3. A base counter is generated by applying PF_{K_3} to the nonce. This base counter is then used to generate the sequence $(S_0, \ldots, S_{n+m-1})$ by repeatedly applying the increment step INC32 to the base counter, which treats each 32-bit block of the base counter as an 32-bit little-endian integer and increases it by one. PF_{K_3} is then again applied to the result of INC32, yielding the block S_0. Further blocks S_i can be generated by calling INC32 on the base counter $i+1$ times before finally applying PF_{K_3}, as shown in Fig. 2a.

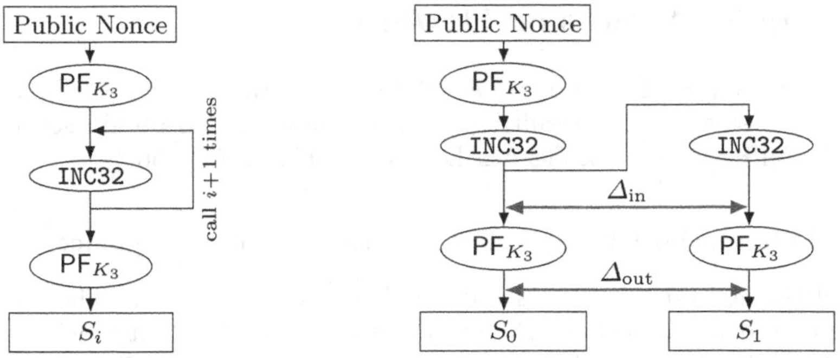

(a) Generation of the sequence S. (b) Differential $\Delta_{\text{in}} \rightarrow \Delta_{\text{out}}$.

Fig. 2. Counter-based differences in the generation of the sequence S.

The sequence $S_0, \ldots, S_{n-1}, S_n, \ldots, S_{n+m-1}$ is then used to mask the associated data blocks $A_0, \ldots, A_{n-1}$ and plaintext blocks $P_0, \ldots, P_{m-1}$, as well as intermediate results of the ciphertext generation process. This construction is inspired by the Integrity Aware Parallelizable Mode (IAPM) [5,6]. To compute the tag T, PF_{K_0} is applied to the XOR of the intermediate results after the first application of PF_{K_2} to each masked block, plus a constant indicating whether the last plaintext block was a full or a partial block. The full construction is illustrated in Fig. 3.

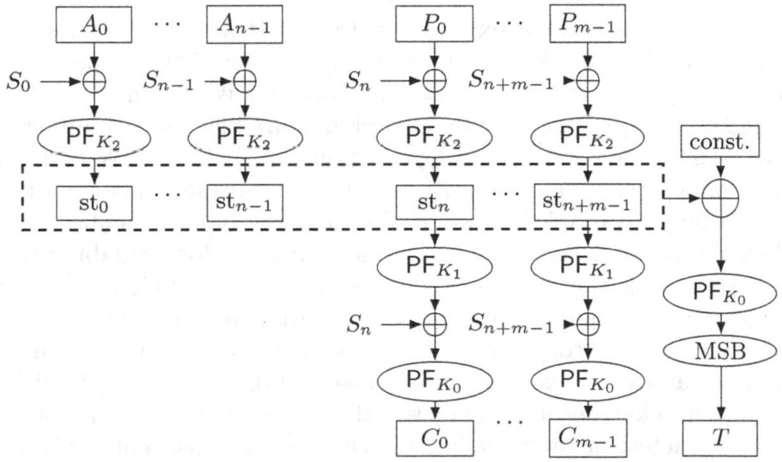

Fig. 3. The FlexAEAD mode for authenticated encryption (simplified, from [13]).

3 Forgery Attacks on FlexAEAD

In this section, we first propose a differential characteristic for PF_{K_3}. Then, we show how to apply the resulting counter differential to obtain several forgery attacks on FlexAEAD-64, FlexAEAD-128, and FlexAEAD-256.

3.1 Differential Characteristic for the Counter Sequence

Recall the generation of the sequence S, as shown in Fig. 2a. The intermediate state is updated by calling INC32, incrementing each 32-bit block of the state. Consider the difference between two states S_i and S_{i+1}: The only difference between the input to the final call to PF_{K_3} is one additional call to INC32. A little-endian addition by 1 behaves like an XOR operation with probability $\frac{1}{2}$ (exactly when the least significant bit of the state is zero). Therefore, the call INC32 behaves like an XOR with a probability of 2^{-2} (2^{-4}, 2^{-8}) for FlexAEAD-64 (FlexAEAD-128, FlexAEAD-256). This process is shown in Fig. 2b.

Consider the input difference Δ_{in} = 01000000 01000000 FlexAEAD-64 (repeated twice for FlexAEAD-128 and four times for FlexAEAD-256). We are interested in differential characteristics for PF starting with this input difference, and use a combined Mixed-Integer Linear Programming (MILP) [9,19] and Constraint Programming (CP)/Satisfiability (SAT) model of the cipher for our search: We first find characteristics truncated to nibble activity with the minimum number of active S-boxes using a MILP model for solvers such as IBM CPLEX or Gurobi. Then, we try to find compatible bitwise differences leading to the highest expected differential probability of the resulting differential characteristic using a precise model of valid transitions in the Differential Distribution Table (DDT) of the AES S-box expressed in the Constraint Programming syntax of the Z3 solver. We remark that the resulting characteristic is not necessarily optimal with respect to its exact probability, but this is not our aim.

For the MILP model, we use binary decision variables for each nibble of the state after each relevant step (S-box layers, XORs, etc.). The nibble permutation can then be modelled trivially, the XORs between the state halves can be modelled using a helper variable per nibble Xor and the branch number of 2, and each S-box can be modelled in a similar way using a helper variable per S-box and the bijectivity of the S-box (i.e., at least one input nibble is active if and only if at least one output nibble is active). Additionally, we use the fixed input difference Δ_{in} as initial constraints. The objective function to be minimized is the number of active S-boxes, which is an easy task for various MILP solvers. The resulting nibble-truncated characteristic can be extended to a full bitwise differential characteristic by modelling the DDT using Constraint Programming. More specifically, we simply list all possible transitions from 8-bit input differences to 8-bit output differences as "hard constraints" and punish transitions with lower probability using Z3's "soft constraints" with appropriate costs. The solver yields a solution that satisfies all hard constraints and minimizes the cost for violating soft constraints, i.e., choosing suboptimal transitions. The resulting differential characteristics for PF are illustrated in Fig. 4.

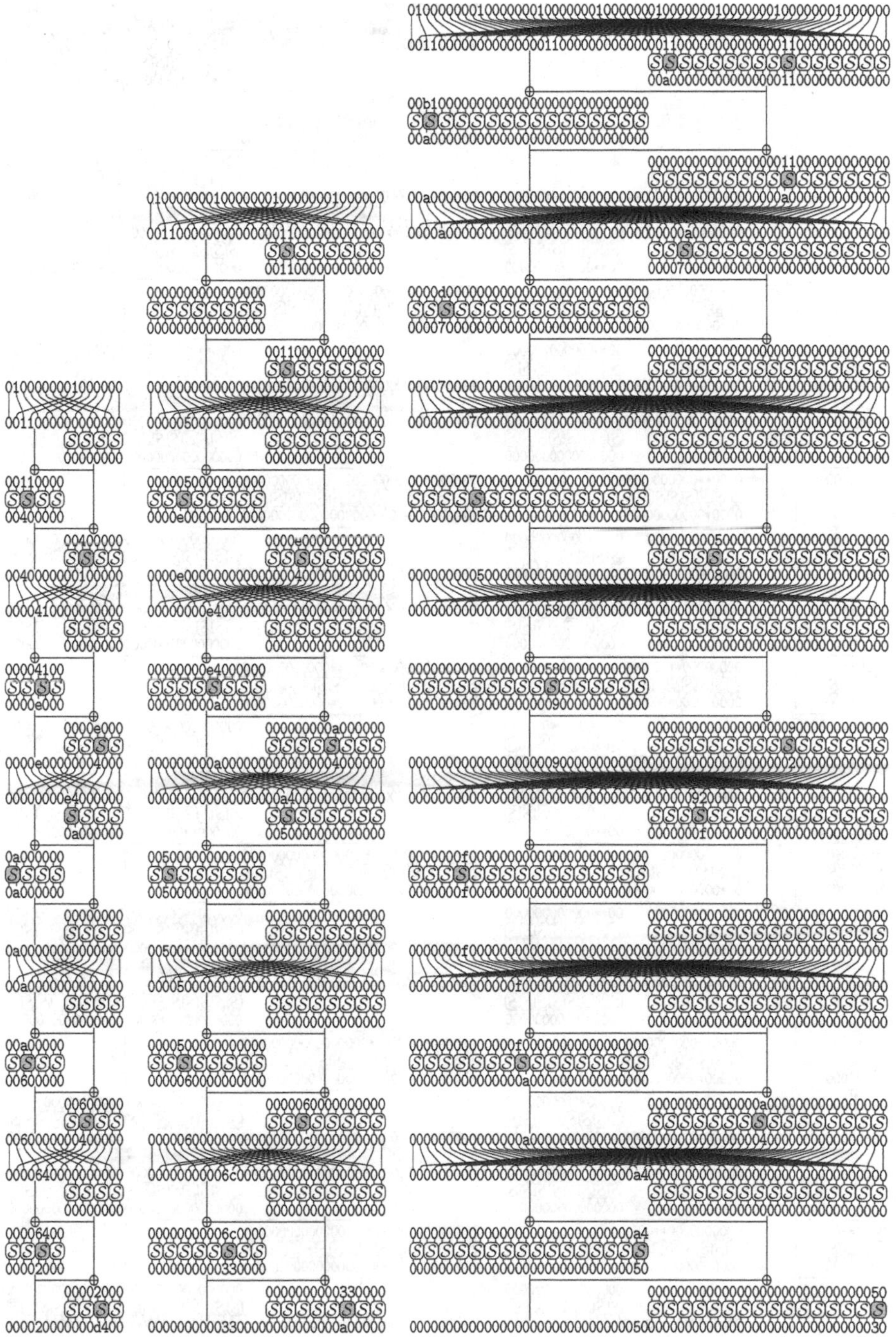

(a) F-64: 2^{-66} (b) FlexAEAD-128: 2^{-79} (c) FlexAEAD-256: 2^{-108}

Fig. 4. Differential characteristics for full-round PF_K in FlexAEAD variants.

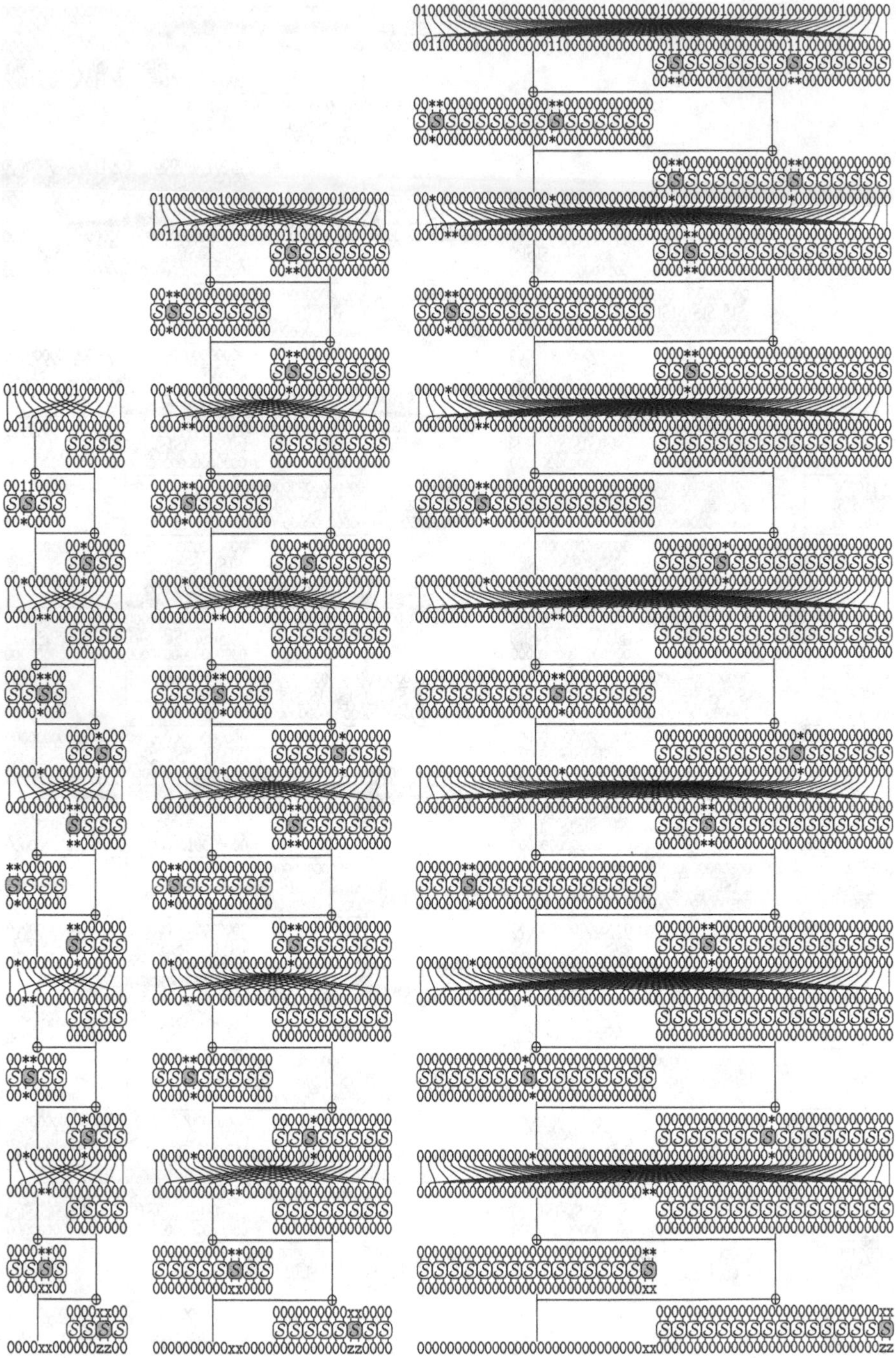

(a) F-64: 2^{-46} (b) FlexAEAD-128: 2^{-54} (c) FlexAEAD-256: 2^{-70}

Fig. 5. Clustered characteristics for full-round PF_K in FlexAEAD variants.

In the following, we always denote the input difference of this characteristic as Δ_{in} and the output difference as Δ_{out}. Under the Markov assumption, the probability of these differential characteristics is 2^{-66} (Fig. 4a for FlexAEAD-64), 2^{-79} (Fig. 4b for FlexAEAD-128), and 2^{-108} (Fig. 4c for FlexAEAD-256), respectively. We remark that the Markov assumption is clearly not well-suited for this keyless construction with limited diffusion.

The round function construction is very prone to clustering of characteristics, as illustrated by the corresponding partially truncated characteristics in Fig. 5, where $*$ denotes a nibble with an unspecified difference, xx is an arbitrary fixed nonzero difference, and zz is the high-probability S-box output difference with $\mathbb{P}[\texttt{xx} \to \texttt{zz}] = 2^{-6}$. Using the estimate that $\mathbb{P}[\texttt{11} \to \texttt{**}] = 1$, $\mathbb{P}[\{\texttt{**}, \texttt{*0}, \texttt{0*}\} \to \texttt{*0}] = \mathbb{P}[\{\texttt{**}, \texttt{*0}, \texttt{0*}\} \to \texttt{0*}] = 2^{-4}$, and $\mathbb{P}[\texttt{**} \to \texttt{xx}] = 2^{-8}$, we obtain estimated probabilities of 2^{-46} (FlexAEAD-64), 2^{-54} (FlexAEAD-128), and 2^{-70} (FlexAEAD-256). Similar clusters for different input differences with maximal probability by updating the cost function of the previous MILP model: For any S-box, let $x_0, x_1 \in \{0, 1\}$ denote the activity of its input nibbles, $y_0, y_1 \in \{0, 1\}$ its output nibbles, and $s \in \{0, 1\}$ the S-box activity helper variable. Instead of summing over s for each S-box for the cost function, minimize the sum over $4 \cdot (2 \cdot s - y_0 - y_1)$, which contributes a cost of 4 (probability 2^{-4}) if the S-box is active and requires one inactive output nibble, and cost 0 otherwise. Additionally, the probability of producing the specific bitwise output difference after the last round needs to be taken into account, which can be approximated by a cost of 4 per active nibble at the output (disregarding small optimizations as used in the final rounds in Fig. 5).

Furthermore, these clusters work not only for a fixed starting difference of 01 in the least significant byte of each counter, but for any single-nibble differences $\{\texttt{01}, \texttt{03}, \texttt{07}, \texttt{0f}\}$. As a consequence, the transition from modular difference $+1$ in each counter to a suitable XOR difference works with high success probability close to 1. A more precise probability estimate could be obtained using tools such as semi-truncated characteristics [3] and exploiting the lack of round keys, but we expect a very similar result. Practical experiments on up to 3 rounds confirm this estimate, see Sect. 4.4.

3.2 Forgery Attacks for FlexAEAD Using the Counter Difference

We can now use these differentials $\Delta_{\text{in}} \to \Delta_{\text{out}}$ in the counter sequence to mount forgery attacks on the full FlexAEAD-64, FlexAEAD-128, and FlexAEAD-256 schemes. In the following, we describe several different approaches.

Changing Associated Data. We query a tag for some plaintext P with associated data $A = A_0 \parallel A_1$, where $A_0 \oplus A_1 = \Delta_{\text{out}}$. With a probability of about 2^{-46} (FlexAEAD-64), 2^{-54} (FlexAEAD-128), or 2^{-70} (FlexAEAD-256), the sequence blocks S_0 and S_1 follow the cluster of differential characteristics, and therefore also fulfill $S_0 \oplus S_1 = \Delta_{\text{out}}$. Then, $A_0 \oplus A_1 \oplus S_0 \oplus S_1 = 0$, so $S_0 \oplus A_0 = S_1 \oplus A_1$, resulting in a contribution of the two associated data blocks to the checksum of $\mathsf{PF}_{K_2}(S_0 \oplus A_0) \oplus \mathsf{PF}_{K_2}(S_1 \oplus A_1) = 0$.

Now, if we swap A_0 and A_1, with the same reasoning, the contribution to the checksum will again be 0, so the original tag is valid for the modified associated data with swapped blocks.

Although the example above assumes a distance of 1 between associated data blocks, we can generalize this property and also find similar differential characteristics for higher distances j. Distances with lower hamming weight and with several suitable XOR differences following the same truncated difference generally result in a better probability. In practical experiments on round-reduced FlexAEAD, we observed an even higher success probability than expected when swapping associated data blocks, such as examples with a non-zero, but constant contribution to the checksum.

Truncating Ciphertext. In a similar fashion to the previous attack, we can also use this strategy to create a forgery targeting the plaintext.

Again, consider the generation of the sequence S, using the same strategy and differential characteristics as in Sect. 3.1. Now query a tag with a plaintext $P = P_0 \,||\, \cdots \,||\, P_{m-2} \,||\, P_{m-1}$, where $P_{m-2} \oplus P_{m-1} = \Delta_{\text{out}}$. With the same reasoning and success probability as before, the combined contribution to the checksum of P_{m-2} and P_{m-1} is 0, since, like in the previous attack, $P_{m-2} \oplus S_{n+m-2} = P_{m-1} \oplus S_{n+m-1}$, and therefore $\mathsf{PF}_{K_2}(S_{n+m-2} \oplus P_{m-2}) \oplus \mathsf{PF}_{K_2}(S_{n+m-1} \oplus P_{m-1}) = 0$.

We can now produce a forgery by truncating the last two ciphertext blocks, since the contribution of the corresponding plaintext blocks to the checksum and therefore the tag is 0, and the number of blocks does not influence the tag.

Reordering Ciphertext. For their submission to the NIST Lightweight Cryptography standardization project, the designers of FlexAEAD updated their design from the previous version FlexAE in order to include associated data and prevent trivial reordering attacks. In this section, we show a forgery based on reordering ciphertexts of a chosen-plaintext query. Again, this attack is based on the same property of the sequence S as the two previous attacks.

Consider a chosen plaintext $P = P_0 \,||\, P_1$, where $P_0 \oplus P_1 = \Delta_{\text{out}}$, and the corresponding ciphertext $C = C_0 \,||\, C_1$ and tag T. As before, this difference of 1 in the block index results in the differential characteristics depicted in Fig. 5. In FlexAEAD, the sequence values S_0 and S_1 are added at two points during the encryption process, so that the internal difference Δ_{out} propagates as shown in Fig. 6. By now swapping the ciphertext blocks C_0 and C_1, we have a valid forgery using the original tag T. If the sequence generation followed the chosen characteristic, the two swapped ciphertext blocks will again have a checksum contribution of 0 during the decryption process. However, the resulting plaintext blocks are unpredictable.

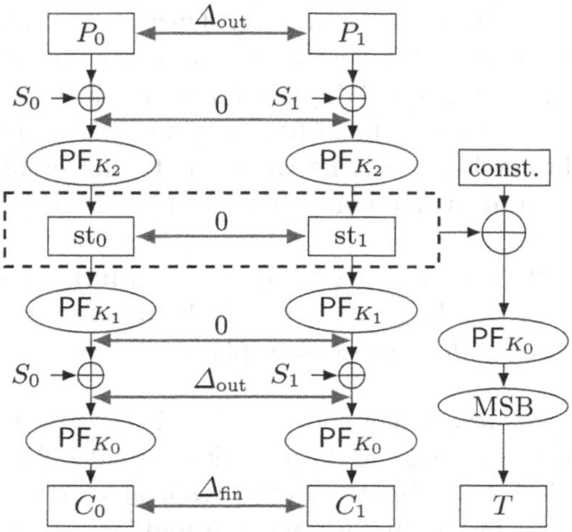

Fig. 6. Propagation of differences in the FlexAEAD encryption function, assuming $S_0 \oplus S_1 = \Delta_{out}$.

4 Discussion and Further Observations on the Mode

The forgery attacks proposed in Sect. 3 exploit high-probability differential characteristics for the primitive PF, and are best prevented by increasing the number of rounds or replacing this primitive entirely. We remark that the designers were aware of the low bounds for PF, but argued that only the bounds for the multiple application $\mathsf{PF}^3 = \mathsf{PF} \circ \mathsf{PF} \circ \mathsf{PF}$ as used to compute C_i from P_i are relevant. As demonstrated in Sect. 3, this is not the case.

In the following, we discuss additional issues with the FlexAEAD mode of operation. These issues are independent of the underlying primitive PF and can be fixed with small tweaks to the mode or by phrasing the security claim for more restrictive message lengths. Finally, we discuss the applicability of our results to FlexAE and their practical verification.

4.1 Domain Separation and Length Issues

Domain Separation between Associated Data and Plaintext. In Fig. 3, observe that the first step of the encryption (i.e., producing part of the checksum) is exactly the same for associated data and the plaintext. Using this observation, we can create a trivial forgery with probability 1 by redeclaring some part of the plaintext to be associated data instead. As an example, given a nonce-associated data-ciphertext-tag tuple (N, A, C, T) with a known plaintext $P = P_0 \,||\, P_1$ (and a corresponding ciphertext $C = C_0 \,||\, C_1$), we can craft a second valid tuple (N^*, A^*, C^*, T^*) with probability 1 by setting

$$N^* = N, \quad A^* = A \,||\, P_0, \quad C^* = C_1, \quad T^* = T.$$

This forgery attack works for all versions of FlexAEAD.

Zero-Length Associated Data and Plaintext. During encryption, the nonce is used to generate the sequence S for each block of associated data and plaintext. If the combined length of associated data and plaintext is 0, the sequence is never used during encryption at all and the final tag does not depend on the nonce. Thus, a forgery is obtained by querying the static tag for empty associated data and plaintext under an arbitrary nonce and then combining it with a different nonce.

To fix this issue, the nonce needs to be included in the computation of the tag, for example by prepending the nonce N before the first associated data block A_0 in the associated data processing phase.

Padding of Associated Data. The associated data is padded using zeros, but the original length of the last associated data block does not influence the tag. Thus, there is no way to distinguish between valid associated data ending in 0 and a padded associated data block. In contrast, the padding of the plaintext has an influence on the final tag value; it appears this was omitted for associated data by mistake, and can easily be fixed. This issue was also observed by Mège [8].

4.2 Other Observations

Overflow of the Internal Counter. During the generation of the sequence S, an internal state is updated repeatedly using the `INC32` function. The internal state repeats after 2^{32} calls, therefore limiting the size of the encrypted payload to 2^{32} blocks. Otherwise, if the associated data or plaintext length is larger than 2^{32}, any two blocks $(A_i, A_{i+2^{32}})$ or $(C_i, C_{i+2^{32}})$ can be swapped to produce a forgery.

This can be addressed by either explicitly imposing a corresponding data length limit as part of the security claim, or by choosing a counter size that does not overflow within the data length limit.

4.3 Applicability to FlexAE

FlexAE, published at IEEE ICC 2017 [11], is the predecessor design of FlexAEAD. It features a slightly simpler mode that omits the step $\mathsf{PF}_{K_1}(\cdot) \oplus S_j$ in the computation of ciphertext block C_j and does not support associated data A. The primitive also shows minor differences, such as 3 slightly different S-boxes, which have no significant impact on the security analysis. The additional steps in FlexAEAD were added by the designers to fix problems in FlexAE; in particular, the ciphertext reordering attack of Sect. 3.2 works with probability 1 for FlexAE.

FlexAE even permits forgeries with zero encryption queries, as illustrated in Fig. 7. The following is a forgery with probability about 2^{-54} for FlexAE-64–128 (or, with similar characteristics, 2^{-86} for FlexAE-128–256, 2^{-150} for FlexAE-256–512, or 2^{-278} for FlexAE-512–1024): Take an arbitrary nonce N and single-block ciphertext C, and select $T = C \oplus \Delta_{\text{out}}$ with $\Delta_{\text{out}} =$ `xx000000 zz000000`, where `xx` is an arbitrary nonzero difference and `zz` is the high-probability S-box output difference with $\mathbb{P}[\texttt{xx} \to \texttt{zz}] = 2^{-6}$. This works based on the differential with input difference $\Delta_{\text{in}} =$ `10101010 10101010` for

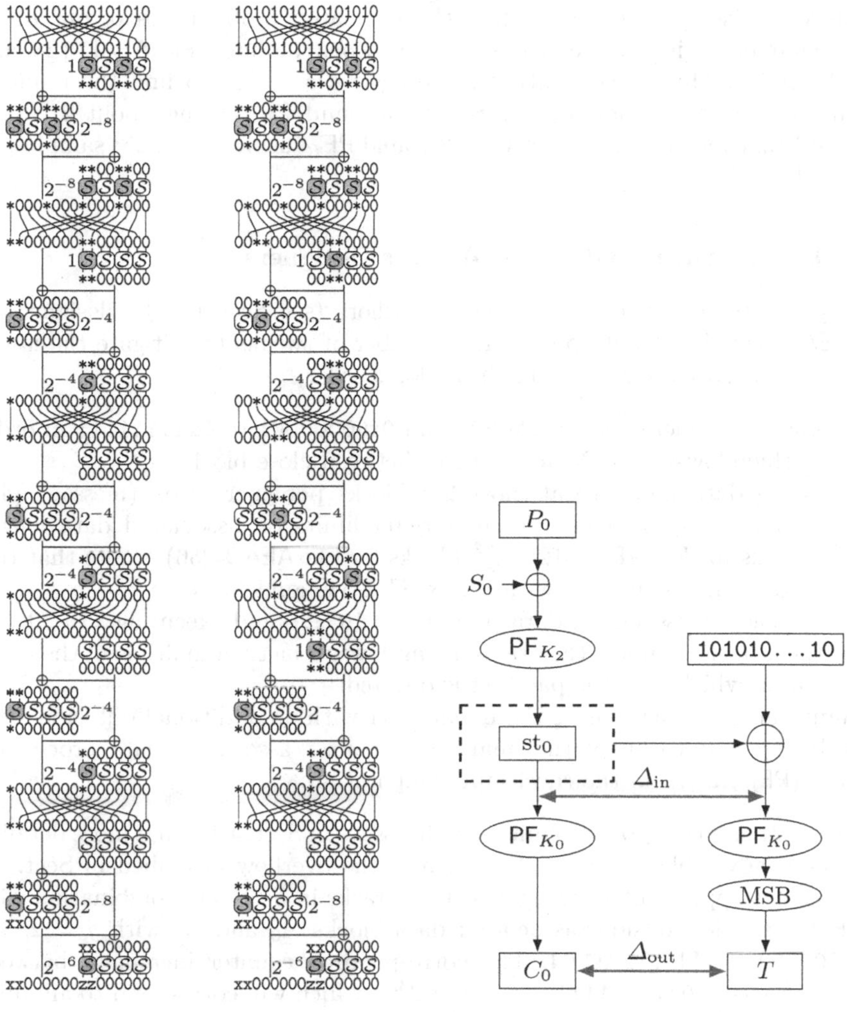

Fig. 7. Zero-query forgery for full FlexAE-64–128 with clusters of probability 2^{-54}.

PF_{K_0} due to the constant addition between the computation of tag T and a single-block ciphertext C. The actual success probability is likely higher; there are several similar clusters contributing to the same differential (see Fig. 7), and the alternative padding constant $(01)^*$ instead of $(10)^*$ gives an alternative compatible Δ_{in} to double the probability.

4.4 Practical Verification

All our practical tests use the reference implementation of FlexAEAD. We successfully verified the domain separation issue (Sect. 4.1) using the full-round version, and we could also confirm that for inputs with zero-length associated data and plaintext blocks, the final tag does not depend on the nonce (Sect. 4.2).

Moreover, we practically verified the estimated probabilities of our differential characteristics for reduced-round versions of both FlexAEAD-128 and FlexAEAD-256. More specifically, on average we are able to find the required output difference for FlexAEAD-128 with 3-round PF_K using about 2^{30} samples, and that for FlexAEAD-256 with 2-round PF_K using about 2^{24} samples, as expected.

4.5 Tweaks Suggested by FlexAEAD's Designers

In response to observations by several authors (see Sect. 1), the designers of FlexAEAD have informally proposed a number of tweaks to mitigate the issues [14]. Proposed tweaks include, in chronologic order,

1. Changing the increment in `INC32` from `0x00000001` to `0x11111111` in order to preclude low-weight XOR-distances between close blocks;
2. Reducing data limits to at most 2^{32} blocks per encryption (message plus associated data) with additional, stricter limits on associated data length (2^{28} blocks for FlexAEAD-128, 2^{23} blocks for FlexAEAD-256) – note that this does not seem compatible with the NIST LWC guidelines;
3. Modifying the associated data padding to $10\ldots0$ and executing PF_{K_2} twice for the last block unless the original length was exactly a multiple of the block length, in which case the padding is omitted;
4. Significantly strengthening the linear layer with an additional diffusion step;
5. Including a function of the final counter after associated data processing, $\mathsf{PF}_{K_2}(\mathsf{PF}_{K_2}(S_n))$, in the checksum computation.

Changes (3) and (5) appear to mitigate the issues in Sect. 4.1, but a more detailed analysis is advisable. Change (2) mitigates the overflow described in Sect. 4.2, but does not appear sufficient against the attacks in Sect. 3 in combination with (1). For example, consider associated data blocks A_0 and A_j with $j = 2^{28} =$ `0x10000000` for FlexAEAD-64. The corresponding counter increment between these blocks is $j \cdot \texttt{0x11111111} \equiv j \pmod{2^{32}}$, which will correspond to an input XOR difference of $\Delta_{\text{in}} =$ `000000*0 000000*0` with very high probability. This leads to an attack with the same success probability as the one in Sect. 3 using a truncated characteristic closely related to the one in Fig. 5a (with mirrored truncated difference patterns at the input to each round). Unless more significant changes such as (4) are considered, it is necessary to apply smaller data limits (a) for all variants and (b) for both associated data and plaintext. In addition, a more detailed analysis of potential tradeoffs with a slightly higher number of active nibbles in Δ_{in} with a lower success probability, but also a sufficiently low distance between the swapped data blocks, is recommended.

Due to the very recent proposal, we have not analyzed the impact of the most significant change (4) in detail, but it appears to significantly improve resistance against differential cryptanalysis and thus against attacks similar to the ones we proposed in Sect. 3.

5 Conclusion

We showed several forgery attacks against the first-round NIST LWC candidate FlexAEAD (also applying to its predecessor FlexAE). Except for the trivial forgery based on domain separation issues, these forgery variants are based on high-probability clusters of differential characteristics in the generation of the internal sequence S. The resulting success probabilities per forgery attempt are summarized as follows. Using a single encryption query with a fixed difference between two consecutive associated data or plaintext blocks, a forgery attempt with swapped or truncated blocks is successful with probability about 2^{-46} (FlexAEAD-64), 2^{-54} (FlexAEAD-128), or 2^{-70} (FlexAEAD-256). Furthermore, we proposed forgery attacks on FlexAE with zero encryption queries and arbitrary single-block ciphertexts with success probability about 2^{-54} (FlexAE-64–128), 2^{-86} (FlexAE-128–256), 2^{-150} (FlexAE-256–512), or 2^{-278} (FlexAE-512–1024).

The set of design tweaks proposed in response by FlexAEAD's designers, including a significantly strengthened linear layer and improved domain separation in the mode, addresses these issues. Further dedicated analysis will be required for a potential final tweaked proposal to validate its improved security properties.

Acknowledgements. We thank the designers of FlexAE and FlexAEAD for their comments on a preliminary version of this analysis on the NIST LWC mailing list.

References

1. Bertoni, G., Daemen, J., Peeters, M., Van Assche, G., Van Keer, R.: Ketje v2. Submission to CAESAR: Competition for Authenticated Encryption. Security, Applicability, and Robustness (Round 3) (2014). http://competitions.cr.yp.to/round3/ketjev2.pdf
2. Daemen, J., Rijmen, V.: The Design of Rijndael: AES - The Advanced Encryption Standard. Information Security and Cryptography. Springer, Heidelberg (2002). https://doi.org/10.1007/978-3-662-04722-4
3. Eichlseder, M., Kales, D.: Clustering related-tweak characteristics: application to MANTIS-6. IACR Trans. Symmetric Cryptol. **2018**(2), 111–132 (2018). https://doi.org/10.13154/tosc.v2018.i2.111-132
4. Eichlseder, M., Kales, D., Schofnegger, M.: Official Comment: FlexAEAD. Posting on the NIST LWC mailing list. https://groups.google.com/a/list.nist.gov/d/msg/lwc-forum/cRjs9x43G2I/KsBQLdDODAAJ
5. Jutla, C.S.: Encryption modes with almost free message integrity. In: Pfitzmann, B. (ed.) EUROCRYPT 2001. LNCS, vol. 2045, pp. 529–544. Springer, Heidelberg (2001). https://doi.org/10.1007/3-540-44987-6_32
6. Jutla, C.S.: Encryption modes with almost free message integrity. J. Cryptol. **21**(4), 547–578 (2008). https://doi.org/10.1007/s00145-008-9024-z
7. Kam, J.B., Davida, G.I.: Structured design of substitution-permutation encryption networks. IEEE Trans. Comput. **28**(10), 747–753 (1979). https://doi.org/10.1109/TC.1979.1675242

8. Mège, A.: Official Comment: FlexAEAD. Posting on the NIST LWC mailing list. https://groups.google.com/a/list.nist.gov/d/msg/lwc-forum/DPQVEJ5oBeU/YXW0QjfjBQAJ
9. Mouha, N., Wang, Q., Gu, D., Preneel, B.: Differential and linear cryptanalysis using mixed-integer linear programming. In: Wu, C.-K., Yung, M., Lin, D. (eds.) Inscrypt 2011. LNCS, vol. 7537, pp. 57–76. Springer, Heidelberg (2012). https://doi.org/10.1007/978-3-642-34704-7_5
10. do Nascimento, E.M.: Algoritmo de Criptografia Leve com Utilização de Autenticação. Ph.D. thesis, Instituto Militar de Engenharia, Rio de Janeiro (2017). http://www.comp.ime.eb.br/pos/arquivos/publicacoes/dissertacoes/2017/2017-Eduardo.pdf
11. do Nascimento, E.M., Xexéo, J.A.M.: A flexible authenticated lightweight cipher using Even-Mansour construction. In: IEEE International Conference on Communications - ICC 2017, pp. 1–6. IEEE (2017). https://doi.org/10.1109/ICC.2017.7996734
12. do Nascimento, E.M., Xexéo, J.A.M.: A lightweight cipher with integrated authentication. In: Simpósio Brasileiro em Segurança da Informação e de Sistemas Computacionais - SBSEG, pp. 25–32. Sociedade Brasileira de Computação (2018). https://portaldeconteudo.sbc.org.br/index.php/sbseg_estendido/article/view/4138
13. do Nascimento, E.M., Xexéo, J.A.M.: FlexAEAD. Submission to Round 1 of the NIST Lightweight Cryptography Standardization Process (2019). https://csrc.nist.gov/CSRC/media/Projects/Lightweight-Cryptography/documents/round-1/spec-doc/FlexAEAD-spec.pdf
14. do Nascimento, E.M., Xexéo, J.A.M.: Official Comment: FlexAEAD. Posting on the NIST LWC mailing list (2019). https://csrc.nist.gov/CSRC/media/Projects/Lightweight-Cryptography/documents/round-1/official-comments/FlexAEAD-official-comment.pdf
15. National Institute of Standards and Technology (NIST): Lightweight cryptography standardization process (2019). https://csrc.nist.gov/projects/lightweight-cryptography
16. Rahman, M., Saha, D., Paul, G.: Attacks against FlexAEAD. Posting on the NIST LWC mailing list. https://groups.google.com/a/list.nist.gov/d/msg/lwc-forum/VLWtGnJStew/X3Fxeg1AQAJ
17. Rahman, M., Saha, D., Paul, G.: Interated truncated differential for internal keyed permutation of FlexAEAD. IACR Cryptology ePrint Archive, Report 2019/539 (2019). https://eprint.iacr.org/2019/539
18. Wu, H., Preneel, B.: AEGIS v1.1. Submission to CAESAR: Competition for Authenticated Encryption. Security, Applicability, and Robustness (Round 3 and Final Portfolio) (2014). http://competitions.cr.yp.to/round3/aegisv11.pdf
19. Wu, S., Wang, M.: Security evaluation against differential cryptanalysis for block cipher structures. IACR Cryptology ePrint Archive, Report 2011/551 (2011)

Key Recovery Attacks on Some Rank Metric Code-Based Signatures

Terry Shue Chien Lau, Chik How Tan(✉), and Theo Fanuela Prabowo

Temasek Laboratories, National University of Singapore,
5A Engineering Drive 1, #09-02, Singapore 117411, Singapore
{tsltlsc,tsltch,tsltfp}@nus.edu.sg

Abstract. Designing secure Code-based signature schemes remains an issue today. In this paper, we focus on schemes designed with the Fiat-Shamir transformations rationale (commit and challenge strategy). We propose two generic key recovery attacks on rank metric code-based signature schemes Veron, TPL and RQCS. More specifically, we exploit the weakness that a support basis or an extended support basis of the secret key could be recovered from the signatures generated in these schemes through different techniques. Furthermore, we are able to determine a support matrix or an extended support matrix for the secret key if the number of equations over the base field is greater than the number of unknown variables in the support matrix. We show that both the design of TPL and RQCS schemes contain these weaknesses, and no reparation of parameters for these schemes is possible to resist our two attacks. Moreover, we show that we can recover a support basis for the secret key used in Veron and that our first attack is successful due to the choice of its proposed parameters. We implement our attacks on Veron, TPL and RQCS signature schemes and manage to recover the secret keys within seconds.

Keywords: Post-quantum cryptography · Digital signature · Code-based cryptography · Key recovery attack

1 Introduction

Post-quantum cryptography has drawn a lot of attention since the discovery of Shor's algorithm to factorize integers in polynomial time [14]. More recently, the National Institute of Standards and Technology (NIST) has initiated a standardization process for quantum-safe key exchange protocols, public-key encryption and digital signature schemes. Code-based cryptography stands as one of the most promising quantum-safe approaches, accounting for 6 out of 17 candidates for encryption and key-establishment. Unfortunately, if we focus on the design of digital signature schemes, none of the code-based schemes made it to Round 2. The design of an efficient and secure signature scheme remains a challenging task in code-based cryptography.

M. Albrecht (Ed.): IMACC 2019, LNCS 11929, pp. 215–235, 2019.
https://doi.org/10.1007/978-3-030-35199-1_11

Recently, the Fiat-Shamir (FS) transformation [7] has been used to construct several new rank metric signature schemes. For instance, Bellini et al. [4] adapted the Veron [17] and CVE [6] identification schemes in the rank metric setting and converted them into signature schemes via the FS transformation. On the other hand, FS rank metric signature schemes such as the TPL signature scheme [16], RQCS signature scheme [15], and Durandal [3] were constructed by adapting the Schnorr approach [13].

Our Contributions. This paper is a generalization of the works published in [2,11][1]. More specifically, we propose two generic key recovery attacks on FS rank metric signature schemes.

Generally for a FS rank metric code-based signature scheme, a signature of length n is generated with some ephemeral keys and the secret key during the signature generation. In order to avoid signature forgery, the secret key and ephemeral keys were chosen such that the rank of the signature generated is less than $\min\{n, m\}$. Our two attacks exploit two weaknesses in which how these FS rank metric code-based signature schemes are designed:

1. Whether the generated signature of low rank would leak any information on a support basis (or extended support basis) for the secret key (or the ephemeral key). If yes, then we are able to determine a support basis (or extended support basis) for the secret key (or the ephemeral key).
2. Let t be the dimension of the support (or dimension of the extended support) for the secret key (or the ephemeral key). If $tn \leq (n-k)m$, then the number of unknown variables (for the support matrix or extended support matrix) is less than or equal to the number of equations available over $\mathbb{F}_q$. Thus, we are able to solve for a support matrix (or an extended support matrix) for the secret key (or the ephemeral key) in polynomial time.

For the first generic attack, we consider the fact that a secret key $\boldsymbol{e} \in \mathbb{F}_{q^m}^n$ of rank r can be written as $\boldsymbol{e} = \boldsymbol{x}M$, where coordinates of $\boldsymbol{x}$ form a support basis for $\boldsymbol{e}$ and M is an $r \times n$ matrix over $\mathbb{F}_q$. We first try to extract a support basis for the secret key $\boldsymbol{e}$ from the signature, and form the vector $\boldsymbol{x}$. Secondly, if $\boldsymbol{e}$ was chosen such that $r \leq (n-k)\frac{m}{n}$, then the number of equations in $\boldsymbol{s} = \boldsymbol{e}H^T = \boldsymbol{x}MH^T$ over $\mathbb{F}_q$ is greater than or equal to the number of unknown variables for its support matrix M: $(n-k)m \geq rn$. So we are able to recover a support matrix $\boldsymbol{M}$, and thus determine $\boldsymbol{e}$.

Our second generic attack is a twist of the first generic attack. Instead of recovering the secret key directly, it first aims to recover the ephemeral key used in the signature generation, and uses this ephemeral key to determine the secret key. This can be achieved by determining a basis of the vector space spanned by the coordinates of the ephemeral key, which is of dimension t. Using the information available from the public key and the signature, if the number

[1] We first published our attack (Algorithm 4 + 1AS) on RQCS signature scheme in [10] on 1 Feb 2019. Xagawa independently published a similar attack on RQCS in [18] on 5 Feb 2019. Later on, we have combined our works with Aragon et al.'s work in [2]. We include the attack on RQCS in this paper for completeness.

of equations is greater than or equal to the number of unknown variables for the extended support matrix, i.e., $(n-k)m \geq tn$, then we are able to recover an extended support matrix for the ephemeral key. Finally, we can compute the ephemeral key using the recovered extended support basis and extended support matrix, and thus recover the secret key.

Using these two generic attacks, we propose some polynomial time attacks on some FS rank metric signature schemes: TPL, RQCS and Veron. For each of these signature schemes, we use different techniques to recover a support basis (or extended support basis) for the secret key (or the ephemeral key). Furthermore, the TPL and RQCS signature schemes are designed such that $r \leq \lfloor \frac{n-k}{4} \rfloor < (n-k)\frac{m}{n}$ (or $t \leq \lfloor \frac{n-k}{2} \rfloor < (n-k)\frac{m}{n}$) and $r < \frac{m+2k-\sqrt{(m-2k)^2+4km}}{2} < (n-k)\frac{m}{n}$ (or $t < \frac{m+2k-\sqrt{(m-2k)^2+4km}}{2} < (n-k)\frac{m}{n}$) respectively. Hence, no reparation of parameters is possible for these two schemes to resist our two attacks. For Veron, all the parameters were proposed such that $r \leq \frac{n-k}{2} < (n-k)\frac{m}{n}$, therefore our first attack works well on Veron. Our practical simulations of the two attacks show that the secret key for all the parameters proposed in TPL, RQCS and Veron can be recovered within seconds.

Organization of the Paper. This paper is organized as follows: Sect. 2 reviews some basic results in rank metric coding theory, and provides an overview for TPL, RQCS and Veron signature schemes. Section 3 presents our first polynomial time attack on TPL, RQCS and Veron, while Sect. 4 presents our second polynomial time attack on TPL and RQCS. The simulation results of these attacks are shown in Sect. 5. We conclude our paper in Sect. 6.

2 Background on Rank Metric Code-Based Cryptography

We recall some definitions and basic results in rank metric coding theory. We also review some rank metric FS signature schemes: TPL, RQCS and Veron signature schemes.

Let $\mathbb{F}_{q^m}$ be a finite field with q^m elements where q is a prime power. We denote the row space of a matrix M by $\langle M \rangle$. We now define the rank of a vector on $\mathbb{F}_{q^m}^n$:

Definition 1. Let $\{\beta_1, \ldots, \beta_m\}$ be a basis of $\mathbb{F}_{q^m}$ over $\mathbb{F}_q$ and $\boldsymbol{x} = (x_1, \ldots, x_n) \in \mathbb{F}_{q^m}^n$. The *rank* of $\boldsymbol{x}$ in $\mathbb{F}_q$, denoted by $\text{rk}(\boldsymbol{x})$, is the rank of the matrix $X = [x_{ij}] \in \mathbb{F}_q^{m \times n}$ where $x_j = \sum_{i=1}^m x_{ij}\beta_i$.

We recall the following result for a vector $\boldsymbol{x}$ of rank r:

Lemma 1 [9, Proposition 3.1]**.** Let $\boldsymbol{x} \in \mathbb{F}_{q^m}^n$ such that $\text{rk}(\boldsymbol{x}) = r$. There exists $\hat{\boldsymbol{x}} = (\hat{x}_1, \ldots, \hat{x}_r) \in \mathbb{F}_{q^m}^r$ with $\text{rk}(\hat{\boldsymbol{x}}) = r$ and $U \in \mathbb{F}_q^{r \times n}$ with $\text{rk}(U) = r$ such that $\boldsymbol{x} = \hat{\boldsymbol{x}}U$. We call $\mathsf{Supp}(\boldsymbol{x}) = \langle x_1, \ldots, x_n \rangle$ the *support* of $\boldsymbol{x}$, U a *support matrix* for $\boldsymbol{x}$, and $\{\hat{x}_1, \ldots, \hat{x}_r\}$ a *support basis* for $\boldsymbol{x}$.

Equivalently, the rank of $\boldsymbol{x}$ is the dimension of $\mathsf{Supp}(\boldsymbol{x})$ over $\mathbb{F}_q$.

Notation. We use the following notations in this paper:

- $\mathcal{H}_{\mathsf{A},\mathsf{B}} : \mathsf{A} \rightarrow \mathsf{B}$ denotes a collision-resistant hash function.
- S_n denotes the set of all $n \times n$ permutation matrices.
- Denote $\mathcal{E}_{m,n,r} = \{\boldsymbol{g} \in \mathbb{F}_{q^m}^n \mid \mathrm{rk}(\boldsymbol{g}) = r\}$.
- Let $\boldsymbol{x} = (x_0, \ldots, x_{n-1}) \in \mathbb{F}_{q^m}^n$. The $n \times n$ circulant matrix generated by $\boldsymbol{x}$ is denoted by $\mathrm{Cir}_n(\boldsymbol{x}) = \left[x_{(i-j) \bmod n}\right]_{i,j} \in \mathbb{F}_{q^m}^{n \times n}$.
- $(\cdot) : \mathbb{F}_{q^m}^n \times \mathbb{F}_{q^m}^n \rightarrow \mathbb{F}_{q^m}^n$ denotes the rotational product between two vectors, i.e., for $\boldsymbol{a}, \boldsymbol{b} \in \mathbb{F}_{q^m}^n$, we have $\boldsymbol{a} \cdot \boldsymbol{b} = \boldsymbol{a}\left[\mathrm{Cir}_n(\boldsymbol{b})\right]^T = \left[\mathrm{Cir}_n(\boldsymbol{a})\boldsymbol{b}^T\right]^T = \boldsymbol{b}\left[\mathrm{Cir}_n(\boldsymbol{a})\right]^T = \boldsymbol{b} \cdot \boldsymbol{a}$.
- Let $i \geq 1$ and $\boldsymbol{a}_i, \boldsymbol{b} \in \mathbb{F}_{q^m}^n$. Define the operator $(\star_i) : \mathbb{F}_{q^m}^{in} \times \mathbb{F}_{q^m}^n \rightarrow \mathbb{F}_{q^m}^{in}$ as $(\boldsymbol{a}_1, \ldots, \boldsymbol{a}_i) \star_i \boldsymbol{b} = (\boldsymbol{a}_1 \cdot \boldsymbol{b}, \ldots, \boldsymbol{a}_i \cdot \boldsymbol{b})$.
- Let X be a finite set. We write $\boldsymbol{x} \xleftarrow{\$} X$ to denote assigning $\boldsymbol{x}$ an element randomly sampled from the uniform distribution on X.
- $\mathsf{size}_{\mathsf{pk}}$, $\mathsf{size}_{\mathsf{sk}}$, and size_{σ} denotes the public key size, secret key size, and signature size respectively.
- Let $\mathbb{F}$ be a field. Suppose $A = \langle a_1, \ldots, a_{d_1}\rangle$ and $B = \langle b_1, \ldots, b_{d_2}\rangle$ are vector subspaces of $\mathbb{F}$ of dimension d_1 and d_2 respectively. The product vector space is defined as $A.B = \langle a_1 b_1, \ldots, a_{d_1} b_{d_2}\rangle$.
- Denote $\begin{bmatrix} n \\ k \end{bmatrix}_q = \prod_{i=0}^{k-1} \frac{q^n - q^i}{q^k - q^i}$.

A digital signature scheme is defined as follows.

Definition 2 (Digital Signature Scheme). A digital signature scheme consists of four polynomial-time algorithms:

- Setup: Taking a security parameter 1^λ as input, it outputs the public parameters param.
- Gen: Taking param as input, it outputs a public key pk and a secret key sk.
- Sign: Taking $(\mathsf{sk}, \mathsf{pk}, \boldsymbol{m})$ as input, where $\boldsymbol{m}$ is a message to be signed, it outputs a signature $\boldsymbol{\sigma}$.
- Vrfy: Taking $(\mathsf{pk}, \sigma, \boldsymbol{m})$ as input, it outputs a bit b where $b = 1$ indicates "accept the signature" and $b = 0$ indicates "reject the signature".

We now recall the rank metric FS signature schemes of our interest in this paper:

1. <u>TPL **Signature Scheme**</u>

$\mathsf{TPL.Setup}$: Taking the security parameter 1^λ as input, generate the public parameters $\mathsf{param} = (m, n, k, d, r_1, r_2, l, l_{\mathcal{H}})$ such that $m > n > k$, $l_{\mathcal{H}} \geq m \geq \left\lceil \frac{l_{\mathcal{H}}}{l} \right\rceil$ and $r_2 \leq r_1 \leq \left\lfloor \frac{d-1}{4} \right\rfloor$. Let $q = 2$.

$\mathsf{TPL.Gen}$: Taking param as input. Let $\mathcal{H}_{\mathsf{A},\mathsf{B}}$ be a collision-resistant hash function where $\mathsf{A} = \left(\mathbb{F}_{q^m}^{n-k}\right)^l \times \{0,1\}^* \times \mathbb{F}_{q^m}^{(n-k)\times n} \times \left(\mathbb{F}_{q^m}^{n-k}\right)^l$ and $\mathsf{B} = \{0,1\}^{l_H}$. Let $H \in \mathbb{F}_{q^m}^{(n-k)\times n}$ be a parity check matrix of a random linear code $\mathcal{C}$ with minimum distance at least d. For $1 \leq i \leq l$, choose random $\boldsymbol{e}_i \xleftarrow{\$} \mathcal{E}_{m,n,r_1}$ where $r_1 \leq \lfloor \frac{d-1}{4} \rfloor$. Compute $\boldsymbol{s}_i = \boldsymbol{e}_i H^T$. Output public key, $\mathsf{pk} = (H, \boldsymbol{s}_1, \ldots, \boldsymbol{s}_l)$ and the secret key, $\mathsf{sk} = (\boldsymbol{e}_1, \ldots, \boldsymbol{e}_l)$.

TPL.Sign: To sign a message $\boldsymbol{m}$, choose random $\boldsymbol{u}_i \xleftarrow{\$} \mathcal{E}_{m,n,r_2}$ for $1 \leq i \leq l$. Compute $\boldsymbol{c} = (c_0, c_1, \ldots, c_{l_\mathcal{H}-1}) = \mathcal{H}(\boldsymbol{u}_1 H^T, \ldots, \boldsymbol{u}_l H^T, \boldsymbol{m}, H, \boldsymbol{s}_1, \ldots, \boldsymbol{s}_l)$ where $c_j \in \mathbb{F}_q$ for $0 \leq j \leq l_\mathcal{H} - 1$. For $1 \leq i \leq l$, define

$$\hat{c}_i := \left(c_{(i-1)m \bmod l_\mathcal{H}}, c_{(i-1)m+1 \bmod l_\mathcal{H}}, \ldots, c_{(i-1)m+m-1 \bmod l_\mathcal{H}}\right)$$

and consider $\hat{c}_i$ as an element in $\mathbb{F}_{q^m}$. Then compute $\boldsymbol{t}_i := \boldsymbol{u}_i + \hat{c}_i \boldsymbol{e}_i$. If the last k coordinates of $\boldsymbol{t}_i$ are all zero for all $1 \leq i \leq l$, then repeat the whole signature generation above. Otherwise output the signature as $(\boldsymbol{c}, \boldsymbol{t}_1, \ldots, \boldsymbol{t}_l)$.

TPL.Vrfy: To verify a signature $(\boldsymbol{c}, \boldsymbol{t}_1, \ldots, \boldsymbol{t}_l)$ with $\mathsf{pk} = (H, \boldsymbol{s}_1, \ldots, \boldsymbol{s}_l)$, the verifier first checks whether the last k coordinates of $\boldsymbol{t}_i$ are all zero for $1 \leq i \leq l$. If it is true, then reject the signature. Otherwise, check whether $\mathrm{rk}(\boldsymbol{t}_i) \stackrel{?}{\leq} r_1 + r_2$ for $1 \leq i \leq l$. If one of them is false, then reject the signature. Otherwise, proceed to compute $\hat{c}_i \in \mathbb{F}_{q^m}$ from $\boldsymbol{c} = (c_0, \ldots, c_{l_\mathcal{H}-1})$ for $1 \leq i \leq l$, and compute $\boldsymbol{v}_i = \boldsymbol{t}_i H^T - \hat{c}_i \boldsymbol{s}_i$. Check whether $\boldsymbol{c} \stackrel{?}{=} \mathcal{H}(\boldsymbol{v}_1, \ldots, \boldsymbol{v}_l, \boldsymbol{m}, H, \boldsymbol{s}_1, \ldots, \boldsymbol{s}_l)$. If it is true, then accept the signature, otherwise, reject the signature.

2. RQCS Signature Scheme

RQCS.Setup: Taking the security parameter 1^λ as input, generate the public parameters $\mathsf{param} = (m, n, w, w_r, w_g)$.

RQCS.Gen: Taking param as input, randomly pick $\boldsymbol{h} \xleftarrow{\$} \mathbb{F}_{q^m}^n$ and $\boldsymbol{x}, \boldsymbol{y} \xleftarrow{\$} \mathcal{E}_{m,n,w}$. Let $\mathcal{H}_{\mathsf{A}, \mathcal{E}_{m,n,w_g}}$ be a collision-resistant hash function, where $\mathsf{A} = \{\boldsymbol{e}_1 + \boldsymbol{h} \cdot \boldsymbol{e}_2 \mid \boldsymbol{e}_1, \boldsymbol{e}_2 \xleftarrow{\$} \mathcal{E}_{m,n,w_r}\} \times \{0,1\}^*$. Compute $\boldsymbol{s} = \boldsymbol{x} + \boldsymbol{h} \cdot \boldsymbol{y}$ and output a pair of keys $(\mathsf{pk}, \mathsf{sk})$. The public key pk is $(\boldsymbol{h}, \boldsymbol{s})$ and the secret key sk is $(\boldsymbol{x}, \boldsymbol{y})$.

RQCS.Sign: Taking a secret key $\mathsf{sk} = (\boldsymbol{x}, \boldsymbol{y})$ and a message $\boldsymbol{m}$ as input, choose randomly $\boldsymbol{r} = (\boldsymbol{r}_1, \boldsymbol{r}_2)$ where $\boldsymbol{r}_1, \boldsymbol{r}_2 \xleftarrow{\$} \mathcal{E}_{m,n,w_r}$. Compute $I = \boldsymbol{r}_1 + \boldsymbol{h} \cdot \boldsymbol{r}_2$ and $\boldsymbol{g} = \mathcal{H}_{\mathsf{A}, \mathcal{E}_{m,n,w_g}}(I, \boldsymbol{m}) \in \mathcal{E}_{m,n,w_g}$, followed by $\boldsymbol{u} = (\boldsymbol{u}_1, \boldsymbol{u}_2) = (\boldsymbol{x}, \boldsymbol{y}) \star_2 \boldsymbol{g} + \boldsymbol{r} = (\boldsymbol{x} \cdot \boldsymbol{g}, \boldsymbol{y} \cdot \boldsymbol{g}) + (\boldsymbol{r}_1, \boldsymbol{r}_2)$. Then output the signature $(\boldsymbol{g}, \boldsymbol{u})$.

RQCS.Vrfy: Taking a public key $\mathsf{pk} = (\boldsymbol{h}, \boldsymbol{s})$, a message $\boldsymbol{m}$, and a signature $(\boldsymbol{g}, \boldsymbol{u})$ as input. Compute $I = \boldsymbol{u}_1 + \boldsymbol{h} \cdot \boldsymbol{u}_2 - \boldsymbol{s} \cdot \boldsymbol{g}$. Accept the signature if and only if $\mathcal{H}_{\mathsf{A}, \mathcal{E}_{m,n,w_g}}(I, \boldsymbol{m}) = \boldsymbol{g}$, $\mathrm{rk}(\boldsymbol{u}_1) \leq w w_g + w_r$, and $\mathrm{rk}(\boldsymbol{u}_2) \leq w w_g + w_r$.

3. Veron Signature Scheme

Veron.Setup: Taking the security parameter 1^λ as input, generate the public parameters $\mathsf{param} = (m, n, k, r)$.

Veron.Gen: Taking param as input, randomly pick $\boldsymbol{x} \xleftarrow{\$} \mathbb{F}_{q^m}^k$ and $\boldsymbol{e} \xleftarrow{\$} \mathcal{E}_{m,n,r}$. Let $\mathcal{H}_{\mathsf{A},\mathsf{B}}$ be a collision-resistant hash function, where $\mathsf{A} = S_n \times \mathbb{F}_{q^m}^n \times \{0,1\}^{\delta h} \times \{0,1\}^*$

and $\mathsf{B} = \{0,1\}^h$. Let $f(v,w)$ be the function that maps the bits v, w to the set $\{0,1,2\}$ following the rule:

$$00 \mapsto 0, \quad 01 \mapsto 1, \quad 10 \mapsto 2, \quad 11 \mapsto \text{ either } 0,\, 1,\, 2 \text{ in a cyclic fashion.}$$

Randomly pick $G \xleftarrow{\$} \mathbb{F}_{q^m}^{k\times n}$. Compute $\boldsymbol{y} = \boldsymbol{x}G + \boldsymbol{e}$ and output a pair of keys $(\mathsf{pk}, \mathsf{sk})$. The public key pk is $(\boldsymbol{y}, G, r)$ and the secret key sk is $(\boldsymbol{x}, \boldsymbol{e})$.

Veron.Sign: Let δ be the number of rounds for the Veron signature. Taking a secret key $\mathsf{sk} = (\boldsymbol{x}, \boldsymbol{y})$ and a message $\boldsymbol{m}$ as input, for $i = 1, \ldots, \delta$, choose randomly $\boldsymbol{u}_i \xleftarrow{\$} \mathbb{F}_{q^m}^k$ and $P_i \xleftarrow{\$} S_n$. Compute

$$c_{i,1} = \mathcal{H}_{\mathsf{A},\mathsf{B}}(P_i), \quad c_{i,2} = \mathcal{H}_{\mathsf{A},\mathsf{B}}(((\boldsymbol{u}_i + \boldsymbol{x})G)P_i), \quad c_{i,3} = \mathcal{H}_{\mathsf{A},\mathsf{B}}((\boldsymbol{u}_i G + \boldsymbol{y})P_i).$$

Let $\mathrm{cmt} = (c_{1,1}, c_{1,2}, c_{1,3}, \ldots, c_{\delta,1}, c_{\delta,2}, c_{\delta,3})$. Then $\mathrm{ch} = \mathcal{H}_{\mathsf{A},\mathsf{B}}(\mathrm{cmt}, \boldsymbol{m})$. For $i = 1, \ldots, \delta$, let $b_i = f(\mathrm{ch}_{2i}, \mathrm{ch}_{2i+1})$. If $b_i = 0$, then $\mathrm{rsp}_i = (P_i, \boldsymbol{u}_i + \boldsymbol{x})$. If $b_i = 1$, then $\mathrm{rsp}_i = (((\boldsymbol{u}_i + \boldsymbol{x})G)P_i, \boldsymbol{e}P_i)$. If $b_i = 2$, then $\mathrm{rsp}_i = (P_i, \boldsymbol{u}_i)$. Then output the signature $(\mathrm{cmt}, \mathrm{rsp})$.

Veron.Vrfy: Taking a public key $\mathsf{pk} = (\boldsymbol{y}, G, r)$, a message $\boldsymbol{m}$, and a signature $(\mathrm{cmt}, \mathrm{rsp})$ as input. Compute $\mathrm{ch} = \mathcal{H}_{\mathsf{A},\mathsf{B}}(\mathrm{cmt}, \boldsymbol{m})$. For $i = 1, \ldots, \delta$ and $j = 1, 2, 3$, compute $c_{i,j} = \mathrm{cmt}_{[(3(i-1)+(j-1))h+1, \ldots, (3(i-1)+j)h]}$ and $b_i = f(\mathrm{ch}_{2i}, \mathrm{ch}_{2i+1})$. For $b_i = 0$, if $c_{i,1} \neq \mathcal{H}_{\mathsf{A},\mathsf{B}}(\mathrm{rsp}_{i,1})$ or $c_{i,2} \neq \mathcal{H}_{\mathsf{A},\mathsf{B}}((\mathrm{rsp}_{i,2}G)\mathrm{rsp}_{i,1})$, then reject the signature. For $b_i = 1$, if $c_{i,2} \neq \mathcal{H}_{\mathsf{A},\mathsf{B}}(\mathrm{rsp}_{i,1})$ or $\mathrm{rk}(\mathrm{rsp}_{i,2}) \neq r$ or $c_{i,3} \neq \mathcal{H}_{\mathsf{A},\mathsf{B}}(\mathrm{rsp}_{i,1} + \mathrm{rsp}_{i,2})$, then reject the signature. For $b_i = 2$, if $c_{i,1} \neq \mathcal{H}_{\mathsf{A},\mathsf{B}}(\mathrm{rsp}_{i,1})$ or $c_{i,3} \neq \mathcal{H}_{\mathsf{A},\mathsf{B}}((\mathrm{rsp}_{i,2}G + \boldsymbol{y})\mathrm{rsp}_{i,1})$, then reject the signature. Else, accept the signature.

Security of TPL, RQCS and Veron Signature Schemes. For these signature schemes, the secret key is a vector of low rank and the syndrome of this secret key is published as the public key. The security of these signature schemes relies on the following problem:

Definition 3 (Rank Syndrome Decoding Problem). Let H be a full rank $(n - k) \times n$ matrix over $\mathbb{F}_{q^m}$, $\boldsymbol{s} \in \mathbb{F}_{q^m}^{n-k}$ and w be an integer. The *Rank Syndrome Decoding* problem $\mathsf{RSD}(q, m, n, k, w)$ is to determine $\boldsymbol{x} \in \mathbb{F}_{q^m}^n$ such that $\mathrm{rk}(\boldsymbol{x}) = w$ and $\boldsymbol{s} = \boldsymbol{x}H^T$.

Classical and Post-quantum Security Level. The security level for a rank metric signature schemes depends on the complexity of solving the underlying RSD problem which the scheme is based on. This complexity contains an exponential term, which should be reduced to its square root when Grover's algorithm is applied using a quantum computer [5]. Therefore, the post-quantum security for rank metric signature schemes were evaluated by taking square root of the exponential term in the (classical) complexity of solving the RSD problem.

Table 1 summarizes the parameters for TPL, RQCS and Veron signature schemes.

Table 1. Proposed parameters for TPL, RQCS and Veron signature schemes. Sec and PQSec refers to the classical and post-quantum security level of the proposed schemes respectively. Note that the sizes are in bits.

Schemes	q	m	n	k	r_1	r_2	$\mathsf{size}_{\mathsf{pk}}$	$\mathsf{size}_{\mathsf{sk}}$	size_{σ}	PQSec
TPL-1	2	570	50	10	10	6	28 496	6 200	8 192	82
TPL-2	2	650	58	10	12	6	37 696	8 496	12 744	98
TPL-3	2	850	78	10	17	8	66 296	14 976	23 200	129

Schemes	q	m	n	w	w_r	w_g	$\mathsf{size}_{\mathsf{pk}}$	$\mathsf{size}_{\mathsf{sk}}$	size_{σ}	Sec
RQCS-1	2	89	67	5	5	5	11 926	1 115	17 889	128
RQCS-2	2	121	97	6	6	6	23 474	1 890	35 211	192
RQCS-3	2	139	101	6	6	6	28 078	2 046	42 117	256

Schemes	q	m	n	k	r	δ	h	$\mathsf{size}_{\mathsf{pk}}$	$\mathsf{size}_{\mathsf{sk}}$	size_{σ}	Sec	PQSec
Veron-1	2	48	35	16	5	137	160	13 971	2 448	389 037	80	-
Veron-2	2	80	64	30	9	219	256	77 124	7 520	1 719 296	-	128
Veron-3	2	96	72	32	12	329	384	105 220	9 984	3 508 508	-	192
Veron-4	2	128	80	32	16	438	512	141 316	14 336	6 800 609	-	256

3 First Polynomial Time Attack on Rank Metric FS Signature Schemes

Notice that the public key of all the rank metric FS signature schemes in Sect. 2 consists of a component of syndrome (or its equivalent form) which is computed using a secret key of low rank. This secret key is used to generate a valid signature. If we are able to recover the secret key, then we are able to forge a valid signature.

3.1 Idea of Attack

We now describe the general idea of our first generic attack on the rank metric signature scheme. Generally, given a syndrome $\boldsymbol{s} \in \mathbb{F}_{q^m}^{n-k}$, we want to determine a vector $\boldsymbol{e} \in \mathcal{E}_{m,n,r}$ such that $\boldsymbol{s} = \boldsymbol{e}H^T$, where $H \in \mathbb{F}_{q^m}^{(n-k)\times n}$ is used in the signature scheme. Since $\text{rk}(\boldsymbol{e}) = r$, recall from Lemma 1 that there exist $\hat{\boldsymbol{e}} = (\hat{e}_1, \ldots, \hat{e}_r) \in \mathcal{E}_{m,r,r}$ and $E \in \mathbb{F}_q^{r\times n}$ with $\text{rk}(E) = r$ such that $\boldsymbol{e} = \hat{\boldsymbol{e}}E$. There are two main steps in our attack:

1. Recover a support basis $\{\hat{e}_1, \ldots, \hat{e}_r\}$ for $\boldsymbol{e}$. This can be achieved by determining a vector subspace spanned by $\langle \hat{e}_1, \ldots, \hat{e}_r \rangle$ through appropriate manipulation of the information retrieved from the signature.
2. Recover a support matrix E for $\boldsymbol{e}$ from $\boldsymbol{s} = \hat{\boldsymbol{e}}EH^T$. This can be achieved by considering the linear system over $\mathbb{F}_q$. We have $m(n-k)$ equations over $\mathbb{F}_q$ and $r \times n$ unknown variables of E over $\mathbb{F}_q$. If $m(n-k) \geq rn$, we can recover the support matrix E in polynomial time.

We now propose our first polynomial time attack on TPL, RQCS, and Veron signature schemes.

3.2 First Attack on TPL Signature Scheme

We first state a generalized version of [12, Lemma 3]. The proof can be found in Appendix A.

Lemma 2. Let $u_1, \ldots, u_k$ be integers such that $0 < u = \sum_{i=1}^{k} u_i \leq \frac{m}{2}$. For $1 \leq i, j \leq k$, let U_i be a u_i-dimensional subspace of $\mathbb{F}_{q^m}$ and $U_i \cap U_j = \{0\}$. Let $r_0 \leq m - u$, $w = \sum_{i=1}^{k} r_i$ and $v = r_0 + w = \sum_{i=0}^{k} r_i$, where each $0 \leq r_i \leq u_i$ for $1 \leq i \leq k$. The number of v-dimensional subspace that intersects each U_i in an r_i-dimensional subspace is $\left(\prod_{i=1}^{k} \begin{bmatrix} u_i \\ r_i \end{bmatrix}_q\right) \begin{bmatrix} m-u \\ r_0 \end{bmatrix}_q q^{r_0(u-w)}$.

We need the following results for our first attack on TPL scheme:

Proposition 1. Let r_x, r_y be integers such that $r_x + r_y \leq \min\{m, n\}$ and $\boldsymbol{x} \in \mathcal{E}_{m,n,r_x}$. Randomly pick a vector $\boldsymbol{y} \xleftarrow{\$} \mathcal{E}_{m,n,r_y}$ and form $\boldsymbol{z} = \boldsymbol{x} + \boldsymbol{y}$. Suppose that $\mathsf{Supp}(\boldsymbol{x}) \cap \mathsf{Supp}(\boldsymbol{y}) = \{0\}$, then the probability that $\mathrm{rk}(\boldsymbol{z}) = r_x + r_y$ is $\begin{bmatrix} n - r_x \\ r_y \end{bmatrix}_q q^{r_y r_x} \left(\begin{bmatrix} n \\ r_y \end{bmatrix}_q\right)^{-1}$.

Theorem 1. Let r_x, r_y be integers such that $r_x + r_y \leq \min\{m, n\}$ and $\boldsymbol{x} \in \mathcal{E}_{m,n,r_x}$. The probability that the vector $\boldsymbol{z} = \boldsymbol{x} + \boldsymbol{y}$ has rank $\mathrm{rk}(\boldsymbol{z}) = r_x + r_y$ for a random $\boldsymbol{y} \xleftarrow{\$} \mathcal{E}_{m,n,r_y}$ is $\begin{bmatrix} m - r_x \\ r_y \end{bmatrix}_q \begin{bmatrix} n - r_x \\ r_y \end{bmatrix}_q q^{2r_y r_x} \left(\begin{bmatrix} m \\ r_y \end{bmatrix}_q \begin{bmatrix} n \\ r_y \end{bmatrix}_q\right)^{-1}$.

Proposition 2. Let r_x, r_y be integers such that $r_x + r_y \leq \min\{m, n\}$, $\boldsymbol{x} \in \mathcal{E}_{m,n,r_x}$, $\boldsymbol{y} \in \mathcal{E}_{m,n,r_y}$ and $\boldsymbol{z} = \boldsymbol{x} + \boldsymbol{y}$ with $\mathrm{rk}(\boldsymbol{z}) = r_x + r_y$. Then $\mathsf{Supp}(\boldsymbol{x}) \subset \mathsf{Supp}(\boldsymbol{z})$.

Now, we describe our first attack on TPL signature scheme. There are two parts in our attack on TPL. The first part is to recover a support basis for the vector $\boldsymbol{e}_i$ from $\boldsymbol{t}_i$ for $i = 1, \ldots, l$ using multiple signatures. The second part is to recover a support matrix for $\boldsymbol{e}_i$ from the public key component H and $\boldsymbol{s}_i$. Once we have recovered a support basis and a support matrix for $\boldsymbol{e}_i$, we can then recover the secret key component $\boldsymbol{e}_i$.

Algorithm 1: First Attack on TPL

Data: w (the number of signatures collected), signatures $\boldsymbol{\sigma}_j = (\boldsymbol{c}_j, \boldsymbol{t}_{j,1}, \ldots, \boldsymbol{t}_{j,l})$ for $1 \le j \le w$, $\mathsf{pk} = (H, \boldsymbol{s}_1, \ldots, \boldsymbol{s}_l)$

Result: The secret key vector $\boldsymbol{e}_1, \ldots, \boldsymbol{e}_l$

`// Step 1: Recover a support basis for` $\boldsymbol{e}_1, \ldots, \boldsymbol{e}_l$

for $i \leftarrow 1$ **to** l **do**

  for $j \leftarrow 1$ **to** w **do**

    Compute $\hat{\boldsymbol{t}}_{j,i} = (\hat{t}_{j,i,1}, \ldots, \hat{t}_{j,i,n}) = (\hat{c}_{j,i})^{-1}\boldsymbol{t}_{j,i}$

  Compute $\mathcal{F}_i = \bigcap_{j=1}^{w} \langle \hat{t}_{j,i,1}, \ldots, \hat{t}_{j,i,n} \rangle$ and a basis $\{\hat{e}_{i,1}, \ldots, \hat{e}_{i,r_1}\}$ for $\mathcal{F}_i$

`// Step 2: Recover a support matrix for` $\boldsymbol{e}_1, \ldots, \boldsymbol{e}_l$

for $i \leftarrow 1$ **to** l **do**

  Solve for E_i from the equation $\boldsymbol{s}_i = (\hat{e}_{i,1}, \ldots, \hat{e}_{i,r_1})E_i H^T$ over $\mathbb{F}_q$

  Compute $\boldsymbol{e}_i \leftarrow (\hat{e}_{i,1}, \ldots, \hat{e}_{i,r_1})E_i$

return $\boldsymbol{e}_1, \ldots, \boldsymbol{e}_l$

Correctness of Algorithm 1. Let $\boldsymbol{\sigma}_1 = (\boldsymbol{c}_1, \boldsymbol{t}_{1,1}, \ldots, \boldsymbol{t}_{1,l})$ be a signature generated in TPL.Sign. Let $\boldsymbol{e}_i = (e_{i,1}, \ldots, e_{i,n})$. Notice that

$$\boldsymbol{t}_{1,i} = \boldsymbol{u}_{1,i} + \hat{c}_{1,i}\boldsymbol{e}_i \Rightarrow \hat{\boldsymbol{t}}_{1,i} = (\hat{t}_{1,i,1}, \ldots, \hat{t}_{1,i,n}) = (\hat{c}_{1,i})^{-1}\boldsymbol{t}_{1,i} = (\hat{c}_i)^{-1}\boldsymbol{u}_{1,i} + \boldsymbol{e}_i.$$

By Theorem 1, for $1 \le i \le l$, the probability that $\mathrm{rk}(\boldsymbol{t}_{1,i}) = r_1 + r_2$ is $p_1' = \begin{bmatrix} m - r_1 \\ r_1 \end{bmatrix}_q \begin{bmatrix} n - r_1 \\ r_2 \end{bmatrix}_q q^{2r_1r_2} \left(\begin{bmatrix} m \\ r_2 \end{bmatrix}_q \begin{bmatrix} n \\ r_2 \end{bmatrix}_q \right)^{-1}$. If $\mathrm{rk}(\boldsymbol{t}_{1,i}) < r_1 + r_2$ (practically this will rarely happen since p_1' is high), then consider another signature which gives us $\mathrm{rk}(\boldsymbol{t}_{1,j}) = r_1 + r_2$. By Proposition 2, we have $\langle e_{i,1}, \ldots, e_{i,n} \rangle \subset \langle \hat{t}_{1,i,1}, \ldots, \hat{t}_{1,i,n} \rangle$. Similarly, for another signature $\boldsymbol{\sigma}_2 = (\boldsymbol{c}_2, \boldsymbol{t}_{2,1}, \ldots, \boldsymbol{t}_{2,l})$, we have $\langle e_{i,1}, \ldots, e_{i,n} \rangle \subset \langle \hat{t}_{2,i,1}, \ldots, \hat{t}_{2,i,n} \rangle$.

By collecting signatures $\boldsymbol{\sigma}_1, \ldots, \boldsymbol{\sigma}_w$ where $w \ge 2$, we have $\langle e_{i,1}, \ldots, e_{i,n} \rangle = \bigcap_{j=1}^{w} \langle \hat{t}_{j,i,1}, \ldots, \hat{t}_{j,i,n} \rangle$. Since $\mathrm{rk}(\boldsymbol{e}_i) = r_1$, we can deduce a basis $\{\hat{e}_1, \ldots, \hat{e}_{r_1}\}$ for the vector space $\langle e_{i,1}, \ldots, e_{i,n} \rangle$.

With a support basis computed, we consider the vector $\boldsymbol{s}_i$ from the public key and form the linear system $\boldsymbol{s}_i = (\hat{e}_1, \ldots, \hat{e}_{r_1})E_i H^T$. Consider the linear system over $\mathbb{F}_q$. Since the number of equations, $m(n-k)$, is greater than the number of unknown variables, $r_1 n$, then we can solve for a support matrix E_i, thus giving us $\boldsymbol{e}_i = (\hat{e}_1, \ldots, \hat{e}_{r_1})E_i$.

Probability of Failure for Algorithm 1. Notice that Algorithm will be successful if $\mathrm{rk}(\boldsymbol{t}_{j,i}) = r_1 + r_2$ for $1 \le j \le w$. Therefore, the probability of failure for Algorithm 1 is at most $p_1 = 1 - (p_1')^{wl}$.

3.3 First Attack on RQCS Signature Scheme

There are two parts in our first attack on RQCS. The first part is to recover a support basis for the vector $\boldsymbol{x}$ and $\boldsymbol{y}$ from $\boldsymbol{u}_1$ and $\boldsymbol{u}_2$ respectively. The second part is to recover a support matrix for $\boldsymbol{x}$ and $\boldsymbol{y}$ from $\mathsf{pk} = (\boldsymbol{h}, \boldsymbol{s})$, since $nm \ge 2wn$.

Once we have recovered a support basis and a support matrix for $\boldsymbol{x}$ and $\boldsymbol{y}$, we can then recover the secret key $\mathsf{sk} = (\boldsymbol{x}, \boldsymbol{y})$.

We are given $\boldsymbol{u_1} = \boldsymbol{x}\left[\mathrm{Cir}_n(\boldsymbol{g})\right]^T + \boldsymbol{r_1}$, $\boldsymbol{u_2} = \boldsymbol{y}\left[\mathrm{Cir}_n(\boldsymbol{g})\right]^T + \boldsymbol{r_2}$, and $\boldsymbol{g}$ with $\mathrm{rk}(\boldsymbol{g}) = w_g$. Here, we present two different algorithms to determine a support basis for $\mathsf{Supp}(\boldsymbol{x})$: the first one, Algorithm $1\mathrm{A}_{\mathsf{RSR}^+}$ applies the Rank Support Recover (RSR) algorithm [1, Algorithm 1] (refer to Appendix F for its specification) on multiple signatures to recover the support basis; the second one, Algorithm 1AS requires only one signature to recover the support basis by modifying RSR algorithm.

Algorithm 2: $1\mathrm{A}_{\mathsf{RSR}^+}(t, \boldsymbol{g_1}, \boldsymbol{u_1}, \ldots, \boldsymbol{g_t}, \boldsymbol{u_t}, w, w_r)$

Data: t, $(\boldsymbol{g_i}, \boldsymbol{u_i})$ for $1 \leq i \leq t$, $w = \dim(\mathsf{Supp}(\boldsymbol{a}))$, $w_r = \dim(\mathsf{Supp}(\boldsymbol{r}))$
Result: A support of $\boldsymbol{a}$, $\mathsf{Supp}(\boldsymbol{a})$

for $i \leftarrow 1$ **to** t **do**
  Compute a basis $\{\lambda_{i,1}, \ldots, \lambda_{i,w_g}\}$ for $\mathsf{Supp}(\boldsymbol{g_i})$
  Compute $\mathcal{G}'_i = \langle 1, \lambda_{i,1}, \ldots, \lambda_{i,w_g} \rangle$
  Compute $\mathcal{F}_{i,a} \leftarrow \mathsf{RSR}(\mathcal{G}'_i, \boldsymbol{u_i}, w + w_r)$
Compute $\mathcal{F}_a = \bigcap_{i=1}^{t} \mathcal{F}_{i,x}$
return $\mathcal{F}_a$

Algorithm 3: $1\mathrm{AS}(\boldsymbol{g}, \boldsymbol{u}, w, w_g)$

Data: $(\boldsymbol{g}, \boldsymbol{u})$, $w = \dim(\mathsf{Supp}(\boldsymbol{a}))$, $w_g = \dim(\mathsf{Supp}(\boldsymbol{g}))$
Result: A support of $\boldsymbol{a}$, $\mathsf{Supp}(\boldsymbol{a})$

Compute a basis $\{\lambda_1, \ldots, \lambda_{w_g}\}$ for $\mathsf{Supp}(\boldsymbol{g})$
for $j \leftarrow 1$ **to** w_g **do**
  Compute $U_j = \langle \lambda_j^{-1} u_1, \ldots, \lambda_j^{-1} u_n \rangle$
Compute $\mathcal{F}_a = \bigcap_{i=1}^{w_g} U_j$
return $\mathcal{F}_a$

Correctness of Algorithm 4. In Step 1(a), $\mathcal{F}_x$ can be recovered by $1\mathrm{A}_{\mathsf{RSR}^+}$-Algorithm or 1AS-Algorithm.

For $1\mathrm{A}_{\mathsf{RSR}^+}$-Algorithm, t signatures are collected. For $1 \leq i \leq t$, let $\mathcal{F}_{i,x} = \mathsf{Supp}(\boldsymbol{x}, \boldsymbol{r_{i,1}})$. Since $\mathcal{G}'_i = \langle \lambda_{i,1}, \ldots, \lambda_{i,w_g}, 1 \rangle$, then the coordinates of $\boldsymbol{u_{i,1}}$ and $\boldsymbol{u_{i,2}}$ generate a subspace of $\mathcal{F}_{i,x} . \mathcal{G}'_i$. As a consequence, the RSR Algorithm will give the desired $\mathcal{F}_{i,x} = \mathsf{Supp}(\boldsymbol{x}, \boldsymbol{r_{i,1}})$. Note that for each $1 \leq i \leq t$, $\mathcal{F}_x = \mathsf{Supp}(\boldsymbol{x}) \subset \mathcal{F}_{i,x}$. The vector space $\mathcal{F}_x$ can be computed by taking the intersections $\mathcal{F}_x = \bigcap_{i=1}^{t} \mathcal{F}_{i,x}$. We can then compute a basis $\{\alpha_1, \ldots, \alpha_w\}$ for $\mathcal{F}_x$.

For 1AS-Algorithm, only 1 signature is required. The probability that $\mathrm{rk}(\boldsymbol{x} \cdot \boldsymbol{g}) < ww_g$ is $q^{-(n - ww_g + 1)}$ [8, Theorem 1]. This implies that $\mathrm{rk}(\boldsymbol{x} \cdot \boldsymbol{g}) = ww_g$ with high probability. By Theorem 1, the probability that $\mathrm{rk}(\boldsymbol{x} \cdot \boldsymbol{g} + \boldsymbol{r_1}) = ww_g + w_r$ is high, i.e., $p''_3 = \begin{bmatrix} m - ww_g \\ w_r \end{bmatrix}_q \begin{bmatrix} n - ww_g \\ w_r \end{bmatrix}_q q^{2ww_g w_r} \left(\begin{bmatrix} m \\ w_r \end{bmatrix}_q \begin{bmatrix} n \\ w_r \end{bmatrix}_q \right)^{-1}$.
By Proposition 2, we have $\langle \alpha_1 \lambda_{1,1}, \ldots, \alpha_w \lambda_{1,w_g} \rangle \subset \langle u_{1,1,1}, \ldots, u_{1,1,n} \rangle$, where

---

Algorithm 4: First Attack on RQCS

Data: t signatures, $\boldsymbol{\sigma}_i = (\boldsymbol{g}_i, \boldsymbol{u}_{i,1}, \boldsymbol{u}_{i,2})$ for $1 \leq i \leq t$, $R = [\mathrm{Cir}_n(\boldsymbol{h})]^T$,
$w_g = \dim(\mathsf{Supp}(\boldsymbol{g}))$, $w = \dim(\mathsf{Supp}(\boldsymbol{x})) = \dim(\mathsf{Supp}(\boldsymbol{y}))$,
$w_r = \dim(\mathsf{Supp}(\boldsymbol{r_1})) = \dim(\mathsf{Supp}(\boldsymbol{r_2}))$
Result: The secret key vector $\boldsymbol{x}$ and $\boldsymbol{y}$

```
// Step 1(a): Recover a support basis for x
```
$\mathcal{F}_x \leftarrow 1\mathrm{A}_{\mathsf{RSR}+}(t, \boldsymbol{g_1}, \boldsymbol{u_{1,1}}, \ldots, \boldsymbol{g_t}, \boldsymbol{u_{t,1}}, w, w_r)$ or $\mathcal{F}_x \leftarrow 1\mathrm{AS}(\boldsymbol{g_1}, \boldsymbol{u_{1,1}}, w, w_g)$
Compute a basis $\{\alpha_1, \ldots, \alpha_w\}$ for $\mathcal{F}_x$
```
// Step 1(b): Recover a support basis for y
```
$\mathcal{F}_y \leftarrow 1\mathrm{A}_{\mathsf{RSR}+}(t, \boldsymbol{g_1}, \boldsymbol{u_{1,2}}, \ldots, \boldsymbol{g_t}, \boldsymbol{u_{t,2}}, w, w_r)$ or $\mathcal{F}_y \leftarrow 1\mathrm{AS}(\boldsymbol{g_1}, \boldsymbol{u_{1,2}}, w, w_g)$
Compute a basis $\{\beta_1, \ldots, \beta_w\}$ for $\mathcal{F}_y$
```
// Step 2: Recover support matrices for x and y
```
$\boldsymbol{\alpha} \leftarrow (\alpha_1, \ldots, \alpha_w)$, $\boldsymbol{\beta} \leftarrow (\beta_1, \ldots, \beta_w)$
Solve for X and Y from the equation $\boldsymbol{s} = \boldsymbol{\alpha} X + \boldsymbol{\beta} Y R$ over $\mathbb{F}_q$
Compute $\boldsymbol{x} \leftarrow \boldsymbol{\alpha} X$ and $\boldsymbol{y} \leftarrow \boldsymbol{\beta} Y$
return $\boldsymbol{x}$, $\boldsymbol{y}$

$\boldsymbol{u_{1,1}} = (u_{1,1,1}, \ldots, u_{1,1,n})$. This gives us $\langle \alpha_1, \ldots, \alpha_w \rangle \subset \langle \alpha_1 \lambda_{1,1} \lambda_{1,j}^{-1}, \ldots, \alpha_w \lambda_{1,w_g} \lambda_{1,j}^{-1} \rangle \subset U_{1,1,j}$ for $1 \leq j \leq w_g$. Therefore, $\mathcal{F}_x = \langle \alpha_1, \ldots, \alpha_w \rangle = \bigcap_{j=1}^{w_g} U_{1,1,j}$.

Note that thc correctness of Step 1(b) follows analogously.

In Step 2, let $\boldsymbol{\alpha} = (\alpha_1, \ldots, \alpha_w)$, $\boldsymbol{\beta} = (\beta_1, \ldots, \beta_w)$. Consider $\boldsymbol{s}$ from the public key and form the linear system $\boldsymbol{s} = \boldsymbol{x} + \boldsymbol{h} \cdot \boldsymbol{y} = \boldsymbol{x} + \boldsymbol{y} R = \boldsymbol{\alpha} X + \boldsymbol{\beta} Y R$. The linear system consists of nm equations over $\mathbb{F}_q$ with a total of $2wn$ unknown variables (from X and Y) to be solved. Since the inequality $m \geq 2w$ is always true in RQCS, we have $nm \geq 2wn$, the number of equations is greater than the number of unknown variables. Then we are able to recover the matrices X and Y in polynomial time.

Probability of Failure for Algorithm 4. If $1\mathrm{A}_{\mathsf{RSR}+}$-Algorithm is used, Step 1(a) and 1(b) of the attack might fail whenever the RSR algorithm fails. It follows that the probability of failure is at most $p_2 = 1 - (1 - p_2')^{2t}$, where $p_2' = \max\{q^{(2-w-w_r)(w_g-2)} \times q^{-(n-(w+w_r)w_g+1)}, q^{-2(n-(w+w_r)w_g+2)}\}$.

If 1AS-Algorithm is used, Step 1(a) and 1(b) of the attack might fail when $\mathcal{F}_x \not\subset U_{1,1,j}$. Note that the probability that $\mathcal{F}_x \subset U_{1,1,j}$ occurs is at least $p_3' = \left(1 - q^{-(n - w w_g + 1)}\right) p_3''$. Thus, the probability of failure is at most $p_3 = 1 - (p_3')^2$.

Therefore, the probability of failure for Algorithm 4 is at most $\max\{p_2, p_3\}$.

3.4 First Attack on Veron Signature Scheme

There are two parts in our attack on Veron. The first part is to recover a support basis for the vector $\boldsymbol{e}$ from $\mathrm{rsp}_{j,2}$ when $b_j = 1$. The second part is to recover a support matrix for $\boldsymbol{e}$ from the public key component G and $\boldsymbol{y}$, if $m(n-k) \geq rn$. Once we have recovered a support basis and a support matrix for $\boldsymbol{e}$, we can recover the secret key component $\boldsymbol{e}$ and $\boldsymbol{x}$.

We now describe our first attack on Veron.

Algorithm 5: First Attack on Veron

Data: signature $sgn = (\mathrm{cmt}, \mathrm{rsp})$, public key $\mathsf{pk} = (\boldsymbol{y}, G, r)$, message $\boldsymbol{m}$, number of rounds for Veron, δ
Result: The secret key vector $\boldsymbol{x}$ and $\boldsymbol{e}$
`// Step 1: Precomputation steps`
Compute $\mathrm{ch} = \mathcal{H}_{\mathsf{A,B}}(\mathrm{cmt}, \boldsymbol{m})$
$i \leftarrow 1$, $tmp \leftarrow 0$
`// Step 2: Recover a support basis for` $\boldsymbol{e}$
while $tmp = 0$ **do**
  Compute $b_i = f(\mathrm{ch}_{2i}, \mathrm{ch}_{2i+1})$
  if $b_i = 1$ **then**
    $tmp \leftarrow 1$, $\boldsymbol{e}' \leftarrow \mathrm{rsp}_{i,2}$
    Compute $\mathcal{F} = \langle e'_1, \ldots, e'_n \rangle$ and a basis $\{\hat{e}_1, \ldots, \hat{e}_r\}$ for $\mathcal{F}$
    break
  else
    $i \leftarrow i + 1$
`// Step 2: Recover support matrix for` $\boldsymbol{e}$
$\hat{\boldsymbol{e}} \leftarrow (\hat{e}_1, \ldots, \hat{e}_r)$
Compute a parity check matrix H for G and $\boldsymbol{s} \leftarrow \boldsymbol{y}H^T$
Solve for E from the equations $\boldsymbol{s} = \hat{\boldsymbol{e}}EH^T$ under $\mathbb{F}_q$
Compute $\boldsymbol{e} \leftarrow \hat{\boldsymbol{e}}E$
`// Step 3: Recover the secret vector` $\boldsymbol{x}$
Compute $\boldsymbol{z} \leftarrow \boldsymbol{y} - \boldsymbol{e}$ and solve for $\boldsymbol{x}$ from the equation $\boldsymbol{z} = \boldsymbol{x}G$ over $\mathbb{F}_{q^m}$
return $\boldsymbol{x}$, $\boldsymbol{e}$

Correctness of Algorithm 5. Let $(\mathrm{cmt}, \mathrm{rsp})$ be a signature generated in Veron.Sign. Following the procedures in Veron.Vrfy, we can compute the challenge $\mathrm{ch} = \mathcal{H}_{\mathsf{A,B}}(\mathrm{cmt}, \boldsymbol{m})$. Notice that there exists an index i such that $b_i = 1$. For such i, consider the rsp_i from the signature, we have $\mathrm{rsp}_{i,2} = \boldsymbol{e}P_i$. Let $\boldsymbol{e} = (e_1, \ldots, e_n)$ and $\boldsymbol{e}P_i = (e'_1, \ldots, e'_n)$. Since $P_i \in S_n$, then we have $\langle e_1, \ldots, e_n \rangle = \langle e'_1, \ldots, e'_n \rangle$. From $\mathcal{F} = \langle e'_1, \ldots, e'_n \rangle$, we can compute a basis $\{\hat{e}_1, \ldots, \hat{e}_r\}$, which is a support basis for $\boldsymbol{e}$.

With a support basis computed, we consider the matrix G from pk and compute a parity check matrix $H \in \mathbb{F}_{q^m}^{(n-k)\times n}$ for G. Using $\boldsymbol{y}$ from pk, compute $\boldsymbol{s} = \boldsymbol{y}H^T = (\boldsymbol{x}G + \boldsymbol{e})H^T = \boldsymbol{e}H^T$. Let $E \in \mathbb{F}_q^{r\times n}$ be a support matrix for $\boldsymbol{e}$, then we can form the linear system $\boldsymbol{s} = (\hat{e}_1, \ldots, \hat{e}_r)EH^T$. Consider the linear system over $\mathbb{F}_q$. Note that the number of equations, $m(n-k)$, is greater than the number of unknown variables, rn. Therefore, we can solve for the matrix E, thus giving us $\boldsymbol{e} = (\bar{e}_1, \ldots, \bar{e}_r)E$. Finally, $\boldsymbol{z} = \boldsymbol{y} - \boldsymbol{e} = \boldsymbol{x}G$. Since $n > k$, we can solve for $\boldsymbol{x}$.

4 Second Polynomial Time Attack on Rank Metric FS Signature Schemes

We now introduce our second generic attack, which is a twist of the first attack. Instead of recovering the secret key, sk for the signature scheme directly, this attack aims to recover the ephemeral key used in signature generation, and then determine the secret key from the generated signature.

4.1 Idea of Attack

We now describe the general idea of our second attack on the rank metric signature scheme. Typically, we are given an invertible function T, a signature $\boldsymbol{\sigma} = \boldsymbol{t} + T(\boldsymbol{e}) \in \mathbb{F}_{q^m}^n$ and a syndrome $\boldsymbol{s} = T(\boldsymbol{e})H^T \in \mathbb{F}_{q^m}^{n-k}$ where $H \in \mathbb{F}_{q^m}^{(n-k)\times n}$ is used in the signature scheme. We need the following result for our attack:

Proposition 3. Let $\boldsymbol{x} \in \mathcal{E}_{m,n,r}$ and $t > r$ be an integer. There exists a vector $\boldsymbol{y} = (y_1, \ldots, y_t) \in \mathcal{E}_{m,t,t}$ such that $\mathsf{Supp}(\boldsymbol{x}) \subset \mathsf{Supp}(\boldsymbol{y})$. We call such $\mathsf{Supp}(\boldsymbol{y})$ an *extended support* of $\boldsymbol{x}$ and $\{y_1, \ldots, y_t\}$ an *extended support basis* for $\boldsymbol{x}$. Moreover, there exists a matrix $V \in \mathbb{F}_q^{t\times n}$ of $\mathrm{rk}(V) = r$ satisfying $\boldsymbol{x} = (y_1, \ldots, y_t)V$. We call such V an *extended support matrix* for $\boldsymbol{x}$.

There are three main steps in our second attack:

1. Let $\boldsymbol{\sigma} = (\sigma_1, \ldots, \sigma_n)$ and $\boldsymbol{t} = (t_1, \ldots, t_n)$ with $\mathrm{rk}(\boldsymbol{\sigma}) = r_\sigma < n$ and $\mathrm{rk}(\boldsymbol{t}) = r_t$ respectively. Determine an extended support basis for $\boldsymbol{t}$. This could be achieved by determining a basis $\{\hat{\sigma}_1, \ldots, \hat{\sigma}_{r_\sigma}\}$ for $\mathsf{Supp}(\boldsymbol{\sigma})$.
2. Recover an extended support matrix E for $\boldsymbol{t}$. Since $\mathsf{Supp}(\boldsymbol{t}) \subset \mathsf{Supp}(\boldsymbol{\sigma})$, there exists an extended support matrix $E \in \mathbb{F}_q^{r_\sigma\times n}$ of rank $\mathrm{rk}(E) = r_t$ such that $\boldsymbol{t} = (\hat{\sigma}_1, \ldots, \hat{\sigma}_{r_\sigma})E$. Then, compute $\boldsymbol{v} = \boldsymbol{\sigma}H^T - \boldsymbol{s} = \boldsymbol{t}H^T = (\hat{\sigma}_1, \ldots, \hat{\sigma}_{r_\sigma})EH^T$. Considering the linear system over $\mathbb{F}_q$, we have $m(n-k)$ equations over $\mathbb{F}_q$ and $r_\sigma \times n$ unknown variables over $\mathbb{F}_q$. If $m(n-k) > r_\sigma n$, then we can recover the support matrix E, and thus compute the ephemeral key $\boldsymbol{t} = (\hat{\sigma}_1, \ldots, \hat{\sigma}_{r_\sigma})E$.
3. Recover the secret key $\boldsymbol{e}$. From $\boldsymbol{\sigma} = \boldsymbol{t} + T(\boldsymbol{e})$, compute $T(\boldsymbol{e}) = \boldsymbol{\sigma} - \boldsymbol{t}$. Finally, compute $\boldsymbol{e} = T^{-1}(T(\boldsymbol{e}))$.

Using this idea, we now propose some polynomial time attacks on TPL and RQCS signature schemes.

Remark 1. The second generic attack aims to recover the ephemeral key, so that the secret key can be determined. However, this attack does not apply on Veron. More specifically, when $b_i = 0$, the information $(P_i, \boldsymbol{u}_i + \boldsymbol{x}, (\boldsymbol{u}_i + \boldsymbol{x})GP_i)$ is available. Although $\boldsymbol{u}_i + \boldsymbol{x}$ is available, we are not able to determine an extended support basis for the ephemeral key $\boldsymbol{u}_i$, as $\mathsf{Supp}(\boldsymbol{u}_i) \not\subset \mathsf{Supp}(\boldsymbol{u}_i + \boldsymbol{x})$. When $b_i = 1$, the information $(((\boldsymbol{u}_i + \boldsymbol{x})G)P_i, \boldsymbol{e}P_i, (\boldsymbol{u}_iG + \boldsymbol{y})P_i)$ is available. As P_i is unknown, we are not able to further extract any useful information regarding the ephemeral key. Whilst the first attack can be applied here as $\mathsf{Supp}(\boldsymbol{e}P_i) = \mathsf{Supp}(\boldsymbol{e})$. When

$b_i = 2$, the information $(P_i, \boldsymbol{u}_i, (\boldsymbol{u}_i G + \boldsymbol{y})P_i)$ is available. Although the ephemeral key $\boldsymbol{u}_i$ is known, we do not have any information on how $\boldsymbol{u}_i$ interacts with the secret key $\boldsymbol{x}$. Therefore, the second generic attack is not applicable to Veron.

4.2 Second Attack on TPL Signature Scheme

There are three parts in our second attack on TPL. The first part is to determine a support basis for the vector $\boldsymbol{t}_i$ for $i = 1, \ldots, l$. The second part is to recover an extended support matrix for the ephemeral $\boldsymbol{u}_i$ from the public key component H and $\boldsymbol{s}_i$. Once we have recovered the vector $\boldsymbol{u}_i$, we can then recover the secret key component $\boldsymbol{e}_i$ using $\boldsymbol{t}_i$.

Algorithm 6: Second Attack on TPL

Data: signature $\boldsymbol{\sigma} = (\boldsymbol{c}, \boldsymbol{t}_1, \ldots, \boldsymbol{t}_l)$ where $\boldsymbol{t}_i = (t_{i,1}, \ldots, t_{i,n})$ for $1 \leq i \leq l$, $\mathsf{pk} = (H, \boldsymbol{s}_1, \ldots, \boldsymbol{s}_l)$

Result: The secret key vector $\boldsymbol{e}_1, \ldots, \boldsymbol{e}_l$

// Step 1: Determine an extended support basis for $\boldsymbol{t}_1, \ldots, \boldsymbol{t}_l$

for $i \leftarrow 1$ **to** l **do**
- Compute $r_{t_i} = \mathrm{rk}(\boldsymbol{t}_i)$ and a basis $\{\hat{t}_{i,1}, \ldots, \hat{t}_{i,r_{t_i}}\}$ for $\mathsf{Supp}(\boldsymbol{t}_i)$

// Step 2: Recover a support matrix for $\boldsymbol{u}_1, \ldots, \boldsymbol{u}_l$

for $i \leftarrow 1$ **to** l **do**
- Compute $\boldsymbol{v}_i = \boldsymbol{t}_i H^T - \hat{c}_i \boldsymbol{s}_i$
- Solve for E_i from the equation $\boldsymbol{v}_i = (\hat{t}_{i,1}, \ldots, \hat{t}_{i,r_{t_i}}) E_i H^T$ over $\mathbb{F}_q$
- Compute $\boldsymbol{u}_i \leftarrow (\hat{t}_{i,1}, \ldots, \hat{t}_{i,r_{t_i}}) E_i$

// Step 3: Recover the secret key vector $\boldsymbol{e}_1, \ldots, \boldsymbol{e}_k$

for $i \leftarrow 1$ **to** l **do**
- Compute $\boldsymbol{e}_i \leftarrow \hat{c}_i^{-1}(\boldsymbol{t}_i - \boldsymbol{u}_i)$

return $\boldsymbol{e}_1, \ldots, \boldsymbol{e}_l$

Correctness of Algorithm 6. Let $\boldsymbol{\sigma} = (\boldsymbol{c}, \boldsymbol{t}_1, \ldots, \boldsymbol{t}_l)$ be a signature generated in TPL.Sign. Let $\boldsymbol{e}_i = (e_{i,1}, \ldots, e_{i,n})$. By Proposition 2, the probability that $\mathsf{Supp}(\boldsymbol{u}_i) \subset \mathsf{Supp}(\boldsymbol{t}_i)$ is p_1'. Let $\{\hat{t}_{i,1}, \ldots, \hat{t}_{i,r_{t_i}}\}$ be a basis of $\mathsf{Supp}(\boldsymbol{t}_i)$, and $\hat{\boldsymbol{t}}_i = (\hat{t}_{i,1}, \ldots, \hat{t}_{i,r_{t_i}})$. There exists $E_i \in \mathbb{F}_q^{r_{t_i} \times n}$ such that $\boldsymbol{u}_i = \hat{\boldsymbol{t}}_i E_i$. Compute $\boldsymbol{v}_i = \boldsymbol{t}_i H^T - \hat{c}_i \boldsymbol{s}_i = \boldsymbol{u}_i H^T = \hat{\boldsymbol{t}}_i E_i H^T$. Then, consider the linear system over $\mathbb{F}_q$. Note that the number of equations, $m(n-k)$, is greater than the number of unknown variables, $r_{t_i} n$. Therefore, we can solve for a support matrix E_i, thus giving us the ephemeral key $\boldsymbol{u}_i = \hat{\boldsymbol{t}}_i E_i$. Once $\boldsymbol{u}_i$ is computed, we have $\hat{c}_i \boldsymbol{e}_i = \boldsymbol{t}_i - \boldsymbol{u}_i$. Finally, compute $\boldsymbol{e}_i = \hat{c}_i^{-1}(\hat{c}_i \boldsymbol{e}_i)$.

Probability of Failure for Algorithm 6. Notice that the algorithm will be successful if $\mathrm{rk}(\boldsymbol{t}_i) = r_1 + r_2$ for $1 \leq i \leq l$. Therefore, the probability of failure for Algorithm 6 is $p_5 = 1 - (p_1)^l$.

4.3 Second Attack on RQCS Signature Scheme

There are three parts in our second attack on RQCS. The first part is to determine a basis for the vector $\boldsymbol{u_1}$ and $\boldsymbol{u_2}$. The second part is to recover an extended support matrix for the ephemeral vector $\boldsymbol{r}$. Once we have recovered the vector $\boldsymbol{r}$, we can then recover the secret key components $\boldsymbol{x}$ and $\boldsymbol{y}$ using $\boldsymbol{u}$ and $\boldsymbol{g}$. Here, we propose two different methods to recover $\boldsymbol{r}$: the first method is to apply the RSR algorithm to recover an extended support basis for $\boldsymbol{r}$; the second method is to recover an extended support basis for $\boldsymbol{r}$ without the RSR algorithm.

Algorithm 7: Second Attack on RQCS

Data: 1 signature $\boldsymbol{\sigma} = (\boldsymbol{g}, \boldsymbol{u_1}, \boldsymbol{u_2})$, $\langle \lambda_1, \dots, \lambda_{w_g} \rangle = \mathsf{Supp}(\boldsymbol{g})$,
$R = [I_n \mid \mathrm{Cir}_n(\boldsymbol{h})]$, $w = \dim(\mathsf{Supp}(\boldsymbol{x})) = \dim(\mathsf{Supp}(\boldsymbol{y}))$,
$w_r = \dim(\mathsf{Supp}(\boldsymbol{r_1})) = \dim(\mathsf{Supp}(\boldsymbol{r_2}))$
Result: The secret key vector $\boldsymbol{x}$ and $\boldsymbol{y}$
// Step 1: Recover an extended support basis for $\boldsymbol{r}$
$\mathcal{F} \leftarrow \mathsf{RSR}(\langle 1, \lambda_1, \dots, \lambda_{w_g} \rangle, \boldsymbol{u}, w + w_r)$ or $\mathcal{F} \leftarrow \mathsf{Supp}(\boldsymbol{u})$
Compute $v \leftarrow \dim(\mathcal{F})$ and a basis $\{\alpha_1, \dots, \alpha_v\}$ for $\mathcal{F}$
// Step 2: Recover an extended support matrix for $\boldsymbol{r}$
$\boldsymbol{\alpha} \leftarrow (\alpha_1, \dots, \alpha_v)$ and compute $I = \boldsymbol{u_1} + \boldsymbol{h} \cdot \boldsymbol{u_2} - \boldsymbol{s} \cdot \boldsymbol{g}$
Solve for X from the equation $I = \boldsymbol{\alpha} X R^T$ over $\mathbb{F}_q$
Compute $\boldsymbol{r} = (\boldsymbol{r_1}, \boldsymbol{r_2}) \leftarrow \boldsymbol{\alpha} X$
// Step 3: Recover the secret key $\boldsymbol{x}$ and $\boldsymbol{y}$
Compute $\boldsymbol{g}''$ such that $\boldsymbol{g} \cdot \boldsymbol{g}'' = (1, 0, \dots, 0) \in \mathbb{F}_{q^m}^n$
Compute $\boldsymbol{x} \leftarrow (\boldsymbol{u_1} - \boldsymbol{r_1}) \cdot \boldsymbol{g}''$ and $\boldsymbol{y} \leftarrow (\boldsymbol{u_2} - \boldsymbol{r_2}) \cdot \boldsymbol{g}''$
return $\boldsymbol{x}$, $\boldsymbol{y}$

Correctness of Algorithm 7. Let $\mathcal{G}' = \langle \lambda_1, \dots, \lambda_{w_g}, 1 \rangle$, the coordinates of $\boldsymbol{u}$ generate a subspace of $\mathcal{F}.\mathcal{G}'$. Therefore, the RSR Algorithm will give the desired $\mathcal{F} = \mathsf{Supp}(\boldsymbol{x}, \boldsymbol{y}, \boldsymbol{r})$, an extended support basis for $\boldsymbol{r}$. Alternatively, the probability that $\mathsf{Supp}(\boldsymbol{r_1}, \boldsymbol{r_2}) \subset \mathsf{Supp}(\boldsymbol{u})$ is $(p_3')^2$. Therefore, a basis $\{\alpha_1, \dots, \alpha_v\}$ of $\mathsf{Supp}(\boldsymbol{u})$ is an extended support basis for $\boldsymbol{r}$, giving us $\mathsf{Supp}(\boldsymbol{r}) \subset \mathcal{F}$.

Let $\boldsymbol{\alpha} = (\alpha_1, \dots, \alpha_v)$, there exists $X \in \mathbb{F}_q^{v \times 2n}$ such that $\boldsymbol{r} = \boldsymbol{\alpha} X$. Compute $I = \boldsymbol{u_1} + \boldsymbol{h} \cdot \boldsymbol{u_2} - \boldsymbol{s} \cdot \boldsymbol{g} = \boldsymbol{r} R^T = \boldsymbol{\alpha} X R^T$. Consider the linear system over $\mathbb{F}_q$. Note that the number of equations, mn, is greater than the number of unknown variables, $2nv$. Therefore, we can solve for an extended support matrix X, thus giving us the ephemeral key $\boldsymbol{r} = \boldsymbol{\alpha} X$.

Let $\boldsymbol{g}'' \in \mathbb{F}_{q^m}^n$ such that $\boldsymbol{g} \cdot \boldsymbol{g}'' = (1, 0, \dots, 0) \in \mathbb{F}_{q^m}^n$. Once $\boldsymbol{r}$ is computed, we have $(\boldsymbol{x}, \boldsymbol{y}) \star_2 \boldsymbol{g} = \boldsymbol{u} - \boldsymbol{r}$. Finally, compute $(\boldsymbol{x}, \boldsymbol{y}) = ((\boldsymbol{x}, \boldsymbol{y}) \star_2 \boldsymbol{g}) \star_2 \boldsymbol{g}'' = (\boldsymbol{x} \cdot \boldsymbol{g}, \boldsymbol{y} \cdot \boldsymbol{g}) \star_2 \boldsymbol{g}'' = (\boldsymbol{x} \cdot \boldsymbol{g} \cdot \boldsymbol{g}'', \boldsymbol{y} \cdot \boldsymbol{g} \cdot \boldsymbol{g}'')$.

Probability of Failure for Algorithm 7. If $\mathcal{F}$ is computed using the RSR Algorithm, then the probability of failure for Algorithm 7 is $p_7 = 1 - (1 - p_2')^2$. Alternatively, if $\mathcal{F} = \mathsf{Supp}(\boldsymbol{u})$, the attack might fail when $\langle r_1, \dots, r_{2n} \rangle \not\subset \mathcal{F}$. Then, the probability of failure for Algorithm 7 is at most $p_8 = 1 - (p_3')^2$.

Therefore, the probability of failure for Algorithm 7 is at most $\max\{p_7, p_8\}$.

5 Experimental Results for Our Attacks

We consider all the parameters of TPL, RQCS and Veron signature schemes given in [4,15,16] respectively and perform simulations for our attacks. The experimental results of our key recovery attacks are presented in Table 2. The experiments were performed using Magma V2.20-5 running on a 3.4 GHz Intel(R) CoreTM i7 processor with 16 GB of memory.

For each parameter, we recorded the time taken (denoted as "KRA Time") to recover the secret key using our algorithms. Table 2 presents the average timing of 100 experiments for each parameter. The claimed classical and post-quantum security level for the schemes are denoted as "Claimed Sec." and "Claimed PQSec." respectively. We use p_f to denote the probability of failure for the attack algorithm used.

Table 2. Simulations results for our key recovery attacks on TPL, RQCS and Veron signature schemes.

Schemes	Number of Signatures Required	Attack Algorithm	Claimed Sec	Claimed PQSec.	KRA Time	p_f
TPL-1	2	Algorithm 1	–	82	2.78 s	2^{-33}
TPL-2			–	98	4.91 s	2^{-39}
TPL-3			–	129	6.25 s	2^{-52}
RQCS-1	2	Algorithm 4 + $1A_{RSR+}$	128	–	3.34 s	2^{-36}
RQCS-2			192	–	7.09 s	2^{-52}
RQCS-3			256	–	8.23 s	2^{-60}
RQCS-1	1	Algorithm 4 + 1AS	128	–	2.58 s	2^{-36}
RQCS-2			192	–	5.48 s	2^{-54}
RQCS-3			256	–	7.12 s	2^{-58}
Veron-1	1	Algorithm 5	80	–	0.86 s	0
Veron-2			–	128	3.17 s	0
Veron-3			–	192	5.25 s	0
Veron-4			–	256	8.44 s	0
TPL-1	1	Algorithm 6	–	82	4.25 s	2^{-33}
TPL-2			–	98	6.08 s	2^{-39}
TPL-3			–	129	8.74 s	2^{-52}
RQCS-1	1	Algorithm 7 with RSR	128	–	5.79 s	2^{-36}
RQCS-2			192	–	12.15 s	2^{-52}
RQCS-3			256	–	14.42 s	2^{-60}
RQCS-1	1	Algorithm 7 without RSR	128	–	4.78 s	2^{-36}
RQCS-2			192	–	10.82 s	2^{-54}
RQCS-3			256	–	13.64 s	2^{-58}

We manage to recover all the secret keys in TPL, RQCS and Veron signature schemes within seconds. For the first generic attack, Algorithm 1 and Algorithm 4 with $1A_{RSR+}$-Algorithm require 2 signatures to recover the secret key. On the other hand, Algorithm 4 with 1AS-Algorithm and Algorithm 5 require only one signature to recover the secret key.

The second generic attack requires only one signature to recover the secret key. However, our second attack takes slightly longer time to recover the secret key for TPL and RQCS signature schemes as compared to the first attack.

6 Conclusion

We have presented two generic key recovery attacks on some rank metric signature schemes constructed via the Fiat-Shamir transformation. In particular, our attacks recover the secret key of the signature scheme, by determining a support basis (or extended support basis) for the secret key (or the ephemeral key). Then, we use the determined basis to recover a support matrix (or extended support matrix) from the signature and the public key. We have implemented our first attack on TPL, RQCS and Veron signature schemes and managed to recover the secret key in seconds. Furthermore, we have also implemented our second attack on TPL and RQCS signature schemes and managed to recover the secret key in seconds.

Overall, our attacks exploit the fact that a support basis or an extended support basis can be recovered through the signature generated in these FS signature schemes. Moreover, the design of TPL and RQCS signature schemes is vulnerable to our attacks, as the rank of the secret key (or the ephemeral key) are always chosen such that the number of equations is greater than the number of unknown variables when solving the linear system for a support matrix or an extended support matrix over the base field $\mathbb{F}_q$. Therefore, the reparation of these schemes by changing their parameters is not possible. However, both our attacks are not applicable on other FS rank metric signature schemes such as Durandal and CVE, as their signatures hide the information for the support basis of their secret key or ephemeral key used in the signature. An interesting open question is the existence of another technique or approach to recover the support basis of the secret keys in these FS rank metric signature schemes.

Acknowledgement. We are grateful to Caroline Fontaine and the anonymous reviewers for their careful reading of our manuscript and their many insightful comments and suggestions which have greatly improved this manuscript.

Appendix

A Proof of Lemma 2.

Lemma 2. Let $u_1, \ldots, u_k$ be integers such that $0 < u = \sum_{i=1}^k u_i \leq \frac{m}{2}$. For $1 \leq i, j \leq k$, let U_i be a u_i-dimensional subspace of $\mathbb{F}_{q^m}$ and $U_i \cap U_j = \{0\}$. Let $r_0 \leq m - u$, $w = \sum_{i=1}^k r_i$ and $v = r_0 + w = \sum_{i=0}^k r_i$, where each $0 \leq r_i \leq u_i$ for $1 \leq i \leq k$. The number of v-dimensional subspace that intersects each U_i in an r_i-dimensional subspace is $\left(\prod_{i=1}^k \begin{bmatrix} u_i \\ r_i \end{bmatrix}_q\right) \begin{bmatrix} m-u \\ r_0 \end{bmatrix}_q q^{r_0(u-w)}$.

Proof. We prove the statement by following the idea of the proof of [12, Lemma 3]. For each $1 \leq i \leq k$, there are $\begin{bmatrix} u_i \\ r_i \end{bmatrix}_q$ subspaces $U_i' \subseteq U_i$ of dimension r_i that can be the intersection space. Now we have to complete the subspace $\bigoplus_{i=1}^k U_i'$ to a v-dimensional vector space V, intersecting each U_i only in U_i'. We have $\sum_{j=1}^{r_0-1}(q^m - q^{u+j})$ choices for the remaining basis vectors. For a fixed basis of $\bigoplus_{i=1}^k U_i'$, the number of bases spanning the same subspace is given by the number of $v \times v$ matrices of the form $\begin{bmatrix} I_w & \mathbf{0} \\ A & B \end{bmatrix}$ where $A \in \mathbb{F}_q^{r_0 \times w}$ and $B \in \mathrm{GL}_{r_0}(\mathbb{F}_q)$. This number is equal to $q^{r_0 w}\,|\mathrm{GL}_{r_0}(\mathbb{F}_q)| = q^{r_0 w}\prod_{j=1}^{r_0-1}(q^{r_0} - q^j)$. Hence the final count is given by

$$\left(\prod_{i=1}^{k}\begin{bmatrix} u_i \\ r_i \end{bmatrix}_q\right)\frac{\prod_{j=1}^{r_0-1}(q^m - q^{u+j})}{q^{r_0 w}\prod_{j=1}^{r_0-1}(q^{r_0} - q^j)} = \left(\prod_{i=1}^{k}\begin{bmatrix} u_i \\ r_i \end{bmatrix}_q\right)\frac{q^{r_0 u}}{q^{r_0 w}}\left(\prod_{j=1}^{r_0-1}\frac{q^{m-u} - q^j}{q^{r_0} - q^j}\right)$$

$$= \left(\prod_{i=1}^{k}\begin{bmatrix} u_i \\ r_i \end{bmatrix}_q\right)\begin{bmatrix} m-u \\ r_0 \end{bmatrix}_q q^{r_0(u-w)}.$$

□

B Proof of Proposition 1.

Proposition 1. Let r_x, r_y be integers such that $r_x + r_y \leq \min\{m, n\}$ and $\boldsymbol{x} \in \mathcal{E}_{m,n,r_x}$. Randomly pick a vector $\boldsymbol{y} \xleftarrow{\$} \mathcal{E}_{m,n,r_y}$ and form $\boldsymbol{z} = \boldsymbol{x} + \boldsymbol{y}$. Suppose that $\mathsf{Supp}(\boldsymbol{x}) \cap \mathsf{Supp}(\boldsymbol{y}) = \{0\}$, then the probability that $\mathrm{rk}(\boldsymbol{z}) = r_x + r_y$ is $\begin{bmatrix} n - r_x \\ r_y \end{bmatrix}_q q^{r_y r_x}\left(\begin{bmatrix} n \\ r_y \end{bmatrix}_q\right)^{-1}$.

Proof. By Lemma 1, we can rewrite $\boldsymbol{x} = (\hat{x}_1, \ldots, \hat{x}_{r_x})A$ and $\boldsymbol{y} = (\hat{y}_1, \ldots, \hat{y}_{r_y})B$ where $\mathrm{rk}(\hat{x}_1, \ldots, \hat{x}_{r_x}) = r_x$ and $\mathrm{rk}(\hat{y}_1, \ldots, \hat{y}_{r_y}) = r_y$. Then

$$\boldsymbol{z} = (\hat{x}_1, \ldots, \hat{x}_{r_x})A + (\hat{y}_1, \ldots, \hat{y}_{r_y})B = (\hat{x}_1, \ldots, \hat{x}_{r_x}, \hat{y}_1, \ldots, \hat{y}_{r_y})\begin{bmatrix} A \\ B \end{bmatrix}.$$

Since $\mathsf{Supp}(\boldsymbol{x}) \cap \mathsf{Supp}(\boldsymbol{y}) = \{0\}$, we have $\mathrm{rk}(\hat{x}_1, \ldots, \hat{x}_{r_x}, \hat{y}_1, \ldots, \hat{y}_{r_y}) = r_x + r_y$. Let $W = \begin{bmatrix} A \\ B \end{bmatrix}$. If $\mathrm{rk}(W) = r_x + r_y$, then $\mathrm{rk}(\boldsymbol{z}) = r_x + r_y$. Hence, we need to calculate the probability that $\mathrm{rk}(W) = r_x + r_y$. Let $\mathcal{A} \subset \mathbb{F}_{q^n}$ with $\dim(\mathcal{A}) = r_x$ and $\mathcal{B} \subset \mathbb{F}_{q^n}$ with $\dim(\mathcal{B}) = r_y$, where each of them is the vector subspace generated by the row space of A and B respectively. If $\mathcal{A} \cap \mathcal{B} = \{0\}$, then each row of W is linearly independent with each other, giving us $\mathrm{rk}(W) = r_x + r_y$. By Lemma 2, the number of $\mathcal{B}$ such that $\mathcal{A} \cap \mathcal{B} = \{0\}$ is $\begin{bmatrix} n - r_x \\ r_y \end{bmatrix}_q q^{r_y r_x}$.

So, the probability that $\mathcal{A} \cap \mathcal{B} = \{0\}$ is $\begin{bmatrix} n - r_x \\ r_y \end{bmatrix}_q q^{r_y r_x} \left(\begin{bmatrix} n \\ r_y \end{bmatrix}_q \right)^{-1}$. Therefore, the probability that $\text{rk}(\boldsymbol{z}) = r_x + r_y$ is equal to the probability that $\text{rk}(W) = r_x + r_y$, which equals to $\begin{bmatrix} n - r_x \\ r_y \end{bmatrix}_q q^{r_y r_x} \left(\begin{bmatrix} n \\ r_y \end{bmatrix}_q \right)^{-1}$. □

C Proof of Theorem 1.

Theorem 1. Let r_x, r_y be integers such that $r_x + r_y \leq \min\{m, n\}$ and $\boldsymbol{x} \in \mathcal{E}_{m,n,r_x}$. The probability that the vector $\boldsymbol{z} = \boldsymbol{x} + \boldsymbol{y}$ has rank $\text{rk}(\boldsymbol{z}) = r_x + r_y$ for a random $\boldsymbol{y} \xleftarrow{\$} \mathcal{E}_{m,n,r_y}$ is $\begin{bmatrix} m - r_x \\ r_y \end{bmatrix}_q \begin{bmatrix} n - r_x \\ r_y \end{bmatrix}_q q^{2r_y r_x} \left(\begin{bmatrix} m \\ r_y \end{bmatrix}_q \begin{bmatrix} n \\ r_y \end{bmatrix}_q \right)^{-1}$.

Proof. By Lemma 2, the number of $\boldsymbol{y}$ such that $\mathsf{Supp}(\boldsymbol{x}) \cap \mathsf{Supp}(\boldsymbol{x}) = \{0\}$ is $\begin{bmatrix} m - r_x \\ r_y \end{bmatrix}_q q^{r_y r_x}$. Thus, the probability that $\mathsf{Supp}(\boldsymbol{x}) \cap \mathsf{Supp}(\boldsymbol{x}) = \{0\}$ is $\begin{bmatrix} m - r_x \\ r_y \end{bmatrix}_q q^{r_y r_x} \left(\begin{bmatrix} m \\ r_y \end{bmatrix}_q \right)^{-1}$. Combining this with the result from Proposition 1, the probability that $\text{rk}(\boldsymbol{z}) = r_x + r_y$ for a random $\boldsymbol{y} \xleftarrow{\$} \mathcal{E}_{m,n,r_y}$ is

$$\mathsf{Pr}[\text{rk}(\boldsymbol{z}) = r_x + r_y] = \begin{bmatrix} m - r_x \\ r_y \end{bmatrix}_q \begin{bmatrix} n - r_x \\ r_y \end{bmatrix}_q q^{2r_y r_x} \left(\begin{bmatrix} m \\ r_y \end{bmatrix}_q \begin{bmatrix} n \\ r_y \end{bmatrix}_q \right)^{-1}.$$

□

D Proof of Proposition 2.

Proposition 2. Let r_x, r_y be integers such that $r_x + r_y \leq \min\{m, n\}$, $\boldsymbol{x} \in \mathcal{E}_{m,n,r_x}$, $\boldsymbol{y} \in \mathcal{E}_{m,n,r_y}$ and $\boldsymbol{z} = \boldsymbol{x} + \boldsymbol{y}$ with $\text{rk}(\boldsymbol{z}) = r_x + r_y$. Then $\mathsf{Supp}(\boldsymbol{x}) \subset \mathsf{Supp}(\boldsymbol{z})$.

Proof. By Lemma 1, we can rewrite $\boldsymbol{x} = (\hat{x}_1, \ldots, \hat{x}_{r_x})A$ and $\boldsymbol{y} = (\hat{y}_1, \ldots, \hat{y}_{r_y})B$ where $\text{rk}(\hat{x}_1, \ldots, \hat{x}_{r_x}) = r_x$ and $\text{rk}(\hat{y}_1, \ldots, \hat{y}_{r_y}) = r_y$. Then

$$\boldsymbol{z} = (\hat{x}_1, \ldots, \hat{x}_{r_x})A + (\hat{y}_1, \ldots, \hat{y}_{r_y})B = (\hat{x}_1, \ldots, \hat{x}_{r_x}, \hat{y}_1, \ldots, \hat{y}_{r_y}) \begin{bmatrix} A \\ B \end{bmatrix}. \quad (1)$$

Similarly, since $\text{rk}(\boldsymbol{z}) = r_x + r_y$, we can rewrite

$$\boldsymbol{z} = \hat{\boldsymbol{z}}Z = (\hat{z}_1, \ldots, \hat{z}_{r_x + r_y})Z \quad (2)$$

where $\text{rk}(\hat{z}) = r_x + r_y$ and $\text{rk}(Z) = r_x + r_y$. Equating (1)=(2), we have

$$(\hat{x}_1, \ldots, \hat{x}_{r_x}, \hat{y}_1, \ldots, \hat{y}_{r_y}) \begin{bmatrix} A \\ B \end{bmatrix} = (\hat{z}_1, \ldots, \hat{z}_{r_x + r_y})Z,$$

which implies that $\langle \hat{x}_1, \ldots, \hat{x}_{r_x}, \hat{y}_1, \ldots, \hat{y}_{r_y} \rangle = \langle \hat{z}_1, \ldots, \hat{z}_{r_x + r_y} \rangle$ and

$$\mathsf{Supp}(\boldsymbol{x}) = \langle \hat{x}_1, \ldots, \hat{x}_{r_x} \rangle \subset \langle \hat{z}_1, \ldots, \hat{z}_{r_x + r_y} \rangle = \mathsf{Supp}(\boldsymbol{z}).$$

□

E Proof of Proposition 3.

Proposition 3. Let $\boldsymbol{x} \in \mathcal{E}_{m,n,r}$ and $t > r$ be an integer. There exists a vector $\boldsymbol{y} = (y_1, \ldots, y_t) \in \mathcal{E}_{m,t,t}$ such that $\mathsf{Supp}(\boldsymbol{x}) \subset \mathsf{Supp}(\boldsymbol{y})$. We call such $\mathsf{Supp}(\boldsymbol{y})$ an *extended support* of $\boldsymbol{x}$ and $\{y_1, \ldots, y_t\}$ an *extended support basis* for $\boldsymbol{x}$. Moreover, there exists a matrix $V \in \mathbb{F}_q^{t\times n}$ of $\mathrm{rk}(V) = r$ satisfying $\boldsymbol{x} = (y_1, \ldots, y_t)V$. We call such V an *extended support matrix* for $\boldsymbol{x}$.

Proof. Since $\boldsymbol{x} \in \mathcal{E}_{m,n,r}$, by Lemma 1, there exists a vector $\hat{\boldsymbol{x}} = (\hat{x}_1, \ldots, \hat{x}_r) \in \mathcal{E}_{m,r,r}$ and a matrix $U \in \mathbb{F}_q^{r\times n}$ with $\mathrm{rk}(U) = r$ such that $\boldsymbol{x} = \hat{\boldsymbol{x}}U$. Let $r' = t - r$, randomly pick r' independent elements $w_1, \ldots, w_{r'} \in \mathbb{F}_{q^m} \setminus \mathsf{Supp}(\boldsymbol{x})$, such that $\mathrm{rk}(\hat{x}_1, \ldots, \hat{x}_r, w_1, \ldots, w_{r'}) = t$. Then we can rewrite the vector $\boldsymbol{x} = \hat{\boldsymbol{x}}U = (\hat{x}_1, \ldots, \hat{x}_r, w_1, \ldots, w_{r'}) \begin{bmatrix} U \\ \mathbf{0}_{r'\times n} \end{bmatrix}$. Finally, let $P \in \mathrm{GL}_t(\mathbb{F}_q)$ and $\hat{\boldsymbol{y}} = (\hat{x}_1, \ldots, \hat{x}_r, w_1, \ldots, w_{r'})$. Then there exists a vector $\boldsymbol{y} = \hat{\boldsymbol{y}}P$ and a matrix $V = P^{-1} \begin{bmatrix} U \\ \mathbf{0}_{r'\times n} \end{bmatrix}$ of $\mathrm{rk}(V) = r$ such that $\boldsymbol{x} = \boldsymbol{y}V$. □

F Rank Support Recovery Algorithm

Let $f = (f_1, \ldots, f_d) \in \mathcal{E}_{m,d,d}$, $e = (e_1, \ldots, e_r) \in \mathcal{E}_{m,r,r}$ and $\boldsymbol{s} = (s_1, \ldots, s_n) \in \mathbb{F}_{q^m}^n$ such that $S := \langle s_1, \ldots, s_n \rangle = \langle f_1e_1, \ldots, f_de_r \rangle$. Given $\boldsymbol{f}$, $\boldsymbol{s}$ and r as input, the Rank Support Recover Algorithm will output a vector space E which satisfies $E = \langle e_1, \ldots, e_r \rangle$. Denote $S_i := f_i^{-1}.S$ and $S_{i,j} := S_i \cap S_j$.

Algorithm 8: Rank Support Recover (RSR) Algorithm

Data: $F = \langle f_1, \ldots, f_d \rangle$, $\boldsymbol{s} = (s_1, \ldots, s_n) \in \mathbb{F}_{q^m}^n$, $r = \dim(E)$

Result: A candidate for the vector space E

Compute $S = \langle s_1, \ldots, s_n \rangle$
Precompute every S_i for $i = 1$ to d
Precompute every $S_{i,i+1}$ for $i = 1$ to $d - 1$
for $i \leftarrow 1$ **to** $d - 2$ **do**
  $tmp \leftarrow S + F.(S_{i,i+1} + S_{i+1,i+2} + S_{i,i+2})$
  if $\dim(tmp) \leq rd$ **then**
    $S \leftarrow tmp$
$E \leftarrow f_1^{-1}.S \cap \ldots \cap f_d^{-1}.S$
return E

References

1. Aguilar Melchor, C., et al.: ROLLO - Rank-Ouroboros, LAKE & Locker. https://pqc-rollo.org/doc/rollo-specification_2018-11-30.pdf
2. Aragon, N., et al.: Cryptanalysis of a rank-based signature with short public keys. Designs, Codes and Cryptography (to appear)

3. Aragon, N., Blazy, O., Gaborit, P., Hauteville, A., Zémor, G.: Durandal: a rank metric based signature scheme. In: Ishai, Y., Rijmen, V. (eds.) EUROCRYPT 2019. LNCS, vol. 11478, pp. 728–758. Springer, Cham (2019). https://doi.org/10.1007/978-3-030-17659-4_25
4. Bellini, E., Caullery, F., Hasikos, A., Manzano, M., Mateu, V.: Code-based signature schemes from identification protocols in the rank metric. In: Camenisch, J., Papadimitratos, P. (eds.) CANS 2018. LNCS, vol. 11124, pp. 277–298. Springer, Cham (2018). https://doi.org/10.1007/978-3-030-00434-7_14
5. Bernstein, D.J.: Grover vs. McEliece. In: Sendrier, N. (ed.) PQCrypto 2010. LNCS, vol. 6061, pp. 73–80. Springer, Heidelberg (2010). https://doi.org/10.1007/978-3-642-12929-2_6
6. Cayrel, P.-L., Véron, P., El Yousfi Alaoui, S.M.: A zero-knowledge identification scheme based on the q-ary syndrome decoding problem. In: Biryukov, A., Gong, G., Stinson, D.R. (eds.) SAC 2010. LNCS, vol. 6544, pp. 171–186. Springer, Heidelberg (2011). https://doi.org/10.1007/978-3-642-19574-7_12
7. Fiat, A., Shamir, A.: How to prove yourself: practical solutions to identification and signature problems. In: Odlyzko, A.M. (ed.) CRYPTO 1986. LNCS, vol. 263, pp. 186–194. Springer, Heidelberg (1987). https://doi.org/10.1007/3-540-47721-7_12
8. Gaborit, P., Ruatta, O., Schrek, J., Zémor, G.: New results for rank-based cryptography. In: Pointcheval, D., Vergnaud, D. (eds.) AFRICACRYPT 2014. LNCS, vol. 8469, pp. 1–12. Springer, Cham (2014). https://doi.org/10.1007/978-3-319-06734-6_1
9. Horlemann-Trautmann, A., Marshall, K., Rosenthal, J.: Extension of Overbeck's attack for Gabidulin based cryptosystems. Des. Codes Cryptogr. **86**(2), 319–340 (2018)
10. Lau, T.S.C., Tan, C.H.: Key recovery attack on Rank Quasi-Cyclic code-based signature scheme. arXiv preprint:1902.00241. https://arxiv.org/abs/1902.00241
11. Lau, T.S.C., Tan, C.H., Prabowo, T.F.: Analysis of TPL signature scheme. IACR Cryptology Archive 2019:303. https://eprint.iacr.org/2019/303
12. Neri, A., Horlemann-Trautmann, A.-L., Randrianarisoa, T., Rosenthal, J.: On the genericity of maximum rank distance and Gabidulin codes. Des. Codes Cryptogr. **86**(2), 341–363 (2018)
13. Schnorr, C.-P.: Efficient signature generation by smart cards. J. Cryptol. **4**(3), 161–174 (1991)
14. Shor, P.W.: Polynomial-time algorithms for prime factorization and discrete logarithms on a quantum computer. SIAM J. Comput. **26**(5), 1484–1509 (1997)
15. Song, Y., Huang, X., Mu, Y., Wu, W.: A new code-based signature scheme with shorter public key. Cryptology ePrint Archive: Report 2019/053. https://eprint.iacr.org/eprint-bin/getfile.pl?entry=2019/053&version=20190125:204017&file=053.pdf
16. Tan, C.H., Prabowo, T.F., Lau, T.S.C.: Rank metric code-based signature. In: Proceedings of the International Symposium on Information Theory and Its Application (ISITA 2018), pp. 70–74 (2018)
17. Véron, P.: Improved identification schemes based on error-correcting codes. Appl. Algebra Eng. Commun. Comput. **8**(1), 57–69 (1997)
18. Xagawa, K.: Cryptanalysis of a new code-based signature scheme with shorter public key in PKC 2019. IACR ePrint:2019/120. https://eprint.iacr.org/2019/120.pdf

On the Security of Multikey Homomorphic Encryption

Hyang-Sook Lee and Jeongeun Park(✉)

Department of Mathematics, Ewha Womans University, Seoul, Republic of Korea
hsl@ewha.ac.kr, jungeun7430@ewhain.net

Abstract. Multikey fully homomorphic encryption (MFHE) scheme enables homomorphic computation on data encrypted under different keys. To decrypt a result ciphertext, all the involved secret keys are required. For multi decryptor setting, decryption is a protocol with minimal interaction among parties. However, all prior schemes supporting the protocol are not secure in public channel against a passive external adversary who can see any public information not joining the protocol. Furthermore, the possible adversaries have not been defined clearly.

In this paper, we revisit the security of MFHE and present a secure one-round decryption protocol. We apply it to one of existing schemes and prove the scheme is secure against possible static adversaries. As an application, we construct a two round multiparty computation without common random string.

Keywords: Security of MFHE · MPC without CRS · Multikey homomorphic encryption

1 Introduction

1.1 Multikey Fully Homomorphic Encryption Schemes

Fully homomorphic encryption (FHE) supports arbitrary computation on encrypted data under the same key. Multikey fully homomorphic encryption (MFHE) is a generalization of FHE, which allows arbitrary computation on encrypted data under *different* keys. The important thing is that all relevant secret keys are required to decrypt a ciphertext. This concept was first proposed by Lopez, Tromer, and Vaikuntanathan [16] in 2012, which is intended to apply to on-the-fly multiparty computation. In fact, MFHE has been an interesting topic for round efficient secure computation with minimal communication cost [4,8,15,17]. There are several results on MFHE [3,8,13,14,18], all of which do not allow any interaction among associated parties before decryption protocol is started. All their schemes assume a common random string (CRS) model, which additionally requires a trusted party who distributes the CRS to every party and can be viewed as an ideal version of multikey homomorphic encryption. A CRS plays a role of linking all the parties' ciphertexts under different

M. Albrecht (Ed.): IMACC 2019, LNCS 11929, pp. 236–251, 2019.
https://doi.org/10.1007/978-3-030-35199-1_12

keys to do correct computation on them. Kim, Lee and Park introduce another scheme to get rid of a role of CRS, which is defined in [9] and also [15] implies the same scheme for the first time. In their scheme, the parties share their public keys after key generation step to relate their keys for their own sake like threshold fully homomorphic encryption scheme [1], but keys are generated independently by each user. On the other hand, each user generates key pair and encrypts its own message using single key encryption then publishes together at once without any interaction in the previous other schemes. Their scheme is for the fixed number of users so that it might loose some dynamic property which lets users join and leave the computation freely.

So far, there are at least two types of MFHE schemes: (1) non-interactive MFHE which does not allow any interaction among parties before decryption (note that the computation is done by a server), (2) interactive MFHE to share public keys after key generation. We call a non-interactive scheme and an interactive scheme to distinguish the two schemes in this paper. The interactive scheme might loose a round efficiency for applying to multiparty computation (MPC) since there is at least one interaction by default. On the other hand, it is possible to remove CRS. However, regardless of schemes, we can think of that the decryption procedure can be divided into two cases. The first case is a single decryptor setting like in [16], where a trusted decryptor exists and holds all parties' secret keys so that no interaction among users is required. Here, only the decryptor gets the output value using all the secret keys. Then, each user just needs to keep its input privacy against one another. The second one is a multi decryptor setting, where all users jointly decrypt a common message with minimal interaction among them. Here, they have to make sure that any information about the function value should not be revealed until the joint decryption protocol is completed. Therefore, Kim, Lee and Park define a new security notion for MFHE, which is called multikey IND-CPA security, for the first time. This is a security for a multikey ciphertext (associated with different keys) against one of users whose key is involved in the ciphertext. It is a reasonable security since the ciphertext may leak some information before decrypted with all relevant secret keys. However, it is not sufficient for MFHE itself. All the existing MFHE schemes for multi decryptor setting employ a decryption protocol called distributed decryption, which is also widely used in threshold FHE [1,2]. More precisely, the distributed decryption protocol consists of two steps:

- **Partial Decryption:** Each user decrypts a common ciphertext partially with its own secret key. It outputs a partial decryption.
- **Final Decryption:** Given all users' partial decryptions, it outputs the plaintext (or evaluated plaintext).

In the protocol, the final decryption algorithm takes only partial decryptions without any key. In other words, the partial decryption is not a ciphertext any more. The final message is decrypted only adding all the partial decryptions. Therefore, anyone who is not joining the protocol but can get all partial decryptions from a transmission channel easily gets the evaluated message by running the final decryption algorithm *for free*. Indeed, this would cause a big problem in industry. For example, there are three companies A, B and C, all of which want to construct the best machine learning model using their clients' information as input. For clients' privacy, each company encrypts each input data with its own key. Then the three companies jointly compute a function to output the best machine learning model via an MFHE scheme with multi decryptor. There is a rival company D which does not join this computation, but also needs a good machine learning model for the same type of data as A, B and C have. If A, B and C use one of existing MFHE schemes, D can learn partial decryption shares from a transmission channel and just run the public algorithm (final decryption) to get the best machine learning model for free. If the above three companies handle a private technique deserving patents, this can be a more critical issue. As such, an MFHE scheme with the above decryption protocol is not secure in a public channel. Up to our best knowledge, all the existing schemes have not considered this situation since most of schemes are constructed for MPC hence they can assume a private channel. In other words, MFHE schemes in public channel have not been studied yet. In fact, it is worth consideration for MFHE itself since "encryption" must protect a plaintext from at least a static adversary in any public channel.

Likewise, an adversarial model and what should be protected from that adversaries are different depending on the decryptor setting in MFHE. However, the existing security definition of MFHE is somewhat ambiguous and not clear enough. Most of previous schemes just check their correctness and apply the IND-CPA security of their base single key homomorphic encryption scheme, even they do not clearly mention which decryptor setting they assume. That is, no particular security definition for MFHE itself has been fully discussed yet.

1.2 Our Contribution

In this paper, we resolve the above problems as a main result. We revisit the security of multikey homomorphic encryption scheme and construct a secure decryption protocol based on an existing multikey homomorphic encryption scheme [13] based on TFHE [5–7]. To do this, we define a possible static adversary and semantic security for MFHE. Then we prove that a MFHE scheme with our protocol is semantically secure. Our idea is that a partial decryption remains a multikey ciphertext still encrypted under the other users' keys even if it is partially decrypted by a user. Therefore, it is still secure against an adversary not holding any key. As an additional result, we obtain a round optimal multiparty computation protocol without CRS. To do this, we convert the non-interactive MFHE [13] with CRS to an interactive MFHE *without CRS* combining two MFHE schemes to get a hybrid scheme. In the hybrid scheme, we use the original (leveled) MFHE of [13] for an encryption of message, and we use the converted interactive scheme for bootstrapping part (encryption of secret key). As a result, we construct a 2 round multiparty computation without CRS via the hybrid scheme.

1.3 Organization

We review some important notions and pre-results in Sect. 2 and introduce a possible adversary and define the semantic security of MFHE in Sect. 3. In Sect. 4, we present our distributed decryption protocol and apply it to a multikey TFHE scheme. As an application of MFHE, we first modify a multikey TFHE to remove CRS, allowing interaction among parties, then combine the two multikey TFHE schemes to construct a 2 round MPC without CRS in Sect. 5.

2 Preliminaries

Notation: We denote λ as the security parameter. We define vectors and matrices in lowercase bold and uppercase bold, respectively. Dot product of two vectors $\mathbf{v}, \mathbf{w}$ is denoted by $< \mathbf{v}, \mathbf{w} >$. For a vector $\mathbf{x}$, $\mathbf{x}[i]$ denotes the i-th component scalar. We denote that $\mathbb{B}$ as the set $\{0, 1\}$ and $\mathbb{T}$ as the real torus $\mathbb{R}/\mathbb{Z}$, the set of real number modulo 1. We denote $\mathbb{Z}_N[X]$ and $\mathbb{T}_N[X]$ by $\mathbb{Z}[X]/(X^N + 1)$ and $\mathbb{R}[X]/(X^N + 1)$ mod 1, respectively. $\mathbb{B}_N[X]$ denotes the polynomials in $\mathbb{Z}_N[X]$ with binary coefficients. For a real $\alpha > 0$, D_α denotes the Gaussian distribution of standard deviation α. In this paper, we use the same notation with [6] for better understanding.

2.1 TFHE Scheme

We describe our base FHE scheme TFHE [6] and its multikey version [13]. The multikey version of TFHE has smaller parameter and ciphertext size, leading to better performance than previous GSW [12]-based multikey schemes [3,4,8,17, 18]. The TFHE scheme [6] is working entirely on real torus $\mathbb{T}$ and $\mathbb{T}_N[X]$ based on TLWE problem and TRLWE problem which are torus variant of LWE problem and RLWE problem respectively, where N is a power of two. It is easy to see that $(\mathbb{T}, +, \cdot)$ (resp. $(\mathbb{T}_N[X], +, \cdot)$) is $\mathbb{Z}$ (resp. $\mathbb{Z}_N[X]$) module.

A TLWE (resp. TRLWE) sample is defined as $(\mathbf{a}, b) \in \mathbb{T}^{kn+1}$ (resp. $\mathbb{T}_N[X]^{k+1}$) for any $k > 0$, where $\mathbf{a}$ is chosen uniformly over $\mathbb{T}^{kn}$ (resp. $\mathbb{T}_N[X]^k$) and $b =< \mathbf{a}, \mathbf{s} > +e$. The vector $\mathbf{s}$ is a secret key which is chosen uniformly from $\mathbb{B}^{kn}$ (resp. $\mathbb{B}_N[X]^k$) and the error e is chosen from Gaussian distribution with standard deviation $\alpha \in \mathbb{R} > 0$. Furthermore, we follow the [6]'s definition of trivial sample as having $\mathbf{a} = \mathbf{0}$ and noiseless sample as having the standard deviation $\alpha = 0$. Here, we denote the message space to $\mathcal{M} \subseteq \mathbb{T}$. A TLWE ciphertext of $\mu \in \mathcal{M}$ is constructed by adding a trivial noiseless TLWE message sample $(0, \ldots, \mu) \in \mathbb{T}^{kn+1}$ to a non-trivial TLWE sample. Therefore, the TLWE ciphertext of μ, say $\mathfrak{c}$, which we will interpret as a TLWE sample (of μ) is $(\mathbf{a}, b) \in \mathbb{T}^{k+1}$, where $b = < \mathbf{a}, \mathbf{s} > +e + \mu$. To decrypt it correctly, we use a linear function $\varphi_{\mathbf{s}}$ called *phase*, which results in $\varphi_{\mathbf{s}}(\mathfrak{c}) = b - < \mathbf{a}, \mathbf{s} >= \mu + e$ and we round it to the nearest element in $\mathcal{M}$. We denote the error as $\mathsf{Err}(\mathfrak{c})$, which is equal to $\varphi_s(\mathfrak{c}) - \mu$. For a TRLWE encryption, it follows the same way over $\mathbb{T}_N[X]$ but a message μ is a polynomial of degree N with coefficients $\in \mathcal{M}$.

From the above definition, we can define the decisional TLWE (resp. TRLWE) problem which is parametrized by an error distribution on $\mathbb{T}_N[X]$ and a function φ_s.

- Decision Problem: distinguish the uniform distribution on $\mathbb{T}^{kn+1}$ (resp. $\mathbb{T}_N^{k+1}$) from TLWE (resp.TRLWE) samples for a fixed TLWE (resp. TRLWE) secret $\mathbf{s}$.

The TLWE (resp. TRLWE) problem is a generalization of LWE (resp. RLWE) problem which is as hard as approximating the shortest vector problem.

2.2 TGSW and an External Product

As we can see, TLWE and TRLWE samples have additive homomorphic property. In order to have FHE scheme, [6] defined TGSW ciphertext which supports external product with TLWE ciphertext to get a TLWE ciphertext encrypting multiplication of messages. For TGSW samples in the ring mode, we use the notation TRGSW which is working as TRLWE and also give the definition of a TRGSW sample only. (for $N = 1$, we can think of TGSW sample).

For any positive integer $B_g(\geq 2), \ell, k$, a TRGSW sample is a matrix $\mathbf{C} = \mathbf{Z} + \mu \cdot \mathbf{H} \in \mathbb{T}_N[X]^{(k+1)\ell \times (k+1)}$, where each row of $\mathbf{Z}$ is a TRLWE sample of zero and $\mathbf{H}$ is a gadget matrix which is defined by

$$\mathbf{H} := \left[\begin{array}{c|c|c} 1/B_g & \dots & 0 \\ \vdots & \ddots & \vdots \\ 1/B_g^{\ell} & \dots & 0 \\ \hline \vdots & \ddots & \vdots \\ \hline 0 & \dots & 1/B_g \\ \vdots & \ddots & \vdots \\ 0 & \dots & 1/B_g^{\ell} \end{array}\right] \in \mathbb{T}_N[X]^{(k+1)\ell \times (k+1)}.$$

i.e. $\mathbf{H} = \mathbf{I}_{k+1} \otimes \mathbf{g}$, where $\mathbf{g} = (1/B_g, \dots, 1/B_g^{\ell})$. There is a decomposition algorithm $\mathbf{g}^{-1}(\cdot)$, which outputs the ℓ-dimensional vector in $\mathbb{Z} \cap (-B_g/2, B_g/2]$, satisfying $< \mathbf{g}^{-1}(a), \mathbf{g} > \approx a$ for $a \in \mathbb{R}$. The message μ is in $\mathbb{Z}_N[X]$. We denote TLWE(μ), TRLWE(μ), and TRGSW(μ) as a ciphertext of each proper message μ of TLWE, TRLWE, and TRGSW, respectively. We also denote a trivial TRGSW(1) (resp. TGSW(1)) as $\mathbf{Z}_t + \mathbf{H}$, where each row of $\mathbf{Z}_t$ is a trivial TRLWE (resp. TLWE) sample. An external product between a TGSW ciphertext and a TLWE ciphertext, denoted as $\boxdot$, is defined as $\mathbf{A} \boxdot \mathbf{b} = \mathbf{H}^{-1}(\mathbf{b}) \cdot \mathbf{A}$, where $\mathbf{A}$ is a TGSW sample of μ_A, $\mathbf{b}$ is a TLWE sample of μ_b and $\mathbf{H}^{-1}(\cdot)$ is the gadget decomposition function $Dec_{\mathbf{H},\beta,\epsilon}$ of [6] with different notation. Then the output of the product is a TLWE($\mu_A \cdot \mu_b$). We denote the error as Err($\mathbf{A}$), which is a list of the $(k+1)\ell$ TLWE errors of each line of $\mathbf{A}$. Then the error growth of the external product between $\mathbf{A}$ and $\mathbf{b}$ is following:

$$\|\mathsf{Err}(\mathbf{A} \boxdot \mathbf{b})\|_\infty \leq (k+1)\ell N\beta \|\mathsf{Err}(\mathbf{A})\|_\infty + \|\mu_A\|_1 (1 + kN)\epsilon + \|\mu_A\|_1 \|\mathsf{Err}(\mathbf{b})\|_\infty$$

2.3 Multikey Version of TFHE

We only describe the *leveled* fully homomorphic mode of Chen, Chillotti and Song's scheme since we focus on decryption algorithm so that we refer [13] for more detail. Their scheme assumes a common random string (CRS) among users and the CRS is used for generating a public key and evaluation keys so we do not care of it in detail here. Their scheme is non-interactive before decryption.

- $\mathsf{MTFHE1.Setup}(1^\lambda)$: It takes security parameter and outputs TLWE parameter params which consists of TLWE dimension n, key distribution χ, error parameter α, and evaluation parameters evparam.
- $\mathsf{MTFHE1.KeyGen}(\mathsf{params})$:
  - Sample $\mathbf{s} = (s_0, \ldots, s_{n-1}) \leftarrow \chi$ and set it as a TLWE secret key sk.
  - construct a public key pk, evaluation keys evk from proper algorithms in [13] with params and evparam.
- $\mathsf{MTFHE1.Enc}(m, \mathbf{s})$: Sample $\mathbf{a} = (a_0, a_1, \ldots, a_{n-1})$ from $\mathbb{T}^n$ uniformly at random. Then take a message bit $m \in \{0, 1\}$ and construct a TLWE sample $(\mathbf{a}, b) \in \mathbb{T}^{n+1}$, where $b = \frac{1}{4}m - < \mathbf{a}, \mathbf{s} > +e \pmod 1$, e is chosen from the Gaussian distribution D_α. Returns a ciphertext $\mathsf{ct} = (\mathbf{a}, b)$.
- $\mathsf{MTFHE1.Dec}(\hat{\mathsf{ct}}, \{sk_j\}_{j\in[k]})$: Taking a (evaluated)ciphertext $\hat{\mathsf{ct}} = (\mathbf{a}_1, \ldots, \mathbf{a}_k, b) \in \mathbb{T}^{kn+1}$ and a concatenation of secret key vectors $(\mathbf{s}_1, \ldots, \mathbf{s}_k, 1) \in \mathbb{T}^{kn+1}$ as input and return the message bit $m \in \{0, 1\}$, which satisfies $b + \sum_{j=1}^{k} < \mathbf{a}_j, \mathbf{s}_j > \approx \frac{1}{4}m \pmod 1$.
- $\mathsf{MTFHE1.NAND}(\hat{\mathsf{ct}}_1, \hat{\mathsf{ct}}_2)$: It takes two ciphertexts $\hat{\mathsf{ct}}_1 \in \mathbb{T}^{k_1 n+1}, \hat{\mathsf{ct}}_2 \in \mathbb{T}^{k_2 n+1}$, where k_1, k_2 are the number of parties who joined the previous evaluations to construct $\hat{\mathsf{ct}}_1, \hat{\mathsf{ct}}_2$, respectively, and the set $[k]$ is the indices of parties who are associated either $\hat{\mathsf{ct}}_1$ or $\hat{\mathsf{ct}}_2$.
  - Extend $\hat{\mathsf{ct}}_1$ and $\hat{\mathsf{ct}}_2$ to make them the same dimensional vectors $\hat{\mathsf{ct}}_1', \hat{\mathsf{ct}}_2' \in \mathbb{T}^{kn+1}$ encrypted under the concatenated secret key $\hat{\mathbf{s}} = (\mathbf{s}_1, \ldots, \mathbf{s}_k) \in \mathbb{Z}^{kn}$. Rearrange $\mathbf{a}_j$s giving each index to each user and putting zero in the empty slots, for $j \in [k]$.
  - Return an evaluated ciphertext $\hat{\mathsf{ct}}' = (\mathbf{0}, \ldots, \mathbf{0}, \frac{5}{8}) - \hat{\mathsf{ct}}_1' - \hat{\mathsf{ct}}_2' \pmod 1$.

  For the bootstrapping part with $\{\mathsf{evk}_j\}_{j\in[k]}$, we do not consider here, so we refer the original paper. We call an evaluated ciphertext multikey ciphertext in this paper. The dimension of a multikey ciphertext increases as a number of homomorphic evaluation increases.

2.4 Distributed Decryption

A multikey homomorphic encryption scheme for multi decryptor setting includes a decryption protocol in which all users jointly decrypt a common evaluated message. The most round efficient distributed decryption [17] has been widely adopted to recent schemes, which is following:

- $\mathsf{PartDec}(\hat{\mathsf{ct}}, \mathsf{sk}_i)$ On inputs a multikey ciphertext $\hat{\mathsf{ct}}$ under a sequence of k users' keys and the i-th secret key sk_i, outputs a partial decryption p_i.

- $\mathsf{FinDec}(p_1, \ldots, p_k)$ Given all parties' partial decryptions $\{p_i\}_{i\in[k]}$, outputs a plaintext (or evaluated plaintext).

The decryption algorithm of MTFHE1 is defined for a single decryptor case. But, they also suggest a distributed decryption protocol following the above for multi decryptor case, hence it is not secure in a public channel.

3 Multikey Fully Homomorphic Encryption Security

Before we define the semantic security of MFHE, we observe possible static (passive) adversaries first. The goal of MFHE for multi decryptor is to protect each user's individual message and the common evaluated message. Then we can see that there are at least two types of static adversaries, one of which is an internal adversary and the other is an external adversary. The internal adversary is one of participants of computation but an external adversary is not. Both can just see messages transmitted over any public channel but hope to learn any information about each user's message. However, the external adversary wants to learn the evaluated message as well. Therefore, a MFHE with multi decryptor has to consider a security for multikey ciphertext against both adversaries and partial decryption against an external adversary. Thanks to the multikey IND-CPA security [9], the multikey ciphertext is guaranteed to be secure against both adversaries. Even if they only care of one of joint users, it is obvious that if a multikey ciphertext is secure against one of secret key owners, it is secure against one not holding any key. So we call it the internal security (of MFHE) in this paper. Then we now define the external security (of MFHE).

For a probabilistic multikey fully homomorphic encryption algorithm, we naturally extend the original indistinguishability under chosen plaintext attack (IND-CPA) to any multikey FHE scheme by the following game between a PPT static external adversary $\mathcal{A}$ and a challenger $\mathcal{C}$. For any multikey FHE encryption scheme $\Pi = (\mathsf{KeyGen}, \mathsf{Enc}, \mathsf{Eval}, \mathsf{Dec})$, any static external adversary $\mathcal{A}$, and any value λ for the security parameter, where $\mathsf{Dec} = (\mathsf{MFHE.PartDec}, \mathsf{MFHE.FinDec})$ is a distributed decryption protocol, MFHE security game is defined as:

1 $\mathcal{A}$ chooses a positive integer k and gives it to the challenger $\mathcal{C}$.
2 $\mathcal{C}$ runs $\mathsf{KeyGen}(1^\lambda)$ to generate k random key pairs $\{(\mathsf{sk}_i, \mathsf{pk}_i)\}_{i\in[k]}$ and k evaluation keys $\{\mathsf{evk}_i\}_{i\in[k]}$. Then it publishes all the public keys $\{\mathsf{pk}_i\}_{i\in[k]}$ and $\{\mathsf{evk}_i\}_{i\in[k]}$ to $\mathcal{A}$ and keeps all the secret keys $\{\mathsf{sk}_i\}_{i\in[k]}$ in secret.
3 The adversary $\mathcal{A}$ is given input 1^λ and oracle access to $\mathsf{Enc}()$ with all public keys and its chosen messages. Then it chooses an index $j \in [k]$ and outputs a pair of message vectors $\mathbf{m_0}, \mathbf{m_1}$ of the same length and a function f (here, each component of a vector is viewed as each user's message). The message vectors are $\mathbf{m_0} = (0, 0, \ldots, 0) \in \{0, 1\}^k$ and $\mathbf{m_1} = (1, 0, \ldots, 0) \in \{0, 1\}^k$ and a funtion f is defined as $f : \{0, 1\}^k \to \{0, 1\}$ which outputs the first component of input vector. Then it gives $\mathbf{m_0}, \mathbf{m_1}$, f, and the index j to $\mathcal{C}$.
4 $\mathcal{C}$ chooses a random bit $b \leftarrow \{0, 1\}$, computes a multikey ciphertext which is an encryption of $f(\mathbf{m_b})$ under k public keys, running Eval. Then it partially

decrypts the ciphertexts using $\{\mathsf{sk}_i\}_{i\in[k]\setminus\{j\}}$. It sends the partial decryption messages to $\mathcal{A}$.

5 The adversary is free to perform any number of additional computations, encryptions by given keys (free access to Enc, Eval). Finally, it outputs a guess for the value of b'. If $b' = b$, $\mathcal{A}$ wins.

We define that for any multikey homomorphic encryption scheme, if the advantage of $\mathcal{A}$ is negligible, then the scheme achieves the external security. As a result, we define semantic security for a MFHE.

Definition 1. *For a multikey homomorphic encryption scheme (*KeyGen, Enc, Eval, Dec*), where* Dec *is run by a single decryptor, it is semantically secure if it achieves the internal security. For a multikey homomorphic encryption scheme for multi decryptor, where* Dec *is a protocol among users, it is semantically secure if it achieves both internal and external security.*

It is possible for a single decryptor who holds every associated secret keys to decrypt a multikey ciphertext by itself. Therefore, achieving the only internal security is enough for its semantic security.

4 Distributed Decryption for Only Joint Users

4.1 Distributed Decryption Protocol

We first formalize the distributed decryption protocol with general algorithms for multikey homomorphic encryption scheme and then construct a specific protocol applying TFHE scheme based on LWE problem. Such a protocol consists of two steps: (1) each user first decrypts a common evaluated ciphertext partially with its secret key and broadcast the partial information, (2) after gathering all the partial decryption from all users, each user decrypts the correct evaluated message finally with its *secret key*, independently. Let k be the number of users.

Definition 2. *A distributed decryption for multikey homomorphic encryption consists of two algorithms:*

- MFHE.PartDec($\hat{\mathsf{ct}}, \mathsf{sk}_i$)*: It takes a common evaluated ciphertext* $\hat{\mathsf{ct}}$ *and* i*-th user's secret key* sk_i *for* $i \in [k]$ *on input. It returns partial decryptions* $p_{i,j}$ *for* $j \in [k]$*. The user keeps* $p_{i,i}$ *secret and broadcasts* $p_{i,j}$ *for* $j \in [k]\setminus\{i\}$.
- MFHE.FinDec($\{p_{j,i}\}_{j\in[k]}, \mathsf{sk}_i$)*: It takes all the partial decrypted messages* $p_{j,i}$ *for* $j \in [k]\setminus\{i\}$ *which are given to the* i*-th user and its own partial decryption message* $p_{i,i}$ *and its secret key* sk_i *on input. It outputs the correct evaluated message.*

Comparing to previous protocol, the number of partial decryption increases linearly on k while the previous one is constant. However, it seems inevitable for keeping privacy. If a scheme is interactive before decryption protocol, it is easy to think of an encryption of a partial decrypted message with other users' public keys since users share their public keys before the computation. Hence the MFHE.PartDec might have another input pk_j for $j \in [k]\backslash\{i\}$. For a non-interactive scheme, server can give all required inputs for distributed decryption such as joint users' public keys and evaluation keys for users' own sake, however, it would not be straightforward to agree on sharing keys among users. Therefore, we introduce a naive protocol preserving the optimal round without having other users' information.

4.2 Specific Protocol with Multikey TFHE Scheme

The multikey ciphertext of [13] scheme is $\hat{\mathsf{ct}} = (\mathbf{a}_1, \ldots, \mathbf{a}_k, b) \in \mathbb{T}^{kn+1}$, which satisfies $b = \frac{1}{4}m - \sum_{j=1}^{k} < \mathbf{a}_j, \mathbf{s}_j > +e \pmod 1$, where k is the number of joint users, $m \in \{0,1\}$. Then the distributed decryption protocol (of the i-th user) is following:

- MTFHE1.PartDec($\hat{\mathsf{ct}}, \mathbf{s}_i$):
  - compute $p_{i,i} = b + < \mathbf{a}_i, \mathbf{s}_i >= \frac{1}{4}m - \sum_{j\neq i}^{k} < \mathbf{a}_j, \mathbf{s}_j > +e \pmod 1 \in \mathbb{T}$
  - $p_{i,i}$ can be viewed as a one component of TLWE ciphertext of j-th user for $j \in [k]\backslash\{i\}$, i.e $p_{i,i} =< \mathbf{a}_j, \mathbf{s}_j > +\mathsf{mess} + e$, where $\mathsf{mess} = \frac{1}{4}m - \sum_{t\neq i,j}^{k} < \mathbf{a}_t, \mathbf{s}_t >$ for $t \in [k]\backslash\{i,j\}$. Then the user does external product between a TLWE sample $(\mathbf{a}_j, p_{i,i})$ and a trivial TGSW(1) which is denoted as $\mathbf{A}_j$ with noise e_j from D_α by the user i.
  - The output of the external product is a TLWE ciphertext of the same message mess, which is $p_{i,j} = (\mathbf{a}_{i,j}, b_{i,j}) \in \mathbb{T}^{n+1}$ and is given to each user j for $j \in [k]\backslash i$.
- MTFHE1.FinDec($\{p_{j,i}\}_{j\in[k]}, \mathbf{s}_i$):
  - It parses $p_{j,i}$ into $\mathbf{a}_{j,i}$ and $b_{j,i}$ and compute $b'_{j,i} = b_{j,i} + < \mathbf{a}_i, \mathbf{s}_i >$ for every $j \in [k]\backslash\{i\}$.
  - It computes $\sum_{j\neq i}^{k} b'_{j,i} - (k-2)p_{i,i} = \frac{1}{4}m + \bar{e}$.
  - if the output is close to $\frac{1}{4}$ the evaluate message 1, otherwise 0.

Note that for $k = 2$ (two users), $b'_{j,i} = b_{j,i} + < \mathbf{a}_i, \mathbf{s}_i >$ itself gives the result for $i \neq j \in [2]$.

Correctness of Decryption. Fix a user i for $i \in [k]$. Then the correctness for the user follows:

$$
\begin{aligned}
&\sum_{j\neq i}^{k} b'_{j,i} - (k-2)p_{i,i} \\
&= \sum_{j\neq i}^{k} (\frac{1}{4}m - \sum_{t\neq i,j} < \mathbf{a}_t, \mathbf{s}_t > +\tilde{e}_j) - (k-2)p_{i,i} \\
&= (k-1)\frac{1}{4}m - \sum_{j\neq i}^{k}(\sum_{t\neq i,j}^{k} < \mathbf{a}_t, \mathbf{s}_t > +\tilde{e}_j) - (k-2)(\frac{1}{4}m - \sum_{j\neq i}^{k} < \mathbf{a}_j, \mathbf{s}_j > +e) \\
&= \frac{1}{4}m - (k-2)\sum_{j\neq i}^{k} < \mathbf{a}_j, \mathbf{s}_j > +(k-2)\sum_{j\neq i}^{k} < \mathbf{a}_j, \mathbf{s}_j > + \sum_{j\neq i}^{k} \tilde{e}_j - (k-2)e \\
&= \frac{1}{4}m + \bar{e}
\end{aligned}
$$

If the magnitude of the error term $\bar{e}$ is less than $\frac{1}{8}$, the decryption works correctly.

Error Growth Estimation. Note that e is $\mathsf{Err}(b)$ and also $\mathsf{Err}(p_{i,i})$. After the external product, e becomes $\tilde{e_j}$ for each $j \in [k]\backslash\{i\}$ then we can say $\tilde{e}_j = e + e_{add_j}$. We can estimate the magnitude of the growth e_{add_j} from the external product noise propagation formula. Finally,

$$\bar{e} = \sum_{j \neq i}^{k} \tilde{e}_j - (k-2)e = (k-1)e + \sum_{j \neq i}^{k} e_{add_j} - (k-2)e = e + \sum_{j \neq i}^{k} e_{add_j},$$

$$\|\bar{e}\|_\infty \leq \|e\|_\infty + (k-1)max_j(\|e_{add_j}\|_\infty) = \|e\|_\infty + 2(k-1)\ell\beta max_j(\|\mathsf{Err}(\mathbf{A}_j)\|_\infty) + 2\epsilon.$$

Therefore, the noise growth after partial decryption procedure is quite small since $\mathsf{Err}(\mathbf{A}_j)$ is the error of a fresh TGSW ciphertext $\mathbf{A}_j$ for $j \in [k]\backslash\{i\}$.

Semantic Security of $\mathsf{MTFHE1}$**.** We prove the semantic security of the above multikey homomorphic encryption scheme.

Theorem 3. *$\mathsf{MTFHE1}$ scheme with the distributed decryption protocol is semantically secure assuming the hardness of the underlying TLWE problem.*

The security against an internal adversary is trivial. Since the evaluated multikey ciphertext is a TLWE ciphertext $(\mathbf{a}_1, \ldots, \mathbf{a}_k, b)$, where $b = \frac{1}{4}m - \sum_{i=1}^{k} < \mathbf{a}_i, \mathbf{s}_i >$ $+e$ which is semantically secure itself by TLWE assumption even if any user partially decrypts it with its own secret key (i.e. $b+ < \mathbf{a}_i, \mathbf{s}_i >$ is also a TLWE ciphertext for $i \in [k]$). We now prove the security of the above scheme against external adversary.

Proof. The security game defined in Sect. 3 follows: After the step 4, all $\mathcal{A}$ has got is a multikey ciphertext $\hat{\mathsf{ct}} = (\mathbf{a}_1, \ldots, \mathbf{a}_k, b)$, $p_{i,j} = (\mathbf{a}_{i,j}, b_{i,j})$ for $i \in [k]\backslash\{j\}$. What $\mathcal{A}$ may perform is to do $\sum_{i \neq j}^{k} p_{i,j} - (k-2)(\mathbf{a}_j, b)$. The result is $(\mathbf{a}'_j, \frac{1}{4}m - < \mathbf{a}'_j, \mathbf{s}_j > +error)$, which is a TLWE ciphertext under $\mathbf{s}_j$. Then $\mathcal{A}$ gives the result to a TLWE distinguisher $\mathcal{D}$ and $\mathcal{A}$ outputs whatever $\mathcal{D}$ outputs. By the TLWE assumption, the advantage of $\mathcal{D}$ is negligible, so is $\mathcal{A}$'s. □

We note that the same technique can be applied to the recent MFHE schemes for batched ciphertext [14] in which the external product would be replaced with a tensor product.

5 Round Optimal MPC Protocol Without a CRS via Two MFHE Schemes

Multikey fully homomorphic encryption (MFHE) scheme is known as achieving a round efficient multi party compuation (MPC) [1,15,17]. Mukherjee and Wichs [17] constructed a round optimal (2 round) MPC with CRS and Kim, Lee, and Park [15] achieved a three round MPC without a CRS via interactive MFHE scheme (against semi-malicious adversaries). There is a 2 round semi malicious secure MPC protocol without CRS assuming the existence of two round oblivious transfer (OT) [11]. Also, if there is a two round MPC protocol without CRS via MFHE, and the ciphertexts and public keys are stored to reuse, it can be done to get a correct output for one round assuming the adversaries are static. Such scenario can be achieved in a hospital. For instance, authorized doctors want to experiment using several patients' data encrypted under individual keys. Once their public keys and encrypted data are registered, doctors can do any computation on them to get a result executing one round MPC via MFHE. However, achieving the full security without CRS takes at least 4 rounds, which is proved in [10].

Assuming CRS in any protocol for multi parties might be a quite strong assumption and does not fit in real situation. Like Kim, Lee and Park's scheme, it seems that alternating a role of CRS can be achieved sharing public keys allowing an interaction among parties as a trade off. We construct an optimal round (two round) MPC protocol without CRS against honest-but curious adversaries, combining non-interactive MFHE scheme with CRS and interactive MFHE scheme without CRS. First, we convert MTFHE1 to an interactive version MTFHE2 then construct a MPC protocol.

5.1 MTFHE2 Scheme Without Common Random String

We convert the non-interactive scheme for bootstrapping part of MTFHE1 to have an interaction before decryption. It means that all parties share their public keys and relate keys to alter the role of common random string. In MTFHE1, a common random string is the common random parameter $\mathbf{a}$. Instead, each party generates its public key independently, then publishes it. It suffices to show how multikey TRGSW ciphertexts (Section 3.2 of [13]) are correctly constructed substituting the common random parameter $\mathbf{a}$ to $\mathbf{a}_i$ for $i \in [k]$, where k is the fixed number of parties, since the common random parameter only has an effect on those procedure. Other algorithms are compatible with our modification. After showing that, we construct MTFHE2 with multi decryptor.

- $\mathsf{mTRGSW.Setup}(1^\lambda)$: It outputs $\mathsf{evparam} = (N, \psi, \alpha, \mathbf{g}, \ell)$, where N is TRLWE dimension, ψ is a key distribution over $\mathbb{Z}_N[X]$, α is an error parameter, and $\mathbf{g}$ and ℓ are TRGSW parameter.
- $\mathsf{mTRGSW.KeyGen}(\mathsf{evparam})$: Sample a secret $z \leftarrow \psi$ and set a vector $\mathbf{z} = (z, 1)$. Sample an error vector $\mathbf{e} \leftarrow D_\alpha^\ell$ over $\mathbb{T}_N[X]$ and a random vector $\mathbf{a} \leftarrow \mathbb{T}_N[X]^\ell$. Set the public key as $\mathbf{P} \leftarrow \mathsf{pk} = [\mathbf{a}, \mathbf{b}] \in \mathbb{T}_N[X]^{\ell \times 2}$, where $\mathbf{b} = -\mathbf{a} \cdot z + \mathbf{e} \pmod 1$. It returns (z, pk).
- $\mathsf{mTRGSW.Enc}(\mu, z, \{\mathsf{pk}_j\}_{j \in [k]}, i)$: It takes a plaintext $\mu \in \mathbb{Z}_N[X]$, a secret $\mathbf{z}$, and all involved parties' public keys, (it is run by a party i) it returns a multikey ciphertext $\hat{\mathbf{C}}_i \in \mathbb{T}_N[X]^{\ell(k+1)\times(k+1)}$. And the procedure is following:
  (1) Sample $\mathbf{c}_0 \leftarrow \mathbb{T}_N[X]^\ell$ and $\mathbf{e}_c \leftarrow D_\alpha^\ell$ uniformly at random. Set $\mathbf{C}_i = [\mathbf{c}_{0,i} | \mathbf{c}_{1,i}]$, where $\mathbf{c}_{1,i} = -z_i \cdot \mathbf{c}_{0,i} + \mathbf{e}_c + \mu \mathbf{g} \pmod 1$.

(2) Sample a randomness $r_j \leftarrow \psi$ and an error matrix $\mathbf{E}_j \leftarrow D_\alpha^{\ell\times 2}$ for $j \in [k]$. Output $\mathbf{D}_j = [\mathbf{d}_{0,j}|\mathbf{d}_{1,j}] = r_j\mathbf{P}_j + \mathbf{E}_j + [\mu\cdot\mathbf{g}|\mathbf{0}] \pmod 1 \in \mathbb{T}_N[X]^{\ell\times 2}$ for $j \in [k]$. And for $j \in [k]\backslash\{i\}$, set $\bar{\mathbf{D}}_j = [\bar{\mathbf{d}}_{0,j}|\bar{\mathbf{d}}_{1,j}] = r_j \cdot \mathbf{P}_i + \bar{\mathbf{E}}_j$, where $\bar{\mathbf{E}}_j \leftarrow D_\alpha^{\ell\times 2}$ uniformly at random.
(3) Sample $\mathbf{f}_0 \leftarrow \mathbb{T}_N[X]^\ell$, $\mathbf{e}_f \leftarrow D_\alpha^\ell$ uniformly at random. Set a ciphertext $\mathbf{F} = [\mathbf{f}_0|\mathbf{f}_1] \in \mathbb{T}_N[X]^{\ell\times 2}$ where $\mathbf{f}_1 = -z_i \cdot \mathbf{f}_0 + \mathbf{e}_f \pmod 1$.

$$\hat{\mathbf{C}}_i := \begin{bmatrix} \mathbf{d}_{0,1} & \cdots & \bar{\mathbf{d}}_{0,1} + \mathbf{f}_0 & \cdots & \mathbf{0} & \mathbf{f}_1 + \mathbf{d}_{1,1} + \bar{\mathbf{d}}_{1,1} \\ \vdots & \ddots & \vdots & \ddots & \vdots & \vdots \\ \mathbf{0} & \cdots & \mathbf{d}_{0,i} & \cdots & \mathbf{0} & \mathbf{d}_{1,i} \\ \vdots & \ddots & \vdots & \ddots & \vdots & \vdots \\ \mathbf{0} & \cdots & \bar{\mathbf{d}}_{0,k} + \mathbf{f}_0 & \cdots & \mathbf{d}_{0,k} & \mathbf{f}_1 + \mathbf{d}_{1,k} + \bar{\mathbf{d}}_{1,k} \\ \mathbf{0} & \cdots & \mathbf{c}_{0,i} & \cdots & \mathbf{0} & \mathbf{c}_{1,i} \end{bmatrix} \in \mathbb{T}_N[X]^{\ell(k+1)\times(k+1)}$$

Note that the (j,j)-th component of $\hat{\mathbf{C}}_i$ is $\mathbf{d}_{0,j}$ for $j \in [k]$. The elements other than the diagonal, the i-th column and $k+1$ th column are zero vectors.

- $\mathsf{mTRGSW.Dec}(\{\mathsf{sk}_j\}_{j\in[k]}, \hat{\mathbf{C}})$: Given all the involved secret keys $\{\mathsf{sk}_j\}$ and a multikey ciphertext $\hat{\mathbf{C}}$, it returns a message μ.

Correctness. Then we check the correctness i.e. $\hat{\mathbf{C}}_i\hat{\mathbf{z}} \approx \mu\mathbf{H}\hat{\mathbf{z}} \pmod 1$, where $\hat{\mathbf{z}}$ is a concatenation of each party's secret vector $(\mathbf{z}_1, \ldots, \mathbf{z}_k, 1)$. The correctness is done with the following equation:

- $z_i \cdot \mathbf{c}_0 + \mathbf{c}_1 + = \mathbf{C}_i\mathbf{z}_i \approx \mu \cdot \mathbf{g} \pmod 1$.
- $z_i \cdot \bar{\mathbf{d}}_{0,j} + \bar{\mathbf{d}}_{1,j} = \bar{\mathbf{D}}_j\mathbf{z}_i \approx 0 \pmod 1$.
- $z_i \cdot \mathbf{f}_0 + \mathbf{f}_1 = \mathbf{F}\mathbf{z}_i \approx 0 \pmod 1$.
- $z_j \cdot \mathbf{d}_{0,j} + \mathbf{d}_{1,j} = \mathbf{D}_j\mathbf{z}_j \approx \mu z_j\mathbf{g} \pmod 1$.

Theorem 4. *The above MFHE scheme* mTRGSW *with a single decryptor is semantically secure by the underlying* TRLWE *assumption.*

Proof. For a single key ciphertext, the two distributions $\{(\mathbf{P}_i, \mathbf{C}_i, \mathbf{D}_i = [\mathbf{d}_{0,i}|\mathbf{d}_{1,i}])\}$ and $\{(\mathbf{P}_u, \mathbf{C}_u, \mathbf{D}_u),\ \mathbf{P}_u, \mathbf{C}_u, \mathbf{D}_u \leftarrow \mathbb{T}_N[X]^{\ell\times 2}$ uniformly at random$\}$ are computationally indistinguishable by the underlying TRLWE problem. Therefor the single key ciphertext for i-th party is semantically secure. Then we consider the internal security for the other information related with other keys. For the j-th user holding z_j and $j \in [k]\backslash\{i\}$, what she can do is $z_j \cdot \mathbf{d}_{0,j} + \mathbf{f}_1 + \mathbf{d}_{1,j} + \bar{\mathbf{d}}_{1,j}$. Then the result is $\mu_i z_j \cdot \mathbf{g} + \mathbf{f}_1\bar{\mathbf{d}}_{1,j}$, which looks totally uniform random element for her. The reason follows:
$(\mathbf{a}_i, \bar{\mathbf{d}}_{0,j} = r_j \cdot \mathbf{a}_i + \bar{\mathbf{e}}_{0,j})$ is computationally indistinguishable with $(\mathbf{a}_i, \mathbf{u})$ by the underlying TRLWE problem, where $\mathbf{u} \leftarrow \mathbb{T}_N[X]^\ell$ uniformly at random, since r_j is a secret chosen by the i-th user. This implies that $\bar{\mathbf{d}}_{0,j} + \mathbf{f}_0$ looks also uniformly random. Thanks to this, $\mathbf{f}_0$ is not revealed at all so that $\mathbf{f}_1$ itself is considered as a uniform element. Then it makes $\mathbf{f}_1 + \bar{\mathbf{d}}_{1,j}$ looks uniformly random. As a result,

no internal adversary can distinguish if the given multikey ciphertext encrypts 0 or 1. In other words, the mTRGSW scheme achieves the internal security so that it is semantically secure by the underlying TRLWE assumption. □

Now, we construct an interactive MFHE scheme MTFHE2 from MTFHE1 and mTRGSW scheme.

- $\mathsf{MTFHE2.Setup}(1^\lambda) \to (\mathsf{params})$: It runs $\mathsf{MTFHE1.Setup}(1^\lambda)$ and we now specify the evparam is included in params. $\mathsf{evparam} \leftarrow \mathsf{mTRGSW.Setup}(1^\lambda)$.
- $\mathsf{MTFHE2.KeyGen}(\mathsf{params}) \to (z, \mathsf{pk}, \mathsf{sk})$: It runs $\mathsf{MTFHE1.KeyGen}(\mathsf{params})$ to get sk and runs $\mathsf{mTRGSW.KeyGen}(\mathsf{evparam})$ to get (z, pk)
- $\mathsf{MTFHE2.Enc}(\mathsf{pk}_1, \ldots, \mathsf{pk}_k, \mathsf{sk}_i, z, \mu)$: It runs $\mathsf{MTFHE1.Enc}(\mu, \mathsf{sk}_i)$ to get a ciphertext ct and runs $\mathsf{mTRGSW}(\mathsf{sk}_i[t], z, \mathsf{pk}_1, \ldots, \mathsf{pk}_k, i)$ to get $\hat{\mathbf{C}}_{i,t}$ for $t \in [n]$. Set $\{\mathbf{C}_{i,t}\}_{t\in[n]}$ as evk_i. It outputs ct and evk
- $\mathsf{MTFHE2.Dec}(\hat{\mathsf{ct}}, \mathsf{sk}_1, \ldots, \mathsf{sk}_k)$: It runs $\mathsf{MTFHE1.Dec}(\hat{\mathsf{ct}}, \mathsf{sk}_1, \ldots, \mathsf{sk}_k)$ and outputs the message μ.
- $\mathsf{MTFHE2.Eval}(\hat{\mathsf{ct}}_1, \hat{\mathsf{ct}}_2, \{\mathsf{evk}_j\}_{j\in[k]})$: It runs $\mathsf{MTFHE1.NAND}(\hat{\mathsf{ct}}_1, \hat{\mathsf{ct}}_2)$ and bootstrapping algorithm of [13] with $\{\mathsf{evk}_j\}_{j\in[k]}$ then outputs the evaluated ciphertext $\hat{\mathsf{ct}}'$.

Note that the decryption protocol is done by MTFHE1.PartDec and MTFHE1.FinDec having an interaction with other parties defined in Sect. 4. We do not cover how bootstrapping procedure works with evk_j since it is exactly the same procedure as the original paper [13]. We have already checked the correctness of mTRGSW ciphertext so that all other algorithms work correctly. This modification allows to get rid of the assumption of the common random parameter (CRS) among all users. However, the number of users should be fixed before the computation, which might be a negative point for some computation.

5.2 2 Round MPC Without a CRS via MTFHE2

We give an optimal round MPC protocol without CRS below. It is not necessary to use our distributed decryption protocol in a MPC protocol for the last step since traditional MPC only cares of input security. Applying what decryption protocol depends on a purpose of a computation.

Let $f : \{0,1\}^k \to \{0,1\}$ be the function to compute.

Preprocessing. Run $\mathsf{params} \leftarrow \mathsf{MTFHE2.Setup}(1^\lambda)$. Make sure that all the parties have params.

Input: For $i \in [k]$, each party U_i holds input $m_i \in \{0,1\}$, and wants to compute $f(m_1, \cdots, m_k)$.

Round I. Each party U_i executes the following steps:

- Generates its public key pk_i and secret keys by running $\mathsf{MTFHE2.KeyGen}(\mathsf{params})$.
- Encrypts a message m_i running MTFHE1.Enc to get a TLWE sample $\mathsf{ct}_i = (\mathbf{a}_i, b_i)$.

- Broadcasts the public key $\mathsf{pk}_i, \mathsf{ct}_i$.

Round II. Once receiving public keys $\{\mathsf{pk}_k\}_{k \neq i}$, each party U_i for $i \in [k]$ executes evaluation procedure with the following steps:
  - Runs $\mathsf{mTRGSW}, \mathsf{Enc}(\mathsf{sk}_i[t], z, \mathsf{pk}_1, \ldots, \mathsf{pk}_k, i)$ to get evk_i.
  - Extends $\{\mathsf{ct}_j\}_{j \in [k]}$ to get $\{\hat{\mathsf{ct}}_j\}_{j \in [k]}$.
    - If the protocol is run for the first time, each party runs $\mathsf{MTFHE1.NAND}(\hat{\mathsf{ct}}_{j1}, \hat{\mathsf{ct}}_{j2})$ to get an evaluted ciphertext for $j1, j2 \in [k]$.
    - else, runs $\mathsf{MTFHE2.Eval}(\hat{\mathsf{ct}}_{j1}, \hat{\mathsf{ct}}_{j2}, \{\mathsf{evk}_j\}_{j \in [k]})$ to get an evaluted ciphertext for $j1, j2 \in [k]$.
  - Runs $\mathsf{MTFHE2.PartDec}(\hat{\mathsf{ct}}, \mathsf{sk}_i)$ to get a partial decryption $p_{i,j}$ for $j \in [k]$.
  - broadcasts $\mathsf{evk}_i, p_{i,j}$.

Output: On receiving all the values $\{p_{j,i}\}_{j \in [k]}$, each party U_i runs the final decryption algorithm to obtain the function value $f(m_1, \cdots, m_k)$:

$$y \leftarrow \mathsf{MTFHE2.FinDec}(\{p_{j,i}\}_{j \in [k]}, \mathsf{sk}_i),$$

and output $y = f(m_1, \cdots, m_k)$.

The above protocol is limited to run a function which has a depth which guarantees that the decryption never fails only for the first time. After that, from the second time, all parties can run the protocol with arbitrary function without predefined depth since the parties share bootstrapping key$\{\mathsf{evk}_j\}_{j \in [k]}$ in the second round. Therefore, once the keys $\{\mathsf{pk}_j\}_{j \in [k]}, \{\mathsf{evk}_j\}_{j \in [k]}$ are published, the protocol does not generate keys for the same number of parties and the parties reuse the keys.

Security. This 2 round MPC protocol is secure against honest but curious adversaries. Honest but curious adversary is a legitimate party in a communication protocol who does not deviate from the defined protocol but will attempt to learn all possible information from legitimately received messages. Then we can see that the security is guaranteed by the semantic security of MTFHE2.

Acknowledgement. Hyang-Sook Lee and Jeongeun Park were supported by the National Research Foundation of Korea (NRF) grant funded by the Korea government (MSIT) (No. NRF-2018R1A2A1A05079095).

References

1. Asharov, G., Jain, A., López-Alt, A., Tromer, E., Vaikuntanathan, V., Wichs, D.: Multiparty computation with low communication, computation and interaction via threshold FHE. In: Pointcheval, D., Johansson, T. (eds.) EUROCRYPT 2012. LNCS, vol. 7237, pp. 483–501. Springer, Heidelberg (2012). https://doi.org/10.1007/978-3-642-29011-4_29
2. Boneh, D., et al.: Threshold cryptosystems from threshold fully homomorphic encryption. In: Shacham, H., Boldyreva, A. (eds.) CRYPTO 2018, Part I. LNCS, vol. 10991, pp. 565–596. Springer, Cham (2018). https://doi.org/10.1007/978-3-319-96884-1_19

3. Brakerski, Z., Perlman, R.: Lattice-based fully dynamic multi-key FHE with short ciphertexts. In: Robshaw, M., Katz, J. (eds.) CRYPTO 2016, Part I. LNCS, vol. 9814, pp. 190–213. Springer, Heidelberg (2016). https://doi.org/10.1007/978-3-662-53018-4_8
4. Chen, L., Zhang, Z., Wang, X.: Batched multi-hop multi-key FHE from Ring-LWE with compact ciphertext extension. In: Kalai, Y., Reyzin, L. (eds.) TCC 2017, Part II. LNCS, vol. 10678, pp. 597–627. Springer, Cham (2017). https://doi.org/10.1007/978-3-319-70503-3_20
5. Chillotti, I., Gama, N., Georgieva, M., Izabachène, M.: Faster fully homomorphic encryption: bootstrapping in less than 0.1 seconds. In: Cheon, J.H., Takagi, T. (eds.) ASIACRYPT 2016, Part I. LNCS, vol. 10031, pp. 3–33. Springer, Heidelberg (2016). https://doi.org/10.1007/978-3-662-53887-6_1
6. Chillotti, I., Gama, N., Georgieva, M., Izabachène, M.: Faster packed homomorphic operations and efficient circuit bootstrapping for TFHE. In: Takagi, T., Peyrin, T. (eds.) ASIACRYPT 2017, Part I. LNCS, vol. 10624, pp. 377–408. Springer, Cham (2017). https://doi.org/10.1007/978-3-319-70694-8_14
7. Chillotti, I., Gama, N., Georgieva, M., Izabachène, M.: TFHE: fast fully homomorphic encryption over the torus. Cryptology ePrint Archive, Report 2018/421 (2018). https://eprint.iacr.org/2018/421
8. Clear, M., McGoldrick, C.: Multi-identity and multi-key leveled FHE from learning with errors. In: Gennaro, R., Robshaw, M. (eds.) CRYPTO 2015, Part II. LNCS, vol. 9216, pp. 630–656. Springer, Heidelberg (2015). https://doi.org/10.1007/978-3-662-48000-7_31
9. Kim, E., Hyang-Sook Lee, J.P.: Towards round-optimal secure multiparty computations: multikey FHE without a CRS. Cryptology ePrint Archive, Report 2018/1156 (2018). https://eprint.iacr.org/2018/1156
10. Garg, S., Mukherjee, P., Pandey, O., Polychroniadou, A.: The exact round complexity of secure computation. In: Fischlin, M., Coron, J.-S. (eds.) EUROCRYPT 2016, Part II. LNCS, vol. 9666, pp. 448–476. Springer, Heidelberg (2016). https://doi.org/10.1007/978-3-662-49896-5_16
11. Garg, S., Srinivasan, A.: Two-round multiparty secure computation from minimal assumptions. In: Nielsen, J.B., Rijmen, V. (eds.) EUROCRYPT 2018, Part II. LNCS, vol. 10821, pp. 468–499. Springer, Cham (2018). https://doi.org/10.1007/978-3-319-78375-8_16
12. Gentry, C., Sahai, A., Waters, B.: Homomorphic encryption from learning with errors: conceptually-simpler, asymptotically-faster, attribute-based. In: Canetti, R., Garay, J.A. (eds.) CRYPTO 2013, Part I. LNCS, vol. 8042, pp. 75–92. Springer, Heidelberg (2013). https://doi.org/10.1007/978-3-642-40041-4_5
13. Hao Chen, I.C., Song, Y.: Multi-key homomophic encryption from tfhe. Cryptology ePrint Archive, Report 2019/116 (2019). https://eprint.iacr.org/2019/116
14. Hao Chen, Wei Dai, M.K., Song, Y.: Efficient multi-key homomorphic encryption with packed ciphertexts with application to oblivious neural network inference. Cryptology ePrint Archive, Report 2019/524 (2019). https://eprint.iacr.org/2019/524
15. Kim, E., Lee, H.-S., Park, J.: Towards round-optimal secure multiparty computations: multikey FHE without a CRS. In: Susilo, W., Yang, G. (eds.) ACISP 2018. LNCS, vol. 10946, pp. 101–113. Springer, Cham (2018). https://doi.org/10.1007/978-3-319-93638-3_7

16. López-Alt, A., Tromer, E., Vaikuntanathan, V.: On-the-fly multiparty computation on the cloud via multikey fully homomorphic encryption. In: Karloff, H.J., Pitassi, T. (eds.) 44th Annual ACM Symposium on Theory of Computing, pp. 1219–1234. ACM Press, New York, 19–22 May 2012. https://doi.org/10.1145/2213977.2214086
17. Mukherjee, P., Wichs, D.: Two round multiparty computation via multi-key FHE. In: Fischlin, M., Coron, J.-S. (eds.) EUROCRYPT 2016, Part II. LNCS, vol. 9666, pp. 735–763. Springer, Heidelberg (2016). https://doi.org/10.1007/978-3-662-49896-5_26
18. Peikert, C., Shiehian, S.: Multi-key FHE from LWE, revisited. In: Hirt, M., Smith, A. (eds.) TCC 2016, Part II. LNCS, vol. 9986, pp. 217–238. Springer, Heidelberg (2016). https://doi.org/10.1007/978-3-662-53644-5_9

RLWE-Based Zero-Knowledge Proofs for Linear and Multiplicative Relations

Ramiro Martínez(✉) and Paz Morillo

Universitat Politècnica de Catalunya, Barcelona, Spain
{ramiro.martinez,paz.morillo}@upc.edu

Abstract. We present efficient Zero-Knowledge Proofs of Knowledge (ZKPoK) for linear and multiplicative relations among secret messages hidden as Ring Learning With Errors (RLWE) samples. Messages are polynomials in $\mathbb{Z}_q[x]/\langle x^n+1\rangle$ and our proposed protocols for a ZKPoK are based on the celebrated paper by Stern on identification schemes using coding problems (Crypto'93). Our 5-move protocol achieves a soundness error slightly above $1/2$ and perfect Zero-Knowledge.

As an application we present Zero-Knowledge Proofs of Knowledge of relations between committed messages. The resulting commitment scheme is perfectly binding with overwhelming probability over the choice of the public key, and computationally hiding under the RLWE assumption. Compared with previous Stern-based commitment scheme proofs we decrease computational complexity, improve the size of the parameters and reduce the soundness error of each round.

Keywords: Zero-Knowledge Proofs of Knowledge · Commitment scheme · Ring Learning With Errors

1 Introduction

The goal of this paper is to present new and more efficient ways of proving linear and multiplicative relations between elements hidden in lattice-based structures, such as commitment schemes, without revealing any additional information about the elements themselves. These kind of proofs play an important role in many applications, from authentication protocols to electronic voting.

Lattice-based cryptography offers a high level of security. Its assumptions rely on the hardness of problems for which there is no known efficient quantum algorithm. This contrasts with classical factorization and discrete logarithm related problems, as they are quantum efficiently solvable by Shor's algorithm [20]. When long term privacy is concerned this is especially important, as public communications could be stored until quantum computers are available.

This work is partially supported by the European Union PROMETHEUS project (Horizon 2020 Research and Innovation Program, grant 780701) and the Spanish Ministry of Economy and Competitiveness, through Project MTM2016-77213-R.

M. Albrecht (Ed.): IMACC 2019, LNCS 11929, pp. 252–277, 2019.
https://doi.org/10.1007/978-3-030-35199-1_13

To handle this issue, new protocols whose security is based on post-quantum safe assumptions are required. Code-based and lattice-based cryptography are two families of primitives widely believed to be quantum-resistant, and extensively used in the literature.

In this article we propose improvements on a classical code-based protocol to use it in a lattice context based on the Ring Learning With Errors (RLWE) problem. Then we apply this construction to build exact proofs of knowledge of a valid opening for a commitment, and to prove that messages inside valid openings of different commitments satisfy linear or multiplicative relations.

1.1 Related Work

In 1993 Stern proposed one of the first post-quantum protocols in his seminal paper on a new identification scheme based on coding theory [24]. His identification protocol was a Zero-Knowledge Proof of Knowledge (ZKPoK) of a solution of an instance of the Syndrome Decoding problem (SD). The syndrome works as a public key and the user can authenticate himself interacting with a verifier and proving knowledge of a solution (a binary vector with small Hamming weight).

The original proposal by Stern was a 3-move protocol with a soundness error of 2/3. Many variants and applications have been published since then, addressing this lack of efficiency and providing new features (different signature schemes, possibility of building secrets with integers module q instead of only bits, applications to lattice-based cryptography, commitment schemes, ...). We describe some of them in the following paragraphs.

In 2007 the use of cyclic codes was proposed in [10], later implemented in [6]. It was adapted to lattices in [14] in 2008, preserving a binary secret. Efficiency was improved in 2010 reducing the soundness error in [9]. And many applications have used it [1,4,7,8,21].

Nevertheless we are particularly interested in the contributions of Jain *et al.* in their paper [12] where they build a commitment scheme based on the Learning Parity with Noise (LPN) problem, proving knowledge of openings, linear and multiplicative relations between committed messages using 3-move and 2/3 soundness error Stern-based protocols. Then in 2013 Ling *et al.* showed in [17] how the original Stern protocol could be run several times in parallel to prove that a solution has small infinity norm (and not only small Hamming weight). Xie *et al.* [25] adapt these techniques to the commitment construction of [12], to be able to prove linear and multiplicative relations between polynomials with coefficients in $\mathbb{Z}_q$. However the size of their proofs require an overhead proportional to $\log^2(q)$. All of them still have a soundness error of 2/3.

In this paper we especially benefit from the adaptation of Stern's protocol to lattices from Ling *et al.* [17], the modification of Cayrel *et al.* [9] for reducing the soundness error increasing the number of rounds and the proposals of Jain *et al.* [12] and Xie *et al.* [25] for proving linear and multiplicative relations, that we further improve.

It is also important to mention the contributions of Benhamouda *et al.* [3] and Baum *et al.* [2], who generalized the commitment idea of [25] without using

Stern's approach. They instead use Fiat-Shamir with aborts, a technique that requires relaxing the definition of commitment (so that the set of valid openings is larger than the set of openings generated by an honest prover, with more elements and less tighter bounds for the error terms) obtaining more efficient proofs with the cost of having stronger restrictions that require larger parameters. Therefore if the relaxed ZKPoK are used as a building block in a different protocol (for example for proving that an encryption public key is well formed), then the restrictions on the parameters imposed by the relaxation might have an impact on the efficiency of other parts of the protocol.

Exact Lattice-Based ZKPoK are therefore an active field of research, with very recent efficient constructions for some lattice statements including linear equations with short solutions and matrix-vector relations [26] by Yang *et al.*, new techniques when a cyclotomic polynomial fully splits in linear factors [5] by Bootle *et al.* and new recent Stern-based contributions for proving integer relations [15] and matrix-vector relations [16] by Libert *et al.*

1.2 Our Contribution

Our contribution is an improvement over the two Stern-based ZKPoK for linear and multiplicative relations from [12,25]. Our ideas on proving multiplicative relations can be easily adapted to any scenario where messages are encoded as RLWE samples. We show how we are able to prove these relations for messages commited using a commitment scheme with Benhamouda *et al.* notation, as it is the most natural adaptation of [12] to the RLWE setting, encoding an element as a lattice point and adding a perturbed random point from a different lattice.

We get rid of the relaxations and limitations that were necessary in Benhamouda *et al.* commitment scheme without needing the quadratic logarithm of q overhead from Xie *et al.* For the linear relation case we apply standard improvements to the original Stern protocol, but adding some original modifications to carefully reduce some constants in the communication cost. For the multiplicative relation we construct a new efficient proof. We achieve this by asking the verifier for two challenges in order to get soundness. Honest-Verifier Zero-Knowledge is obtained as we explicitly provide a perfect simulator for each protocol. Notice that simulations can skip the generation of never opened auxiliary commitments, as they can just be computed as commitments to 0, indistinguishable from honestly computed commitments.

Many applications demand to evaluate arbitrary arithmetic circuits on secret elements. Fully Homomorphic Encryption could be a solution (which can be achieved with lattices by means of the Gentry *et al.* scheme [11]). An alternative is to apply our proofs for linear and multiplicative relations to prove knowledge of valid evaluations of the gates. The first lattice-based Attributed Based Signature scheme for unbounded circuits [13] uses this strategy with the ZKPoK from [25]. Directly replacing their construction with our proposal greatly improves the efficiency of the signature scheme.

Our proposal is a 5-move protocol with a soundness error slightly above 1/2. It allows us to prove exact knowledge of the secret inside a RLWE sample, that is, the secret is a polynomial with coefficients in $\mathbb{Z}_q$. The proposed commitment scheme is perfectly binding with overwhelming probability over the choice of the public key and computationally hiding under the RLWE assumption, widely believe to be post-quantum.

The organization of this paper is as follows. We explain the notation and the basic primitives that we are going to use in Sect. 2. We present the commitment in Sect. 3, along with a proof of knowledge of a valid opening in Subsect. 3.1. We then give proofs of a linear relation and a multiplicative relation in Subsects. 3.2 and 3.3, respectively. We finally end with some comparisons and conclusions in Sect. 4.

2 Preliminaries

2.1 Notation

Column vectors are denoted with lower-case bold letters $\boldsymbol{a}$ and row vectors as transposed column vectors $\boldsymbol{a}^\top$. We denote by $\mathbb{1}_n$ the vector of dimension n with all its coordinates equal to 1. Matrices are represented using upper-case bold letters $\boldsymbol{M}$. Let q be prime, given a vector $\boldsymbol{v} \in \mathbb{Z}_q^n$ we define the infinity norm as $\|\boldsymbol{v}\|_\infty = \max_{1 \le i \le n} |v_i|$ where v_i are the coordinates of vector $\boldsymbol{v}$ taking $\left[-\left\lfloor \frac{q}{2} \right\rfloor, \dots, 0, \dots, \left\lfloor \frac{q}{2} \right\rfloor\right]$ as representatives.

When a is sampled uniformly at random from set A we write $a \xleftarrow{\$} A$, $a \xleftarrow{\$} D$ when a is sampled according to a probability distribution D and $a \xleftarrow{\$} \mathcal{A}$ when a is the output of a probabilistic algorithm $\mathcal{A}$.

PPT denotes the class of Probabilistic Polynomial-Time algorithms.

A function f is *negligible* if $|f(n)| \in \mathcal{O}(n^{-c})$, $\forall c \in \mathbb{Z}^+$.

A function f is *overwhelming* if $|f(n) - 1| \in \mathcal{O}(n^{-c})$, $\forall c \in \mathbb{Z}^+$.

When an honest prover should send an element a we denote by $\widetilde{a}$ the element actually disclosed by the (possibly malicious) prover and we call $\widehat{a}$ to the element alleged to play the same role in the simulated conversation.

2.2 Zero-Knowledge Proofs

In this paper we use Public Coin Honest-Verifier Zero-Knowledge Proofs of Knowledge. Let $\mathcal{R} \subset \{0,1\}^* \times \{0,1\}^*$ be a binary relation with one restriction. If $(x, w) \in \mathcal{R}$ satisfies the relation then the size $|w|$ is at most $p(|x|)$ for some fixed polynomial p.

Definition 1 (Zero-Knowledge Proofs of Knowledge). *A* $(2n+1)$-move Public Coin Honest-Verifier Zero-Knowledge Proof of Knowledge *is a protocol between a prover $\mathcal{P}$ and a verifier $\mathcal{V}$ in which, given an x, $\mathcal{P}$ tries to convince $\mathcal{V}$ that he knows a witness w such that $(x, w) \in \mathcal{R}$. We use the following notation ZKP$\left[\, w \,\middle|\, (x, w) \in \mathcal{R} \,\right]$.*

$\mathcal{P}$ and $\mathcal{V}$ engage in an interaction where $\mathcal{P}$ consecutively sends a message a_i answered by $\mathcal{V}$ with a random challenge b_i for i from 1 to n. Finally $\mathcal{P}$ gives a final answer z and $\mathcal{V}$ accepts or rejects the proof checking the conversation $(x, \{a_i\}_i, \{b_i\}_i, z)$. And has the following properties:

- ***Completeness:*** *if an honest prover $\mathcal{P}$ knows a valid witness w such that $(x, w) \in \mathcal{R}$ and follows the protocol, then an honest verifier $\mathcal{V}$ always accepts the conversation.*
- ***k-Special Soundness:*** *from k accepted conversations $\left\{(x, \{a_{i,j}\}_i, \{b_{i,j}\}_i, z)\right\}_{j=1}^{k}$, and $\{b_{i,j}\}_i \neq \{b_{i,j'}\}_i$ for $j \neq j'$, it is possible to efficiently extract a witness w such that $(x, w) \in \mathcal{R}$.*
- ***Honest-Verifier Zero-Knowledge:*** *there exists a polynomial-time simulator that takes as input x and random $\{b_i\}_i$ and outputs an accepted conversation $(x, \{a_i\}_i, \{b_i\}_i, z)$ with the same probability distribution as conversations between honest $\mathcal{P}$ and $\mathcal{V}$.*

This is a variant of standard Σ-protocols, as it is also pointed out by of Jain *et al.* [12] and Xie *et al.* [25].

k-Special Soundness means that a prover able to answer k challenges is honest, as in this case a witness could be extracted. If the challenge space is large enough we get the desired soundness in one shot. In Stern's protocol and some of its variants it is only possible to extract a valid witness from answers to all possible challenges (three in his particular protocol), then the prover could cheat with all but one (and therefore the protocol has 2/3 soundness error). In our case, increasing the number of challenges, we prove how to obtain a valid witness from valid answers to approximately one half of the possible challenges, reducing the soundness error and therefore reducing the number of repetitions required.

2.3 Ring Learning with Errors

Considering a ring $R = \mathbb{Z}[x] / \langle f(x) \rangle$ and $R_q = R/qR$, principal ideals $\langle a(x) \rangle \subseteq R_q$ can be identified with lattices generated by structured matrices $\boldsymbol{A}$ that only depend on polynomials $a(x)$ and $f(x)$, called *ideal lattices* [19].

The ideal lattice $\mathcal{L}(\boldsymbol{a})$ generated by a vector of polynomials $\boldsymbol{a} \in R_q^k$ is then $\mathcal{L}(\boldsymbol{a}) = \{\boldsymbol{a}r | r \in R_q\}$. We choose $f(x)$ to be $x^n + 1$, with n a power of 2, and then $R_q = \mathbb{Z}_q[x] / \langle x^n + 1 \rangle$, as it gives nice security reductions.

Definition 2 (Ring Learning With Errors($\mathsf{RLWE}_{n,q,\chi}$)). *Let χ be a distribution over R (tipically a Gaussian distribution). The decisional* ring learning with errors *assumption states that $\{(a_i, a_i \cdot s + e_i)\}$ is indistinguishable from $\{(a_i, u_i)\}$ for any polynomial number of samples where $a_i \xleftarrow{\$} R_q$, $e_i \xleftarrow{\$} \chi$, $u_i \xleftarrow{\$} R_q$ and $s \in R_q$ is secret.*

The search RLWE *assumption states that no PPT adversary can recover s from a polynomial number of samples with a non-negligible probability.*

Hardness of RLWE. If parameters are chosen properly the RLWE problem becomes as hard as well known hard ideal lattice problems such as the ideal Shortest Vector Problem (SVP) [18]. With a discrete Gaussian error distribution χ where its standard deviation $\sigma \geq \omega(\sqrt{\log n})$, and for any ring, there exists a quantum reduction from the $\gamma(n)$-SVP problem to the RLWE problem to within an approximation factor $\gamma(n) = \mathcal{O}(\sqrt{n} \cdot q/\sigma)$. Additionaly, RLWE becomes no easier to solve even if the secret s is chosen from the error distribution, rather than uniformly [18].

2.4 Stern Identification Scheme

The original Zero-Knowledge interactive identification scheme by Stern allows a prover to convince a verifier that given a parity check matrix $\boldsymbol{H} \in \mathbb{F}_2^{n \times m}$ and a syndrome $\boldsymbol{y} \in \mathbb{F}_2^n$ he knows a binary vector $\boldsymbol{e} \in \mathbb{F}_2^m$ of small fixed Hamming weight $\|\boldsymbol{e}\|_{\mathsf{H}} = w$ such that it has this syndrome $\boldsymbol{y} = \boldsymbol{He}$.

The original Stern protocol [24] hides $\boldsymbol{e}$ with a masking vector $\boldsymbol{x} \xleftarrow{\$} \mathbb{F}_2^n$, a masking syndrome $\boldsymbol{y}' \in \mathbb{F}_2^{n-k}$ (an honest prover will compute $\boldsymbol{y}' = \boldsymbol{Hx}$) and a permutation $\pi \xleftarrow{\$} \mathfrak{S}_n$. Notice that $\boldsymbol{x} + \boldsymbol{e}$ reveals no information about $\boldsymbol{e}$, while $\pi(\boldsymbol{e})$ only reveals its Hamming weight, which is already known.

Ling *et al.* [17] propose to use a bounded infinity norm secret. In order to prove this restriction on the norm they show that the secret element has a fixed length binary decomposition. To hide the binary decomposition they extend it so that it has the same number of -1, 0 and 1. Then running the protocol in parallel for each of the vectors of the decomposition allows to prove knowledge of a solution of a general instance of the Inhomogeneous Short Integer Solution (ISIS) problem. We have to adapt their setting to the dual version and prove knowledge of a solution of a RLWE problem.

In order to prove that something has small norm we prove that it can be written with a constant number of bits. An ad-hoc basis could be used, but we prefer to keep notation simple and decompose the elements in binary assuming that the bound is a power of two.

The paper of Cayrel *et al.* [9] combines the secret and the masking element with a random challenge $\alpha \in \mathbb{Z}_q$ to obtain $(\pi(\boldsymbol{x} + \alpha\boldsymbol{e}))$, reducing the communication cost and the soundness error. We extend their approach with more challenges so that we can prove knowledge of linear and multiplicative relations.

3 Commitment Scheme

Definition 3 (Comitment Scheme). *A* commitment scheme *consists of three algorithms:*

- ***Gen****: the generator algorithm takes a security parameter* 1^λ *and outputs a public key pk.* $pk \xleftarrow{\$} \mathsf{Gen}\left(1^\lambda\right)$
- ***Com****: the commitment algorithm takes as input a message m and a public key pk and produces a commitment* $\mathbf{c}$ *and an opening d.* $(\mathbf{c}, d) \xleftarrow{\$} \mathsf{Com}\,(m; pk)$
- ***Ver****: the verification algorithm takes as input a commitment* $\mathbf{c}$*, a message m, an opening d and a public key pk and accepts, returns* 1*, or rejects, returns* 0. $\mathsf{Ver} : \{(\mathbf{c}, m, d; pk)\} \rightarrow \{0, 1\}$

We say that a commitment scheme is secure *if it satisfies the following three properties:*

- ***Correctness**: if the commitment has been built correctly and the valid message and opening are published the verifier algorithm always accepts:*

$$\left(pk \xleftarrow{\$} \mathsf{Gen}\left(1^{\lambda}\right), (\mathbf{c}, d) \xleftarrow{\$} \mathsf{Com}\left(m; pk\right)\right) \implies 1 \leftarrow \mathsf{Ver}\left(\mathbf{c}, m, d; pk\right).$$

- ***Perfectly Binding**: a commitment can only be opened to one message:*

$$1 \leftarrow \mathsf{Ver}\left(\mathbf{c}, m, d; pk\right) \wedge 1 \leftarrow \mathsf{Ver}\left(\mathbf{c}, m', d'; pk\right) \implies m = m'.$$

- ***Computationally Hiding**: a well constructed commitment* $\mathbf{c}$ *does not leak any relevant information about the message* m*. For any PPT adversary* $(\mathcal{A}_1, \mathcal{A}_2)$*:*

$$\left|\Pr\left[b = b' \middle| \begin{array}{c} pk \xleftarrow{\$} \mathsf{Gen}(1^{\lambda}),\ (m_0, m_1, aux) \xleftarrow{\$} \mathcal{A}_1(pk) \\ b \xleftarrow{\$} \{0,1\},\ (\mathbf{c}, d) \xleftarrow{\$} \mathsf{Com}(m_b; pk),\ b' \xleftarrow{\$} \mathcal{A}_2(\mathbf{c}, aux) \end{array}\right] - \frac{1}{2}\right| \in negl(\lambda).$$

Now we define a lattice-based commitment scheme, for this we can encode a message $m \in R_q$ as the coordinates of a point in an ideal lattice defined by $\boldsymbol{a} \in R_q^k$. To hide this lattice point $\boldsymbol{a}m$ we add a RLWE sample from another lattice $\boldsymbol{b}r + \boldsymbol{e}$, where $\boldsymbol{b} \in R_q^k$ defines this other lattice, the randomness $r \xleftarrow{\$} R_q$ is chosen uniformly at random and the error term $\boldsymbol{e} \xleftarrow{\$} \chi^{nk}$ is chosen from the appropriate bounded discrete Gaussian distribution.

This structure $\boldsymbol{a}m + \boldsymbol{b}r + \boldsymbol{e}$ is used by Benhamouda *et al.* in [3], and it is very similar to the one proposed by Xie *et al.* in [25]. As we use their structure we can use some of the parameters proposed by Benhamouda *et al.*

The degree of the polynomial $n = 2^{\kappa}$ is a power of two, usually $\kappa = 9$ or $\kappa = 10$. γ is an integer parameter controlling the size of the modulus q, a prime number such that $q \equiv 3 \mod 8$ and $q \geq n^{\gamma}$. Integer k would be the multiplicative overhead (the length of $\boldsymbol{a}$ as a vector of polynomials). Finally as in their case our errors obtained from χ will have a standard deviation $\sigma \in \mathcal{O}(n^{3/4})$ and will be bounded by $n = 2^{\kappa}$. We will restrict our coefficients to $[-2^{\kappa}, \ldots, 2^{\kappa})$ but abuse notation and just write $\|\boldsymbol{e}\|_{\infty} < 2^{\kappa}$.

While the commitment algorithm Com we present in this paper is the same as the one that was presented in [3] our proofs of openings and relations do not require any relaxation (in our case the set of valid openings is exactly the set of openings obtained following the commitment algorithm). Therefore our proposal is different as a commitment scheme, our verification algorithm Ver is simpler and our parameter conditions required to prove security are less strict.

Proposition 1. *If $n \geq 16$, $\gamma \geq 3$ and $k \geq \frac{8\gamma+4}{2\gamma-5}$ then the following is a secure commitment scheme under the assumption that RLWE is hard.*

- Gen*: the generator algorithm takes a security parameter 1^λ and outputs a public key $pk = (\boldsymbol{a}, \boldsymbol{b}) \in (R_q^k)^2$, where $R_q = \mathbb{Z}_q[x] / \langle x^n + 1 \rangle$ and k are defined so that the difficulty of solving the RLWE problem is related to 1^λ. In particular the size of n is also related to 1^λ.*
  $(\boldsymbol{a}, \boldsymbol{b}) \stackrel{\$}{\leftarrow} \mathsf{Gen}(1^\lambda)$
- Com*: the commitment algorithm takes as input a message $m \in R_q$ and a public key $pk = (\boldsymbol{a}, \boldsymbol{b})$ and produces a commitment $\boldsymbol{c} = \boldsymbol{a}m + \boldsymbol{b}r + \boldsymbol{e}$ and an opening $d = (m, r, \boldsymbol{e})$, where $r \stackrel{\$}{\leftarrow} R_q$ and $\boldsymbol{e} \stackrel{\$}{\leftarrow} \chi^{nk}$ conditioned to have infinity norm smaller than $n = 2^\kappa$.*
  $(\boldsymbol{c} = \boldsymbol{a}m + \boldsymbol{b}r + \boldsymbol{e}, d = (m, r, \boldsymbol{e})) \stackrel{\$}{\leftarrow} \mathsf{Com}(m; pk = (\boldsymbol{a}, \boldsymbol{b}))$
- Ver*: the verification algorithm takes as input a commitment $\boldsymbol{c}$, a message m, an opening $d = (m, r, \boldsymbol{e})$ and a public key $pk = (\boldsymbol{a}, \boldsymbol{b})$ and accepts if $(\boldsymbol{c} = \boldsymbol{a}m + \boldsymbol{b}r + \boldsymbol{e}) \wedge (\|\boldsymbol{e}\|_\infty < 2^\kappa)$, or rejects otherwise.*
  $\mathsf{Ver} : \{(\boldsymbol{c}, m, d; pk)\} \rightarrow \{0, 1\}$

It satisfies the properties of a secure commitment scheme from Definition 3.

Proof. We can check that all properties are verified.

- **Correctness**: it immediate follows by the definitions of Com and Ver.
- **Binding**: a commitment can only be correctly opened to one message. It is perfectly binding with overwhelming probability as:

$$1 \leftarrow \mathsf{Ver}(\boldsymbol{c}, m', d'; pk) \wedge 1 \leftarrow \mathsf{Ver}(\boldsymbol{c}, m'', d''; pk) \implies m' = m''$$

  We redo here the proof from [3] since our simpler verification algorithm implies that we require less restrictions on the parameters.
  Two accepted openings to the same commitment would be:

$$\boldsymbol{c} = \boldsymbol{a}m' + \boldsymbol{b}r' + \boldsymbol{e}'$$
$$\boldsymbol{c} = \boldsymbol{a}m'' + \boldsymbol{b}r'' + \boldsymbol{e}''$$

  Therefore if $m' \neq m''$ we have that $\boldsymbol{a}(m' - m'') + \boldsymbol{b}(r' - r'') + (\boldsymbol{e}' - \boldsymbol{e}'') = 0$.
  If $q \equiv 3 \mod 8$, with overwhelming probability over the choice of $\boldsymbol{a}$ and $\boldsymbol{b}$, there are no $m, r \in R_q$ and $\boldsymbol{e} \in R_q^k$ small such that $\boldsymbol{a}m + \boldsymbol{b}r + \boldsymbol{e} = 0$ holds and $m \neq 0$.
  We bound the probability that this solution exists. For a fixed m, r and $\boldsymbol{e}$ we count the proportion of pairs $(\boldsymbol{a}, \boldsymbol{b})$ for which the equality holds. In order to estimate the overall probability of choosing a pair $(\boldsymbol{a}, \boldsymbol{b})$ such that there exists a solution we use a union bound adding up all previous probabilities. We finally see that it is negligible if parameters are carefully selected.
  Fixed m, r and $\boldsymbol{e}$ for each $\boldsymbol{b}$ we have $\boldsymbol{a}m = -\boldsymbol{b}r - \boldsymbol{e}$. In each component $a_j m = -b_j r - e_j$. $q \equiv 3 \mod 8$ implies that $x^n + 1$ splits into two irreducible

polynomials $p_1(x), p_2(x)$ of degree $n/2$ (lemma 3 in [22]). We know that $m \not\equiv 0 \mod x^n + 1$, therefore $m \not\equiv 0 \mod p_1(x)$ or $m \not\equiv 0 \mod p_2(x)$.
In either case we know that $a_j m$ takes at least $q^{n/2}$ different values. There are $q^{n/2}$ equivalence classes $\mod p_i(x)$ and only one of them is $-b_j r - e_j \mod p_i(x)$, therefore at most $1/q^{n/2}$ of the possible a_j hold the equation. As this is independently true for each j we have that the probability of $(\boldsymbol{a}, \boldsymbol{b})$ to fit the equation for these particular m, r and e is at most $1/q^{nk/2}$.
If we want to consider the possibility that there exists a solution we can bound this probability with a union bound. There are q^n possible m, q^n possible r and $(2n)^{nk}$ possible $\boldsymbol{e}$. Therefore if $(\boldsymbol{a}, \boldsymbol{b}) \xleftarrow{\$} \text{Gen}(1^\lambda)$:

$$\Pr_{(\boldsymbol{a},\boldsymbol{b})}\left[\exists m, r, \boldsymbol{e} \,\middle|\, \begin{array}{c} \boldsymbol{a}m + \boldsymbol{b}r + \boldsymbol{e} = 0 \\ \wedge \|\boldsymbol{e}\|_\infty \leq n \end{array}\right] \leq \frac{q^{2n}(2n)^{nk}}{q^{nk/2}} \in negl(1^\lambda).$$

The condition $n \geq 16$ implies $(2n) \leq n^{5/4}$:

$$\begin{aligned} \frac{q^{2n}(2n)^{nk}}{q^{nk/2}} &\leq \frac{q^{2n} n^{5nk/4}}{q^{nk/2}} \\ &\leq \frac{q^{2n} q^{5nk/(4\gamma)}}{q^{nk/2}} \\ &= q^{n(2+5k/(4\gamma)-k/2)} \end{aligned}$$

because $\gamma \geq 3$ and $k \geq \frac{8\gamma+4}{2\gamma-5} \geq \frac{8\gamma}{2\gamma-5}$ we know that $2 + 5k/(4\gamma) - k/2 \leq 0$:

$$q^{n(2+5k/(4\gamma)-k/2)} \leq n^{n\gamma(2+5k/(4\gamma)-k/2)}$$

because $\gamma \geq 3$ and $k \geq \frac{8\gamma+4}{2\gamma-5}$ we know that $\gamma(2 + 5k/(4\gamma) - k/2) \leq -1$:

$$\begin{aligned} n^{n\gamma(2+5k/(4\gamma)-k/2)} &\leq n^{-n} = 2^{-n\kappa} \\ &\leq \frac{1}{2^n} \end{aligned}$$

- **Hiding**: a well constructed commitment **c** does not leak any relevant information about the message m.
  It is computationally hiding as $\boldsymbol{b}r + \boldsymbol{e}$ are k RLWE samples, indistinguishable from independent uniformly random polynomials under the $\mathsf{RLWE}_{n,q,\chi}$ assumption. Any adversary able to break the hiding property would then also be able to solve the decisional $\mathsf{RLWE}_{n,q,\chi}$. Notice that the probability that $\boldsymbol{e} \xleftarrow{\$} \chi^{nk}$ has $\|\boldsymbol{e}\|_\infty > n$ is negligible and then original and conditioned probability distributions are statistically indistinguishable.

□

3.1 Knowledge of a Valid Opening

We first propose an Interactive Honest-Verifier Zero-Knowledge Proof of Knowledge of a valid opening for the commitment presented before. The difficult part is to prove that the error term is small enough, for which we adapt Stern-based protocols to this particular RLWE based commitment. While SD problem and ISIS problem are very similar, in order to prove that the commitment has been constructed with a RLWE sample we need several auxiliary elements. What we obtain is a 5-move protocol with a soundness error of $\frac{q+1}{2q}$, really close to $1/2$ as q is usually a very large prime.

Let $\boldsymbol{a} = (a_1, \ldots, a_k), \boldsymbol{b} = (b_1, \ldots, b_k) \in R_q^k$, a message $m \in R_q$, a random element r in R_q and $\boldsymbol{e} \in R_q^k$ a vector of polynomials with their coefficients sampled from a discrete Gaussian distribution conditioned to have norm smaller than $n = 2^\kappa$. We want to prove knowledge of a valid opening for the commitment $\boldsymbol{c} = \boldsymbol{a}m + \boldsymbol{b}r + \boldsymbol{e}$.

We identify a polynomial u with a vector $\boldsymbol{u}$ that has as elements the coefficients of the polynomial. For convenience we also identify a vector of polynomials with the concatenation of its associated vectors.

$$\begin{aligned} \varphi : \mathbb{Z}_q^n &\longrightarrow R_q \\ \boldsymbol{u} = (u_0, u_1, \ldots, u_{n-1}) &\longmapsto u = u_0 + u_1 x + \cdots + u_{n-1} x^{n-1} \\ \phi : \mathbb{Z}_q^{nk} &\longrightarrow R_q^k \\ \boldsymbol{u} = (u_0, \ldots, u_{nk-1}) &\longmapsto \boldsymbol{u} = (\varphi(u_0, \ldots, u_{n-1}), \ldots, \varphi(u_{n(k-1)}, \ldots, u_{nk-1})) \end{aligned}$$

Lets consider the vector $\bar{\boldsymbol{e}} = \phi^{-1}(\boldsymbol{e}) + 2^\kappa \mathbb{1}_{nk}$ and its binary decomposition $\bar{\boldsymbol{e}} = \sum_{j=0}^{\kappa} 2^j \bar{\boldsymbol{e}}_j$, $\bar{\boldsymbol{e}}_j \in \{0,1\}^{nk}$ (notice that $\bar{\boldsymbol{e}}$ has only positive representatives because we have added $2^\kappa \mathbb{1}_{nk}$). From now on index j will always belong to $[0, \ldots, \kappa]$. Choose extensions $\boldsymbol{e}'_j = (\bar{\boldsymbol{e}}_j || \boldsymbol{e}''_j) \in \mathcal{B}_{nk}$, where $\mathcal{B}_{nk} \subset \{0,1\}^{2nk}$ are vectors with the same number of 0 and 1's. The extended error term is $\boldsymbol{e}' = \sum_j 2^j \boldsymbol{e}'_j$. Let $\boldsymbol{I}'$ be an nk-identity matrix attached to nk columns of 0's.

Then we have: $\boldsymbol{c} = \boldsymbol{a}m + \boldsymbol{b}r + \phi((\boldsymbol{I}' \sum_j 2^j \boldsymbol{e}'_j) - 2^\kappa \mathbb{1}_{nk})$.

With this notation we can define an interactive protocol to prove knowledge of a valid opening for commitment $\boldsymbol{c}$. This extension is an adaptation of the idea from Ling *et al.* in [17] to the dual ring setting (we also shift the error to only have 0's and 1's, while their protocol also included −1's, this way we only have a factor two overhead instead of a factor three). Notice that each error decomposition element in $\mathcal{B}_{nk}$ with the same number of 0 and 1's can be completely randomized with a permutation, as it was done in the original Stern protocol with fixed Hamming weight vectors.

The complex structure of the commitment scheme requires more subtle details than the original Stern proposal, but the underlying intuition is the same. We want to prove knowledge of some elements $m, r, \boldsymbol{e}$, of some masking elements $\mu, \rho, \boldsymbol{f}$ and a of vector of polynomials $\boldsymbol{y}$ such that:

(a) $\pi_j(\boldsymbol{e}'_j) \in \mathcal{B}_{nk}$
(b) $\boldsymbol{y} = \boldsymbol{a}\mu + \boldsymbol{b}\rho + \boldsymbol{f}$
(c) $\boldsymbol{y} + \boldsymbol{c} = \boldsymbol{a}(\mu + m) + \boldsymbol{b}(\rho + r) + (\boldsymbol{f} + \boldsymbol{e})$, where $\boldsymbol{e} = \phi(\boldsymbol{I}' \sum_j 2^j \boldsymbol{e}'_j - 2^\kappa \mathbb{1}_{nk})$

All three properties imply knowledge of a valid opening for the commitment. In order to improve efficiency we can add one more round where we ask the verifier for an element $\alpha \in \mathbb{Z}_q$ and then prove only these two properties:

(a) $\pi_j(\boldsymbol{e}'_j) \in \mathcal{B}_{nk}$
(b') $\boldsymbol{y} + \alpha\boldsymbol{c} = \boldsymbol{a}(\mu + \alpha m) + \boldsymbol{b}(\rho + \alpha r) + (\boldsymbol{f} + \alpha\boldsymbol{e})$, where $\boldsymbol{e} = \phi(\boldsymbol{I}' \sum_j 2^j \boldsymbol{e}'_j - 2^\kappa \mathbb{1}_{nk})$

Since the relevant elements were commited in the first round (using an auxiliary commitment scheme) before α was chosen we can ensure with high probability that property (b') implies both properties (b) and (c). This is an adaptation of the idea used in [9] and allows us to reduce the soundness error to almost 1/2.

With this intuition in mind we can provide our protocol (1) for proving knowledge of valid openings. Let (aCom, aVer) denote an auxiliary commitment scheme that can be instantiated using our construction or a different one.

Proposition 2. *Protocol 1 describes a Public Coin Honest-Verifier ZKPoK, as it satisfies the properties of completeness, soundness and zero-knowledge.*

Completeness: Immediate as all relations hold by construction.

Soundness: If a (possibly malicious) prover $\widetilde{\mathcal{P}}$ is able to provide accepted answers to δ rounds of interaction with an honest verifier $\mathcal{V}$ with probability $(q+1/2q)^\delta + \epsilon$, were ϵ is non-negligible, then he is able to efficiently extract a witness with probability $2(\epsilon/3)^3$.

Let $\omega \in \Omega$ be the random coins used by the prover in its interaction with the verifier. We call $T(\omega)$ to the execution tree of all possible interactions between $\widetilde{\mathcal{P}}$ and $\mathcal{V}$ depending on the verifier challenges. Many authors [9] that face similar problems simply argue that a probability larger than $\left(\frac{q+1}{2q}\right)^\delta + \epsilon$ implies that there is a node with at least $q+2$ accepted answers, meaning that there exist c_1, c_2, two α, α' and $\boldsymbol{g}_j, \boldsymbol{g}'_j$ that induce accepted answers for both $b = 0$ and $b = 1$, from which it is possible to extract a witness.

However, merely proving existence implies that the extractor should explore the whole tree rewinding the prover $\widetilde{\mathcal{P}}$ until he finds this particular node. It is possible to do so in polynomial-time if q is polynomial in the security parameter and the number of nodes in $T(\omega)$ is $\mathcal{O}(q^\delta)$, but is very inefficient and provides us bounds $\mathcal{O}(q^\delta/\epsilon)$ that are far from tight.

$$\text{ZKP}\left[m,r,e \,\middle|\, \begin{matrix} c=am+br+e \\ \|e\|_\infty < 2^\kappa \end{matrix} \right] \tag{1}$$

$\mathcal{P}((\boldsymbol{a},\boldsymbol{b}),\boldsymbol{c};m,r,\boldsymbol{e})$		$\mathcal{V}((\boldsymbol{a},\boldsymbol{b}),\boldsymbol{c}))$
$\pi_0,\ldots,\pi_{\kappa-1} \xleftarrow{\$} \mathfrak{S}_{2nk}$		
$\boldsymbol{f}_0,\ldots,\boldsymbol{f}_{\kappa-1} \xleftarrow{\$} \mathbb{Z}_q^{2nk}$		
$\mu,\rho \xleftarrow{\$} R_q$		
$(c_1,d_1)=\mathsf{aCom}\left(\{\pi_j\}_j,\boldsymbol{a}\mu+\boldsymbol{b}\rho+\phi(\boldsymbol{I}'\sum_j 2^j \boldsymbol{f}_j)\right)$		
$(c_2,d_2)=\mathsf{aCom}\left(\{\pi_j(\boldsymbol{f}_j)\}_j,\{\pi_j(\boldsymbol{e}'_j)\}_j\right)$		
	$\xrightarrow{c_1,c_2}$	
		$\alpha \xleftarrow{\$} \mathbb{Z}_q$
	$\xleftarrow{\alpha}$	
$\boldsymbol{g}_j=\pi_j(\boldsymbol{f}_j+\alpha\boldsymbol{e}'_j)$		
	$\xrightarrow{\{\boldsymbol{g}_j\}_j}$	
		$b \xleftarrow{\$} \{0,1\}$
	$\xleftarrow{b}$	
if $b=0$		
$\widetilde{\pi}_j=\pi_j$		
$\widetilde{\boldsymbol{y}}=\boldsymbol{a}\mu+\boldsymbol{b}\rho+\phi(\boldsymbol{I}'\sum_j 2^j \boldsymbol{f}_j)$		
$\widetilde{s}=\rho+\alpha r$		
$\widetilde{d}=d_1$		
$ans=(\{\widetilde{\pi}_j\}_j,\widetilde{\boldsymbol{y}},\widetilde{s},\widetilde{d})$		
if $b=1$		
$\widetilde{\boldsymbol{e}}'_j=\pi_j(\boldsymbol{e}'_j)$		
$\widetilde{d}=d_2$		
$ans=(\{\widetilde{\boldsymbol{e}}'_j\}_j,\widetilde{d})$		
	$\xrightarrow{ans}$	
		if $b=0$
		$1 \overset{?}{\leftarrow} \mathsf{aVer}\left(c_1,(\{\widetilde{\pi}_j\}_j,\widetilde{\boldsymbol{y}}),\widetilde{d}\right)$
		$\widetilde{\boldsymbol{y}}+\alpha(\boldsymbol{c}+\phi(2^\kappa \mathbb{1}_{nk}))-\boldsymbol{b}\widetilde{s}-\phi(\boldsymbol{I}'\sum_j 2^j \widetilde{\pi}_j^{-1}(\boldsymbol{g}_j)) \overset{?}{\in} \mathcal{L}(\boldsymbol{a})$
		if $b=1$
		$1 \overset{?}{\leftarrow} \mathsf{aVer}\left(c_2,(\{\boldsymbol{g}_j-\alpha\widetilde{\boldsymbol{e}}'_j\}_j,\{\widetilde{\boldsymbol{e}}'_j\}_j),\widetilde{d}\right)$
		$\widetilde{\boldsymbol{e}}'_j \overset{?}{\in} \mathcal{B}_{nk}$

We prefer to analyze it as Stern did in an extension of its original paper [23], that gives us a more detailed insight and requires at most an expected number of $\mathcal{O}(1/\epsilon^3)$ attempts to find such a node and extract a witness. For this to be true we have to assume that q is large enough so that $\log\left(\frac{q}{q+1}\right) > -1/9$ (which only implies $q \geq 13$). We start defining a subset of the possible random coins:

$$X = \left\{\omega \in \Omega \;\middle|\; T(\omega) \text{ has at least } (q+1)^\delta + \frac{\epsilon}{2}(2q)^\delta \text{ branches at level } \delta\right\}$$

Claim. X has probability at least $\epsilon/2$.

Proof. Assume $\Pr[X] < \frac{\epsilon}{2}$. Then we arrive at a contradiction with the fact that $\widetilde{\mathcal{P}}$ has a success probability of more than $\left(\frac{q+1}{2q}\right)^\delta + \epsilon$.

$$\begin{aligned}\Pr\left[\widetilde{\mathcal{P}}(\omega)\right] &= \Pr\left[\widetilde{\mathcal{P}}(\omega)\middle|\omega \in X\right]\Pr\left[X\right] + \Pr\left[\widetilde{\mathcal{P}}(\omega)\middle|\omega \notin X\right]\Pr\left[\Omega \setminus X\right] \\ &\leq \Pr\left[X\right] + \Pr\left[\widetilde{\mathcal{P}}(\omega)\middle|\omega \notin X\right]\end{aligned}$$

We are under the assumption of $\Pr[X] < \epsilon/2$:

$$< \frac{\epsilon}{2} + \Pr\left[\widetilde{\mathcal{P}}(\omega)\middle|\omega \notin X\right]$$

If $\omega \notin X$ there are less than $(q+1)^\delta + \frac{\epsilon}{2}(2q)^\delta$ branches and $(2q)^\delta$ possible challenges:

$$< \frac{\epsilon}{2} + \left(\frac{q+1}{2q}\right)^\delta + \frac{\epsilon}{2}\left(\frac{2q}{2q}\right)^\delta = \left(\frac{q+1}{2q}\right)^\delta + \epsilon$$

And we have found the contradiction. Therefore $\Pr[X] \geq \epsilon/2$. □

From now on consider $T(\omega)$ with $\omega \in X$. For any index $0 \leq d \leq \delta$ we denote by n_d the number of vertices at level d, and for $0 \leq d < \delta$ we define $\gamma_d = n_{d+1}/n_d$.

$$\prod_{d=0}^{\delta-1} \gamma_d \geq (q+1)^\delta + \frac{\epsilon}{2}(2q)^\delta$$

Taking binary logarithms:

$$\begin{aligned}\sum_{d=0}^{\delta-1} \log(\gamma_d) &\geq \log\left((q+1)^\delta + \frac{\epsilon}{2}(2q)^\delta\right) \\ &\geq \log\left(\left(1-\frac{\epsilon}{2}\right)(q+1)^\delta + \frac{\epsilon}{2}(2q)^\delta\right)\end{aligned}$$

By convexity of the log function:

$$\geq \delta\left(\left(1-\frac{\epsilon}{2}\right)\log(q+1) + \frac{\epsilon}{2}\log(2q)\right)$$

This implies that there exists an $0 \leq i \leq \delta - 1$ such that:

$$\begin{aligned}\log(\gamma_i) &\geq \left(1-\frac{\epsilon}{2}\right)\log(q+1) + \frac{\epsilon}{2}\log(2q) \\ &= \log(q+1) + \frac{\epsilon}{2}\left(1 + \log\left(\frac{q}{q+1}\right)\right)\end{aligned}$$

Given that $\log\left(\frac{q}{q+1}\right) \geq -1/9$:

$$\geq \log(q+1) + 4\epsilon/9$$

Undoing logarithms:

$$\begin{aligned}\gamma_i &\geq 2^{\log(q+1)+4\epsilon/9} = (q+1)2^{4\epsilon/9} \\ &\geq (q+1)(1 + \frac{4\epsilon}{9}\ln(2)) \\ &\geq (q+1) + \frac{8(q+1)\epsilon}{27} \\ &\geq (q+1) + \frac{8(q-1)\epsilon}{27}\end{aligned}$$

If we define $n_{i,\leq q+1}$ as the number of nodes on level i that have less or equal than $q+1$ children and $n_{i,>q+1}$ as the number of nodes on level i that have more than $q+1$ children we can also bound γ_i:

$$\begin{aligned}\gamma_i &\leq \frac{(q+1)n_{i,\leq q+1} + (2q)n_{i,>q+1}}{n_{i,\leq q+1} + n_{i,>q+1}}\\ &= (q+1) + (q-1)\frac{n_{i,>q+1}}{n_{i,\leq q+1} + n_{i,>q+1}}\end{aligned}$$

Combining all we have:

$$\begin{aligned}(q+1) + \frac{8(q-1)\epsilon}{27} &\leq (q+1) + (q-1)\frac{n_{i,>q+1}}{n_{i,\leq q+1} + n_{i,>q+1}}\\ \frac{8\epsilon}{27} &\leq \frac{n_{i,>q+1}}{n_{i,\leq q+1} + n_{i,>q+1}}\end{aligned}$$

That is, the fraction of nodes with $q+2$ children or more is larger than $8\epsilon/27$. Therefore, we know that ω belongs to X with probability at least $\epsilon/2$. We know that $T(\omega)$ has at least $(q+1)^\delta + {}^{\epsilon}\!/\!_{2}(2q)^\delta$ branches, that is, the probability of choosing a successful branch is $\left(\frac{q+1}{2q}\right)^\delta + \frac{\epsilon}{2}$. Once we have chosen at random a successful branch, if we look at its level i the probability of finding a node with at least $q+2$ children is at least ${}^{8\epsilon}\!/\!_{27}$. Combining all these probabilities we have that the probability of a success is greater than $({}^{\epsilon}\!/\!_{2})({}^{\epsilon}\!/\!_{2})({}^{8\epsilon}\!/\!_{27}) = 2({}^{\epsilon}\!/\!_{3})^3$. By the pigeonhole principle we can find commitments c_1, c_2, two α, α' and $\boldsymbol{g}_j, \boldsymbol{g}'_j$ that induce accepted answers. Define $\Delta_\alpha = \alpha - \alpha' \neq 0$.

The binding property of c_1, c_2 ensures that openings to $\widetilde{\pi}_j$, $\widetilde{\boldsymbol{y}}$ and $\widetilde{\boldsymbol{e}}'_j$ are fixed.

$$\begin{aligned}\boldsymbol{a}\widetilde{t} &= \widetilde{\boldsymbol{y}} + \alpha(\boldsymbol{c} + \phi(2^\kappa \mathbb{1}_{nk})) - \boldsymbol{b}\widetilde{s} - \phi(\boldsymbol{I}' \textstyle\sum_j 2^j \widetilde{\pi}_j^{-1}(\boldsymbol{g}_j))\\ \boldsymbol{a}\widetilde{t}' &= \widetilde{\boldsymbol{y}} + \alpha'(\boldsymbol{c} + \phi(2^\kappa \mathbb{1}_{nk})) - \boldsymbol{b}\widetilde{s}' - \phi(\boldsymbol{I}' \textstyle\sum_j 2^j \widetilde{\pi}_j^{-1}(\boldsymbol{g}'_j))\\ \Delta_\alpha \boldsymbol{c} &= \boldsymbol{a}(\widetilde{t} - \widetilde{t}') + \boldsymbol{b}(\widetilde{s} - \widetilde{s}') + \phi(\boldsymbol{I}' \textstyle\sum_j 2^j \widetilde{\pi}_j^{-1}(\boldsymbol{g}_j - \boldsymbol{g}'_j) - \Delta_\alpha 2^\kappa \mathbb{1}_{nk})\\ \widetilde{\boldsymbol{e}}'_j &= \Delta_\alpha^{-1}(\boldsymbol{g}_j - \boldsymbol{g}'_j)\\ \boldsymbol{c} &= \boldsymbol{a}(\Delta_\alpha^{-1}(\widetilde{t} - \widetilde{t}')) + \boldsymbol{b}(\Delta_\alpha^{-1}(\widetilde{s} - \widetilde{s}')) + \phi(\boldsymbol{I}' \textstyle\sum_j 2^j \widetilde{\pi}_j^{-1}(\widetilde{\boldsymbol{e}}'_j) - 2^\kappa \mathbb{1}_{nk})\end{aligned}$$

As these elements come from accepted answers we know that $\widetilde{\boldsymbol{e}}'_j \in \mathcal{B}_{nk} \subset \{0,1\}^{2nk}$ and therefore $\phi(\boldsymbol{I}' \sum_j 2^j \widetilde{\pi}_j^{-1}(\widetilde{\boldsymbol{e}}'_j) - 2^\kappa \mathbb{1}_{nk})$ has norm smaller than 2^κ. Then $(\Delta_\alpha^{-1}(\widetilde{t} - \widetilde{t}'), \Delta_\alpha^{-1}(\widetilde{s} - \widetilde{s}'), \phi(\boldsymbol{I}' \sum_j 2^j \widetilde{\pi}_j^{-1}(\widetilde{\boldsymbol{e}}'_j) - 2^\kappa \mathbb{1}_{nk}))$ is a valid opening.

Zero-Knowledge:

Case $b = 0$

$\widehat{t}, \widehat{s} \xleftarrow{\$} R_q, \quad \widehat{\boldsymbol{g}}_j \xleftarrow{\$} \mathbb{Z}_q^{2nk}, \quad \widehat{\pi}_j \xleftarrow{\$} \mathfrak{S}_{2nk}$

$c_1 = \mathsf{aCom}(\{\widehat{\pi}_j\}_j, \boldsymbol{a}\widehat{t} + \boldsymbol{b}\widehat{s}$

$+ \phi(\boldsymbol{I}' \sum_j 2^j \widehat{\pi}_j^{-1}(\widehat{\boldsymbol{g}}_j)) - \alpha(\boldsymbol{c} + \phi(2^\kappa \mathbb{1}_{nk})))$

$\mathcal{P}$ reveals $\{\widehat{\boldsymbol{g}}_j\}_j$, $\{\widetilde{\pi}_j = \widehat{\pi}_j\}_j$, $\widetilde{s} = \widehat{s}$, $\widetilde{\boldsymbol{y}} = \boldsymbol{a}\widehat{t} + \boldsymbol{b}\widehat{s} + \phi(\boldsymbol{I}' \sum_j 2^j \widehat{\pi}_j^{-1}(\widehat{\boldsymbol{g}}_j)) - \alpha\boldsymbol{c}$.
Indistinguishable from a real conversation with the same $\pi_j = \widehat{\pi}_j$ and where $\mu = \widehat{t} - \alpha m$, $\rho = \widehat{s} - \alpha r$ and $\boldsymbol{f}_j = \widehat{\pi}_j^{-1}(\widehat{\boldsymbol{g}}_j) - \alpha \boldsymbol{e}'_j$.

Case $b = 1$

$\widehat{\boldsymbol{e}}'_j \xleftarrow{\$} \mathcal{B}_{nk}, \quad \widehat{\boldsymbol{f}}_j \xleftarrow{\$} \mathbb{Z}_q^{2nk}, \quad \widehat{\pi}_j \xleftarrow{\$} \mathfrak{S}_{2nk}$

$c_2 = \mathsf{aCom}(\{\widehat{\pi}_j(\widehat{\boldsymbol{f}}_j)\}_j, \{\widehat{\pi}_j(\widehat{\boldsymbol{e}}'_j)\}_j)$

$\widehat{\boldsymbol{g}}_j = \widehat{\pi}_j(\widehat{\boldsymbol{f}}_j + \alpha\widehat{\boldsymbol{e}}'_j)$

$\mathcal{P}$ reveals $\{\widehat{\boldsymbol{g}}_j\}_j$, $\{\widetilde{\boldsymbol{e}}'_j = \widehat{\pi}_j(\widehat{\boldsymbol{e}}'_j)\}_j$.

Equivalent to an honest conversation were π_j is such that $\pi_j(\boldsymbol{e}'_j) = \widehat{\pi}_j(\widehat{\boldsymbol{e}}'_j)$ and $\boldsymbol{f}_j = \pi_j^{-1}(\widehat{\pi}_j(\widehat{\boldsymbol{f}}_j))$.

Notice that in both cases simulated conversations follow the same distribution as honest conversations.

3.2 Linear Relation

The analyzed commitment scheme is not homomorphic, since the sum of two commitments may not be a commitment to the sum as the errors may grow. However it is possible to prove knowledge of openings to different commitments proving that the committed messages satisfy a given linear relation. As in the proof for the opening we have $\boldsymbol{a}, \boldsymbol{b} \in R_q^k$, messages $m_1, m_2, m_3 \in R_q$ such that $m_3 = \lambda_1 m_1 + \lambda_2 m_2$ with $\lambda_1, \lambda_2 \in R_q$, random elements r_1, r_2, r_3 in R_q and $\boldsymbol{e}_1, \boldsymbol{e}_2, \boldsymbol{e}_3 \in R_q^k$ vectors of polynomials with their coefficients sampled from a discrete Gaussian distribution conditioned to have norm smaller than $n = 2^\kappa$. We want to prove knowledge of valid openings for the commitments $\boldsymbol{c}_i = \boldsymbol{a}m_i + \boldsymbol{b}r_i + \boldsymbol{e}_i$ satisfying the relation. From now on index i will belong to $\{1, 2, 3\}$.

Consider the extended error decomposition terms $\boldsymbol{e}'_{ij} \in \mathcal{B}_{nk}$ so that:

$$\boldsymbol{c}_i = \boldsymbol{a}m_i + \boldsymbol{b}r_i + \phi(\boldsymbol{I}' \textstyle\sum_j 2^j \boldsymbol{e}'_{ij} - 2^\kappa \mathbb{1}_{nk}).$$

With this notation we can define the interactive protocol (2) to prove knowledge of valid openings for commitments $\boldsymbol{c}_i$ holding the required relation.

This can be done analogously as the previous case, reproducing protocol (1) three times in parallel imposing that the message masking elements hold the same linear relation. μ_3 is computed as $\mu_3 = \lambda_1\mu_1 + \lambda_2\mu_2$ and in case $b = 0$ the verifier needs to check whether $\widetilde{t}_3 = \lambda_1\widetilde{t}_1 + \lambda_2\widetilde{t}_2$.

Proposition 3. *Protocol 2 describes a Public Coin Honest-Verifier ZKPoK, as it satisfies the properties of completeness, soundness and zero-knowledge.*

Completeness: The relation $\widehat{t}_3 = \lambda_1\widehat{t}_1 + \lambda_2\widehat{t}_2$ is satisfied as $\widehat{t}_i = \mu_i + \alpha m_i$, m_i hold the relation and μ_3 is computed such that it holds the relation too.

Soundness: If a (possibly malicious) prover $\widetilde{\mathcal{P}}$ is able to provide accepted answers to δ rounds of interaction with an honest verifier $\mathcal{V}$ with probability

$(q+1/2q)^\delta + \epsilon$, were ϵ is non-negligible, then he is able to efficiently extract a witness. The same argument for the knowledge of a valid opening applies here and provides us with three valid openings

$$\{(\Delta_\alpha^{-1}(\widetilde{t}_i - \widetilde{t}'_i), \Delta_\alpha^{-1}(\widetilde{s}_i - \widetilde{s}'_i), \phi(\boldsymbol{I}' \textstyle\sum_j 2^j \widetilde{\pi}_{ij}^{-1}(\widetilde{\boldsymbol{e}}'_{ij}) - 2^\kappa \mathbb{1}_{nk}))\}_i.$$

We know that $\widetilde{t}_3 = \lambda_1\widetilde{t}_1 + \lambda_2\widetilde{t}_2$ and the same applies to $\widetilde{t}'_3 = \lambda_1\widetilde{t}'_1 + \lambda_2\widetilde{t}'_2$. Therefore we have that the required linear relation holds:

$$\Delta_\alpha^{-1}(\widetilde{t}_3 - \widetilde{t}'_3) = \lambda_1\Delta_\alpha^{-1}(\widetilde{t}_1 - \widetilde{t}'_1) + \lambda_2\Delta_\alpha^{-1}(\widetilde{t}_2 - \widetilde{t}'_2).$$

Zero-Knowledge: The same simulator for protocol 1 works repeated 3 times, with the only exception that in case $b = 0$ we randomly choose $\widehat{t}_1, \widehat{t}_2 \xleftarrow{\$} R_q$ but $\widehat{t}_3$ is computed as $\widehat{t}_3 = \lambda_1\widehat{t}_1 + \lambda_2\widehat{t}_2$.

3.3 Multiplicative Relation

In this subsection we present the main contribution of this paper, an efficient proof of knowledge of a multiplicative relation. That is, index i belongs again to $\{1, 2, 3\}$ and we have $\boldsymbol{c}_i = \boldsymbol{a}m_i + \boldsymbol{b}r_i + \boldsymbol{e}_i$ three valid commitments where $m_3 = m_1 \cdot m_2$. We want to prove knowledge of valid openings for the commitments $\boldsymbol{c}_i$ satisfying this relation.

If we mask the messages $(m_1+\mu_1)$ and $(m_2+\mu_2)$ with random $\mu_1, \mu_2 \xleftarrow{\$} R_q$, as we did before, and then multiply them, some crossed terms appear: $(m_1 + \mu_1)(m_2+\mu_2) = m_3 + (m_1\mu_2 + m_2\mu_1) + \mu_1\mu_2$. Following the notation from [3] we define $m_+ = m_1\mu_2 + m_2\mu_1$ and $m_\times = \mu_1\mu_2$. If we want to get $m_3 = m_1m_2$ we need to prove a similar equality involving two challenges $\alpha, \beta \xleftarrow{\$} \mathbb{Z}_q$ chosen by the verifier. In [3] they use a challenge to prove the relation, while [9] introduces the challenge to reduce the soundness error of each round as we did in Sect. 3.1. The particular requirements of our proofs, where we try to achieve both goals at the same time, imply that we need a much more involved analysis in order to prove the soundness of this strategy. This efficient interactive protocol to prove knowledge of a valid opening for commitments $\boldsymbol{c}_i$ holding the required relation is the main contribution of this paper.

The multiplicative relation protocol (3) can also be seen as parallel executions of protocol (1), this time taking into account the crossed terms.

Proposition 4. *Protocol 3 describes a Public Coin Honest-Verifier ZKPoK, as it satisfies the properties of completeness, soundness and zero-knowledge.*

Completeness: We should check the alternative openings of commitment c_5.

$$\begin{aligned} &\beta\widetilde{t}_\times + \alpha\beta\widetilde{t}_+ + \alpha^2\widetilde{t}_3 - \beta\widetilde{t}_1\widetilde{t}_2 \\ &= \beta(\mu_\times + m_\times - \mu_1\mu_2) + \alpha\beta(\mu_+ + m_+ - \mu_1 m_2 - \mu_2 m_1) + \alpha^2(\mu_3 + \beta(m_3 - m_1m_2)) \\ &= (\beta\mu_\times) + \alpha(\beta\mu_+) + \alpha^2(\mu_3) \end{aligned}$$

Soundness: If a (possibly malicious) prover $\widetilde{\mathcal{P}}$ is able to provide accepted answers to δ rounds of interaction with an honest verifier $\mathcal{V}$ with probability $((q^2 + 3q - 2)/(2q^2))^\delta + \epsilon$, were ϵ is non-negligible, then he is able to efficiently extract a witness. If q is such that $\log(q^2/(q^2+3q-2)) \geq -1/9$ (which is true if $q \geq 37$) we should be able to find more than q^2+3q-2 accepted answers (by an argument analogous to the one explained in Sect. 3.1).

$$\mathrm{ZKP}\left[m_i, r_i, \boldsymbol{e}_i \;\middle|\; \begin{array}{c} \boldsymbol{c}_i = \boldsymbol{a}m_i + \boldsymbol{b}r_i + \boldsymbol{e}_i \\ \|\boldsymbol{e}_i\|_\infty < 2^\kappa, \\ m_3 = \lambda_1 m_1 + \lambda_2 m_2 \end{array}\right] \qquad (2)$$

$$\mathrm{ZKP}\left[m_i, r_i, \boldsymbol{e}_i \;\middle|\; \begin{array}{c} \boldsymbol{c}_i = \boldsymbol{a}m_i + \boldsymbol{b}r_i + \boldsymbol{e}_i \\ \|\boldsymbol{e}_i\|_\infty < 2^\kappa, m_3 = m_1 m_2 \end{array}\right] \qquad (3)$$

$$\mathcal{P}((\boldsymbol{a},\boldsymbol{b}),\boldsymbol{c}_i; m_i, r_i, \boldsymbol{e}_i) \qquad\qquad \mathcal{V}((\boldsymbol{a},\boldsymbol{b}),\boldsymbol{c}_i))$$

$\pi_{i0},\dots,\pi_{i(\kappa-1)} \xleftarrow{\$} \mathfrak{S}_{2nk}$

$\boldsymbol{f}_{i0},\dots,\boldsymbol{f}_{i(\kappa-1)} \xleftarrow{\$} \mathbb{Z}_q^{2nk}$

$\mu_1,\mu_2,\rho_1,\rho_2,\rho_3 \xleftarrow{\$} R_q$

$\mu_3 = \lambda_1\mu_1 + \lambda_2\mu_2$

$(c_1,d_1) = \mathsf{aCom}\left(\{\pi_{ij}\}_{i,j}, \{\boldsymbol{a}\mu_i + \boldsymbol{b}\rho_i + \phi(\boldsymbol{I}'\sum_j 2^j \boldsymbol{f}_{ij})\}_i\right)$

$(c_2,d_2) = \mathsf{aCom}\left(\{\pi_{ij}(\boldsymbol{f}_{ij})\}_{i,j}, \{\pi_{ij}(\mathbf{e}'_{ij})\}_{i,j}\right)$

$\xrightarrow{c_1, c_2}$

$\alpha \xleftarrow{\$} \mathbb{Z}_q$

$\xleftarrow{\alpha}$

$\boldsymbol{g}_{ij} = \pi_{ij}(\boldsymbol{f}_{ij} + \alpha\mathbf{e}'_{ij})$

$\xrightarrow{\{\boldsymbol{g}_{ij}\}_{i,j}}$

$b \xleftarrow{\$} \{0,1\}$

$\xleftarrow{b}$

if $b=0$

$\widetilde{\pi}_{ij} = \pi_{ij}$

$\widetilde{\boldsymbol{y}}_i = \boldsymbol{a}\mu_i + \boldsymbol{b}\rho_i + \phi(\boldsymbol{I}'\sum_j 2^j \boldsymbol{f}_{ij})$

$\widetilde{s}_i = \rho_i + \alpha r_i$

$\widetilde{d} = d_1$

$ans = (\{\widetilde{\pi}_{ij}\}_{i,j}, \{\widetilde{\boldsymbol{y}}_i\}_i, \{\widetilde{s}_i\}_i, \widetilde{d})$

if $b=1$

$\widetilde{\mathbf{e}}'_{ij} = \pi_{ij}(\mathbf{e}'_{ij})$

$\widetilde{d} = d_2$

$ans = (\{\widetilde{\mathbf{e}}'_{ij}\}_{i,j}, \widetilde{d})$

$\xrightarrow{ans}$

if $b=0$

$1 \overset{?}{\leftarrow} \mathsf{aVer}\left(c_1, (\{\widetilde{\pi}_{ij}\}_{i,j}, \{\widetilde{\boldsymbol{y}}_i\}_i), \widetilde{d}\right)$

$\widetilde{\boldsymbol{y}}_i + \alpha(\boldsymbol{c}_i + \phi(2^\kappa \mathbb{1}_{nk})) - \boldsymbol{b}\widetilde{s}_i - \phi(\boldsymbol{I}'\sum_j 2^j \widetilde{\pi}_{ij}^{-1}(\boldsymbol{g}_{ij})) \overset{?}{\in} \mathcal{L}(\boldsymbol{a})$

$\widetilde{t}_3 \overset{?}{=} \lambda_1\widetilde{t}_1 + \lambda_2\widetilde{t}_2$

if $b=1$

$1 \overset{?}{\leftarrow} \mathsf{aVer}\left(c_2, (\{\boldsymbol{g}_{ij} - \alpha\widetilde{\mathbf{e}}'_{ij}\}_{i,j}, \{\widetilde{\mathbf{e}}'_{ij}\}_{i,j}), \widetilde{d}\right)$

$\widetilde{\mathbf{e}}'_{ij} \overset{?}{\in} \mathcal{B}_{nk}$

$$\mathcal{P}((\boldsymbol{a},\boldsymbol{b}),\boldsymbol{c}_i; m_i, r_i, \boldsymbol{e}_i) \qquad\qquad \mathcal{V}((\boldsymbol{a},\boldsymbol{b}),\boldsymbol{c}_i)$$

$\pi_{i0},\dots,\pi_{i(\kappa-1)} \xleftarrow{\$} \mathfrak{S}_{2nk}$

$\boldsymbol{f}_{i0},\dots,\boldsymbol{f}_{i(\kappa-1)} \xleftarrow{\$} \mathbb{Z}_q^{2nk}$

$\mu_i, \mu_\times, \mu_+, \rho_i \xleftarrow{\$} R_q$

$m_\times = \mu_1\mu_2, \quad m_+ = \mu_1 m_2 + \mu_2 m_1$

$(c_1,d_1) = \mathsf{aCom}\left(\{\pi_{ij}\}_{i,j}, \{\boldsymbol{a}\mu_i + \boldsymbol{b}\rho_i + \phi(\boldsymbol{I}'\sum_j 2^j \boldsymbol{f}_{ij})\}_i\right)$

$(c_2,d_2) = \mathsf{aCom}\left(\mu_3, \mu_\times, \mu_+\right)$

$(c_3,d_3) = \mathsf{aCom}\left(\{\pi_{ij}(\boldsymbol{f}_{ij})\}_{i,j}, \{\pi_{ij}(\mathbf{e}'_{ij})\}_{i,j}\right)$

$(c_4,d_4) = \mathsf{aCom}\left(\mu_\times + m_\times, \mu_+ + m_+\right)$

$\xrightarrow{c_1, c_2, c_3, c_4}$

$\alpha, \beta \xleftarrow{\$} \mathbb{Z}_q$

$\xleftarrow{\alpha, \beta}$

$\delta_1 = \alpha, \quad \delta_2 = \alpha, \quad \delta_3 = \beta$

$\boldsymbol{g}_{ij} = \pi_{ij}(\boldsymbol{f}_{ij} + \delta_i\mathbf{e}'_{ij})$

$(c_5,d_5) = \mathsf{aCom}\left((\beta\mu_\times) + \alpha(\beta\mu_+) + \alpha^2(\mu_3)\right)$

$\xrightarrow{\{\boldsymbol{g}_{ij}\}_{i,j}, c_5}$

$b \xleftarrow{\$} \{0,1\}$

$\xleftarrow{b}$

if $b=0$

$\widetilde{\pi}_{ij} = \pi_{ij}$

$\widetilde{\boldsymbol{y}}_i = \boldsymbol{a}\mu_i + \boldsymbol{b}\rho_i + \phi(\boldsymbol{I}'\sum_j 2^j \boldsymbol{f}_{ij})$

$\widetilde{t}_\times = \mu_\times + m_\times, \quad \widetilde{t}_+ = \mu_+ + m_+, \quad \widetilde{s}_i = \rho_i + \delta_i r_i$

$\widetilde{d}_1 = d_1, \quad \widetilde{d}_4 = d_4, \quad \widetilde{d}_5 = d_5$

$ans = (\{\widetilde{\pi}_{ij}\}_{i,j}, \{\widetilde{\boldsymbol{y}}_i\}_i, \widetilde{t}_\times, \widetilde{t}_+, \{\widetilde{s}_i\}_i, \widetilde{d}_1, \widetilde{d}_4, \widetilde{d}_5)$

if $b=1$

$\widetilde{\mathbf{e}}'_{ij} = \pi_{ij}(\mathbf{e}'_{ij})$

$\widetilde{\mu}_3 = \mu_3, \quad \widetilde{\mu}_\times = \mu_\times, \quad \widetilde{\mu}_+ = \mu_+$

$\widetilde{d}_2 = d_2, \quad \widetilde{d}_3 = d_3, \quad \widetilde{d}_5 = d_5$

$ans = (\{\widetilde{\mathbf{e}}'_{ij}\}_{i,j}, \widetilde{\mu}_3, \widetilde{\mu}_\times, \widetilde{\mu}_+, \widetilde{d}_2, \widetilde{d}_3, \widetilde{d}_5)$

$\xrightarrow{ans}$

if $b=0$

$1 \overset{?}{\leftarrow} \mathsf{aVer}\left(c_1, (\{\widetilde{\pi}_{ij}\}_{i,j}, \{\widetilde{\boldsymbol{y}}_i\}_i), \widetilde{d}_1\right)$

$1 \overset{?}{\leftarrow} \mathsf{aVer}\left(c_4, (\widetilde{t}_\times, \widetilde{t}_+), \widetilde{d}_4\right)$

$1 \overset{?}{\leftarrow} \mathsf{aVer}\left(c_5, \beta\widetilde{t}_\times + \alpha\beta\widetilde{t}_+ + \alpha^2\widetilde{t}_3 - \beta\widetilde{t}_1\widetilde{t}_2, \widetilde{d}_5\right)$

$\widetilde{\boldsymbol{y}}_i + \delta_i(\boldsymbol{c}_i + \phi(2^\kappa \mathbb{1}_{nk})) - \boldsymbol{b}\widetilde{s}_i - \phi(\boldsymbol{I}'\sum_j 2^j \widetilde{\pi}_{ij}^{-1}(\boldsymbol{g}_{ij})) \overset{?}{\in} \mathcal{L}(\boldsymbol{a})$

if $b=1$

$1 \overset{?}{\leftarrow} \mathsf{aVer}\left(c_2, (\widetilde{\mu}_3, \widetilde{\mu}_\times, \widetilde{\mu}_+), \widetilde{d}_2\right)$

$1 \overset{?}{\leftarrow} \mathsf{aVer}\left(c_3, (\{\boldsymbol{g}_{ij} - \alpha\widetilde{\mathbf{e}}'_{ij}\}_{i,j}, \{\widetilde{\mathbf{e}}'_{ij}\}_{i,j}), \widetilde{d}_3\right)$

$1 \overset{?}{\leftarrow} \mathsf{aVer}\left(c_5, (\beta\widetilde{\mu}_\times) + \alpha(\beta\widetilde{\mu}_+) + \alpha^2(\widetilde{\mu}_3), \widetilde{d}_5\right)$

$\widetilde{\mathbf{e}}'_{ij} \overset{?}{\in} \mathcal{B}_{nk}$

Then the pigeonhole principle ensures that we can find six pairs $(\alpha^{(1)},\beta^{(1)})$, $(\alpha^{(2)},\beta^{(2)})$, $(\alpha^{(3)},\beta^{(3)})$, $(\alpha^{(4)},\beta^{(4)})$, $(\alpha^{(5)},\beta^{(5)})$, $(\alpha^{(6)},\beta^{(6)})$, with all $\alpha^{(l)}$ different for $l \in \{1,2,3\}$, all $\alpha^{(l)}$ different for $l \in \{4,5,6\}$ and $\beta^{(1)} = \beta^{(2)} = \beta^{(3)} \neq \beta^{(4)} = \beta^{(5)} = \beta^{(6)}$ that induce accepted answers for both $b = 0$ and $b = 1$.

Assume there only exist one β for which there exists at least 3 different $\alpha^{(i)}$ with accepted answers for $b = 0$ and $b = 1$. This particular β belongs to at most $2q$ answers, 2 for each possible α. All other β' contribute each of them with at most $q+2$, only one b accepted for each possible α except two of them. If we add everything up we get $2q + (q-1)(q+2) = q^2 + 3q - 2$, but we had strictly more valid answers.

The binding property of all commitments ensures that openings to the same elements are equal. Therefore we have fixed $\widetilde{\pi}_{ij}$, $\widetilde{\boldsymbol{y}}_i$, $\widetilde{\mu}_3$, $\widetilde{\mu}_\times$, $\widetilde{\mu}_+$, $\widetilde{\boldsymbol{e}}'_{ij}$, $\widetilde{t}_\times$ and $\widetilde{t}_+$. For each pair $(\alpha^{(l)},\beta^{(l)})$ we have $\boldsymbol{g}_{ij}^{(l)}$.

We know that $\widetilde{\boldsymbol{y}}_i + \delta_i^{(l)}(\boldsymbol{c}_i + \phi(2^\kappa \mathbb{1}_{nk})) - \boldsymbol{b}_i\widetilde{s}_i^{(l)} - \phi(\boldsymbol{I}'\sum_j 2^j \widetilde{\pi}_{ij}^{-1}(\boldsymbol{g}_{ij}^{(l)})) \in \mathcal{L}(\boldsymbol{a})$ and call $\widetilde{t}_i^{(l)}$ to its coordinates. Let l and l' in $\{1,2,3,4,5,6\}$ such that $\Delta_{\delta_i} = \delta_i^{(l)} - \delta_i^{(l')} \neq 0$. Then we will be able to compute valid openings of $\boldsymbol{c}_i$:

$$
\begin{aligned}
\boldsymbol{a}\widetilde{t}_i^{(l)} &= \widetilde{\boldsymbol{y}}_i + \delta_i^{(l)}(\boldsymbol{c}_i + \phi(2^\kappa \mathbb{1}_{nk})) - \boldsymbol{b}\widetilde{s}_i^{(l)} - \phi(\boldsymbol{I}'\textstyle\sum_j 2^j \widetilde{\pi}_{ij}^{-1}(\boldsymbol{g}_{ij}^{(l)}))\\
\boldsymbol{a}\widetilde{t}_i^{(l')} &= \widetilde{\boldsymbol{y}}_i + \delta_i^{(l')}(\boldsymbol{c}_i + \phi(2^\kappa \mathbb{1}_{nk})) - \boldsymbol{b}\widetilde{s}_i^{(l')} - \phi(\boldsymbol{I}'\textstyle\sum_j 2^j \widetilde{\pi}_{ij}^{-1}(\boldsymbol{g}_{ij}^{(l')}))\\
\Delta_{\delta_i}\boldsymbol{c}_i &= \boldsymbol{a}(\widetilde{t}_i^{(l)} - \widetilde{t}_i^{(l')}) + \boldsymbol{b}(\widetilde{s}_i^{(l)} - \widetilde{s}_i^{(l')}) + \phi(\boldsymbol{I}'\textstyle\sum_j 2^j \widetilde{\pi}_{ij}^{-1}(\boldsymbol{g}_{ij}^{(l)} - \boldsymbol{g}_{ij}^{(l')}) - \Delta_{\delta_i}2^\kappa \mathbb{1}_{nk})\\
\widetilde{\boldsymbol{e}}'_{ij} &= \Delta_{\delta_i}^{-1}(\boldsymbol{g}_{ij}^{(l)} - \boldsymbol{g}_{ij}^{(l')})\\
\boldsymbol{c}_i &= \boldsymbol{a}(\Delta_{\delta_i}^{-1}(\widetilde{t}_i^{(l)} - \widetilde{t}_i^{(l')})) + \boldsymbol{b}(\Delta_{\delta_i}^{-1}(\widetilde{s}_i^{(l)} - \widetilde{s}_i^{(l')})) + \phi(\boldsymbol{I}'\textstyle\sum_j 2^j \widetilde{\pi}_{ij}^{-1}(\widetilde{\boldsymbol{e}}'_{ij}) - 2^\kappa \mathbb{1}_{nk})
\end{aligned}
$$

As these elements come from accepted answers we know that $\widetilde{\boldsymbol{e}}'_{ij} \in \mathcal{B}_{nk} \subset \{0,1\}^{2nk}$ and therefore $\phi(\boldsymbol{I}'\sum_j 2^j \widetilde{\pi}_{ij}^{-1}(\widetilde{\boldsymbol{e}}'_{ij}) - 2^\kappa \mathbb{1}_{nk})$ has norm smaller than 2^κ. This implies that $(\Delta_{\delta_i}^{-1}(\widetilde{t}_i^{(l)} - \widetilde{t}_i^{(l')}), \Delta_{\delta_i}^{-1}(\widetilde{s}_i^{(l)} - \widetilde{s}_i^{(l')}), \phi(\boldsymbol{I}'\sum_j 2^j \widetilde{\pi}_{ij}^{-1}(\widetilde{\boldsymbol{e}}'_{ij}) - 2^\kappa \mathbb{1}_{nk}))$ are valid openings.

We know that these openings do not depend on (l) and (l'), as the commitment scheme is binding. Therefore we can call them $(\overline{m}_i = \Delta_{\delta_i}^{-1}(\widetilde{t}_i^{(l)} - \widetilde{t}_i^{(l')}), \widetilde{r}_i = \Delta_{\delta_i}^{-1}(\widetilde{s}_i^{(l)} - \widetilde{s}_i^{(l')}), \widetilde{e}_i = \phi(\boldsymbol{I}'\sum_j 2^j \widetilde{\pi}_{ij}^{-1}(\widetilde{\boldsymbol{e}}'_{ij}) - 2^\kappa \mathbb{1}_{nk}))$. It only remains to prove that $\overline{m}_3 = \overline{m}_1\overline{m}_2$.

We can define $\overline{\mu}_i^{(l)} = \widetilde{t}_i^{(l)} - \delta_i^{(l)}\overline{m}_i$ and $\widetilde{\rho}_i^{(l)} = \widetilde{s}_i^{(l)} - \delta_i^{(l)}\widetilde{r}_i$.

Claim. This newly defined elements do not depend on l and we can omit the superindex (l) as $\overline{\mu}_i = \overline{\mu}_i^{(l)} = \overline{\mu}_i^{(l')}$ and $\widetilde{\rho}_i = \widetilde{\rho}_i^{(l)} = \widetilde{\rho}_i^{(l')}$ for any pair l and l'.

Proof. Assume that we have l and l' such that $\overline{\mu}_i^{(l)} \neq \overline{\mu}_i^{(l')}$ or $\widetilde{\rho}_i^{(l)} \neq \widetilde{\rho}_i^{(l')}$.

We could rewrite the expression of $\boldsymbol{a}\widetilde{t}_i^{(l)}$ in terms of this new variables.

$$\begin{aligned}
\boldsymbol{a}\widetilde{t}_i^{(l)} &= \widetilde{\boldsymbol{y}}_i + \delta_i^{(l)}(\boldsymbol{c}_i + \phi(2^{\kappa}\mathbb{1}_{nk})) - \boldsymbol{b}\widetilde{s}_i^{(l)} - \phi(\boldsymbol{I}'\textstyle\sum_j 2^j \widetilde{\pi}_{ij}^{-1}(\boldsymbol{g}_{ij}^{(l)}))\\
\boldsymbol{a}(\overline{\mu}_i^{(l)} + \delta_i^{(l)}\overline{m}_i) &= \widetilde{\boldsymbol{y}}_i + \delta_i^{(l)}(\boldsymbol{a}\overline{m}_i + \boldsymbol{b}\widetilde{r}_i + \phi(\boldsymbol{I}'\textstyle\sum_j 2^j \widetilde{\pi}_{ij}^{-1}(\widetilde{\boldsymbol{e}}'_{ij})))\\
&\quad - \boldsymbol{b}(\widetilde{\rho}_i^{(l)} + \delta_i^{(l)}\widetilde{r}_i) - \phi(\boldsymbol{I}'\textstyle\sum_j 2^j \widetilde{\pi}_{ij}^{-1}(\boldsymbol{g}_{ij}^{(l)}))\\
\boldsymbol{a}\overline{\mu}_i^{(l)} + \boldsymbol{b}\widetilde{\rho}_i^{(l)} &= \widetilde{\boldsymbol{y}}_i - \phi(\boldsymbol{I}'\textstyle\sum_j 2^j \widetilde{\pi}_{ij}^{-1}(\boldsymbol{g}_{ij}^{(l)} - \delta_i^{(l)}\widetilde{\boldsymbol{e}}'_{ij}))
\end{aligned}$$

Notice that $\boldsymbol{g}_{ij}^{(l)} - \delta_i^{(l)}\widetilde{\boldsymbol{e}}'_{ij}$ is open to $\widetilde{\boldsymbol{f}}_{ij}$, that was commited before $\alpha^{(l)}$ and $\beta^{(l)}$ were chosen and therefore does not depend on l:

$$\boldsymbol{a}\overline{\mu}_i^{(l)} + \boldsymbol{b}\widetilde{\rho}_i^{(l)} = \widetilde{\boldsymbol{y}}_i - \phi(\boldsymbol{I}'\textstyle\sum_j 2^j \widetilde{\pi}_{ij}^{-1}(\widetilde{\boldsymbol{f}}_{ij})).$$

Since the right handside does not depend on l nor l' from two equations we get:

$$\boldsymbol{a}(\overline{\mu}_i^{(l)} - \overline{\mu}_i^{(l')}) + \boldsymbol{b}(\widetilde{\rho}_i^{(l)} - \widetilde{\rho}_i^{(l')}) = 0. \tag{4}$$

We can apply a similar argument as we do in Proposition 1 to prove that the commitment was binding. In this particular case there exist nonzero elements satisfying equation (4) with probability:

$$\Pr_{(\boldsymbol{a},\boldsymbol{b})}\left[\exists \mu, \rho \text{ (not both 0)} \middle| \boldsymbol{a}\mu + \boldsymbol{b}\rho = 0\right] \le \frac{q^{2n}}{q^{kn/2}} \in negl(1^{\lambda}).$$

Then both differences have to be 0 and the elements do not depend on l. □

We can also define $\widetilde{m}_{\times} = \widetilde{t}_{\times} - \widetilde{\mu}_{\times}, \widetilde{m}_{+} = \widetilde{t}_{+} - \widetilde{\mu}_{+}$. This time there is no dependence with l as the elements were committed previously. With all these discussions now we are ready to prove the relation $\overline{m}_3 = \overline{m}_1\overline{m}_2$.

$$\alpha^{(l)^2}(\widetilde{\mu}_3) + \alpha^{(l)}(\beta^{(l)}\widetilde{\mu}_{+}) + (\beta^{(l)}\widetilde{\mu}_{\times}) = \beta^{(l)}\widetilde{t}_{\times} + \alpha^{(l)}\beta^{(l)}\widetilde{t}_{+} + \alpha^{(l)^2}\widetilde{t}_3 - \beta^{(l)}\widetilde{t}_1\widetilde{t}_2$$

$$\begin{pmatrix} \alpha^{(l)^2}(\widetilde{\mu}_3 - \overline{\mu}_3 + \beta^{(l)}(\overline{m}_1\overline{m}_2 - \overline{m}_3)) \\ +\alpha^{(l)}(\beta^{(l)}(\overline{\mu}_1\overline{m}_2 + \overline{\mu}_2\overline{m}_1 - \widetilde{m}_{+})) \\ +(\beta^{(l)}(\overline{\mu}_1\overline{\mu}_2 - \widetilde{m}_{\times})) \end{pmatrix} = 0$$

If we restrict ourselves to the cases with equal β we can see this expression as a two degree polynomial in α (the coefficients were committed before the challenges were chosen), that is equal to 0 for three evaluations $\alpha^{(1)}, \alpha^{(2)}, \alpha^{(3)}$ or $\alpha^{(4)}, \alpha^{(5)}, \alpha^{(6)}$. This implies that it is the 0 polynomial and that all its coefficients are 0, providing us with the equalities $\widetilde{\mu}_3 - \overline{\mu}_3 + \beta^{(l)}(\overline{m}_1\overline{m}_2 - \overline{m}_3) = 0$. Given that this equality is satisfied by two different β we have that $(\beta^{(l)} - \beta^{(l')})(\overline{m}_1\overline{m}_2 - \overline{m}_3) = 0$ and finally $\overline{m}_3 = \overline{m}_1\overline{m}_2$ as we wanted to prove, the relation holds for the extracted witness.

Zero-Knowledge:

Case $b = 0$

$\widehat{t}_i, \widehat{s}_i \xleftarrow{\$} R_q, \quad \widehat{t}_\times, \widehat{t}_+ \xleftarrow{\$} R_q$

$\widehat{\boldsymbol{g}}_{ij} \xleftarrow{\$} \mathbb{Z}_q^{2nk}, \quad \widehat{\pi}_{ij} \xleftarrow{\$} \mathfrak{S}_{2nk}$

$$c_1 = \mathsf{aCom}\Big(\{\widehat{\pi}_{ij}\}_{i,j}, \{\boldsymbol{a}\widehat{t}_i + \boldsymbol{b}\widehat{s}_i + \phi(\boldsymbol{I}' \textstyle\sum_j 2^j \widehat{\pi}_{ij}^{-1}(\widehat{\boldsymbol{g}}_{ij})) - \delta_i(\boldsymbol{c}_i + \phi(2^\kappa \mathbb{1}_{nk}))\}_i\Big)$$

$$c_4 = \mathsf{aCom}(\widehat{t}_\times, \widehat{t}_+)$$

$$c_5 = \mathsf{aCom}(\beta\widehat{t}_\times + \alpha\beta\widehat{t}_+ + \alpha^2\widehat{t}_3 - \beta\widehat{t}_1\widehat{t}_2)$$

$\mathcal{P}$ reveals $\{\widehat{\boldsymbol{g}}_{ij}\}_{i,j}$, $\{\widetilde{\pi}_{ij} = \widehat{\pi}_{ij}\}_{i,j}$, $\{\widetilde{\boldsymbol{y}}_i = \boldsymbol{a}\widehat{t}_i + \boldsymbol{b}\widehat{s}_i + \phi(\boldsymbol{I}' \sum_j 2^j \widehat{\pi}_{ij}^{-1}(\widehat{\boldsymbol{g}}_{ij})) - \delta_i(\boldsymbol{c}_i + \phi(2^\kappa \mathbb{1}_{nk}))\}_i, \widetilde{t}_\times, \widetilde{t}_+$, $\{\widetilde{s}_i\}_i$. Indistinguishable from a real conversation with the same $\pi_{ij} = \widehat{\pi}_{ij}$ and where $\mu_i = \widehat{t}_i - \delta_i m_i$, $\mu_\times = \widehat{t}_\times - m_\times$, $\mu_+ = \widehat{t}_+ - m_+$, $\rho_i = \widehat{s}_i - \delta_i r_i$ and $\boldsymbol{f}_{ij} = \widehat{\pi}_{ij}^{-1}(\widehat{\boldsymbol{g}}_{ij}) - \delta_i \boldsymbol{e}'_{ij}$.

Case $b = 1$

$\widehat{\mu}_3, \widehat{\mu}_\times, \widehat{\mu}_+ \xleftarrow{\$} R_q, \quad \widehat{\boldsymbol{e}}'_{ij} \xleftarrow{\$} \mathcal{B}_{nk}$

$\widehat{\boldsymbol{f}}_{ij} \xleftarrow{\$} \mathbb{Z}_q^{2nk}, \quad \widehat{\pi}_{ij} \xleftarrow{\$} \mathfrak{S}_{2nk}$

$$c_2 = \mathsf{aCom}(\widehat{\mu}_3, \widehat{\mu}_\times, \widehat{\mu}_+)$$

$$c_3 = \mathsf{aCom}(\{\widehat{\pi}_{ij}(\widehat{\boldsymbol{f}}_{ij})\}_{i,j}, \{\widehat{\pi}_{ij}(\widehat{\boldsymbol{e}}'_{ij})\}_{i,j})$$

$$c_5 = \mathsf{aCom}(\beta\widehat{\mu}_\times + \alpha\beta\widehat{\mu}_+ + \alpha^2\widehat{\mu}_3)$$

$$\widehat{\boldsymbol{g}}_{ij} = \widehat{\pi}_{ij}(\widehat{\boldsymbol{f}}_{ij} + \delta_i \widehat{\boldsymbol{e}}'_{ij})$$

$\mathcal{P}$ reveals $\{\widehat{\boldsymbol{g}}_{ij}\}_{i,j}$, $\widetilde{\mu}_3 = \widehat{\mu}_3$, $\widetilde{\mu}_\times = \widehat{\mu}_\times$, $\widetilde{\mu}_+ = \widehat{\mu}_+$, $\{\widetilde{\boldsymbol{e}}'_{ij} = \widehat{\pi}_{ij}(\widehat{\boldsymbol{e}}'_{ij})\}_{i,j}$. Equivalent to an honest conversation with equal $\mu_3 = \widehat{\mu}_3, \mu_\times = \widehat{\mu}_\times, \mu_+ = \widehat{\mu}_+$ and were π_{ij} is such that $\pi_{ij}(\boldsymbol{e}'_{ij}) = \widehat{\pi}_{ij}(\widehat{\boldsymbol{e}}'_{ij})$ and $\boldsymbol{f}_{ij} = \pi_{ij}^{-1}(\widehat{\pi}_{ij}(\widehat{\boldsymbol{f}}_{ij}))$.

Notice again that simulated conversations follow the proper distributions.

4 Comparisons and Conclusions

4.1 Comparisons with Other Proposals

In this subsection we compare our proposal of Zero-Knowledge proofs for commitments with those presented by Xie *et al.* [25] and Benhamouda *et al.* [3]. All these commitments are adaptations of the LPN commitment scheme of Jain *et al.* [12] to the RLWE problem.

We first compare the size of the commitments (Table 1). Benhamouda *et al.* directly adapt the structure from [12], and we use their same notation for commiting to a polynomial of degree n with coefficients in $\mathbb{Z}_q$. The commitment is a vector of k polynomials. Xie *et al.* do not commit to a single polynomial but to l polynomials of smaller degree d. Their commitment is made of m polynomials of degree d, but as their construction requires m to be linear in l, the size is asymptotically the same.

Table 1. Commitment size

	Xie *et al.*	Benhamouda *et al.*	our proposal
Commitment Size (in bits)	$md \log q$	$kn \log q$	$kn \log q$

In order to be able to relate these sizes we have to compare the restrictions on the parameters (Table 2). Xie *et al.* impose that the overhead factor (the ratio between the size of the commitment and the size of the original message) has to be of the order of the logarithm of the security parameter. We can directly compare our and Benhamouda *et al.* proposal as we both require this ratio k to be greater than a quotient related to a constant γ, where $q \geq n^\gamma$. Our restriction is weaker and we also require a smaller minimum value for γ. This is really important as it allows us to choose the size of q with more flexibility.

Table 2. Parameter restrictions

	Xie *et al.*	Benhamouda *et al.*	Our proposal
overhead factor	$m/l \in \omega(\log \lambda)$	$k > \frac{18\gamma}{3\gamma-16}$	$k > \frac{8\gamma+4}{2\gamma-5}$
n and q relation	–	$\gamma \geq 6$	$\gamma \geq 3$

In Fig. 1, for a fixed value $n = 2^{10}$, we represent the size of the commitment of Xie *et al.*, Benhamouda *et al.* and ours for different values of γ (that is, different values of q since $q \geq n^\gamma$).

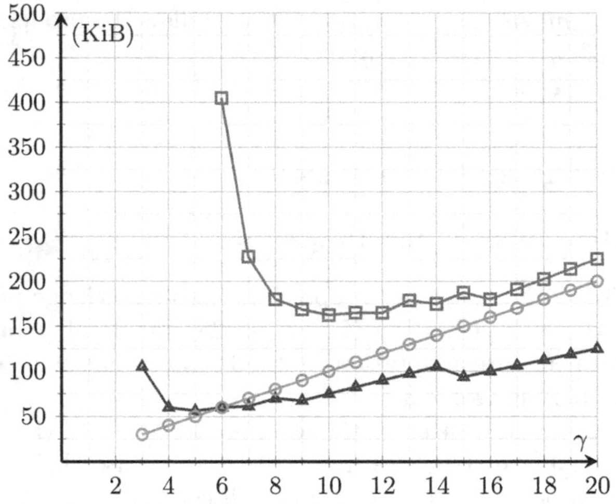

Fig. 1. Commitment's size of Xie et al. (—○—), Benhamouda et al. (—□—) and our proposal (—△—)

Finally we can compare the communication cost of the Zero-Knowledge Proofs of multiplicative relations (Table 3), as this is the most interesting case and the major contribution of this paper. In Table 4 we compare soundness and completeness properties for one round of each protocol.

We separately show what are the initial communication costs (in bits), the cost per round (in bits), the number of auxiliary commitments, the number of openings of these auxiliary commitments and the number of seeds for the pseudorandom generation of the permutations. The last three items depend on the final implementation. Random seeds could be 256 bit strings. If the auxiliary commitment scheme is implemented using a hash function (secure in the random oracle model) then the size of each of these auxiliary commitments could also be 256 bits.

Table 3. Communication cost (in bits)

	Benhamouda *et al.*	Xie *et al.*	our proposal
initial com.	–	$md\log^3 q + 2md\log^2 q$	–
round cost	$(8k+7)n\log q +$ $n/2 + 16\kappa/3 - 8$	$(12\kappa+2)md\log^3 q + 8ld\log^3 q +$ $\frac{\kappa^2+2\kappa+3}{3}(14md\log q)$	$(3(\kappa+1)k + 1.5k + 4)n\log q +$ $6(\kappa+1)kn + 2\log q + 1$
aux. com.	1	$3(\log^2 q + 1)$	5
openings	1	$2(\log^2 q + 1)$	3
seeds	–	$2(\kappa\log^2 q + \log^2 q + \kappa)$	$3(\kappa+1)$

Table 4. Soundness and completeness

	Benhamouda *et al.*	Xie *et al.*	our proposal
soundness error	negligible	$\frac{2}{3}$	$\frac{q^2+3q-2}{2q^2}$
extracted error gap	$\mathcal{O}\left(n^{4/3}/2\right)$	1	1

It should be taken into account that the cost per round has to be multiplied by the number of rounds required to achieve soundness, that depends on the desired level of soundness and the soundness error per round exposed in Table 4. In this final table we also include what we call the extracted error gap, that is, the quotient between the bound on the error of the RLWE samples obtained by the extractor and the original bound on the error known by the prover.

Compared with the Stern-based protocol of Xie *et al.* we have a similar commitment size but significantly reduce the cost of the proofs. Notice that md is comparable to kn, therefore we reduce the size of the proof by a factor $\log^2 q$ and we also improve the constants. We also reduce the number of rounds, as our soundness error per round is aproximately $1/2$ instead of $2/3$. Xie *et al.* needed to decompose the original message into bits, while we only need to decompose the error. Then we do not need any initial communication (they had to commit to the decompositions of the messages before starting the rounds), and we also reduce in the same proportion the number of auxiliar commitments, openings of auxiliar commitments and random seeds for the permutations, that are common in all Stern-based protocols.

On the other hand our commitment scheme is smaller than Benhamouda *et al.* for the same value of n and q, but they have a smaller communication cost, as its proof has a smaller cost per round and only needs one round. There is a trade-off between the size of the commitment and the communication cost. The running time of their proofs depends on the secret elements that are used, and that has to be taken into account in an interactive setting to avoid timing attacks. We don't have this issue, which makes the implementation more direct. We only need the modulus q to be greater than n^3 while they require $q \geq n^6$.

Just taking into account the size of the proofs it could still be more efficient to use a larger q and their negligible soundness error technique, however, if these proofs are just part of a different protocol then been forced to use a larger q for the whole protocol might not be compensated by their more efficient commitment proofs and our more flexible scheme could be the best option.

The same applies if the relation proofs are used not just for commitments but for any messages hidden in RLWE samples where the bounds on the size of the error matters (for example in proofs about public keys of encryption schemes). One could increase the size of all parameters in order to take into account the extracted error gap, or one could use our slightly more expensive but exact ZKPoK and avoid modifications on the parameters of the rest of the protocol.

It would be interesting to study the benefits and costs of applying our proofs to other constructions that currently use Fiat-Shamir with aborts, such as the commitment scheme using more structured lattice assumptions (Module-LWE and Module-SIS) from [2], and we left it as future work.

4.2 Final Conclusions

To sum up, we have proposed a new protocol for proving linear and multiplicative relations between secret elements hidden inside RLWE samples. The direct applications are new Zero-Knowledge Proofs for proving knowledge of the evaluations of arithmetic circuits with committed inputs.

Xie *et al.* [25] proposed exact Stern-based proofs for lattice-based commitments, but they had a factor $\log(q)^2$ overhead to the messages. We are able to build exact proofs with a constant factor overhead, thus further improving efficiency. Besides that, our scheme is compatible with the techniques that reduce the soundness error to $1/2$, so that it requires less repetitions to achieve the same confidence level. Several constructions using Xie *et al.* Zero-Knowledge Proofs for relations between committed messages (as the recently presented lattice-based Attributed Based Signature scheme for unbounded circuits [13]) could benefit from this improvement directly replacing their proofs with our proposal.

Our scheme can be directly compared to the one proposed by Benhamouda *et al.* [3]. While their proofs do not require repetitions our proposal achieves the same security level with smaller commitments, as we do not generalize the definition of opening of the commitment. It is also more robust and easy to implement, as in our protocol the prover is always able to answer with a valid response, without any abort probability. And finally we require a significantly smaller modulus q for our construction to be sound. This implies that our schemes can still be used as a building block in larger protocols where it would be much less efficient (or even unfeasible) to increase the modulus q for the whole protocol. That could be the case for electronic voting, where heavy ZKPoK could be performed on some servers but votes have to be encrypted using resource constrained voting devices.

We think that these properties represent a major improvement on constructions based on Stern protocol and might be useful in applications that heavily require this kind of proofs, as electronic voting. We think that our ideas are flexible enough to be applied as building blocks for other different constructions besides commitment schemes. We consider that it would be interesting to implement the protocol presented in this paper and leave it as future work.

References

1. Aguilar Melchor, C., Cayrel, P.L., Gaborit, P., Laguillaumie, F.: A new efficient threshold ring signature scheme based on coding theory. IEEE Trans. Inf. Theory **57**(7), 4833–4842 (2011). https://doi.org/10.1109/TIT.2011.2145950
2. Baum, C., Damgård, I., Lyubashevsky, V., Oechsner, S., Peikert, C.: More efficient commitments from structured lattice assumptions. In: Catalano, D., De Prisco, R. (eds.) SCN 2018. LNCS, vol. 11035, pp. 368–385. Springer, Cham (2018). https://doi.org/10.1007/978-3-319-98113-0_20
3. Benhamouda, F., Krenn, S., Lyubashevsky, V., Pietrzak, K.: Efficient zero-knowledge proofs for commitments from learning with errors over rings. In: Pernul, G., Ryan, P.Y.A., Weippl, E. (eds.) ESORICS 2015. LNCS, vol. 9326, pp. 305–325. Springer, Cham (2015). https://doi.org/10.1007/978-3-319-24174-6_16
4. Bettaieb, S., Schrek, J.: Improved lattice-based threshold ring signature scheme. In: Gaborit, P. (ed.) PQCrypto 2013. LNCS, vol. 7932, pp. 34–51. Springer, Heidelberg (2013). https://doi.org/10.1007/978-3-642-38616-9_3
5. Bootle, J., Lyubashevsky, V., Seiler, G.: Algebraic techniques for short(er) exact lattice-based zero-knowledge proofs. In: Boldyreva, A., Micciancio, D. (eds.) CRYPTO 2019. LNCS, vol. 11692, pp. 176–202. Springer, Cham (2019). https://doi.org/10.1007/978-3-030-26948-7_7
6. Cayrel, P.-L., Gaborit, P., Prouff, E.: Secure implementation of the stern authentication and signature schemes for low-resource devices. In: Grimaud, G., Standaert, F.-X. (eds.) CARDIS 2008. LNCS, vol. 5189, pp. 191–205. Springer, Heidelberg (2008). https://doi.org/10.1007/978-3-540-85893-5_14
7. Cayrel, P.-L., Lindner, R., Rückert, M., Silva, R.: Improved zero-knowledge identification with lattices. In: Heng, S.-H., Kurosawa, K. (eds.) ProvSec 2010. LNCS, vol. 6402, pp. 1–17. Springer, Heidelberg (2010). https://doi.org/10.1007/978-3-642-16280-0_1
8. Cayrel, P.-L., Lindner, R., Rückert, M., Silva, R.: A lattice-based threshold ring signature scheme. In: Abdalla, M., Barreto, P.S.L.M. (eds.) LATINCRYPT 2010. LNCS, vol. 6212, pp. 255–272. Springer, Heidelberg (2010). https://doi.org/10.1007/978-3-642-14712-8_16
9. Cayrel, P.-L., Véron, P., El Yousfi Alaoui, S.M.: A zero-knowledge identification scheme based on the q-ary syndrome decoding problem. In: Biryukov, A., Gong, G., Stinson, D.R. (eds.) SAC 2010. LNCS, vol. 6544, pp. 171–186. Springer, Heidelberg (2011). https://doi.org/10.1007/978-3-642-19574-7_12

10. Gaborit, P., Girault, M.: Lightweight code-based identification and signature. In: 2007 IEEE International Symposium on Information Theory, pp. 191–195 (2007). https://doi.org/10.1109/ISIT.2007.4557225
11. Gentry, C., Sahai, A., Waters, B.: Homomorphic encryption from learning with errors: conceptually-simpler, asymptotically-faster, attribute-based. In: Canetti, R., Garay, J.A. (eds.) CRYPTO 2013. LNCS, vol. 8042, pp. 75–92. Springer, Heidelberg (2013). https://doi.org/10.1007/978-3-642-40041-4_5
12. Jain, A., Krenn, S., Pietrzak, K., Tentes, A.: Commitments and efficient zero-knowledge proofs from learning parity with noise. In: Wang, X., Sako, K. (eds.) ASIACRYPT 2012. LNCS, vol. 7658, pp. 663–680. Springer, Heidelberg (2012). https://doi.org/10.1007/978-3-642-34961-4_40
13. El Kaafarani, A., Katsumata, S.: Attribute-based signatures for unbounded circuits in the ROM and efficient instantiations from lattices. In: Abdalla, M., Dahab, R. (eds.) PKC 2018. LNCS, vol. 10770, pp. 89–119. Springer, Cham (2018). https://doi.org/10.1007/978-3-319-76581-5_4
14. Kawachi, A., Tanaka, K., Xagawa, K.: Concurrently secure identification schemes based on the worst-case hardness of lattice problems. In: Pieprzyk, J. (ed.) ASIACRYPT 2008. LNCS, vol. 5350, pp. 372–389. Springer, Heidelberg (2008). https://doi.org/10.1007/978-3-540-89255-7_23
15. Libert, B., Ling, S., Nguyen, K., Wang, H.: Lattice-based zero-knowledge arguments for integer relations. In: Shacham, H., Boldyreva, A. (eds.) CRYPTO 2018. LNCS, vol. 10992, pp. 700–732. Springer, Cham (2018). https://doi.org/10.1007/978-3-319-96881-0_24
16. Libert, B., Ling, S., Mouhartem, F., Nguyen, K., Wang, H.: Zero-knowledge arguments for matrix-vector relations and lattice-based group encryption. Theor. Comput. Sci. **759**, 72–97 (2019). https://doi.org/10.1016/j.tcs.2019.01.003
17. Ling, S., Nguyen, K., Stehlé, D., Wang, H.: Improved zero-knowledge proofs of knowledge for the ISIS problem, and applications. In: Kurosawa, K., Hanaoka, G. (eds.) PKC 2013. LNCS, vol. 7778, pp. 107–124. Springer, Heidelberg (2013). https://doi.org/10.1007/978-3-642-36362-7_8
18. Lyubashevsky, V., Peikert, C., Regev, O.: On ideal lattices and learning with errors over rings. In: Gilbert, H. (ed.) EUROCRYPT 2010. LNCS, vol. 6110, pp. 1–23. Springer, Heidelberg (2010). https://doi.org/10.1007/978-3-642-13190-5_1
19. Peikert, C., et al.: A decade of lattice cryptography. Found. Trends Theor. Comput. Sci. **10**(4), 283–424 (2016). https://doi.org/10.1561/0400000074
20. Shor, P.W.: Polynomial-time algorithms for prime factorization and discrete logarithms on a quantum computer. SIAM J. Comput. **26**(5), 1484–1509 (1997). https://doi.org/10.1137/S0097539795293172
21. Silva, R., Cayrel, P.L., Lindner, R.: A lattice-based batch identification scheme. In: 2011 IEEE Information Theory Workshop, pp. 215–219, October 2011. https://doi.org/10.1109/ITW.2011.6089381
22. Stehlé, D., Steinfeld, R., Tanaka, K., Xagawa, K.: Efficient public key encryption based on ideal lattices. In: Matsui, M. (ed.) ASIACRYPT 2009. LNCS, vol. 5912, pp. 617–635. Springer, Heidelberg (2009). https://doi.org/10.1007/978-3-642-10366-7_36
23. Stern, J.: A new paradigm for public key identification. IEEE Trans. Inf. Theory **42**(6), 1757–1768 (1996). https://doi.org/10.1109/18.556672
24. Stern, J.: A new identification scheme based on syndrome decoding. In: Stinson, D.R. (ed.) CRYPTO 1993. LNCS, vol. 773, pp. 13–21. Springer, Heidelberg (1994). https://doi.org/10.1007/3-540-48329-2_2

25. Xie, X., Xue, R., Wang, M.: Zero knowledge proofs from Ring-LWE. In: Abdalla, M., Nita-Rotaru, C., Dahab, R. (eds.) CANS 2013. LNCS, vol. 8257, pp. 57–73. Springer, Cham (2013). https://doi.org/10.1007/978-3-319-02937-5_4
26. Yang, R., Au, M.H., Zhang, Z., Xu, Q., Yu, Z., Whyte, W.: Efficient lattice-based zero-knowledge arguments with standard soundness: construction and applications. In: Boldyreva, A., Micciancio, D. (eds.) CRYPTO 2019. LNCS, vol. 11692, pp. 147–175. Springer, Cham (2019). https://doi.org/10.1007/978-3-030-26948-7_6

Cryptanalysis of a Protocol for Efficient Sorting on SHE Encrypted Data

Shyam Murthy(✉) and Srinivas Vivek

IIIT Bangalore, Bangalore, India
shyam.sm@iiitb.org, srinivas.vivek@iiitb.ac.in

Abstract. Sorting on encrypted data using Somewhat Homomorphic Encryption (SHE) schemes is currently inefficient in practice when the number of elements to be sorted is very large. Hence alternate protocols that can efficiently perform computation and sorting on encrypted data is of interest. Recently, Kesarwani et al. (EDBT 2018) proposed a protocol for efficient sorting on data encrypted using an SHE scheme in a model where one of the two non-colluding servers is holding the decryption key. The encrypted data to be sorted is transformed homomorphically by the first server using a randomly chosen monotonic polynomial with possibly large coefficients, and then the non-colluding server holding the decryption key decrypts, sorts, and conveys back the sorted order to the first server without learning the actual values except possibly for the order.

In this work we demonstrate an attack on the above protocol that allows the non-colluding server holding the decryption key to recover the original plaintext inputs (up to a constant difference). Though our attack runs in time exponential in the size of plaintext inputs and degree of the polynomial but polynomial in the size of coefficients, we show that our attack is feasible for 32-bit inputs, hence accounting for several real world scenarios. Of independent interest is our algorithm for recovering the integer inputs (up to a constant difference) by observing only the integer polynomial outputs.

Keywords: Somewhat Homomorphic Encryption · Comparison · Sorting · Polynomial reconstruction · Low-depth circuit

1 Introduction

Cloud hosting solutions that offer pay-as-you-use models provide elasticity and cost-efficiency thus attracting users from varied domains. Cloud providers also offer services and computation capabilities on stored data thereby offloading such overheads from their customers. However, these services can compromise the privacy of the stored data. Hence while data has to be in encrypted form, to be able to make use of the services offered by the cloud, there should be ways to perform meaningful operations on encrypted data. One such service is to search for k-Nearest Neighbours (k-NN) (according to a given metric) of an encrypted

M. Albrecht (Ed.): IMACC 2019, LNCS 11929, pp. 278–294, 2019.
https://doi.org/10.1007/978-3-030-35199-1_14

δ-tuple in a database containing n encrypted δ-tuples. k-NN is a basic algorithm used in data mining, machine learning, pattern recognition, etc. Many *efficient* solutions have been proposed for determining k-NN on private data [WCKM09, XLY13, CGLB14, SHSK15, ZHT16], and [ESJ14], [KKN+18] give solutions based on homomorphic encryption schemes.

Secure Sorting and k-NN Protocol from [KKN+18]. Suppose a (possibly very large) data set consists of points in a multi-dimensional vector space with the Euclidean distance as metric and that are stored in encrypted form in the cloud for privacy reasons by a client. Also suppose that the client wishes the server to compute k-NN on this encrypted data by providing an encrypted query point. One obvious approach is to use Fully/Somewhat Homomorphic Encryption (F/SHE) schemes [Gen09, BGV12, GSW13, CGGI19] to perform the computing of the Euclidean distances, sorting and then the computing of the indices of the k-NNs on the encrypted data. But with the current F/SHE schemes it is impractical to even handle data that merely consists of a few hundred elements [ÇDSS15, CS15, ÇS19].

At EDBT 2018, Kesarwani et al. [KKN+18] proposed a secure way to solve the k-NN problem on SHE encrypted data in a model where there is a non-colluding pair of Cloud A and B, *a.k.a.* the federated cloud setting. In this setting, the participating clouds do not collaborate with each other. A client uses Cloud A as storage to store n data points encoded as integer values with each of the δ coordinates encrypted in separate ciphertexts. A user (querier) provides an encrypted query point in a similar format. Server A homomorphically computes the square of the Euclidean distances between the query and the data points in n different ciphertexts using an SHE scheme. The result of the computation is also in encrypted form. Once the distances to the given query point are computed as n ciphertexts, the Server A homomorphically evaluates a monotonic polynomial p of degree d having positive integer coefficients, randomly permutes the order of the ciphertexts and sends them to the Server B. The Server B has access to the full decryption key, who decrypts the received data and sorts the (transformed) plaintext distances, computes the indices of the k-NNs and sends back the indices to Server A which then maps them back to the original encrypted indices and sends the same to the client. The authors of [KKN+18] demonstrate that their method takes only a few minutes when the number of elements is as large as 200,000 and the dimension is 2. It is also claimed in [KKN+18][Section 4.2] that the Server B will not learn anything other than the value of k and the number of equidistant points from the query point. Moreover, the authors claim that if the size of squared plaintext distances is 16 bits, then a polynomial of degree $d = 9$ suffices to ensure that an adversary will only be able to recover the plaintext distances with probability as small as 2^{-160}.

It may be noted that though the protocol of [KKN+18] has been described specifically in the context of securely evaluating k-NN, their technique of transforming inputs through a random monotonic polynomial has applications in many settings where sorting of SHE encrypted data is needed. Moreover, this protocol may be of interest in scenarios where both computation and then sorting on encrypted data is needed. It may be noted that if sorting is the only functionality required, then order-preserving or order-revealing encryption schemes would suffice for the purpose [BCLO09,BLR+15].

Polynomial Recovery from Only the Outputs. As is evident from the above description of the k-NN (and the sorting) protocol from [KKN+18] on encrypted data, one way of formalizing the cryptanalysis of this protocol is to formulate it as the problem of recovering inputs of a randomly chosen monotonic polynomial with positive coefficients by observing *only* the corresponding outputs. Here the adversary is the Server B who is keen to learn more about the transformed input distances than just their ordering. Formally, let $p(x) = a_0+a_1 \cdot x+a_2 \cdot x^2+\ldots+a_d \cdot x^d$ be a polynomial of degree d, where each of the integer coefficients a_i is picked uniform randomly and independently in the range $[1, 2^\alpha - 1]$. The polynomial is evaluated (homomorphically) on the (encrypted) unknown n integer inputs $x_i \in [0, 2^\beta - 1]$ $(i = 1, 2, \ldots, n)$. The adversary is provided only n outputs $p(x_i)$. It may be assumed that it knows the parameters d, α and β as assumed in [KKN+18]. The goal is to recover the inputs x_i. In the context of Secure k-NN problem, recovering x_i would correspond to recovering the squares of the Euclidean distances between the query point and data set points.

The problem of polynomial reconstruction, posed in different flavours, has received good attention in the past. A well-known technique for this is the Lagrange interpolation. The problem of polynomial reconstruction also occurs in the context of decoding error-correcting codes with many well-known techniques to recover polynomials even when a sufficiently small fraction of the input-output pairs are error prone [Ber68,GS99,GRS00], and many follow up works. But we would like to emphasize that, to the best of our knowledge, in all the previous works both the input to and the output of the polynomials are given. But in the present setting, only the outputs are provided and we are *not* provided the inputs (except that we only know the range where the inputs come and the degree of polynomial). The goal is to recover the inputs and, consequently, the polynomial itself.

We observe that given only the polynomial outputs there may be many polynomial/input combinations (in the given input range) that result in the same outputs. This is because if $p(x)$ and x_i are the chosen polynomial and the n integer inputs, respectively, then, any polynomial of the form $p(x + c)$ (c, a constant) will result in the same outputs for $x_i - c$ provided all the $x_i - c$ lie in the given interval. So the best we could hope to recover for the current problem is to recover the inputs up to a constant difference. Of course, there are other possibilities too and the number of such equivalent solutions will likely be significantly small if the number of outputs is much larger than the degree of the polynomial. This is indeed the case for the secure k-NN problem when the input data set is very large.

Our Contribution. We give an algorithm (cf. Algorithm 1) to the above defined polynomial reconstruction problem where the goal is to recover the inputs (up to a constant difference) of the randomly chosen monotonic polynomial with positive integer coefficients by observing only their outputs assuming the number of evaluation points is much greater in number compared to the degree of the polynomial. Once $(d + 1)$ inputs are recovered, the degree d *integer* polynomial can be reconstructed using the Lagrange interpolation technique. This result invalidates the security claim in [KKN+18][Theorem 4.2] regarding the leakage profile for Server B. In particular, the Server B will be able to learn the square of the Euclidean distances (up to a constant difference) between the query point and the data set points. It may not be able to tell the exact distance to a given point due to random re-ordering but will be able to know all such values. Such an information can potentially help the adversary to narrow down further if it has access to extra information about the underlying data set or query point.

There can be many solutions to the above polynomial reconstruction problem, and hence we will output one solution that satisfies all the output points, (there is also a possibility to enumerate all the solutions). But as discussed above, when the number of output values is far bigger than the input degree, the number of equivalent solutions will likely be small. Our algorithm readily extends to recovering any integer polynomial (not necessarily a monotonic integer polynomial) and any input range (not necessarily $[0, 2^{\beta} - 1]$). The proposed algorithm (heuristically) runs in time exponential in the size of the inputs (β) and degree (d) of the chosen polynomial, but *polynomially* dependent on the size of the random coefficients (α). We would like to note that in many real world scenarios the inputs are/can be encoded as integers of 16- or 32-bits length and our method is feasible for inputs of such size. Note also that in SHE applications d is required to be not large as well. This is because bigger values of d imply deeper circuits w.r.t. homomorphic multiplications and hence more slow. For the concrete parameters suggested in [KKN+18][Section 4.2], i.e., $\beta = 16$ and $d = 9$, we can recover the inputs (up to a constant difference) for $\alpha = 16$ in a few seconds. We tested our attack using real-world data as well as with uniform random data chosen within the input range, and this is described in detail in Sect. 3.

Lastly, we investigate in Sect. 4 another variant of the protocol of [KKN+18] where the (homomorphically) transformed polynomial outputs are perturbed by a noise, yet maintaining the monotonicity. In this case our previously mentioned attack will not work. But we show that it is still possible to recover ratios of the inputs.

2 Cryptanalysis of a Secure *k*-NN Protocol

In Sect. 2.1 we describe the Secure k-Nearest Neighbour protocol from [KKN+18] and formulate our attack as the polynomial reconstruction problem given only the outputs. We describe our method for polynomial reconstruction and attack on the k-NN protocol in Sect. 2.2. In Sect. 2.3 we provide a heuristic running time analysis of our method. This is followed by an optimisation of our attack in Sect. 2.4.

2.1 Protocol from [KKN+18]

The Secure k-Nearest Neighbour (Secure k-NN) protocol from [KKN+18] makes use of a non-colluding federated two cloud setting (Fig. 1). The data owner outsources his/her database in an encrypted form using an SHE scheme for storage in the Cloud A, whereby the cloud is not privy to the data, thus preserving confidentiality of the data. Each of the n data points are of δ-dimensions. Cloud A provides storage for the database and provides services on the encrypted database homomorphically. One of these services is computation of k-NN of a given δ-dimension query point. End users are clients who are trusted entities for accessing the database and hence possess the secret decryption key shared by the data owner. These users who wish to avail of the computation services provided by Server A form a δ-dimensional query point q, encrypts the same and provides it to Server A.

When Server A receives the query, it homomorphically computes the square of the Euclidean Distances (ED) between the δ-dimensional query point and each of the n data points; if the query point is of the form $q = (q_1, q_2, \ldots, q_\delta)$ and the kth data point is of the form $(k_1, k_2, \ldots, k_\delta)$, then the Euclidean distance between this k^{th} data point and q is $ED_k^2 = (q_1 - k_1)^2 + (q_2 - k_2)^2 + \ldots (q_\delta - k_\delta)^2$. This needs to be computed for each of the n data points in an encrypted manner. Because this ED computation is of multiplicative depth 1, it can be efficiently evaluated using an SHE scheme. The plaintext data points and the query point are encoded as tuples of integers. Note that in the context of F/SHE schemes, fixed-point values too are (exactly) encoded using essentially the scaled-integer representation [CSVW16]. Since the Server A does not possess the decryption key, it will not be able to efficiently uncover the underlying plaintext information of either the query point or the data points. It now picks a monotonic polynomial $p(x)$ of degree d of the form $a_0 + a_1 \cdot x + a_2 \cdot x^2 + \ldots + a_d \cdot x^d$ for some chosen $d \in \mathbb{N}$, where each of the *integer* coefficients a_i are picked uniform randomly and independently in the range $[1, 2^\alpha - 1]$, for example in the range $[1, 2^{32} - 1]$ as done in [KKN+18][Section 3.4]. This polynomial is then evaluated homomorphically for each of the Euclidean distances and the output ciphertexts are re-ordered using a permutation σ picked uniformly at random, before sending them to Server B for sorting.

Server B possesses the decryption key using which it will decrypt the values received from Server A and sorts them. As the decrypted values are outputs of a random polynomial, the original distances as computed by Server A are "hidden" from Server B. Server B would then send the indices of k-NNs to Server A which would then apply σ^{-1} to the received ordering of the indices and forward the same to the client. The client would decrypt the encrypted indices of the k-NNs of the query point q.

The Server B (and also A) is assumed to be honest but curious. It will perform the computations correctly but is keen to learn more about the distances between the query point and the data set points. After decryption, the Server B would observe only the outputs of the polynomial evaluation (and *not* the input

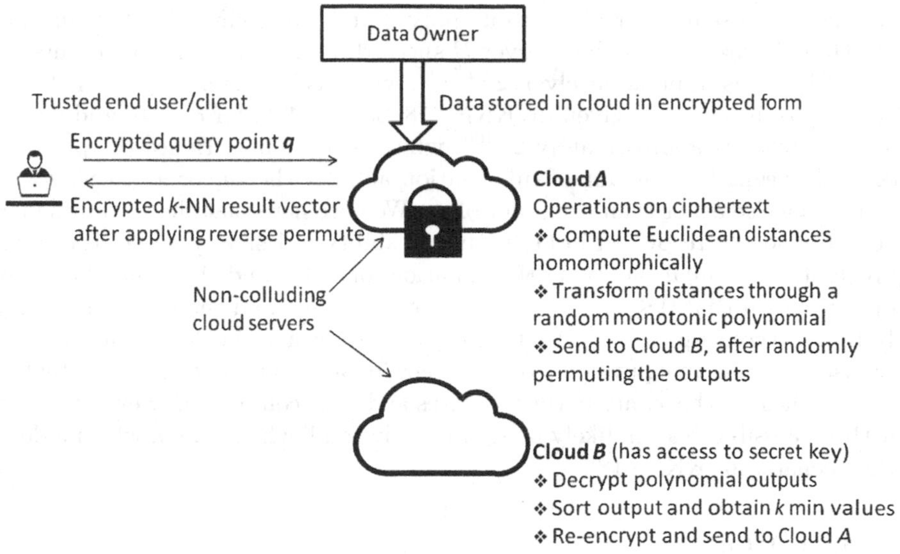

Fig. 1. Secure k-NN Setting from [KKN+18]

squared distances). That is, it only sees the values on the L.H.S. of the following set of equations:

$$\begin{aligned} p(x_1) &= a_0 + a_1 \cdot x_1 + a_2 \cdot x_1^2 + \ldots + a_d \cdot x_1^d \\ p(x_2) &= a_0 + a_1 \cdot x_2 + a_2 \cdot x_2^2 + \ldots + a_d \cdot x_2^d \\ &\vdots \\ p(x_n) &= a_0 + a_1 \cdot x_n + a_2 \cdot x_n^2 + \ldots + a_d \cdot x_n^d \end{aligned} \tag{1}$$

It is assumed that the adversary B knows the degree d as it is usually small since homomorphic evaluation of polynomials in encrypted form are efficient only for small degree. It also knows the range $[1, \ldots, 2^\alpha - 1]$ for the unknown coefficients a_i, and the range $[0, \ldots, 2^\beta - 1]$ for the unknown inputs x_i. For our attack, we need not know the exact values for the above three parameters, just an upper bound on them would suffice. Also note that all the parameters above take non-negative integer values.

As noted before, Server A evaluates the polynomial $p(x)$ at n (squared Euclidean distance) integer values $x_1, \ldots, x_n$, and we can assume without loss of generality that $0 \le x_1 \le x_2 \le \ldots \le x_n$. Since $p(x)$ is monotonic the ordering of $p(x_i)$ is identical to the ordering of x_i (except possibly when there is equality). If $a_0 \le x_1$, then for any given tuple of coefficients $(a_0, a_1, \ldots, a_d)$, there will be a set of positive real roots $(\chi_1, \chi_2, \ldots, \chi_d)$ to (1). Hence the authors of [KKN+18] seem to argue that if the range for a_i is large enough, then it will be infeasible to search for all possible polynomials satisfying (1). The authors claim that the probability that Server B successfully recovers the coefficients a_i, followed by x_i, is approximately $1/2^{\alpha \cdot (d+1)}$, which is negligible when α is large. Referring to the example given in [KKN+18, Section 4.2], for $\alpha = 16$ and $d = 9$, this probability is approximately 2^{-160}, which is negligible. Hence the protocol leaks only negligible amount of information about either a_i or x_i to Server B and nothing else other than the order of x_i. We note here that the x_i values may never be uniquely recovered in (1) with probability $= 1$ since $p(x + c)$ is also an equivalent polynomial satisfying the equation for $c \in \mathbb{Z}$ and there may be many values of c such that $0 \leq x_i - c < 2^{\beta}$. Hence the inputs and the polynomial may only be recovered up to a constant difference. Other non-linear transformations may also result in an equivalent solution. For instance, $p(\sqrt{x})$ can be a potential solution when all the x_i are perfect squares and $p(x)$ contains only even powers. But these possibilities will likely be significantly small when $n \gg d$, which indeed is the scenario in [KKN+18].

2.2 Our Attack

Our key idea is to dramatically reduce the search space of x_i by using the fact that all the roots should be non-negative integers, not just non-negative real values. The pseudocode of our method is given in Algorithm 1 on Page 10 and is described in the steps below.

Step 1 - Guess the Differences $(x_i - x_j)$**:** Consider the two equations from (1) for $p(x_i)$ and $p(x_j)$, where $i > j$:

$$p(x_i) - p(x_j) = (x_i - x_j)(\cdot). \tag{2}$$

Let $L_{i,j} = (p(x_i) - p(x_j)) \geq 0$ (as $p(x_i) \geq p(x_j)$), and $D_{i,j}$ be the set of positive divisors of $L_{i,j}$ that are less than 2^{β}. From (2) we have that $(x_i - x_j)$ is a "small" divisor of $L_{i,j}$. Note that $0 \leq |x_i - x_j| < 2^{\beta}$. So we can *sieve* all the divisors of $L_{i,j}$ of value less than 2^{β}. In the sieve method, the quotient of $L_{i,j}/(x_i - x_j)$ is divided by its smallest prime factor and the process of dividing the quotient by its smallest prime factor is continued until we get 1. This is where we crucially use the fact that the inputs and the outputs are represented as integers, and that the (plaintext) input space is small enough to enumerate. The list $D_{i,j}$ constitutes the guesses for the differences of the (unknown but to be determined) values x_i. It turns out that for many values of $L_{i,j}$ there may be too many divisors that are less than 2^{β}, so we need to sample larger number of output values (i.e., larger n) and carefully pick up d number of $L_{i,j}$'s such that the value of each $D_{i,j}$ is a small positive integer (say, $\leq \psi$) whereby the search space for the guesses becomes feasible to enumerate. There is another condition on how we choose the set of d many $L_{i,j}$. Namely, we must be able to determine the required $d + 1$ many x_i from the given guesses for the differences when one of the free variable, say, x_1 is assigned a value. In other words, the corresponding equations must be linearly independent. Because of the existence of one free variable, the input values can only be determined up to a constant difference. Hence we may assign $x_1 = 0$ if the coefficients of the resulting polynomial are within the given range and this polynomial is consistent with the remaining output values.

Each of the $D_{i,j}$ sets can be visualized as entries of a lower triangular matrix with element $D[i][j]$ represented by the set $D_{i,j}$. One way to determine the d independent set of equations is to stick on to elements of Column 1 of the D matrix for simplicity. We walk the elements of the matrix examining the number of divisors of each of the $D_{i,1}$ lists. As soon as $D_{i,1}$ is greater than ψ, we discard the elements in the particular row $D[i]$. This is continued until we get at least d valid rows in the D matrix. We again note here that the ith row element of Column 1 of D matrix contains sets of divisors for each of $(p(x_i) - p(x_1))$ for $2 \leq i \leq n$ respectively. In Step 2 we look for a consistent set of divisors from Column 1 and in Step 3 we use these d guesses of x_i together with x_1 to compute the required degree d polynomial using Lagrange interpolation and check whether this polynomial is consistent with the remaining $n-d-1$ output values.

Step 2 - Consistency Check of the Guessed Differences: In Step 1 we would have obtained d rows of divisors of polynomial differences in the D matrix that contains the set of guesses for each of the d differences among the unknown inputs. In this step we try to filter out as many guessed tuples as possible before executing the Step 3. This is because the Step 3 below consists of performing Lagrange interpolation and then checking the validity of the constructed polynomial on the remaining inputs and these steps are quite expensive to perform for all the guessed tuples. We iterate over every d-tuple of divisors/guesses in Column 1 of the D matrix and examine to check if that guessed divisor is *consistent* as explained below. For integers i, j with $D_{i,1}$, $D_{j,1}$ representing the set of divisors in Rows i and j in Column 1 of D and given divisors $d_i \in D_{i,1}$ and $d_j \in D_{j,1}$, then d_i and d_j are said to be *consistent* if $(d_i - d_j) \in D_{i,j}$. This is so because if $(x_i - x_1)$ is a divisor of $L_{i,1}$ and $(x_j - x_1)$ is a divisor of $L_{j,1}$ then $(x_i - x_j)$ must be present in $D_{i,j}$, which is evident in the way $L_{i,j}$ is obtained from (2). Only the consistent values are considered and copied to an array *state*[]. In summary, the output of this step is the array *state* where each of its elements is a consistent divisor of $L_{j,1}$ obtained as above, and it is consistent with every value of $state[j], i \neq j$.

Step 3 - Find a Probable Polynomial and Verify Its Suitability: Lagrange interpolation using the $(d+1)$ number of (x, y) tuples is used to compute a degree d polynomial. The x values are based on values found in Step 2 and the corresponding y values are the corresponding polynomial outputs, such that if x_i is a divisor of $L_{i,1}$ then y_i is the ith polynomial output enumerated in order. Since the x values are guesses based on differences of d values of $(x_i - x_1)$, the polynomial obtained by setting x_1 to 0 can actually be a potential polynomial solution. If the polynomial coefficients do not happen to lie within $[1,2^{\alpha})$, we can iterate over successive integer values of x from 0 up to $(2^{\beta} - 1)$, using it as an offset for each of the $(d + 1)$ values of x to get solutions that indeed satify the needed bounds. Once a candidate polynomial is identified, using the remaining $(n - d - 1)$ points we verify the correctness by computing the roots of this polynomial and checking if they are all in the range $[0, 2^\beta)$. If these verification steps are successful, then the algorithm outputs the coefficients of a polynomial that takes the same values as those of the n input points, and these points are unique up to a constant difference. In other words, the differences of the Euclidean distances are thus recovered in the most likely scenario.

2.3 Running Time Analysis

It looks difficult to do a tight analysis as we need to know the distribution of the divisors of the polynomial outputs evaluated at independent and uniformly random inputs. Hence we only provide a heuristic bound on the expected running time.

Our method makes use of the sieving method to find divisors, in the given range, of the polynomial differences. We then use Lagrange interpolation over $(d + 1)$ points to find a polynomial, and then find roots for $c = (n - d - 1)$ polynomials that satisfy the validity checks mentioned in Step 3 of Algorithm 1. While the first polynomial output by Lagrange interpolation is very likely the candidate polynomial, we may need to iterate over more values of x_1 (bounded by 2^β) until the polynomial coefficients lie in the range $[1,2^\alpha)$ and all the x_i are in $[0,2^\beta)$.

Suppose we consider ψ as a small integer bound on the number of divisors for each of the d polynomial differences. Then the bound on the size of the search space for the divisors is ψ^d. The number of divisors of an integer N is bounded by $N^{O\left(\frac{1}{\log \log N}\right)}$; and on the average case it is $\log N$ [Tao08]. Though we only consider divisors bounded by 2^β, for ease of analysis we use the $\log N$ expected bound. Based on this, we can set the value of ψ to be approximately equal to $\alpha + d\beta$, whereby the expected value of search space size is $O(\alpha + d\beta)^d$. We then find the consistent set of divisors as described in Step 2 of Algorithm 1 and the worst case scenario to assume is that all the d-tuple divisors/guesses are consistent. Using each of the ψ^d many d-tuple divisors/guesses, in the worst case, we need to iterate over 2^β values of x_1 doing a Lagrange interpolation for $(d + 1)$ points and root finding for c polynomials. With Lagrange interpolation being a $O(d^2 \cdot (\alpha + d\beta)^2)$ algorithm and so is the cost of a root finding, then the total cost for Step 3 comes to $\tilde{O}(\alpha + d\beta)^d \cdot 2^\beta \cdot n)$.

The heuristic expected running time of Algorithm 1 is $\tilde{O}((\alpha + d\beta)^d \cdot 2^\beta \cdot n)$.

2.4 Further Optimisation

In Algorithm 1, in the worst case, we need to enumerate over ψ^d many d-tuples of divisors/guesses. We provide here a way to choose the divisor sets such that the enumeration complexity is as small as possible.

We refer to (1) giving the polynomial outputs. We compute differences $p(x_i) - p(x_j)$, where $p(x_i) \geq p(x_j)$ if $x_i \geq x_j$. These ${}^nC_2$ values can be represented as lower a triangular matrix L, with elements $L_{i,j}$ as described in Step 1 of Algorithm 1, is given below :

Algorithm 1: Integer Polynomial Reconstruction From Only the Outputs

```
Procedure Main(Polynomial outputs : {p(x_1), ..., p(x_n)}) :
    D = GuessTheDifference({p(x_1), ..., p(x_n)}, ψ)
    state = CheckConsistency(D)
    Q = FindCandidatePolynomial(state, {p(x_1), ..., p(x_n)})
    return Q

Procedure GuessTheDifference(Polynomial outputs : {p(x_1), ..., p(x_n)}, ψ) :
    for i = 2 to (n) do
        for j = 1 to (i − 1) do
            Use the sieve method to obtain all the (positive) divisors less than 2^β of
            L_{i,j} = (p(x_i) − p(x_j)) /* p(x_i) > p(x_j) */
            D_{i,j} := Set of all divisors of L_{i,j} less than 2^β
        end
    end
    /* We now have D: a lower triangular matrix */
    valid_row_count = 0 /* Count rows in which all row elements have their divisor count
    less than ψ */
    forall the D_i do
        forall the D_{i,j} elements in D_i do
            if Sizeof(D_{i,j}) > ψ then
                /* Number of factors of D_{i,j} more than threshold */
                Discard row D_i /* Mark D_{i,1} as -1 */
                Break out of this loop and start enumeration on row D_{i+1}
            end
        end
        valid_row_count++
        if valid_row_count == d then
            /* We now have d valid rows in D matrix */
            break /* Out of outer loop */
        end
    end
    Compact D matrix by removing all rows having first element = -1.
    /* First row of D contains 0s, next (d + 1) rows contain valid values */
    return D /* Set of divisors matrix */

Procedure CheckConsistency(Set of positive divisors matrix D) :
    for i = 3 to (d + 2) do
        for j = (i − 1) downto 2 do
            ∀(d_i, d_j) where d_i ∈ D_{i,1} and d_j ∈ D_{j,1} and d_i ≠ 0, d_j ≠ 0
            if (d_i − d_j) ∉ D_{i,j} then
                Set d_i = 0 in D_{i,1}
            end
        end
    end
    forall the d_j ≠ 0 ∈ D_{2,1} do
        for i = 3 to (d + 2) do
            if d_i ≠ 0 and (d_i − d_j) ∉ D_{i,1} then
                Set d_j = 0 in D_{2,1}
            end
        end
    end
    Iterate over D_i and populate state[i] with non-zero divisor of D_{i,0} where i is suitably
    offset to populate state[] starting from index 0
    return state[] /* Divisor set consistent over all elements ∈ L */

/* Continued on next page */
```

Procedure `FindCandidatePolynomial`(*Consistent Divisor set* $\{state\}$, *Polynomial outputs* $\{p(x_1), \ldots, p(x_n)\}$) :

```
for ν = 0 to (2^β − 1) do
    for i = 0 to d do
        Form a set of tuples G := {(a, b) : a = (ν + state[i]) and b = p(x_i)}
    end
    Use Lagrange interpolation on G to get polynomial Q
    Verify if 1 ≤ coefficient of Q < 2^α is true for all coefficients of Q
    Verify if Q has non-negative integer roots, which are < 2^β, with respect
    to the remaining (n − d − 1) polynomial outputs, namely, p(x_{d+2}) to
    p(x_n).
    If all the above verification steps are successful, return Q
end
return 0
```

$$L = \begin{pmatrix} 0 & 0 & 0 & \ldots & 0 \\ p(x_2) - p(x_1) & 0 & 0 & \ldots & 0 \\ p(x_3) - p(x_1) & p(x_3) - p(x_2) & 0 & \ldots & 0 \\ \vdots & & & & \\ p(x_n) - p(x_1) & p(x_n) - p(x_2) & p(x_n) - p(x_3) \ldots & p(x_n) - p(x_{n-1}) & 0 \end{pmatrix}$$

The number of divisors for each of the differences up to a bound ψ are obtained by sieving, represented as a matrix D where the element D_{ij} represents the set of divisors (with values $< 2^\beta$) of $(p(x_i) - p(x_j))$.

$$D = \begin{pmatrix} 0 & 0 & 0 & \ldots & 0 \\ D_{2,1} & 0 & 0 & \ldots & 0 \\ D_{3,1} & D_{3,2} & 0 & \ldots & 0 \\ \vdots & & & & \\ D_{n,1} & D_{n,2} & D_{n,3} & \ldots \; D_{n,n-1} & 0 \end{pmatrix}$$

We now need to find the set of d many D_{ij} elements of the matrix D such that $\prod D_{ij}$ is minimum, in other words, the product of the number of guesses is minimum. This set of elements in the matrix D can be visualized as a complete undirected graph on n vertices wherein the number of elements in D_{ij} is the edge cost between nodes V_i and V_j. Now finding the minimum $\prod D_{ij}$ is akin to finding the d-Minimum Spanning Tree (i.e., a minimum weight tree with d edges only) in the graph, where the weight of the tree is represented by the product of the weights. The requirement that the subgraph is a tree comes from the linear independence requirement of the corresponding set of equations. Essentially, we are transforming the problem of finding the small search space of divisors to the problem of finding a d-minimum spanning tree having the least cost (in terms of divisor product) across all divisors sets of matrix D yet satisfying the linear independence condition. It is shown in [RSM+96] that the d-MST problem is NP-hard for points in the Euclidean plane. The same paper provides an approximation algorithm to find d-MST with performance ratio of $2\sqrt{d}$ for a general edge-weighted graph, with non-negative edge weights. Note that this approximation algorithm also works for multiplication of edge weights (weights greater than 1) since by extraction of logarithms this can be trivially turned into addition of edge weights. Using this algorithm, we can carefully select $d < n$ nodes having close to the minimum enumeration complexity. In order to make our search space feasible to guess the differences $(x_i - x_j)$ with $x_i \geq x_j$. From the d-MST so obtained, we can now go on to find the set of divisors $(x_i - x_j)$ such that they are consistent as explained in Sect. 2.2 and continue with finding the polynomial coefficients using Lagrange interpolation as described in Algorithm 1. However, we did not implement this optimisation in our code as the concrete running time was already small enough. But for larger instances this optimisation will be useful.

3 Experiments and Results

We have performed two sets of experiments using the SAGE library [The19]. Our source code is available at [MV]. One set consists of choosing random values within given bounds for x_i and a_i, computing the outputs of a degree d polynomial, and trying to recover the coefficients of the polynomial, namely the a_i values using only the polynomial output values. The second set consists of using data available from the UCI Machine learning repository [DG17] which is a real-world hospital data obtained from a hospital in Caracas, Venezuela.

All our experiments were run on a Lenovo ThinkStation P920 workstation having a 2.3 GHz Intel®Xeon® processor with 12 cores. The algorithms for sieving, consistency check and polynomial verification were exactly same in both the cases, the only difference being in the datasets as described in the respective sections below. As in [KKN+18], we have chosen the degree of the polynomial $d = 9$.

3.1 Experiments with Random Values

We set the bound for a_i and x_i as given in Table 1 with the values being uniform random and independently chosen from the respective ranges. We computed the polynomial with a_i as coefficients and computed $n = 40$ outputs for the x_i values. These n values were the input to our algorithm. The choice of $n = 40$ was based on observations from the experiments; in majority of the instances we could bound the number of divisors to less than 20 thereby making the search space significantly less than 20^{10}. We then used the divisor set and $(d+1)$ polynomial outputs to compute a possible polynomial using Lagrange interpolation which we then used to verify successfully against the remaining $(n - d - 1)$ output values. We note that our search space is significantly less than the estimate of

2^{160} in [KKN+18]. It looks like many further optimization could be done to reduce the search space. When we increased β to 32 for x_i, SAGE encountered an out-of-memory error while performing Lagrange interpolation. But we think it should still be feasible to run this instance too.

Table 1. Run times for polynomial reconstruction for random parameters.

α (in bits)	β (in bits)	Run time (in seconds)
16	16	4
16	24	288
16	28	552
24	16	8
24	24	374
24	28	1283
32	16	9
32	24	241
32	28	1676

3.2 Experiments with Real World Data

We used the cervical cancer (risk factors) data set, same as the one used by [KKN+18], also available from the UCI Machine learning repository [DG17]. This data set consists of information pertaining to 858 patients, each consisting of 32 attributes comprising of demographic information, habits and historic medical records. The dataset had a few missing values due to privacy concerns and these were set to 0. Values with fractional part were rounded off to the nearest integer. We repeated the experiment with different random polynomials and were able to recover the polynomial successfully up to the differences. We also tested with 16, 24 and 32 bit values of α and have tabulated the time taken by SAGE to compute the polynomial in each of the cases. $\beta = 16$ was suffice to encode this data. Time for execution is given seconds and is averaged over 5 runs in each case.

Our results invalidate the security claims in [KKN+18][Theorem 4.2] regarding the leakage profile for Server B. For the parameters mentioned in [KKN+18] [Sect. 4.2], i.e., $d = 9$ and the (squared plaintext) distances are in the range $[0, 2^{\beta})$, where, $\beta = 16$. For the parameters mentioned there, with only $n = 40$ output values, we could recover the coefficients of the polynomial (up to a constant difference) within a few minutes as given in Table 2.

Because of the random re-ordering of the distances, Server B will not learn the exact distance of the query point to a specified point (say the ith point in the original order). Nevertheless, in many real world scenarios the data set is publicly available and this, and perhaps other auxilliary information, may potentially be used in combination with our results to leak information about the query point.

Table 2. Run times for polynomial reconstruction for a real world data.

α (in bits)	β (in bits)	Run time (in seconds)
16	16	2.25
24	16	73.81
32	16	109.87

4 Attack on the Secure k-NN Protocol in the Noisy Setting

In this section we give another attack on the protocol of [KKN+18] if one tries to overcome our attack from Sect. 2 by perturbing the polynomial outputs by adding noisy error terms. This modified protocol is not mentioned in [KKN+18] but we consider it here for completeness.

In the original solution given in [KKN+18], in order to hide the Euclidean distance values, Server A chooses a monotonic polynomial and homomorphically evaluates this polynomial on its computed distances and permutes the order before sending them to Server B. Now, instead of sending these (encrypted) polynomial outputs as it is, if they are perturbed with some noise such that the ordering is still maintained, it will make our attack in Sect. 2 unsuccessful in recovering the polynomial or the inputs, as the attack relies on the exact difference of the polynomial outputs. It is easy to see that the error value can only be as large as the sum of all the coefficients except the constant term. Let $P(x) = a_0 + a_1 \cdot x + \ldots + a_d \cdot x^d$ be the chosen monotonic polynomial, then, $P(0) = a_0$, $P(1) = a_0 + a_1 + \ldots + a_d$ and the maximum value of the added noise needs to be less than $(P(1) - P(0))$ so as to maintain the original ordering of polynomial outputs, meaning the perturbation error may only be chosen from the set $[0, 1, \ldots, (a_1 + \ldots + a_d)]$. This safe choice of the error term is due to the fact that the polynomial output values are encrypted and hence it is not possible for the Server A to inspect the value and accordingly choose the error term. The range of perturbation error terms still depends on the size of the coefficient space that can potentially be very large (unlike the plaintext space as assumed). The attack presented in the previous section will not work in this new setting because in the attack we rely on the exact differences of the polynomial outputs.

In this new setting, we next show that it is still possible to leak ratios of the inputs to the Server B, although recovering the exact values (even up to to a constant difference) may be challenging. But still a lot more information about the inputs is leaked than just a single bit. Let two of the values that the Adversary B obtains after decryption be $F(x_i) = P(x_i) + e_i$ and $F(x_j) = P(x_j) + e_j$, where e_i and e_j are the random error terms such that $0 \leq e_i, e_j < \sum_{k=1}^{d} a_k$ and $1 \leq a_k < 2^\alpha$. Consider the ratio $F(x_i)/F(x_j)$ with $0 \leq x_j \leq x_i < 2^\beta$:

$$\frac{F(x_i)}{F(x_j)} = \frac{(\sum_{k=0}^{d} a_k) + a_1 \cdot x_i + \ldots + a_d \cdot x_i^d}{(\sum_{k=0}^{d} a_k) + a_1 \cdot x_j + \ldots + a_d \cdot x_j^d}. \tag{3}$$

Note that each $F(x_k) > 0$. When x_i and x_j are sufficiently large we obtain that the ratio in (3) is approximately close to $(x_i/x_j)^d$. By taking the dth root of this value, we can recover the ratio (x_i/x_j). Note also that if the error terms e_k were not significantly small than the leading terms (which, fortunately, is *not* the case), then we would not be able to recover the ratios.

5 Conclusion and Future Work

In this paper we give an attack on the protocol of [KKN+18] for Secure k-NN on encrypted data. This attack is based on our algorithm for integer polynomial reconstruction given only the outputs. While, by just using the outputs, it is not possible to accurately determine the coefficients or the inputs, we show that we can feasibly recover the inputs (up to a constant difference) of size about 32 bits when the number of outputs is much bigger than the degree of the polynomial. Our experiments were conducted both on uniformly randomly selected values as well as a real-world dataset. Since many of the datasets are available in the public domain it may possible for an adversary to derive more information about the exact values using our method together with some other available metadata.

Our method for polynomial reconstruction runs in exponential time in plaintext space β and degree d of the chosen polynomial. In many real-world scenarios both these parameters will be small. Future work can look at having a better algorithm and/or have a lower bound analysis of the time required for this polynomial reconstruction problem. Finally, an FHE solution that can perform efficient sorting and searching on large datasets would eliminate the need for service providers to be entrusted with decryption keys, thereby providing a more secure cloud computation environment.

Acknowledgements. We thank Sonata Software Limited, Bengaluru, India for funding this work. We also thank Debdeep Mukhopadhyay and Sikhar Patranabis for helpful discussions.

References

[BCLO09] Boldyreva, A., Chenette, N., Lee, Y., O'Neill, A.: Order-preserving symmetric encryption. In: Joux, A. (ed.) EUROCRYPT 2009. LNCS, vol. 5479, pp. 224–241. Springer, Heidelberg (2009). https://doi.org/10.1007/978-3-642-01001-9_13

[Ber68] Berlekamp, E.R.: Algebraic Coding Theory, vol. 8. McGraw-Hill, New York (1968)

[BGV12] Brakerski, Z., Gentry, C., Vaikuntanathan, V.: (Leveled) fully homomorphic encryption without bootstrapping. In: Proceedings of the 3rd Innovations in Theoretical Computer Science Conference, ITCS 2012, pp. 309–325. ACM, New York (2012)

[BLR+15] Boneh, D., Lewi, K., Raykova, M., Sahai, A., Zhandry, M., Zimmerman, J.: Semantically secure order-revealing encryption: multi-input functional encryption without obfuscation. In: Oswald, E., Fischlin, M. (eds.) EUROCRYPT 2015. LNCS, vol. 9057, pp. 563–594. Springer, Heidelberg (2015). https://doi.org/10.1007/978-3-662-46803-6_19

[ÇDSS15] Çetin, G.S., Doröz, Y., Sunar, B., Savaş, E.: Depth optimized efficient homomorphic sorting. In: Lauter, K., Rodríguez-Henríquez, F. (eds.) LATINCRYPT 2015. LNCS, vol. 9230, pp. 61–80. Springer, Cham (2015). https://doi.org/10.1007/978-3-319-22174-8_4

[CGGI19] Chillotti, I., Gama, N., Georgieva, M., Izabachène, M.: TFHE: fast fully homomorphic encryption over the torus. J. Cryptol. (2019)

[CGLB14] Choi, S., Ghinita, G., Lim, H.-S., Bertino, E.: Secure kNN query processing in untrusted cloud environments. IEEE Trans. Knowl. Data Eng. **26**, 2818–2831 (2014)

[CS15] Chatterjee, A., Sengupta, I.: Searching and Sorting of Fully Homomorphic Encrypted Data on cloud. IACR Cryptology ePrint Archive 2015/981 (2015)

[ÇS19] Çetin, G.S., Sunar, B.: Homomorphic rank sort using surrogate polynomials. In: Lange, T., Dunkelman, O. (eds.) LATINCRYPT 2017. LNCS, vol. 11368, pp. 311–326. Springer, Cham (2019). https://doi.org/10.1007/978-3-030-25283-0_17

[CSVW16] Costache, A., Smart, N.P., Vivek, S., Waller, A.: Fixed-point arithmetic in SHE schemes. In: Avanzi, R., Heys, H. (eds.) SAC 2016. LNCS, vol. 10532, pp. 401–422. Springer, Cham (2017). https://doi.org/10.1007/978-3-319-69453-5_22

[DG17] Dua, D., Graff, C.: UCI Machine Learning Repository (2017)

[ESJ14] Elmehdwi, Y., Samanthula, B.K., Jiang, W.: Secure k-nearest neighbor query over encrypted data in outsourced environments. In: IEEE 30th International Conference on Data Engineering, ICDE 2014, Chicago, IL, USA, 31 March–4 April 2014, pp. 664–675 (2014)

[Gen09] Gentry, C.: A fully homomorphic encryption scheme. Ph.D. thesis, Stanford University, Stanford, CA, USA (2009). AAI3382729

[GRS00] Goldreich, O., Rubinfeld, R., Sudan, M.: Learning polynomials with queries: the highly noisy case. SIAM J. Discrete Math. **13**(4), 535–570 (2000)

[GS99] Guruswami, V., Sudan, M.: Improved decoding of reed-solomon and algebraic-geometry codes. IEEE Trans. Inf. Theory **45**(6), 1757–1767 (1999)

[GSW13] Gentry, C., Sahai, A., Waters, B.: Homomorphic encryption from learning with errors: conceptually-simpler, asymptotically-faster, attribute-based. In: Canetti, R., Garay, J.A. (eds.) CRYPTO 2013. LNCS, vol. 8042, pp. 75–92. Springer, Heidelberg (2013). https://doi.org/10.1007/978-3-642-40041-4_5

[KKN+18] Kesarwani, M., et al.: Efficient secure k-nearest neighbours over encrypted data. In: Proceedings of the 21th International Conference on Extending Database Technology, EDBT 2018, Vienna, Austria, 26–29 March 2018, pp. 564–575 (2018)

[MV] Murthy, S., Vivek, S.: http://github.com/shyamsmurthy/knn_polynomial_recovery. Accessed 22nd Sept 2019. 15:30

[RSM+96] Ravi, R., Sundaram, R., Marathe, M.V., Rosenkrantz, D.J., Ravi, S.S.: Spanning trees - short or small. SIAM J. Discrete Math. **9**(2), 178–200 (1996)

[SHSK15] Songhori, E.M., Hussain, S.U., Sadeghi, A.-R., Koushanfar, F.: Compacting privacy-preserving k-nearest neighbor search using logic synthesis. In: 2015 52nd ACM/EDAC/IEEE Design Automation Conference (DAC), pp. 1–6 (2015)

[Tao08] Tao, T.: Blog: the divisor bound (2008). https://terrytao.wordpress.com/2008/09/23/the-divisor-bound/. Accessed 19 July 2019. at 15:30

[The19] The Sage Developers: SageMath, the Sage Mathematics Software System (Version 8.4) (2019). https://www.sagemath.org

[WCKM09] Wong, W.K., Cheung, D.W., Kao, B., Mamoulis, N.: Secure kNN Computation on encrypted databases. In: Proceedings of the 2009 ACM SIGMOD International Conference on Management of Data, SIGMOD 2009, pp. 139–152. ACM, New York (2009)

[XLY13] Xiao, X., Li, F., Yao, B.: Secure nearest neighbor revisited. In: Proceedings of the 2013 IEEE International Conference on Data Engineering (ICDE 2013), ICDE 2013, pp. 733–744, Washington, DC, USA. IEEE Computer Society (2013)

[ZHT16] Zhu, Y., Huang, Z., Takagi, T.: Secure and controllable k-NN query over encrypted cloud data with key confidentiality. J. Parallel Distrib. Comput. **89**(C), 1–12 (2016)

Quantum-Secure (Non-)Sequential Aggregate Message Authentication Codes

Shingo Sato[1(✉)] and Junji Shikata[1,2]

[1] Graduate School of Environment and Information Sciences, Yokohama National University, Yokohama, Japan
sato-shingo-cz@ynu.jp, shikata-junji-rb@ynu.ac.jp

[2] Institute of Advanced Sciences, Yokohama National University, Yokohama, Japan

Abstract. Recently, the post-quantum cryptography becomes the object of attention, since quantum algorithms breaking the existing cryptosystems have been proposed and the development of quantum computers has been promoted. In fact, quantum-secure systems have been studied in both areas of public key cryptography and symmetric key cryptography. This paper studies quantum security of message authentication codes (MACs) with advanced functionality of compressing multiple tags, so-called aggregate message authentication codes (AMACs) and sequential aggregate message authentication codes (SAMACs).

In this paper, we present AMAC/SAMAC schemes meeting quantum security in the model where adversaries can submit quantum queries. Specifically, we first formalize the quantum security for AMAC/SAMAC schemes. Second, we propose AMAC/SAMAC schemes satisfying the quantum security. Regarding AMACs, we show that Katz-Lindell scheme meets the quantum security. Regarding SAMACs, since the existing schemes are insecure, we newly present two generic constructions: One is constructed from quantum pseudorandom functions, and the other is constructed from randomized pseudorandom generators and (classical) pseudorandom functions.

1 Introduction

1.1 Background

Message authentication codes (MACs) are fundamental and important primitives in symmetric cryptography for message authentication by generating MAC tags on messages. Aggregate MACs (AMACs) are MACs that can compress multiple MAC tags on multiple messages into short tags. When many MAC tags are sent to a receiver via a network, AMACs are effective since it is possible to reduce the total size of MAC tags. In [13], Katz and Lindell formalized the model and security of AMACs for the first time, and proposed a generic construction starting from any MACs. Sequential aggregate MAC (SAMACs) are AMACs that can check validity of the order of sequential messages. We can consider several applications of SAMACs such as mobile ad-hoc networks (MANETs),

M. Albrecht (Ed.): IMACC 2019, LNCS 11929, pp. 295–316, 2019.
https://doi.org/10.1007/978-3-030-35199-1_15

border gateway protocol security (BGPSec), and others for resource-constrained devices. In [8], Eikemeier et al. defined the model and security of SAMACs, and they proposed a generic construction from any MACs and pseudorandom permutations. In [10], Hirose and Kuwakado formalized forward security of SAMACs and proposed a generic construction from any pseudorandom function (PRF) and any pseudorandom generator. Tomita et al. [19] defined sequential aggregate authentication codes with information-theoretic (one-time) security, and they proposed constructions of SAMACs.

Recently, the post-quantum cryptography becomes the object of attention, since quantum algorithms breaking the existing cryptosystems have been proposed and the development of quantum computers has been promoted. In fact, quantum-secure systems have been studied in both areas of public key cryptography and symmetric key cryptography. For public key cryptography, it is known that by using quantum algorithms, we can break cryptographic systems based on the integer factoring and discrete logarithm problems [16,17], and post-quantum cryptography received much attention for this reason. In addition, the post-quantum cryptography standardization project is currently in progress by the NIST (National Institute of Standards Technology) [15]. In symmetric key cryptography, it is also important to study quantum security. In particular, we focus on the security model where adversaries are allowed to submit quantum queries to oracles, which we call quantum query model, since we would like to establish quantum-secure systems in a stronger sense. It is known that there exist quantum attacks against MAC schemes such as CBC-MAC, PMAC, and Carter-Wegman MAC in this model [4,12]. In prior work, various MAC schemes satisfying the security in the quantum query model have been proposed. In [4], Boneh and Zhandry defined the security of MACs in this model for the first time. They also proposed several MAC schemes meeting this security: a variant of Carter-Wegman MAC, pseudorandom functions meeting the quantum security defined in [21], and a q-time MAC scheme, where q is the number of classical/quantum queries to the tagging oracle. In [18], Song and Yun showed that NMAC and HMAC met the quantum security of pseudorandom functions defined in [21], if the underlying pseudorandom functions meet the quantum security. However, no paper reports about MACs with advanced functionality of compressing multiple tags, AMACs and SAMACs.

1.2 Our Contribution

Our purpose in this paper is to propose quantum-secure AMAC/SAMAC schemes, namely secure AMAC/SAMAC schemes in the quantum query model. To the best of our knowledge, security of AMACs/SAMACs in this model has not been dealt with in the literature. In this paper, we formalize a model and security of AMACs/SAMACs in the quantum query model. Then, we show generic constructions of AMAC/SAMAC schemes that satisfy the security in the quantum query model. Specifically, the contribution of this paper is described as follows.

1. In Sect. 3, we formalize quantum security of AMACs in the quantum query model. In addition, we show that the generic construction of AMAC from any

MACs by Katz and Lindell [13] is quantum-secure, if the underlying MACs meets quantum security defined in [4].

2. In Sect. 4, we formalize quantum security of SAMACs in the quantum query model. Our security formalization includes the existing security definition in [8] in the classical query model, and hence our formalization is considered to be reasonable. In terms of quantum security, we analyze security of known SAMACs, and the results are summarized in Table 1. In particular, we can break the security of SAMACs of [8,19] by using quantum algorithms proposed in [4,12] (see Appendix A for attacking algorithms).
3. In Sect. 5, we propose two generic constructions of SAMACs, SAMAC_1 and SAMAC_2. SAMAC_1 is constructed from any quantum secure pseudorandom function (QPRF), while SAMAC_2 is constructed from any randomized pseudorandom generator (PRG) and any classical PRF. The features of those constructions are explained as follows.
   SAMAC_1 uses a deterministic PRF satisfying the security in the quantum query model. In particular, we can apply the quantum-secure PRF of [18,21] to SAMAC_1, since those are deterministic. More specifically, we can apply NMAC/HMAC to SAMAC_1 as a quantum PRF, since these MACs are shown to be quantum PRFs in [18].
   SAMAC_2 uses a randomized function (i.e., PRG). The advantage of using randomized primitives lies in constructing quantum-secure SAMAC schemes based on assumed computationally hard problems for quantum computers such as the learning parity with noise (LPN) problem. Since LPN-based cryptography has been studied in constructing various cryptographic systems such as public key encryption [7,14], oblivious transfer [5], symmetric key encryption [2], MACs [6], and randomized PRGs/PRFs [2,20], it is even interesting to consider quantum-secure SAMACs from LPN-based primitives. LPN-based primitives consist of randomized algorithms, and hence, those can be applied to SAMAC_2. In particular, we can apply randomized PRGs [2,20] based on the LPN problem to SAMAC_2 (see Appendix B for the detailed description).

2 Preliminaries

We use the following notation: For a positive integer n, let $[n] := \{1, 2, \ldots, n\}$. For positive integers n_1, n_2 such that $n_1 < n_2$, let $[n_1, n_2] := \{n_1, n_1+1, \ldots, n_2\}$. For n values $x_1, x_2, \ldots, x_n$, let $\{x_i\}_{i \in n}$ be a set $\{x_1, \ldots, x_n\}$ and let $(x_i)_{i \in [n]}$ be a sequence $(x_1, \ldots, x_n)$. For a set $\mathcal{X}$, let $|\mathcal{X}|$ be the number of elements in $\mathcal{X}$. For a set $\mathcal{X}$ and an element $x \in \mathcal{X}$, we write $|x|$ as the bit-length of x. A function $\epsilon = \epsilon(\lambda)$ is negligible if for a large enough λ and all polynomial $p(\lambda)$, it holds that $\epsilon(\lambda) < 1/p(\lambda)$. In this paper, we write $\mathsf{negl}(\lambda) := \epsilon(\lambda)$ for a negligible function ϵ, and $\mathsf{poly}(\lambda)$ means a polynomial of λ. For a randomized algorithm $\mathcal{A}$ and the input x of $\mathcal{A}$, we write $\mathcal{A}(x; r)$ as a deterministic algorithm, where r is randomness used by $\mathcal{A}$. Probabilistic polynomial-time algorithm is abbreviated as PPTA.

Table 1. Security of SAMAC Schemes in the Quantum Query Model: The term "Primitive" means cryptographic primitives required in the generic constructions, "Quantum Security" means security in the quantum query model, and "Attacking algorithm" means a quantum algorithm which makes the target scheme insecure in the quantum query model. PRP means a pseudorandom permutation, A-code means an authentication code with information theoretic (one-time) security, (Q)PRF means a (quantum) pseudorandom function, RPRG means a randomized pseudorandom generator, and PIH means pairwise independent hashing.

Scheme	Primitive	Quantum Security	Attacking algorithm
[8]	MAC	insecure	Quantum algorithm against CBC-MAC
	PRP		(see Section 5.1 in [12])
[19] Scheme 1	A-code	insecure	Quantum algorithm against PIH
[19] Scheme 2	A-code		(see the proof of Lemma 6.3 in [4])
SAMAC_1	QPRF	secure	n/a
SAMAC_2	RPRG	secure	n/a
	PRF		

In addition, we use the following notation for quantum computation as in [4]. We write an n-qubit state $|\psi\rangle$ as a linear combination $|\psi\rangle = \sum_{x\in\{0,1\}^n} \psi_x|x\rangle$ with a basis $\{|x\rangle\}_{x\in\{0,1\}^n}$ and amplitudes $\psi_x \in \mathbb{C}$ such that $\sum_{x\in\{0,1\}^n} |\psi_x|^2 = 1$. When $|\psi\rangle$ is measured, the state x is observed with probability $|\psi_x|^2$. Suppose that we have superposition $|\psi\rangle = \sum_{x\in\mathcal{X},y\in\mathcal{Y},z\in\mathcal{Z}} \psi_{x,y,z}|x,y,z\rangle$, where $\mathcal{X}$ and $\mathcal{Y}$ are finite sets and $\mathcal{Z}$ is a work space. For an oracle $O : \mathcal{X} \to \mathcal{Y}$, we write quantum access to O as a mapping $|\psi\rangle \mapsto \sum_{x\in\mathcal{X},y\in\mathcal{Y},z\in\mathcal{Z}} \psi_{x,y,z}|x, y + O(x), z\rangle$, where $+ : \mathcal{Y} \times \mathcal{Y} \to \mathcal{Y}$ is a certain group operation on $\mathcal{Y}$. Quantum polynomial-time algorithm is abbreviated as QPA.

2.1 Pseudorandom Function and Pseudorandom Generator

A function $\mathsf{PRF} : \mathcal{K} \times \mathcal{X} \to \mathcal{Y}$, where for a security parameter λ, $\mathcal{K} = \mathcal{K}(\lambda)$ is a key space, $\mathcal{X} = \mathcal{X}(\lambda)$ is a domain, and $\mathcal{Y} = \mathcal{Y}(\lambda)$ is a range, is a *pseudorandom function (PRF)*, if the following $\mathsf{Adv}^{\mathrm{pr}}_{\mathcal{D},\mathsf{PRF}}(\lambda)$ is negligible for any PPTA,

$$\mathsf{Adv}^{\mathrm{pr}}_{\mathcal{D},\mathsf{PRF}}(\lambda) := \left|\Pr\left[\mathcal{D}^{\mathsf{PRF}_{\mathsf{k}}(\cdot)}(1^\lambda) \to 1\right] - \Pr\left[\mathcal{D}^{\mathsf{RF}(\cdot)}(1^\lambda) \to 1\right]\right|,$$

where $\mathsf{PRF}_{\mathsf{k}}(\cdot)$ is an oracle which, on input $x \in \mathcal{X}$, outputs $\mathsf{PRF}(\mathsf{k}, x)$, and $\mathsf{RF}(\cdot)$ is an oracle which, on input $x \in \mathcal{X}$, outputs a value $\mathsf{RF}(x)$ of a random function $\mathsf{RF} : \mathcal{X} \to \mathcal{Y}$.

In addition, a quantum PRF (QPRF) is defined in a similar way as above by assuming that $\mathcal{D}$ is any QPA allowed to issue quantum superposition of queries to oracles.

Consider a function $G : \mathcal{X} \to \mathcal{Y}$, where for a security parameter λ, $\mathcal{X} = \mathcal{X}(\lambda)$ is a domain, and $\mathcal{Y} = \mathcal{Y}(\lambda)$ is a range. And, we assume that $|x| < |y|$ holds for all $x \in \mathcal{X}$ and all $y \in \mathcal{Y}$, where $|x|$ and $|y|$ are the bit-lengths of x and y, respectively. Then, G is said to be a *pseudorandom generator (PRG)*, if the following $\mathsf{Adv}^{\mathrm{prg}}_{\mathcal{A},G}(\lambda)$ is negligible for any PPTA $\mathcal{A}$,

$$\mathsf{Adv}^{\mathrm{prg}}_{\mathcal{A},G}(\lambda) := \left|\Pr[\mathcal{A}(G(x)) \to 1 \mid x \xleftarrow{U} \mathcal{X}] - \Pr[\mathcal{A}(y) \to 1 \mid y \xleftarrow{U} \mathcal{Y}]\right|.$$

In addition, a PRG $G : \mathcal{X} \to \mathcal{Y}$ with a randomness space $\mathcal{R}$ is called a *randomized PRG*, if the following $\mathsf{Adv}^{\mathrm{prg}}_{\mathcal{A},G}(\lambda)$ is negligible for any PPTA $\mathcal{A}$,

$$\mathsf{Adv}^{\mathrm{prg}}_{\mathcal{A},G}(\lambda) := \left|\Pr[\mathcal{A}(G(x;r)) \to 1 \mid x \xleftarrow{U} \mathcal{X}; r \xleftarrow{R} \mathcal{R}] - \Pr[\mathcal{A}(y) \to 1 \mid y \xleftarrow{U} \mathcal{Y}]\right|.$$

Note that for a randomized PRG G with a randomness space $\mathcal{R}$ and any seed $x \in \mathcal{X}$, we write $G(x;r)$ as a deterministic function, where randomness $r \in \mathcal{R}$ might not be uniformly distributed.

2.2 Quantum Security of MAC

We describe a message authentication code (MAC) and its security in the quantum query model following [4]. A MAC scheme consists of a tuple of three polynomial-time algorithms $(\mathsf{KGen}, \mathsf{Tag}, \mathsf{Vrfy})$: Let λ be a security parameter, let $\mathcal{K} = \mathcal{K}(\lambda)$ be a key space, let $\mathcal{M} = \mathcal{M}(\lambda)$ be a message space, and let $\mathcal{T} = \mathcal{T}(\lambda)$ be a tag space.

Key Generation. KGen is a randomized algorithm which, on input a security parameter 1^λ, outputs a secret key $\mathsf{k} \in \mathcal{K}$.

Tagging. Tag is a deterministic or randomized algorithm which, on input a secret key $\mathsf{k} \in \mathcal{K}$ and a message $m \in \mathcal{M}$, outputs a tag $\mathsf{t} \in \mathcal{T}$.

Verification. Vrfy is a deterministic algorithm which, on input a secret key $\mathsf{k} \in \mathcal{K}$, a message $m \in \mathcal{M}$, and a tag $\mathsf{t} \in \mathcal{T}$, outputs 1 (accept) or 0 (reject).

As correctness of MACs, we require that a MAC scheme $(\mathsf{KGen}, \mathsf{Tag}, \mathsf{Vrfy})$ meets the following: For all secret keys $\mathsf{k} \leftarrow \mathsf{KGen}(1^\lambda)$ and all messages $m \in \mathcal{M}$, it holds that $1 \leftarrow \mathsf{Vrfy}(\mathsf{k}, m, \mathsf{t})$, where $\mathsf{t} \leftarrow \mathsf{Tag}(\mathsf{k}, m)$.

As security of MACs in the quantum query model, the notion of *existential unforgeability against quantum chosen message attacks* called EUF-qCMA *security* was formalized in [4].

Definition 1 (EUF-qCMA **security** [4]). *A MAC scheme* $\mathsf{MAC} = (\mathsf{KGen}, \mathsf{Tag}, \mathsf{Vrfy})$ *meets* EUF-qCMA *security, if for any QPA* $\mathcal{A}$ *against* MAC, $\mathsf{Adv}^{\mathrm{qcma}}_{\mathcal{A},\mathsf{MAC}}(\lambda) := \Pr[\mathcal{A}\ wins]$ *is negligible, where* $[\mathcal{A}\ wins]$ *is an event that* $\mathcal{A}$ *wins in the following game:*

Setup: *A challenger generates a secret key* $\mathsf{k} \leftarrow \mathsf{KGen}(1^\lambda)$.

Queries: *When $\mathcal{A}$ submits a quantum query (i.e., a superposition of messages) $|\psi\rangle = \sum_{m \in \mathcal{M}, t \in \mathcal{T}, z} \psi_{m,t,z} |m, t, z\rangle$ to the tagging oracle, it chooses randomness r used in* Tag *algorithm, where it does not need to choose randomness r if* Tag *is deterministic. Then, it returns*

$$\sum_{m \in \mathcal{M}, t \in \mathcal{T}, z} \psi_{m,t,z} |m, t \oplus \mathsf{Tag}(\mathsf{k}, m; r), z\rangle.$$

Let q be the number of queries which $\mathcal{A}$ submits to the tagging oracle.

Output: *$\mathcal{A}$ outputs $(q+1)$ message/tag pairs $(m_1, \mathsf{t}_1), \ldots, (m_{q+1}, \mathsf{t}_{q+1})$. $\mathcal{A}$ wins if the following holds:*
- *$1 \leftarrow \mathsf{Vrfy}(\mathsf{k}, m_i, \mathsf{t}_i)$ for all $i \in [q+1]$.*
- *$m_i \neq m_j$ for any distinct $i, j \in [q+1]$.*

3 Quantum-Secure AMAC

3.1 Quantum Security of AMAC

In this section, we formalize quantum security of AMACs by taking into account the quantum security of MACs in [4] and (classical) security of AMACs in [13]. An AMAC scheme consists of four polynomial-time algorithms (KGen, Tag, Agg, AVrfy): Let λ be a security parameter, and let $n = \mathsf{poly}(\lambda)$ be the number of tagging users. $\mathcal{ID} = \{\mathsf{id}_i\}_{i \in [n]} \in \left(\{0,1\}^{\mathcal{O}(\lambda)}\right)^n$ is an ID space, $\mathcal{K} = \mathcal{K}(\lambda)$ is a key space, $\mathcal{M} = \mathcal{M}(\lambda)$ is a message space, and $\mathcal{T} = \mathcal{T}(\lambda)$ is a tag space.

Key Generation. KGen is a randomized algorithm which, on input a security parameter 1^λ and an ID $\mathsf{id} \in \mathcal{ID}$, outputs a secret key $\mathsf{k}_{\mathsf{id}} \in \mathcal{K}$. We write $\mathsf{k}_{\mathsf{id}} \leftarrow \mathsf{KGen}(1^\lambda, \mathsf{id})$.

Tagging. Tag is an algorithm which, on input a secret key $\mathsf{k}_{\mathsf{id}} \in \mathcal{K}$ and a message $m \in \mathcal{M}$, outputs a tag $\mathsf{t} \in \mathcal{T}$. We write $\mathsf{t} \leftarrow \mathsf{Tag}(\mathsf{k}_{\mathsf{id}}, m)$.

Aggregation. Agg is a deterministic algorithm which, on input a set of arbitrary ℓ pairs of IDs and tags $T = \{(\mathsf{id}_{j_i}, \mathsf{t}_i)\}_{i \in [\ell]}$ $(\ell \leq n)$, outputs an aggregate tag τ. We write $\tau \leftarrow \mathsf{Agg}(T)$.

Verification. AVrfy is a deterministic algorithm which, on input a set of secret keys $K = \{\mathsf{k}_{\mathsf{id}_i}\}_{i \in [n]}$, a set of arbitrary ℓ pairs of IDs and messages $M = \{(\mathsf{id}_{j_i}, m_i)\}_{i \in [\ell]}$, and an aggregate tag τ, outputs 1 (accept) or 0 (reject). We write $1/0 \leftarrow \mathsf{AVrfy}(K, M, \tau)$.

We require that an AMAC scheme $\mathsf{AMAC} = (\mathsf{KGen}, \mathsf{Tag}, \mathsf{Agg}, \mathsf{AVrfy})$ meets correctness as follows: For any set $K = \{\mathsf{k}_{\mathsf{id}_i}\}_{i \in [n]}$ of secret keys ($\forall \mathsf{id}_i \in \mathcal{ID}$, $\mathsf{k}_{\mathsf{id}_i} \leftarrow \mathsf{KGen}(1^\lambda, \mathsf{id}_i)$), and any set M of ID/message pairs, it holds that $1 \leftarrow \mathsf{AVrfy}(K, M, \tau)$, where $\tau \leftarrow \mathsf{Agg}(\{\mathsf{id}_{j_i}, \mathsf{t}_i\}_{i \in [\ell]})$, where $\mathsf{t}_i \leftarrow \mathsf{Tag}(\mathsf{k}_{\mathsf{id}_{j_i}}, m_i)$ for $i \in [\ell]$ $(1 \leq \ell \leq n)$.

As security of AMACs in the quantum query model, we define *aggregate unforgeability against quantum chosen message attacks*, which we call aggUF-qCMA security, as follows.

Definition 2 (aggUF-qCMA **security**). *An AMAC scheme* $\mathsf{AMAC} = (\mathsf{KGen}, \mathsf{Tag}, \mathsf{Agg}, \mathsf{AVrfy})$ *meets* aggUF-qCMA *security, if for any QPA* $\mathcal{A}$ *against* AMAC, $\mathsf{Adv}^{\mathrm{agguf-qcma}}_{\mathcal{A},\mathsf{AMAC}}(\lambda) := \Pr[\mathcal{A}\ wins]$ *is negligible, where* $[\mathcal{A}\ wins]$ *is an event that* $\mathcal{A}$ *wins in the following game:*

Setup: *Generate secret keys* $\mathsf{k}_{\mathsf{id}_i} \leftarrow \mathsf{KGen}(1^\lambda, \mathsf{id}_i)$ *for all* $\mathsf{id}_i \in \mathcal{ID}$. *Set a list* $\mathcal{L}_{\mathsf{Cor}} \leftarrow \{\emptyset\}$.

Queries: $\mathcal{A}$ *is allowed to submit queries to the following oracles* $O_{\mathsf{Cor}}, O_{\mathsf{Tag}}$*:*
- O_{Cor}*: Given a query* $\mathsf{id} \in \mathcal{ID}$*, it returns the corresponding key* k_{id} *and sets* $\mathcal{L}_{\mathsf{Cor}} \leftarrow \mathcal{L}_{\mathsf{Cor}} \cup \{\mathsf{id}\}$.
- O_{Tag}*: Given* $\mathsf{id} \in \mathcal{ID}$ *and a query* $|\psi\rangle = \sum_{m\in\mathcal{M},t\in\mathcal{T},z} \psi_{m,t,z}|m,t,z\rangle$ *to the tagging oracle* O_{Tag}*, it chooses randomness* r *used in* Tag *algorithm, where it needs not to choose randomness* r *if* Tag *is deterministic. Then, it returns* $\sum_{m\in\mathcal{M},t\in\mathcal{T},z} \psi_{m,t,z}|m, t\oplus\mathsf{Tag}(\mathsf{k}_{\mathsf{id}}, m; r), z\rangle$*. Let* q *be the number of queries which* $\mathcal{A}$ *submits to* O_{Tag}.

Output: $\mathcal{A}$ *outputs* q *ID/message/tag triplets* $(\mathsf{id}^{(1)}, m^{(1)}, \mathsf{t}^{(1)}), \ldots, (\mathsf{id}^{(q)}, m^{(q)}, \mathsf{t}^{(q)})$*, where* $\mathsf{id}^{(i)} \in \mathcal{ID}$ *for all* $i \in [q]$*, and* (M, τ)*, where* $M = \{(\mathsf{id}_{j_i}, m_i)\}_{i\in[\ell]}$ $(1 \le \ell \le n)$ *is a set of arbitrary* ℓ *pairs of IDs and messages and* τ *is an aggregate tag. Then,* $\mathcal{A}$ *wins if the following holds:*
- $1 \leftarrow \mathsf{AVrfy}(\mathsf{k}_{\mathsf{id}^{(i)}}, (\mathsf{id}^{(i)}, m^{(i)}), \mathsf{t}^{(i)})$ *for all* $i \in [q]$*, and* $1 \leftarrow \mathsf{AVrfy}(K, M, \tau)$.
- *There exists some* $(\mathsf{id}, m) \in M$ *such that* $\mathsf{id} \notin \mathcal{L}_{\mathsf{Cor}}$ *and* $(\mathsf{id}, m) \notin \{(\mathsf{id}^{(1)}, m^{(1)}), \ldots, (\mathsf{id}^{(q)}, m^{(q)})\}$.

Definition 2 is regarded as an extension from both security notions of the quantum security of MACs in [4] and (classical) security of AMACs in [13] from the following reasons:

- Consider a special case $n = \ell = 1$ in Definition 2. Suppose that, in a aggUF-qCMA security game, a QPA $\mathcal{A}$ finally outputs q ID/message/tag triplets $(\mathsf{id}^{(1)}, m^{(1)}, \mathsf{t}^{(1)}), \ldots, (\mathsf{id}^{(1)}, m^{(q)}, \mathsf{t}^{(q)})$ for the same ID, and (M, τ), where $M = \{m\}$ is a set consisting of a single element and τ is a single tag. Then, $\mathcal{A}$ wins, if $1 \leftarrow \mathsf{AVrfy}(\mathsf{k}_{\mathsf{id}^{(1)}}, (\mathsf{id}^{(1)}, m^{(i)}), \mathsf{t}^{(i)})$ for all $i \in [q]$ and $1 \leftarrow \mathsf{AVrfy}(\mathsf{k}_{\mathsf{id}^{(1)}}, m, t)$, and $m \notin \{m^{(1)}, \ldots, m^{(q)}\}$. This is the same as Definition 1, and hence Definition 2 is regarded as an extension from quantum security of MACs in [4].
- Consider a special case where PPTA $\mathcal{A}$ obtains valid q triplets $(\mathsf{id}^{(1)}, m^{(1)}, \mathsf{t}^{(1)}), \ldots, (\mathsf{id}^{(q)}, m^{(q)}, \mathsf{t}^{(q)})$ by having access to the oracle O_{Tag} with classical queries $(\mathsf{id}^{(1)}, m^{(1)}), \ldots, (\mathsf{id}^{(q)}, m^{(q)})$. Suppose that, in aggUF-qCMA security game, $\mathcal{A}$ outputs q ID/message/tag triplets $(\mathsf{id}^{(1)}, m^{(1)}, \mathsf{t}^{(1)}), \ldots, (\mathsf{id}^{(1)}, m^{(q)}, \mathsf{t}^{(q)})$ which he obtained, and (M, τ), where $M = \{(\mathsf{id}_{j_i}, m_i)\}_{i\in[\ell]}$ $(1 \le \ell \le n)$ is a set of arbitrary ℓ pairs of IDs and messages and τ is an aggregate tag. Then, $\mathcal{A}$ wins, if $1 \leftarrow \mathsf{AVrfy}(K, M, \tau)$ and there is some $(\mathsf{id}, m) \in M$ such that $\mathsf{id} \notin \mathcal{L}_{\mathsf{Cor}}$ and $(\mathsf{id}, m) \notin \{(\mathsf{id}^{(1)}, m^{(1)}), \ldots, (\mathsf{id}^{(q)}, m^{(q)})\}$. This is the same as the security definition of AMACs in [13], and ours is an extension of it.

3.2 Katz-Lindell Construction

We show that the Katz-Lindell construction [13] of AMACs meets aggUF-qCMA security. Let $\mathsf{MAC} = (\mathsf{KGen_{MAC}}, \mathsf{Tag_{MAC}}, \mathsf{Vrfy_{MAC}})$ be a deterministic MAC scheme. The Katz-Lindell construction $\mathsf{AMAC_{KL}} = (\mathsf{KGen}, \mathsf{Tag}, \mathsf{Agg}, \mathsf{AVrfy})$ is described as follows:

- $\mathsf{k_{id}} \leftarrow \mathsf{KGen}(1^\lambda, \mathsf{id})$: Generate a key $\mathsf{k} \leftarrow \mathsf{KGen_{MAC}}(1^\lambda)$, and output $\mathsf{k_{id}} := \mathsf{k}$ for an ID $\mathsf{id} \in \mathcal{ID}$.
- $\mathsf{t} \leftarrow \mathsf{Tag}(\mathsf{k_{id}}, m)$: Given a message $m \in \mathcal{M}$, output $\mathsf{t} \leftarrow \mathsf{Tag_{MAC}}(\mathsf{k_{id}}, m) \in \mathcal{T}$.
- $\tau \leftarrow \mathsf{Agg}(\{(\mathsf{id}_{j_1}, \mathsf{t}_1), \dots, (\mathsf{id}_{j_\ell}, \mathsf{t}_\ell)\})$: Output $\tau := \mathsf{t}_1 \oplus \cdots \oplus \mathsf{t}_\ell \in \mathcal{T}$.
- $1/0 \leftarrow \mathsf{AVrfy}(K, M, \tau)$: Given an ID/message set $M = \{(\mathsf{id}_{j_i}, m_i)\}_{i \in [\ell]}$ and an aggregate tag τ, do the following:
  1. $\tilde{\tau} \leftarrow \mathsf{Agg}(\{(\mathsf{id}_{j_1}, \tilde{\mathsf{t}}_1), \dots, (\mathsf{id}_{j_\ell}, \tilde{\mathsf{t}}_\ell)\})$, where $\tilde{\mathsf{t}}_i \leftarrow \mathsf{Tag}(\mathsf{k}_{\mathsf{id}_{j_i}}, m_i)$.
  2. Output 1 if $\tau = \tilde{\tau}$, or output 0 otherwise.

We show the following theorem which states quantum security of the construction $\mathsf{AMAC_{KL}}$.

Theorem 1. *If a deterministic* MAC *meets* EUF-qCMA *security,* $\mathsf{AMAC_{KL}}$ *satisfies* aggUF-qCMA *security.*

Proof. Let $\mathcal{A}$ be a QPA against $\mathsf{AMAC_{KL}}$. We prove the theorem by constructing a PPTA $\mathcal{F}$ breaking the EUF-qCMA security of MAC, in the following way: Given a tagging oracle in EUF-qCMA game, it chooses $\mathsf{id}^* \in \mathcal{ID}$ uniformly at random and generates $\mathsf{k_{id}}$ for all $\mathsf{id} \in \mathcal{ID}$ and a list $\mathcal{L}_{\mathsf{Cor}} \leftarrow \emptyset$. When $\mathcal{A}$ submits queries to O_{Cor} and O_{Tag}, it simulates these oracles as follows:

- O_{Cor}: Take id as input. Abort this game if $\mathsf{id} = \mathsf{id}^*$. Return the corresponding key $\mathsf{k_{id}}$ and set $\mathcal{L}_{\mathsf{Cor}} \leftarrow \mathcal{L}_{\mathsf{Cor}} \cup \{\mathsf{id}\}$ if $\mathsf{id} \neq \mathsf{id}^*$.
- O_{Tag}: Take $(\mathsf{id}, \sum_{m \in \mathcal{M}, t \in \mathcal{T}, z} \psi_{m,t,z} |m, t, z\rangle)$ as input. If $\mathsf{id} = \mathsf{id}^*$, submit the given quantum query to the tagging oracle and return the received quantum superposition. If $\mathsf{id} \neq \mathsf{id}^*$, return $\sum_{m,t,z} \psi_{m,t,z} |m, t \oplus \mathsf{Tag}(\mathsf{k_{id}}, m), z\rangle$.

When $\mathcal{A}$ outputs $(\mathsf{id}^{(1)}, m^{(1)}, \mathsf{t}^{(1)}), \dots, (\mathsf{id}^{(q)}, m^{(q)}, \mathsf{t}^{(q)})$, and (M, τ), $\mathcal{F}$ checks the following:

- For all $\mathsf{id}^{(i)} \neq \mathsf{id}^*$ $(i \in [q])$, we have $1 \leftarrow \mathsf{AVrfy}(\mathsf{k}_{\mathsf{id}^{(i)}}, (\mathsf{id}^{(i)}, m^{(i)}), \mathsf{t}^{(i)})$, and
- there exists some ID/message pair $(\mathsf{id}^*, m^*) \in M$ such that $(\mathsf{id}^*, m^*) \notin \{(\mathsf{id}^{(1)}, m^{(1)}), \dots, (\mathsf{id}^{(q)}, m^{(q)})\}$.

If the output of $\mathcal{A}$ meets these conditions, $\mathcal{F}$ sets $\mathsf{t}^* \leftarrow \tau$ and computes $\mathsf{t}^* \leftarrow \mathsf{t}^* \oplus \mathsf{t}^{(i)}$ for all $(\mathsf{id}^{(i)}, m^{(i)}) \neq (\mathsf{id}^*, m^*)$ $(i \in [q])$. Then, it outputs (m^*, t^*) and all (m, t) such that $(\mathsf{id}^*, m', \mathsf{t}') \in \{(\mathsf{id}^{(i)}, m^{(i)}, \mathsf{t}^{(i)})\}_{i \in [q]}$. If the output of $\mathcal{A}$ does not meet the conditions above, $\mathcal{F}$ aborts this game.

The output of $\mathcal{F}$ is a forgery in EUF-qCMA security game, since the one-more forgery (m^*, t^*) is not in $\{(m^{(1)}, \mathsf{t}^{(1)}), \dots, (m^{(q)}, \mathsf{t}^{(q)})\}$ and the other pairs can be obtained in the straightforward way. Besides, the probability that $\mathcal{A}$ wins without finding a forgery for MACs is at most $1/|\mathcal{T}|$. Thus, we obtain $\mathsf{Adv}^{\mathrm{agguf-qcma}}_{\mathcal{A},\mathsf{AMAC_{KL}}}(\lambda) \leq n \cdot \mathsf{Adv}^{\mathrm{qcma}}_{\mathcal{F},\mathsf{MAC}}(\lambda) + 1/|\mathcal{T}|$, and the proof is completed. □

4 Quantum Security for SAMACs

We define a model of history-free SAMACs and formalize security in the quantum query model, since all existing SAMACs [8,10,19] are history-free. The ordinary SAMACs generate each aggregate tag depending on the local message of a tagging user, a sequence of previous messages, and an aggregate-so-far tag. On the other hand, history-free SAMACs generate each aggregate tag depending only on a local message and an aggregate-so-far tag.

A SAMAC scheme consists of a tuple of three polynomial-time algorithms $(\mathsf{KGen}, \mathsf{STag}, \mathsf{SVrfy})$: Let λ be a security parameter, let $n = \mathsf{poly}(\lambda)$ be the number of tagging users, and a permutation $\sigma : [n] \to [n]$ denotes order information. $\mathcal{ID} = \{\mathsf{id}_i\}_{i\in[n]} \in \left(\{0,1\}^{\mathcal{O}(\lambda)}\right)^n$ is an ID space, $\mathcal{K} = \mathcal{K}(\lambda)$ is a key space, $\mathcal{M} = \mathcal{M}(\lambda)$ is a message space, and $\mathcal{T} = \mathcal{T}(\lambda)$ is a tag space.

Key Generation. KGen is a randomized algorithm which, on input a security parameter 1^λ and an ID $\mathsf{id} \in \mathcal{ID}$, outputs a secret key $\mathsf{k}_{\mathsf{id}} \in \mathcal{K}$. We write $\mathsf{k}_{\mathsf{id}} \leftarrow \mathsf{KGen}(1^\lambda, \mathsf{id})$.

Tagging. STag is an algorithm which, on input a secret key $\mathsf{k}_{\mathsf{id}} \in \mathcal{K}$, a message $m \in \mathcal{M}$, and an aggregate-so-far tag $\tau' \in \mathcal{T}$, outputs an aggregate tag $\tau \in \mathcal{T}$. We write $\tau \leftarrow \mathsf{STag}(\mathsf{k}_{\mathsf{id}}, m, \tau')$. Note that the first tagging user generates an aggregate tag on a local message and an empty symbol $\emptyset_\tau \in \mathcal{T}$ as an aggregate-so-far tag.

Verification. SVrfy is a deterministic algorithm which, on input a set of secret keys $K = \{\mathsf{k}_{\mathsf{id}_i}\}_{i\in[n]}$, a sequence of arbitrary ℓ ID/message pairs $M = ((\mathsf{id}_{\sigma(i)}, m_i))_{i\in[\ell]}$, an aggregate-so-far tag $\tau' \in \mathcal{T}$, and an aggregate tag $\tau \in \mathcal{T}$, outputs 1 (accept) or 0 (reject). We write $1/0 \leftarrow \mathsf{SVrfy}(K, (M, \tau'), \tau)$.

We require that a SAMAC scheme $\mathsf{SAMAC} = (\mathsf{KGen}, \mathsf{STag}, \mathsf{SVrfy})$ meets correctness in the following way: For any set $K = \{\mathsf{k}_{\mathsf{id}_i}\}_{i\in[n]}$ of secret keys ($\forall \mathsf{id}_i \in \mathcal{ID}$, $\mathsf{k}_{\mathsf{id}_i} \leftarrow \mathsf{KGen}(1^\lambda, \mathsf{id}_i)$), any sequence M of ID/message pairs, and any aggregate-so-far tag $\tau' \in \mathcal{T}$, it holds that $1 = \mathsf{SVrfy}(K, (M, \tau'), \tau)$, where $\tau \leftarrow \mathsf{STag}(\mathsf{k}_{\mathsf{id}_{\sigma(\ell)}}, m_\ell, \mathsf{STag}(\ldots \mathsf{STag}(\mathsf{k}_{\mathsf{id}_{\sigma(1)}}, m_1, \tau') \ldots))$.

As security of SAMACs in the quantum query model, we define *sequential aggregate unforgeability against quantum chosen message attacks*, which we call saggUF-qCMA *security*.

First, we define a sequential aggregation algorithm SeqAgg_K and a closure $\mathsf{Closure}$ in order to define saggUF-qCMA security. For a SAMAC scheme $\mathsf{SAMAC} = (\mathsf{KGen}, \mathsf{STag}, \mathsf{SVrfy})$, a deterministic or randomized algorithm SeqAgg_K with secret keys $K = \{\mathsf{k}_{\mathsf{id}_i}\}_{i\in[n]}$ is defined as follows:

Definition 3 (Sequential Aggregation Algorithm). *Given a permutation $\sigma : [n] \to [n]$, a sequence of messages $\boldsymbol{m} = (m_1, \ldots, m_\ell)$, and an aggregate-so-far tag $\tau' \in \mathcal{T}$, a sequential aggregation algorithm outputs the aggregate tag*

$$\tau \leftarrow \mathsf{STag}(\mathsf{k}_{\mathsf{id}_{\sigma(\ell)}}, m_\ell, \mathsf{STag}(\ldots m_2, \mathsf{STag}(\mathsf{k}_{\mathsf{id}_{\sigma(1)}}, m_1, \tau') \ldots))$$

on the given messages/tag sequence $((m_1, \ldots, m_\ell), \tau')$. Then, we write $\tau \leftarrow \mathsf{SeqAgg}_K(\sigma, \boldsymbol{m}, \tau')$ as the sequential aggregation algorithm.

And, we define Closure in the same way as the closure defined in [8].

Definition 4 (Closure). *We introduce a set* Trivial *to define* Closure. *Let* $\mathcal{L}_{\mathsf{Tag}}$ *be a set of pairs* $((M,\tau'),\tau)$, *where* $M = ((\mathsf{id}_{\sigma(i)}, m_i))_{i\in[\ell]}$ *is a sequence of ID/message pairs,* τ' *is an aggregate-so-far tag, and* τ *is an aggregate tag on* (M,τ'). *Let* $\mathcal{L}_{\mathsf{Cor}}$ *be a set of corrupted IDs.* Trivial *is defined as follows:*

$$\mathsf{Trivial}_{\mathcal{L}_{\mathsf{Tag}},\mathcal{L}_{\mathsf{Cor}}}(M,\tau) := \{M\} \cup \bigcup_{((\hat{M},\tau),\hat{\tau})\in\mathcal{L}_{\mathsf{Tag}}} \mathsf{Trivial}_{\mathcal{L}_{\mathsf{Tag}},\mathcal{L}_{\mathsf{Cor}}}(M \parallel \hat{M},\hat{\tau}) \cup \bigcup_{\substack{\forall \bar{m}\in\mathcal{M},\bar{\tau}\in\mathcal{T},\\ \mathsf{id}\in\mathcal{L}_{\mathsf{Cor}}}} \mathsf{Trivial}_{\mathcal{L}_{\mathsf{Tag}},\mathcal{L}_{\mathsf{Cor}}}(M \parallel (\mathsf{id},\bar{m}),\bar{\tau}).$$

Closure *is defined as follows: Let* $\emptyset_m$ *be an empty symbol in* $\mathcal{M}$ *and let* $\emptyset_\tau$ *be an empty symbol in* $\mathcal{T}$, *then define* $\mathsf{Closure}(\mathcal{L}_{\mathsf{Tag}},\mathcal{L}_{\mathsf{Cor}}) := \{\mathsf{Trivial}_{\mathcal{L}_{\mathsf{Tag}},\mathcal{L}_{\mathsf{Cor}}}(\emptyset_m,\emptyset_\tau)\}$.

Then, we define saggUF-qCMA security by using SeqAgg_K and Closure.

Definition 5 (**saggUF-qCMA security**). *A SAMAC scheme* SAMAC = (KGen, STag, SVrfy) *meets* saggUF-qCMA *security, if for any QPA* $\mathcal{A}$ *against* SAMAC, $\mathsf{Adv}^{\mathrm{sagguf-qcma}}_{\mathcal{A},\mathsf{SAMAC}}(\lambda) := \Pr[\mathcal{A}\ wins]$ *is negligible, where* $[\mathcal{A}\ wins]$ *is an event that* $\mathcal{A}$ *wins in the following game:*

Setup: *Generate secret keys* $\mathsf{k}_{\mathsf{id}_i} \leftarrow \mathsf{KGen}(1^\lambda, \mathsf{id}_i)$ *for all* $\mathsf{id}_i \in \mathcal{ID}$. *Set a list* $\mathcal{L}_{\mathsf{Cor}} \leftarrow \{\emptyset\}$.

Corrupt: *When* $\mathcal{A}$ *submits a query* $\mathsf{id} \in \mathcal{ID}$ *to corrupt oracle* O_{Cor}, O_{Cor} *returns the corresponding key* k_{id} *and sets* $\mathcal{L}_{\mathsf{Cor}} \leftarrow \mathcal{L}_{\mathsf{Cor}} \cup \{\mathsf{id}\}$.

Tagging: $\mathcal{A}$ *submits a permutation* $\sigma : [n] \to [n]$ *(classical data) and a superposition of message/previous-tag pairs*

$$\sum_{\boldsymbol{m}\in\mathcal{M}^\ell,\tau'\in\mathcal{T},t\in\mathcal{T},z} \psi_{\boldsymbol{m},\tau',t,z}|(\boldsymbol{m},\tau'),t,z\rangle$$

to tagging oracle O_{Tag}, *where* ℓ *is an integer such that* $1 \le \ell \le n$, *a permutation* $\sigma : [n] \to [n]$ *is order-information of IDs, and* $\boldsymbol{m} = (m_i)_{i\in[\ell]}$ *is a sequence of messages. Then,* O_{Tag} *chooses randomness* r *used in* STag *algorithm, where it does not need to choose* r *if* STag *is deterministic, and returns*

$$\sum_{\boldsymbol{m}\in\mathcal{M}^\ell,\tau'\in\mathcal{T},t\in\mathcal{T},z} \psi_{\boldsymbol{m},\tau',t,z}|(\boldsymbol{m},\tau'),t \oplus \mathsf{SeqAgg}_K(\sigma,\boldsymbol{m},\tau';r),z\rangle.$$

$\mathcal{A}$ *submits at most* q *queries to* O_{Tag} *and it is not allowed to issue queries to* O_{Cor} *after submitting queries to* O_{Tag}.

Output: $\mathcal{A}$ *outputs* $(q+1)$ *tuples of ID/message pairs, aggregate-so-far tags, and aggregate tags* $((M_1,\tau'_1),\tau_1),\ldots,((M_{q+1},\tau'_{q+1}),\tau_{q+1})$. $\mathcal{A}$ *wins if the following holds:*
- *For all* $i \in [q+1]$, $1 \leftarrow \mathsf{SVrfy}(K,(M_i,\tau'_i),\tau_i)$ *holds.*

– *For all* $i \in [q+1]$, $(M_i, \tau'_i) \notin \mathsf{Closure}(\mathcal{L}^{(i)}_{\mathsf{Tag}}, \mathcal{L}_{\mathsf{Cor}})$ *holds, where* $\mathcal{L}^{(i)}_{\mathsf{Tag}} := \{((M_j, \tau'_j), \tau_j)\}_{j\in[q+1]} \backslash \{((M_i, \tau'_i), \tau_i)\}$.

We explain that Definition 5 can be viewed as an extension from both of the quantum security of MACs (Definition 1) in [4] and the classical security of SAMACs in [8].

- Consider a special case where the number of IDs is 1 (i.e., $n = 1$) in Definition 5. Suppose that, in an saggUF-qCMA security game, a QPA $\mathcal{A}$ outputs q tuples of ID/message pairs, aggregate-so-far tags, and aggregate tags $((\mathsf{id}_1, m_1), \tau'_1, \tau_1), \ldots, ((\mathsf{id}_1, m_{q+1}), \tau'_{q+1}, \tau_{q+1})$ for the same ID id_1. Then, $\mathcal{A}$ wins if $1 \leftarrow \mathsf{SVrfy}(\mathsf{k}_{\mathsf{id}_1}, (m_i, \tau'_i), \tau_i)$ and $((\mathsf{id}_1, m_i), \tau'_i) \notin \mathsf{Closure}(\mathcal{L}^{(i)}_{\mathsf{Tag}}, \emptyset)$ for all $i \in [q+1]$, where $\mathsf{Closure}(\mathcal{L}^{(i)}_{\mathsf{Tag}}, \emptyset) = \{(\mathsf{id}_1, m_j), \tau'_j)\}_{j\in[q+1]} \backslash \{(\mathsf{id}_1, m_i), \tau'_i)\}$. This is the same as Definition 1 since we can view $m_i \| \tau'_i$ as messages for all $i \in [q+1]$, and the outputted messages $m_i \| \tau'_i$ are different one another. Hence, Definition 5 is regarded as an extension of the quantum security of MACs in [4].
- Consider a special case where PPTA $\mathcal{A}$ obtains valid q tuples of ID/message pairs, aggregate-so-far tags, and aggregate tags $((M_1, \tau'_1), \tau_1), \ldots, ((M_q, \tau'_q), \tau_q)$ by having access to the oracle O_{Tag} with classical queries $(M_1, \tau'_1), \ldots, (M_q, \tau'_q)$. Suppose that, in an saggUF-qCMA security game, a PPTA $\mathcal{A}$ finally outputs q tuples of ID/message pairs, aggregate-so-far tags, and aggregate tags $((M_1, \tau'_1), \tau_1), \ldots, ((M_q, \tau'_q), \tau_q)$ which he obtained, and $((M_{q+1}, \tau'_{q+1}), \tau_{q+1})$, where $M_{q+1} = ((\mathsf{id}_{\sigma(i)}, m_i))_{i\in[\ell]}$ $(1 \leq \ell \leq n)$ is a sequence of arbitrary ℓ pairs of IDs and messages and τ_{q+1} is an aggregate tag on (M_{q+1}, τ'_{q+1}). Then, $\mathcal{A}$ wins if we have $1 \leftarrow \mathsf{SVrfy}(K, (M_{q+1}, \tau'_{q+1}), \tau_{q+1})$ and $(M_{q+1}, \tau'_{q+1}) \notin \mathsf{Closure}(\mathcal{L}^{(q+1)}_{\mathsf{Tag}}, \mathcal{L}_{\mathsf{Cor}})$. This is the same as the security definition of SAMACs in [8], and ours is an extension of it.

In terms of quantum security mentioned above, we analyze security of known SAMACs, and the results are summarized in Table 1. In particular, we can break the security of SAMACs of [8,19] by using quantum algorithms proposed in [4,12], and this fact is explained in details in Appendix A. In the next section, we propose secure constructions of SAMACs in terms of quantum security mentioned above.

5 Quantum-Secure Constructions of SAMACs

We propose two generic constructions SAMAC_1 and SAMAC_2 of (history-free) SAMACs and show that these constructions meet saggUF-qCMA security.

5.1 SAMAC_1

We construct a generic construction SAMAC_1 starting from any QPRF. The idea is as follows: Regarding [8], it is shown that there exists a SAMAC if there exists a partial invertible MAC which can recover partial messages from MAC tags and the other parts of messages. The paper [8] generally presented a partial invertible MAC from the ordinary MACs and pseudorandom permutations. However, in order to construct SAMACs, it is enough to use a PRF. This is because it is known that (quantum) PRFs can be used as EUF-(q)CMA secure MACs [3,4]. Hence, it is possible to construct a quantum-secure SAMAC if a PRF meets the quantum security.

Let $\mathsf{PRF} : \mathcal{K} \times \mathcal{X} \to \mathcal{T}$ be a QPRF. Then, $\mathsf{SAMAC}_1 = (\mathsf{KGen}, \mathsf{STag}, \mathsf{SVrfy})$ is constructed as follows:

- $\mathsf{k}_{\mathsf{id}} \leftarrow \mathsf{KGen}(1^\lambda, \mathsf{id})$: Choose a secret key $\mathsf{k} \in \mathcal{K}$ uniformly at random, and output $\mathsf{k}_{\mathsf{id}} := \mathsf{k}$.
- $\tau \leftarrow \mathsf{STag}(\mathsf{k}_{\mathsf{id}}, m, \tau')$: Compute $\tau \leftarrow \mathsf{PRF}(\mathsf{k}_{\mathsf{id}}, m \parallel \tau')$, and output τ.
- $1/0 \leftarrow \mathsf{SVrfy}(K, (M, \tau'), \tau)$: Given a sequence $M = ((\mathsf{id}_{\sigma(i)}, m_i))_{i \in [\ell]}$ and an aggregate-so-far tag τ', do the following:
  1. $\tilde{\tau} \leftarrow \mathsf{STag}(\mathsf{k}_{\mathsf{id}_{\sigma(\ell)}}, m_\ell, \mathsf{STag}(\ldots \mathsf{STag}(\mathsf{k}_{\mathsf{id}_{\sigma(1)}}, m_1, \tau') \ldots))$.
  2. Output 1 if $\tau = \tilde{\tau}$, or output 0 otherwise.

Theorem 2. *If* PRF *is a quantum pseudorandom function, then* SAMAC_1 *satisfies* $\mathsf{saggUF\text{-}qCMA}$ *security.*

Proof. Let $\mathcal{A}$ be a QPA against SAMAC_1, let $|\tau|$ be the bit-length of aggregate tags, and let q be the number of queries which $\mathcal{A}$ issues to O_{Tag}.

We consider any QPA $\mathcal{A}$ which outputs one-more forgery for an ID/message sequence including a target subsequence $M^*_{j,k} := ((\mathsf{id}^*_j, m^*_j), \ldots, (\mathsf{id}^*_k, m^*_k))$ defined as follows: We assume that $\mathcal{A}$ outputs one-more forgery for a sequence $((M_{i^*}, \tau'_{i^*}), \tau_{i^*})$ $(i^* \in [q+1])$. The target subsequence $M^*_{j,k}$ is included in M_{i^*} and satisfies the following:

- It is not in $\mathsf{Trivial}_{\mathcal{L}^{(i^*)}_{\mathsf{Tag}}, \mathcal{L}_{\mathsf{Cor}}}(\emptyset_m, \emptyset_\tau)$.
- It contains only not corrupted IDs.
- There do not exist j', k' such that $1 \le j \le j' \le k' \le k$ and $((\mathsf{id}^*_{j'}, m_{j'}), \ldots, (\mathsf{id}^*_{k'}, m_{k'})) \in \mathsf{Trivial}_{\mathcal{L}^{(i^*)}_{\mathsf{Tag}}, \mathcal{L}_{\mathsf{Cor}}}(\emptyset_m, \emptyset_\tau)$.
- There do not exist j', k' such that $1 \le j' \le j \le k'$ and $((\mathsf{id}^*_{j'}, m_{j'}), \ldots, (\mathsf{id}^*_{k'}, m_{k'})) \in \mathsf{Trivial}_{\mathcal{L}^{(i^*)}_{\mathsf{Tag}}, \mathcal{L}_{\mathsf{Cor}}}(\emptyset_m, \emptyset_\tau)$.
- There do not exist j', k' such that $1 \le j' \le k \le k' \le \ell^*$ and $((\mathsf{id}^*_{j'}, m_{j'}), \ldots, (\mathsf{id}^*_{k'}, m_{k'})) \in \mathsf{Trivial}_{\mathcal{L}^{(i^*)}_{\mathsf{Tag}}, \mathcal{L}_{\mathsf{Cor}}}(\emptyset_m, \emptyset_\tau)$, where ℓ^* is the maximum of the length of an ID/message sequence.

And then, we classify the event that $\mathcal{A}$ wins in the security game as some events by using target subsequence, and prove that the probabilities that these events occur are negligible. Regarding $\mathcal{A}$'s output $\{((M_i, \tau'_i), \tau_i)\}_{i \in [q+1]}$, we consider the following events:

- [Coll]: $\mathcal{A}$ outputs $\{((M_i, \tau'_i), \tau_i)\}_{i \in [q+1]}$ by finding a collision pair $(m \parallel \tau', \hat{m} \parallel \hat{\tau}')$ of SAMAC_1 for an ID $\mathsf{id} \in \mathcal{ID}$.

- [Suff]: $\mathcal{A}$ outputs $\{((M_i, \tau'_i), \tau_i)\}_{i\in[q+1]}$ such that there exists a target sequence $M^*_{j,k}$ in a sequence M_{i^*} ($i^* \in [q+1]$), which is a suffix of an ID/message sequence in $\mathcal{A}$'s output.
- [Pref]: $\mathcal{A}$ outputs $\{((M_i, \tau'_i), \tau_i)\}_{i\in[q+1]}$ such that there exists a target sequence $M^*_{j,k}$ in a sequence M_{i^*} ($i^* \in [q+1]$), which is a prefix of an ID/message sequence in $\mathcal{A}$'s output.
- [New]: $\mathcal{A}$ outputs $\{((M_i, \tau'_i), \tau_i)\}_{i\in[q+1]}$ such that there exists a target sequence $M^*_{j,k}$ in a sequence M_{i^*} ($i^* \in [q+1]$), which is neither suffix nor prefix of an ID/message sequence in $\mathcal{A}$'s output.

Then, we have the following advantage:

$$\begin{aligned}\mathsf{Adv}^{\mathrm{sagguf-qcma}}_{\mathcal{A},\mathsf{SAMAC}_1}(\lambda) \leq & \Pr[\mathsf{Coll}] + \Pr[\mathsf{Suff} \mid \overline{\mathsf{Coll}}] \\ & + \Pr[\mathsf{Pref} \mid \overline{\mathsf{Coll}} \wedge \overline{\mathsf{Suff}}] + \Pr[\mathsf{New} \mid \overline{\mathsf{Coll}} \wedge \overline{\mathsf{Suff}} \wedge \overline{\mathsf{Pref}}].\end{aligned}$$

Event [Coll]: By using $\mathcal{A}$ which outputs a forgery meeting the condition of [Coll], we construct a PPT algorithm $\mathcal{D}_c$ breaking a PRF in the following way: It is given the oracle O_{PRF} in the security game of QPRFs.

Setup: Set secret keys as follows:
1. $\mathsf{id}^* \xleftarrow{U} \mathcal{ID}$ and assign O_{PRF} to the PRF of id^*.
2. For all $\mathsf{id} \in \mathcal{ID}\backslash\{\mathsf{id}^*\}$, $\mathsf{k_{id}} \leftarrow \mathsf{KGen}(1^\lambda, \mathsf{id})$.

Corrupt: For each query id, return the key $\mathsf{k_{id}}$ and set $\mathcal{L}_{\mathsf{Cor}} \leftarrow \mathcal{L}_{\mathsf{Cor}} \cup \{\mathsf{id}\}$.
Tagging: For each query $(\sigma, \sum \psi_{\boldsymbol{m},\tau',t,z}|(\boldsymbol{m}, \tau'), t, z\rangle)$, simulate as follows:
1. Compute each $\mathsf{STag}(\mathsf{k}_{\mathsf{id}_{\sigma(i)}}, \cdot, \cdot)$ algorithm, in the following way:
   - If $\mathsf{id}_{\sigma(i)} = \mathsf{id}^*$, generate a tag by using $O_{\mathsf{PRF}}(\cdot)$.
   - If $\mathsf{id}_{\sigma(i)} \neq \mathsf{id}^*$, generate a tag by using $\mathsf{PRF}(\mathsf{k}_{\mathsf{id}_{\sigma(i)}}, \cdot)$.
2. Return $\sum \psi_{\boldsymbol{m},\tau',t,z}|(\boldsymbol{m}, \tau'), t \oplus \mathsf{SeqAgg}_K(\sigma, \boldsymbol{m}, \tau'), z\rangle$.

Output: When $\mathcal{A}$ outputs $\{((M_i, \tau'_i), \tau_i)\}_{i\in[q+1]}$, do the following:
1. For all (M, τ') including id^*, compute aggregate tags generated by id^*.
2. Find a pair $(M, \tau'), (\hat{M}_j, \hat{\tau}')$ such that $(M, \tau') \neq (\hat{M}, \hat{\tau}')$ and $O_{\mathsf{PRF}}(M \parallel \tau') = O_{\mathsf{PRF}}(\hat{M} \parallel \hat{\tau}')$.
3. If there exists such a pair, output 1. Otherwise, output 0.

$\mathcal{D}_c$ simulates the environment of $\mathcal{A}$ completely since it has secret keys and the oracle in the security game of PRFs. If $\mathcal{A}$ can find a collision of PRF, $\mathcal{D}_c$ can also break the security of PRF obviously. Because the probability that $\mathcal{A}$ finds a collision in the straightforward way is $\mathcal{O}\left(q^3 \cdot 2^{-|\tau|}\right)$ from [22], we have $\Pr[\mathsf{Coll}] \leq n(q+1) \cdot \mathsf{Adv}^{\mathrm{qpr}}_{\mathcal{D}_c,\mathsf{PRF}}(\lambda) + \mathcal{O}\left(q^3 \cdot 2^{-|\tau|}\right)$. ■

Event [$\mathsf{Suff}|\overline{\mathsf{Coll}}$]: We consider the case where id^*_{j-1} is corrupted for a target sequence $M^*_{j,k}$, or the case where id^*_j is the first order of another sequence including $M^*_{j,k}$. In these cases, $M^*_{j,k}$ is not any suffix of other ID/message-sequences. Thus, the event [Suff] does not happen. If id^*_{j-1} is not corrupted, $M^*_{j-1,k}$ must be the target subsequence from the condition that event [Coll] does not happen. By replying this, however, the obtained $M^*_{1,k}$ does not meet the condition of target subsequences. From this contradiction, event $[\mathsf{Suff}|\overline{\mathsf{Coll}}]$ does not happen. That is, $\Pr[\mathsf{Suff}|\overline{\mathsf{Coll}}] = 0$ holds. ■

Event $[\mathsf{Pref}|\overline{\mathsf{Coll}} \wedge \overline{\mathsf{Suff}}]$: We construct $\mathcal{D}_p$ breaking a QPRF in the same way as the algorithm above $\mathcal{D}_c$ except for the process in **Output** phase. When $\mathcal{A}$ outputs $\{((M_i, \tau_i'), \tau_i)\}_{i\in[q+1]}$ in **Output** phase, it does the following:

1. Find a pair $((M^*, \tau'^*), \tau^*)$ such that M^* includes a target sequence $M_{j,k}^*$ meeting the condition of $[\mathsf{Pref}|\overline{\mathsf{Coll}} \wedge \overline{\mathsf{Suff}}]$, and id^* equals to id_k^* of $M_{j,k}^*$.
2. Generate an aggregate tag $\bar{\tau}^*$ on (M^*, τ'^*) by using O_{PRF}.
3. If $\tau^* = \bar{\tau}^*$, output 1. Otherwise, output 0.

$\mathcal{D}_p$ simulates the view of $\mathcal{A}$ and breaks the quantum security of PRF. Then, we have $\Pr[\mathsf{Pref}|\overline{\mathsf{Coll}} \wedge \overline{\mathsf{Suff}}] \leq n(q+1) \cdot \mathsf{Adv}_{\mathcal{D}_p,\mathsf{PRF}}^{\mathrm{qpr}}(\lambda) + 2^{-|\tau|/2}$. ■

Event $[\mathsf{New}|\overline{\mathsf{Coll}} \wedge \overline{\mathsf{Suff}} \wedge \overline{\mathsf{Pref}}]$: In the same way as the proof in $[\mathsf{Pref}|\overline{\mathsf{Coll}} \wedge \overline{\mathsf{Suff}}]$, we can show that the event happens with negligible probability. It is possible to construct a PPT algorithms $\mathcal{D}_n$ in the same way as $\mathcal{D}_p$ except for the way to choose the target sequence. That is, $\mathcal{D}_n$ chooses a target sequence which is neither suffix nor prefix of another ID/message-sequence and checks whether it is a valid tag. Hence, we have $\Pr[\mathsf{New}|\overline{\mathsf{Coll}} \wedge \overline{\mathsf{Suff}} \wedge \overline{\mathsf{Pref}}] \leq n(q+1) \cdot \mathsf{Adv}_{\mathcal{D}_n,\mathsf{PRF}}^{\mathrm{qpr}}(\lambda) + \frac{1}{2^{|\tau|/2}}$. ■

From the above, we obtain the following advantage:

$$\mathsf{Adv}_{\mathcal{A},\mathsf{SAMAC}_1}^{\mathrm{sagguf-qcma}}(\lambda) \leq 3n(q+1) \cdot \mathsf{Adv}_{\mathcal{D},\mathsf{PRF}}^{\mathrm{qpr}}(\lambda) + \mathcal{O}\left(q^3 \cdot 2^{-|\tau|}\right).$$

Therefore, the proof is completed. □

In order to obtain quantum-secure constructions of SAMACs based on SAMAC_1, we can apply the quantum-secure PRF of [18,21] to SAMAC_1, since those are deterministic. More specifically, we can apply NMAC/HMAC to SAMAC_1 as a quantum PRF, since these MACs are shown to be quantum PRFs in [18].

5.2 SAMAC$_2$

We construct an SAMAC scheme SAMAC_2 starting from any randomized PRG and any PRF. This scheme is based on the GGM (quantum) pseudorandom function [9,21]. The difference between the GGM construction and ours is that a deterministic PRG is used in the GGM construction, whereas a randomized PRG is used in SAMAC_2.

Although one may think that we can realize quantum-secure SAMAC schemes by applying randomized PRGs to the GGM pseudorandom function, there exists a problem. This problem is that each tagging user has to append a randomness to his/her aggregate tag. Namely, a tagging user generates an aggregate tag $\tau_1 = (r_1, GGM(\mathsf{k}_1, m_1\|\tau'; r_1))$, and the next user generates his/her tag $\tau_2 = (r_1, r_2, GGM(\mathsf{k}_2, m_2\|\tau_1; r_2))$ so that a verifier can check whether

(m_1, m_2, τ') and $GGM(\mathsf{k}_2, m_2 \| \tau_1; r_2)$ are valid. Here, a function $GGM(\cdot)$ is the GGM pseudorandom function, r_1, r_2 are randomness used in underlying PRGs, $\mathsf{k}_1, \mathsf{k}_2$ are the seeds of PRGs, m_1, m_2 are local messages, and τ' is an aggregate-so-far tag. In this case, the size of aggregate tags increases every time tagging users generate aggregate tags. Therefore, the size depends on the number of tagging users.

In order to resolve this problem, we utilize a value $r \leftarrow \mathsf{PRF}(\mathsf{k}_{\mathsf{PRF}}, c)$ as randomness, where $\mathsf{PRF}(\mathsf{k}_{\mathsf{PRF}}, \cdot)$ is a classical PRF, and c is a counter value which is a component of tags. This counter value is shared among tagging users and updated after sending an aggregate tag to a verifier. And, each counter value is used only once for a sequential aggregate tag. The value r is used as follows: r is the randomness used in randomized PRGs. The tag-size does not depend on the number of tagging users, since it is possible to obtain each r from a counter c and each PRF PRF.

Note that it is natural to use (counter) values shared among tagging users in the model of SAMACs, since users are synchronized basically and the same situation using common values has been considered in previous works such as counter-based aggregate MACs [8], and synchronized aggregate signatures [1,11]. We use the following primitives and parameters:

- Let $G : \mathcal{X} \times \mathcal{R} \to \mathcal{X}^2$ be a randomized PRG with a set $\mathcal{R}$ of randomness used in G. Then, we write $G(x) = (G_0(x), G_1(x))$, where G_0, G_1 are functions from $\mathcal{X}$ to $\mathcal{X}$.
- Let $\mathsf{PRF} : \mathcal{K} \times \mathcal{C} \to \mathcal{R}$ be a (classical) PRF.
- Let c be a counter value in a space $\mathcal{C}$.
- $\mathcal{L}_c \leftarrow \emptyset$ is a list of counter values and shared among tagging users.

$\mathsf{SAMAC}_2 = (\mathsf{KGen}, \mathsf{STag}, \mathsf{SVrfy})$ is constructed as follows:

- $\mathsf{k}_{\mathsf{id}} \leftarrow \mathsf{KGen}(1^\lambda, \mathsf{id})$: Choose $x \in \mathcal{X}$ and $\mathsf{k}_{\mathsf{PRF}} \in \mathcal{K}$ uniformly at random. Output $\mathsf{k}_{\mathsf{id}} := (x, \mathsf{k}_{\mathsf{PRF}})$.
- $\tau \leftarrow \mathsf{STag}(\mathsf{k}_{\mathsf{id}}, m, \tau')$: Generate an aggregate tag as follows.
  1. Split τ' into (c, y').
  2. $(r_i)_{i \in [\mu]} \leftarrow \mathsf{PRF}(\mathsf{k}_{\mathsf{PRF}}, c) \in \mathcal{R}^\mu$.
  3. $(z_i)_{i \in [\mu]} \leftarrow m \parallel y' \in \{0,1\}^\mu$.
  4. $y \leftarrow G_{z_1}(\ldots G_{z_{\mu-1}}(G_{z_\mu}(x; r_\mu); r_{\mu-1}) \ldots; r_1)$.
  5. Output $\tau := (c, y)$.
- $1/0 \leftarrow \mathsf{SVrfy}(K, (M, \tau'), \tau)$: Verify a message/previous-tag pair (M, τ') and an aggregate tag τ, as follows.
  1. $\tilde{\tau} \leftarrow \mathsf{STag}(\mathsf{k}_{\mathsf{id}_{\sigma(\ell)}}, m_\ell, \mathsf{STag}(\ldots \mathsf{STag}(\mathsf{k}_{\mathsf{id}_{\sigma(1)}}, m_1, \tau') \ldots))$.
  2. Output 1 if $\tau = \tilde{\tau}$ and $c \notin \mathcal{L}_c$, or output 0 otherwise.

The following theorem holds regarding SAMAC_2.

Theorem 3. *If G is a randomized pseudorandom generator and* PRF *is a pseudorandom function, then* SAMAC_2 *satisfies* $\mathsf{saggUF\text{-}qCMA}$ *security.*

Proof. Let $\mathcal{A}$ be a QPA against SAMAC_2. In the process of STag algorithm, let $F\left(x, (z_i)_{i\in[\mu]}; (r_i)_{i\in[\mu]}\right) := G_{z_1}(\ldots G_{z_{\mu-1}}(G_{z_\mu}(x; r_\mu); r_{\mu-1})\ldots; r_1)$ be a PRF, where x is a key, and $\left((z_i)_{i\in[\mu]}; (r_i)_{i\in[\mu]}\right)$ is the input of F.

If F is a QPRF, the resulting SAMAC SAMAC_2 meets $\mathsf{saggUF\text{-}qCMA}$ security from Theorem 2. To this end, we show that the function F is a QPRF if G is a randomized PRG.

First, we consider that for $i \in [\mu]$, $\mathcal{A}_{\mathsf{PRF}}$ is given an oracle $F_i\left((z_j, r_j)_{j\in[\mu]}\right) := G_{z_1}(\ldots G_{z_i}(P((z_j, r_j)_{j\in[i+1,\mu]}); r_i)\ldots; r_1)$, where $P : \{0,1\}^{\mu-i} \times \mathcal{R}^{\mu-i} \to \mathcal{X}$ is a random function. Notice that the case of $i = \mu$ is the same as the game that $\mathcal{A}_{\mathsf{PRF}}$ is given the truly PRF F. Let p_i be the probability $\Pr[\mathcal{A}_{\mathsf{PRF}}^{F_i} \to 1]$ for $i \in \{0, 1, \ldots, \mu\}$ and let $\epsilon := |p_0 - p_\mu|$. Then, we have $\epsilon = \left|\sum_{i\in\{0,1,\ldots,\mu-1\}} (p_i - p_{i+1})\right|$.

Next, we construct an algorithm $\mathcal{D}$ which distinguishes a random function $\mathsf{RF} : \{0,1\}^{\mu-1} \times \mathcal{R}^{\mu-1} \to \mathcal{X}^2$ and a function $G \circ \mathsf{RF}$ for a random function $\mathsf{RF} : \{0,1\}^{\mu-1} \times \mathcal{R}^{\mu-1} \to \mathcal{X} \times \mathcal{R}$. $\mathcal{D}$ breaking PRG G is as follows:

- Choose $i \in \{0, 1, \ldots, \mu - 1\}$ at random.
- Let $P^{(i)} : \{0,1\}^{\mu-i-1} \times \mathcal{R}^{\mu-i-1} \to \mathcal{X}^2$ be the oracle $P^{(i)}(z; r) = P(0^i z; 0^i r)$.
- Write $P^{(i)}$ as $(P_0^{(i)}, P_1^{(i)})$ where $P_b^{(i)} : \{0,1\}^{\mu-i-1} \times \mathcal{R}^{\mu-i-1} \to \mathcal{X}$ for each $b \in \{0,1\}$ is the left-hand side ($b = 0$) or the right-hand side ($b = 1$) of $P^{(i)}(\cdot)$.
- Construct the oracle $F((z_j)_{j\in[\mu]})$ as follows: Choose $(r_j)_{j\in[\mu]} \in \mathcal{R}^\mu$ at random, and compute $G_{z_1}(\ldots, G_{z_i}(P_{z_{i+1}}^{(i)}\left((z_j)_{j\in[i+2,n]}; (r_j)_{j\in[i+2,n]}\right); r_i)\ldots; r_1)$.
- When $\mathcal{A}_{\mathsf{PRF}}^F$ outputs the guessing bit, output this bit.

Let $\mathcal{D}_i$ be an algorithm $\mathcal{D}$ which chooses $i \in \{0, \ldots, \mu - 1\}$. We analyze the algorithm $\mathcal{D}_i$. If the given P is a random function, then $P^{(i)}(z; r) = P(0^i z; 0^i r)$ is also truly random, and $\mathcal{D}_i$ simulates the environment of Game_i. If given oracle P is $G \circ \mathsf{RF}$ for a random function RF, $\mathcal{D}_i$ simulates Game_{i+1} since P_b is $G_b \circ \mathsf{RF}$ for $b \in \{0,1\}$. For each $i \in \{0, \ldots, \mu - 1\}$, we have $\Pr_{P=\mathsf{RF}}\left[\mathcal{D}_i^P(1^\lambda) \to 1\right] - \Pr_{P=G\circ\mathsf{RF}}\left[\mathcal{D}_i^P(1^\lambda) \to 1\right] = p_i - p_{i+1}$. Then, we obtain the following advantage:

$$\begin{aligned}
\mathsf{Adv}_{\mathcal{D},G}^{\mathrm{prg}}(\lambda) &= \left|\Pr_{P=\mathsf{RF}}\left[\mathcal{D}^P(1^\lambda) \to 1\right] - \Pr_{P=G\circ\mathsf{RF}}\left[\mathcal{D}^P(1^\lambda) \to 1\right]\right| \\
&= \frac{1}{\mu}\left|\sum_{i\in\{0,\ldots,\mu-1\}} \left(\Pr_{P=\mathsf{RF}}\left[\mathcal{D}_i^P(1^\lambda) \to 1\right] - \Pr_{P=G\circ\mathsf{RF}}\left[\mathcal{D}_i^P(1^\lambda) \to 1\right]\right)\right| \\
&= \frac{1}{\mu}\left|\sum_{i\in\{0,\ldots,\mu-1\}} (p_i - p_{i+1})\right| = \frac{\epsilon}{\mu}.
\end{aligned}$$

Therefore, $\epsilon = \mu \cdot \mathsf{Adv}_{\mathcal{D},G}^{\mathrm{prg}}(\lambda)$ holds, and F is a QPRF.

Thus, by using the standard hybrid argument, we can replace the QPRFs of targeted tagging users by random functions, and it is possible to prove Theorem 3 in the same way as the proof of Theorem 2. Hence, we obtain $\mathsf{Adv}_{\mathcal{A},\mathsf{SAMAC}_2}^{\mathsf{sagguf-qcma}}(\lambda) \leq 3n^2(q+1)\mu \cdot \mathsf{Adv}_{\mathcal{D},G}^{\mathrm{prg}}(\lambda) + \mathcal{O}\left(q^3 \cdot 2^{-|\tau|/2}\right)$. Therefore, the proof of Theorem 3 is completed. □

The advantage of using randomized primitives lies in constructing quantum-secure SAMAC schemes based on assumed computationally hard problems for quantum computers such as the learning parity with noise (LPN) problem. Since LPN-based cryptography has been studied in constructing various cryptographic systems such as public key encryption [7,14], oblivious transfer [5], symmetric key encryption [2], MACs [6], and randomized PRGs/PRFs [2,20], it is even interesting to consider quantum-secure SAMACs from LPN-based primitives. LPN-based primitives consist of randomized algorithms, and hence, those can be applied to SAMAC_2. In particular, we can apply randomized PRGs [2,20] based on the LPN problem to our SAMAC_2. The detailed description about it is given in Appendix B.

6 Conclusion

In this paper, we have shown secure AMAC/SAMAC schemes in the quantum query model. For this, we formalized the security of AMACs and SAMACs in the quantum query model, which are called aggUF-qCMA security and saggUF-qCMA security, respectively. Note that the existing SAMAC schemes in [8,19] are broken in our security model, and hence, we have investigated and shown AMAC and SAMAC schemes that meet the security in the quantum query model. Specifically, regarding AMACs, we have proved that the Katz-Lindel construction [13] meets aggUF-qCMA security if the underlying MACs meet EUF-qCMA security. Regarding SAMACs, we have proposed two generic constructions SAMAC_1 and SAMAC_2: SAMAC_1 is constructed from any quantum PRF, and SAMAC_2 is constructed from any randomized PRG and any PRF. In particular, we can realize concrete SAMAC_1 schemes by applying NMAC/HMAC, while we can provide a concrete SAMAC_2 scheme from LPN-based randomized PRGs [20].

Acknowledgements. The authors would like to thank the anonymous referees for their helpful comments. This research was conducted under a contract of Research and Development for Expansion of Radio Wave Resources funded by the Ministry of Internal Affairs and Communications, Japan.

Appendix A: Attacks against the Existing Schemes

We describe the attack against the existing sequential aggregate authentication schemes of [8,19].

A.1: The Attack against the Scheme of [8]

The algorithm breaking the scheme of [8] follows the quantum attack against CBC-MAC of [12]. First, we define Simon's algorithm used by the one against the scheme of [8]. Simon's algorithm is a quantum algorithm solving the following problem.

Definition 6 (Simon's Problem). *Given a Boolean function* $f : \{0,1\}^n \rightarrow \{0,1\}^n$ *and the promise that there exists* $s \in \{0,1\}^n$ *such that for any* $(x, y) \in \{0,1\}^n$, $[f(x) = f(y)] \Leftrightarrow [x \oplus y \in \{0^n, s\}]$, *the goal is to find* s.

Simon's algorithm is as follows:

1. Set the following $2n$-qubit: $\frac{1}{\sqrt{2^n}} \sum_{x \in \{0,1\}^n} |x\rangle|0\rangle$.
2. A quantum query to the function f maps this state to $\frac{1}{\sqrt{2^n}} \sum_{x \in \{0,1\}^n} |x\rangle |f(x)\rangle$.
3. Measure the second register in the computational basis and obtain a value $f(z)$. Then, from the promise $f(x) = f(x \oplus s)$, the first register is as follows:
$$\frac{1}{\sqrt{2}}(|z\rangle + |z \oplus s\rangle).$$
4. Apply the Hadamard transformation to the first register and get
$$\frac{1}{\sqrt{2}} \frac{1}{\sqrt{2^n}} \sum_{y \in \{0,1\}^n} (-1)^{y \cdot z}(1 + (-1)^{y \cdot s})|y\rangle.$$
5. Measure the register and obtain a vector y.

The obtained vector y meets $y \cdot s = 0$ since if the amplitude of y such that $y \cdot s = 1$ is 0. By replying the above process, we have $\mathcal{O}(n)$ vectors y such that $y \cdot s = 0$. Therefore, we can recover s.

Let $\varepsilon(f, s) := \max_{t \in \{0,1\}^n \setminus \{0,s\}} \Pr_x[f(x) + f(x \oplus t)]$ for a function $f : \{0,1\}^n \rightarrow \{0,1\}^n$ meeting the promise of Simon's algorithm ($f(x \oplus s) = f(x)$ for all x). From [12], the success probability of Simon's algorithm is as follows.

Proposition 1 (Theorem 1 in [12]). *Let* $f : \{0,1\}^n \rightarrow \{0,1\}^n$ *be a function such that* $f(x \oplus s) = f(x)$ *for all* x, *and let* c *be a positive integer. If* $\varepsilon(f, s) \leq p_0 < 1$ *holds for probability* p_0, *then Simon's algorithm returns* s *with* cn *queries, with probability at least* $1 - \left(2\left(\frac{1+p_0}{2}\right)^c\right)^n$.

Next, we describe the SAMAC scheme $\mathsf{SAMAC}_{ex} = (\mathsf{KGen}, \mathsf{STag}, \mathsf{SVrfy})$ of [8] as follows: Let $(\mathsf{KGen}, \mathsf{Tag}, \mathsf{Vrfy})$ be a deterministic MAC with a tag space $\mathcal{T}$, and let $\mathsf{PRP} : \mathcal{K}_{\mathsf{PRP}} \times \mathcal{T} \rightarrow \mathcal{T}$ be a pseudorandom permutation.

- $\mathsf{k_{id}} \leftarrow \mathsf{KGen}(1^\lambda, \mathsf{id})$: Generate keys $\mathsf{k_{MAC}} \leftarrow \mathsf{MAC.KGen}$ and $\mathsf{k_{PRP}} \stackrel{U}{\leftarrow} \mathcal{K}_{\mathsf{PRP}}$. Output $\mathsf{k_{id}} := (\mathsf{k_{MAC}}, \mathsf{k_{PRP}})$.
- $\tau \leftarrow \mathsf{STag}(\mathsf{k_{id}}, m, \tau')$:
  Compute $t \leftarrow \mathsf{Tag}(\mathsf{k_{MAC}}, m)$, and then output $\tau \leftarrow \mathsf{PRP}(\mathsf{k_{PRP}}, t \oplus \tau')$.
- $1/0 \leftarrow \mathsf{SVrfy}(K, (M, \tau'), \tau)$:
  Compute $\tilde{\tau} \leftarrow \mathsf{STag}(\mathsf{k_{id_{\sigma(\ell)}}}, m_\ell, \mathsf{STag}(\ldots, \mathsf{STag}(\mathsf{k_{id_{\sigma(1)}}}, m_1, \tau') \ldots))$. Output 1 if $\tau = \tilde{\tau}$, or output 0 otherwise.

Finally, we describe the attack against SAMAC_{ex}. We fix two arbitrary messages $m_0, m_1 \in \mathcal{M}$ ($m_0 \neq m_1$), and the function of Simon's problem is defined as follows:

$$f : \{0,1\} \times \mathcal{M} \to \mathcal{T}$$
$$(b, \tau') \mapsto \mathsf{PRP}(\mathsf{k}_{\mathsf{PRP}}, \tau' \oplus \mathsf{Tag}(\mathsf{k}_{\mathsf{MAC}}, m_b))$$

For $s = 1 \parallel \mathsf{Tag}(\mathsf{k}_{\mathsf{MAC}}, m_0) \oplus \mathsf{Tag}(\mathsf{k}_{\mathsf{MAC}}, m_1)$, the function f meets the promise of Simon's problem:

$$f(0,x) = \mathsf{PRP}(\mathsf{k}_{\mathsf{PRP}}, \tau' \oplus \mathsf{Tag}(\mathsf{k}_{\mathsf{MAC}}, m_1)),$$
$$f(1,x) = \mathsf{PRP}(\mathsf{k}_{\mathsf{PRP}}, \tau' \oplus \mathsf{Tag}(\mathsf{k}_{\mathsf{MAC}}, m_0)),$$
$$f(b,x) = f(b \oplus 1, x \oplus \mathsf{Tag}(\mathsf{k}_{\mathsf{MAC}}, m_0) \oplus \mathsf{Tag}(\mathsf{k}_{\mathsf{MAC}}, m_1)).$$

Then, we can generate the following forgery against SAMAC_{ex}:

1. Fix m_0, m_1 as the messages of a message block, and let a previous tag $\tau' = 0^n \in \mathcal{T}$ denote a n-bit string of 0.
2. Submit a classical query $m_0 \parallel 0^n$ to the tagging oracle of saggUF-qCMA security game, and receive the aggregate tag τ.
3. By using Simon's algorithm with $O(n)$ quantum queries, we obtain $s = \mathsf{Tag}(\mathsf{k}_{\mathsf{MAC}}, m_0) \oplus \mathsf{Tag}(\mathsf{k}_{\mathsf{MAC}}, m_1)$.
4. Output a forgery $(m_1 \parallel \mathsf{Tag}(\mathsf{k}_{\mathsf{MAC}}, m_0) \oplus \mathsf{Tag}(\mathsf{k}_{\mathsf{MAC}}, m_1), \tau)$ as a valid aggregate tag.

The above forgery is valid, since $m_1 \parallel \mathsf{Tag}(\mathsf{k}_{\mathsf{MAC}}, m_0) \oplus \mathsf{Tag}(\mathsf{k}_{\mathsf{MAC}}, m_1)$ has never been queried.

A.2: The Attack against the Scheme of [19]

We describe two schemes presented in [19]. Let $\mathbb{F}_p$ be a finite field with a prime power p. The first construction is given as follows:

- $\mathsf{k}_{\mathsf{id}} \leftarrow \mathsf{KGen}(1^\lambda, \mathsf{id})$: Output a secret key $\mathsf{k}_{\mathsf{id}} := (a, b) \xleftarrow{U} \mathbb{F}_p^2$.
- $\tau \leftarrow \mathsf{STag}(\mathsf{k}_{\mathsf{id}}, m, \tau')$: On input a message $m \in \mathbb{F}_p$ and an aggregate-so-far tag $\tau' \in \mathbb{F}_p$, output a tag $\tau := a \cdot m + b + \tau' \in \mathbb{F}_p$.
- $1/0 \leftarrow \mathsf{SVrfy}(K, (M, \tau'), \tau)$: Compute $\tilde{\tau} \leftarrow \mathsf{STag}(K, (M, \tau'))$. Output 1 if $\tau = \tilde{\tau}$, or output 0 otherwise.

And, the second construction is described as follows:

- $\mathsf{k}_{\mathsf{id}} \leftarrow \mathsf{KGen}(1^\lambda, \mathsf{id})$: Output a secret key $\mathsf{k}_{\mathsf{id}} := (a, b, c) \xleftarrow{U} \mathbb{F}_p^3$.
- $\tau \leftarrow \mathsf{STag}(\mathsf{k}_{\mathsf{id}}, m, \tau')$: On input a message $m \in \mathbb{F}_p$, an ID $\mathsf{id} \in \mathbb{F}_p$, and an aggregate-so-far tag $\tau' = (s', t') \in \mathbb{F}_p^2$, output a tag $\tau := (a \cdot m + b + s', a \cdot \mathsf{id} + c + t') \in \mathbb{F}_p^2$.
- $1/0 \leftarrow \mathsf{SVrfy}(K, (M, \tau'), \tau)$: Compute $\tilde{\tau} \leftarrow \mathsf{STag}(K, (M, \tau'))$. Output 1 if $\tau = \tilde{\tau}$, or output 0 otherwise.

Regarding both schemes, we can view aggregate tags as the values of pairwise independent hash functions $h(x) = ax + b$ with $a, b \in \mathbb{F}_p$. In the straightforward way, we can apply the quantum algorithm in the proof of Lemma 6.3 in [4]. In this case, adversaries can get secret keys $(a, b) \in \mathbb{F}_p^2$ with non-negligible probability and generate forgeries obviously even if they submit only one quantum query. Therefore, the schemes of [19] do not meet the one-time security formalized in Sect. 4.

Appendix B: Concrete Construction of SAMAC_2

We describe our concrete SAMAC_2 scheme based on the learning parity with noise (LPN) problem by using the randomized PRG of [20].

B.1: LPN Problem

We first define an oracle $\Lambda_{t,n}(\cdot)$ that outputs LPN samples in the following way: Let Ber_t be the Bernoulli distribution over $\{0,1\}$ with bias $t \in (0, 1/2)$. For parameters $t \in (0, 1/2)$ and $n \geq 1$, an oracle $\Lambda_{t,n}(s)$ takes $s \in \{0,1\}^n$ as input and outputs samples $(a, a \cdot s \oplus e) \in \{0,1\}^n \times \{0,1\}$ by sampling $a \overset{U}{\leftarrow} \{0,1\}^n$ and $e \leftarrow \mathsf{Ber}_t$. In addition, an oracle U_n outputs uniformly random samples over $\{0,1\}^n \times \{0,1\}$. The LPN assumption is defined as follows:

Definition 7 (Learning Parity with Noise). *The (decisional)* $\mathsf{LPN}_{t,n}$ *assumption holds if for any PPT algorithm* $\mathcal{D}$*, the advantage*

$$\left|\Pr\left[\mathcal{D}^{\Lambda_{t,n}(s)} \to 1 \mid s \overset{U}{\leftarrow} \{0,1\}^n\right] - \Pr\left[\mathcal{D}^{U_n} \to 1\right]\right|$$

is negligible.

B.2: Concrete Construction of SAMAC_2

We describe a concrete scheme $\mathsf{SAMAC}_{\mathsf{LPN}} = (\mathsf{KGen}, \mathsf{STag}, \mathsf{SVrfy})$. The randomized PRG based on LPN is $G_a(s; e) = a \cdot s \oplus e$, where $a \in \{0,1\}^{\delta n \times n}$ and $s \in \{0,1\}^n$ are uniformly random, and $e \in \{0,1\}^{\delta n}$ is a sample drawn from the Bernoulli distribution with a parameter t. We use the following public parameters and primitives based on a security parameter λ.

- $t \in (0, 1/2)$ is a parameter for the error distribution Ber_t.
- An integer n is a LPN parameter based on λ.
- An integer $v = \mathcal{O}(\log n)$ denotes the block-size of messages, and then let $\delta := 2^v$.
- A positive integer $\mu = dv$ denotes the bit-length of message/tag pairs, where d is a positive integer.
- $G_a : \{0,1\}^n \to \{0,1\}^{\delta n}$ is a randomized PRG with a uniformly random parameter $a \in \{0,1\}^{\delta n \times n}$ and a randomness space $\mathsf{Ber}_t^{\delta n}$. G_a is described as $G_a(s; e) = a \cdot s \oplus e$, where e is drawn from $\mathsf{Ber}_t^{\delta n}$.

- $\mathsf{SAMP} : \{0,1\}^n \to \mathsf{Ber}_t^{\delta^2 n}$ denotes a (deterministic) sampling function which, on input randomness in $\{0,1\}^n$, outputs a value over $\mathsf{Ber}_t^{\delta n}$.
- $\mathsf{PRF} : \mathcal{K} \times \mathcal{X} \to \{0,1\}^n$ is a classical PRF.
- c is a counter value and $\mathcal{L}_c \leftarrow \{\emptyset\}$ is a list of counter values.

$\mathsf{SAMAC_{LPN}}$ is constructed as follows:

- $\mathsf{k_{id}} \leftarrow \mathsf{KGen}(1^\lambda, \mathsf{id})$: Generate a key as follows:
  1. $s \xleftarrow{U} \{0,1\}^n$, $\mathsf{k_{PRF}} \xleftarrow{U} \mathcal{K}$.
  2. Output $\mathsf{k_{id}} := (s, \mathsf{k_{PRF}})$.
- $\tau \leftarrow \mathsf{STag}(\mathsf{k_{id}}, m, \tau')$: Split τ' into $(c, \boldsymbol{y}')$ and generate an aggregate tag in the following way:
  1. $e^{(0\ldots00)} \parallel e^{(0\ldots01)} \parallel \cdots \parallel e^{(1\ldots11)} \leftarrow \mathsf{SAMP}(\mathsf{PRF}(\mathsf{k_{PRF}}, c))$.
  2. $(z_i)_{i\in[\mu]} \leftarrow m \parallel y' \in \{0,1\}^\mu$.
  3. $y \leftarrow G_a^{(z_{(d-1)v+1}\ldots z_{dv})}(\ldots G_a^{(z_{v+1}\ldots z_{2v})}(G_a^{(z_1\ldots z_v)}(s; e^{(z_1\ldots z_v)}); e^{(z_{v+1}\ldots z_{2v})})\ldots)$.
  4. Output $\tau := (c, y)$.
- $1/0 \leftarrow \mathsf{SVrfy}(K, (M, \tau'), \tau)$: Verify $((M, \tau'), \tau)$ in the following way:
  1. Output 0 if $c \in \mathcal{L}_c$.
  2. $\tilde{\tau} \leftarrow \mathsf{STag}(\mathsf{k}_{\mathsf{id}_{\sigma(\ell)}}, m_\ell, \mathsf{STag}(\ldots \mathsf{STag}(\mathsf{k}_{\mathsf{id}_{\sigma(1)}}, m_1, \tau')\ldots))$.
  3. Output 1 and set $\mathcal{L}_c \leftarrow \mathcal{L}_c \cup \{c\}$ if $\tau = \tilde{\tau}$, or output 0 otherwise.

We can obtain the following result about security. The proof can be given in the same way as that of Theorem 3.

Corollary 1. *If* $\mathsf{LPN}_{t,n}$ *assumption holds and* PRF *is a pseudorandom function, then* $\mathsf{SAMAC_{LPN}}$ *meets* saggUF-qCMA *security.*

References

1. Ahn, J.H., Green, M., Hohenberger, S.: Synchronized aggregate signatures: new definitions, constructions and applications. In: ACM Conference on Computer and Communications Security, pp. 473–484. ACM (2010)
2. Applebaum, B., Cash, D., Peikert, C., Sahai, A.: Fast cryptographic primitives and circular-secure encryption based on hard learning problems. In: Halevi, S. (ed.) CRYPTO 2009. LNCS, vol. 5677, pp. 595–618. Springer, Heidelberg (2009). https://doi.org/10.1007/978-3-642-03356-8_35
3. Bellare, M., Kilian, J., Rogaway, P.: The security of the cipher block chaining message authentication code. J. Comput. Syst. Sci. **61**(3), 362–399 (2000)
4. Boneh, D., Zhandry, M.: Quantum-secure message authentication codes. In: Johansson, T., Nguyen, P.Q. (eds.) EUROCRYPT 2013. LNCS, vol. 7881, pp. 592–608. Springer, Heidelberg (2013). https://doi.org/10.1007/978-3-642-38348-9_35
5. David, B., Dowsley, R., Nascimento, A.C.A.: Universally composable oblivious transfer based on a variant of LPN. In: Gritzalis, D., Kiayias, A., Askoxylakis, I. (eds.) CANS 2014. LNCS, vol. 8813, pp. 143–158. Springer, Cham (2014). https://doi.org/10.1007/978-3-319-12280-9_10

6. Dodis, Y., Kiltz, E., Pietrzak, K., Wichs, D.: Message authentication, revisited. In: Pointcheval, D., Johansson, T. (eds.) EUROCRYPT 2012. LNCS, vol. 7237, pp. 355–374. Springer, Heidelberg (2012). https://doi.org/10.1007/978-3-642-29011-4_22
7. Döttling, N., Müller-Quade, J., Nascimento, A.C.A.: IND-CCA secure cryptography based on a variant of the LPN problem. In: Wang, X., Sako, K. (eds.) ASIACRYPT 2012. LNCS, vol. 7658, pp. 485–503. Springer, Heidelberg (2012). https://doi.org/10.1007/978-3-642-34961-4_30
8. Eikemeier, O., et al.: History-free aggregate message authentication codes. In: Garay, J.A., De Prisco, R. (eds.) SCN 2010. LNCS, vol. 6280, pp. 309–328. Springer, Heidelberg (2010). https://doi.org/10.1007/978-3-642-15317-4_20
9. Goldreich, O., Goldwasser, S., Micali, S.: How to construct random functions (extended abstract). In: FOCS, pp. 464–479. IEEE Computer Society (1984)
10. Hirose, S., Kuwakado, H.: Forward-secure sequential aggregate message authentication revisited. In: Chow, S.S.M., Liu, J.K., Hui, L.C.K., Yiu, S.M. (eds.) ProvSec 2014. LNCS, vol. 8782, pp. 87–102. Springer, Cham (2014). https://doi.org/10.1007/978-3-319-12475-9_7
11. Hohenberger, S., Waters, B.: Synchronized aggregate signatures from the RSA assumption. In: Nielsen, J.B., Rijmen, V. (eds.) EUROCRYPT 2018. LNCS, vol. 10821, pp. 197–229. Springer, Cham (2018). https://doi.org/10.1007/978-3-319-78375-8_7
12. Kaplan, M., Leurent, G., Leverrier, A., Naya-Plasencia, M.: Breaking symmetric cryptosystems using quantum period finding. In: Robshaw, M., Katz, J. (eds.) CRYPTO 2016. LNCS, vol. 9815, pp. 207–237. Springer, Heidelberg (2016). https://doi.org/10.1007/978-3-662-53008-5_8
13. Katz, J., Lindell, A.Y.: Aggregate message authentication codes. In: Malkin, T. (ed.) CT-RSA 2008. LNCS, vol. 4964, pp. 155–169. Springer, Heidelberg (2008). https://doi.org/10.1007/978-3-540-79263-5_10
14. Kiltz, E., Masny, D., Pietrzak, K.: Simple chosen-ciphertext security from low-noise LPN. In: Krawczyk, H. (ed.) PKC 2014. LNCS, vol. 8383, pp. 1–18. Springer, Heidelberg (2014). https://doi.org/10.1007/978-3-642-54631-0_1
15. NIST: Post-quantum cryptography: post-quantum cryptography standardzation (2017)
16. Shor, P.W.: Algorithms for quantum computation: discrete logarithms and factoring. In: Proceedings of IEEE Symposium on Foundations of Computer Science, pp. 124–134. IEEE (1994)
17. Shor, P.W.: Polynomial-time algorithms for prime factorization and discrete logarithms on a quantum computer. SIAM J. Comput. **26**(5), 1484–1509 (1997)
18. Song, F., Yun, A.: Quantum security of NMAC and related constructions. In: Katz, J., Shacham, H. (eds.) CRYPTO 2017. LNCS, vol. 10402, pp. 283–309. Springer, Cham (2017). https://doi.org/10.1007/978-3-319-63715-0_10
19. Tomita, S., Watanabe, Y., Shikata, J.: Sequential aggregate authentication codes with information theoretic security. In: CISS, pp. 192–197. IEEE (2016)
20. Yu, Y., Steinberger, J.: Pseudorandom functions in almost constant depth from low-noise LPN. In: Fischlin, M., Coron, J.-S. (eds.) EUROCRYPT 2016. LNCS, vol. 9666, pp. 154–183. Springer, Heidelberg (2016). https://doi.org/10.1007/978-3-662-49896-5_6
21. Zhandry, M.: How to construct quantum random functions. In: FOCS. pp. 679–687. IEEE Computer Society (2012)
22. Zhandry, M.: A note on the quantum collision and set equality problems. Quantum Inf. Comput. **15**(7–8), 557–567 (2015)

SO-CCA Secure PKE in the Quantum Random Oracle Model or the Quantum Ideal Cipher Model

Shingo Sato[1(✉)] and Junji Shikata[1,2]

[1] Graduate School of Environment and Information Sciences, Yokohama National University, Yokohama, Japan
sato-shingo-cz@ynu.jp, shikata-junji-rb@ynu.ac.jp

[2] Institute of Advanced Sciences, Yokohama National University, Yokohama, Japan

Abstract. Selective opening (SO) security is one of the most important securities of public key encryption (PKE) in a multi-user setting. Even though messages and random coins used in some ciphertexts are leaked, SO security guarantees the confidentiality of the other ciphertexts. Actually, it is shown that there exist PKE schemes which meet the standard security such as indistinguishability against chosen ciphertext attacks (IND-CCA security) but do not meet SO security against chosen ciphertext attacks. Hence, it is important to consider SO security in the multi-user setting. On the other hand, many researchers have studied cryptosystems in the security model where adversaries can submit quantum superposition queries (i.e., quantum queries) to oracles. In particular, IND-CCA secure PKE and KEM schemes in the quantum random oracle model have been intensively studied so far.

In this paper, we show that two kinds of constructions of hybrid encryption schemes meet simulation-based SO security against chosen ciphertext attacks (SIM-SO-CCA security) in the quantum random oracle model or the quantum ideal cipher model. The first scheme is constructed from any IND-CCA secure KEM and any simulatable data encapsulation mechanism (DEM). The second one is constructed from any IND-CCA secure KEM based on Fujisaki-Okamoto transformation and any strongly unforgetable message authentication code (MAC). We can apply any IND-CCA secure KEM scheme to the first one if the underlying DEM scheme meets simulatability, whereas we can apply any DEM scheme meeting integrity to the second one if the underlying KEM is based on Fujisaki-Okamoto transformation.

Keywords: Post-quantum cryptography · Simulation-based selective opening security · Quantum random oracle model · Quantum ideal cipher model

M. Albrecht (Ed.): IMACC 2019, LNCS 11929, pp. 317–341, 2019.
https://doi.org/10.1007/978-3-030-35199-1_16

1 Introduction

1.1 Background

As one of the most important securities of public key encryption (PKE), securities against chosen ciphertext attacks, which is called *CCA* security, have been studied. However, as the security of PKE in the multi-user setting, the notion of securities against selective opening attacks, which is called SO security, was introduced by Bellare, Hofheinz and Yilek in [4]. SO security guarantees that even though an adversary gets secret information such as messages and random coins used in some ciphertexts, the other ciphertexts meet confidentiality. In a real world, there exist such situations where secret information of some ciphertexts is leaked because of factors except for cryptosystems such as vulnerability in implementation and side-channel attacks. Actually, it is shown that there exist PKE schemes which meet *CCA* security but do not satisfy SO security [3,22,23]. Hence, it is important to consider SO security. In particular, several SO secure PKE schemes have been proposed so far: PKE [4,16,17,21,33], hybrid encryption [14,18,32], identity-based encryption [7,30], and lattice-based PKE [11,31]. SO security is roughly classified as simulation-based SO (SIM-SO) security and indistinguishability-based SO (IND-SO) security. In this paper, we consider SIM-SO security against chosen ciphertext attacks called SIM-SO-CCA security, since it seems that it is harder to achieve SIM-SO security [8,21] and several works aimed at proposing SIM-SO-CCA secure PKE schemes in the past [14,17,18,21,31–33]. Hence, it is natural to consider SIM-SO-CCA security as our goal in the multi-user setting.

On the other hand, we consider the model where adversaries can submit quantum superposition queries (i.e., quantum queries) to oracles. In particular, secure cryptosystems in the quantum random oracle model (QROM) have been intensively studied. The QROM, whose notion was introduced by [9], is a model where any users can issue quantum queries to random oracles. There exist several works related to PKE schemes in the QROM: PKE [9,36], key encapsulation mechanism (KEM) [20,25–28,35], digital signatures (DSs) [10,13,19,29]. Moreover, almost all PKE/KEM and DS schemes submitted to the post-quantum cryptography standardization process of NIST (National Institute of Standards and Technology) satisfy securities in the QROM. Therefore, it is interesting and important to consider secure PKE schemes in the QROM. PKE/KEM schemes in the QROM that have already been proposed are summarized as follows. A PKE scheme constructed from trapdoor permutations meets indistinguishability against chosen ciphertext attacks (called IND-CCA security) in the QROM [9]. [36] proved that Fujisaki-Okamoto (FO) transformation [15] and OAEP [6] with additional hash satisfy IND-CCA security in the QROM. [20] analyzed FO-based KEM schemes. Based on the proof technique of [9,35] proposed a tightly secure KEM scheme starting from any disjunct-simulatable deterministic PKE scheme. [26] revisited FO-based KEM schemes with implicit rejection and proved that they meet tighter IND-CCA security without additional hash. [27] proposed IND-CCA secure KEM schemes with explicit rejection. [25] gave a tighter security proof for the KEM scheme based on FO transformation by utilizing the proof techniques proposed in [2]. [28] also gave tighter security proofs for generic constructions of KEM by utilizing the techniques in [2].

1.2 Our Contribution

Our goal is to present SIM-SO-CCA secure PKE schemes obtained from KEM schemes in the QROM or the quantum ideal cipher model (QICM). Our main motivation is that we would like to transform any PKE/KEM schemes submitted to the post-quantum cryptography standardization to SIM-SO-CCA secure PKE without loss of efficiency in terms of key-size, ciphertext-size, and time-complexity.

In the classical random oracle model, classical ideal cipher model, or the standard model (i.e., the model without random oracles or ideal ciphers), several SIM-SO-CCA secure PKE schemes constructed from KEM schemes have been studied. Liu and Paterson proposed a SIM-SO-CCA secure PKE scheme constructed from KEM schemes secure against tailored constrained chosen ciphertext attacks and strengthened cross authentication codes (XACs) [32]. Heuer et al. proposed a SIM-SO-CCA secure construction by combining KEM secure against plaintext checking attacks and message authentication codes (MACs) [17]. Heuer and Poettering proved that a PKE scheme in the KEM/DEM framework meets SIM-SO-CCA security in the classical ideal cipher model if a KEM scheme satisfies IND-CCA security and a DEM scheme satisfies both of simulatability and one-time integrity of chosen ciphertext attacks, which is called OT-INT-CTXT security [18]. Lyu et al. proposed a tightly secure PKE starting from any KEM scheme meeting both of multi-encapsulation pseudorandom security and random encapsulation rejection security, and any XAC [33]. Table 1 shows the above primitives and security models of the existing constructions.

In the QROM or QICM, how to construct PKE schemes meeting SIM-SO-CCA security is not obvious because of the following reason: In the classical random oracle model or classical ideal cipher model, the security proofs of existing schemes [18,32] utilize the lists of query/response pairs submitted to random oracles or ideal ciphers. In the QROM and QICM, we cannot use such lists, since it is impossible to record query/response pairs in principle due to the quantum no-cloning theorem. Hence, it is worth to consider secure PKE schemes in the models where quantum queries are issued.

As for the PKE schemes obtained from KEM schemes in the standard model [32,33], ciphertext-size and time-complexity of encryption and decryption algorithms linearly depend on the bit-length of messages. Since we are aiming at constructing practical PKE schemes, we do not focus on these schemes in this paper due to the lack of efficiency in terms of ciphertext-size and time-complexity.

In this paper, we propose two constructions of SIM-SO-CCA secure PKE schemes from KEM schemes and symmetric key encryption (SKE) schemes. The details are explained as follows:

1. The first scheme PKE_1^{hy} is the KEM/DEM scheme [12]. We prove that this scheme meets SIM-SO-CCA security in the QICM if the underlying KEM

Table 1. SIM-SO-CCA secure PKE constructed from KEM schemes: IND-tCCCA means indistinguishability against tailored constrained chosen ciphertext attacks. mPR-CCCA means multi-encapsulation pseudorandom security against constrained chosen ciphertext attacks. RER means random encapsulation rejection security. XAC means cross authentication code. IND-CPA means indistinguishability against chosen message attacks. FO-based KEM means $\mathsf{FO}^{\not\perp}$, $\mathsf{FO}^{\not\perp}_m$, $\mathsf{QFO}^{\not\perp}$, and $\mathsf{QFO}^{\not\perp}_m$. Standard model denotes the security model without random oracles and ideal ciphers.

Scheme	Primitives	Security Model
[32]	IND-tCCCA secure KEM	Standard Model
	XAC	
[17]	OW-PCA secure KEM	Random Oracle Model
	sUF-OT-CMA secure MAC	
[18]	IND-CCA secure KEM	Ideal Cipher Model
	Simulatable DEM	
[33]	mPR-CCCA and RER secure KEM	Standard Model
	XAC	
PKE_1^{hy}	IND-CCA secure KEM	Quantum Ideal Cipher Model
	Simulatable DEM	
PKE_2^{hy}	FO-based KEM (from IND-CPA secure PKE)	Quantum Random Oracle Model
	sUF-OT-CMA secure MAC	

scheme satisfies IND-CCA security, and the underlying DEM scheme satisfies both of simulatability [18] and one-time integrity of chosen ciphertext attacks (OT-INT-CTXT security) [5]. The advantage of this scheme is that we can apply any IND-CCA secure KEM scheme such as any PKE/KEM schemes submitted to the post-quantum cryptography standardization, and we can obtain a SIM-SO-CCA secure PKE schemes in the QICM. In addition, almost all standardized DEM schemes satisfy simulatability and OT-INT-CTXT security. Hence, we can realize concrete PKE schemes in the QICM.

2. The second one PKE_2^{hy} is a concrete scheme constructed from any FO-based KEM scheme such as $\mathsf{FO}^{\not\perp}$, $\mathsf{FO}^{\not\perp}_m$, $\mathsf{QFO}^{\not\perp}$, and $\mathsf{QFO}^{\not\perp}_m$, which are categorized in [20], and any MAC meeting strong unforgetability against one-time chosen message attacks called sUF-OT-CMA security. The underlying KEM scheme

is FO-based KEM with implicit rejection. That is, these schemes output a random key which is not encapsulated if a given ciphertext is invalid.
We require that the underlying PKE scheme in $\mathsf{FO}^{\not\perp}$, $\mathsf{FO}^{\not\perp}_m$, $\mathsf{QFO}^{\not\perp}$, or $\mathsf{QFO}^{\not\perp}_m$ is injective and satisfies indistinguishability against chosen plaintext attacks called IND-CPA security. In addition, almost all KEM schemes submitted to the NIST post-quantum cryptography standardization are classified as $\mathsf{FO}^{\not\perp}$, $\mathsf{FO}^{\not\perp}_m$, $\mathsf{QFO}^{\not\perp}$, or $\mathsf{QFO}^{\not\perp}_m$. Hence, the advantage of PKE_2^{hy} is that a lot of PKE/KEM schemes submitted to the post-quantum standardization can satisfy SIM-SO-CCA security without demanding any special property such as simulatability for the underlying SKE.

The difference between PKE_1^{hy} and PKE_2^{hy} is given as follows:

- Any IND-CCA secure KEM scheme can be applied to PKE_1^{hy} while a particular KEM scheme (i.e., $\mathsf{FO}^{\not\perp}$, $\mathsf{FO}^{\not\perp}_m$, $\mathsf{QFO}^{\not\perp}$, or $\mathsf{QFO}^{\not\perp}_m$) can be applied to PKE_2^{hy}.
- PKE_1^{hy} requires that the underlying DEM scheme satisfies a special property such as simulatability while PKE_2^{hy} does not require that the underlying MAC satisfies such a special property.

In Sects. 3.1 and 3.2, we describe concrete primitives which can be applied to PKE_1^{hy} and PKE_2^{hy}, respectively.

2 Preliminaries

For a positive integer n, let $[n]$ be a set $\{1, 2, \ldots, n\}$. For a set $\mathcal{X}$, let $|\mathcal{X}|$ be the number of elements in $\mathcal{X}$ (the size of $\mathcal{X}$). For a set $\mathcal{X}$ and an element $x \in \mathcal{X}$, we write $|x|$ as the bit-length of x. We write that a function $\epsilon = \epsilon(\lambda)$ is negligible, if for a large enough λ and all polynomial $p(\lambda)$, it holds that $\epsilon(\lambda) < 1/p(\lambda)$. For a randomized algorithm A and any input x of A, $\mathsf{A}(x; r)$ denotes a deterministic algorithm, where r is a random coin used in A. In this paper, probabilistic polynomial-time is abbreviated as PPT, and quantum polynomial-time is abbreviated as QPT.

2.1 Quantum Computation

We define an n-qubit state as $|\varphi\rangle = \sum_{x\in\{0,1\}^n} \psi_x|x\rangle$ with a basis $\{|x\rangle\}_{x\in\{0,1\}^n}$ and amplitudes $\psi_x \in \mathbb{C}$ such that $\sum_{x\in\{0,1\}^n} |\psi_x|^2 = 1$. If $|\varphi\rangle = \sum_{x\in\{0,1\}^n} \psi_x|x\rangle$ is measured in the computational basis, $|\varphi\rangle$ will become a classical state $|x\rangle$ with probability $|\psi_x|^2$. For a quantum oracle $\mathsf{O} : \mathcal{X} \to \mathcal{Y}$, submitting a quantum query $\sum_{x\in\mathcal{X},y\in\mathcal{Y}} \psi_{x,y}|x, y\rangle$ to O (quantum access to O) is written as

$$\sum_{x\in\mathcal{X},y\in\mathcal{Y}} \psi_{x,y}|x, y\rangle \mapsto \sum_{x\in\mathcal{X},y\in\mathcal{Y}} \psi_{x,y}|x, y \oplus \mathsf{O}(x)\rangle.$$

The quantum random oracle model (QROM) is defined as the model where quantum adversaries can submit quantum queries to random oracles. The quantum ideal (block) cipher model (QICM) which was introduced in [24] is defined as follows: A block cipher with a key space $\mathcal{K}$ and a message space $\mathcal{X}$ is defined as a mapping $E : \mathcal{K} \times \mathcal{X} \to \mathcal{X}$ which is a permutation over $\mathcal{X}$ for any key in $\mathcal{K}$. In the QICM, quantum adversaries are allowed to issue quantum queries to oracles $E^+ : \mathcal{K} \times \mathcal{X} \to \mathcal{X}$ and $E^- : \mathcal{K} \times \mathcal{X} \to \mathcal{X}$ such that for any $\mathsf{k} \in \mathcal{K}$ and any $x, y \in \mathcal{X}$, the response of $E^-(\mathsf{k}, y)$ is x meeting $E^+(\mathsf{k}, x) = y$. In this paper, QROM (resp. QICM) denote the security model where quantum adversaries are allowed to issue quantum queries to random oracles (resp. ideal ciphers), but submit only classical queries to the other oracles.

Semi-classical Oracle. We describe semi-classical oracle which was introduced in [2] and utilize this oracle for our security proofs. We consider quantum access to an oracle with a domain $\mathcal{X}$. A semi-classical oracle O_S^{SC} for a subset $S \subseteq \mathcal{X}$ uses an indicator function $f_S : \mathcal{X} \to \{0,1\}$ with the subset S which evaluates 1 if $x \in S$ is given, and evaluates 0 otherwise. When O_S^{SC} is given a quantum query $\sum_{x \in \mathcal{X}} \psi_x |x\rangle|0\rangle$ with the input register Q and the output register R, it maps

$$\sum_{x \in \mathcal{X}} \psi_{x,z} |x\rangle|0\rangle \mapsto \sum_{x \in \mathcal{X}} \psi_x |x\rangle|f_S(x)\rangle,$$

and measures the register R. Then, the quantum query $\sum_{x \in \mathcal{X}} \psi_x |x\rangle|0\rangle$ collapses to either $\sum_{x \in \mathcal{X} \setminus S} \psi'_x |x\rangle|0\rangle$ or $\sum_{x \in S} \psi'_x |x\rangle|1\rangle$. Let Find be the event that O_S^{SC} returns $\sum_{x \in S} \psi'_x |x\rangle|1\rangle$ for a quantum query $\sum_{x \in S} \psi_x |x\rangle$. For a quantum oracle H with domain $\mathcal{X}$ and a subset $S \subseteq \mathcal{X}$, let $\mathsf{H} \setminus S$ be an oracle which first queries O_S^{SC} and then H.

By using semi-classical oracles, [2] proved the following propositions. We notice that for query depth d and the number of queries q, we use q such that $q \geq d$ in the same way as Theorem 2.8 in [25].

Proposition 1 (Theorem 1 in [2]). *Let $S \subseteq \mathcal{X}$ be random. Let $\mathsf{H} : \mathcal{X} \to \mathcal{Y}$, $\mathsf{G} : \mathcal{X} \to \mathcal{Y}$ be random functions such that $\mathsf{H}(x) = \mathsf{G}(x)$ for all $x \in \mathcal{X} \setminus S$, and let z be a random bit-string (S, H, G and z may have an arbitrary joint distribution). Let A be any quantum algorithm issuing at most q quantum queries to oracles. Then, it holds that*

$$\left|\Pr[1 \leftarrow \mathsf{A}^{\mathsf{H}}(z)] - \Pr[1 \leftarrow \mathsf{A}^{\mathsf{G}}(z)]\right| \leq 2\sqrt{q \cdot \Pr[\mathsf{Find} \mid 1 \leftarrow \mathsf{A}^{\mathsf{H} \setminus S}(z)]}.$$

Proposition 2 (Corollary 1 in [2]). *Let A be any quantum algorithm issuing at most q quantum queries to a semi-classical oracle with domain $\mathcal{X}$. Suppose that $S \subseteq \mathcal{X}$ and $z \in \{0,1\}^*$ are independent. Then, it holds that* $\Pr[\mathsf{Find} \mid \mathsf{A}^{O_S^{SC}}(z)] \leq 4q \cdot P_{\max}$*, where* $P_{\max} = \max_{x \in X} \Pr[x \in S]$.

2.2 Cryptosystems

Public Key Encryption. A public key encryption (PKE) scheme consists of a tuple of three polynomial-time algorithms $(\mathsf{KGen}, \mathsf{Enc}, \mathsf{Dec})$ with a message space $\mathcal{M} = \mathcal{M}(\lambda)$ for a security parameter λ.

Key Generation KGen is a randomized algorithm which, on input a security parameter 1^λ, outputs a public key pk and a secret key sk.

Encryption Enc is a randomized or deterministic algorithm which, on input a public key pk and a message $m \in \mathcal{M}$, outputs a ciphertext c.

Decryption Dec is a deterministic algorithm which, on input a secret key sk and a ciphertext c, outputs a message $\mu \in \mathcal{M}$ or an invalid symbol $\perp$.

A PKE scheme $(\mathsf{KGen}, \mathsf{Enc}, \mathsf{Dec})$ meets δ-correctness [20] if the expectation $\mathbf{E}[\max_{m\in\mathcal{M}} \Pr[\mathsf{Dec}(\mathsf{sk}, \mathsf{c}) \neq m \mid \mathsf{c} \leftarrow \mathsf{Enc}(\mathsf{pk}, m)]]$ taken over $(\mathsf{pk}, \mathsf{sk}) \leftarrow \mathsf{KGen}(\lambda)$ is at most δ.

We define IND-CPA security as follows:

Definition 1 (IND-CPA **security**). *A PKE scheme* $\mathsf{PKE} = (\mathsf{KGen}, \mathsf{Enc}, \mathsf{Dec})$ *meets* IND-CPA *security if for any PPT adversary* A *against* PKE*, the advantage* $\mathsf{Adv}^{\text{ind-cpa}}_{\mathsf{PKE},\mathsf{A}}(\lambda) := |2 \cdot \Pr[\mathsf{A}\ wins] - 1|$ *is negligible in* λ*, where* $[\mathsf{A}\ wins]$ *is the event that* A *wins in the following game:*

Key Generation: *A challenger generates* $(\mathsf{pk}, \mathsf{sk}) \leftarrow \mathsf{KGen}(\lambda)$.

Challenge: *When* A *submits* (m_0, m_1) *such that* $|m_0| = |m_1|$*, the challenger returns* $\mathsf{c}^* \leftarrow \mathsf{Enc}(\mathsf{pk}, m_b)$ *for* $b \xleftarrow{U} \{0,1\}$.

Output: A *outputs the guessing bit* $b' \in \{0,1\}$. A *wins if* $b = b'$ *holds.*

SIM-SO-CCA security is defined as follows.

Definition 2 (SIM-SO-CCA **security**). *A PKE scheme* $\mathsf{PKE} = (\mathsf{KGen}, \mathsf{Enc}, \mathsf{Dec})$ *meets* SIM-SO-CCA *security if for any PPT algorithms* $\mathsf{A} = (\mathsf{A}_0, \mathsf{A}_1)$, $\mathsf{S} = (\mathsf{S}_0, \mathsf{S}_1)$ *and any relation* R*, the advantage* $\mathsf{Adv}^{\text{sim-so-cca}}_{\mathsf{PKE},\mathsf{A},\mathsf{S},R}(\lambda)$ *is negligible in* λ. $\mathsf{Adv}^{\text{sim-so-cca}}_{\mathsf{PKE},\mathsf{A},\mathsf{S},R}(\lambda)$ *is defined as follow:*

$$\mathsf{Adv}^{\text{sim-so-cca}}_{\mathsf{PKE},\mathsf{A},\mathsf{S},R}(\lambda) := \left|\Pr[\mathsf{Exp}^{\text{real-so-cca}}_{\mathsf{PKE},\mathsf{A}}(\lambda) \to 1] - \Pr[\mathsf{Exp}^{\text{ideal-so-cca}}_{\mathsf{PKE},\mathsf{S}}(\lambda) \to 1]\right|,$$

where the two experiments $\mathsf{Exp}^{\text{real-so-cca}}_{\mathsf{PKE},\mathsf{A}}(\lambda)$ *and* $\mathsf{Exp}^{\text{ideal-so-cca}}_{\mathsf{PKE},\mathsf{S}}(\lambda)$ *are defined in Fig. 1.*

Key Encapsulation Mechanism. A key encapsulation mechanism (KEM) scheme consists of three polynomial-time algorithms $(\mathsf{KGen}, \mathsf{Encap}, \mathsf{Decap})$ with a key space $\mathcal{K} = \mathcal{K}(\lambda)$ for a security parameter λ.

Key Generation. KGen is a randomized algorithm which, on input a security parameter 1^λ, outputs a public key pk and a secret key sk.

Encapsulation. Encap is a randomized algorithm which, on input a public key pk, outputs a ciphertext c and a key $\mathsf{k} \in \mathcal{K}$.

Decapsulation. Decap is a deterministic algorithm which, on input a secret key sk and a ciphertext c, outputs a key $\mathsf{k} \in \mathcal{K}$ or an invalid symbol $\perp$.

$\mathsf{Exp}^{\text{real-so-cca}}_{\mathsf{PKE,A}}(\lambda)$	$\mathsf{Exp}^{\text{ideal-so-cca}}_{\mathsf{PKE,S}}(\lambda)$
$I \leftarrow \emptyset$	$I \leftarrow \emptyset$
$(\mathsf{pk}, \mathsf{sk}) \leftarrow \mathsf{KGen}(1^\lambda)$	
$(\mathcal{M}_\mathrm{D}, \mathsf{st}) \leftarrow \mathsf{A}_0(\mathsf{pk})$	$(\mathcal{M}_\mathrm{D}, \mathsf{st}) \leftarrow \mathsf{S}_0(1^\lambda)$
$(m_1, \ldots, m_n) \overset{U}{\leftarrow} \mathcal{M}_\mathrm{D}$	$(m_1, \ldots, m_n) \overset{U}{\leftarrow} \mathcal{M}_\mathrm{D}$
$(r_1, \ldots, r_n) \overset{U}{\leftarrow} \mathcal{R}$	
$\forall i \in [n], \mathsf{c}_i = \mathsf{Enc}(\mathsf{pk}, m_i; r_i)$	
$out \leftarrow \mathsf{A}_1^{\mathsf{OPEN},\mathsf{DEC}}(\mathsf{st}, \mathsf{c}_1, \ldots, \mathsf{c}_n)$	$out \leftarrow \mathsf{S}_1^{\mathsf{OPEN}}(\mathsf{st}, \lvert m_1 \rvert, \ldots, \lvert m_n \rvert)$
return $R(\mathcal{M}_\mathcal{D}, m_1, \ldots, m_n, I, out)$	**return** $R(\mathcal{M}_\mathcal{D}, m_1, \ldots, m_n, I, out)$

$\mathsf{OPEN}(i)$	$\mathsf{OPEN}(i)$
$I \leftarrow I \cup \{i\}$	$I \leftarrow I \cup \{i\}$
return (m_i, r_i)	**return** m_i

$\mathsf{DEC}(\mathsf{c})$

if $\mathsf{c} \in \{\mathsf{c}_i\}_{i \in [n]}$, **return** $\perp$
$m \leftarrow \mathsf{Dec}(\mathsf{sk}, \mathsf{c})$
return $m \in \mathcal{M} \cup \{\perp\}$

Fig. 1. Experiments in Real-SIM-SO-CCA and Ideal-SIM-SO-CCA Games

A KEM scheme (KGen, Encap, Decap) meets δ-correctness if for any $(\mathsf{pk}, \mathsf{sk}) \leftarrow \mathsf{KGen}(1^\lambda)$, it holds that $\mathsf{k} = \mathsf{Decap}(\mathsf{sk}, \mathsf{c})$ with at least probability $1 - \delta$, where $(\mathsf{c}, \mathsf{k}) \leftarrow \mathsf{Encap}(\mathsf{pk})$. Then, it is required that KEM schemes satisfy δ-correctness with a negligible function δ for λ.

As a security of KEM, IND-CCA security is defined as follows.

Definition 3 (IND-CCA security). *A KEM scheme* KEM $=$ (KGen, Encap, Decap) *meets* IND-CCA *security if for any PPT adversary* A *against* KEM*, the advantage* $\mathsf{Adv}^{\text{ind-cca}}_{\mathsf{KEM,A}}(\lambda) := \lvert 2 \cdot \Pr[\mathsf{A}\ wins] - 1 \rvert$ *is negligible in* λ. [A *wins*] *is the event that* A *wins in the following game:*

Setup: *A challenger generates* $(\mathsf{pk}, \mathsf{sk}) \leftarrow \mathsf{KGen}(\lambda)$ *and sends* pk *to* A.
Oracle Access: A *is allowed to access the following oracles:*

- Challenge()*: Given a challenge request, the challenger computes* $(\mathsf{c}^*, \mathsf{k}_0) \leftarrow \mathsf{Encap}(\mathsf{pk})$ *and chooses* $\mathsf{k}_1 \in \mathcal{K}$ *uniformly at random. It returns* $(\mathsf{c}^*, \mathsf{k}_b)$ *for* $b \overset{U}{\leftarrow} \{0, 1\}$.
- DEC(c)*: Given a ciphertext query* c*, a decapsulation oracle* DEC(c) *returns* $\mathsf{k}' \leftarrow \mathsf{Decap}(\mathsf{sk}, \mathsf{c}) \in \mathcal{K} \cup \{\perp\}$. A *is not allowed to submit* c^* *to* $\mathsf{DEC}(\cdot)$.

Output: A *outputs the guessing bit* $b' \in \{0, 1\}$. A *wins if* $b = b'$ *holds.*

Data Encapsulation Mechanism. A data encapsulation mechanism (DEM) scheme consists of two polynomial-time algorithms (Enc, Dec) with a key space $\mathcal{K} = \mathcal{K}(\lambda)$ and a message space $\mathcal{M} = \mathcal{M}(\lambda)$ for a security parameter λ.

Encapsulation. Enc is an algorithm which, on input a secret key $\mathsf{k} \in \mathcal{K}$ and a message $m \in \mathcal{M}$, outputs a ciphertext c.

Decryption. Dec is a deterministic algorithm which, on input a secret key $\mathsf{k} \in \mathcal{K}$, a ciphertext c, outputs a message $m \in \mathcal{M}$ or an invalid symbol $\perp$.

We require that DEM schemes meet correctness as follows: A DEM scheme $(\mathsf{Enc}, \mathsf{Dec})$ meets correctness if for any $\mathsf{k} \in \mathcal{K}$ and any $m \in \mathcal{M}$, it holds that $m = \mathsf{Dec}(\mathsf{k}, \mathsf{c})$, where $\mathsf{c} \leftarrow \mathsf{Enc}(\mathsf{k}, m)$.

As a security of DEM, we define *one-time integrity of chosen ciphertext attacks* which is called OT-INT-CTXT security [5].

Definition 4 (OT-INT-CTXT security). *A DEM scheme* $\mathsf{DEM} = (\mathsf{Enc}, \mathsf{Dec})$ *meets* OT-INT-CTXT *security if for any PPT adversary* A *against* DEM*, the advantage* $\mathsf{Adv}^{\text{int-ctxt}}_{\mathsf{A},\mathsf{DEM}}(\lambda) := \Pr[\mathsf{A}\ wins]$ *is negligible in* λ*, where* $[\mathsf{A}\ wins]$ *is the event that* A *wins in the following game:*

Setup: *A challenger chooses a key* $\mathsf{k} \in \mathcal{K}$ *uniformly at random, and sets* $\mathsf{win} \leftarrow 0$ *and* $C \leftarrow \emptyset$.

Oracle Access: A *is allowed to the following oracles:*

- $\mathsf{ENC}(m)$: *If* $C \neq \emptyset$*, an encryption oracle* $\mathsf{ENC}(m)$ *returns* $\perp$*. Otherwise, it returns* $\mathsf{c} \leftarrow \mathsf{Enc}(\mathsf{k}, m)$*, and sets* $C \leftarrow C \cup \{\mathsf{c}\}$.
- $\mathsf{VRFY}(\mathsf{c})$: *Given a ciphertext query* c*, a verification oracle* $\mathsf{VRFY}(\mathsf{c})$ *runs* $m' \leftarrow \mathsf{Dec}(\mathsf{k}, m)$*. If* $m' \neq \perp$ *and* $\mathsf{c} \notin C$*, it sets* $\mathsf{win} \leftarrow 1$*. It returns* 1 *if* $m' \neq \perp$*, and returns* 0 *otherwise.*

Final: A *wins if* $\mathsf{win} = 1$.

In this paper, we view DEM as block cipher-based DEM which uses a block-cipher as a black-box. In addition, we view the key space $\mathcal{K}$ of DEM schemes as a product set $\mathcal{K} = \mathcal{K}' \times \mathcal{K}''$, where $\mathcal{K}'$ is the key space of a block cipher, and $\mathcal{K}''$ is the key space of encryption using a block cipher as a black-box.

To define simulatable DEM, oracle DEM and permutation-driven DEM are defined following [18].

Definition 5 (Oracle DEM). *A DEM scheme* $(\mathsf{O.Enc}^{\pi}, \mathsf{O.Dec}^{\pi})$ *with a key space* $\mathcal{K}$ *and a message space* $\mathcal{M}$ *is an oracle DEM scheme for a domain* $\mathcal{X}$ *if* $(\mathsf{O.Enc}, \mathsf{O.DEM})$ *has access to a permutation* π *on* $\mathcal{D}$*, and if for all permutations* $\pi : \mathcal{X} \rightarrow \mathcal{X}$*, all* $\mathsf{k} \in \mathcal{K}$*, and all* $m \in \mathcal{M}$*, it holds that* $m = \mathsf{Dec}^{\pi}(\mathsf{k}, \mathsf{c})$*, where* $\mathsf{c} \leftarrow \mathsf{Enc}^{\pi}(\mathsf{k}, m)$*, as the correctness of the DEM* $(\mathsf{O.Enc}^{\pi}, \mathsf{O.Dec}^{\pi})$.

Definition 6 (Permutation-Driven DEM). *A DEM scheme* $\mathsf{DEM} = (\mathsf{Enc}, \mathsf{Dec})$ *with a key space* $\mathcal{K} = \mathcal{K}' \times \mathcal{K}''$ *and a message space* $\mathcal{M}$ *is a* $(\mathcal{K} \times \mathcal{X})$*-permutation-driven DEM if the following conditions hold:*

- DEM *is an oracle DEM* $(\mathsf{O.Enc}^{\pi}, \mathsf{O.Dec}^{\pi})$ *for a domain* $\mathcal{X}$ *with a block cipher* $\{E_{\mathsf{k}'} : \mathcal{X} \rightarrow \mathcal{X}\}_{\mathsf{k}' \in \mathcal{K}'}$ *as the permutation* π *over* $\mathcal{X}$.
- *For any key* $(\mathsf{k}', \mathsf{k}'') \in \mathcal{K}$*, any message* $m \in \mathcal{M}$*, and any ciphertexts* c*, it holds that* $\mathsf{Enc}((\mathsf{k}', \mathsf{k}''), m) = \mathsf{O.Enc}^{E_{\mathsf{k}'}}(\mathsf{k}'', m)$ *and* $\mathsf{Dec}((\mathsf{k}', \mathsf{k}''), \mathsf{c}) = \mathsf{O.Dec}^{E_{\mathsf{k}'}}(\mathsf{k}'', \mathsf{c})$.

Then, the simulatability of oracle DEM [18] is defined as follows.

Definition 7 (Simulatability of Oracle DEM). *Let* $\mathsf{DEM} = (\mathsf{Enc}, \mathsf{Dec})$ *with a key space* $\mathcal{K} = \mathcal{K}' \times \mathcal{K}''$ *and a message space* $\mathcal{M}$ *be an oracle DEM scheme for a domain* $\mathcal{X}$*. And, we assume that* DEM *has the following algorithms* Fake *and* Make*:*

- Fake*: A randomized algorithm which, given a key* $\mathsf{k}'' \in \mathcal{K}''$ *and the bit-length* $|m|$ *of messages, outputs a ciphertext* c *and a state* st*.*
- Make*: A randomized algorithm which, given a state* st *and a message* $m \in \mathcal{M}$*, outputs a relation* $\tilde{\pi} \in \mathcal{X} \times \mathcal{X}$ *which has functions* $\tilde{\pi}^+ : \mathcal{X} \to \mathcal{X}$ *and* $\tilde{\pi}^- : \mathcal{X} \to \mathcal{X}$ *such that if* $(\alpha, \beta) \in \tilde{\pi}$, $\alpha = \tilde{\pi}^+(\beta)$ *and* $\beta = \tilde{\pi}^-(\alpha)$ *hold.*

The oracle DEM scheme DEM *meets* ϵ*-simulatablility if for all* $\mathsf{k} = (\mathsf{k}', \mathsf{k}'') \in \mathcal{K}$*, all* $m \in \mathcal{M}$*, and the set* $\Pi^m_{\mathsf{k}''} := \{\tilde{\pi} \mid (\mathsf{c}, \mathsf{st}) \leftarrow \mathsf{Fake}(\mathsf{k}'', |m|); \tilde{\pi} \leftarrow \mathsf{Make}(\mathsf{st}, m)\}$*, the following conditions hold:*

- *The set* $\Pi^m_{\mathsf{k}''}$ *can be extended to a set of uniformly distributed permutations on* $\mathcal{X}$*.*
- *For any permutation* π *extended* $\Pi^m_{\mathsf{k}''}$*, it holds that* $\Pr[\mathsf{c} \neq \mathsf{O.Enc}^{\pi}(\mathsf{k}'', m)] \leq \epsilon$*, where* $\mathsf{c} \leftarrow \mathsf{Fake}(\mathsf{k}'', |m|)$*.*
- *The time-complexity of algorithms* $\mathsf{Fake}(\mathsf{k}', |m|)$ *and* $\mathsf{Make}(\mathsf{st}, m)$ *does not exceed the time-complexity of algorithm* $\mathsf{Enc}(\mathsf{k}, m)$ *without counting that of oracles which is accessed by* $\mathsf{Enc}(\cdot)$*.*

Message Authentication Code. A message authentication code (MAC) consists of two polynomial time algorithms (Tag, Vrfy) with a key space $\mathcal{K} = \mathcal{K}(\lambda)$ and a message space $\mathcal{M} = \mathcal{M}(\lambda)$ for a security parameter λ.

Tagging. Tag is an algorithm which, on input a secret key $\mathsf{k} \in \mathcal{K}$ and a message $m \in \mathcal{M}$, outputs a tag τ.

Verification. Vrfy is a deterministic algorithm which, on input a secret key $\mathsf{k} \in \mathcal{K}$, a message m ,and a tag τ, outputs 1 or 0.

It is required that MAC schemes meet correctness as follows: A MAC scheme $\mathsf{MAC} = (\mathsf{Tag}, \mathsf{Vrfy})$ with a key space $\mathcal{K}$ and a message space $\mathcal{M}$ meets correctness if for all $\mathsf{k} \in \mathcal{K}$ and all $m \in \mathcal{M}$, it holds that $1 = \mathsf{Vrfy}(\mathsf{k}, m, \tau)$, where $\tau \leftarrow \mathsf{Tag}(\mathsf{k}, m)$.

Strong unforgeability against one-time chosen message attacks (sUF-OT-CMA security) of MACs is defined as follows.

Definition 8 (sUF-OT-CMA security). *A MAC scheme* $\mathsf{MAC} = (\mathsf{Tag}, \mathsf{Vrfy})$ *meets* sUF-OT-CMA *security if for any PPT adversary* A *against* MAC*, the advantage* $\mathsf{Adv}^{\text{suf-cma}}_{\mathsf{A},\mathsf{MAC}} := \Pr[\mathsf{A}\ \textit{wins}]$ *is negligible, where* [A *wins*] *is the event that* A *wins in the following game:*

Setup: *A challenger chooses a key* $\mathsf{k} \in \mathcal{K}$ *uniformly at random and sets* $T \leftarrow \emptyset$ *and* $\mathsf{win} \leftarrow 0$*.*

Oracle Access: A *is allowed to the following oracles:*

- $\mathsf{TAG}(m)$: *If* $T \neq \emptyset$, *a tagging oracle* $\mathsf{TAG}(m)$ *returns* $\perp$. *Otherwise, it returns* $\tau \leftarrow \mathsf{Tag}(\mathsf{k}, m)$ *and sets* $T \leftarrow T \cup \{(m, \tau)\}$.
- $\mathsf{VRFY}(m, \tau)$: *Given a message and a tag* (m, τ), *a verification oracle* $\mathsf{VRFY}(m, \tau)$ *returns* $b \leftarrow \mathsf{Vrfy}(\mathsf{k}, m, \tau)$. *If* $b = 1$ *and* $(m, \tau) \notin T$, *it sets* $\mathsf{win} \leftarrow 1$.

Final: A *wins if* $\mathsf{win} = 1$.

3 SIM-SO-CCA Secure PKE from KEM Schemes

3.1 KEM/DEM Framework

In this section, we focus on the standard KEM/DEM scheme PKE_1^{hy} starting from any IND-CCA secure KEM and any simulatable DEM, and prove that PKE_1^{hy} meets SIM-SO-CCA security in the QICM. This security proof is based on the proof of Theorem 2 in [18]. However, it is not obvious that it satisfies SIM-SO-CCA security in the QICM because the proof in [18] uses the list of query/response pairs issued to ideal cipher oracles and we cannot apply this technique due to the quantum no-cloning theorem. To resolve this problem, we utilize a semi-classical oracle to check whether quantum queries meeting a condition are submitted to ideal cipher oracles or not, instead of using the list of ideal cipher oracles.

It is possible to construct concrete SIM-SO-CCA secure PKE schemes in the QICM. This is because several DEM schemes such as CTR-DEM, CBC-DEM, CCM-DEM, and hidden-shift CBC-DEM meet simulatability [1,18]. As a quantum (ideal) block cipher, hidden-shift Even-Mansour ciphers in [1] may be used.

To construct PKE_1^{hy} with a message space $\mathcal{M}$, we use the following primitives: Let $\mathsf{KEM} = (\mathsf{KGen}^{asy}, \mathsf{Encap}, \mathsf{Decap})$ be a KEM scheme with a key space $\mathcal{K} = \mathcal{K}' \times \mathcal{K}''$ and a randomness space $\mathcal{R}^{asy}$. Let $\mathsf{DEM} = (\mathsf{Enc}^{sym}, \mathsf{Dec}^{sym})$ be a DEM scheme with a key space $\mathcal{K} = \mathcal{K}' \times \mathcal{K}''$ and a message space $\mathcal{M}$.

The PKE scheme $\mathsf{PKE}_1^{hy} = (\mathsf{KGen}, \mathsf{Enc}, \mathsf{Dec})$ is described as follows:

- $(\mathsf{pk}, \mathsf{sk}) \leftarrow \mathsf{KGen}(1^\lambda)$: Generate $(\mathsf{pk}^{asy}, \mathsf{sk}^{asy}) \leftarrow \mathsf{KGen}^{asy}(1^\lambda)$ and output $\mathsf{pk} := \mathsf{pk}^{asy}$ and $\mathsf{sk} := \mathsf{sk}^{asy}$.
- $\mathsf{c} \leftarrow \mathsf{Enc}(\mathsf{pk}, m)$: Encrypt a message $m \in \mathcal{M}$ as follows:
  1. $(e, \mathsf{k}) \leftarrow \mathsf{Encap}(\mathsf{pk}^{asy})$, and $d \leftarrow \mathsf{Enc}^{sym}(\mathsf{k}, m)$.
  2. Output $\mathsf{c} := (e, d)$.
- $m/\perp \leftarrow \mathsf{Dec}(\mathsf{sk}, \mathsf{c})$: Decrypt a ciphertext $\mathsf{c} = (e, d)$ as follows:
  1. $\mathsf{k} \leftarrow \mathsf{Decap}(\mathsf{sk}^{asy}, e)$.
  2. Output $m' \leftarrow \mathsf{Dec}^{sym}(\mathsf{k}, d)$ if $\mathsf{k} \neq \perp$, and output $\perp$ otherwise.

Theorem 1. *If a KEM scheme* KEM *meets* IND-CCA *security, and a* $(\mathcal{K}, \mathcal{X})$*-permutation-driven DEM scheme* DEM *with an oracle DEM scheme* (O.Enc, O.Dec) *for a domain* $\mathcal{X}$ *and a block cipher* E *meets both of* ϵ_{sim}*-simulatability and* OT-INT-CTXT *security, then* PKE_1^{hy} *satisfies* SIM-SO-CCA *security in the quantum ideal cipher model.*

Proof. Let A be a QPT adversary against PKE_1^{hy}. Let q_d be the number of accessing $\mathsf{DEC}(\cdot)$, and q_e be the total number of accessing $E^+(\cdot)$ and $E^-(\cdot)$. For $J \subseteq [n]$, let $K'_J := \{\mathsf{k}'_j \mid j \in J\}$. Let $\mathsf{D}_1, \mathsf{D}_2$ be PPT algorithms against KEM and let F be a PPT algorithm against DEM. We write $E_{\mathsf{k}'}(\cdot) = E(\mathsf{k}', \cdot)$ for an ideal cipher E with a key k'.

For each $i \in \{0, 1, 2, 3, 4\}$, we consider a security game Game_i, and let W_i be the event that A outputs *out* such that $R(\mathcal{M}_{\mathrm{D}}, m_1, \ldots, m_n, I, out) = 1$ in Game_i. Let ϵ be a probability that A distinguishes any two distinct games.

Game_0: This game is the same as $\mathsf{Real\text{-}SIM\text{-}SO\text{-}CCA}$ security game. We have $\Pr[\mathsf{Exp}^{\text{real-so-cca}}_{\mathsf{PKE}^{hy},\mathsf{A}}(\lambda) \to 1] = \Pr[W_0]$. ■

Game_1: This game is the same as Game_1 except that DEC oracle returns $\perp$ if a query (e, d) such that $e \in \{e_i\}_{i \in [n] \setminus I}$ is submitted.

We show $|\Pr[W_0] - \Pr[W_1]| \leq n \cdot (\mathsf{Adv}^{\text{ind-cca}}_{\mathsf{KEM},\mathsf{D}_1}(\lambda) + \mathsf{Adv}^{\text{int-ctxt}}_{\mathsf{DEM},\mathsf{F}}(\lambda))$. Let Bad be the event that A submits a ciphertext query (e, d) such that $e \in \{e_i\}_{i \in [n] \setminus I}$ and $\mathsf{Dec}(\mathsf{sk}, (e, d)) \neq \perp$. Unless Bad occurs, Game_1 is equal to Game_0. Besides, we consider the following events: Let Bad_1 be the event that Bad happens in Game_1, and let Bad_2 be the same event as Bad_1 except that for $i \in [n] \setminus I$, keys k_i are chosen uniformly at random.

To show $|\Pr[\mathsf{Bad}_1] - \Pr[\mathsf{Bad}_2]| \leq n \cdot \mathsf{Adv}^{\text{ind-cca}}_{\mathsf{KEM},\mathsf{D}_1}(\lambda)$, we construct a PPT algorithm D_1 breaking the $\mathsf{IND\text{-}CCA}$ security of KEM in the following way: At the beginning of the security game, D_1 takes pk^{asy} as input. It sets $i^* \xleftarrow{U} [n]$ and chooses a random polynomial f_E of degree $2q_e - 1$ over $GF(2^\kappa)$ uniformly at random as a $2q_e$-wise independent hash function, where κ is the bit-length of elements in $\mathcal{K}' \times \mathcal{X}$. Then, it sets $I \leftarrow \emptyset$ and sends $\mathsf{pk} := \mathsf{pk}^{asy}$ to A. When A submits $\mathcal{M}_{\mathrm{D}}$, it does the following for each $i \in [n]$:

1. If $i = i^*$, request a challenge $(e_{i^*}, \mathsf{k}_{i^*})$ in $\mathsf{IND\text{-}CCA}$ game. Otherwise, compute $(e_i, \mathsf{k}_i) \leftarrow \mathsf{Encap}(\mathsf{pk}; r_i)$, where $r_i \in \mathcal{R}^{asy}$ is sampled at random.
2. $d_i \leftarrow \mathsf{Enc}^{sym}(\mathsf{k}_i, m_i)$, where $m_i \xleftarrow{U} \mathcal{M}_D$.

Then, it returns $((e_i, d_i))_{i \in [n]}$ to A. D_1 simulates oracles as follows:

- $E^+(\mathsf{k}', \alpha)$: Return $f_E(\mathsf{k}' \parallel \alpha)$.
- $E^-(\mathsf{k}', \beta)$: Compute the set R of all roots of the polynomial $f_E - \beta$ and return α such that $\mathsf{k}' \parallel \alpha \in R$.
- $\mathsf{DEC}(\mathsf{c})$: Take $\mathsf{c} = (e, d)$ as input. In the case of $e = e_{i^*}$, halt and output 1 if $\perp \neq \mathsf{Dec}^{sym}(\mathsf{k}_{i^*}, d)$, and return $\perp$ otherwise. In the case of $e \neq e_{i^*}$, submit e to the given decapsulation oracle and receive k. Return $\perp$ if $\mathsf{k} = \perp$, and return $\mathsf{Dec}^{sym}(\mathsf{k}, d)$ if $\mathsf{k} \neq \perp$.
- $\mathsf{OPEN}(i)$: Set $I \leftarrow I \cup \{i\}$. Abort if $i = i^*$. Return (m_i, r_i) if $i \neq i^*$.

Note that quantum ideal ciphers E^+ and E^- can be simulated by using $2q_e$-wise independent hash functions from Theorem 6.1 in [37]. When A outputs *out*, D_1 outputs 0 if Bad does not happen.

D_1 simulates the view of A completely. If A submits a decryption query meeting the condition of Bad, it can distinguish the two games, and D_1 breaks IND-CCA security with at least probability ϵ/n. Thus, we get the bound.

To show $\Pr[\mathsf{Bad}_2] \leq n \cdot \mathsf{Adv}_{\mathsf{DEM},\mathsf{F}}^{\text{int-ctxt}}(\lambda)$, we construct a PPT algorithm F breaking OT-INT-CTXT security as follows: It is given the two oracles $\mathsf{ENC}(\cdot)$ and $\mathsf{VRFY}(\cdot)$ in OT-INT-CTXT game. At the beginning of the security game, F generates $(\mathsf{pk}, \mathsf{sk}) \leftarrow \mathsf{KGen}(1^\lambda)$ and chooses $i^* \in [n]$ uniformly at random. When A submits $\mathcal{M}_\mathrm{D}$, it does the following for each $i \in [n]$:

1. $(e_i, \mathsf{k}_i) \leftarrow \mathsf{Encap}(\mathsf{pk}; r_i)$, where $r_i \in \mathcal{R}^{asy}$ is sampled at random.
2. $m_i \xleftarrow{U} \mathcal{M}_\mathrm{D}$.
3. If $i = i^*$, $d_{i^*} \leftarrow \mathsf{ENC}(m_{i^*})$. Otherwise, $d_i \leftarrow \mathsf{Enc}^{sym}(\mathsf{k}_i, m_i)$.

Then, it returns $((e_i, d_i))_{i \in [n]}$. F simulates oracles $E^+(\cdot,\cdot)$, $E^-(\cdot,\cdot)$, and $\mathsf{OPEN}(\cdot)$ in the same way as the above algorithm D_1. $\mathsf{DEC}(\cdot)$ is simulated as follows: If $e = e_{i^*}$ for a given $\mathsf{c} = (e, d)$, it submits (e, d) to $\mathsf{VRFY}(\cdot)$. F halts if it returns 1, and returns $\perp$ otherwise. If $e \neq e_{i^*}$, F computes $\mathsf{k} \leftarrow \mathsf{Decap}(\mathsf{sk}^{asy}, e)$ and returns $\mathsf{Dec}^{sym}(\mathsf{k}, d) \in \mathcal{M} \cup \{\perp\}$. When A outputs *out*, F aborts this game if Bad does not happen.

The success condition of F is identical to the condition that Bad occurs. Hence, it wins in OT-INT-CTXT game if A outputs a ciphertext query (e, d) such that $e \neq e_{i^*}$ and oracle $\mathsf{VRFY}(d)$ returns 1. The success probability of F is at least $\Pr[\mathsf{Bad}_2]/n$.

Therefore, we have $|\Pr[W_0] - \Pr[W_1]| \leq n \cdot (\mathsf{Adv}_{\mathsf{PKE}^{hy},\mathsf{D}_1}^{\text{ind-cca}}(\lambda) + \mathsf{Adv}_{\mathsf{DEM},\mathsf{F}}^{\text{int-ctxt}}(\lambda))$ in the straightforward way. ■

$\ddot{E}^+$ (resp. $\ddot{E}^-$) is an ideal cipher oracle such that $\ddot{E}^+(\mathsf{k}', \alpha)$ (resp. $\ddot{E}^-(\mathsf{k}', \beta)$) is sampled from $\mathcal{X}$ uniformly at random if $\mathsf{k}' \in \{\mathsf{k}'_i\}_{i \in [n] \setminus I}$, and $\ddot{E}^+(\mathsf{k}', \alpha) = E^+(\mathsf{k}', \alpha)$ (resp. $\ddot{E}^-(\mathsf{k}', \beta) = E^-(\mathsf{k}', \beta)$) holds otherwise.

Game_2: This game is the same as Game_1 except that at the beginning of the security game, the challenger computes $(e_i, \mathsf{k}_i) \leftarrow \mathsf{Encap}(\mathsf{pk})$ for $i \in [n]$ ($\mathsf{k}_i = (\mathsf{k}'_i, \mathsf{k}''_i)$), and oracles E^+ and E^- are replaced by $\ddot{E}^+ \backslash S$ and $\ddot{E}^- \backslash S$ for $S = \{\mathsf{k}'_i\}_{i \in [n] \setminus I}$, respectively.

We show $|\Pr[W_1] - \Pr[W_2]| \leq 2\sqrt{nq \cdot \mathsf{Adv}_{\mathsf{KEM},\mathsf{D}_2}^{\text{ind-cca}}(\lambda)} + 4q\sqrt{n/|\mathcal{K}'|}$. Let Bad' be the event that a semi-classical oracle O_S^{SC} returns $|1\rangle$ when A submits a query to an oracle $E^+(\cdot,\cdot)$ or $E^-(\cdot,\cdot)$. Besides, we consider the following events: Let Bad'_1 be the event that Bad' happens in Game'_2, and let Bad'_2 be the same event as Bad'_1 except that for $i \in [n] \backslash I$, keys k_i are chosen uniformly at random. From Proposition 1 and the hybrid argument, we have $|\Pr[W_1] - \Pr[W_2]| \leq 2\sqrt{q \cdot \Pr[\mathsf{Bad}'_1]} \leq 2\sqrt{q\,|\Pr[\mathsf{Bad}'_1] - \Pr[\mathsf{Bad}'_2]| + q \cdot \Pr[\mathsf{Bad}'_2]}$.

We show $|\Pr[\mathsf{Bad}'_1] - \Pr[\mathsf{Bad}'_2]| \leq n \cdot \mathsf{Adv}_{\mathsf{KEM},\mathsf{D}_2}^{\text{ind-cca}}(\lambda)$ by constructing a PPT algorithm D_2 breaking IND-CCA security. Notice that running $(e_i, \mathsf{k}_i) \leftarrow \mathsf{Encap}(\mathsf{pk}; r_i)$ at the beginning of the game is a conceptual modification. D_2 is constructed as follows: Given $(\mathsf{pk}^{asy}, e^*, \mathsf{k}^*)$, it chooses $i^* \in [n]$ uniformly at random, sets $(e_{i^*}, \mathsf{k}_{i^*}) := (e^*, \mathsf{k}^*)$, and generates $(e_i, \mathsf{k}_i) \leftarrow \mathsf{Encap}(\mathsf{pk}^{asy}; r_i)$ for all $i \in [n] \backslash \{i^*\}$, where r_i is sampled from $\mathcal{R}^{asy}$ at random. And then, it sets $I \leftarrow \emptyset$ and sends $\mathsf{pk} := \mathsf{pk}^{asy}$ to A. When A submits $\mathcal{M}_\mathrm{D}$, it computes $d_i \leftarrow \mathsf{Enc}^{sym}(\mathsf{k}_i, m_i)$, where $m_i \overset{U}{\leftarrow} \mathcal{M}_\mathrm{D}$ for $i \in [n]$ and returns $((e_i, d_i))_{i\in[n]}$ to A. When A issues a quantum query $\sum_{\mathsf{k}'\in\mathcal{K}',x\in\mathcal{X}} \psi_{\mathsf{k}',x}|\mathsf{k}', x\rangle$ to E^+ or E^-, D_2 submits $\sum_{\mathsf{k}'\in\mathcal{K}',x\in\mathcal{X}} \psi_{\mathsf{k}',x}|\mathsf{k}', x\rangle|0\rangle$ to a semi-classical oracle O_S^{SC}. It halts and outputs 1 if O_S^{SC} returns a quantum superposition state $\sum_{\mathsf{k}'\in\mathcal{K}',x\in\mathcal{X}} \psi'_{\mathsf{k}',x}|\mathsf{k}', x\rangle|1\rangle$. It returns a quantum state by accessing E^+ or E^- otherwise. In addition, D_2 simulates the following oracles:

- $\mathsf{DEC}(\mathsf{c})$: Take $\mathsf{c} = (e, d)$ as input. If $e \in \{e_i\}_{i\in[n]\setminus I}$, return $\perp$. If $e \notin \{e_i\}_{i\in[n]\setminus I}$, submit e to the given decapsulation oracle and receive k. Return $\perp$ if $\mathsf{k} = \perp$, and return $\mathsf{Dec}^{sym}(\mathsf{k}', d)$ if $\mathsf{k} \neq \perp$.
- $\mathsf{OPEN}(i)$: Set $I \leftarrow I \cup \{i\}$. If $i = i^*$, abort this game. If $i \neq i^*$, set $E_{\mathsf{k}'_i} \leftarrow \emptyset$ and return (m_i, r_i) if $i \neq i^*$.

When A outputs a value *out*, D_2 aborts this game if Bad' does not occur. Then, D_2 simulates the environment of A completely. If A submits a quantum query including the valid key k_i of e_i to E^+ or E^-, A can distinguish the two games, and D_2 breaks the IND-CCA security of KEM. The success probability of D_2 is at least ϵ/n.

In addition, we have $\Pr[\mathsf{Bad}'_2] \leq 4nq_e/|\mathcal{K}'|$ from Proposition 2. Therefore, we obtain the following inequality

$$|\Pr[W_1] - \Pr[W_2]| \leq 2\sqrt{q\left(n \cdot \mathsf{Adv}^{\text{ind-cca}}_{\mathsf{KEM},\mathsf{D}_2}(\lambda) + \frac{4qn}{|\mathcal{K}'|}\right)}$$
$$\leq 2\sqrt{nq_e \cdot \mathsf{Adv}^{\text{ind-cca}}_{\mathsf{KEM},\mathsf{D}_2}(\lambda)} + 4q\sqrt{\frac{n}{|\mathcal{K}'|}},$$

and the proof is completed. ■

Game_3: This game is the same as Game_2 except that the game is aborted if the challenger generates $(e_i, (\mathsf{k}'_i, \mathsf{k}''_i)) \leftarrow \mathsf{Encap}(\mathsf{pk})$ such that $\mathsf{k}'_i \in K'_{[i-1]}$ for $i \in [n]$.

The probability of choosing $\mathsf{k}'_i \in K'_{[i-1]}$ by running $\mathsf{Encap}(\mathsf{pk})$ for $i \in [n]$ is at most $n^2/|\mathcal{K}'|$. Thus, we have $|\Pr[W_2] - \Pr[W_3]| \leq n^2/|\mathcal{K}'|$. ■

Game_4: This game is the same as Game_3 except that for all $i \in [n]$, we replace replace Enc^{sym} algorithm by $(\mathsf{Fake}, \mathsf{Make})$. Namely, the process of the challenger and OPEN oracle is modified as follows: Given $\mathcal{M}_\mathrm{D}$, the challenger runs $(d_i, \mathsf{st}_i) \leftarrow \mathsf{Fake}(\mathsf{k}''_i, |m_i|)$ and returns (e_i, d_i) for each $i \in [n]$. In addition, OPEN oracle is modified as follows:

1. $I \leftarrow I \cup \{i\}$.
2. $m_i \overset{U}{\leftarrow} \mathcal{M}_\mathrm{D}$.
3. $\tilde{\pi} \leftarrow \mathsf{Make}(\mathsf{st}_i, m_i)$ and oracles $\ddot{E}^+(\mathsf{k}'_i, \cdot), \ddot{E}^-(\mathsf{k}'_i, \cdot)$ follow this relation $\tilde{\pi}$.
4. Abort this game if $d_i \neq \mathsf{O.Enc}^{E_{\mathsf{k}'_i}}(\mathsf{k}''_i, m_i)$.
5. Return (m_i, r_i).

We show $|\Pr[W_3] - \Pr[W_4]| \leq n \cdot \epsilon_{sim}$. From the simulatability of DEM, A cannot distinguish d_i in the two games. In the process of OPEN oracle, we can define a relation $\tilde{\pi}$ in this phase since A cannot find $\mathsf{k}_i' \in \{\mathsf{k}_i'\}_{i\in[n]\setminus I}$ from the game-hop of Game_2. In addition, for each $i \in [n]$, the probability that the aborting event happens in OPEN oracle is negligible in λ from the simulatability of DEM. Hence, we have the inequality. ■

Finally, we prove $\Pr[\mathsf{Exp}^{\text{ideal-so-cca}}_{\mathsf{PKE}^{hy},\mathsf{S}}(\lambda) \to 1] = \Pr[W_4]$. We construct a simulator S in the following way: It is given $\overline{\mathsf{OPEN}}$ oracle in $\mathsf{Ideal\text{-}SIM\text{-}SO\text{-}CCA}$ game. At the beginning of the security game, S generates $(\mathsf{pk}, \mathsf{sk}) \leftarrow \mathsf{KGen}(1^\lambda)$ and $(e_i, \mathsf{k}_i) \leftarrow \mathsf{Encap}(\mathsf{pk}; r_i)$ for $i \in [n]$. When A submits $\mathcal{M}_{\mathrm{D}}$, it receives $|m_i|$ from the challenger of $\mathsf{Ideal\text{-}SIM\text{-}SO\text{-}CCA}$ game, generates $d_i \leftarrow \mathsf{Fake}(\mathsf{k}_i'', |m_i|)$ for $i \in [n]$, and returns $((e_i, d_i))_{i\in[n]}$. In the same way as the game-hop of Game_4, S simulates $\ddot{E}^+$ and $\ddot{E}^-$ by using a $2q_e$-wise independent hash function and algorithms $(\mathsf{Fake}, \mathsf{Make})$. It simulates oracles $\mathsf{DEC}(\cdot)$ and $\mathsf{OPEN}(\cdot)$ as follows:

- $\mathsf{DEC}(\mathsf{c})$: Take $\mathsf{c} = (e, d)$ as input and do the following.
  1. Return $\perp$ if $e \in \{e_i\}_{i\in[n]\setminus I}$.
  2. $\mathsf{k} \leftarrow \mathsf{Decap}(\mathsf{sk}, e)$.
  3. Return $\perp$ if $\mathsf{k} = \perp$. Return $\mathsf{Dec}^{sym}(\mathsf{k}, d) \in \mathcal{M} \cup \{\perp\}$ otherwise.
- $\mathsf{OPEN}(i)$: Take $i \in [n]$ as input and do the following:
  1. $I \leftarrow I \cup \{i\}$.
  2. Receive $m_i \leftarrow \overline{\mathsf{OPEN}}(i)$.
  3. $\tilde{\pi} \leftarrow \mathsf{Make}(\mathsf{st}_i, m_i)$ and oracles $\ddot{E}^+(\mathsf{k}_i', \cdot), \ddot{E}^-(\mathsf{k}_i', \cdot)$ follow this relation $\tilde{\pi}$.
  4. Abort this game if $d_i \neq \mathsf{O.Enc}^{E_{\mathsf{k}_i'}}(\mathsf{k}_i'', m_i)$.
  5. Return (m_i, r_i).

When A outputs out, S halts and outputs $R(\mathcal{M}_{\mathrm{D}}, m_1, \ldots, m_n, I, out)$.

S completely simulates Game_4 by using only the given oracle $\overline{\mathsf{OPEN}}$. Thus, we have $\Pr[\mathsf{Exp}^{\text{ideal-so-cca}}_{\mathsf{PKE}_1^{hy},\mathsf{S}}(\lambda) \to 1] = \Pr[W_4]$.

Therefore, we obtain the following advantage

$$\mathsf{Adv}^{\text{sim-so-cca}}_{\mathsf{PKE}_1^{hy},\mathsf{A},\mathsf{S},R}(\lambda) \leq n \cdot \mathsf{Adv}^{\text{ind-cca}}_{\mathsf{KEM},\mathsf{D}_1}(\lambda) + 2\sqrt{nq_e \cdot \mathsf{Adv}^{\text{ind-cca}}_{\mathsf{KEM},\mathsf{D}_2}(\lambda)} + n \cdot \mathsf{Adv}^{\text{int-ctxt}}_{\mathsf{DEM},\mathsf{F}}(\lambda)$$
$$+ n \cdot \epsilon_{sim} + 4q_e\sqrt{\frac{n}{|\mathcal{K}'|}} + \frac{n^2}{|\mathcal{K}'|}.$$

From the discussion above, the proof is completed. □

3.2 PKE from FO-Based KEM Schemes

We describe a PKE scheme PKE_2^{hy} constructed from an FO-based KEM $\mathsf{FO}^{\not\perp}$ and a MAC, and prove that this scheme meets $\mathsf{SIM\text{-}SO\text{-}CCA}$ security in the QROM. Concretely, we use the FO-based KEM scheme $\mathsf{FO}^{\not\perp}$ and any $\mathsf{sUF\text{-}OT\text{-}CMA}$ secure MAC. As KEM schemes, we can apply not only $\mathsf{FO}^{\not\perp}$ but also other FO-based schemes $\mathsf{FO}_m^{\not\perp}$, $\mathsf{QFO}^{\not\perp}$, and $\mathsf{QFO}_m^{\not\perp}$, which are classified in [20]. In this paper, we select $\mathsf{FO}^{\not\perp}$ to construct PKE_2^{hy}. This is because PKE_2^{hy} does not need other primitives such as pseudorandom functions unlike $\mathsf{FO}_m^{\not\perp}$. Besides, it does not need to append additional hash [20,36] to ciphertexts while $\mathsf{QFO}^{\not\perp}$ and $\mathsf{QFO}_m^{\not\perp}$ need additional hash. Notice that in the same way as the security proof of PKE_2^{hy}(Theorem 2), it is possible to prove the security of PKE_2^{hy} using $\mathsf{FO}_m^{\not\perp}$, $\mathsf{QFO}^{\not\perp}$, or $\mathsf{QFO}_m^{\not\perp}$, instead of $\mathsf{FO}^{\not\perp}$.

Concretely, we can apply CRYSTALS-Kyber, SABER, SIKE, and LEDAkem to the KEM scheme $\mathsf{FO}^{\not\perp}$, and apply FrodoKEM, NewHope, ThreeBears, and more other schemes [34] to $\mathsf{FO}_m^{\not\perp}$, $\mathsf{QFO}^{\not\perp}$, or $\mathsf{QFO}_m^{\not\perp}$. As concrete MAC schemes, we can use deterministic MACs standardized by NIST.

To construct PKE_2^{hy} with a message space $\mathcal{M}$, we use the following primitives: Let $\mathsf{PKE}^{asy} = (\mathsf{KGen}^{asy}, \mathsf{Enc}^{asy}, \mathsf{Dec}^{asy})$ be a PKE scheme with a message space $\mathcal{M}^{asy}$, a randomness space $\mathcal{R}^{asy}$, and a ciphertext space $\mathcal{C}^{asy}$. And, PKE^{asy} meets δ-correctness. Let $\mathsf{MAC} = (\mathsf{Tag}, \mathsf{Vrfy})$ be a MAC scheme with a key space $\mathcal{K}^{mac}$. Let $\mathsf{H} : \mathcal{M}^{asy} \times \mathcal{C}^{asy} \to \mathcal{K}^{sym} \times \mathcal{K}^{mac}$, $\mathsf{G} : \mathcal{M}^{asy} \to \mathcal{R}^{asy}$ be random oracles, where $\mathcal{K}^{sym} = \mathcal{M}$ is a key space.

$\mathsf{PKE}_2^{hy} = (\mathsf{KGen}, \mathsf{Enc}, \mathsf{Dec})$ is constructed as follows:

- $(\mathsf{pk}, \mathsf{sk}) \leftarrow \mathsf{KGen}(1^\lambda)$: Generate $(\mathsf{pk}^{asy}, \mathsf{sk}^{asy}) \leftarrow \mathsf{KGen}^{asy}(1^\lambda)$ and $s \xleftarrow{U} \mathcal{M}^{asy}$. Then, output $\mathsf{pk} := \mathsf{pk}^{asy}$ and $\mathsf{sk} := (\mathsf{sk}^{asy}, s)$.
- $\mathsf{c} \leftarrow \mathsf{Enc}(\mathsf{pk}, m)$: Encrypt $m \in \mathcal{M}$ as follows:
  1. $r \xleftarrow{U} \mathcal{M}^{asy}$.
  2. $e \leftarrow \mathsf{Enc}^{asy}(\mathsf{pk}^{asy}, r; \mathsf{G}(r))$.
  3. $(\mathsf{k}^{sym}, \mathsf{k}^{mac}) \leftarrow \mathsf{H}(r, e)$.
  4. $d \leftarrow \mathsf{k}^{sym} \oplus m$, $\tau \leftarrow \mathsf{Tag}(\mathsf{k}^{mac}, d)$.
  5. Output $\mathsf{c} := (e, d, \tau)$.
- $m/\perp \leftarrow \mathsf{Dec}(\mathsf{sk}, \mathsf{c})$: Decrypt $\mathsf{c} = (e, d, \tau)$ as follows:
  1. $r' \leftarrow \mathsf{Dec}^{asy}(\mathsf{sk}^{asy}, e)$.
  2. $(\mathsf{k}^{sym}, \mathsf{k}^{mac}) \leftarrow \mathsf{H}(s, e)$ if $e \neq \mathsf{Enc}^{asy}(\mathsf{pk}^{asy}, r'; \mathsf{G}(r'))$.
  3. $(\mathsf{k}^{sym}, \mathsf{k}^{mac}) \leftarrow \mathsf{H}(r', e)$ otherwise.
  4. Output $m := d \oplus \mathsf{k}^{sym}$ if $\mathsf{Vrfy}(\mathsf{k}^{mac}, d, \tau) = 1$, and output $\perp$ otherwise.

As the security of PKE_2^{hy}, Theorem 2 holds.

Theorem 2. *If a PKE scheme* PKE^{asy} *with* δ*-correctness meets* IND-CPA *security and a MAC scheme* MAC *meets* sUF-OT-CMA *security, then* PKE_2^{hy} *satisfies* SIM-SO-CCA *security in the quantum random oracle model.*

Proof. Let A be a QPT adversary against PKE_2^{hy}. Let q_d be the number of accessing $\mathsf{DEC}(\cdot)$, q_h be the number of accessing $\mathsf{H}(\cdot)$, q_g be the number of accessing $\mathsf{G}(\cdot)$. For a subset $J \subseteq [n]$, let $K_J^{sym} := \{\mathsf{k}_j^{sym} \mid j \in J\}$. Notice that we can view $\mathsf{FO}^{\not\perp}$ in Fig. 2 as the KEM scheme in PKE_2^{hy}.

$(\mathsf{pk},\mathsf{sk}) \leftarrow \mathsf{KGen}(1^\lambda)$

1 : $(\mathsf{pk}^{asy},\mathsf{sk}^{asy}) \leftarrow \mathsf{KGen}^{asy}(1^\lambda)$.
2 : $s \xleftarrow{U} \mathcal{M}^{asy}$.
3 : **return** $\mathsf{pk} := \mathsf{pk}^{asy}$ *and* $\mathsf{sk} := (\mathsf{sk}^{asy}, s)$

$(e,\mathsf{k}) \leftarrow \mathsf{Encap}(\mathsf{pk})$	$\mathsf{k} \leftarrow \mathsf{Decap}(\mathsf{sk}, e)$
1 : $r \xleftarrow{U} \mathcal{M}^{asy}$	1 : $r' \leftarrow \mathsf{Dec}^{asy}(\mathsf{sk}^{asy}, e)$
2 : $e \leftarrow \mathsf{Enc}^{asy}(\mathsf{pk}^{asy}, r; \mathsf{G}(r))$	2 : **if** $e \neq \mathsf{Enc}^{asy}(\mathsf{pk}, r'; \mathsf{G}(r'))$:
3 : $\mathsf{k} \leftarrow \mathsf{H}(r, e)$	**return** $\mathsf{k} := \mathsf{H}(s, e)$
4 : **return** (e, k)	3 : **return** $\mathsf{k} := \mathsf{H}(r', e)$

Fig. 2. KEM scheme $\mathsf{FO}^{\not\perp}$ in PKE_2^{hy}

For $i \in \{0, 1, \ldots, 9\}$, we consider a security game Game_i, and let W_i be the event that A outputs *out* such that $R(\mathcal{M}_{\mathrm{D}}, m_1, \ldots, m_n, I, out) = 1$ in Game_i. Let ϵ be a probability that A distinguishes any two distinct games.

Game_0: This game is the same as Real-SIM-SO-CCA security game. Thus, we have $\Pr[\mathsf{Exp}^{\text{real-so-cca}}_{\mathsf{PKE}_2^{hy},\mathsf{A}}(\lambda) \to 1] = \Pr[W_0]$. ■

Game_1: This game is the same as Game_0 except that DEC oracle computes $(\mathsf{k}^{sym}, \mathsf{k}^{mac}) \leftarrow \mathsf{H}'_q(e)$ instead of $(\mathsf{k}^{sym}, \mathsf{k}^{mac}) \leftarrow \mathsf{H}(s, e)$ if $e \neq \mathsf{Enc}^{asy}(\mathsf{pk}, r'; \mathsf{G}(r'))$, where $\mathsf{H}'_q : \mathcal{C}^{asy} \to \mathcal{K}^{sym} \times \mathcal{K}^{mac}$ is a random oracle. By using Lemma 4 in [26], we have $|\Pr[W_1] - \Pr[W_2]| \leq 2q_h/\sqrt{|\mathcal{M}^{asy}|}$. ■

We define $\mathsf{G}' : \mathcal{M}^{asy} \to \mathcal{R}^{asy}$ as a random oracle which, on input $r \in \mathcal{M}^{asy}$, returns a value sampled from the uniform distribution over a set of "good" random coins $\mathcal{R}^{asy}_{good}(\mathsf{pk}^{asy}, \mathsf{sk}^{asy}, r) = \{\hat{r} \in \mathcal{R}^{asy} \mid \mathsf{Dec}^{asy}(\mathsf{sk}^{asy}, \mathsf{Enc}^{asy}(\mathsf{pk}, r; \hat{r}))\}$. Let $\delta(\mathsf{pk}^{asy}, \mathsf{sk}^{asy}, r) = |\mathcal{R}^{asy} \setminus \mathcal{R}^{asy}_{good}(\mathsf{pk}^{asy}, \mathsf{sk}^{asy}, r)|/|\mathcal{R}^{asy}|$ denote the fraction of bad random coins, and let $\delta(\mathsf{pk}^{asy}, \mathsf{sk}^{asy}) = \max_{r \in \mathcal{M}^{asy}} \delta(\mathsf{pk}^{asy}, \mathsf{sk}^{asy}, r)$. And then, we have $\delta = \mathbf{E}[\delta(\mathsf{pk}^{asy}, \mathsf{sk}^{asy})]$ as the expectation of $\delta(\mathsf{pk}^{asy}, \mathsf{sk}^{asy})$, which is taken over $(\mathsf{pk}^{asy}, \mathsf{sk}^{asy}) \leftarrow \mathsf{KGen}^{asy}(1^\lambda)$.

Game_2: This game is the same as Game_1 except that we replace the random oracle $\mathsf{G}(\cdot)$ by $\mathsf{G}' : \mathcal{M}^{asy} \to \mathcal{R}^{asy}$. In the same way as the proof of Theorem 1 in [28], we get $|\Pr[W_1] - \Pr[W_2]| \leq 2q_g\sqrt{\delta}$. ■

Game_3: This game is the same as Game_2 except that the random oracle $\mathsf{H}(r, e)$ returns $\mathsf{H}_q(\mathsf{Enc}^{asy}(\mathsf{pk}, r; \mathsf{G}(r)))$ if $e = \mathsf{Enc}^{asy}(\mathsf{pk}, r; \mathsf{G}(r))$, and returns $\mathsf{H}'(r, e)$ otherwise. $\mathsf{H}_q : \mathcal{C}^{asy} \to \mathcal{K}^{sym} \times \mathcal{K}^{mac}$ and $\mathsf{H}' : \mathcal{M}^{asy} \times \mathcal{C}^{asy} \to \mathcal{K}^{sym} \times \mathcal{K}^{mac}$ are random oracles.

Since $\mathsf{G}'(\cdot)$ oracle returns "good" random coins, $\mathsf{Enc}^{asy}(\mathsf{pk}, \cdot; \mathsf{G}(\cdot))$ is injective. Hence, we can view $\mathsf{H}_q(\mathsf{Enc}^{asy}(\mathsf{pk}, \cdot; \mathsf{G}(\cdot)))$ as a perfect random oracle, and $\Pr[W_3] = \Pr[W_2]$ holds. ■

Game_4: This game is the same as Game_3 except that DEC oracle is modified as follows: Take $\mathsf{c} = (e, d, \tau)$ as input and compute $(\mathsf{k}^{sym}, \mathsf{k}^{mac}) \leftarrow \mathsf{H}_q(e)$. Then, return $m \leftarrow \mathsf{k}^{sym} \oplus d$ if $\mathsf{Vrfy}(\mathsf{k}^{mac}, d, \tau) = 1$, and return $\perp$ otherwise.

In the case where $e = \mathsf{Enc}^{asy}(\mathsf{pk}, r; \mathsf{G}(r))$ holds, both Decap oracles in Hybrid_3 and Hybrid_4 return the same value. In the case where $e \neq \mathsf{Enc}^{asy}(\mathsf{pk}, r; \mathsf{G}(r))$ holds, A cannot distinguish Game_3 and Game_4 since both H oracles in the two games return uniformly random values. Thus, we have $\Pr[W_4] = \Pr[W_3]$. ■

Game_5: This game is the same as Game_4 except that we replace the random oracle $\mathsf{G}'(\cdot)$ by $\mathsf{G}(\cdot)$. In the same way as the game-hop of Game_2, we have $|\Pr[W_4] - \Pr[W_5]| \leq 2q_g\sqrt{\delta}$. ■

We define $\ddot{\mathsf{G}}$ (resp. $\ddot{\mathsf{H}}$) as a random oracle such that for $r \in \{r_i\}_{i\in[n]\setminus I}$, the value $\ddot{\mathsf{G}}(r)$ (resp. $\ddot{\mathsf{H}}(r, e)$) is sampled from $\mathcal{R}^{asy}$ (resp. $\mathcal{K}^{sym} \times \mathcal{K}^{mac}$) uniformly at random, and for $r \notin \{r_i\}_{i\in[n]\setminus I}$, $\ddot{\mathsf{G}}(r) = \mathsf{G}(r)$ (resp. $\ddot{\mathsf{H}}(r, e) = \mathsf{H}(r, e)$) holds.

Game_6: This game is the same as Game_5 except that at the beginning of the security game, the challenger computes (e_i, k_i) for $i \in [n]$, and oracles H and G are replaced by $\ddot{\mathsf{H}}\backslash S$ and $\ddot{\mathsf{G}}\backslash S$ for $S = \{r_i\}_{i\in[n]\setminus I}$, respectively, before A queries to OPEN oracle.

In the similar way as the proof of Theorem 1 in [28], the following lemma holds.

Lemma 1. *For any QPT algorithm* A *against* PKE_2^{hy} *that makes at most* q_g *queries to* G *and at most* q_h *queries to* H, *there exists a PPT algorithm* D *against* PKE^{asy} *such that*

$$|\Pr[W_5] - \Pr[W_6]| \leq 2\sqrt{n(q_g + q_h)\mathsf{Adv}^{\text{ind-cpa}}_{\mathsf{PKE}^{asy},\mathsf{D}}(\lambda)} + 4(q_g + q_h)\sqrt{\frac{n}{|\mathcal{M}^{asy}|}}.$$

For readability, the proof of Lemma 1 is given in Appendix A. $|\Pr[W_5] - \Pr[W_6]|$ is negligible in λ if PKE^{asy} meets IND-CPA security. ■

Game_7: This game is the same as Game_6 except that DEC oracle returns $\perp$ if a query (e, d, τ) such that $e \in \{e_i\}_{i\in[n]\setminus I}$ is submitted.

Let Bad be the event that A submits a ciphertext query (e, d, τ) such that $e \in \{e_i\}_{i\in[n]\setminus I}$ and $\mathsf{Vrfy}(\mathsf{k}^{mac}, d, \tau) = 1$. Besides, we consider the following events: Let Bad_1 be the event that Bad happens in Game_7, and let Bad_2 be the same event as Bad_1 except that keys k_i are chosen uniformly at random for all $i \in [n]$.

In the similar way as the proof of Lemma 1, we have

$$|\Pr[\mathsf{Bad}_1] - \Pr[\mathsf{Bad}_2]| \leq 4\sqrt{n(q_g + q_h)\mathsf{Adv}^{\text{ind-cpa}}_{\mathsf{PKE}^{asy},\mathsf{D}'}(\lambda)}.$$

Next, we show $\Pr[\mathsf{Bad}_2] \leq n \cdot \mathsf{Adv}^{\text{suf-cma}}_{\mathsf{MAC},\mathsf{F}}(\lambda)$. We construct a PPT algorithm F breaking sUF-OT-CMA security as follows: It is given oracles TAG and VRFY in sUF-OT-CMA game. At the beginning of the security game, F generates $(\mathsf{pk}, \mathsf{sk}) \leftarrow \mathsf{KGen}(1^\lambda)$ and chooses $i^* \in [n]$ uniformly at random. Then, it sets $I \leftarrow \emptyset$ and sends pk to A. When A submits $\mathcal{M}_{\mathrm{D}}$, it does the following for every $i \in [n]$:

1. $e_i \leftarrow \mathsf{Enc}^{asy}(\mathsf{pk}; r_i; \mathsf{G}(r_i))$, where $r_i \in \mathcal{M}^{asy}$ is sampled at random.

2. $m_i \xleftarrow{U} \mathcal{M}_{\mathrm{D}}$ and $(\mathsf{k}_i^{sym}, \mathsf{k}_i^{mac}) \leftarrow \mathsf{H}(r_i, e_i)$.
3. If $i = i^*$, choose $d_{i^*} \xleftarrow{U} \mathcal{K}^{sym}$ and let $\tau_{i^*} := \mathsf{TAG}(d_{i^*})$. Otherwise, $d_i \leftarrow \mathsf{k}_i^{sym} \oplus m_i$ and $\tau_i \leftarrow \mathsf{Tag}(\mathsf{k}_i^{mac}, d_i)$.

Then, it returns $\{(e_i, d_i, \tau_i)\}_{i \in [n]}$. F simulates oracles in the following way: From Theorem 6.1 in [37], random oracles H and G can be simulated by using a $2q_h$-wise pairwise independent hash function and $2q_g$-wise independent hash function, respectively. The other oracles are simulated as follows:

- $\mathsf{DEC}(\mathsf{c})$: Take $\mathsf{c} = (e, d, \tau)$ as input. If $e = e_{i^*}$, submit (d, τ) to VRFY oracle. Halt if VRFY returns 1, and return $\perp$ otherwise. If $e \neq e_{i^*}$, return $\mathsf{Dec}(\mathsf{sk}, \mathsf{c}) \in \mathcal{M} \cup \{\perp\}$.
- $\mathsf{OPEN}(i)$: Set $I \leftarrow I \cup \{i\}$. Abort this game if $i = i^*$. Return (m_i, r_i) if $i \neq i^*$.

Finally, when A outputs *out*, F aborts if Bad does not occur. Then, the success condition of F is identical to the condition that Bad occurs. Hence, F wins in sUF-OT-CMA game if A submits a ciphertext query (e, d, τ) such that $e = e_{i^*}$ and $\mathsf{VRFY}(d, \tau)$ returns 1, and the success probability of F is at least $\Pr[\mathsf{Bad}_2]/n$.

Therefore, we obtain

$$|\Pr[W_6] - \Pr[W_7]| \leq 4\sqrt{n(q_g + q_h)\mathsf{Adv}^{\text{ind-cpa}}_{\mathsf{PKE}^{asy},\mathsf{D}'}(\lambda)} + n \cdot \mathsf{Adv}^{\text{suf-cma}}_{\mathsf{MAC},\mathsf{F}}(\lambda),$$

and $|\Pr[W_6] - \Pr[W_7]|$ is negligible in λ if PKE^{asy} and MAC meet IND-CPA security and sUF-OT-CMA security, respectively. ■

Game_8: This game is the same as Game_7 except that the game is aborted if for $i \in [n]$, the challenger chooses $r_i \in \mathcal{M}^{asy}$ such that $\mathsf{k}_i^{sym} \in K_{[i-1]}^{sym}$, where $(\mathsf{k}_i^{sym}, \mathsf{k}_i^{mac}) = \mathsf{H}(r_i, e_i)$.

The probability of choosing $\mathsf{k}_i^{sym} \in K_{[i-1]}^{sym}$ is at most $n^2/|\mathcal{K}^{sym}|$ from the collision resistance of random oracles. ■

Game_9: This game is the same as Game_8 except that the challenge phase and OPEN oracle are modified as follows: When A submits $\mathcal{M}_{\mathrm{D}}$, the challenger chooses $d_i \in \mathcal{K}^{sym}$ uniformly at random, computes $\tau_i \leftarrow \mathsf{Tag}(\mathsf{k}_i^{mac}, d_i)$ and returns (e_i, d_i, τ_i) for $i \in [n]$. In addition, OPEN oracle does the following:

1. $I \leftarrow I \cup \{i\}$.
2. $m_i \xleftarrow{U} \mathcal{M}_{\mathrm{D}}$.
3. Let $\mathsf{H}(r_i, e_i) := (d_i \oplus m_i, \mathsf{k}_i^{mac})$.
4. Return (m_i, r_i).

Game_9 is identical to Game_8. Any QPT adversary A cannot distinguish d_i in the two games since both ciphertexts in these games are uniformly random and A cannot find $r \in \{r_i\}_{i \in [n] \setminus I}$ before querying OPEN oracle. For this reason, it is possible to define $\mathsf{H}(r_i, e_i)$ when A submits i to OPEN oracle. Hence, we have $\Pr[W_9] = \Pr[W_8]$. ■

Finally, we prove $\Pr[\mathsf{Exp}^{\text{ideal-so-cca}}_{\mathsf{PKE}_2^{hy},\mathsf{S}}(\lambda) \rightarrow 1] = \Pr[W_9]$ by constructing a simulator S in the following way: It is given $\overline{\mathsf{OPEN}}$ oracle. At the beginning of

$\mathsf{Ideal\text{-}SIM\text{-}SO\text{-}CCA}$ security game, S generates $(\mathsf{pk}, \mathsf{sk}) \leftarrow \mathsf{KGen}(1^\lambda)$ and e_i for $i \in [n]$. And then, it sets $I \leftarrow \emptyset$ and sends pk to A. When A submits $\mathcal{M}_{\mathrm{D}}$, it chooses $d_i \in \mathcal{M}_{\mathrm{D}}$ uniformly at random, and computes $\tau_i \leftarrow \mathsf{Tag}(\mathsf{k}_i^{mac}, d_i)$ for $i \in [n]$. And then it returns $((e_i, d_i, \tau_i))_{i \in [n]}$. It simulates random oracles by using a $2q_h$-wise independent hash function and a $2q_g$-wise independent hash function. Oracles $\mathsf{DEC}(\cdot)$ and $\mathsf{OPEN}(\cdot)$ are simulated as follows:

- $\mathsf{DEC}(\mathsf{c})$: Take $\mathsf{c} = (e, d, \tau)$ as input and do the following.
  1. Return $\perp$ if $e \in \{e_i\}_{i \in [n] \setminus I}$.
  2. $r' \leftarrow \mathsf{Dec}^{asy}(\mathsf{sk}, e)$.
  3. Return $\perp$ if $e \neq \mathsf{Enc}^{asy}(\mathsf{pk}^{asy}, r; \mathsf{G}(r))$.
  4. $(\mathsf{k}^{sym}, \mathsf{k}^{mac}) \leftarrow \mathsf{H}(r', e)$
  5. Return $m \leftarrow \mathsf{k}^{sym} \oplus d$ if $\mathsf{Vrfy}(\mathsf{k}^{mac}, d, \tau) = 1$. Return $\perp$ otherwise.
- $\mathsf{OPEN}(i)$: Take $i \in [n]$ as input and do the following:
  1. $I \leftarrow I \cup \{i\}$.
  2. Receive m_i by accessing the given $\overline{\mathsf{OPEN}}(i)$.
  3. Let $\mathsf{H}(r_i, e_i) := (d_i \oplus m_i, \mathsf{k}_i^{mac})$.
  4. Return (m_i, r_i).

When A outputs out, S halts and outputs $R(\mathcal{M}_{\mathrm{D}}, m_1, \ldots, m_n, I, out)$. Because S can simulate the view of A only with $\overline{\mathsf{OPEN}}$ oracle, we have $\Pr[\mathsf{Exp}^{\text{ideal-so-cca}}_{\mathsf{PKE}_2^{hy}, \mathsf{S}}(\lambda) \to 1] = \Pr[W_9]$.

From the discussion above, we obtain

$$\begin{aligned}
\mathsf{Adv}^{\text{sim-so-cca}}_{\mathsf{PKE}_2^{hy}, \mathsf{A}, \mathsf{S}, R}(\lambda) \leq & 6\sqrt{n(q_g + q_h)\mathsf{Adv}^{\text{ind-cpa}}_{\mathsf{PKE}^{asy}, \mathsf{D}}(\lambda)} + n \cdot \mathsf{Adv}^{\text{suf-cma}}_{\mathsf{MAC}, \mathsf{F}}(\lambda) \\
& + 4(q_g + q_h)\sqrt{\frac{n}{|\mathcal{M}^{asy}|}} + \frac{2q_h}{\sqrt{|\mathcal{M}^{asy}|}} + 4q_g\sqrt{\delta} + \frac{n^2}{|\mathcal{K}^{sym}|} \\
\leq & 6\sqrt{n(q_g + q_h)\mathsf{Adv}^{\text{ind-cpa}}_{\mathsf{PKE}^{asy}, \mathsf{D}}(\lambda)} + n \cdot \mathsf{Adv}^{\text{suf-cma}}_{\mathsf{MAC}, \mathsf{F}}(\lambda) \\
& + (4q_g + 6q_h)\sqrt{\frac{n}{|\mathcal{M}^{asy}|}} + 4q_g\sqrt{\delta} + \frac{n^2}{|\mathcal{K}^{sym}|},
\end{aligned}$$

and complete the proof. □

4 Conclusion

We presented two $\mathsf{SIM\text{-}SO\text{-}CCA}$ secure PKE schemes constructed from KEM schemes in the quantum random oracle model or quantum ideal cipher model. The first one PKE_1^{hy} meets the security in the quantum ideal cipher model. It is constructed from any $\mathsf{IND\text{-}CCA}$ secure KEM and any simulatable DEM with $\mathsf{OT\text{-}INT\text{-}CTXT}$ security. On the other hand, the second one PKE_2^{hy} meets the security in the quantum random oracle model. It is constructed from an FO-based KEM $\mathsf{FO}^{\not\perp}$ and any $\mathsf{sUF\text{-}OT\text{-}CMA}$ secure MAC. The differences between these schemes are as follows: It is possible to apply any $\mathsf{IND\text{-}CCA}$ secure KEM scheme to PKE_1^{hy}, while PKE_2^{hy} uses a particular KEM scheme $\mathsf{FO}^{\not\perp}$ to PKE_2^{hy}.

In addition, it is possible to apply any deterministic MAC scheme to PKE_2^{hy}, while the underlying DEM scheme in PKE_1^{hy} needs to meet not only integrity but also simulatability.

Acknowledgements. The authors would like to thank the anonymous referees for their helpful comments.

Appendix A: Proof of Lemma 1

We prove Lemma 1. We use the same notations defined in the proof of Theorem 2. For $i \in \{0, 1, \ldots, 4\}$, we consider games Hybrid_i, and let H_i be the event that A outputs *out* such that $R(\mathcal{M}_\mathrm{D}, m_1, \ldots, m_n, I, out) = 1$ in Hybrid_i, Find_i be the event that a semi-classical oracle O_S^{SC} returns $\sum_{x \in S, y \in \mathcal{Y}} \psi'_{x,y} |x, y\rangle |1\rangle$ for a quantum query $\sum_{x \in \mathcal{M}^{asy}, y \in \mathcal{Y}} \psi_{x,y} |x, y\rangle$ to the random oracle G (resp. H), where $S = \{r_i\}_{i \in [n] \setminus I}$ and $\mathcal{Y} = \mathcal{R}^{asy}$ (resp. $\mathcal{Y} = \mathcal{C}^{asy} \times \mathcal{K}^{sym} \times \mathcal{K}^{mac}$).

Furthermore, in the same way as the proof in Theorem 2, random oracles $\ddot{\mathsf{G}}$ and $\ddot{\mathsf{H}}$ are defined. Namely, $\ddot{\mathsf{G}}$ (resp. $\ddot{\mathsf{H}}$) is a random oracle such that $\ddot{\mathsf{G}}(r)$ (resp. $\ddot{\mathsf{H}}(r, e)$) is sampled from $\mathcal{R}^{asy}$ (resp. $\mathcal{K}^{sym} \times \mathcal{K}^{mac}$) uniformly at random if $r \in \{r_i\}_{i \in [n] \setminus I}$, and $\ddot{\mathsf{G}}(r) = \mathsf{G}(r)$ (resp. $\ddot{\mathsf{H}}(r, e) = \mathsf{H}(r, e)$) holds otherwise.

Hybrid_0: This game is the same as Game_5 in Theorem 2. Then, we have $\Pr[H_0] = \Pr[W_5]$. ■

Hybrid_1: This game is the same as Hybrid_0 except that we replace G and H by $\ddot{\mathsf{G}} \backslash S$ and $\ddot{\mathsf{H}} \backslash S$, respectively, where $S = \{r_i\}_{i \in [n] \setminus I}$. From Proposition 1, we have $|\Pr[H_0] - \Pr[H_1]| \leq 2\sqrt{(q_g + q_h) \Pr[\mathsf{Find}_1]}$. Notice that we also have $\Pr[H_1] = \Pr[W_6]$. ■

Hybrid_2: This game is the same as Hybrid_1 except that for all $i \in [n]$, we replace $\hat{r}_i \xleftarrow{U} \mathcal{R}^{asy}$ and $(\mathsf{k}_i^{sym}, \mathsf{k}_i^{mac}) \xleftarrow{U} \mathcal{K}^{sym} \times \mathcal{K}^{mac}$ instead of $\hat{r}_i \leftarrow \mathsf{G}(r_i)$ and $(\mathsf{k}_i^{sym}, \mathsf{k}_i^{mac}) \leftarrow \mathsf{H}(r_i, e_i)$, respectively. We have $\Pr[\mathsf{Find}_2] = \Pr[\mathsf{Find}_1]$ because we do not focus on the output of A. ■

Hybrid_3: This game is the same as Hybrid_2 except that we replace $\ddot{\mathsf{G}}$ and $\ddot{\mathsf{H}}$ by G and H, respectively. Because there is no difference between the view of A in the two games by this change, $\Pr[\mathsf{Find}_3] = \Pr[\mathsf{Find}_2]$ holds. ■

Hybrid_4: This game is the same as Hybrid_3 except that we replace r_i by r'_i for all $i \in [n]$. Notice that we do not replace the set $S = \{r_i\}_{i \in [n] \setminus I}$ by $\{r'_i\}_{i \in [n] \setminus I}$.

From Proposition 2, we get $\Pr[\mathsf{Find}_4] \leq 4n(q_g + q_h)/|\mathcal{M}^{asy}|$. In addition, We show $|\Pr[\mathsf{Find}_3] - \Pr[\mathsf{Find}_4]| \leq n \cdot \mathsf{Adv}_{\mathsf{PKE},\mathsf{D}}^{\text{ind-cpa}}(\lambda)$ by constructing the following PPT algorithm D breaking IND-CPA security of PKE^{asy}: Given a public key pk^{asy}, D chooses $i^* \in [n]$, $r_{i^*}, r'_{i^*} \in \mathcal{M}^{asy}$, and $\mathsf{k}_{i^*} \in \mathcal{K}$ uniformly at random. It submits (r_i, r_i') to the challenger in IND-CPA game and receives e_{i^*}. And then, it computes $e_i \leftarrow \mathsf{Enc}^{asy}(\mathsf{pk}, r_i, \mathsf{G}(r_i))$ and $\mathsf{k}_i \leftarrow \mathsf{H}_q(e_i)$ for $i \in [n]\backslash\{i^*\}$. In order to simulate a random oracle G (resp. H_q), D chooses a $2q_g$-wise independent hash function (resp. a $2q_h$-wise independent hash function) at random. It sets $I \leftarrow \emptyset$ and sends $\mathsf{pk} := \mathsf{pk}^{asy}$ to A.

When A submits $\mathcal{M}_{\mathrm{D}}$, D chooses $m_i \overset{U}{\leftarrow} \mathcal{M}_{\mathrm{D}}$ and computes $d_i \leftarrow \mathsf{k}_i^{sym} \oplus m_i$ and $\tau_i \leftarrow \mathsf{Tag}(\mathsf{k}_i^{mac}, d_i)$ for $i \in [n]$. Then, it returns $((e_i, d_i, \tau_i))_{i \in [n]}$.

D simulates oracles in the following way: When A issues a quantum query $\sum_{r \in \mathcal{M}^{asy}, y \in \mathcal{Y}} \psi_{r,y}|r, y\rangle$ to the random oracle G (resp. H) for $\mathcal{Y} = \mathcal{R}^{asy}$ (resp. $\mathcal{Y} = \mathcal{C}^{asy} \times \mathcal{K}^{sym} \times \mathcal{K}^{mac}$), D submits $\sum_{r \in \mathcal{M}^{asy}, y \in \mathcal{Y}} \psi_{r,y}|r, y\rangle|0\rangle$ to a semi-classical oracle O_S^{SC}. It halts and outputs 1 if O_S^{SC} returns the quantum superposition state $\sum_{r \in \mathcal{M}^{asy}, y \in \mathcal{Y}} \psi'_{r,y}|r, y\rangle|1\rangle$. It returns a quantum state by accessing G (resp. H) otherwise.

- $\mathsf{DEC}(\mathsf{c})$: Take $\mathsf{c} = (e, d, \tau)$ as input and do the following.
  1. $(\mathsf{k}^{sym}, \mathsf{k}^{mac}) \leftarrow \mathsf{H}_q(e)$.
  2. Return $m \leftarrow \mathsf{k}^{sym} \oplus d$ if $\mathsf{Vrfy}(\mathsf{k}^{mac}, d, \tau) = 1$. Return $\perp$ otherwise.
- $\mathsf{OPEN}(i)$: Set $I \leftarrow I \cup \{i\}$. Abort if $i = i^*$. Return (m_i, r_i) otherwise.

When A outputs a value *out* and halts, D outputs 0. D simulates the view of A in Game_3 (resp. Game_4) if the challenger chooses r_i (resp. r_i'). Then, the success probability of D is at least ϵ/n, and we have the inequality.

Therefore, we obtain

$$|\Pr[\mathsf{Find}_3] - \Pr[\mathsf{Find}_4]| + \Pr[\mathsf{Find}_4] \leq n \cdot \mathsf{Adv}_{\mathsf{PKE,D}}^{\text{ind-cpa}}(\lambda) + \frac{4n(q_g + q_h)}{|\mathcal{M}^{asy}|}.$$

■

From the discussion above, we obtain the following inequality

$$\begin{aligned} |\Pr[W_5] - \Pr[W_6]| &\leq 2\sqrt{(q_g + q_h)\Pr[\mathsf{Find}_1]} \\ &\leq 2\sqrt{n(q_g + q_h)\mathsf{Adv}_{\mathsf{PKE,D}}^{\text{ind-cpa}}(\lambda) + 4n\frac{(q_g + q_h)^2}{|\mathcal{M}^{asy}|}} \\ &\leq 2\sqrt{n(q_g + q_h)\mathsf{Adv}_{\mathsf{PKE,D}}^{\text{ind-cpa}}(\lambda)} + 4(q_g + q_h)\sqrt{\frac{n}{|\mathcal{M}^{asy}|}}. \end{aligned}$$

Therefore, we complete the proof. □

References

1. Alagic, G., Russell, A.: Quantum-secure symmetric-key cryptography based on hidden shifts. In: Coron, J.-S., Nielsen, J.B. (eds.) EUROCRYPT 2017. LNCS, vol. 10212, pp. 65–93. Springer, Cham (2017). https://doi.org/10.1007/978-3-319-56617-7_3

2. Ambainis, A., Hamburg, M., Unruh, D.: Quantum security proofs using semi-classical oracles. In: Boldyreva, A., Micciancio, D. (eds.) CRYPTO 2019. LNCS, vol. 11693, pp. 269–295. Springer, Cham (2019). https://doi.org/10.1007/978-3-030-26951-7_10
3. Bellare, M., Dowsley, R., Waters, B., Yilek, S.: Standard security does not imply security against selective-opening. In: Pointcheval, D., Johansson, T. (eds.) EUROCRYPT 2012. LNCS, vol. 7237, pp. 645–662. Springer, Heidelberg (2012). https://doi.org/10.1007/978-3-642-29011-4_38
4. Bellare, M., Hofheinz, D., Yilek, S.: Possibility and impossibility results for encryption and commitment secure under selective opening. In: Joux, A. (ed.) EUROCRYPT 2009. LNCS, vol. 5479, pp. 1–35. Springer, Heidelberg (2009). https://doi.org/10.1007/978-3-642-01001-9_1
5. Bellare, M., Namprempre, C.: Authenticated encryption: relations among notions and analysis of the generic composition paradigm. J. Cryptol. **21**(4), 469–491 (2008)
6. Bellare, M., Rogaway, P.: Optimal asymmetric encryption. In: De Santis, A. (ed.) EUROCRYPT 1994. LNCS, vol. 950, pp. 92–111. Springer, Heidelberg (1995). https://doi.org/10.1007/BFb0053428
7. Bellare, M., Waters, B., Yilek, S.: Identity-based encryption secure against selective opening attack. In: Ishai, Y. (ed.) TCC 2011. LNCS, vol. 6597, pp. 235–252. Springer, Heidelberg (2011). https://doi.org/10.1007/978-3-642-19571-6_15
8. Bellare, M., Yilek, S.: Encryption schemes secure under selective opening attack. IACR Cryptology ePrint Archive 2009/101 (2009)
9. Boneh, D., Dagdelen, Ö., Fischlin, M., Lehmann, A., Schaffner, C., Zhandry, M.: Random oracles in a quantum world. In: Lee, D.H., Wang, X. (eds.) ASIACRYPT 2011. LNCS, vol. 7073, pp. 41–69. Springer, Heidelberg (2011). https://doi.org/10.1007/978-3-642-25385-0_3
10. Boneh, D., Zhandry, M.: Secure signatures and chosen ciphertext security in a quantum computing world. In: Canetti, R., Garay, J.A. (eds.) CRYPTO 2013. LNCS, vol. 8043, pp. 361–379. Springer, Heidelberg (2013). https://doi.org/10.1007/978-3-642-40084-1_21
11. Boyen, X., Li, Q.: All-but-many lossy trapdoor functions from lattices and applications. In: Katz, J., Shacham, H. (eds.) CRYPTO 2017. LNCS, vol. 10403, pp. 298–331. Springer, Cham (2017). https://doi.org/10.1007/978-3-319-63697-9_11
12. Cramer, R., Shoup, V.: Design and analysis of practical public-key encryption schemes secure against adaptive chosen ciphertext attack. IACR Cryptology ePrint Archive 2001/108 (2001)
13. Don, J., Fehr, S., Majenz, C., Schaffner, C.: Security of the Fiat-Shamir transformation in the quantum random-oracle model. In: Boldyreva, A., Micciancio, D. (eds.) CRYPTO 2019. LNCS, vol. 11693, pp. 356–383. Springer, Cham (2019). https://doi.org/10.1007/978-3-030-26951-7_13
14. Fehr, S., Hofheinz, D., Kiltz, E., Wee, H.: Encryption schemes secure against chosen-ciphertext selective opening attacks. In: Gilbert, H. (ed.) EUROCRYPT 2010. LNCS, vol. 6110, pp. 381–402. Springer, Heidelberg (2010). https://doi.org/10.1007/978-3-642-13190-5_20
15. Fujisaki, E., Okamoto, T.: Secure integration of asymmetric and symmetric encryption schemes. J. Cryptology **26**(1), 80–101 (2013)

16. Hemenway, B., Libert, B., Ostrovsky, R., Vergnaud, D.: Lossy encryption: constructions from general assumptions and efficient selective opening chosen ciphertext security. In: Lee, D.H., Wang, X. (eds.) ASIACRYPT 2011. LNCS, vol. 7073, pp. 70–88. Springer, Heidelberg (2011). https://doi.org/10.1007/978-3-642-25385-0_4
17. Heuer, F., Jager, T., Kiltz, E., Schäge, S.: On the selective opening security of practical public-key encryption schemes. In: Katz, J. (ed.) PKC 2015. LNCS, vol. 9020, pp. 27–51. Springer, Heidelberg (2015). https://doi.org/10.1007/978-3-662-46447-2_2
18. Heuer, F., Poettering, B.: Selective opening security from simulatable data encapsulation. In: Cheon, J.H., Takagi, T. (eds.) ASIACRYPT 2016. LNCS, vol. 10032, pp. 248–277. Springer, Heidelberg (2016). https://doi.org/10.1007/978-3-662-53890-6_9
19. Hiromasa, R.: Digital signatures from the middle-product LWE. In: Baek, J., Susilo, W., Kim, J. (eds.) ProvSec 2018. LNCS, vol. 11192, pp. 239–257. Springer, Cham (2018). https://doi.org/10.1007/978-3-030-01446-9_14
20. Hofheinz, D., Hövelmanns, K., Kiltz, E.: A modular analysis of the Fujisaki-Okamoto transformation. In: Kalai, Y., Reyzin, L. (eds.) TCC 2017. LNCS, vol. 10677, pp. 341–371. Springer, Cham (2017). https://doi.org/10.1007/978-3-319-70500-2_12
21. Hofheinz, D., Jager, T., Rupp, A.: Public-key encryption with simulation-based selective-opening security and compact ciphertexts. In: Hirt, M., Smith, A. (eds.) TCC 2016. LNCS, vol. 9986, pp. 146–168. Springer, Heidelberg (2016). https://doi.org/10.1007/978-3-662-53644-5_6
22. Hofheinz, D., Rao, V., Wichs, D.: Standard security does not imply indistinguishability under selective opening. In: Hirt, M., Smith, A. (eds.) TCC 2016. LNCS, vol. 9986, pp. 121–145. Springer, Heidelberg (2016). https://doi.org/10.1007/978-3-662-53644-5_5
23. Hofheinz, D., Rupp, A.: Standard versus selective opening security: separation and equivalence results. In: Lindell, Y. (ed.) TCC 2014. LNCS, vol. 8349, pp. 591–615. Springer, Heidelberg (2014). https://doi.org/10.1007/978-3-642-54242-8_25
24. Hosoyamada, A., Yasuda, K.: Building quantum-one-way functions from block ciphers: Davies-Meyer and Merkle-Damgård constructions. In: Peyrin, T., Galbraith, S. (eds.) ASIACRYPT 2018. LNCS, vol. 11272, pp. 275–304. Springer, Cham (2018). https://doi.org/10.1007/978-3-030-03326-2_10
25. Hövelmanns, K., Kiltz, E., Schäge, S., Unruh, D.: Generic authenticated key exchange in the quantum random oracle model. IACR Cryptology ePrint Archive 2018/928 (2018)
26. Jiang, H., Zhang, Z., Chen, L., Wang, H., Ma, Z.: IND-CCA-secure key encapsulation mechanism in the quantum random oracle model, revisited. In: Shacham, H., Boldyreva, A. (eds.) CRYPTO 2018. LNCS, vol. 10993, pp. 96–125. Springer, Cham (2018). https://doi.org/10.1007/978-3-319-96878-0_4
27. Jiang, H., Zhang, Z., Ma, Z.: Key encapsulation mechanism with explicit rejection in the quantum random oracle model. In: Lin, D., Sako, K. (eds.) PKC 2019. LNCS, vol. 11443, pp. 618–645. Springer, Cham (2019). https://doi.org/10.1007/978-3-030-17259-6_21
28. Jiang, H., Zhang, Z., Ma, Z.: Tighter security proofs for generic key encapsulation mechanism in the quantum random oracle model. In: Ding, J., Steinwandt, R. (eds.) PQCrypto 2019. LNCS, vol. 11505, pp. 227–248. Springer, Cham (2019). https://doi.org/10.1007/978-3-030-25510-7_13

29. Kiltz, E., Lyubashevsky, V., Schaffner, C.: A concrete treatment of Fiat-Shamir signatures in the quantum random-oracle model. In: Nielsen, J.B., Rijmen, V. (eds.) EUROCRYPT 2018. LNCS, vol. 10822, pp. 552–586. Springer, Cham (2018). https://doi.org/10.1007/978-3-319-78372-7_18
30. Lai, J., Deng, R.H., Liu, S., Weng, J., Zhao, Y.: Identity-based encryption secure against selective opening chosen-ciphertext attack. In: Nguyen, P.Q., Oswald, E. (eds.) EUROCRYPT 2014. LNCS, vol. 8441, pp. 77–92. Springer, Heidelberg (2014). https://doi.org/10.1007/978-3-642-55220-5_5
31. Libert, B., Sakzad, A., Stehlé, D., Steinfeld, R.: All-but-many lossy trapdoor functions and selective opening chosen-ciphertext security from LWE. In: Katz, J., Shacham, H. (eds.) CRYPTO 2017. LNCS, vol. 10403, pp. 332–364. Springer, Cham (2017). https://doi.org/10.1007/978-3-319-63697-9_12
32. Liu, S., Paterson, K.G.: Simulation-based selective opening CCA security for PKE from key encapsulation mechanisms. In: Katz, J. (ed.) PKC 2015. LNCS, vol. 9020, pp. 3–26. Springer, Heidelberg (2015). https://doi.org/10.1007/978-3-662-46447-2_1
33. Lyu, L., Liu, S., Han, S., Gu, D.: Tightly SIM-SO-CCA secure public key encryption from standard assumptions. In: Abdalla, M., Dahab, R. (eds.) PKC 2018. LNCS, vol. 10769, pp. 62–92. Springer, Cham (2018). https://doi.org/10.1007/978-3-319-76578-5_3
34. NIST: National institute for standards and technology: post quantum crypto project (2019). https://csrc.nist.gov/projects/post-quantum-cryptography/round-2-submissions
35. Saito, T., Xagawa, K., Yamakawa, T.: Tightly-secure key-encapsulation mechanism in the quantum random oracle model. In: Nielsen, J.B., Rijmen, V. (eds.) EUROCRYPT 2018. LNCS, vol. 10822, pp. 520–551. Springer, Cham (2018). https://doi.org/10.1007/978-3-319-78372-7_17
36. Targhi, E.E., Unruh, D.: Post-quantum security of the Fujisaki-Okamoto and OAEP transforms. In: Hirt, M., Smith, A. (eds.) TCC 2016. LNCS, vol. 9986, pp. 192–216. Springer, Heidelberg (2016). https://doi.org/10.1007/978-3-662-53644-5_8
37. Zhandry, M.: Secure identity-based encryption in the quantum random oracle model. In: Safavi-Naini, R., Canetti, R. (eds.) CRYPTO 2012. LNCS, vol. 7417, pp. 758–775. Springer, Heidelberg (2012). https://doi.org/10.1007/978-3-642-32009-5_44

Distributing Any Elliptic Curve Based Protocol

Nigel P. Smart[1,2](✉) and Younes Talibi Alaoui[2]

[1] University of Bristol, Bristol, UK
[2] KU Leuven, Leuven, Belgium
{nigel.smart,younes.talibialaoui}@kuleuven.be

Abstract. We show how to perform a full-threshold n-party actively secure MPC protocol over a subgroup of order p of an elliptic curve group $E(K)$. This is done by utilizing a full-threshold n-party actively secure MPC protocol over $\mathbb{F}_p$ in the pre-processing model (such as SPDZ), and then locally mapping the Beaver triples from this protocol into equivalent triples for the elliptic curve. This allows us to transform essentially *any* (algebraic) one-party protocol over an elliptic curve, into an n-party one. As an example we show how to transform a general Σ-protocol over elliptic curves and the shuffle protocol of Abe into an n-party protocol. This latter application requires us to also give an MPC protocol to derive the switches in a Waksman network from a generic permutation, which may be of independent interest.

1 Introduction

Over the years there have been a number of protocols developed for elliptic curves, starting with basic protocols such as encryption and signature, through to zero-knowledge proofs, and secure shuffles. In some application instances one wants to perform these protocols where the secret data of a party is not held by a single party but held by a set of parties via a secret sharing scheme. Obvious examples include distributed decryption and distributed signing protocols. Indeed the case of distributed signatures for EC-DSA has recently undergone a renewed interest, see [8,14–16], due to applications to block-chain. In addition, general distributed cryptographic solutions for decryption and signature operations are becoming more in vogue, as evidenced by the recent NIST workshop in this space[1].

There are however a large number of other protocols which applications may require to be distributed in this manner. For example take a simple elliptic curve based Sigma-protocol to prove equality of two discrete logarithms, see [18][Chapter 21]. If the application requires the two discrete logarithms to be secret shared, then the protocol to produce the proof must be executed in a

[1] https://www.nist.gov/news-events/events/2019/03/nist-threshold-cryptography-workshop-2019.

M. Albrecht (Ed.): IMACC 2019, LNCS 11929, pp. 342–366, 2019.
https://doi.org/10.1007/978-3-030-35199-1_17

distributed manner. In this work we present a *simple* method to produce n-party actively secure distributed elliptic curve based protocols.

Our method applies to what we term *algebraic* protocols over $E(K)$. These are protocols which do not involve non-algebraic operations on secret data. Thus EC-DSA signing is an algebraic protocol as the non-algebraic operation (the hash-function operation) is performed on public data, but EC-IES decryption is not as the key-derivation needs to be applied on secret data. Thus our technique is unable to deal with the issues raised in [17]. Despite this restriction our model captures a number of useful cryptographic protocols.

We take the underlying elliptic curve as $E(K)$ where the (cryptographically interesting) subgroup order is a prime p. For such protocols we need to secret share both finite field elements in $\mathbb{F}_p$, and elliptic curve group elements in $E(K)$. In both cases we do this via an additive secret sharing scheme. Linear operations in $\mathbb{F}_p$ and in $E(K)$ are then able to be performed for free, and the problem then comes in performing the non-linear operations. For non-linear operations in $\mathbb{F}_p$ (i.e. multiplication) we utilize the idea of Beaver triples from general Multi-Party Computation (MPC) protocols (such as [7]), and thus our protocol is in the offline/online paradigm. For non-linear operations in $E(K)$, which are point multiplications of a secret shared point by a secret shared field element, we can utilize *the same* Beaver triples. Thus supporting additively secret shared elements in $E(K)$ can be accomplished using *the same* offline phase as is needed to perform MPC over $\mathbb{F}_p$.

To achieve active security we utilize the methodology of the SPDZ protocol [7] and its improvements, e.g. [6]. This protocol is a so-called MPC-with-abort system, in that if a dishonest party deviates from the protocol then the honest parties will abort with overwhelming probability. In SPDZ for each field element $x \in \mathbb{F}_p$ which is secret shared, we also secret share a MAC-value $\alpha \cdot x$ for some global secret shared MAC value α. We then translate this to the elliptic curve sharing by not only additively sharing an element $P \in E(K)$, but also additively sharing its MAC value $[\alpha]P$, for *the same* MAC key α as used to authenticate the shares over $\mathbb{F}_p$.

The first part of this paper is devoted to giving the details of this MPC protocol over elliptic curves, and the associated security proofs. We then give three applications, the first to show how distributed EC-DSA signing can be performed using this protocol. The online time for this EC-DSA signing operation will be very fast, the only drawback being the offline time inherited from the SPDZ protocol for generating authenticated Beaver triples over $\mathbb{F}_p$. Our second application shows how to perform a simple distributed Sigma protocol for an OR-proof, using the same methodology.

We then turn to a more complex application. In a number of applications one has a set of ElGamal ciphertexts and one wishes to perform a secure shuffle on them. The traditional method for doing this is to pass them through a sequence of so-called Mix-Nets. Each mixer applies their own private shuffle, and provides a zero-knowledge proof, that their mix has been performed correctly. The final recipient of the mix needs to verify *each* individual zero-knowledge proof. Thus if we have n-mixers we have a proof n times larger than that produced by a single mixer. Another way of achieving the same security, but with a smaller zero-knowledge proof, would be for the mixers to produce the mix in a distributed manner and generate a single *joint* proof of correctness of the mix. We show how the mix protocol of Abe [2] can be performed in such a distributed manner using our underlying MPC protocol.

Given a permutation as a Waksman network [20], with each Waksman switch secret shared, we show how to generate in a distributed manner the proof presented by Abe. This is essentially a more complex version of the Sigma protocol for equality of two discrete logarithms discussed earlier. We note, that more efficient proofs of correct shuffle have been given since Abe's work, see for example [4,9–11], but we concentrate on this one as it shows how our elliptic curve MPC protocol can be applied to more complex higher level protocols. Our solution is more efficient than an equivalent solution to the problem of n-mixers discussed by [1].

A problem with Abe's mixer is how to generate the secret shared Waksman network. Simply generating the switch values at random does not produce a uniformly random permutation (as was noticed in [3]). We can easily produce a secret shared uniformly random permutation, by each party P_i generating a permutation σ_i, sharing it, and then using as the secret-shared final permutation the product permutation $\sigma = \sigma_1 \cdots \sigma_n$. However, the question then remains how to convert the secret-shared permutation σ, given by (say) a permutation matrix, into a set of switches for a Waksman network. There is a classical algorithm to do this, which appears to require solving a set of non-linear equations. However, by closely examining this algorithm we see that one can perform the conversion from a permutation matrix to Waksman switches using a relatively simple algorithm which is suitable for implementation via an MPC system. Our algorithm for obtaining the Waksman switches in secret shared form is actively secure, if the underlying MPC system used is actively secure (which is what we assume throughout this work).

We end this introduction by re-iterating that our MPC system is in the full threshold paradigm, where active security is obtained by authenticating a share using a global shared MAC key. We note that our methodology can also be applied in the case of Q2 access structures (for example honest majority threshold access structures) if we accept MPC-with-abort. In such systems one can obtain similar authentication of the shares by utilizing the error detection properties of the underlying error correcting code associated to the secret sharing scheme, see [19] for a discussion of MPC for Q2 access structures in the case of MPC-with-abort. It can be easily seen that minor adaptations to our MPC protocol over elliptic curves will also enable one to support such Q2 access structures. Our methodology can also be applied to protocols over any finite abelian group of prime order, and not just elliptic curves. We concentrate on elliptic curves to make the presentation more down to earth.

2 Preliminaries

In this section we present some basic notation and the underlying MPC protocols we will make extensive use of.

Notation: We assume that all the parties $\mathcal{P}_1, \ldots, \mathcal{P}_n$ are probabilistic polynomial time Turing machines. We let $[n]$ denote the interval $[1, \ldots, n]$. We let $a \leftarrow X$ denote randomly assigning a value a from a set X, where we assume a uniform distribution on X. If A is an algorithm, we let $a \leftarrow A$ denote assignment of the output, where the probability distribution is over the random tape of A; we also let $a \leftarrow b$ be a shorthand for $a \leftarrow \{b\}$, i.e. to denote normal variable assignment. If $\mathcal{D}$ is a probability distribution over a set X then we let $a \leftarrow \mathcal{D}$ denote sampling from X with respect to the distribution $\mathcal{D}$.

We let $\mathcal{G} \subseteq E(K)$ denote a subgroup of large prime order of an elliptic curve E over a finite field K. Let the order of $\mathcal{G}$ be p. Any (non-zero) element of $\mathcal{G}$ can be taken as a generator, however we assume that a specific generator P is given as part of the group description. An element $Q \in \mathcal{G}$ can be multiplied by an element $x \in \mathbb{F}_p$ to produce another element $R \in \mathcal{G}$. We call this operation the point multiplication between a point Q and a multiplier x, and we write it as $R \leftarrow [x] \cdot Q$.

The SPDZ Protocol: Our protocols will be built on top of a number of existing functionalities/protocols. The main two being an ideal commitment functionality $\mathcal{F}_{\mathsf{Commit}}$ (given in the full versioni) and the SPDZ MPC protocol [7] for performing actively secure MPC over $\mathbb{F}_p$ for full-threshold adversaries. The SPDZ protocol processes data using an authenticated secret sharing scheme defined over a finite field $\mathbb{F}_p$, where p is prime.

We describe the variant of authentication and checking presented in [6]. The secret sharing scheme is defined as follows: Each party $\mathcal{P}_i$ holds a share of a global MAC key $\alpha_i \in \mathbb{F}_p$, where the global MAC key is defined to be $\alpha = \sum_i \alpha_i$. A data element $x \in \mathbb{F}_p$ is held in secret shared form as a tuple $\{x_i, \gamma_i\}_{i \in [n]}$, such that $x = \sum_i x_i$ and $\sum \gamma_i = \alpha \cdot x$. We denote a value x held in such a secret shared form as $\langle x \rangle_F$. If we wish to denote the specific value on which γ_i is a MAC share then we write $\gamma_i[x]$.

The SPDZ protocol implements the functionality given in Fig. 1. The functionality permits the secure computation of any function f on parties' inputs, assuming that any (reactive) function f is expressed in term of additions and multiplications over a finite field. Parties can also choose to whom the output of f is sent.

As explained earlier, SPDZ is an MPC-with-abort system. In such a system, an adversary can always deviate from the protocol, however, honest parties will abort when this happens with overwhelming probability. This behavior explains why $\mathcal{F}_{\mathsf{Online}}[\mathsf{SPDZ}]$ is written as such. That is, within the output stage, an adversary can choose between not sending Deliver, which translates the fact that they

Functionality $\mathcal{F}_{\mathsf{Online}}[\mathsf{SPDZ}]$

Initialize: On input $(init, p)$ from all parties, the functionality stores $(domain, p)$.

Input: On input $(input, \mathcal{P}_i, varid, x)$ from $\mathcal{P}_i$ and $(input, \mathcal{P}_i, varid, ?)$ from all other parties, with *varid* a fresh identifier, the functionality stores $(varid, x)$.

Add: On command $(add, varid_1, varid_2, varid_3)$ from all parties (if $varid_1, varid_2$ are present in memory and $varid_3$ is not), the functionality retrieves $(varid_1, x)$, $(varid_2, y)$ and stores $(varid_3, x + y)$.

Multiply: On input $(multiply, varid_1, varid_2, varid_3)$ from all parties (if $varid_1, varid_2$ are present in memory and $varid_3$ is not), the functionality retrieves $(varid_1, x)$, $(varid_2, y)$ and stores $(varid_3, x \cdot y)$.

Triple: On input $(triple, varid_1, varid_2, varid_3)$ from all parties (if none of the $varid_i$ are stored in memory), the functionality generates a uniformly random $a, b \in \mathbb{F}_p$ and computes $c = a \cdot b$ and then stores $(varid_1, a)$, $(varid_2, b)$ and $(varid_3, c)$

Output: On input $(output, varid, i)$ from all honest parties (if *varid* is present in memory), the functionality retrieves $(varid, y)$ and outputs it to the environment. The functionality waits for an input from the environment. If it is Deliver then y is output to all players if $i = 0$, or y is output to player i if $i \neq 0$. If the adversarial input is not equal to Deliver then $\varnothing$ is output to all players.

Fig. 1. The ideal functionality for MPC over $\mathbb{F}_p$

can deviate from protocol during the online phase, and sending Deliver, which means that the adversary is following the protocol so far.

The SPDZ protocol works in an offline-online manner, the precise offline protocol will not concern us in this work. The main goal of the SPDZ offline phase is to produce random triples $(\langle a\rangle_F, \langle b\rangle_F, \langle c\rangle_F)$ such that $c = a \cdot b$. It is convenient in some protocols to assume that the Beaver triples produced in the offline phase are also available to the user of the online phase. Thus we have a command in the online functionality that exports this data.

The online protocol $\Pi_{\mathsf{Online}}[\mathsf{SPDZ}]$ is given in Fig. 2, and can be shown (see e.g. [6]) that it realises the $\mathcal{F}_{\mathsf{Online}}[\mathsf{SPDZ}]$ functionality in the $(\mathcal{F}_{\mathsf{Offline}}[\mathsf{SPDZ}], \mathcal{F}_{\mathsf{Commit}})$-hybrid model. The online protocol makes use of a crucial sub-protocol, called $\Pi_{\mathsf{MACCheck}}[\mathsf{SPDZ}]$, which we have given in Fig. 3. This sub-protocol is executed (in batches) on every opened value throughout the computation, in order to check if the adversary is trying to deviate from the protocol without being caught.

Since $\langle\cdot\rangle_F$ is a linear secret sharing scheme it is easy to compute linear functions on the share values. In particular given $\langle x\rangle_F$ and $\langle y\rangle_F$ and three field constants $a, b, c \in \mathbb{F}_p$ we can compute the sharing of $z = a \cdot x + b \cdot y + c$ locally by each player computing

$$
\begin{aligned}
z_1 &\leftarrow a \cdot x_i + b \cdot y_i + c && \text{for } i = 1\\
z_i &\leftarrow a \cdot x_i + b \cdot y_i && \text{for } i \neq 1\\
\gamma_i[z] &\leftarrow a \cdot \gamma_i[x] + b \cdot \gamma_i[y] + \alpha_i \cdot c && \text{for all } i.
\end{aligned}
$$

Protocol $\Pi_{\mathsf{Online}}[\mathsf{SPDZ}]$

Initialize: The parties call $\mathcal{F}_{\mathsf{Offline}}$ to get the shares α_i of the MAC key, a number of multiplication triples $(\langle a\rangle_F, \langle b\rangle_F, \langle c\rangle_F)$ and mask values $(r_i, \langle r_i\rangle_F)$ as needed for the circuit being evaluated. If $\mathcal{F}_{\mathsf{Offline}}$ aborts then abort, otherwise the operations specified below are performed according to the circuit.

Input: To share his input x_i, player i takes an available mask value $(r_i, \langle r_i\rangle_F)$ and does the following:
1. Broadcast $e \leftarrow x_i - r_i$.
2. The players compute $\langle x_i\rangle_F \leftarrow \langle r_i\rangle_F + e$.

Add: On input $(\langle x\rangle_F, \langle y\rangle_F)$, the players locally compute $\langle x+y\rangle_F \leftarrow \langle x\rangle_F + \langle y\rangle_F$.

Multiply: On input $(\langle x\rangle_F, \langle y\rangle_F)$, the players do the following:
1. Take one multiplication triple $(\langle a\rangle_F, \langle b\rangle_F, \langle c\rangle_F)$ and open $\langle x\rangle_F - \langle a\rangle_F, \langle y\rangle_F - \langle b\rangle_F$ to get s and t respectively.
2. Locally each player computes $\langle z\rangle_F \leftarrow \langle c\rangle_F + s\cdot\langle b\rangle_F + t\cdot\langle a\rangle_F + s\cdot t$

Triple: Here the players simply take one multiplication triple $(\langle a\rangle_F, \langle b\rangle_F, \langle c\rangle_F)$ off the pre-computed list obtained in the offline phase.

Output: This procedure is entered once the players have finished the circuit evaluation, but still the final output $\langle y\rangle_F$ has not been opened.
1. The players call the MACCheck[SPDZ] protocol on input all opened values so far.
2. The players open $\langle y\rangle_F$ and call MACCheck[SPDZ] on input y to verify its MAC.

Fig. 2. Operations for secure function evaluation

Protocol $\Pi_{\mathsf{MACCheck}}[\mathsf{SPDZ}]$

Usage: Each player has input α_i and $(\gamma_i[a_j])$ for $j = 1, \ldots, t$. All players have a public set of opened values $\{a_1, \ldots, a_t\}$; the protocol either succeeds or outputs failure if an inconsistent MAC value is found.

MACCheck($\{a_1, \ldots, a_t\}$):
1. All players $\mathcal{P}_i$ sample s_i and asks $\mathcal{F}_{\mathsf{Commit}}$ to broadcast $\tau_i^s \leftarrow \mathsf{Comm}(s_i)$.
2. Every player $\mathcal{P}_i$ calls $\mathcal{F}_{\mathsf{Commit}}$ with $\mathsf{Open}(\tau_i^s)$ all players obtain s_j for all j.
3. Set $s \leftarrow s_1 \oplus \cdots \oplus s_n$.
4. Players using s sample a random vector $\mathbf{r}$ from $\mathbb{F}_p^t$; note all players obtain the same vector as they have agreed on the seed s.
5. Each player computes the public value $a \leftarrow \sum_{j=1}^t r_j \cdot a_j$.
6. P_i computes $v_i \leftarrow \sum_{j=1}^t r_j \cdot \gamma_i[a_j]$, and $w_i \leftarrow v_i - \alpha_i \cdot a$.
7. P_i asks $\mathcal{F}_{\mathsf{Commit}}$ to broadcast $\tau_i^w \leftarrow \mathsf{Comm}(w_i)$.
8. Every player calls $\mathcal{F}_{\mathsf{Commit}}$ with $\mathsf{Open}(\tau_i^w)$, all players obtain w_i for all i.
9. If $w_1 + \cdots + w_n \neq 0_{\mathbb{F}_p}$, the players output $\varnothing$ and abort.

Fig. 3. Method to check MACs on partially opened values

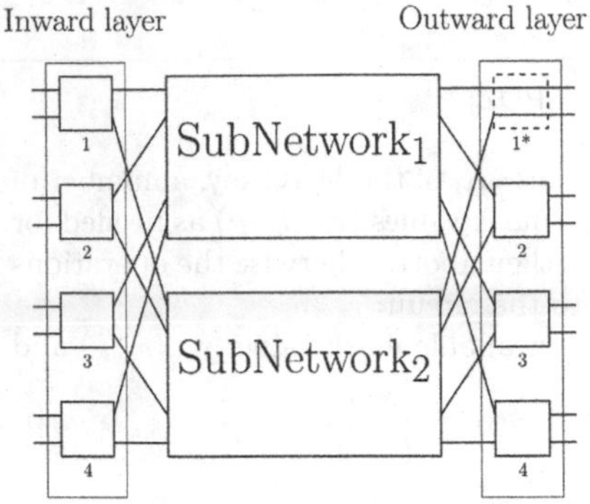

Fig. 4. Waksman network of size 8

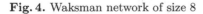

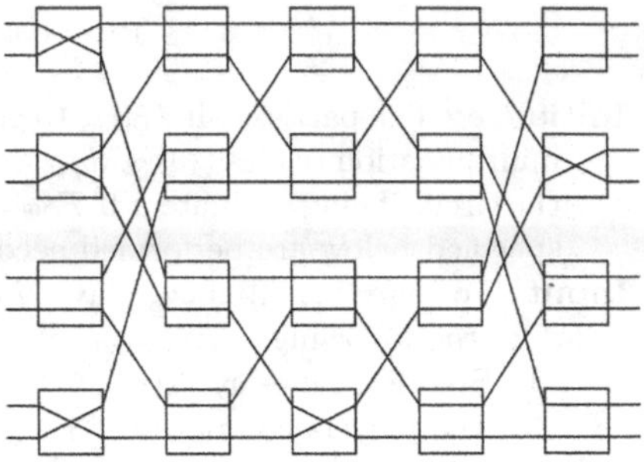

Fig. 5. A realization of the permutation $\tilde{\pi}$

Waksman Networks: A Waksman network [20] is a circuit with m input and output wires, to make our discussion cleaner we will assume m is a power of two. Within the circuit, inputs are shuffled with respect to a permutation. The building blocks of a Waksman network are switches; where a switch is a circuit with two input and output wires, with a hardwired bit called the control bit. If the control bit equals one, the switch swaps its inputs, otherwise, the switch simply forwards its inputs to the output wires.

The construction of a Waksman network follows a recursive structure (Fig. 4), that is to say a Waksman network contains:

- One inward layer.
- One outward layer.
- Two parallel subnetworks of size $\frac{m}{2}$, linked in a butterfly manner to the inward and outward layers.

The inward layer contains $\frac{m}{2}$ switches, whereas the outward layer contains $\frac{m}{2} - 1$ switches. That is, the missing switch (switch 1*) is fixed by setting its control bit to be zero. The inner networks are constructed in a similar manner, and there are $2 \cdot \log_2(m) - 1$ layers in total. Thus the total number of switches within the whole network is $m \cdot \log_2(m) - m + 1$. Given any permutation, there is a classical algorithm to determine a set of control bits realizing it. That is to say, this algorithm takes as input the permutation, and outputs a control bit for every switch, such that the resulting Waksman network realizes this permutation. In our work (for ease of implementing the algorithm to create a Waksman network in a data-oblivious manner) we use a more relaxed definition of a Waksman network in which the first gate of the outer layer is not fixed to be an empty switch. This increases the total number of switches in a network by $m/2 - 1$ to the value $m \cdot \log_2(m) - m/2$.

As an example consider the permutation matrix

$$\tilde{M} = \begin{bmatrix} 0&1&0&0&0&0&0&0 \\ 1&0&0&0&0&0&0&0 \\ 0&0&0&0&0&0&0&1 \\ 0&0&0&1&0&0&0&0 \\ 0&0&0&0&1&0&0&0 \\ 0&0&0&0&0&1&0&0 \\ 0&0&1&0&0&0&0&0 \\ 0&0&0&0&0&0&1&0 \end{bmatrix}$$

realizing the permutation $\tilde{\pi} \in S_8$. This can be represented by the Waksman network in Fig. 5. One immediately sees an advantage of using a Waksman network to represent a permutation on a vector v. Instead of evaluating π on v by a matrix vector product, we apply a series of transpositions on v using the permutation networks. This is more efficient in terms of operations performed. That is, the matrix based approach requires m^2 multiplications to apply a permutation on a vector, whereas a network based approach using (our modified) Waksman network, would require at most $m \cdot \log_2(m) - m/2$ swaps. In terms of an MPC based implementation of the network for secret shared control bits, one swap consists of two multiplications.

3 Multiparty Computation Over Elliptic Curve Groups

Our goal in this section is to define a protocol to perform efficient actively secure (with abort) MPC in the context of elliptic curve calculations. This will enable us to efficiently transfer any algebraic ECC based cryptographic protocols into the distributed domain. Such protocols require us to perform arithmetic not only in the elliptic curve group, but also over the finite field given by the order of the large prime subgroup (the so-called exponent group, even though it is a field). Our basic strategy is to use the SPDZ protocol to conduct the MPC in the exponent group, and to use a similar protocol with *the same MAC key* to define the MPC protocol to work in the elliptic curve group itself.

The functionality we aim to produce a secure realisation of is $\mathcal{F}_{\mathsf{Online}}[\mathsf{ECC}]$, given in Fig. 6. This functionality permits the parties to compute over elliptic curve points, and as explained earlier, this essentially requires doing computation over a finite field, as well as over an elliptic curve group. Therefore, one immediately notes that this is essentially an extension of the $\mathcal{F}_{\mathsf{Online}}[\mathsf{SPDZ}]$ functionality in that we have added an additional set of variables corresponding to elliptic curve points. Given this similarity it should not be surprising that we utilize the same secret sharing as in SPDZ to share values in the exponent group.

In our realisation of this functionality, an elliptic curve data element $Q \in \mathcal{G}$ is held in secret shared form as a tuple $\{Q_i, \Gamma_i\}_{i \in [n]}$, such that $Q = \sum_i Q_i$ and $\sum \Gamma_i = [\alpha] \cdot Q$ where α is the same MAC key as used in the secret sharing $\langle \cdot \rangle_F$. We denote a value Q held in such a secret shared form as $\langle Q \rangle_E$. Again if we want to denote the specific value on which Γ_i is a MAC share we will write $\Gamma_i[Q]$.

Functionality $\mathcal{F}_{\mathsf{Online}}[\mathsf{ECC}]$

Initialize: On input $(init, \mathcal{G})$ from all parties, the functionality stores $(domain, \mathcal{G})$. Two lists of identifiers are established, one called field identifiers and one called curve identifiers.

Input-F: On input $(inputF, \mathcal{P}_i, varid, x)$ with $x \in \mathbb{F}_p$ from $\mathcal{P}_i$ and $(input, \mathcal{P}_i, varid, ?_{\mathbb{F}_p})$ from all other parties, with *varid* a fresh identifier, the functionality stores $(varid, x)$ in the list of field identifiers.

Input-G: On input $(inputG, \mathcal{P}_i, varid, Q)$ with $Q \in \mathcal{G}$ from $\mathcal{P}_i$ and $(input, \mathcal{P}_i, varid, ?_{\mathcal{G}})$ from all other parties, with *varid* a fresh identifier, the functionality stores $(varid, P)$ in the list of curve identifiers.

Add-F: On command $(addF, varid_1, varid_2, varid_3)$ from all parties where $varid_1, varid_2$ are in the list of field identifiers and $varid_3$ is not, the functionality retrieves $(varid_1, x)$, $(varid_2, y)$ from the list of field identifiers and stores $(varid_3, x + y)$ in the list of field identifiers.

Add-G: On command $(addG, varid_1, varid_2, varid_3)$ from all parties where $varid_1, varid_2$ are in the list of curve identifiers and $varid_3$ is not, the functionality retrieves $(varid_1, Q)$, $(varid_2, R)$ from the list of curve identifiers and stores $(varid_3, Q + R)$ in the list of curve identifiers.

Multiply-F: On command $(multiplyF, varid_1, varid_2, varid_3)$ from all parties where $varid_1, varid_2$ are in the list of field identifiers and $varid_3$ is not, the functionality retrieves $(varid_1, x)$, $(varid_2, y)$ from the list of field identifiers and stores $(varid_3, x \cdot y)$ in the list of field identifiers.

Triple: On input $(triple, varid_1, varid_2, varid_3)$ from all parties (if none of the $varid_i$ are stored in memory), the functionality generates a uniformly random $a, b \in \mathbb{F}_p$ and computes $c = a \cdot b$ and then stores $(varid_1, a)$, $(varid_2, b)$ and $(varid_3, c)$ in the list of field identifiers.

Multiply-G-P: On command $(multiplyGP, varid_1, Q, varid_2)$ from all parties where $varid_1$ is in the list of field identifiers, $Q \in \mathcal{G}$, and $varid_2$ is a fresh identifier from the list of the curve identifiers, the functionality retrieves $(varid_1, x)$, from the list of field identifiers and stores $(varid_2, [x] \cdot Q)$.

Multiply-G-S: On command $(multiplyGS, varid_1, varid_2, varid_3)$ from all parties where $varid_1$ is in the list of field identifiers and $varid_2$ is in the list of curve identifiers and $varid_3$ is not, the functionality retrieves $(varid_1, x)$, $(varid_2, Q)$ from the respective lists and stores $(varid_3, [x] \cdot Q)$.

Output-F: On input $(outputF, varid, i)$ from all honest parties (if *varid* is present in the list of field identifiers), the functionality retrieves $(varid, y)$ from the set of field identifiers and outputs it to the environment. The functionality waits for an input from the environment. If this input is $\mathsf{Deliver}$ then y is output to all players if $i = 0$, or y is output to player i if $i \neq 0$. If the adversarial input is not equal to $\mathsf{Deliver}$ then $\varnothing$ is output to all players.

Output-G: On input $(outputG, varid, i)$ from all honest parties (if *varid* is present in the list of curve identifiers), the functionality retrieves $(varid, R)$ from the set of curve identifiers and outputs it to the environment. The functionality waits for an input from the environment. If this input is $\mathsf{Deliver}$ then R is output to all players if $i = 0$, or R is output to player i if $i \neq 0$. If the adversarial input is not equal to $\mathsf{Deliver}$ then $\varnothing$ is output to all players.

Fig. 6. The ideal functionality for MPC over $\mathcal{G} \subseteq E(K)$ with $\#\mathcal{G} = p$

Again, as $\langle \cdot \rangle_E$ is a linear secret sharing scheme it is easy to compute linear functions on the share values. In particular given $\langle Q \rangle_E$ and $\langle R \rangle_E$, two field constants $a, b \in \mathbb{F}_p$ and one public curve point S we can compute the sharing of $T = [a] \cdot Q + [b] \cdot R + S$ locally by each player computing

$$\begin{aligned} T_0 &\leftarrow [a] \cdot Q_i + [b] \cdot R_i + S && \text{for } i = 0 \\ T_i &\leftarrow [a] \cdot Q_i + [b] \cdot R_i && \text{for } i \neq 0 \\ \Gamma_i[T] &\leftarrow [a] \cdot \Gamma_i[Q] + [b] \cdot \Gamma_i[R] + [\alpha_i] \cdot S && \text{for all } i. \end{aligned}$$

One can also compute $U = [a] \cdot Q$ when a is shared and Q is public, with only local computation. This can be done by having each player locally compute

$$\begin{aligned} U_i &\leftarrow [a_i] \cdot Q && \text{for all } i. \\ \Gamma_i[U] &\leftarrow [\gamma_i[a]] \cdot Q && \text{for all } i. \end{aligned}$$

Which we write as

$$\langle U \rangle_E \leftarrow [\langle a \rangle_F] \cdot Q. \tag{1}$$

The only complex part is then to perform non-linear operations, namely to compute the point multiplication of a secret shared element in $\mathbb{F}_q$ by a secret shared elliptic curve point. An operation which we write as

$$\langle U \rangle_E \leftarrow [\langle a \rangle_F] \cdot \langle Q \rangle_E. \tag{2}$$

3.1 MACCheck Protocol

Before presenting our protocol for performing the arithmetic operation in Eq. (2), we first modify the SPDZ MACCheck protocol so that it also checks the MAC values on the authenticated sharings of elliptic curve points. This is done in Fig. 7. The intuition behind correctness and soundness of this protocol, comes from the fact that we took the MAC check protocol from SPDZ operating over elements in $\mathbb{F}_p$, and replicated it for elements of $\mathcal{G}$. Then, we combined these two checks in order to execute the protocol only once. So we perform the MAC check in a single operation on both opened elements in $\mathbb{F}_p$ and opened elements in $\mathcal{G}$. Thus at step 7 we map the share $v_i - \alpha_i \cdot a$ of player i to the point $[v_i - \alpha_i \cdot a] \cdot P$ over $\mathcal{G}$. This makes the protocol inherit the correctness and soundness properties from the one in SPDZ. This is captured in the following theorem, the proof of which is given in the full version.

Theorem 1. *The protocol $\Pi_{\mathsf{MACCheck}}[\mathsf{ECC}]$ is correct and sound. That is, it accepts if all values $\{a_1, \dots, a_t\}$ and $\{A_1, \dots, A_u\}$ along with their corresponding MACs were correctly computed, and it rejects except with negligible probability if at least one value or MAC was not correctly computed.*

Protocol $\Pi_{\mathsf{MACCheck}}[\mathsf{ECC}]$

Usage: Each player has input α_i, $(\gamma_i[a_j])$ for $j = 1, \ldots, t$ and $(\Gamma_i[A_k])$ for $k = 1, \ldots, u$. All players have two public sets of opened values : $\{a_1, \ldots, a_t\}$ over $\mathbb{F}_p$, and $\{A_1, \ldots, A_u\}$ over $\mathcal{G}$; the protocol either succeeds or outputs failure if an inconsistent MAC value is found.

$\mathsf{MACCheck}(\{a_1, \ldots, a_t\}, \{A_1, \ldots, A_u\})$:

1. Every player $\mathcal{P}_i$ samples a seed s_i and asks $\mathcal{F}_{\mathsf{Commit}}$ to broadcast $\tau_i^s \leftarrow \mathsf{Comm}(s_i)$.
2. Every player $\mathcal{P}_i$ calls $\mathcal{F}_{\mathsf{Commit}}$ with $\mathsf{Open}(\tau_i^s)$ and all players obtain s_j for all j.
3. Set $s \leftarrow s_1 \oplus \cdots \oplus s_n$.
4. Players using s sample a random vector $\mathbf{r}$ from $\mathbb{F}_p^{t+u}$; note all players obtain the same vector as they have agreed on the seed s.
5. Each player computes the public values $a \leftarrow \sum_{j=1}^{t} r_j \cdot a_j$ and $A \leftarrow \sum_{k=1}^{u} [r_{k+t}] \cdot A_k$
6. Player i computes $v_i \leftarrow \sum_{j=1}^{t} r_j \cdot \gamma_i[a_j]$, and $\Gamma_i \leftarrow \sum_{k=1}^{u} [r_{k+t}] \cdot \Gamma_i[A_k]$
7. Player i computes $W_i \leftarrow [v_i - \alpha_i \cdot a] \cdot P + \Gamma_i - [\alpha_i] \cdot A$, where P is the generator of $\mathcal{G}$
8. Player i asks $\mathcal{F}_{\mathsf{Commit}}$ to broadcast $\tau_i^W \leftarrow \mathsf{Comm}(W_i)$.
9. Every player calls $\mathcal{F}_{\mathsf{Commit}}$ with $\mathsf{Open}(\tau_i^W)$, and all players obtain W_i for all i.
10. If $W_1 + \cdots + W_n \neq 0_{\mathcal{G}}$, the players output $\varnothing$ and abort.

Fig. 7. Method to check MACs on partially opened values

3.2 MPC Online Protocol

We introduce now in Fig. 8 our protocol for the online phase. Similar to $\mathcal{F}_{\mathsf{Online}}[\mathsf{ECC}]$, which was constructed by extending $\mathcal{F}_{\mathsf{Online}}[\mathsf{SPDZ}]$, we do the same here while realizing $\mathcal{F}_{\mathsf{Online}}[\mathsf{ECC}]$. That is, the sub-functionalities **Initialize**, **Input-F**, **Add-F**, and **Multiply-F**, will be realized the same way as in the protocol $\Pi_{\mathsf{Online}}[\mathsf{SPDZ}]$. For the remaining functionalities, we will realize them using essentially the same techniques as in the SPDZ protocol.

- **Input-G** is realized using the same trick as used to implement **Input-F**. That is, assuming player i holds $(R_i, \langle R_i \rangle_E)$, this player can share a point $Q_i \in \mathcal{G}$ by broadcasting $E = Q_i - R_i$, then players compute $\langle Q_i \rangle_E = \langle R_i \rangle_E + E$ to obtain a share of Q_i. However, as we are using only the preprocessing of SPDZ, we need to somehow provide $(R_i, \langle R_i \rangle_E)$ to player i, using only the generated data from $\mathcal{F}_{\mathsf{Offline}}[\mathsf{SPDZ}]$. This can be done using the generator P, That is, from a SPDZ input mask $(r_i, \langle r_i \rangle_F)$, one can obtain a mask $(R_i, \langle R_i \rangle_E)$ by setting $\langle R_i \rangle_E \leftarrow [\langle r_i \rangle_F] \cdot P$, which requires only local computation.
- **Add-G** is realized similarly to **Add-F**. That is, players will locally compute $\langle Q + R \rangle_E \leftarrow \langle Q \rangle_E + \langle R \rangle_E$.
- **Multiply-G-P** is realized by having players locally compute $\langle R \rangle_E \leftarrow \langle x \rangle_F \cdot Q$.

Protocol $\Pi_{\mathsf{Online}}[\mathsf{ECC}]$

Initialize: The parties call $\mathcal{F}_{\mathsf{Offline}}$ to get the shares α_i of the MAC key, a number of multiplication triples $(\langle a\rangle_F, \langle b\rangle_F, \langle c\rangle_F)$, and mask values $(r_i, \langle r_i\rangle_F)$ as needed for the circuit being evaluated. If $\mathcal{F}_{\mathsf{Offline}}$ aborts then abort, otherwise the operations specified below are performed according to the circuit.

Input-F: To share his input x_i, player i takes an available mask value $(r_i, \langle r_i\rangle_F)$ and does the following:

1. Broadcast $e \leftarrow x_i - r_i$.
2. The players compute $\langle x_i\rangle_F \leftarrow \langle r_i\rangle_F + e$.

Input-G: To share his input Q_i, Player i takes an available mask value $(r_i, \langle r_i\rangle_F)$ and does the following:

1. Broadcast $E \leftarrow Q_i - [r_i] \cdot P$.
2. The players compute $\langle Q_i\rangle_E \leftarrow [\langle r_i\rangle_F] \cdot P + E$ using Multiply-G-P.

Add-F: On input $(\langle x\rangle_F, \langle y\rangle_F)$, the players locally compute $\langle x+y\rangle_F \leftarrow \langle x\rangle_F + \langle y\rangle_F$.

Add-G: On input $(\langle Q\rangle_E, \langle R\rangle_E)$, the players locally compute $\langle Q+R\rangle_E \leftarrow \langle Q\rangle_E + \langle R\rangle_E$.

Multiply-F: On input $(\langle x\rangle_F, \langle y\rangle_F)$, the players do the following:

1. Take one multiplication triple $(\langle a\rangle_F, \langle b\rangle_F, \langle c\rangle_F)$ and open $\langle x\rangle_F - \langle a\rangle_F, \langle y\rangle_F - \langle b\rangle_F$ to get s and t respectively.
2. Locally each player sets $\langle x \cdot y\rangle_F \leftarrow \langle c\rangle_F + s \cdot \langle b\rangle_F + t \cdot \langle a\rangle_F + s \cdot t$

Triple: Here the players simply take one multiplication triple $(\langle a\rangle_F, \langle b\rangle_F, \langle c\rangle_F)$ off the pre-computed list obtained in the offline phase.

Multiply-G-P: On input $(\langle x\rangle_F, Q)$, where Q is a public point in $\mathcal{G}$, the players locally compute $\langle [x] \cdot Q\rangle_E \leftarrow [\langle x\rangle_F] \cdot Q$ using the operation defined in (1) .

Multiply-G-S: On input $(\langle x\rangle_F, \langle Q\rangle_E)$, the players do the following:

1. Take one multiplication triple $(\langle a\rangle_F, \langle b\rangle_F, \langle c\rangle_F)$, locally compute $\langle U\rangle_E \leftarrow [\langle b\rangle_F] \cdot P$ and $\langle V\rangle_E \leftarrow [\langle c\rangle_F] \cdot P$ using Multiply-G-P.
2. Open $\langle x\rangle_F - \langle a\rangle_F, \langle Q\rangle_E - \langle U\rangle_E$ to get s and T respectively.
3. Locally each player sets $\langle [x] \cdot Q\rangle_E \leftarrow \langle V\rangle_E + [s] \cdot \langle U\rangle_E + [\langle a\rangle_F] \cdot T + [s] \cdot T$

Output-F: This procedure is entered once the players have finished the circuit evaluation, but still the final output $\langle y\rangle_F$ has not been opened.

1. The players call the MACCheck[ECC] protocol on input all opened values so far.
2. The players open $\langle y\rangle_F$ and call MACCheck[ECC] on input y to verify its MAC.

Output-G: This procedure is entered once the players have finished the circuit evaluation, but still the final output $\langle R\rangle_E$ has not been opened.

1. The players call the MACCheck[ECC] protocol on input all opened values so far.
2. The players open $\langle R\rangle_E$ and call MACCheck[ECC] on input R to verify its MAC.

Fig. 8. Operations for secure function evaluation

- **Multiply-G-S** is realized using the Beaver trick. That is, assuming players hold a triple $(\langle a\rangle_F, \langle U\rangle_E, \langle V\rangle_E)$ such that $V = [a]\cdot U$, to compute $[\langle x\rangle_F]\cdot\langle Q\rangle_E$, players open $\langle x-a\rangle_F$ and $\langle Q-U\rangle_E$ to obtain s and T. Then the product can be obtained by setting $\langle [x]\cdot Q\rangle_E \leftarrow \langle V\rangle_E + [s]\cdot\langle U\rangle_E + [\langle a\rangle_F]\cdot T + [s]\cdot T$. However, the SPDZ preprocessing doesn't provide this type of triples, nonetheless, we still can obtain them locally by taking a SPDZ-triple $(\langle a\rangle_F, \langle b\rangle_F, \langle c\rangle_F)$ and having players locally compute $\langle U\rangle_E = \langle b\rangle_F \cdot P$ and $\langle V\rangle_E = \langle c\rangle_F \cdot P$. This results in a triple $(\langle a\rangle_F, \langle U\rangle_E, \langle V\rangle_E)$, which is a valid triple since $V = [c]\cdot P = [a\cdot b]\cdot P = [a]\cdot U$.
- **Output-F** and **Output-G** are realized the same way as in SPDZ, where we call here the MAC check protocol $\Pi_{\mathsf{MACCheck}}[\mathsf{ECC}]$ that we defined in the previous section, operating over all opened values in $\mathbb{F}_p$ and $\mathcal{G}$ so far, then we open the final output y (resp. R) and call $\Pi_{\mathsf{MACCheck}}[\mathsf{SPDZ}]$ (resp. $\Pi_{\mathsf{MACCheck}}[\mathsf{ECC}]$).

Thus we have the following theorem, the proof of which is given in the full version.

Theorem 2. *The protocol* $\Pi_{\mathsf{Online}}[\mathsf{ECC}]$ *securely implements* $\mathcal{F}_{\mathsf{Online}}[\mathsf{ECC}]$ *in the* $\mathcal{F}_{\mathsf{Offline}}[\mathsf{SPDZ}]$ *hybrid model.*

4 Simple Example Applications

In this section we present two toy applications of our methodology to perform MPC over elliptic curves, distributed EC-DSA signing and a distributed zero-knowledge proof.

EC-DSA Signing

Given a secret key $x \in \mathbb{F}_p$ for a public key $Q = [x]\cdot P$, for P an element of order q in $E(K)$, a hash function H with codomain $\mathbb{F}_p$, and a message m, the EC-DSA operation is given by:

1. $k \leftarrow \mathbb{F}_p$.
2. $R \leftarrow [k]\cdot P$.
3. $r \leftarrow \mathsf{x}-\mathsf{coord}(R) \pmod p$.
4. $e \leftarrow H(m)$.
5. $s \leftarrow (e + x\cdot r)/k \pmod p$.
6. Output (r, s).

Fig. 9. EC-DSA signing operation

Distributed EC-DSA: The EC-DSA signing operation is given in Fig. 9. To produce a distributed version we assume that the secret key x is already secret shared $\langle x \rangle_F$ using our secret sharing scheme. For simplicity we ignore the unlikely event that $r = 0$ in our description. The associated distributed version is given in Fig. 10. The protocol requires three multiplication triples from the offline phase (one to produce the initial sharings of $(\langle k \rangle_F, \langle b \rangle_F, \langle k \cdot b \rangle_F)$ and two to enable the secure computation of $\langle u \rangle_F$ and $\langle v \rangle_F$. Note, that we have correctness since the s produced by the distributed EC-DSA protocol is equal to $s = v/c = (u \cdot b)/(k \cdot b) = (e + x \cdot r)/k$. The trivial simulation of the distributed protocol appears to leak a minor amount of information. In particular the execution of the distributed protocol reveals R, whereas the ideal functionality for distributed signing will only reveal $r = \mathsf{x-coord}(R) \pmod p$. However, the verification operation recovers R in any case, thus this is not an actual leak of information.

Distributed EC-DSA Signing

1. Call **Triple** on $\mathcal{F}_{\mathsf{Online}}[\mathsf{ECC}]$ so as to obtain $(\langle k \rangle_F, \langle b \rangle_F, \langle c \rangle_F)$ where $c = k \cdot b$.
2. Compute $\langle R \rangle_E \leftarrow [\langle k \rangle_F] \cdot P$ by calling **Multiply-G-P** on $\mathcal{F}_{\mathsf{Online}}[\mathsf{ECC}]$.
3. Open $\langle R \rangle_E$ so all parties obtain R by calling **Output-G** on $\mathcal{F}_{\mathsf{Online}}[\mathsf{ECC}]$.
4. $r \leftarrow \mathsf{x-coord}(R) \pmod p$.
5. $e \leftarrow H(m)$.
6. $\langle u \rangle_F \leftarrow e + \langle x \rangle_F \cdot \langle r \rangle_F$ using **Multiply-F**.
7. $\langle v \rangle_F \leftarrow \langle u \rangle_F \cdot \langle b \rangle_F$ using **Multiply-F**.
8. Open $\langle c \rangle_F$ using **Output-F**.
9. $\langle s \rangle_F \leftarrow \langle v \rangle_F / c$.
10. Open $\langle s \rangle_F$ using **Output-F**.
11. Output (r, s).

Fig. 10. Distributed EC-DSA signing operation

In practice the specialist threshold EC-DSA protocols of [8,14–16] *may* be preferable than our general one. This is because whilst our protocol is especially simple in the online phase, and so will be able respond to requests much faster than the specialist protocols, the downside comes from needing to perform the offline phase. Thus the preferred protocol depends on whether the application supports offline processing. For intermittent signing operations, such as in an individual crypto wallet, the offline costs could be prohibitive. But for applications on an crypto-currency exchange the offline cost could be a cost worth bearing in order to respond faster to signing requests as they arise.

Distributed OR-Proof: The above EC-DSA application did not use the full power of our MPC over elliptic curves, in particular we did not make use of any non-linear operations on the elliptic curve. Here we present a more complex example, which will be useful later when we consider the MixNet proof of Abe, and which does present an application of these additional non-linear operations.

Suppose we want to give a non-interactive zero-knowledge proof the statement $\mathcal{L} = \{ x_b : T_0 = [x_0] \cdot P \text{ or } T_1 = [x_1] \cdot P \}$, where $x_b \in \mathbb{F}_p$, for $b \in \{0, 1\}$, is the secret value. Non-interactive zero-knowledge proofs of such statements are trivial to obtain, in the random oracle model, using the OR-proof technique for Sigma protocols [5]. To fix notation for what follows it can make more sense to consider the statement as being given by $\{ b, x_b : T_b = [x_b] \cdot P \}$, where $b \in \{0, 1\}$, $x_b \in \mathbb{F}_p$ are the secret values. In Fig. 11 we give the standard non-interactive proof for such a statement, again we assume a hash function with codomain $\mathbb{F}_p$.

Non-Interactive Zero-Knowledge Proof of the Statement $\mathcal{L}$.

Proof The proof proceeds as follows:

1. If $b = 0$ then
   (a) $k_0, e_1, s_1 \leftarrow \mathbb{F}_p$.
   (b) $R_0 \leftarrow [k_0] \cdot P$.
   (c) $R_1 \leftarrow [s_1] \cdot P - [e_1] \cdot T_1$.
   (d) $e \leftarrow H(R_0, R_1, T_0, T_1, P)$.
   (e) $e_0 \leftarrow e - e_1$.
   (f) $s_0 \leftarrow k_0 + e_0 \cdot x_0$.
2. Else
   (a) $k_1, e_0, s_0 \leftarrow \mathbb{F}_p$
   (b) $R_0 \leftarrow [s_0] \cdot P - [e_0] \cdot T_0$.
   (c) $R_1 \leftarrow [k_1] \cdot P$.
   (d) $e \leftarrow H(R_0, R_1, T_0, T_1, P)$.
   (e) $e_1 \leftarrow e - e_0$.
   (f) $s_1 \leftarrow k_1 + e_1 \cdot x_1$.
3. Output (e_0, e_1, s_0, s_1).

Verify Verification of the above proof is done as follows:

1. $R_0 \leftarrow [s_0] \cdot P - [e_0] \cdot T_0$, $R_1 \leftarrow [s_1] \cdot P - [e_1] \cdot T_1$.
2. $e \leftarrow H(R_0, R_1, T_0, T_1, P)$.
3. Reject if $e \neq e_0 + e_1$.

Fig. 11. Non-interactive ZKPoK for the statement $\mathcal{L}$

If we assume the secret inputs to the zero-knowledge proof are now distributed via our secret sharing scheme $\langle b \rangle_F, \langle x_b \rangle_F$, then we need to execute the above protocol using our elliptic curve based MPC protocol. We make use of the standard trick of multiplexing between two values depending on a hidden bit b, via $y_b \leftarrow b \cdot y_1 + (1 - b) \cdot y_0$. Our distributed protocol then can be described as in Fig. 12. Note, that operations of the form $\langle x \rangle_F \leftarrow \mathbb{F}_p$ can be performed by utilizing the first two elements in a Beaver triple produced in the offline phase. Notice how in lines 4, 5 and 6 we use non-linear secret-shared operations on the curve.

Distributed Non-Interactive Zero-Knowledge Proof of the Statement $\mathcal{L}$.

1. $\langle k_u \rangle_F, \langle e_v \rangle_F, \langle s_v \rangle_F \leftarrow \mathbb{F}_p$
2. $\langle R_u \rangle_E \leftarrow [\langle k_u \rangle_F] \cdot P$.
3. $\langle T_v \rangle_E \leftarrow [\langle b \rangle_F] \cdot T_0 + [1 - \langle b \rangle_F] \cdot T_1$.
4. $\langle R_v \rangle_E \leftarrow [\langle s_v \rangle_F] \cdot P - [\langle e_v \rangle_F] \cdot \langle T_v \rangle_E$.
5. $\langle R_0 \rangle_E \leftarrow [\langle b \rangle_F] \cdot \langle R_v \rangle_E + [1 - \langle b \rangle_F] \cdot \langle R_u \rangle_E$
6. $\langle R_1 \rangle_E \leftarrow [\langle b \rangle_F] \cdot \langle R_u \rangle_E + [1 - \langle b \rangle_F] \cdot \langle R_v \rangle_E$
7. Open $\langle R_0 \rangle_E$ and $\langle R_1 \rangle_E$.
8. $e \leftarrow H(R_0, R_1, T_0, T_1, P)$.
9. $\langle e_u \rangle_F \leftarrow e - \langle e_v \rangle_F$.
10. $\langle s_u \rangle_F \leftarrow \langle k_u \rangle_F + \langle e_v \rangle_F \cdot \langle x_b \rangle_F$.
11. $\langle e_0 \rangle_F \leftarrow [\langle b \rangle_F] \cdot \langle e_v \rangle_F + [1 - \langle b \rangle_F] \cdot \langle e_u \rangle_F$
12. $\langle e_1 \rangle_F \leftarrow [\langle b \rangle_F] \cdot \langle e_u \rangle_F + [1 - \langle b \rangle_F] \cdot \langle e_v \rangle_F$
13. $\langle s_0 \rangle_F \leftarrow [\langle b \rangle_F] \cdot \langle s_v \rangle_F + [1 - \langle b \rangle_F] \cdot \langle s_u \rangle_F$
14. $\langle s_1 \rangle_F \leftarrow [\langle b \rangle_F] \cdot \langle s_u \rangle_F + [1 - \langle b \rangle_F] \cdot \langle s_v \rangle_F$
15. Open $\langle e_0 \rangle_F$, $\langle e_1 \rangle_F$, $\langle s_0 \rangle_F$ and $\langle s_1 \rangle_F$.
16. Output (e_0, e_1, s_0, s_1).

Fig. 12. Distributed non-interactive ZKPoK for the statement $\mathcal{L}$

5 Application to MixNets

The rest of the paper is devoted to applying the above techniques to providing a more efficient (in terms of bandwidth and verification time) for a standard ElGamal based shuffle due to Abe [2]. As remarked in the introduction more efficient single party shuffles are now known, here we are focused on providing a general n-party shuffle.

Secure shuffling consists of randomly shuffling a vector of m elements $\mathbf{v}$ using a uniformly random permutation $\pi \in S_m$ unknown to the adversary. Secure shuffling is used in several contexts such as Oblivious-RAM, secure voting, etc. Within any context, we can distinguish three sets of parties, the parties A that provide input elements $\mathbf{v}$, the parties B that shuffle $\mathbf{v}$ to get $\mathbf{v}'$, and the parties C that will use $\mathbf{v}'$. These sets are not necessarily disjoint sets. That is, it depends on the context whether a party is part of more than one set.

Prior MPC use in shuffles has primarily considered two cases: In the first case, used in [13], the data donors A provide the sensitive data $\mathbf{v}$ to the computing parties (where here $B = C$) via secret sharing. The parties in B then shuffle the secret shared data with respect to a uniformly random permutation π to get $\mathbf{v}'$, and then perform computation on $\mathbf{v}'$ on behalf of a client. The permutation $\pi \in S_m$ is generated by each party $i \in B$ locally generating their own permutation π_i and then secret sharing this, with the final permutation being computed via the product $\pi = \prod \pi_i$. If the permutations are represented as permutation matrices this can be achieved by simply multiplying the secret shared permutation matrices. Active security being obtained by performing the obvious checks on the final matrix representing π, i.e. that all entries are in $\{0, 1\}$ and that the row and column sums are all equal to one.

In [12] the case of $A = B = C$ is considered for an application of Oblivious-RAM within an MPC calculation. Parties are already assumed to have secret shares of the values to be shuffled. In order to hide the data access pattern on $\mathbf{v}$, that is which component of $\mathbf{v}$ is queried at any specific point, $\mathbf{v}$ is shuffled with a uniformly random permutation. To generate π, every party i generates their own permutation π_i and (locally) transforms it into control bits for a Waksman network. Then every party secret shares its control bits among the other parties, and all permutations are evaluated in sequence. The switch with respect to a control bit being evaluated using the traditional multiplex $(x, y) \longrightarrow ((1-b)\cdot x + b \cdot y, b \cdot x + (1-b)\cdot y)$. To ensure active security, we check whether control bits b are in $\{0, 1\}$ by opening $b \cdot (b-1)$.

In traditional MixNets one has that the sets A, B and C are disjoint. A MixNet works by A entering a set of input ciphertexts, consider for example ElGamal style ciphertexts over our elliptic curve group $\mathcal{G}$, i.e. the vector $\mathbf{v} = (v_i)$ consists of values of the form

$$v_i = (M_i + [k_i] \cdot Q, [k_i] \cdot P)$$

for some ElGamal public key $Q = [x] \cdot P$. We then want to shuffle these ciphertexts and output a new set of ciphertexts $\mathbf{v}'$ which are the result of the shuffle. Here we utilize the malleability of ElGamal ciphertexts to transform an encryption of a message M_i into another ciphertext encrypting the same message. Traditionally each Mixer in the MixNet performs a shuffle and provides a zero-knowledge proof that the resulting output ciphertexts are in fact the permuted (and randomized) input ciphertexts. Then the data is passed onto another Mixer which does the same operation. Thus B consists of a number of parties all of whom operate in sequence. The receiving parties C need to verify *all* of the zero-knowledge proofs from each Mixer.

In this work we examine whether one can treat B as a single multi-party mixer, and thus end up with a single zero-knowledge proof. To do this we examine the MixNet protocol of Abe [2], and cast it not as a single player protocol but as a multi-party protocol. Our protocol consists of two stages. In the first stage we generate a secret-shared permutation π, then in the second stage we utilize the permutation π to shuffle the ciphertexts and produce the zero-knowledge proofs.

Stage 1: Producing the Shared Permutation: In this stage each of our n parties generates a random permutation π_i, represented as a permutation matrix. They enter it into the MPC system, and the parties then multiply the permutation matrices together to form a permutation π. We then need to derive switches for a Waksman network producing the same permutation as π. We leave this step to the next section. Note that we cannot generate shared random bits and use these as the control bits for a Waksman network, as this does not result in a uniformly random permutation, as was observed in [3].

Stage 2: Producing the Ciphertext Permutation and Proof: To perform the second step we can concentrate on what happens at a single switching gate in the Waksman network. Let the control bit for this gate be secret shared as $\langle b \rangle_F$, where $b \in \{0,1\}$, and we assume the input ciphertexts are given by

$$v_0 = (A_0, B_0) = (M_0 + [k_0] \cdot Q, [k_0] \cdot P),$$
$$v_1 = (A_1, B_1) = (M_1 + [k_1] \cdot Q, [k_1] \cdot P).$$

for some unknown messages M_0, M_1 and ephemeral keys k_0 and k_1. In Abe's MixNet the output of the switching gate will be the values

$$v'_b = (\overline{A}_b, \overline{B}_b) = (A_0 + [r_0] \cdot Q, B_0 + [r_0] \cdot P),$$
$$v'_{1-b} = (\overline{A}_{1-b}, \overline{B}_{1-b}) = (A_1 + [r_1] \cdot Q, B_1 + [r_1] \cdot P),$$

plus a zero-knowledge proof of the statement that

$$\Big(\log_Q(\overline{A}_0 - A_0) = \log_P(\overline{B}_0 - B_0) = r_0$$
$$\text{AND} \quad \log_Q(\overline{A}_1 - A_1) = \log_P(\overline{B}_1 - B_1) = r_1 \Big)$$
$$\text{OR} \quad \Big(\log_Q(\overline{A}_0 - A_1) = \log_P(\overline{B}_0 - B_1) = r_1$$
$$\text{AND} \quad \log_Q(\overline{A}_1 - A_0) = \log_P(\overline{B}_1 - B_0) = r_0 \Big)$$

given the secret input r_0 and r_1. This is (again) a relatively standard Sigma protocol proof, and we have already seen how to produce an (albeit simpler) zero-knowledge proof for an OR statement of equality of discrete logarithms in Sect. 4. For the values of r_0 and r_1 we take a Beaver triple $(\langle r_0 \rangle_F, \langle r_1 \rangle_F, \langle r_2 \rangle_F)$ from the pre-processing. These values of $\langle r_0 \rangle_F$ and $\langle r_1 \rangle_F$ are also used to generate the zero-knowledge proof. Thus we only need to produce the values of $\overline{A}_b$, $\overline{B}_b$ etc., which can be derived from the assignments

$$\langle C_0 \rangle_E \leftarrow A_0 + [\langle r_0 \rangle_F] \cdot Q,$$
$$\langle D_0 \rangle_E \leftarrow B_0 + [\langle r_0 \rangle_F] \cdot P,$$
$$\langle C_1 \rangle_E \leftarrow A_1 + [\langle r_1 \rangle_F] \cdot Q,$$
$$\langle D_1 \rangle_E \leftarrow B_1 + [\langle r_1 \rangle_F] \cdot P,$$
$$\langle \overline{A}_0 \rangle_E \leftarrow [1 - \langle b \rangle_F] \cdot \langle C_0 \rangle_E + [\langle b \rangle_F] \cdot \langle C_1 \rangle_E,$$
$$\langle \overline{B}_0 \rangle_E \leftarrow [1 - \langle b \rangle_F] \cdot \langle D_0 \rangle_E + [\langle b \rangle_F] \cdot \langle D_1 \rangle_E,$$
$$\langle \overline{A}_1 \rangle_E \leftarrow [1 - \langle b \rangle_F] \cdot \langle C_1 \rangle_E + [\langle b \rangle_F] \cdot \langle C_0 \rangle_E,$$
$$\langle \overline{B}_1 \rangle_E \leftarrow [1 - \langle b \rangle_F] \cdot \langle D_1 \rangle_E + [\langle b \rangle_F] \cdot \langle D_0 \rangle_E.$$

We can then open $(\langle \overline{A}_0 \rangle_E, \langle \overline{B}_0 \rangle_E, \langle \overline{A}_1 \rangle_E, \langle \overline{B}_1 \rangle_E)$, and produce the zero-knowledge proof as well.

6 Generating the Waksman Control Bits

We are now left with the final problem of giving an algorithm which on input of a secret-shared permutation matrix, outputs the secret-shared control bits of the associated Waksman network. Recall we simplify the algorithm, and the network, by not having the fixed switch in the first gate of each output layer (thus increasing the number of gates by $m/2-1$ from a traditional Waksman network). There is a classical algorithm for this [20], but it is not obvious how to translate this to work in a data-oblivious manner. Thus in this section we show how to perform this transformation obliviously. We let M denote the permutation matrix which we start with, whose i-th row and j-th column element we refer to as $M_{i,j}$. We assume that (the shared value of) M is guaranteed on input to be a permutation matrix; which can be checked by opening the column and row sums and checking them to be equal to m, as well as opening $M_{i,j} \cdot (M_{i,j} - 1)$ and verifying it is equal to zero for all i and j.

In what follows, to explain the algorithm used to do this conversion from the matrix to control bits, and how we realized it with MPC, we will use a running example which is the permutation $\tilde{\pi}$ of matrix given earlier:

$$\tilde{M} = \begin{bmatrix} 0\,1\,0\,0\,0\,0\,0\,0 \\ 1\,0\,0\,0\,0\,0\,0\,0 \\ 0\,0\,0\,0\,0\,0\,0\,1 \\ 0\,0\,0\,1\,0\,0\,0\,0 \\ 0\,0\,0\,0\,1\,0\,0\,0 \\ 0\,0\,0\,0\,0\,1\,0\,0 \\ 0\,0\,1\,0\,0\,0\,0\,0 \\ 0\,0\,0\,0\,0\,0\,1\,0 \end{bmatrix}$$

The high level idea behind the algorithm uses the fact that a Waksman network has a recursive structure, hence finding the control bits for a given permutation π can be done recursively. From π we determine two permutations π^1, π^2 for the two subnetworks, as well as control bits for the inward and outward layers, such that the composition of these realizes π. Then we apply the same process on π^1, π^2 and so on, till a control bit is determined for every switch. The process proceeds in the three steps:

- **Step One:** The first step consists of taking the $m \times m$ permutation matrix M of π, and merging coordinates corresponding to the same input or output switch, e.g., the first and second rows correspond to the first inward switch thus they will be merged. The first and second columns correspond to the first outward switch, they will be merged as well. Thus, this will result in an $m/2 \times m/2$ matrix M' such that $M'_{i,j} = M_{2\cdot i-1,2\cdot j-1} + M_{2\cdot i,2\cdot j-1} + M_{2\cdot i-1,2\cdot j} + M_{2\cdot i,2\cdot j}$. For instance, for the permutation $\tilde{\pi}$, $\tilde{M}'$ will be

$$\tilde{M}' = \begin{bmatrix} 2\,0\,0\,0 \\ 0\,1\,0\,1 \\ 0\,0\,2\,0 \\ 0\,1\,0\,1 \end{bmatrix}$$

- **Step Two:** In the second step, we construct two permutation matrices M^1 and M^2 such that $M^1_{i,j} + M^2_{i,j} = M'_{i,j}$. Those matrices will be the ones corresponding respectively to π^1 and π^2, the permutations of the two sub networks. For our example, $\tilde{M}^1$ and $\tilde{M}^2$ can be (one has a choice obviously)

$$\tilde{M}^1 = \begin{bmatrix} 1&0&0&0 \\ 0&1&0&0 \\ 0&0&1&0 \\ 0&0&0&1 \end{bmatrix} \qquad \tilde{M}^2 = \begin{bmatrix} 1&0&0&0 \\ 0&0&0&1 \\ 0&0&1&0 \\ 0&1&0&0 \end{bmatrix}$$

- **Step Three:** The last step is then setting the control bits for the inward and outward layers. The algorithm does this by identifying the coordinates of the entries in M, that correspond to the entries in M^1 which are equal to one. So for our example $\tilde{M}^1_{2,2} = 1$ as this entry corresponds to the one in position $(4, 4)$ of $\tilde{M}$, therefore the coordinates $(4, 4)$ are identified. Note that for some entries, two coordinates can be identified instead of one, which is the case for $\tilde{M}^1_{1,1}$ and $\tilde{M}^1_{3,3}$ in our example. When this happens, one of the coordinates is identified (which one does not matter for the algorithm) As such, for example, the coordinates $(2, 1), (4, 4), (5, 5)$ and $(8, 7)$ could be identified.
  Then within each of these coordinates, if there is an even component, the associated switch to this component is identified and its control bit is set to be one. So for our example, the coordinates $(2, 1)$ contain an even component (in the first position) and thus the associated switch to this even component is the switch one, i.e. $2/2$, in the inward layer, i.e. control one bit is set to one.
  Similarly, the coordinates $(4, 4)$, and $(8, 7)$ contain even components, and so the associated switches to these even components are $2 = 4/2$ and $4 = 8/2$ in the inward layer and $2 = 4/2$ in the outward layer, and their associated control bits are also set to one.
  The control bit of all the remaining switches in the inward and outward layers are set to zero.

This process is repeated recursively on the sub networks, until we reach the subnetworks of size 2 which are simply switches. For such switches, if the corresponding matrix is the identity matrix, we set the switch to be zero, otherwise, we set it to be one. Figure 5 illustrates the resulting realization of the permutation $\tilde{\pi}$.

Making the Algorithm Suitable for MPC Implementation: Recall, our aim is to transform a secret shared permutation matrix M of π, into secret shared control bits realizing it. We can achieve this if we somehow manage to transform the above algorithm into arithmetic operations.

The first step of the algorithm is easy to transform, as constructing M' is by definition done by summing up entries from M of known coordinates, and is thus a local operation when M is presented in secret shared form.

The last step is also relatively easy to transform; it consists of comparing entries from M^1 with entries from M, then checking whether coordinates contain even components. As such, the control bit b_k^{in} for the switch k in the inward layer and b_k^{out} in the outer layer can be computed as

$$b_k^{in} = \sum_{j=1}^{j=m/2} M^1_{k,j} \cdot (M_{2\cdot k, 2\cdot j-1} + M_{2\cdot k, 2\cdot j}),$$

$$b_k^{out} = \sum_{i=1}^{i=m/2} M^1_{i,k} \cdot (M_{2\cdot i-1, 2\cdot k} \cdot (1 - M_{2\cdot i, 2\cdot k-1}) + M_{2\cdot i, 2\cdot k}).$$

The control bit corresponding to a subnetwork of size two can be computed as

$$b^{mid} = M_{1,2},$$

as we have $M = I_2$ if no switch occurs and M is the off-diagonal 2×2 matrix if a switch occurs.

The second step is the most intricate one to transform, given that we need to split a secret shared matrix M' into two secret-shared permutation matrices M^1 and M^2. Our idea for this step is to express constraints on M^1 and M^2 into equations, where variables are entries of M^1 and M^2. Therefore, solving these equations identifies M^1 and M^2. This solution is then accomplished by making use of the fact that the entries are integers in $\{0, 1\}$, which constrains their possible value considerably.

The first constraint on M^1 and M^2 is that they sum up to M', i.e. for $i, j \in \{1, \ldots, m/2\}$ we have

$$M^1_{i,j} + M^2_{i,j} = M'_{i,j}$$

The second constraint on M^1 and M^2 is that they are permutation matrices, which translates into the set of linears equations for $j \in \{1, \ldots, m/2\}$ and $k \in \{1, 2\}$

$$\sum_{i=1}^{m/2} M^k_{i,j} = 1 \quad \text{and} \quad \sum_{i=1}^{m/2} M^k_{j,i} = 1,$$

as well as the quadratic equations for $i, j \in \{1, \ldots, m/2\}$ and $k \in \{1, 2\}$

$$M^k_{i,j} \cdot (M^k_{i,j} - 1) = 0.$$

To find M^1 and M^2, the strategy will be to solve the linear equations, while allowing entries $M^k_{i,j}$ to have values only in $\{0, 1\}$, which thus caters for the quadratic equations.

We do this by first initializing the matrices M^1, M^2, O^1 and O^2 by having their entries equal to zero. The matrices M^1 and M^2 will contain at the end the permutation matrices of π^1 and π^2, as soon as we fix an entry in $M^k_{i,j}$ we set $O^k_{i,j}$ equal to one. This is represented by the algorithm $\mathsf{Init}(M^1, M^2, O^1, O^2)$ in Fig. 13.

The next step of the process consists of setting entries $M^k_{i,j}$ that have only one solution, see the function $\mathsf{StartFix}(M', M^1, M^2, O^1, O^2)$ in Fig. 13. When we have $M'_{i,j} = 0$ (resp. 2) then we know that the values $M^k_{i,j}$ must be equal to zero (resp. one), since these are the only ways integers in $\{0, 1\}$ can add up to zero (resp. two).

For our example, after the execution of StartFix our values of $\tilde{O}_1$ and $\tilde{O}_2$ become

$$\tilde{O}^1 = \begin{bmatrix} 1\,1\,1\,1 \\ 1\,0\,1\,0 \\ 1\,1\,1\,1 \\ 1\,0\,1\,0 \end{bmatrix} \qquad \tilde{O}^2 = \begin{bmatrix} 1\,1\,1\,1 \\ 1\,0\,1\,0 \\ 1\,1\,1\,1 \\ 1\,0\,1\,0 \end{bmatrix}$$

If M^k are not fully determined at this stage, we need to deal with entries corresponding to one's in M'. Having a one in $M'_{i,j}$ means that one of the entries $M^1_{i,j}, M^2_{i,j}$ is equal to one, and the other equals zero. We will take (as a free choice) coordinates (i, j) of the first entry in M' that is equal to one, and we will set $M^1_{i,j}$ to be one. See procedure MakeChoice in Fig. 13. In our example, after making such a choice, $\tilde{O}_1$ and $\tilde{O}_2$ become

$$\tilde{O}^1 = \begin{bmatrix} 1\,1\,1\,1 \\ 1\,1\,1\,0 \\ 1\,1\,1\,1 \\ 1\,0\,1\,0 \end{bmatrix} \qquad \tilde{O}^2 = \begin{bmatrix} 1\,1\,1\,1 \\ 1\,1\,1\,0 \\ 1\,1\,1\,1 \\ 1\,0\,1\,0 \end{bmatrix}$$

Making a choice will fix one entry in M^k, and fixing an entry in M^k will allow us to fix other entries, see sub-procedure Update in Fig. 13. For our example, after executing Update, all entries $\tilde{O}^k_{i,j}$ are equal to one and therefore M^1, M^2 are fully determined. However, executing Update only once does not always guarantee to fix all entries that can be fixed with respect to the choice made, in addition making one choice does not guarantee that all entries will be fixed. That is, some permutations require repeated application of MakeChoice and Update until all the values $\tilde{O}^k_{i,j}$ are equal to one. Then we need to determine the bounds of how many times we should iterate these steps.

At the end of the execution of StartFix, in each row i (resp. column j) of M^k, either $m/2 - 2$ entries are fixed (which is the case where the row i (resp. column j) in M' contained two one's), or $m/2$ entries are fixed (which is the case where the row i (resp. the column j) in M' contained an entry that is equal to two). Thus, at most n entries in M^k remain unfixed.

Recall once we make a choice to fix one entry in M^k, this allows us to fix other entries. That is, at least row i and column j in M^k will now contain only one entry that is not fixed, respectively $M^k_{i,f}$ and $M^k_{f',j}$. This is because each row (resp. column) in O^k can contain at most two zero entries before fixing the value (i, j). These two entries will themselves fix one entry in row f' and one entry in column f (if $f = f'$ only one entry will be fixed). Therefore, making a choice and updating with respect to it will fix at least four other entries, with the minimum occurring when $f = f'$. Thus, we will need to execute MakeChoice at most $m/4$ times.

$\mathsf{Init}(M^1, M^2, O^1, O^2)$:
1. For $k \in \{1, 2\}$ and $i, j \in \{1, \ldots, \frac{m}{2}\}$:
   (a) $M^k_{i,j} \leftarrow 0$, $O^k_{i,j} \leftarrow 0$.

$\mathsf{StartFix}(M', M^1, M^2, O^1, O^2)$:
1. For $i, j \in \{1, \ldots, \frac{m}{2}\}$:
   (a) If $(M'_{i,j} = 0)$ then set $O^1_{i,j} \leftarrow 1$, $O^2_{i,j} \leftarrow 1$.
   (b) If $(M'_{i,j} = 2)$ then set $M^1_{i,j} \leftarrow 1$, $O^1_{i,j} \leftarrow 1$, $M^2_{i,j} \leftarrow 1$, $O^2_{i,j} \leftarrow 1$.

$\mathsf{MakeChoice}(M', M^1, M^2, O^1, O^2)$:
1. For $i, j \in \{1, \ldots, \frac{m}{2}\}$
   (a) If $(M'_{i,j} = 1$ and $O^1_{i,j} = 0)$ then set $M^1_{i,j} \leftarrow 1$, $M^2_{i,j} \leftarrow 0$, $O^1_{i,j} \leftarrow 1$, $O^2_{i,j} \leftarrow 1$ and return.

$\mathsf{Update}(M^1, M^2, O^1, O^2)$:
1. For $i, j \in \{1, \ldots, \frac{m}{2}\}$:
   (a) If $(O^1_{i,j} = 0)$
      i. If $(\prod_{k=1, k\neq j}^{\frac{m}{2}} O^1_{i,k} = 1)$ then set $M^1_{i,j} \leftarrow 1 - (\sum_{k=1, k\neq j}^{\frac{m}{2}} M^1_{i,k})$, $O^1_{i,j} \leftarrow 1$, $M^2_{i,j} \leftarrow 1 - M^1_{i,j}$ and $O^2_{i,j} \leftarrow 1$.
   (b) If $(O^1_{i,j} = 0)$
      i. If $(\prod_{k=1, k\neq i}^{\frac{m}{2}} O^1_{k,j} = 1)$ then set $M^1_{i,j} \leftarrow 1 - (\sum_{k=1, k\neq i}^{\frac{m}{2}} M^1_{k,j})$, $O^1_{i,j} \leftarrow 1$, $M^2_{i,j} \leftarrow 1 - (M^1_{i,j})$ and $O^2_{i,j} \leftarrow 1$.

$\mathsf{Waksman\text{-}Sub}(M')$:
1. $\mathsf{Init}(M^1, M^2, O^1, O^2)$.
2. $\mathsf{StartFix}(M', M^1, M^2, O^1, O^2)$.
3. For $c \in \{1, \ldots, \frac{m}{4}\}$
   (a) $\mathsf{MakeChoice}(M', M^1, M^2, O^1, O^2)$.
      i. For $k \in \{1, \ldots, m + 1 - 4 \cdot c\}$
         A. $\mathsf{Update}(M^1, M^2, O^1, O^2)$.

Fig. 13. Waksman algorithm step 2 sub-procedures

Assuming that the first execution of Update after MakeChoice will fix at least three entries, and each execution of Update after the first execution will at least fix one entry of the entries that can be fixed. Also the choice we made may fix the whole of the matrices M^k. Thus, we will need to execute Update $m+1-4\cdot c$ times where c is the number of choices already made. This gives the final procedure for the second step in sub-algorithm Waksman-Sub in Fig. 13.

Transforming the Algorithm: Having produced an (almost) data-oblivious methodology to generate a Waksman network we now need to transform it into a fully data-oblivious methodology by replacing all operations with algebraic operations. Again steps one and three are trivial, thus we are left with step two. The key step is dealing with the conditional operations, but this can be easily transformed into algebraic operations as follows.

At various points we need to determine whether a value in $\{0, 1, 2\}$ is equal to zero, one or two. This can be done via algebraic operations using three simple quadratic functions, namely

$$\begin{aligned} Q_0(x) &= (x-1)\cdot(x-2)/2, \\ Q_1(x) &= -x\cdot(x-2), \\ Q_2(x) &= x\cdot(x-1)/2. \end{aligned}$$

Given these functions converting Fig. 13 into a secret shared format is relatively simple; which we give in the full version.

Acknowledgements. The authors would like to thank Tim Wood, for insightful discussions and suggestions. This work has been supported in part by ERC Advanced Grant ERC-2015-AdG-IMPaCT, by the Defense Advanced Research Projects Agency (DARPA) and Space and Naval Warfare Systems Center, Pacific (SSC Pacific) under contracts No. N66001-15-C-4070 and FA8750-19-C-0502, and by the FWO under an Odysseus project GOH9718N. Any opinions, findings and conclusions or recommendations expressed in this material are those of the author(s) and do not necessarily reflect the views of the ERC, DARPA or FWO.

References

1. Abe, M.: Universally verifiable mix-net with verification work independent of the number of mix-servers. In: Nyberg, K. (ed.) EUROCRYPT 1998. LNCS, vol. 1403, pp. 437–447. Springer, Heidelberg (1998). https://doi.org/10.1007/BFb0054144
2. Abe, M.: Mix-networks on permutation networks. In: Lam, K.-Y., Okamoto, E., Xing, C. (eds.) ASIACRYPT 1999. LNCS, vol. 1716, pp. 258–273. Springer, Heidelberg (1999). https://doi.org/10.1007/978-3-540-48000-6_21
3. Abe, M., Hoshino, F.: Remarks on mix-network based on permutation networks. In: Kim, K. (ed.) PKC 2001. LNCS, vol. 1992, pp. 317–324. Springer, Heidelberg (2001). https://doi.org/10.1007/3-540-44586-2_23
4. Bayer, S., Groth, J.: Efficient zero-knowledge argument for correctness of a shuffle. In: Pointcheval, D., Johansson, T. (eds.) EUROCRYPT 2012. LNCS, vol. 7237, pp. 263–280. Springer, Heidelberg (2012). https://doi.org/10.1007/978-3-642-29011-4_17
5. Cramer, R., Damgård, I., Schoenmakers, B.: Proofs of partial knowledge and simplified design of witness hiding protocols. In: Desmedt, Y.G. (ed.) CRYPTO 1994. LNCS, vol. 839, pp. 174–187. Springer, Heidelberg (1994). https://doi.org/10.1007/3-540-48658-5_19
6. Damgård, I., Keller, M., Larraia, E., Pastro, V., Scholl, P., Smart, N.P.: Practical covertly secure MPC for dishonest majority – or: breaking the SPDZ limits. In: Crampton, J., Jajodia, S., Mayes, K. (eds.) ESORICS 2013. LNCS, vol. 8134, pp. 1–18. Springer, Heidelberg (2013). https://doi.org/10.1007/978-3-642-40203-6_1

7. Damgård, I., Pastro, V., Smart, N., Zakarias, S.: Multiparty computation from somewhat homomorphic encryption. In: Safavi-Naini, R., Canetti, R. (eds.) CRYPTO 2012. LNCS, vol. 7417, pp. 643–662. Springer, Heidelberg (2012). https://doi.org/10.1007/978-3-642-32009-5_38
8. Doerner, J., Kondi, Y., Lee, E., Shelat, A.: Secure two-party threshold ECDSA from ECDSA assumptions. In: 2018 IEEE Symposium on Security and Privacy, pp. 980–997. IEEE Computer Society Press, May 2018
9. Fauzi, P., Lipmaa, H., Siim, J., Zając, M.: An efficient pairing-based shuffle argument. In: Takagi, T., Peyrin, T. (eds.) ASIACRYPT 2017, Part II. LNCS, vol. 10625, pp. 97–127. Springer, Cham (2017). https://doi.org/10.1007/978-3-319-70697-9_4
10. Fauzi, P., Lipmaa, H., Zając, M.: A shuffle argument secure in the generic model. In: Cheon, J.H., Takagi, T. (eds.) ASIACRYPT 2016, Part II. LNCS, vol. 10032, pp. 841–872. Springer, Heidelberg (2016). https://doi.org/10.1007/978-3-662-53890-6_28
11. González, A., Ráfols, C.: New techniques for non-interactive shuffle and range arguments. In: Manulis, M., Sadeghi, A.-R., Schneider, S. (eds.) ACNS 2016. LNCS, vol. 9696, pp. 427–444. Springer, Cham (2016). https://doi.org/10.1007/978-3-319-39555-5_23
12. Keller, M., Scholl, P.: Efficient, oblivious data structures for MPC. In: Sarkar, P., Iwata, T. (eds.) ASIACRYPT 2014, Part II. LNCS, vol. 8874, pp. 506–525. Springer, Heidelberg (2014). https://doi.org/10.1007/978-3-662-45608-8_27
13. Laur, S., Willemson, J., Zhang, B.: Round-efficient oblivious database manipulation. In: Lai, X., Zhou, J., Li, H. (eds.) ISC 2011. LNCS, vol. 7001, pp. 262–277. Springer, Heidelberg (2011). https://doi.org/10.1007/978-3-642-24861-0_18
14. Lindell, Y.: Fast secure two-party ECDSA signing. In: Katz, J., Shacham, H. (eds.) CRYPTO 2017, Part II. LNCS, vol. 10402, pp. 613–644. Springer, Cham (2017). https://doi.org/10.1007/978-3-319-63715-0_21
15. Lindell, Y., Nof, A.: Fast secure multiparty ECDSA with practical distributed key generation and applications to cryptocurrency custody. In: Lie, D., Mannan, M., Backes, M., Wang, X. (eds.) ACM CCS 2018, pp. 1837–1854. ACM Press, October 2018
16. Lindell, Y., Nof, A., Ranellucci, S.: Fast secure multiparty ECDSA with practical distributed key generation and applications to cryptocurrency custody. IACR Cryptology ePrint Archive 2018, 987 (2018). https://eprint.iacr.org/2018/987
17. Shoup, V., Gennaro, R.: Securing threshold cryptosystems against chosen ciphertext attack. In: Nyberg, K. (ed.) EUROCRYPT 1998. LNCS, vol. 1403, pp. 1–16. Springer, Heidelberg (1998). https://doi.org/10.1007/BFb0054113
18. Smart, N.P.: Cryptography Made Simple. ISC. Springer, Heidelberg (2016). https://doi.org/10.1007/978-3-319-21936-3
19. Smart, N.P., Wood, T.: Error detection in monotone span programs with application to communication-efficient multi-party computation. In: Matsui, M. (ed.) CT-RSA 2019. LNCS, vol. 11405, pp. 210–229. Springer, Cham (2019). https://doi.org/10.1007/978-3-030-12612-4_11
20. Waksman, A.: A permutation network. J. ACM **15**(1), 159–163 (1968)

Author Index

Printed in the United States
By Bookmasters